Higher
HUMAN
BIOLOGY

SECOND EDITION

Team Co-ordinator:

James Torrance

Writing Team:

James Torrance, James Fullarton,
Clare Marsh, James Simms,
Caroline Stevenson

Diagrams by James Torrance

HODDER
GIBSON
AN HACHETTE UK COMPANY

Orders: please contact Bookpoint Ltd, 130 Milton Park, Abingdon, Oxon
OX14 4SB. Telephone: (44) 01235 827720, Fax: (44) 01235 400454. Lines are
open from 9.00–5.00, Monday to Saturday, with a 24 hour message answering
service. You can also order through our website at www.hoddereducation.co.uk

British Library Cataloguing in Publication Data
A catalogue record for this title is available from The British Library

Published by Hodder Gibson, 2a Christie St. Paisley, Scotland PA1 1NB

ISBN-13 978-0-340-80461-2

First published 2002
Impression number   11
                     2010

ISBN-13 978-0-340-80460-5

First published 2002
Impression number   13
Year   2011

Illustrated by James Torrance
Printed and bound in Great Britain by CPI Group (UK) Ltd, Croydon, CR0 4YY
for Hodder Gibson, an imprint of Hodder Education, an Hachette UK Company,
338 Euston Road, London NW1 3BH

Contents

Preface ■■■■■■■■■■■■■■■■■■■■■■■

This book has been written to articulate closely with Standard Grade Biology. It is intended to act as a valuable resource for pupils studying Higher Grade Human Biology.

The book provides a concise set of notes which adheres closely to the SQA Higher Still syllabus for Higher Grade Human Biology (first examined in 2000). Each section of the book matches a unit of the syllabus; each chapter corresponds to a content area. The book contains several special features:

Testing your knowledge

Key questions incorporated into the text of every chapter and designed to continuously assess *Knowledge and Understanding*. These will be especially useful as homework and as instruments of diagnostic assessment to check that full understanding of course content has been achieved.

Applying your knowledge

A variety of questions at the end of each chapter designed to give students practice in exam questions and to foster the development of *Problem-solving Skills* (selection of relevant information, presentation of information, processing of information, planning experimental procedures, drawing valid conclusions and making predictions). These questions will be especially useful as extensions to class work and as homework.

What you should know

Summaries of key facts and concepts as 'cloze' tests accompanied by appropriate word banks. These feature at regular intervals throughout the book and provide an excellent source of material for consolidation and revision prior to the SQA examination.

CELL FUNCTION AND INHERITANCE

1 Structure and variety of proteins

Structure

Proteins are organic compounds. In addition to always containing the chemical elements **carbon** (C), **hydrogen** (H), **oxygen** (O) and **nitrogen** (N), they often contain **sulphur** (S). These elements are built into molecules called **amino acids**.

Peptide bonds

Each protein is built up from a large number of amino acids of which there are about twenty different types. These sub-units are joined together into chains by strong chemical links called **peptide bonds**. Each chain is called a **polypeptide** and it normally consists of hundreds of amino acid molecules linked together.

The amino acids are built into a particular genetically determined sequence during the process of protein synthesis (see chapter 3). This sequence is known as the **primary structure** of the protein.

Hydrogen bonds

Weak chemical links known as **hydrogen bonds** form between certain amino acids in a polypeptide chain causing the chain to become coiled into a spiral (helix) as shown in figure 1.1. This is referred to as the protein's **secondary structure**.

Further linkages

The protein's **tertiary structure** is established when its polypeptides become further linked together by various types of cross-connection. These include bridges between sulphur atoms and additional hydrogen bonding.

The types of connection that occur at this stage are important since they determine the final structure of the protein enabling it to carry out its **specific function**. These further linkages lead to the formation of a fibrous or globular protein as shown in figure 1.1.

Variety and roles of proteins

An enormous number of different proteins is found in living things. A human being possesses over 10 000 different proteins.

Fibrous proteins

A **fibrous** protein is formed by several spiral-shaped polypeptide molecules becoming linked together in parallel by cross-bridges forming between them. This gives the molecule of structural protein a rope-like structure (see figure 1.1).

Many types of fibrous protein exist, each possessing structural properties which suit it to the role that it plays in the organism's body (see table 1.1).

Muscular contraction

Skeletal muscle consists of fibres containing many smaller **myofibrils**. Each myofibril is divided into compartments called **sarcomeres** by membranous partitions as shown in figure 1.2.

fibrous protein	structural properties	tissue rich in this protein	function of this protein
elastin	strong and elastic	wall of large arteries	flexible support
collagen	strong and inelastic	bone	rigid support
		tendon and ligament	attachment
keratin	strong and inelastic	hair	protection
actin and myosin	contractile	muscle	movement

Table 1.1 Fibrous proteins

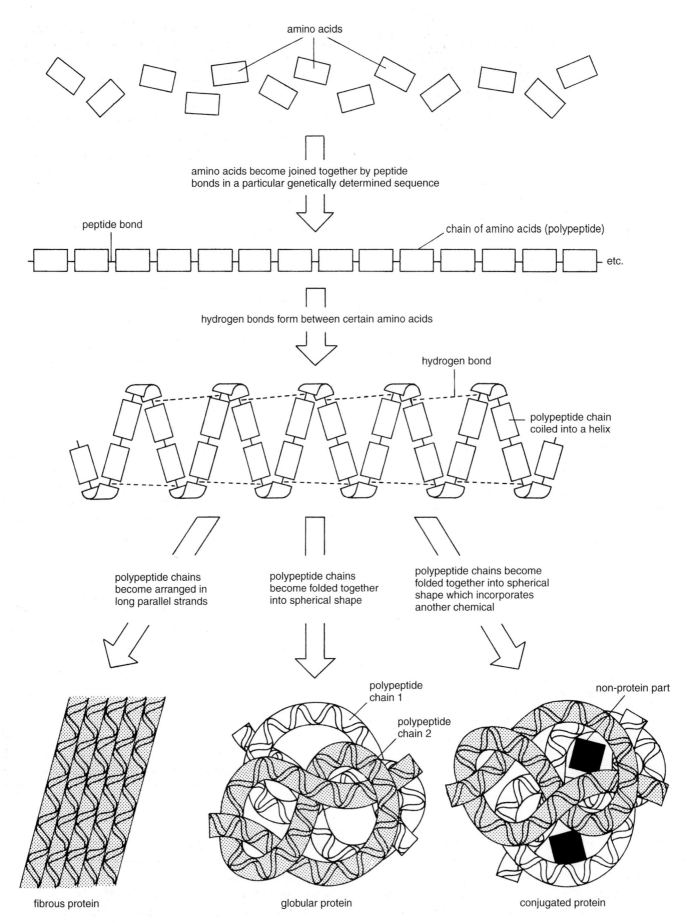

amino acids

amino acids become joined together by peptide
bonds in a particular genetically determined sequence

peptide bond

chain of amino acids (polypeptide)

etc.

hydrogen bonds form between certain amino acids

hydrogen bond

polypeptide chain
coiled into a helix

polypeptide chains
become arranged in
long parallel strands

polypeptide chains
become folded together
into spherical shape

polypeptide chains become
folded together into spherical
shape which incorporates
another chemical

polypeptide
chain 1

polypeptide
chain 2

non-protein part

fibrous protein

globular protein

conjugated protein

Figure 1.1 Structure of proteins

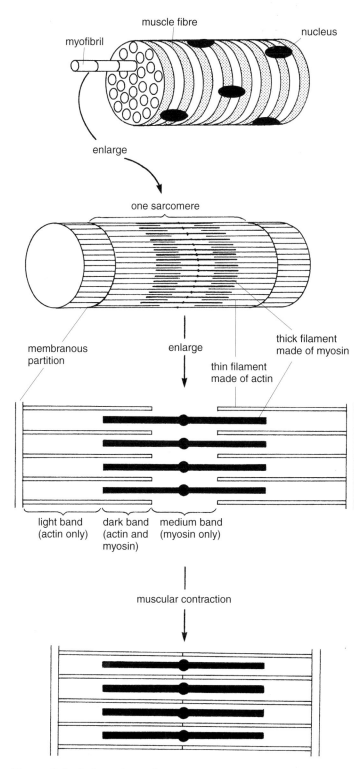

Figure 1.2 Actin and myosin

each membranous partition and fit between the thick filaments. This arrangement of filaments produces the **striated** (striped) effect typical of skeletal muscle tissue viewed under a microscope.

When a muscle fibre contracts, each of its sarcomeres becomes shorter. This reduction in length is brought about by the actin filaments sliding over the myosin filaments and moving towards the centre of the sarcomere, thereby increasing the amount of overlap between the two types of filament.

Globular proteins

A molecule of **globular** protein consists of several polypeptide chains folded together into a roughly spherical shape like a tangled ball of string (see figure 1.1). The exact form that the folding takes depends on the types of further linkage that form between amino acids on the same and adjacent polypeptide chains.

Globular proteins are vital components of all living cells and play a variety of roles.

Enzymes

All **enzymes** (biological catalysts) are made of globular protein. Each is folded in a particular way to expose an active surface which readily combines with a specific substrate (see figure 1.3). Since intracellular enzymes speed up the rate of biochemical processes such as photosynthesis, respiration and protein synthesis, they are essential for the maintenance of life.

Hormones

These are **chemical messengers** made by endocrine glands (see Appendix 1) and transported in an animal's blood to 'target' tissues where they exert a specific effect. Some hormones are made of globular protein and exert a regulatory effect on the animal's growth and metabolism. A few examples are given in table 1.2.

Antibodies

Although Y-shaped rather than spherical, **antibodies** are also a type of globular protein. They are made by white blood cells called **lymphocytes** and defend the body against antigens (see chapter 7).

Transport proteins

Some globular proteins are responsible for the transport of substances from one part of the body to another. For example, **transferrin** binds with iron entering the bloodstream from the gut or released during the destruction of red blood cells and transports it to the bone marrow for re-use.

The term filament means a slender, thread-like structure. Each myofibril contains two types of filament. **Thick** filaments, each composed of many molecules of the fibrous protein **myosin**, are found in the centre of a sarcomere lying parallel to its longitudinal axis. **Thin** filaments, each composed of many molecules of the fibrous protein **actin**, extend across the sarcomere from

3

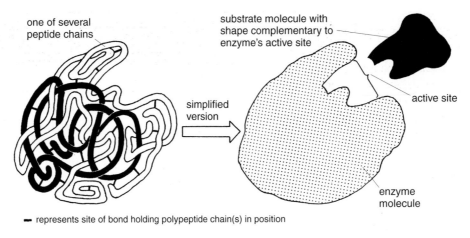

one of several
peptide chains

substrate molecule with
shape complementary to
enzyme's active site

simplified
version

active site

enzyme
molecule

— represents site of bond holding polypeptide chain(s) in position

Figure 1.3 Enzyme structure

hormone	secretory (endocrine) gland	role of hormone
secretin	wall of small intestine	Stimulates release of pancreatic juice.
growth hormone (somatotrophin)	anterior pituitary	Promotes growth of long bones.
prolactin	anterior pituitary	Stimulates milk production in nursing mothers.
insulin	pancreas	Promotes conversion of glucose to glycogen.
glucagon	pancreas	Promotes conversion of glycogen to glucose.

Table 1.2 Hormones composed of globular protein

Structural protein

Globular protein is one of the two components which make up the **membrane** surrounding a living cell (see p 45). Similarly it forms an essential part of all membranes possessed by structures within the cell such as the nucleus. This type of protein therefore plays a vital structural role in every living cell.

Conjugated proteins

Each **conjugated** protein consists of a globular protein associated with a non-protein chemical (see figure 1.1).

A **glycoprotein** is composed of protein and carbohydrate. An example is mucus, the slimy, viscous substance secreted by epithelial cells to lubricate or protect parts of the body.

A **lipoprotein** is a complex molecule consisting of protein and lipid. The products of fat digestion absorbed from the small intestine are coated with lipoprotein before being transported round the body (see p 169).

Haemoglobin is the oxygen-transporting pigment in blood. It is a conjugated protein consisting of the globular protein globin associated with haem, a non-protein part containing iron (see p 160). **Cytochrome**, which plays a key role in the cell's aerobic respiratory pathway (see p 32), is also a conjugated protein which contains iron.

Proteins play a wide variety of roles. Some form part of the cell's structure, some defend the body, some transport essential materials whilst others regulate biochemical reactions and metabolic processes.

Testing your knowledge

1 a) (i) Give the symbols of the four chemical
           elements always present in the amino acids
           that make up a protein.
       (ii) Approximately how many different types of
             amino acid are found in proteins? (3)

   b) (i) Identify the type of bonds that join amino
           acids into the polypeptide chain primary
           structure.
       (ii) Which type of bonds give the further
             linkages that produce secondary and tertiary
             structures? (2)

2 Copy and complete table 1.3 (where F = fibrous,
   G = globular and C = conjugated protein). (8)

name of protein	type of protein (F, G or C)	role of this protein
actin and myosin		
antibody		
catalase		
cytochrome		
haemoglobin		
insulin		
keratin		
transferrin		

Table 1.3

Applying your knowledge

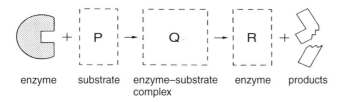

enzyme   substrate   enzyme–substrate   enzyme   products
                       complex

Figure 1.4

1 Figure 1.4 is incomplete. It represents the action of
   an enzyme on its substrate. Draw a complete version
   of the diagram by replacing boxes P, Q and R with
   the omitted molecules. (3)

2 Figure 1.5 shows three different types of protein.

   a) Which of these is
       (i) a globular protein;
       (ii) a conjugated protein;
       (iii) a fibrous protein;
       (iv) composed of only one polypeptide chain? (4)

   b) (i) Which diagram represents collagen?
       (ii) Explain how you arrived at your answer.
       (iii) State ONE way in which collagen's structure
              is suited to its function. (3)

   c) (i) Which diagram represents a molecule of
           myoglobin, a red oxygen-carrying pigment
           found in vertebrate muscle?

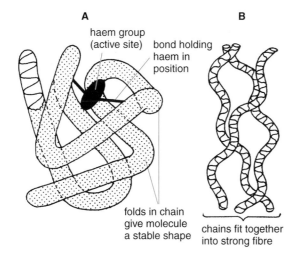

A
haem group
(active site)   bond holding
                 haem in
                 position

folds in chain
give molecule
a stable shape

B

chains fit together
into strong fibre

C
active site

Figure 1.5

Continued ➤

Applying your knowledge

    (ii) Explain your choice of answer.
    (iii) State ONE way in which the molecular structure of myoglobin enables it to carry out its function efficiently. (3)

d) **(i)** Which diagram represents a molecule of enzyme?
    (ii) Explain how you arrived at your answer. (2)

3 Some amino acids can be synthesised by the body from simple compounds; others cannot be synthesised and must be supplied in the diet. The latter type are called the **essential amino acids**.

The graph in figure 1.6 shows the results of an experiment using rats where group 1 was fed zein (maize protein), group 2 was fed casein (milk protein) and group 3 was fed a varied diet.

a) One of the proteins contains all of the essential amino acids whereas the other lacks two of them. Identify each protein and explain how you arrived at your answer. (4)

b) **(i)** State which protein was given to the rats in group 3 during the first six days of the experiment.
    (ii) Suggest TWO different ways in which their diet could have been altered from day 6 onwards to account for the results shown in the graph. (3)

c) By how many grams did the average body weight of the rats in group 2 increase over the 20-day period? (1)

d) Calculate the percentage decrease in average body weight shown by the rats in group 1 over the 20-day period. (1)

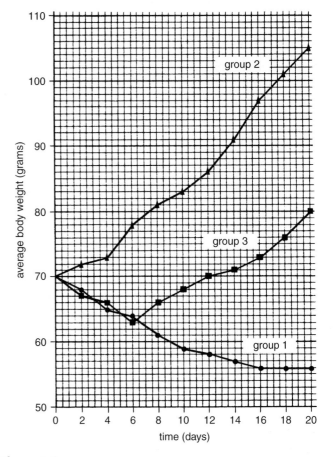

Figure 1.6

4 Write an essay on the various functions of proteins. (10)

② Role of enzymes

Biological catalyst

A **catalyst** is a substance which increases the rate of a chemical reaction by lowering the amount of energy needed to make the reaction proceed. The catalyst itself is not changed at the end of the reaction.

Enzymes are biological catalysts which speed up the rate of biochemical reactions. In the absence of enzymes, biochemical pathways such as respiration and photosynthesis would proceed so slowly that life as we know it would cease to exist.

Location

Many different enzymes are produced by and are present in all living cells. Every biochemical reaction that occurs in a living organism is catalysed by an enzyme. Some of these processes occur inside cells and are controlled by **intracellular** enzymes (e.g. cytochrome oxidase plays a key role in aerobic respiration – see p 33). Other reactions occur outside cells under the influence of **extracellular** enzymes (e.g. pepsin promotes the digestion of protein in the stomach).

Structure

All enzyme molecules are made of **protein**. Most enzymes are simple globular proteins and consist of one or more polypeptide chains folded together like a tangled ball of string (see p 2). A few enzymes are made of conjugated protein (i.e. a globular protein attached to a non-protein part).

At some point on the surface of an enzyme molecule there is an **active site** which has a particular shape. This is determined by the chemical structure of, and type of bonding between, amino acids in the polypeptide chains which make up the enzyme molecule.

Mechanism of action

An enzyme is able to act on only one type of substance (its **substrate**) since this is the only substance whose molecules exactly fit the enzyme's active site. The enzyme is said therefore to be **specific** to its substrate and the substrate's molecular shape is said to be **complementary** to the enzyme's active site.

Enzymes are thought to operate by a 'lock-and-key' mechanism. This model of enzyme action proposes that the substrate combines with the enzyme at its active site in a precise way just as a lock and key fit together. Figure 2.1 shows how the two combine briefly as the enzyme-substrate complex, allowing the reaction to occur. The end products become detached from the active site leaving the enzyme **unaltered** and free to combine with another molecule of substrate.

Some enzymes promote the **breaking down** of complex molecules to simpler ones (see figure 2.1); others promote the **building up** of complex molecules from simpler ones (see figure 2.2).

Factors affecting enzyme action

To function efficiently an enzyme requires a suitable temperature, a suitable pH and an adequate supply of substrate. Inhibitors (see p 10) may bring the enzyme's action to a partial or even complete halt.

Effect of temperature

The graph in figure 2.3 summarises the general effect of temperature on enzyme activity in humans.

Denaturation

Increase in temperature makes an enzyme's atoms vibrate. At temperatures above 40 °C, its atoms vibrate so much

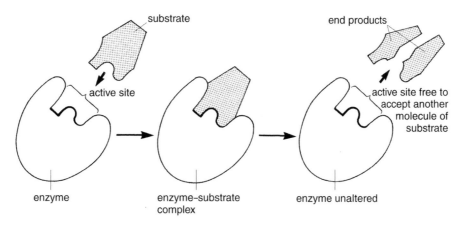

Figure 2.1 Lock and key mechanism of enzyme action (degradation of complex substrate)

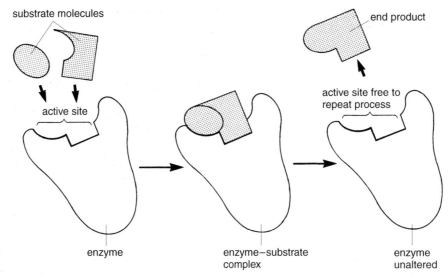

Figure 2.2 Lock and key mechanism of enzyme action (synthesis of complex product)

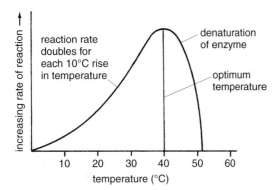

Figure 2.3 Effect of temperature on enzyme activity

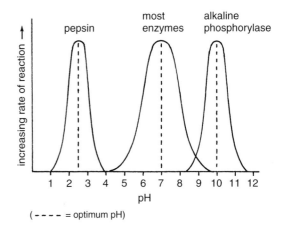

Figure 2.4 Effect of pH on enzymes

that some of the chemical bonds (e.g. hydrogen bonds) that hold the enzyme together in its specific shape, start to break. The enzyme's constituent polypeptide molecules start to unravel and soon its active site is lost. An enzyme in this state is said to be **denatured**.

Effect of pH

Each enzyme works best at a particular pH (its optimum pH) as shown in figure 2.4. Many enzymes function within a working pH range of about 5–9 with an **optimum** at pH 7 (neutral). However there are exceptions. Pepsin secreted by the stomach's gastric glands works best in strongly acidic conditions of pH 2.5; alkaline phosphorylase which plays a role in bone formation works best at pH 10.

Effect of enzyme concentration

The enzyme-substrate complex formed during an enzyme-controlled reaction exists for only a brief moment. Following the release of the products, the

enzyme's active site becomes free allowing it to combine with another molecule of substrate and so on.

The number of substrate molecules which can be acted upon by an enzyme molecule in a given time is called its **turnover number**. This varies from about 4000 substrate molecules per second in the case of catalase to around 100 per second for the slowest enzyme.

An increase in **concentration** (i.e. number of molecules) **of enzyme** results in an increase in rate of reaction since more and more substrate molecules are being acted upon. This relationship is summarised by the graph in figure 2.5.

This upward trend continues as a straight line provided that excess substrate is present. However, if the concentration of substrate is limited, then the graph levels off since some enzyme molecules fail to find substrate molecules to act upon.

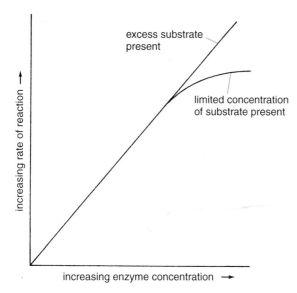

Figure 2.5 Effect of increasing enzyme concentration

The effect of increasing enzyme concentration is summarised at molecular level in a simplified way in figure 2.6.

Effect of substrate concentration

Investigating the effect of substrate concentration on enzyme activity

Catalase is an enzyme made by living cells (e.g. liver). It catalyses the breakdown of hydrogen peroxide to water and oxygen as in the equation:

$$\text{hydrogen peroxide} \xrightarrow{\text{catalase}} \text{water} + \text{oxygen}$$
$$(2H_2O_2) \qquad\qquad (2H_2O) \quad (O_2)$$

In the experiment shown in figure 2.7, the one variable factor is the concentration of the **substrate** (hydrogen peroxide). When an equal mass of fresh liver is added to each cylinder, the results shown in the diagram are produced. The height of the froth of oxygen bubbles indicates the activity of the enzyme at each substrate concentration.

From the experiment it is concluded that increase in substrate concentration results in increased enzyme activity until a point is reached (in cylinder G) where some factor other than substrate concentration has become the limiting factor.

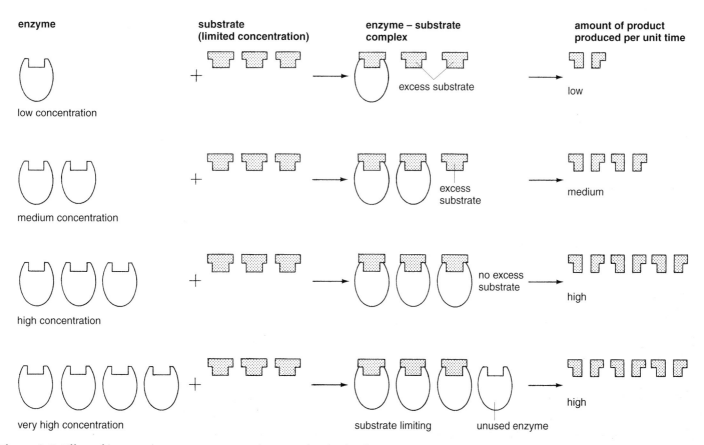

Figure 2.6 Effect of increase in enzyme concentration at molecular level

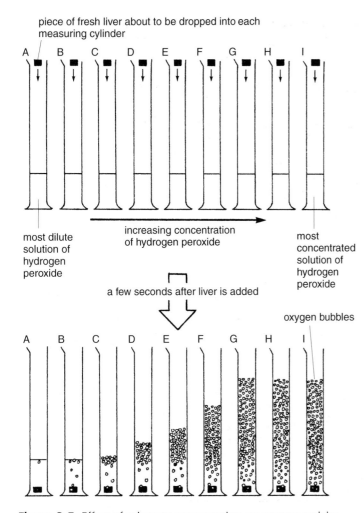

Figure 2.7 Effect of substrate concentration on enzyme activity

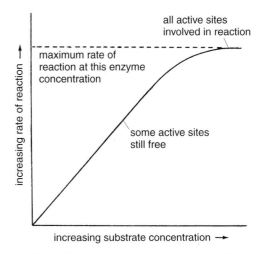

Figure 2.8 Effect of increasing substrate concentration

Explanation

The graph in figure 2.8 shows the effect of increasing substrate concentration on the rate of an enzyme-controlled reaction for a limited concentration of enzyme.

At low concentrations of substrate the reaction rate is low since there are too few substrate molecules present to make maximum use of all the active sites on the enzyme molecules.

An increase in substrate concentration results in an increase in reaction rate since more and more active sites become involved.

This upward trend in the graph continues as a straight line until a point is reached where further increase in substrate concentration fails to make the reaction go any faster. At this point all the active sites are occupied (the enzyme concentration has become the limiting factor). The graph levels off since there are now more substrate molecules present than there are free active sites with which to combine. The effect of increasing substrate concentration is summarised at molecular level in a simplified way in figure 2.9.

Effect of inhibitors

An **inhibitor** is a substance which decreases the rate of an enzyme-controlled reaction and may even bring it to a halt. Inhibitors can be divided into two types: **competitive** and **non-competitive**.

Competitive inhibitors

Molecules of a competitive inhibitor compete with molecules of the substrate for the active sites on the enzyme. The inhibitor is able to do this because its molecular structure is **similar** to that of the substrate and it can attach itself to the enzyme's active site as shown in figure 2.10.

Since active sites **blocked** by competitive inhibitor molecules cannot become occupied by substrate molecules, the rate of the reaction is reduced.

Effect of concentration of competitive inhibitor

For a limited concentration of substrate and enzyme, an increase in concentration of competitive inhibitor has the effect on reaction rate shown in figure 2.11.

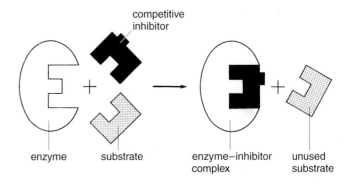

Figure 2.10 Action of a competitive inhibitor

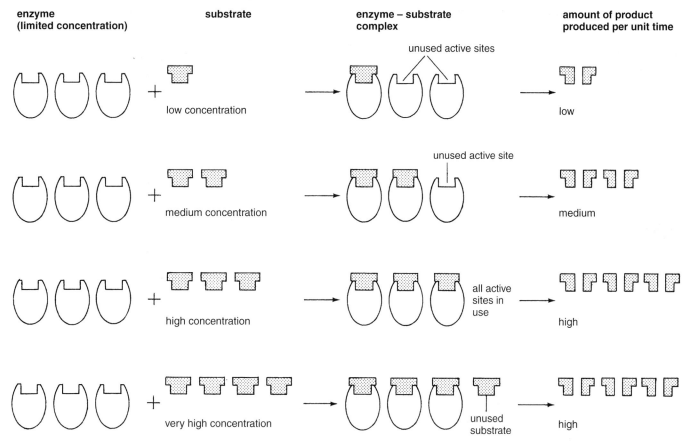

Figure 2.9 Effect of increasing substrate concentration at a molecular level

At low concentrations of inhibitor, the reaction rate is high since few active sites are blocked by the inhibitor and substrate molecules have no difficulty finding free active sites on the enzyme molecules.

However as the concentration of competitive inhibitor increases, the reaction rate decreases owing to the reduced number of unblocked active sites available to substrate molecules.

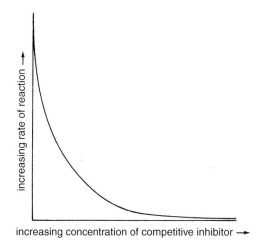

Figure 2.11 Effect of increasing concentration of competitive inhibitor

Non-competitive inhibitors

These do not combine with the enzyme's active site. Instead a non-competitive inhibitor becomes attached to some other region of the enzyme molecule. This results in the active site being **altered indirectly** as shown in figure 2.12. The substrate is therefore unable to combine with the enzyme.

Cyanide acts in this way by attaching itself to the non-protein iron part of the enzyme cytochrome oxidase. This inhibits the process of aerobic respiration. Heavy metals such as mercury, copper and lead are further examples of non-competitive inhibitors.

Effect of increasing substrate concentration

The graph in figure 2.13 compares the effect of increasing substrate concentration on rate of reaction for a limited amount of enzyme affected by a limited amount of inhibitor.

In graph line 1 (the control), increase in substrate concentration brings about an increase in reaction rate until a point is reached where all the active sites on the enzyme molecules are occupied (see also figure 2.8) and then the graph levels off.

In graph line 2, increase in substrate concentration brings about a gradual increase in reaction rate. Although the

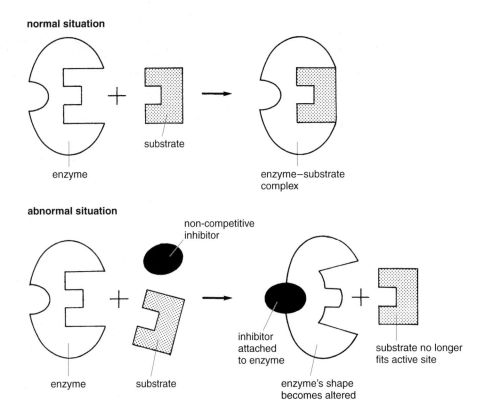

Figure 2.12 Action of a non-competitive inhibitor

competitive inhibitor is competing for and occupying some of the enzyme's active sites, the true substrate is also occupying some of the sites. As substrate molecules increase in concentration and outnumber those of the competitive inhibitor, more and more active sites become occupied by true substrate rather than inhibitor molecules. The reaction rate continues to increase until all the active sites are occupied (almost all of them by substrate).

In graph line 3, most of the enzyme molecules have been altered (at some position other than the active site) by the **non-competitive** inhibitor and rendered inactive. However a very few enzyme molecules remain unaffected and the reaction proceeds at a low rate. Increase in substrate concentration fails to increase reaction rate

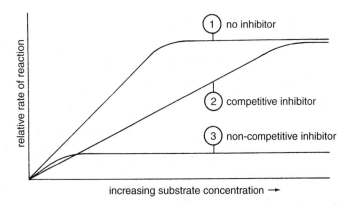

Figure 2.13 Comparative effects of increasing substrate concentration in the presence of inhibitors

since the few active sites that are operational are already working at maximum capacity.

Summary

The degree of inhibition of an enzyme by a competitive inhibitor is affected by both the concentration of the inhibitor and the concentration of the substrate present.

The degree of inhibition of an enzyme by a non-competitive inhibitor depends on the concentration of the inhibitor only.

Investigating the effect of copper nitrate on catalase activity

Five measuring cylinders are set up as shown in figure 2.14. After the liver has been allowed to soak in the copper nitrate solutions for 10 minutes, an equal volume of substrate (hydrogen peroxide) is added to each cylinder.

The froth of oxygen bubbles produced in the cylinders is found to decrease in volume with increasing concentration of copper nitrate solution. No froth is produced at all at the highest concentration of copper nitrate.

Table 2.1 gives a summary of design features and precautions adopted in this investigation to ensure that good scientific practice and safety procedures are observed throughout.

It is concluded from the results that very low concentrations of copper nitrate do **not inhibit** the

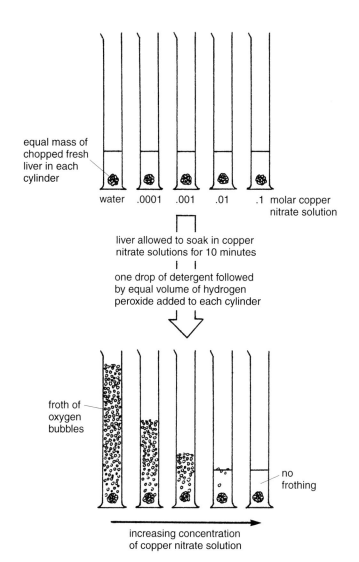

equal mass of chopped fresh liver in each cylinder

water .0001 .001 .01 .1 molar copper nitrate solution

liver allowed to soak in copper nitrate solutions for 10 minutes

one drop of detergent followed by equal volume of hydrogen peroxide added to each cylinder

froth of oxygen bubbles

no frothing

increasing concentration of copper nitrate solution

Figure 2.14 Effect of copper nitrate on activity of catalase

action of the enzyme catalase. Low concentrations of copper nitrate cause **partial** inhibition since only some enzyme molecules are affected; high concentrations cause **complete** inhibition since all enzyme molecules are affected. (Very low concentrations of copper activate some enzymes – see co-factors p 14).

Testing your knowledge

1 a) Why is an enzyme described as a *biological catalyst*? (1)

b) What is the difference between an *intracellular* and an *extracellular* enzyme? (1)

c) What determines the shape of an enzyme's active site? (1)

d) Explain why an enzyme is said to be *specific* in its relationship with its substrate. (1)

2 a) (i) In general, what effect does an increase in concentration of an enzyme have on reaction rate when the substrate is present in excess? Explain why.

(ii) What effect does an increase in concentration of enzyme have on reaction rate when a limited concentration of substrate is present? Explain why. (2)

b) (i) What effect does an increase in concentration of substrate have on reaction rate when the enzyme is present in excess? Explain why.

(ii) What effect does an increase in concentration of substrate have on reaction rate when a limited concentration of enzyme is present? Explain why. (2)

3 a) Define the term *inhibitor* with respect to enzymes. (1)

b) (i) What property of a competitive inhibitor enables it to compete with the substrate?

(ii) What effect does an increase in concentration of competitive inhibitor have on reaction rate when the concentration of substrate present is limited? Explain why. (3)

c) Describe how a non-competitive inhibitor acts on an enzyme. (2)

design feature or precaution	reason
Equal volumes of solutions and equal masses of liver used.	To ensure that the concentration of copper nitrate solution is the only variable factor under investigation.
Liver allowed to soak for 10 minutes.	To give copper nitrate time to affect molecules of catalase.
Protective gloves and goggles worn.	To prevent harmful chemicals making contact with eyes and skin.
One drop of detergent added to each measuring cylinder.	To promote and sustain froth of oxygen bubbles allowing volume to be measured easily.
Experiment repeated several times.	To ensure that the results are reliable.

Table 2.1 Design features

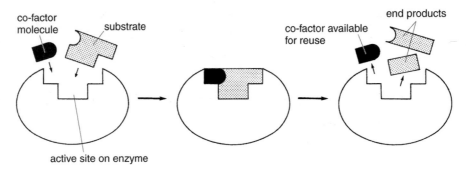

Figure 2.15 Action of enzyme co-factor

Activation of enzymes

Co-factors

In order to function and bring about their catalytic effect, many enzymes require the presence of a non-protein substance called a **co-factor**. In some cases the co-factor is thought to activate the enzyme by enabling the substrate to fit at the enzyme's active site (see figure 2.15).

Some co-factors are mineral ions such as **zinc**, **iron**, **copper** and **magnesium**. Other co-factors are called **co-enzymes**. Many of these contain a vitamin as the main part of their molecular structure. **Vitamin B**, for example, is required to make the co-enzymes involved in the transfer of hydrogen during aerobic respiration (see p 33). Vitamins are therefore essential ingredients of the diet. They are only needed in small quantities since co-enzymes are continuously reused.

Other enzymes

A number of digestive enzymes are produced in an inactive form. On being secreted into the gut cavity (lumen) they are converted to an active form by **enzyme activators**.

Trypsinogen and chymotrypsinogen are two proteases (protein-digesting enzymes) made by the pancreas. They remain inactive (otherwise they would digest the pancreas itself) until they come into contact with the enzyme enteropeptidase made by the wall of the small intestine.

In the gut lumen, enteropeptidase converts inactive trypsinogen to active trypsin. Trypsin then converts inactive chymotrypsinogen to active chymotrypsin (see figure 2.16). Trypsin and chymotrypsin in their active state in the small intestine continue the process of protein digestion begun by pepsin in the stomach.

Inborn errors of metabolism

All of the chemical processes that occur in the human body and keep it alive are known collectively as its **metabolism**. Cell metabolism refers to the biochemical reactions that occur within a cell. Some of these involve the **breaking down** of a substance (e.g. oxidation of glucose during aerobic respiration); others bring about the **building up** of a substance (e.g. synthesis of protein).

A **metabolic pathway** normally consists of several stages each of which involves the conversion of one metabolite to another during a breaking down or building up process.

Each stage in a metabolic reaction is controlled by an enzyme as shown in the imaginary example in figure 2.17. Each enzyme is made of protein whose structure and synthesis is determined by genetic information held in a particular gene (see chapter 3). However if a **fault** occurs in the genetic information due to mutation (see chapter 13), the enzyme is not produced in its normal functional state. In the absence of the enzyme some essential step in the pathway cannot proceed and an intermediate metabolite is often found to accumulate and lead to problems. Two examples of such **inborn errors of metabolism** are listed in table 2.2. Further details of the metabolic pathway involved are given in chapter 13.

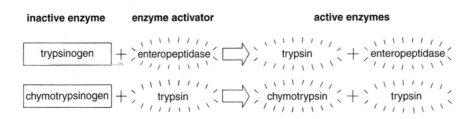

Figure 2.16 Activation of enzymes by enzymes

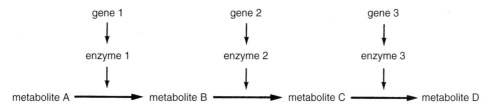

Figure 2.17 Enzyme control of a metabolic pathway

enzyme absent	disorder caused	effect of disorder
phenylalanine hydroxylase	phenylketonuria (PKU)	Accumulation of phenylalanine which is converted into poison and affects brain cells.
melanocyte tyrosinase	albinism	Lack of formation of melanin, the pigment which gives skin, eyes and hair their colour.

Table 2.2 Inborn errors of metabolism

Testing your knowledge

1 a) (i) Name TWO mineral ions that are important enzyme activators.
   (ii) Briefly describe the means by which many such co-factors are thought to play their role. (3)

b) Despite being essential ingredients in the diet, vitamins are only required in tiny quantities. Explain why. (1)

c) Name the enzyme activators that convert
   (i) trypsinogen and
   (ii) chymotrypsinogen to their active forms. (2)

2 a) Define the term *metabolism*. (2)

b) By what type of substance is each stage in a metabolic reaction controlled? (1)

c) (i) What causes an inborn error of metabolism?
   (ii) Why is an intermediate often found to accumulate as a result?
   (iii) Give ONE example of a disorder resulting from an inborn error of metabolism. (3)

Applying your knowledge

1 Figure 2.18 shows the stages that occur during an enzyme-controlled reaction.

a) What name is given to the complex indicated by the letter Z? (1)

b) Using the THREE letters given, indicate the correct sequence in which the three stages would occur if:

   (i) the enzyme promotes the breakdown of a complex molecule to simpler ones;

   (ii) the enzyme promotes the build-up of a complex molecule from simpler ones. (2)

2 One gram of roughly chopped raw liver was added to hydrogen peroxide solution at different pH values and the time taken to collect one cm^3 of oxygen was noted in each case. The results are given in table 2.3.

a) Present the results as a line graph (in the form of a curve). (2)

Continued ➤

Applying your knowledge

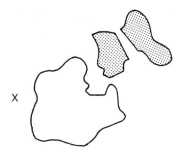

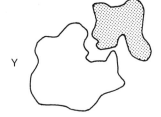

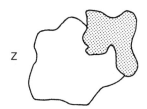

Figure 2.18

pH of hydrogen peroxide solution	time to collect 1cm³ of oxygen (seconds)
6	105
7	78
8	57
9	45
10	52
11	66
12	99

Table 2.3

4 The graph shown in figure 2.19 summarises the results from an experiment involving an enzyme-controlled reaction.

    a) **(i)** In this experiment, the enzyme concentration was kept constant. From the graph, identify the factor that was varied by the experimenter.

           (ii) What effect did an increase in this factor have over region AB of the graph? (2)

    b) Suggest which factor became limiting at point C on the graph. (1)

    c) Which letter on the graph represents the situation where
        (i) almost all of the active sites;
        (ii) none of the active sites;
        (iii) about half of the active sites on enzyme molecules are freely available for attachment to substrate molecules? (3)

    b) From your graph state the pH value at which the enzyme was
    (i) most active;
    (ii) least active. (2)

    c) Of the pH values used in this experiment, which is the optimum for the enzyme present in the liver cells? (1)

    d) How could you obtain an even more accurate measurement of the optimum pH at which this enzyme works? (1)

3 Explain each of the following in terms of enzymes:

    a) Fevers which raise the body temperature to over 42 °C are normally fatal to human beings. (2)

    b) Vinegar (an acid) is used to preserve food against attack by micro-organisms. (2)

    c) Cheese kept in a warm room turns mouldy much more quickly than cheese kept in a refrigerator. (2)

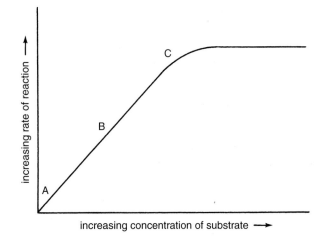

Figure 2.19

Continued ➤

Applying your knowledge

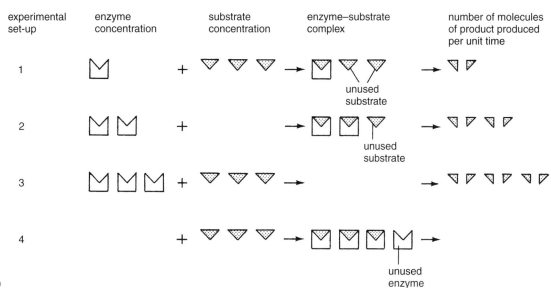

Figure 2.20

d) Suggest what could be done to increase the rate of the reaction beyond the level it has reached at C. (1)

5 Figure 2.20 represents, at molecular level, the effect of increasing enzyme concentration on the rate of an enzyme-controlled reaction.

a) Copy and complete the diagram to include the missing molecules. (4)

b) From the information in the diagram, state which factor was
(i) varied;
(ii) kept constant during the series of experiments. (2)

c) **(i)** Which piece of information given in the diagram could be used as a measure of reaction rate?
(ii) What effect did increasing concentration of enzyme have on reaction rate in experimental set-ups 1, 2 and 3? (2)

d) What factor was limiting in experimental set-up 4 that held its reaction rate at the same level as that in set-up 3? (1)

6 The flow diagram shown in figure 2.21 represents a complete biochemical pathway.

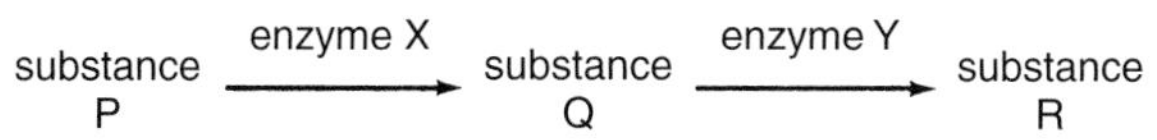

substance → enzyme X → substance → enzyme Y → substance
P   Q   R

Figure 2.21

a) Name enzyme X's
(i) substrate;
(ii) end product. (2)

b) Name enzyme Y's
(i) substrate;
(ii) end product. (2)

c) Enzyme X is known to be affected by a certain inhibitor. If equal concentrations of substances P, Q and R are put into a flask containing enzymes X and Y and a high concentration of the inhibitor is added, what will happen to the concentrations of substances P, Q and R? (3)

d) Some people suffer an inborn error of metabolism and are unable to produce enzyme Y. Predict the concentrations of substances P, Q and R that will be present in the body of a person suffering this disorder. (3)

7 Give an account of the factors that affect enzyme activity under the headings:

(i) concentration of enzyme; (3)
(ii) concentration of substrate; (3)
(iii) inhibition. (4)

3 Nucleic acids and protein synthesis

Structure of DNA

Chromosomes are thread-like structures found inside the nucleus of a cell. They contain **deoxyribonucleic acid (DNA)**. A molecule of DNA consists of two strands each made of repeating units called **nucleotides**.

Each DNA nucleotide (see figure 3.1) is made of a molecule of **deoxyribose sugar** joined to a **phosphate** group and a **base**. Since DNA possesses four different bases (**adenine, thymine, guanine** and **cytosine**) it has four different types of nucleotide.

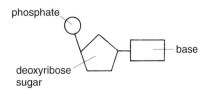

Figure 3.1 Structure of a DNA nucleotide

A strong **chemical bond** forms between the phosphate group of one nucleotide and the deoxyribose sugar of another. These bonds are not easily broken and join neighbouring nucleotide units into a permanent strand as shown in figure 3.2.

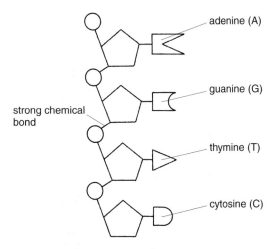

Figure 3.2 Strand of DNA nucleotides

Two of these strands become joined together by weaker **hydrogen bonds** forming between their bases. However this union is temporary in that hydrogen bonds can be easily broken when this becomes necessary (e.g. during transcription of DNA into RNA – see p 20).

Each base can only join with one other type of base: adenine (A) always bonds with thymine (T), and guanine (G) always bonds with cytosine (C). A–T and G–C are called **base pairs**. Each member of a pair is complementary to its partner.

Double helix

The resultant double-stranded molecule is DNA and its two strands are arranged as shown in figure 3.3. This twisted coil is called a **double helix**. It is like a spiral ladder in which the sugar-phosphate 'backbones' form the uprights and the base pairs form the rungs.

Testing your knowledge

1. **a)** What name is given to each of the repeating units that make up a strand of DNA? (1)

   b) How many strands are present in a molecule of DNA? (1)

2. **a)** Name the THREE parts of a DNA nucleotide. (3)

   b) Which type of bond joins nucleotides into a strand of DNA? (1)

   c) Name each type of base molecule found in DNA and give the base-pairing rule. (3)

   d) Which type of bond forms between the bases of adjacent strands of a DNA molecule? (1)

3. **a)** What name is given to the twisted coil arrangement typical of a DNA molecule? (1)

   b) If DNA is like a spiral ladder, which part of it corresponds to the ladder's
   (i) rungs;
   (ii) uprights? (1)

Structure of RNA

The second type of nucleic acid is called **ribonucleic acid (RNA)**. RNA also consists of nucleotides (see figure 3.4).

Although RNA's structure (see figure 3.5) closely resembles that of DNA, a molecule of RNA differs from a molecule of DNA in three important ways as summarised in table 3.1.

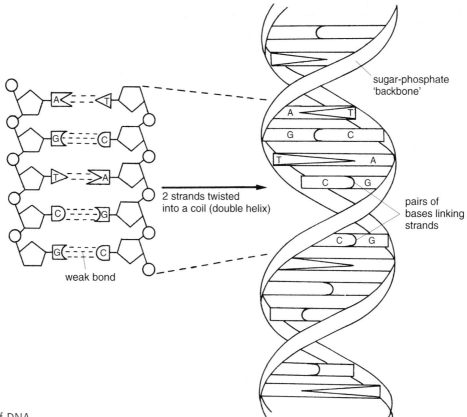

Figure 3.3 Structure of DNA

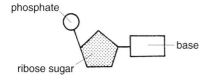

Figure 3.4 Structure of an RNA nucleotide

	RNA	DNA
number of nucleotide strands present in one molecule	one	two
complementary base partner of adenine	uracil	thymine
sugar present in a nucleotide molecule	ribose	deoxyribose (each molecule contains one fewer oxygen atom than ribose)

Table 3.1 Differences between RNA and DNA

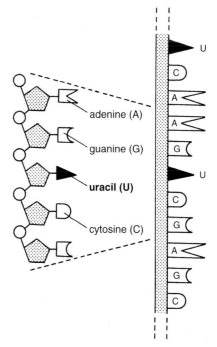

Figure 3.5 Structure of RNA

Sequence of DNA bases

The chemical components of DNA remain constant from species to species. However the DNA of one species differs from that of another in quantity and in the order in which the bases (A, T, G and C) occur along its length. It is this **sequence of bases** along the DNA strands which is unique to the organism. It contains the **genetic instructions** which control the organism's inherited characteristics.

Enzymes

Inherited characteristics are the result of many biochemical processes controlled by **enzymes**. In humans, for example, certain enzymes govern the biochemical pathways which lead to the formation of hair of a certain texture, eyes of a particular colour and so on.

Every enzyme is made of protein. Its exact molecular structure, shape and ability to carry out its function all depend on the sequence of the amino acids in its polypeptide chain(s).

This critical order is determined by the sequence of the bases in the organism's DNA. By this means DNA controls the structure of enzymes and, in doing so, determines the organism's **inherited characteristics**.

Genetic code

The information present in DNA takes the form of a molecular code language called the **genetic code**. The sequence of bases along a DNA strand represents a sequence of 'codewords'.

DNA possesses only four different bases yet proteins contain about twenty different types of amino acid. The relationship cannot be one base coding for one amino acid since this would only allow four amino acids to be coded. Even two bases per amino acid would give only sixteen (4^2) different 'codewords'.

Codon

However if the bases are taken in groups of three then this gives 64 (4^3) different combinations (see Appendix 2). It is now known that each amino acid is coded for by one (or more) of these 64 **triplets** of bases. Each triplet is called a **codon**. The codon is the basic unit of the genetic code (triplet code).

Thus a species' genetic information is encoded in its DNA with each strand bearing a series of base triplets arranged in a **specific order** for coding the particular proteins needed by that species.

Testing your knowledge

1 State THREE ways in which RNA and DNA differ in structure and chemical composition. (3)

2 In what way does the DNA of one species differ from that of another, which makes each species unique? (1)

3 What do an enzyme's structure, shape and ability to carry out its function all depend on? (1)

4 a) With reference to the relationship between the genetic code and the protein synthesised, why is it not possible that
 (i) one base corresponds to one amino acid?
 (ii) two bases correspond to one amino acid? (2)

 b) How many bases in the genetic code do correspond to one amino acid? (1)

 c) What name is given to the groups of bases that make up the genetic code? (1)

Protein synthesis

Transcription of DNA into mRNA

The genetic information carried on a section of DNA makes contact with structures responsible for protein synthesis in the cell's cytoplasm via a messenger. This go-between is called **messenger RNA** (**mRNA**) and it is formed (transcribed) from one of the DNA strands using free RNA nucleotides present in the cell's nucleus.

The process of **transcription** is illustrated in figure 3.6.

Stage 1 shows the DNA strands becoming unwound. Stage 2 is a little further ahead of stage 1. Here weak hydrogen bonds between two bases are breaking and causing the DNA strands to separate.

At stage 3, pairing of bases enables a free RNA nucleotide to find its complementary nucleotide on the DNA strand which is being transcribed. At stage 4, weak hydrogen bonds are forming between two complementary bases.

At stage 5, a little further ahead in the process, a strong chemical bond is forming between the sugar of one RNA nucleotide and the phosphate of the next one in the chain. This linking of nucleotides into a chain is controlled by an enzyme called RNA polymerase.

At stage 6, the weak hydrogen bonds between the DNA and RNA bases are breaking allowing the molecule of transcribed mRNA to become separated from the DNA template. Stage 7 shows transcribed mRNA ready to begin its journey out of the nucleus and into the cytoplasm.

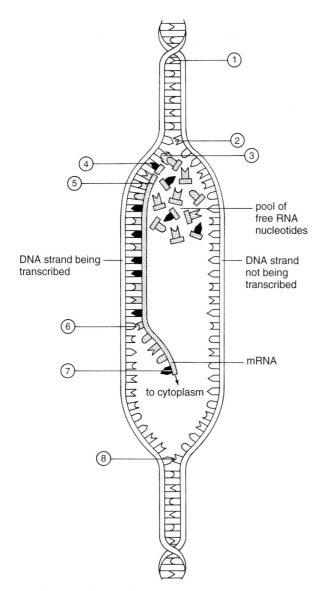

DNA strand being transcribed

pool of free RNA nucleotides

DNA strand not being transcribed

mRNA

to cytoplasm

Figure 3.6 Transcription of mRNA

At stage 8, weak hydrogen bonds between the two DNA strands reunite them and the molecule becomes wound up into a double helix once more. Although transcription of RNA has been presented as a series of stages, in reality it is a continuous process.

mRNA

The completed molecule of mRNA leaves the nucleus through a pore in the nuclear membrane and enters the cytoplasm as shown in figure 3.7. Each triplet of bases on mRNA is called a **codon**.

tRNA

A second type of RNA is found in the cell's cytoplasm. This is called **transfer RNA (tRNA)** (see figure 3.7). Each molecule of tRNA has one of its triplets of bases exposed. This triplet, known as an **anticodon**, corresponds to a particular amino acid. Each tRNA

molecule picks up the appropriate amino acid from the cytoplasm at its site of attachment. Every cell has at least twenty different types of tRNA, one for each type of amino acid.

Nucleolus

One or more **nucleoli** are found within the nucleus (see figure 3.11). These dense spherical structures are composed of RNA, DNA and protein but lack membranes. They control the synthesis of RNA and other components needed to build ribosomes. The component parts of ribosomes pass out of the nucleus through pores and become assembled in the cytoplasm.

Ribosomes

Ribosomes are small, almost spherical structures found in all cells. Some occur freely in the cytoplasm, others are found attached to the endoplasmic reticulum (see p 23).

They are the site of the **translation** of mRNA into protein. Each ribosome contains enzymes essential for the process of protein formation.

Translation of RNA into protein

A ribosome becomes attached to one end of the mRNA molecule about to be translated. Inside the ribosome there are sites for the attachment of tRNA molecules, two at a time (see figure 3.8).

This arrangement allows the **anticodon** of the first tRNA molecule to form weak hydrogen bonds with the complementary **codon** on the **mRNA**. When the second tRNA molecule repeats this process, the first two amino acid molecules are brought into line with one another. They become joined together by a strong **peptide bond** whose formation is controlled by an enzyme present in the ribosome.

The first tRNA becomes disconnected from its amino acid and from the mRNA and leaves the ribosome. The ribosome moves along the mRNA strand allowing the anticodon of the third tRNA to move into place and link with its complementary codon on the mRNA. This allows the third amino acid to become bonded to the second one and so on along the chain.

Thus the process of translation brings about the alignment of amino acids in a certain order at the ribosome, where they form a **polypeptide chain**. The completed polypeptide (normally consisting of very many amino acids) is then released into the cytoplasm.

Formation of completed protein may involve folding or rearrangement of the polypeptide chain. Sometimes a number of polypeptide chains combine to form a **protein molecule**.

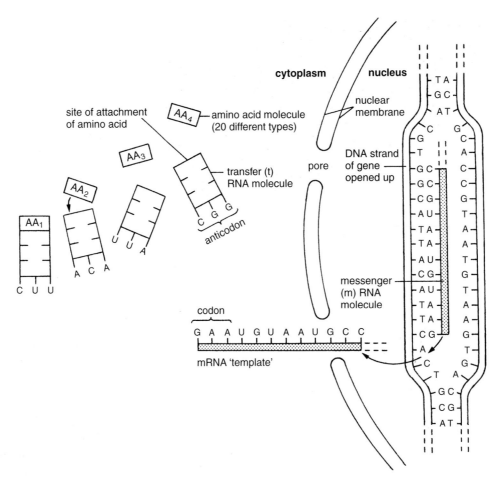

Figure 3.7 Two types of RNA

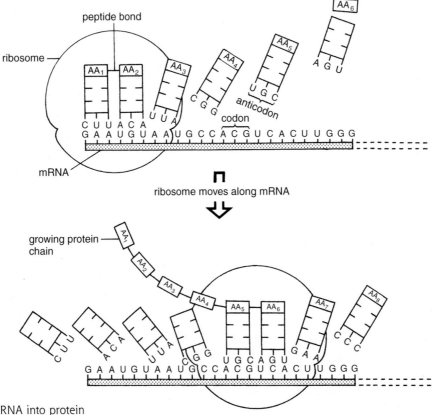

Figure 3.8 Translation of RNA into protein

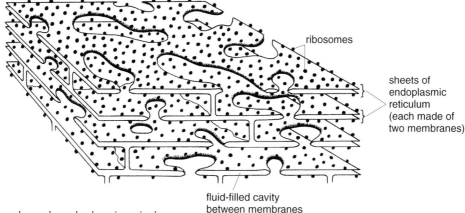

ribosomes

sheets of
endoplasmic
reticulum
(each made of
two membranes)

fluid-filled cavity
between membranes

Figure 3.9 Ribosomes and rough endoplasmic reticulum

Each tRNA molecule becomes attached to another molecule of its amino acid ready to repeat the process. The mRNA is often reused to produce further molecules of the same polypeptide.

Protein synthesised in free ribosomes is for use within the cell; protein made in ribosomes attached to the endoplasmic reticulum is for export.

Endoplasmic reticulum

Rough ER

The **rough endoplasmic reticulum (rough ER)** is illustrated in figure 3.9 and figure 3.11. It is composed of a system of flattened sacs and tubules encrusted with ribosomes on the outer surfaces of their membranes. Rough ER is continuous with the outer nuclear membrane and provides a **large surface area** upon which chemical reactions can occur. It is present throughout the cell and acts as a pathway for the transport of materials.

The rough ER is the route taken by proteins that are to be secreted by a cell. When such a protein is synthesised in a ribosome on the surface of the rough ER, the emerging polypeptide chain is 'injected' into the ER. It then undergoes the coiling and folding processes involved in the formation of the protein's specific structure. Secretory proteins are then passed on to the Golgi apparatus (see below).

Smooth ER

The **smooth endoplasmic reticulum** (see figure 3.11) lacks ribosomes. Like rough ER, it is also composed of a system of cavities and tubules, and plays various roles depending on the type of cell. For example it is the site of enzyme reactions in cells which produce steroid hormones and the site of the resynthesis of triglycerides in epithelial cells of the small intestine (see p 169).

Golgi apparatus

The **Golgi apparatus** (or Golgi body) is composed of a group of flattened fluid-filled sacs (see figure 3.10 and figure 3.11).

Vesicles (tiny fluid-filled sacs) containing newly synthesised protein become pinched off from the rough ER. These vesicles fuse with the outermost sac of the Golgi apparatus and the protein is passed from sac to sac by means of vesicles. During this time the Golgi apparatus processes the protein, for example by adding a carbohydrate part to it to make it into a glycoprotein.

Vesicles containing the finished product (e.g. mucus, digestive enzyme, hormone etc.) become pinched off at the ends of the Golgi apparatus. Figure 3.10 shows how these vesicles move towards and fuse with the cell membrane. The contents of a vesicle are then discharged to the outside. This **secretion** of intracellular products by the cell is called **exocytosis** (see p 49).

Golgi bodies are especially numerous and active in secretory cells such as the gastric gland cells in the stomach wall (which produce mucus and the enzyme pepsin) and certain cells in the pancreas (which produce the hormone insulin).

Lysosomes

The Golgi apparatus is also the source of small structures called **lysosomes** (see figure 3.11). These arise in the same way as secretory vesicles but remain within the cell. They contain digestive **enzymes** which break down worn out cell structures and play a key role in **phagocytosis** (see p 52).

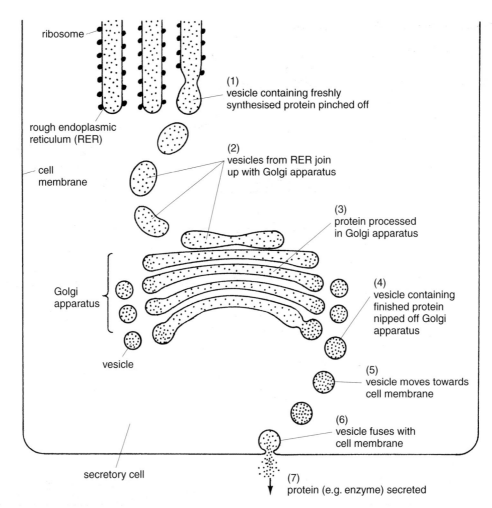

Figure 3.10 Processing and secretion of a protein

Ultrastructure of a cell

Magnification

Magnification is the apparent enlargement of an object. By magnifying material, a microscope allows structures which are invisible to the naked eye to be examined. Whereas the maximum useful magnification possible using a **light microscope** is approximately 1500 times, an **electron microscope** can achieve a useful magnification of over 500 000 times.

Electron micrograph

An image of material viewed under an electron microscope can be recorded as a black and white photograph called an **electron micrograph**. Figure 3.11, which is based on several electron micrographs, shows how the electron microscope reveals the presence in a cell of tiny structures which cannot be seen using a light microscope. Many of these specialised structures are called **organelles** and they make up the cell's **ultrastructure**. Table 3.2 gives a summary of the roles of the organelles that have featured in chapter 3.

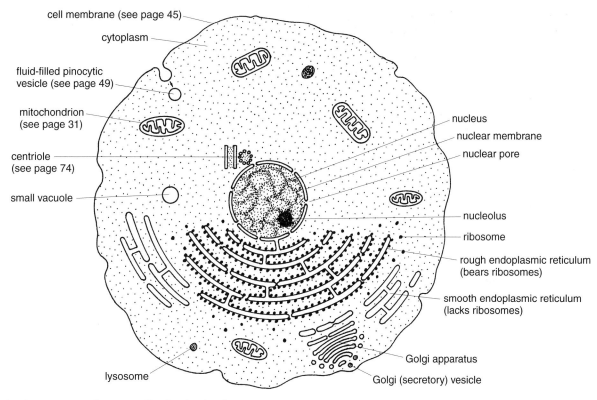

cell membrane (see page 45)

cytoplasm

fluid-filled pinocytic
vesicle (see page 49)

mitochondrion
(see page 31)

centriole
(see page 74)

small vacuole

nucleus

nuclear membrane

nuclear pore

nucleolus

ribosome

rough endoplasmic reticulum
(bears ribosomes)

smooth endoplasmic reticulum
(lacks ribosomes)

Golgi apparatus

Golgi (secretory) vesicle

lysosome

Figure 3.11 Ultrastructure of a generalised animal cell

organelle	role
nucleus	contains DNA which holds the genetic instructions for the manufacture of proteins and the control of inherited characteristics
nucleolus	controls the synthesis of RNA and other components needed to build ribosomes
ribosome	acts as site where tRNA and mRNA meet and protein is synthesised
rough endoplasmic reticulum (RER)	provides both a large surface area upon which chemical reactions can occur and a pathway for the transport of materials
smooth endoplasmic reticulum (SER)	plays various roles e.g. site of enzyme reactions that produce steroid hormones
Golgi apparatus	processes and packages complex molecules ready for discharge from the cell
Golgi vesicle	carries complex molecules to the plasma membrane for discharge
lysosome	contains enzymes that digest worn-out organelles and micro-organisms

Table 3.2 Role of cell's organelles

Testing your knowledge

1 Study figure 3.6 carefully and then answer the following questions

 a) What type of bond is breaking at stage 2? (1)

 b) Name the type of bond formed and the types of molecule involved during
  (i) stage 4;
  (ii) stage 5. (4)

 c) What happens to a molecule of transcribed mRNA? (1)

2 a) What name is given to a triplet of bases on a molecule of

 (i) mRNA;
 (ii) tRNA? (2)

 b) To what type of molecule does each tRNA triplet correspond? (1)

3 a) What name is given to the conversion of the genetic message (held by RNA) into protein? (1)

 b) What type of bond forms between adjacent amino acids brought together by their tRNAs at a ribosome? (1)

 c) What is formed as the ribosome continues to move along the mRNA molecule? (1)

Applying your knowledge

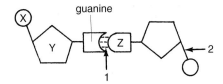

Figure 3.12

1 Figure 3.12 shows the molecular structure of two of the chemical units from which DNA is built.

 a) Name this type of basic unit from which nucleic acids are constructed. (1)

 b) Identify chemical molecules X, Y and Z. (3)

 c) Redraw the diagram and then expand it to include the bases adenine and thymine connected to the appropriate molecules. (2)

 d) Which of the numbered arrows indicates
  (i) strong chemical bonding;
  (ii) weak hydrogen bonding? (1)

 e) Name a structural feature of an inactive DNA molecule which the diagram above fails to illustrate. (1)

2 A DNA molecule is found to contain 10 000 base molecules of which 20% are thymine.

 a) What percentage of the bases are cytosine? (1)

 b) How many of the bases are adenine? (1)

3 The stages in the following list refer to the process of transcription of mRNA from DNA. Arrange them into the correct sequence starting with E. (1)

A Bases along each DNA strand become exposed.
B Adjacent RNA nucleotides become joined to one another to form mRNA.
C DNA strands become separated as hydrogen bonds break between base pairs.
D Completed molecule of mRNA becomes detached from DNA template.
E A specific region of a DNA molecule unwinds.
F Hydrogen bonds form between bases of DNA strands which then rewind.
G Each base on the DNA strand attracts its complementary base on a free RNA nucleotide.

4 Figure 3.13 shows part of a secretory cell viewed under an electron microscope.

 a) Name parts A–I. (4)

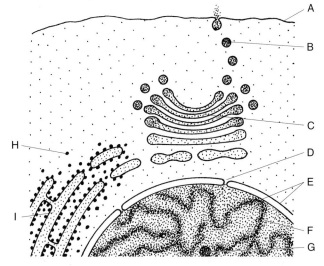

Figure 3.13

Continued ➤

Applying your knowledge

b) (i) Identify the type of chemical that would be present in B.
   (ii) State which letter indicates the site at which synthesis of this substance from its sub-units occurs. (2)

c) State the functions of structures C, G and I. (3)

5 Figure 3.14 shows the method by which the genetic code is transmitted during protein synthesis. Table 3.3 gives some of the triplets which correspond to certain amino acids.

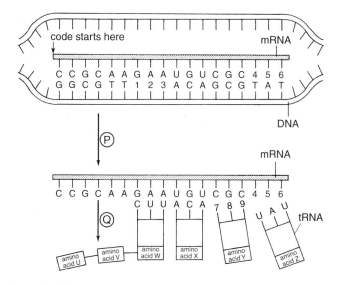

Figure 3.14

a) Identify bases 1–9. (2)

b) Name processes P and Q. (1)

c) Copy and complete table 3.3. (2)

d) Give the triplet of bases that would be exposed on a molecule of tRNA to which valine would become attached. (1)

amino acid	codon	anticodon
alanine		CGC
arginine	CGC	
cysteine		ACA
glutamic acid	GAA	
glutamine		GUU
glycine	GGC	
isoleucine		UAU
leucine	CUU	
proline		GGC
threonine	ACA	
tyrosine		AUA
valine	GUU	

Table 3.3

e) Use your table to identify amino acids U, V, W, X, Y and Z. (2)

f) (i) Work out the mRNA code for part of a polypeptide chain with the amino acid sequence: threonine-leucine-alanine-glycine. (1)
   (ii) State the genetic code on the DNA strand from which this mRNA would be formed. (1)

6 Give an account of protein synthesis under the headings:

(i) transcription; (5)
(ii) translation. (5)

What you should know
(Chapters 1–3)

(See table 3.4 for word bank.)

1 Enzymes are biological _____ which speed up the rate of a biochemical reaction. _____ enzymes work inside cells; _____ enzymes function outside cells.

2 A molecule of enzyme is composed of _____ . It has an active site which is _____ to the molecular structure of its substrate, like a lock and key.

3 To function efficiently an enzyme requires a suitable temperature, an appropriate pH and an adequate supply of _____ .

Continued ➤

What you should know
(Chapters 1–3)

4 An inhibitor is a substance that _____ or halts the rate of an enzyme-controlled reaction. A _____ inhibitor is affected by both concentration of inhibitor and concentration of substrate; a non-competitive inhibitor is affected by concentration of _____ only.

5 Many enzymes require the presence of a _____ to function properly; some enzymes are activated by other _____.

6 Each stage in a _____ pathway is controlled by an enzyme. If a genetic fault occurs, an enzyme may be absent causing an inborn _____ of metabolism.

7 In addition to carbon, hydrogen and oxygen, proteins always contain _____.

8 A protein consists of sub-units called _____ which are joined together by _____ bonds to form polypeptides.

9 A molecule of _____ protein consists of _____ chains arranged in parallel. It has a structural function.

10 A molecule of _____ protein consists of polypeptide chains folded into a spherical shape. Some are structural in function; others act as enzymes, hormones or _____.

11 A molecule of _____ protein consists of globular protein associated with a non-protein part.

12 DNA consists of two strands twisted into a double _____. Each strand is composed of _____. Each nucleotide consists of _____ sugar, phosphate and one of four types of base (_____, thymine, _____ or cytosine).

13 Adenine always pairs with _____; guanine always pairs with _____.

14 RNA consists of a single strand of nucleotides. _____ is found in place of thymine; _____ replaces deoxyribose.

15 The bases along a DNA strand take the form of a molecular language called the genetic _____. Each _____ of bases codes for a particular amino acid.

16 Messenger RNA (mRNA) is _____ from a strand of DNA and carries this genetic message from the nucleus out into the cytoplasm. At a _____ mRNA meets molecules of _____ RNA (tRNA) each carrying a specific amino acid.

17 Protein synthesis occurs in ribosomes; mRNA's triplets of bases, called _____, are 'read' and matched by tRNA's _____. This enables peptide _____ to form between adjacent amino acids.

18 Rough _____ reticulum (ER) bears ribosomes on its surface; smooth ER lacks ribosomes.

19 Freshly synthesised protein is transported via the rough ER to the _____ apparatus where it is processed and packaged into _____.

20 Some protein is _____ out of the cell by vesicles moving towards and fusing with the plasma membrane.

adenine	deoxyribose	nucleotides
amino acids	endoplasmic	peptide
antibodies	enzymes	polypeptide
anticodons	error	protein
bonds	extracellular	ribose
catalysts	fibrous	ribosome
code	globular	secreted
codons	Golgi	substrate
co-factor	guanine	thymine
competitive	helix	transcribed
complementary	inhibitor	transfer
conjugated	intracellular	triplet
cytosine	metabolic	uracil
decreases	nitrogen	vesicles

Table 3.4 Word bank for chapters 1–3

4 ATP and energy transfer

Effect of adenosine triphosphate (ATP) on muscle fibre

In the experiment shown in figure 4.1, only **ATP** is found to bring about contraction of the muscle fibres. It is therefore concluded that ATP is able to provide immediately the **energy** required for muscle contraction whereas glucose, despite being an energy-rich compound, is unable to do so.

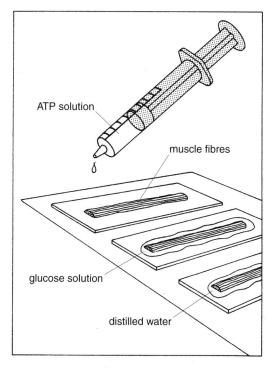

Figure 4.1 Investigating effect of ATP on muscle

Structure of ATP

A molecule of adenosine triphosphate (ATP) is composed of **adenosine** and three **inorganic phosphate** (Pi) groups as shown in figure 4.2.

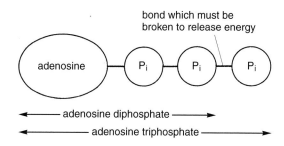

Figure 4.2 Structure of ATP

Energy stored in an ATP molecule is released when the bond attaching the terminal phosphate is broken by enzyme action. This results in the formation of adenosine diphosphate (ADP) and inorganic phosphate (Pi).

On the other hand, energy is required to regenerate ATP from ADP and inorganic phosphate by an enzyme-controlled process called **phosphorylation**.

This reversible reaction is summarised by the equation:

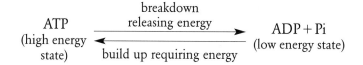

Production of ATP

When an energy-rich substance such as glucose is broken down in a living cell, it releases energy which is used to produce ATP.

When glucose is burned in a dish in the laboratory, its energy is released in one quick burst of heat and light. However, in a living cell, the breakdown of glucose during cell respiration is a **gradual** process involving many enzyme-controlled steps. This **orderly** release of energy is the ideal means by which the chemical energy needed to regenerate ATP from ADP + Pi is made available.

Role of ATP

Many molecules of ATP are present in every living cell. Since ATP can rapidly revert to ADP + Pi, it is able to make energy available for energy-requiring processes (e.g. muscular contraction, synthesis of protein and nucleic acids, active transport of molecules and transmission of nerve impulses).

ATP is important because it acts as the **link** between energy-releasing reactions and energy-consuming reactions. It provides the means by which chemical energy is transferred from one type of reaction to the other in a living cell, as shown in figure 4.3.

Since ATP breakdown is **coupled** with energy-demanding reactions, this promotes the transfer of energy to the new chemical bonds (e.g. those joining amino acids together) and helps to reduce the amount of energy that is lost as heat.

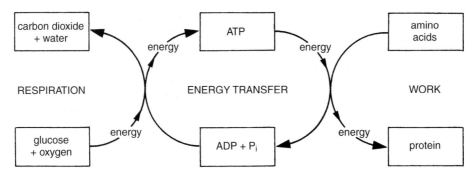

Figure 4.3 Transfer of chemical energy by ATP

Turnover of ATP molecules

It has been estimated that some active cells require approximately two million molecules of ATP per second to satisfy their energy requirements. This is made possible by the fact that a **rapid turnover** of ATP molecules constantly occurs in a cell. At any given moment some ATP molecules are undergoing breakdown and releasing the energy needed for cellular processes while others are being **regenerated** from ADP + Pi using energy released during cell respiration.

Constant quantity of ATP

In the human body a rise in level of activity by working cells (e.g. exercising muscle) leads to an increased demand being made on the supply of ATP molecules to break down and release energy. This is rapidly followed by an increase in rate of tissue respiration which produces the energy needed to regenerate the ATP that has been used up.

Since ATP is manufactured at the same rate as it is used up, there is no need for the body to possess vast stores of ATP. The quantity of ATP present in the body is found to remain fairly **constant** at about 50 g despite the fact that the body may be using up and regenerating ATP at a rate of about 400 g/hour.

Oxidation and reduction

Oxidation is the removal of electrons from a substance. In a metabolic pathway this can involve the removal of hydrogen from the substrate which is then said to have become oxidised (see figure 4.4).

Reduction is the addition of electrons to a substance. In a metabolic pathway this can involve the addition of hydrogen to the substrate which is then said to have become reduced.

Oxidation and reduction are described as **coupled reactions**. Normally an atom or molecule becomes oxidised by donating electrons (and hydrogen) to another atom or molecule which becomes reduced.

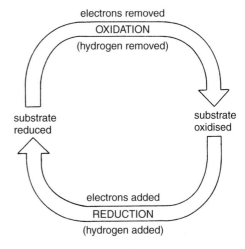

Figure 4.4 Oxidation and reduction

Chemistry of respiration

Respiration is the process by which chemical energy is released from a foodstuff by **oxidation**. It occurs in every living cell and involves the regeneration of the high energy compound ATP by a complex series of metabolic reactions.

Glycolysis

In the cytoplasm of a living cell, the process of cell respiration begins with a molecule of **6-carbon glucose** being broken down by a series of enzyme-controlled steps to form two molecules of **3-carbon pyruvic acid** (see figure 4.5).

This process of 'glucose-splitting' is called **glycolysis**. It requires energy from two molecules of ATP to activate the process but later in the pathway sufficient energy is released to form four molecules of ATP giving a **net gain of 2 ATP**.

During glycolysis, hydrogen released from the respiratory substrate becomes temporarily bound to a **co-enzyme** molecule which acts as a hydrogen acceptor. The co-enzyme involved is normally **NAD** (full name – nicotinamide adenine dinucleotide). For the sake of simplicity any co-enzyme which acts as a hydrogen acceptor in the respiratory pathway will be referred to as NAD and represented in its reduced state as $NADH_2$. At no point in the pathway does hydrogen exist as free atoms or molecules.

The process of glycolysis does not require oxygen but the hydrogen bound to a reduced co-enzyme only produces further molecules of ATP at a later stage in the process if oxygen is present. In the absence of oxygen, anaerobic respiration occurs (see p 33).

Mitochondria

When oxygen is present, **aerobic respiration** occurs in the cell's **mitochondria** (see figure 4.6).

Mitochondria are sausage-shaped organelles present in the cytoplasm of living cells. The inner membrane of each mitochondrion is folded into many plate-like extensions (**cristae**) which present a large surface area

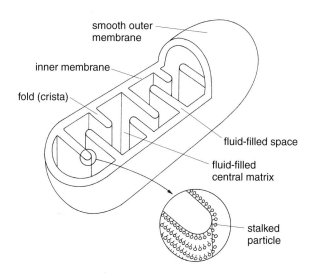

smooth outer membrane
inner membrane
fold (crista)
fluid-filled space
fluid-filled central matrix
stalked particle

Figure 4.6 Mitochondrion

upon which respiratory processes can take place. The cristae project into the fluid-filled interior (**matrix**) which contains enzymes.

Electron micrographs reveal that each crista bears many **stalked particles**. These are the site of ATP production. Cells requiring much energy such as sperm, liver, muscle and nerve cells contain numerous mitochondria which possess many cristae.

Fate of pyruvic acid

Pyruvic acid produced during glycolysis diffuses into the matrix of a mitochondrion where it is converted into a **2-carbon** compound called **acetyl co-enzyme A (acetyl CoA)**. This reaction is accompanied by the release of hydrogen which again becomes bound to NAD, the co-enzyme acting as a hydrogen acceptor.

Testing your knowledge

1 a) (i)   What substance results from the breakdown of a glucose molecule during glycolysis?
       (ii) How many molecules of ATP are gained by the cell as a result? (2)

   b) How many carbon atoms are present in a molecule of:
       (i)   pyruvic acid;
       (iii) glucose? (2)

2 a) Name the type of organelle responsible for aerobic respiration. (1)

   b) What is the fluid-filled inner cavity of this organelle called? (1)

   c) What name is given to the folded extentions of this organelle's inner membrane which present a large surface area? (1)

3 Pyruvic acid is converted to acetyl CoA on entering a mitochondrion.

   a) How many carbon atoms are present in one molecule of acetyl CoA? (1)

   b) (i)   What TWO substances are released during the breakdown of pyruvic acid?
       (ii) Which of these becomes bound to a coenzyme molecule? (3)

Krebs cycle

The Krebs cycle is the aerobic phase of respiration. It is also known as the **citric acid cycle** (and the **tricarboxylic acid cycle**).

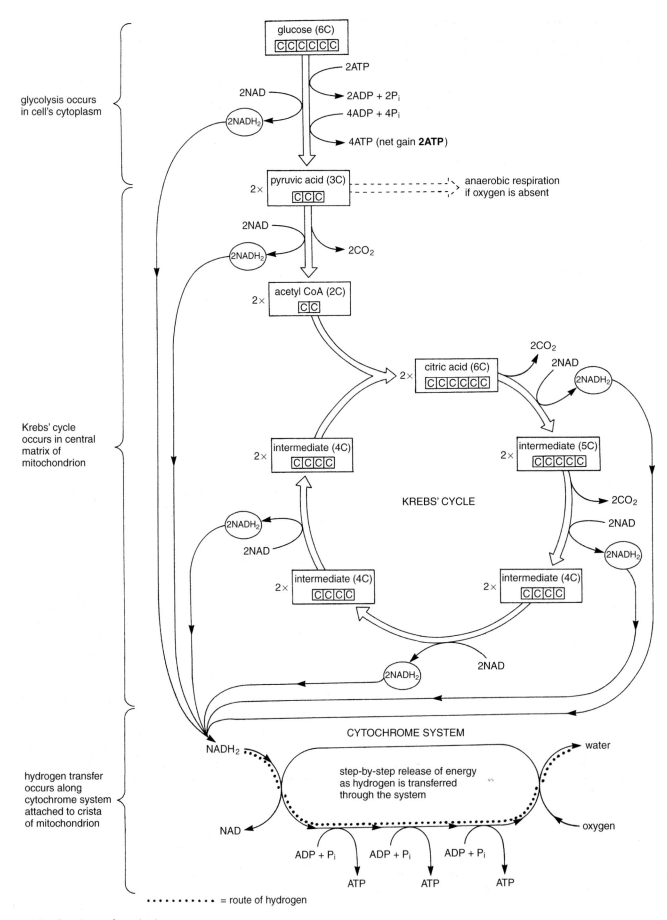

Figure 4.5 Chemistry of respiration

Each molecule of 2-carbon acetyl CoA combines with a molecule of a **4-carbon compound** present in the matrix of the mitochondrion to form **6-carbon citric acid** (which is a tricarboxylic acid). This is gradually converted back to the 4-carbon compound by a cyclic series of enzyme-controlled reactions which bring about the release of carbon (as carbon dioxide) and hydrogen from the respiratory substrate (see figure 4.5).

Enzymes controlling the release of carbon to form carbon dioxide are called **decarboxylases**. The carbon dioxide formed diffuses out of the cell as a waste product.

Enzymes controlling the release of hydrogen are called **dehydrogenases**.

Hydrogen transfer system

There are six points along the pathway where hydrogen is released and becomes temporarily bound to NAD, the co-enzyme molecule. Reduced co-enzyme ($NADH_2$) transfers hydrogen to a chain of carriers called the **cytochrome system**. Every mitochondrion possesses many of these systems attached to each of its cristae.

Transfer of hydrogen from $NADH_2$ along the cytochrome system releases sufficient energy to produce **3 ATP**. This process is called **oxidative phosphorylation**. The complete oxidation of one glucose molecule yields a total of **38 ATP** (2 ATP during glycolysis + 36 ATP during oxidative phosphorylation).

Role of oxygen

Oxygen is the final hydrogen acceptor. Hydrogen and oxygen combine under the action of the enzyme **cytochrome oxidase** to form **water**. Although oxygen only plays its part at the very end of the pathway, its presence is essential for hydrogen to pass along the cytochrome system. In the absence of oxygen, the oxidation process cannot proceed beyond glycolysis.

Electron transfer system

The cytochrome system is described above as the hydrogen transfer system. However it is more accurate to refer to it as the **electron transfer system** because strictly speaking it is electrons (from the hydrogen) that release energy while they are being transferred along the carrier system. This energy is used to regenerate ATP from ADP and Pi.

Function of aerobic respiration

Aerobic respiration (summarised in figure 4.7) is a metabolic pathway with a series of enzyme-controlled reactions by which a respiratory substrate such as 6-carbon glucose is oxidised to form carbon dioxide

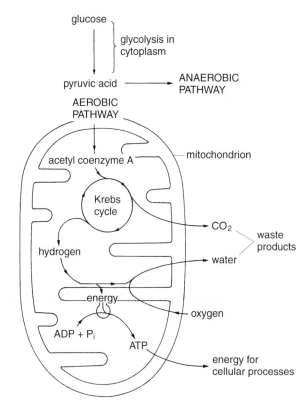

Figure 4.7 Summary of the chemistry of aerobic respiration

accompanied by the production of ATP from ADP + Pi. This **regeneration of ATP** for use in other cellular processes is the key function of respiration.

Anaerobic respiration

Anaerobic respiration is the process by which a little energy is derived from the **partial breakdown** of sugar in the absence of oxygen. Since oxygen is unavailable to the cell, the electron (hydrogen) transfer system and the Krebs cycle cannot operate in any of the cell's mitochondria. Only glycolysis can occur.

Each glucose molecule undergoes partial breakdown to pyruvic acid and yields only two molecules of ATP. The hydrogen released cannot go on to make ATP in the absence of oxygen. An alternative metabolic pathway takes place in the cell's cytoplasm. The following equation summarises this process in animal cells such as skeletal muscle tissue.

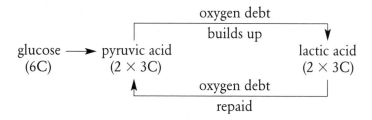

During **lactic acid** formation, the body accumulates an **oxygen debt**. This is repaid when oxygen becomes available and lactic acid is converted back to pyruvic acid which then enters the aerobic pathway.

Anaerobic respiration is a less efficient process since it produces only **2 ATP** per molecule of glucose compared with 38 ATP formed by aerobic respiration. The majority of living cells thrive on oxygen and respire aerobically. They only resort to anaerobic respiration to obtain a little energy for survival while oxygen is absent.

Testing your knowledge

1 a) How many carbon atoms are present in a molecule of citric acid? (1)

   b) In which region of a mitochondrion is citric acid formed? (1)

   c) (i)   What name is given to the cycle of reactions by which citric acid is gradually converted back to a 4-carbon compound?
       (ii) What happens to the hydrogen released during this cycle? (2)

2 a) What is the function of the cytochrome system? (1)

   b) Where is the cytochrome system located in a mitochondrion (1)

   c) Name the high-energy compound whose synthesis depends on energy released when hydrogen passes along the cytochrome system. (1)

   d) Identify the final hydrogen acceptor in the aerobic phase of respiration. (1)

3 a) With reference to oxygen, explain the difference between aerobic and anaerobic respiration. (1)

   b) State the number of ATP molecules formed from the breakdown of one glucose molecule during each type of respiration. (1)

Applying your knowledge

time (min)	length of muscle sample (mm)
0	50.0
1	48.0
2	46.5
3	44.8
4	42.3
5	40.7
6	40.7

Table 4.1

1 Table 4.1 shows the results of an experiment set up to investigate the effect of ATP solution on the length of a sample of skeletal muscle from a cow.

   a) Making the best use of a sheet of graph paper, present the data as a line graph. (2)

   b) (i)   Between which two times did decrease in length occur at the fastest rate?
       (ii) Between which two times did no decrease in length occur? (2).

   c) Give an equation to represent the chemical reaction involving ATP that occurs in the muscle cells enabling them to contract. (2)

   d) It could be argued that the muscle sample was going to decrease in length whether or not ATP was added. In what way should the experiment be altered to make the results valid? (1)

2 Metabolism (the sum of all the chemical changes that occur in a living organism) falls into two parts: **anabolism** which consists of energy-requiring reactions involving synthesis of complex molecules, and **catabolism** consisting of energy-yielding reactions in which complex molecules are broken down. **Transfer of energy** from catabolic reactions to anabolic reactions is brought about by **ATP**.

Figure 4.8 is based on the information in the above paragraph.

   a) Copy the diagram and add four arrow heads to show the directions in which the two coupled reactions occur. (2)

Continued ➤

Applying your knowledge

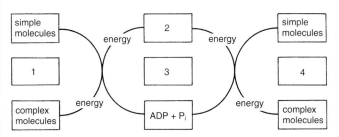

Figure 4.8

b) Complete boxes 1–4 using each of the terms given in bold print in the passage. (4)

3 Figure 4.9 shows a simplified version of the chemistry of respiration in an animal cell.

a) State the number of carbon atoms present in a molecule of each of the substances represented by boxes Q, R, S, T, U and V. (3)

b) Identify substances Q, R, S, T and W. (5)

c) The various stages in the pathway are labelled using the letters A–I.
   (i) At which of these stages is most ATP synthesised per molecule of glucose?
   (ii) Identify another stage at which ATP is also synthesised (though in a much smaller quantity).
   (iii) Which of the lettered stages occurs in the cell's cytoplasm?
   (iv) Which stages occur in the central matrix of a mitochondrion? (4)

4 Give TWO reasons why a drop in pH occurs in the skeletal muscle tissue of a human during intensive physical training. (2)

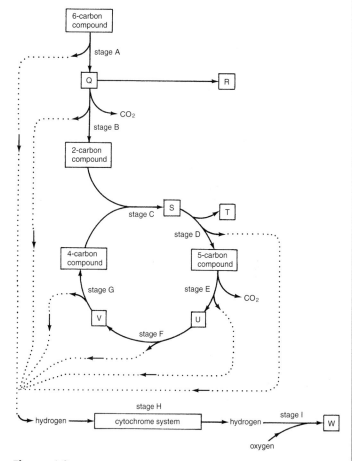

Figure 4.9

5 Sources of energy

Carbohydrates

Carbohydrates (e.g. sugar, starch and glycogen) are compounds whose molecules all contain the chemical elements **carbon** (C), **hydrogen** (H) and **oxygen** (O).

Monosaccharides

A **monosaccharide** ('single' sugar) is a simple sugar. Two examples of 6-carbon monosaccharides are **glucose** and **fructose**. Their molecular structure is often represented in a simple way as a six-sided unit (see figure 5.1).

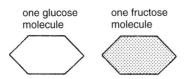

Figure 5.1 Monosaccharides

Monosaccharides are soluble in water. Many of them are described as **reducing sugars** because they have reducing properties. This means that they can donate electrons to other substances. For example, in the presence of reducing sugars, Cu^{2+} ions in Benedict's solution are reduced to Cu^+ ions giving a brick-red precipitate of copper (I) oxide.

Disaccharides

A **disaccharide** ('double' sugar) is a sugar consisting of two monosaccharide molecules joined together. Two examples are **maltose** and **sucrose** as shown in figure 5.2. Disaccharides are soluble in water.

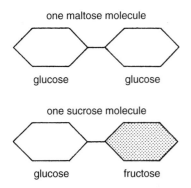

Figure 5.2 Disaccharides

Maltose is described as a reducing sugar since it has reducing properties like monosaccharides and gives a positive result when tested with Benedict's solution.

Sucrose is a **non-reducing sugar** since it does not have reducing properties. However if it is boiled with dilute acid, it becomes broken down (hydrolysed) into its component monosaccharide molecules which do have reducing properties.

Polysaccharides

A **polysaccharide** is a carbohydrate composed of many monosaccharide molecules joined together. Polysaccharide molecules are large and insoluble in water.

Starch

This polysaccharide consists of a long chain of glucose molecules (see figure 5.3). The complete molecule may contain a thousand or more monosaccharide units. The molecules of some forms of starch bear side branches. Starch is the form in which plants store carbohydrate.

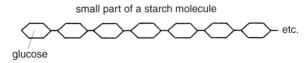

Figure 5.3 Starch – a polysaccharide

Glycogen

This polysaccharide has a molecular structure similar to the branched form of starch (see also p 171). Like starch its molecules are large and insoluble in water. This means that they cannot diffuse out of the cell and that they do not affect the cell's osmotic balance. This makes glycogen an ideal storage material. It exists as granules which are particularly abundant in human liver and muscle cells.

Energy

All of the above carbohydrates are rich sources of **energy**. Whereas a molecule of monosaccharide (e.g. glucose) is able to undergo glycolysis and enter the respiratory pathway outlined in chapter 4, disaccharides and polysaccharides must be broken down first by enzyme action to monosaccharides before they can release their energy.

Investigating the identity of an unknown carbohydrate

Great care should be taken and goggles worn when carrying out the following **tests for carbohydrates**, since several of the chemicals are potentially dangerous. Any splashes of chemicals on the skin should be washed off immediately with cold water. An appropriate control (e.g. water) should be included in each investigation.

Solubility in water test

A small sample of the carbohydrate powder is added to **water**. If it dissolves it is a monosaccharide or disaccharide sugar. If it forms a cloudy suspension and fails to become a true solution it is a polysaccharide.

Benedict's test

A few drops of **Benedict's reagent** are added to a sample of the carbohydrate solution (or suspension) and the mixture brought to the boil in a water bath. The formation of a **brick-red** (orange) precipitate indicates the presence of reducing sugar (e.g. glucose, fructose, maltose and lactose).

Acid hydrolysis

When a soluble carbohydrate fails to give a positive result with Benedict's reagent, a few drops of dilute hydrochloric **acid** are added to a fresh sample of the carbohydrate and boiled for 2–3 minutes. A few drops of Benedict's reagent are then added and the sample returned to the boil.

The formation of a brick-red precipitate indicates the presence of reducing sugar formed as a result of acid hydrolysis of the non-reducing disaccharide sucrose. It is therefore concluded that the original carbohydrate sample is sucrose.

Barfoed's test

A few drops of **Barfoed's reagent** are added to a sample of the carbohydrate solution (or suspension) and the mixture brought to the boil in a water bath. The rapid formation of a **brick-red** precipitate indicates the presence of a reducing monosaccharide sugar (e.g. glucose or fructose). A slight brick-red colour after 10–15 minutes of boiling indicates the presence of the disaccharide sugar maltose (but not lactose or sucrose).

Clinistix test

A **clinistix reagent strip** is dipped into a sample of the carbohydrate solution (or suspension). A **purple-blue** colour produced within 10 seconds indicates the presence of glucose. This is a specific test for glucose.

Iodine test

A few drops of **iodine solution** are added to a sample of the carbohydrate solution (or suspension). A **blue-black** colour indicates the presence of starch; a **purple-red** colour indicates the presence of glycogen.

Identification

Table 5.1 gives the results of these tests on seven different carbohydrates. This information can be used to construct a key as shown in figure 5.4, which then allows an unknown carbohydrate (belonging to this group of 7) to be identified. For example a white powder which is soluble in water forming a solution which fails to give a positive result with Benedict's reagent unless it has been hydrolysed by acid would be sucrose.

carbohydrate	test				
	solubility	Benedict's reagent	Barfoed's reagent	Clinistix	iodine solution
glucose	soluble	brick-red ppte	brick-red ppte rapidly	purple-blue	–
fructose	soluble	brick-red ppte	brick-red ppte rapidly	–	–
maltose	soluble	brick-red ppte	faint brick-red eventually	–	–
lactose	soluble	brick-red ppte	–	–	–
sucrose	soluble	brick-red ppte after acid hydrolysis	–	–	–
starch	insoluble	–	–	–	blue-black
glycogen	insoluble	–	–	–	purple-red

Table 5.1 Summary of results (ppte = precipitate)

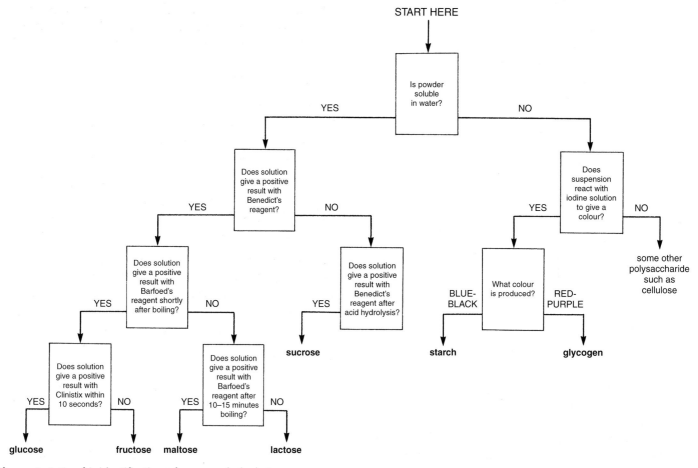

Figure 5.4 Key for identification of seven carbohydrates

Testing your knowledge

1 a) Name TWO monosaccharides. (2)

   b) Explain the meaning of the term *reducing sugar*. (2)

   c) (i) Name a disaccharide that is a non-reducing sugar.
      (ii) By what means can this sugar be broken down into its components that do have reducing properties? (2)

   d) (i) What is meant by the term *polysaccharide*?
      (ii) Give TWO examples. (3)

2 Why are carbohydrates regarded as an important part of the human diet? (1)

3 a) Describe how a solution could be tested for the presence of reducing monosaccharide sugar. (2)

   b) Describe the specific test for glucose. (2)

Lipids

The term **lipids** refers to a diverse group of organic compounds which includes simple lipids such as **fats** and **oils** and more complex substances such as **phospholipids** and **steroids**.

Like carbohydrates, lipids contain the chemical elements **carbon** (C), **hydrogen** (H) and **oxygen** (O). However the proportion of oxygen in a lipid molecule is much smaller than that in a carbohydrate. Lipids are insoluble in water.

Simple lipids

Fats (solid at room temperature) and oils (liquid at room temperature) are also known as **triglycerides** since their molecular structure consists of a molecule of glycerol combined with 3 fatty acid molecules (see figure 5.5).

Phospholipid

A typical phospholipid molecule contains two molecules of fatty acid linked to one of glycerol as before. However the third position on the glycerol molecule is occupied by a **phosphate** group (see figure 5.6).

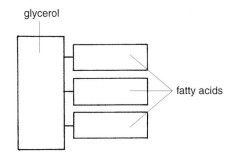

Figure 5.5 Molecule of simple lipid

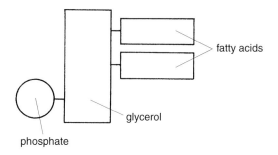

Figure 5.6 Molecule of phospholipid

The two ends of a molecule of phospholipid possess different properties. The phosphate ('head') end of the molecule is **hydrophilic** ('water-loving') and therefore soluble in water. The fatty acid ('tail') end of the molecule is **hydrophobic** ('water-hating') and therefore insoluble in water. This is summarised in figure 5.7 which shows a simpler way of representing a phospholipid molecule.

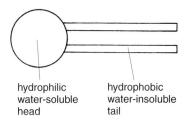

Figure 5.7 Simplified diagram of phospholipid

Steroids

Although steroids are classified as lipids, they have a completely different structure from simple lipids and phospholipids. Each molecule of a steroid has a basic structure composed of three 6-carbon rings joined to one 5-carbon ring (see figure 5.8).

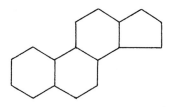

Figure 5.8 Basic structure of a steroid

Cholesterol is an example of a steroid. It provides the basic molecular structure from which other steroids such as **bile** and **sex hormones** are formed.

Roles of lipids

Energy store

Fat is deposited in fatty (adipose) tissue (see p 172). Like glycogen, it is insoluble in water and structurally compact making it a convenient form in which to store **energy**.

When required to release its energy, a molecule of fat (triglyceride) is broken down by enzyme action into glycerol and fatty acids which become available for use in aerobic respiration by liver, muscle and other tissues.

Glycerol becomes converted into a 3-carbon sugar and then into pyruvic acid (see figure 5.9). Pyruvic acid enters a mitochondrion and generates ATP in the normal way. Each molecule of **fatty acid** is broken down into many molecules of acetyl CoA in the matrix of a mitochondrion. Acetyl CoA enters the Krebs cycle and produces ATP as before.

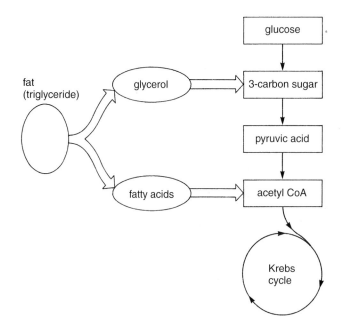

Figure 5.9 Fat as a respiratory substrate

Fat liberates more than double the quantity of energy released by the same mass of carbohydrate. Each part of the biochemical pathway represented by a white arrow in figure 5.9 can be reversed and therefore excessive intake of glucose is stored as fat.

Thermal and nerve insulation

In addition to acting as a site of food storage, the layer of subcutaneous fat beneath the dermis of the skin serves as an **insulator** and helps to conserve body heat.

39

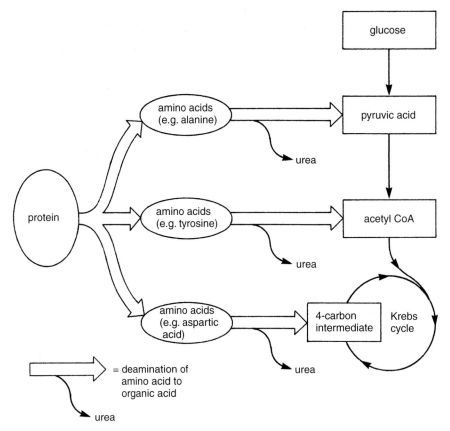

Figure 5.10 Protein as a respiratory substrate

The sheath around each nerve fibre (see p 218) consists of fatty material called **myelin** which acts as a layer of insulation and greatly increases the speed at which nerve impulses can be transmitted along a nerve fibre.

Fat pads

Pads of fat in the palms of the hands and soles of the feet protect underlying structures by acting as **cushions**. The kidneys are also protected and supported by fat pads.

Vitamin transport

Vitamins A, D, E and **K** are fat-soluble. Their absorption from the alimentary canal depends on the presence of bile salts. They are incorporated into **micelles** (see p 168) along with digested fat and passed into the lymphatic system. Lipoproteins bring about the **transport** of lipids and fat-soluble vitamins in lymph and blood plasma.

Hormones

The **sex hormones** testosterone, oestrogen and progesterone are steroids. Their roles are described in chapter 15.

Major components of plasma membrane

Phospholipids are one of the basic building blocks of **cell membranes** (see p 44). The steroid cholesterol is also an important component of membranes.

Proteins

Proteins in the diet are broken down to their component amino acids by the action of digestive enzymes. Amino acids in excess of the body's requirements for protein synthesis cannot be stored. They undergo **deamination** (see p 175) forming urea and organic acids such as pyruvic acid and Krebs cycle intermediates. These acids then enter the biochemical pathway (see figure 5.10) and act as respiratory substrates regenerating ATP in the usual way. A certain amount of energy is always derived from **excess dietary protein**.

Starvation

Tissue protein is used as a source of energy only during prolonged starvation when reserves of glycogen and fat have become exhausted. Skeletal muscle and other tissues rich in protein are used up to provide energy during the crisis. The person becomes emaciated and death soon follows.

Marathon running

The foods used in this lengthy athletic event (49.195 km) are glucose, glycogen and fat (triglyceride) as shown in figure 5.11.

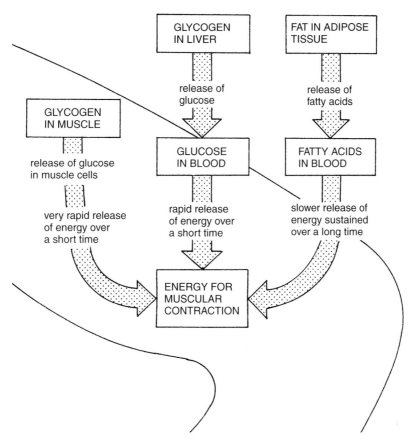

Figure 5.11 Fuelling a marathon

During the first few minutes of the race, readily available glucose from **muscle glycogen** is the main fuel used to generate energy. However, as the race continues and rate of blood flow increases, **blood-borne** fuels carried to the exercising muscles become the dominant sources of energy. Blood glucose (largely from liver glycogen) and slower-acting fatty acids provide most of the energy over the next 30 minutes or so. In the later stages of the race, **fatty acids** become increasingly important as supplies of glucose decrease.

A marathon runner therefore depends on a combination of carbohydrate and fat. The relative contribution made by each fuel depends on availability. The athlete may decide to 'load up' with carbohydrate during pre-race meals. He or she may consume an **approved refreshment** of glucose solution after 11 km and thereafter at intervals of 5 km. Under these circumstances the degree of dependency on fat reserves is greatly reduced.

● Testing your knowledge ●

1 a) (i)   Draw a diagram of a molecule of simple lipid.
       (ii) Explain why this substance is also known as a triglyceride. (3)

   b) Draw a diagram of a molecule of phospholipid to illustrate the ONE way in which it differs from that of a simple lipid (2).

2 a) Name TWO steroids that are formed from cholesterol. (2)

   b) Which releases more energy per unit mass, glucose or lipid? (1)

3 Name an organic acid resulting from deamination of an amino acid that can act as a respiratory substrate. (1)

4 During marathon running, which class of food is the main source of fuel:
   (i)   at the start;
   (ii) towards the end of the race? (2)

Applying your knowledge

test	heat or no heat	result when test is positive	carbohydrate present
solubility in water			
Benedict's reagent		brick-red ppte	
acid hydrolysis + Benedict's reagent			sucrose
Barfoed's reagent	heat		
Clinistix			
iodine solution			starch
		purple-red	

Table 5.2 (ppte = precipitate)

1 Copy and complete table 5.2 which refers to various tests used to identify carbohydrates. (8)

2 **a)** With reference to the key in figure 5.4, identify the carbohydrate which is found to
   (i) be insoluble in water and react with iodine solution giving a purple-red colour;
   (ii) give a positive result with Benedict's reagent without needing acid hydrolysis, dissolve in water and give a positive result to Barfoed's test after 15 minutes. (2)

   b) Describe the procedure that should be followed to demonstrate that a given sample of sugar is the monosaccharide fructose. (4)

3 Figure 5.12 shows a simplified version of the relationship between carbohydrate and two other classes of foodstuff which can act as alternative sources of energy.

   a) Identify blanks 1–5. (5)

   b) Which class of food cannot be stored by the human body in its original chemical form? (1)

   c) Which class of food is stored in adipose tissue? (1)

   d) Which class of food is richest in energy? (1)

   e) A person can survive for many days in the total absence of food. How is this possible? (2)

4 The data in table 5.3 refer to a man about to run a marathon.

   a) The man's average energy expenditure during the race was found to be 105 kJ per minute. Calculate how long each fuel would have lasted if it had been the only fuel used during the event. (4)

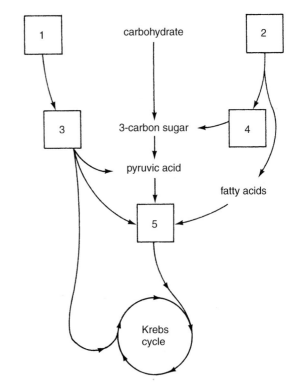

Figure 5.12

   b) The man took 180 minutes to complete the race.
   (i) Which food on its own could have easily fuelled the whole race?
   (ii) Why then is there any need for muscle glycogen to be available as a fuel? (2)

5 Give an account of the varied roles played by lipids within the human body. (10)

Continued ➤

Applying your knowledge

fuel	location	mass of fuel (g)	total energy contained in fuel (kJ)
triglyceride	adipose tissue	10 000	378 000
glycogen	liver	93.75	1575
glycogen	muscle	350	5880
glucose	bloodstream	6.25	105

Table 5.3

What you should know
(Chapters 4–5)

(See table 5.4 for word bank.)

1 ATP is a high _____ compound which is able to release and _____ chemical energy when it is required for cellular processes.

2 ATP is regenerated from ADP and inorganic _____ by the process of _____ using energy released during respiration.

3 The quantity of ATP in the body remains fairly _____ since ATP is manufactured at the same rate as it is used up.

4 _____ is the removal of electrons (and hydrogen) from a substance; _____ is the addition of electrons (and hydrogen) to a substance.

5 _____ is a biochemical pathway common to aerobic and anaerobic respiration. It involves the breakdown of glucose to _____ in the _____ of a cell with the net gain of 2 ATP.

6 In the presence of oxygen, aerobic _____ occurs in the central _____ of mitochondria where the respiratory substrate is oxidised during the _____ cycle and hydrogen is released.

7 The hydrogen becomes temporarily bound to _____ which transfers it to the cytochrome system on the _____ of mitochondria where energy is released and used to form ATP.

8 As a result of _____ respiration, one molecule of glucose yields 38 ATP. _____ and CO_2 are the final metabolic products.

9 In the absence of oxygen, _____ respiration occurs and one molecule of glucose yields 2 ATP with _____ as the metabolic product.

10 Carbohydrates are composed of _____, hydrogen and _____. They are rich in energy.

11 Monosaccharides and _____ are soluble carbohydrates of relatively small molecular size; _____ are _____ carbohydrates of large molecular size.

12 Lipids (fats) are also composed of carbon, hydrogen and oxygen. They act as a _____ of energy. Fat liberates more than _____ the energy released by an equal mass of carbohydrate.

13 Lipid provides thermal and nerve _____. Pads of fat on hands and feet act as _____. Fats aid the transport of fat-soluble _____. Steroid hormones are composed of fat-related molecules.

14 Excess _____ protein provides the body with some of its energy; _____ protein is not a source of energy except during prolonged _____.

aerobic	energy	polysaccharides
anaerobic	glycolysis	pyruvic acid
carbon	insoluble	reduction
co-enzyme	insulation	respiration
constant	Krebs	starvation
cristae	lactic acid	store
cushions	matrix	tissue
cytoplasm	oxidation	transfer
dietary	oxygen	vitamins
disaccharides	phosphate	water
double	phosphorylation	

Table 5.4 Word bank for chapters 4–5

6 Cell membrane and transport of materials

All living cells are surrounded by a thin boundary called a **cell membrane** (plasma membrane) which regulates the flow of materials into and out of the cell.

Cell **organelles** (e.g. nucleus, mitochondria, Golgi apparatus and lysosomes – see page 52) are also bounded by membranes. Exceptions to this rule are nucleoli and ribosomes.

Investigating the chemical nature of the cell membrane

The cell sap present in the central vacuole of a beetroot cell (see figure 6.1) contains red pigment. 'Bleeding' (the escape of this red sap from a cell) indicates that the cell's plasma and vacuolar membranes have been damaged.

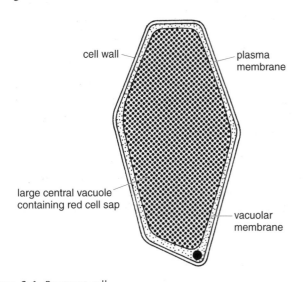

Figure 6.1 Beetroot cell

In the experiment shown in figure 6.2, four identical cylinders of fresh beetroot are prepared using a cork borer. The cylinders are thoroughly washed in distilled water to remove traces of red cell sap from outer damaged cells. The figure shows the results of subjecting the cylinders to various conditions.

Bleeding is found to occur in B, C and D showing that the membranes have been destroyed. Molecules of protein are known to become denatured when exposed to acid or high temperatures. Molecules of lipid are known to be soluble in alcohol.

It is therefore concluded that the cell membrane contains **protein** (as indicated by B and D whose denatured protein has allowed red cell sap to leak out) and **lipid** (as indicated by C whose lipid molecules

have dissolved in alcohol permitting the pigment to escape).

Structure of the plasma membrane

The plasma membrane is now known to consist of **protein** and **phospholipid** molecules. Although the precise arrangement of these molecules is still unknown, most evidence supports the **fluid mosaic model** of cell membrane structure (see figure 6.3). This proposes that the plasma membrane consists of a fluid bilayer of constantly moving phospholipid molecules containing a patchy mosaic of protein molecules.

Phospholipid bilayer

One end of a **phospholipid** molecule is **hydrophilic** and the other end is **hydrophobic** (see p 39). In the company of other similar molecules, phospholipid molecules arrange themselves into a bilayer.

The **water-soluble** hydrophilic heads (see figure 6.3) make up the two outside surfaces of the bilayer where they form hydrogen bonds with water molecules. One layer of heads forms the outside of the cell membrane in contact with extracellular fluid and the other layer forms

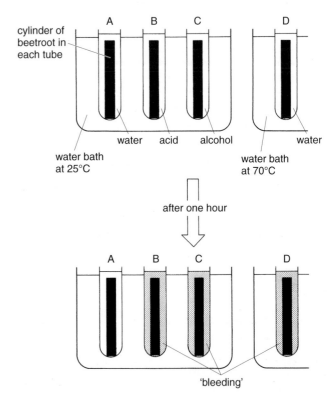

Figure 6.2 Investigating the chemical nature of the cell membrane

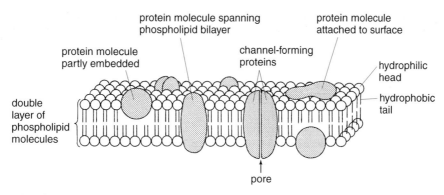

protein molecule spanning
phospholipid bilayer

protein molecule
partly embedded

channel-forming
proteins

protein molecule
attached to surface

hydrophilic
head

hydrophobic
tail

double
layer of
phospholipid
molecules

pore

Figure 6.3 Fluid mosaic model of plasma membrane

the inside of the membrane in contact with the intracellular fluid.

The **water-insoluble** hydrophobic tails point inward to the centre of the bilayer since they are attracted to those in the opposite layer.

The steroid **cholesterol** is also a component of the plasma membrane. For the sake of simplicity it has been omitted from the diagram but its molecules are envisaged as being interspersed amongst the hydrophobic tails of the phospholipids.

This arrangement of phospholipid molecules is **fluid** yet at the same time it forms a **stable** and effective **boundary** round the cell. It allows tiny molecules such as water to pass through it rapidly. Larger molecules such as glucose depend on the membrane's protein molecules for entry to or exit from the cell.

Proteins

The **protein** molecules in the plasma membrane vary in size and structure. Some extend partly into the phospholipid layer while others extend across it from one side to the other. Some of these enclose narrow channels making the membrane porous. The fluid nature of the membrane allows some movement of proteins.

The protein molecules also vary in function in that they:

◆ provide structural **support**;

◆ contain **channels** allowing transport of small molecules through the membrane;

◆ act as **carriers** which actively 'pump' molecules across the membrane;

◆ serve as **enzymes** catalysing biochemical reactions in and on the membrane;

◆ act as **receptors** for hormones arriving at the outer surface of the membrane;

◆ serve as **antigenic markers** which identify the cell's blood or tissue type.

Membrane systems within a cell

The membranes possessed by the cell's various organelles (see page 25) tend to vary from one another in function and arrangement.

The nucleus, for example, has a double membrane perforated by pores which allow the exit of mRNA for protein synthesis. The inner membrane of a mitochondrion is convoluted giving it a large surface area upon which the biochemical processes of aerobic respiration can occur. The membranes of the endoplasmic reticulum and Golgi apparatus become pinched off releasing vesicles containing protein. The membrane round a lysosome isolates digestive enzymes until they are required.

Despite this diversity of function, all of these membranes have the same basic structure as the plasma membrane and operate as **selective barriers**, each contributing in its own way to the integrated working of the cell.

Constant cell environment

For a cell to function efficiently, its internal environment must remain fairly **constant** with respect to the concentration of water and soluble substances present in its cytoplasm.

If, for example, carbon dioxide produced during respiration continued to build up in concentration, the cell's pH would drop and many intracellular enzymes would fail to catalyse the biochemical pathways upon which life depends.

Similarly if oxygen continued to be used up without being replenished, the cell would eventually be unable to respire aerobically.

A constant environment is successfully maintained within the cell by the cell membrane **regulating** the entry and exit of materials as required. It does this by allowing **selective communication** between intracellular and extracellular environments.

45

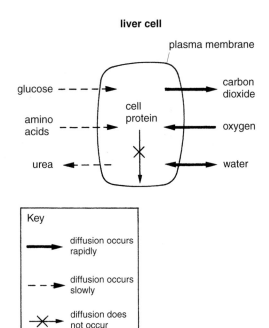

Figure 6.4 Diffusion into and out of a cell

Modes of transport

The movement of small molecules or ions (electrically charged particles) into or out of a cell normally occurs as a result of **diffusion, osmosis** or **active transport** depending upon the nature of the substance involved. In addition some cells engulf and take in large molecules by **endocytosis**; others discharge secretory products by **exocytosis**.

Diffusion

Diffusion is the net movement of molecules or ions from a region of high concentration to a region of low concentration of that type of molecule or ion.

The difference that exists between two regions before diffusion occurs is called the **concentration gradient**. During diffusion, molecules and ions always move along a concentration gradient from a high to a low concentration.

Diffusion is a basic cell process which is **passive** (does not require energy). It is the means by which useful substances such as oxygen enter a cell, and waste materials such as carbon dioxide leave it.

Role of plasma membrane in diffusion

The plasma membrane possesses very tiny pores (see figure 6.3) and is freely permeable to small molecules such as oxygen, carbon dioxide and water. However it is not equally permeable to all substances. This is shown in figure 6.4 which illustrates diffusion in a liver cell. Larger molecules such as urea, amino acids and glucose diffuse through it more slowly. Even larger molecules such as protein are unable to pass through by diffusion. The plasma membrane is said therefore to be **selectively permeable**.

Osmosis

Osmosis is the net movement of water molecules from a region of higher water concentration (HWC) to a region of lower water concentration (LWC) through a selectively permeable membrane.

Role of plasma membrane in osmosis

Whenever a cell is in contact with a solution of differing water concentration, osmosis occurs. This is made possible by the fact that the plasma membrane is selectively permeable. It allows the rapid movement of water molecules through it (but only allows larger molecules to move across slowly or not at all). The direction in which net movement of water molecules occurs depends upon the water concentration of the liquid in which the cell is immersed compared with that of the cell contents.

Osmosis in red blood cells

When red blood cells are placed in **water**, osmosis occurs causing net movement of water molecules from the region of higher water concentration (outside the cell) to the region of lower water concentration (the cell cytoplasm). This results in the cells **bursting** (see figure 6.5).

When red blood cells are placed in salt solution with a **lower** water concentration than that of the cell contents, osmosis brings about net movement of water molecules out of the cells causing them to **shrink**.

When red blood cells are placed in salt solution that is **isotonic** (of equal water concentration) to their

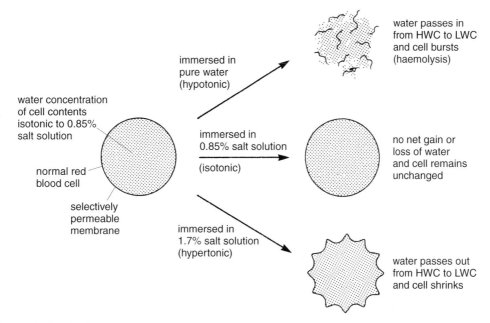

Figure 6.5 Osmosis in a red blood cell

cytoplasm, they remain **unaltered**. Movement of water molecules into the cell exactly equals their movement in the opposite direction and no net gain or loss occurs. This is the situation that exists in the body where blood plasma is isotonic to the cytoplasm of red blood cells.

It is essential that the water (and solute) concentration of blood plasma and body cells is maintained at the same steady state so that the body is not damaged by cells shrinking or bursting.

Active transport

Active transport is the movement of molecules or ions across the plasma membrane from a low to a high concentration i.e. against a concentration gradient.

Active transport works in the opposite direction to the passive process of diffusion and requires **energy**.

Consider the two situations shown in figure 6.6. Ion type A is being actively transported into the cell whereas ion type B is being actively transported out of the cell.

Role of plasma membrane in active transport

Recent studies suggest that certain protein molecules present in the plasma membrane act as **carrier** molecules. These protein molecules 'recognise' specific ions and transfer them across the plasma membrane (see figure 6.7). The energy required for this active process is supplied by **ATP** formed during respiration.

Sodium/potassium pump

Active transport carriers are often called '**pumps**'. Some carrier molecules have a dual role in that they **exchange** one type of ion for another. An example of this is the

sodium/potassium pump. The same carrier molecule (an enzyme that converts ATP to ADP + Pi) actively pumps sodium ions out of the cell and potassium ions into the cell each against its concentration gradient. The resulting difference in ionic concentrations maintained by the pump is especially important for the functioning of nerve cells.

Conditions required for active transport

Factors such as **temperature**, availability of **oxygen** and concentration of **respiratory substrate** (e.g. glucose)

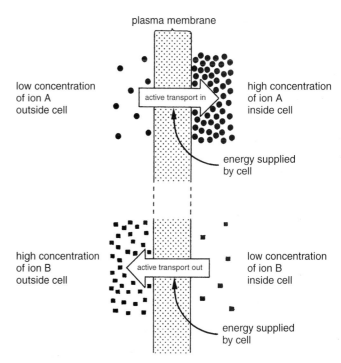

Figure 6.6 Active transport of two different ions

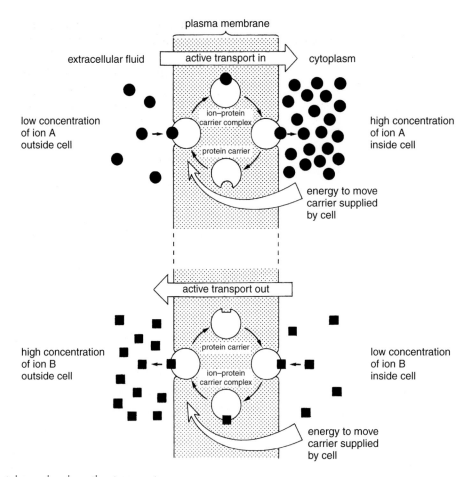

Figure 6.7 Role of protein carriers in active transport

which directly affect a cell's respiration rate also affect the rate of active transport.

Figures 6.8 and 6.9 show the effects of increasing temperature and oxygen concentration on the rate of active uptake of a type of ion by living cells.

Increase in temperature brings about an increase in ion uptake until, at high temperatures, enzymes become denatured and the cell dies.

Increase in oxygen concentration results in increased rate of ion uptake until some other factor such as sugar (the respiratory substrate) becomes limiting and makes the rate of ion uptake level off.

Gross movements of the cell membrane

Membrane transport systems involving proteins can cope adequately with the transport of relatively small

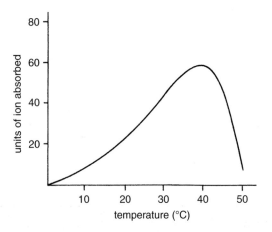

Figure 6.8 Effect of temperature on ion uptake

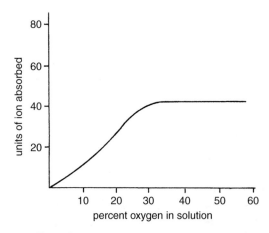

Figure 6.9 Effect of oxygen concentration on ion uptake

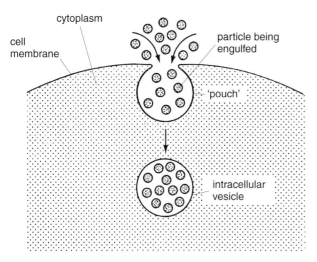

Figure 6.10 Endocytosis

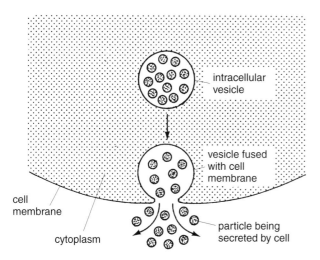

Figure 6.11 Exocytosis

particles such as ions and molecules into and out of the cell. However there are some occasions when the cell needs to take in or pass out large particles. Such movements are beyond the scope of the protein transport systems; they require **gross movements** of the whole membrane.

Endocytosis

Endocytosis is the process by which a cell engulfs and takes in relatively large particles or quantities of material. This involves the plasma membrane folding inwards to form a 'pouch' (see figure 6.10). When this becomes closed off and detached from the cell membrane, it is called an **intracellular vesicle**.

There are two types of endocytosis. The engulfing of large solid particles (e.g. bacteria by white blood cells) is called **phagocytosis** ('cell-eating'). The contents of the vesicle are then digested (see p 52). The formation of small liquid-filled vesicles by the cell membrane is called **pinocytosis** ('cell-drinking'). Endocytosis is the means by which a cell often acquires hormones, lipids and proteins.

Exocytosis

Exocytosis is the reverse of endocytosis. Vesicles formed inside the cell fuse with the plasma membrane (see figure 6.11) allowing their contents to be expelled from the cell. By this means intracellular products such as enzymes, glycoproteins, hormones and chemotransmitters can be secreted by the cell.

Testing your knowledge

3 Decide whether each of the following statements is true or false and then use T or F to indicate your choice. Where a statement is false, give the word that should have been used in place of the word in bold print. (5)

a) Molecules of carbon dioxide move out of a respiring cell by **diffusion**.

b) The carrier molecules that pump ions across a membrane are made of **phospholipid**.

c) Red blood cells **shrink** when placed in concentrated salt solution.

d) Phagocytosis and pinocytosis are two examples of **exocytosis**.

e) During **osmosis**, energy is needed to move molecules against a concentration gradient.

Applying your knowledge

1 Figure 6.12 shows a possible arrangement of the molecules in a plasma membrane.

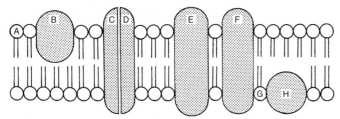

Figure 6.12

a) What name is given to this model? (1)

b) Identify molecule types A and B. (2)

c) (i) Which lettered structures enclose a narrow channel?
   (ii) What is the function of such a channel? (2)

2 Figure 6.13 shows the direction of movement of two different substances through the plasma membrane of an animal cell.

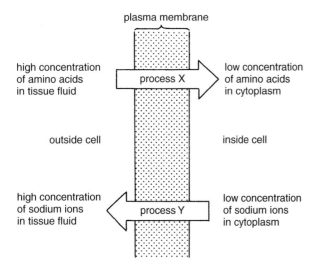

Figure 6.13

a) (i) Name process X and Y.
   (ii) Which of these processes requires energy?
   (iii) Which process will be unaffected by a decrease in oxygen concentration in the cell's environment? (4)

b) (i) Predict what will happen to the rate of process Y if the temperature of the cell is reduced to 4 °C for several hours.
   (ii) Give a reason for your answer. (2)

3 It is possible that some protein carrier molecules actively transport materials by rotating within the plasma membrane. Starting with A, arrange the stages shown in figure 6.14 to give the correct sequence in which this would occur. (1)

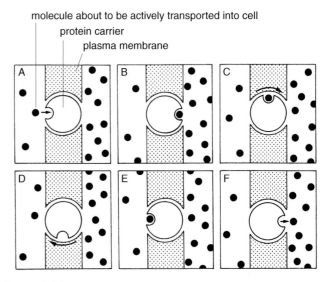

Figure 6.14

Continued ➤

Applying your knowledge

ion	concentration (mmol/l)		relative size of ion compared with potassium
	intracellular	extracellular	
potassium	137.5	2.5	1
sodium	13.0	104.0	1.47
chloride	3.0	90.0	0.96

Table 6.2

4 The data in table 6.2 refer to ions present inside and outside muscle cells in the body of an amphibian.

The graph in figure 6.15 represents the results of an experiment set up to investigate the effect of oxygen concentration on uptake of potassium ions and consumption of sugar by muscle cells in a tissue culture.

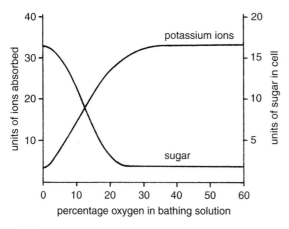

Figure 6.15

a) Identify the region of
  (i) high sodium concentration;
  (ii) low sodium concentration;
  (iii) high potassium concentration;
  (iv) low potassium concentration.
  (v) Explain how these differences in ionic concentration are maintained. (3)

b) By how many more times is the concentration of potassium inside a cell greater than that outside? (1)

c) Which type of ion will tend to diffuse into the cell more rapidly? Explain your answer. (1)

d) In what way does the data support the theory that a plasma membrane is selective with respect to the active transport of ions out of the cell? (2)

e) (i) From the graph in figure 6.15, state the effect that an increase in oxygen concentration from 0 to 30% has on the rate of ion uptake. (1)
  (ii) Suggest why ion uptake levels off beyond 30% oxygen. (1)
  (iii) What relationship exists between units of ion absorbed and units of sugar remaining in the cell? Suggest why. (1)

5 Give an account of the functions of phospholipids and proteins within a cell membrane. (10)

7 Cellular response in defence

Immunity is the ability of the body to resist infection by a disease-causing organism (pathogen) or to overcome the organism if it succeeds in invading and infecting the body. Immunity can be **innate** or **acquired**.

Innate immunity

This form of immunity is **inborn** and **unchanging**. It is comprised of several non-specific defence mechanisms including:

◆ presence of skin acting as effective barrier;

◆ lethal effect of stomach acid on pathogens;

◆ lethal effect of lysozyme (enzyme in tears) on bacteria;

◆ production of interferon which helps to prevent the multiplication of viruses;

◆ phagocytosis.

Phagocytosis ('cell-eating')

This is the process by which foreign bodies such as bacteria are engulfed and destroyed. Examples of phagocytic cells are **monocytes** (a type of white blood cell) and **macrophages** (large cells derived from monocytes). Macrophages are found throughout the body in the connective tissue (cellular and fibrous 'background' material in which specialised structures such as nerves and blood vessels are embedded).

The process of phagocytosis is illustrated in figure 7.1. A phagocytic cell detects chemicals released by a bacterium and moves along a concentration gradient (from low to high) towards it. The phagocyte adheres to the bacterium and engulfs it in a vacuole formed by an in-folding of the cell membrane.

A phagocyte's cytoplasm contains a rich supply of organelles called **lysosomes** which contain digestive enzymes. Some of these lysosomes fuse with the vacuole and release their enzymes into it. The bacterium becomes digested and the breakdown products are absorbed by the phagocyte.

During infection hundreds of phagocytes migrate to the infected area and engulf many bacteria by phagocytosis. Dead bacteria and phagocytes often accumulate at a site of injury forming **pus**.

Large numbers of macrophages are also found in the liver, spleen and lymph nodes. They are fixed to the inside lining of channels within these organs and are

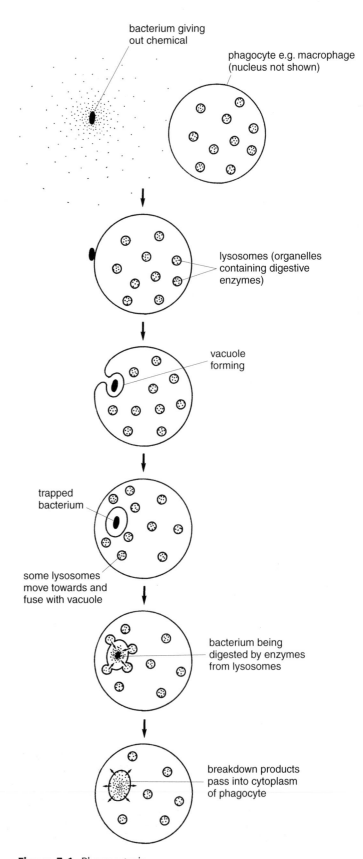

Figure 7.1 Phagocytosis

immobile. However they operate in exactly the same way as mobile phagocytes by removing foreign bodies from passing blood or lymph by phagocytosis.

Acquired immunity

This form of immunity is **acquired** (naturally or artificially) during the person's lifetime. It depends on the action of antibodies to combat antigens.

Antigens and antibodies

An **antigen** is a complex molecule such as a protein or polysaccharide which is recognised as alien by the body's **lymphocytes** (a type of white blood cell). The antigen's presence stimulates lymphocytes to produce special protein molecules called antibodies.

An **antibody** is a Y-shaped molecule as shown in figure 7.2. Each of its arms bears a **receptor (binding) site** which is specific to a particular antigen. The human body possesses thousands of different types of lymphocyte each capable of responding to one specific antigen and producing the appropriate antibody.

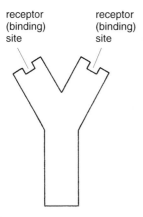

receptor (binding) site   receptor (binding) site

Figure 7.2 Antibody

Naturally acquired immunity

T cells and B cells

Lymphocytes are derived originally from unspecialised cells in the bone marrow. Some of them pass to the thymus (a gland in the lower neck) and to the lymph nodes where they produce self-replacing colonies. Lymphocytes from the thymus are called **T-lymphocytes** (T cells); the others are called **B-lymphocytes** (B cells).

Action of B-lymphocytes

When B cells are stimulated by the presence of an antigen (e.g. a virus whose coat of protein acts as an antigen) they multiply rapidly. Some become memory cells (see below); others mass produce the required antibody. The antibodies pass into lymph and blood plasma and combine at their receptor sites with the antigen rendering it harmless (see figure 7.3). The mobilisation of free cell products (antibodies) to deal with foreign material is called the **humoral response**.

Action of T-lymphocytes

When a human cell becomes infected by a micro-organism, microbial proteins released inside the host cell may move to the cell's surface and act as antigens. These are recognised by a type of T-lymphocyte known as a **killer T cell**. Killer T cells destroy the infected cell by coming into direct contact with it and releasing a chemical which perforates the cell membrane (see figure 7.4).

The mobilisation of killer T cells to deal directly with foreign material is called the **cell-mediated response**. This type of T cell also acts against cancer cells and brings about rejection of transplanted tissue.

A second type of T-lymphocyte is known as a **helper T cell**. These do not kill pathogens directly. However they are important because they patrol the body and, on recognising alien antigens on the surfaces of viruses, they activate B cells, killer T cells and macrophages.

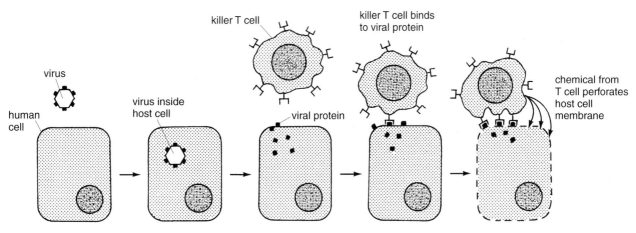

killer T cell

killer T cell binds to viral protein

chemical from T cell perforates host cell membrane

virus

human cell

virus inside host cell

viral protein

Figure 7.4 Action of killer T cells

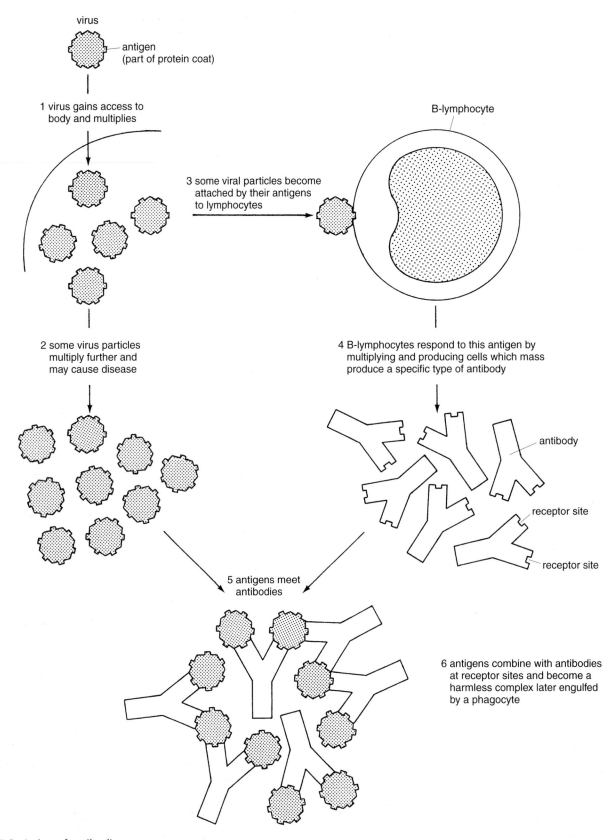

virus

antigen
(part of protein coat)

1 virus gains access to
body and multiplies

B-lymphocyte

3 some viral particles become
attached by their antigens
to lymphocytes

2 some virus particles
multiply further and
may cause disease

4 B-lymphocytes respond to this antigen by
multiplying and producing cells which mass
produce a specific type of antibody

antibody

receptor site

receptor site

5 antigens meet
antibodies

6 antigens combine with antibodies
at receptor sites and become a
harmless complex later engulfed
by a phagocyte

Figure 7.3 Action of antibodies

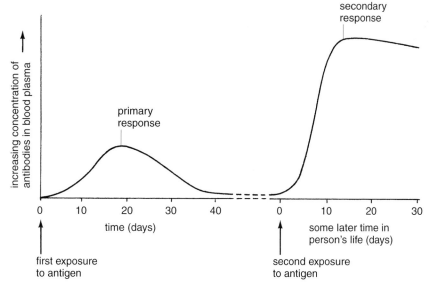

Figure 7.5 Primary and secondary response

Immunological memory

Primary and secondary responses

When a person is infected by a pathogen for the first time, a latent period elapses before a significant level of antibodies appears in the bloodstream. This is called the **primary response** (see figure 7.5). The primary response is often not quick enough or large enough to prevent the person from suffering the disease.

If the person survives, subsequent exposure to the same antigen at a later date results in the **secondary response**. This time antibody production is much more rapid, a higher concentration is reached and it is maintained for a longer time. As a result the disease is usually prevented.

Memory cells

Following the first exposure to an antigen, some B- and T-lymphocytes specific to the antigen remain in the body as **memory cells**. The next time that the body is exposed to the pathogen, these can be quickly stimulated to produce clones of antibody-forming B cells and killer T cells. The person has acquired immunity by **natural** means.

Artificially acquired immunity

Inoculation is the deliberate introduction of the causative agent of a disease into the body in order to induce immunity. **Vaccination** is a form of inoculation. The agent is introduced by injection or ingestion and it initiates the immune response. It may be a **harmless** form of the pathogen (see p 63 for smallpox/cowpox example), a **weakened** version of the pathogen (see p 63 for polio example) or a **dead** microbe whose antigens remain unaltered (e.g. cholera vaccine). It may instead contain a **treated** version of the microbial toxin (poison) that normally causes the disease (e.g. tetanus vaccine).

In each case the agent induces the production of B and T cells and the formation of antibodies, but does not cause the disease. Some B and T cells persist in the body as memory cells. These initiate the secondary response if the person is exposed to the normal disease-causing antigen at a later date. The person has acquired immunity by **artificial** means.

Vaccination is often unsuccessful against certain viral diseases because the virus **mutates** rapidly and produces new strains. Some of these have antigens to which the body has no immunity.

Active and passive immunity

Active immunity refers to protection gained as a result of the person's body producing its **own antibodies**. This can be by natural means following exposure to the disease-causing antigen or by artificial means in response to receipt of a vaccine.

Passive immunity refers to protection gained as a result of the person receiving **ready-made antibodies** produced by another person or animal. Such passive immunity occurs **naturally** when antibodies cross the placenta from mother to fetus and from mother's milk to suckling baby. This gives the new-born child protection for a short time until its own immune system develops.

Passive immunity is brought about **artificially** by extracting antibodies that have been made by one mammal (e.g. a horse) and injecting them into another (e.g. a human). Someone suffering tetanus, for example, is given an injection of tetanus antitoxins (antibodies which render disease-causing toxins harmless).

type of acquired immunity	mode of acquisition	example of disease against which body is made immune
natural active immunity	Infection by pathogen leading to production of memory cells able to give secondary response.	chickenpox
artificial active immunity	Receipt of vaccine leading to production of memory cells able to give secondary response.	poliomyelitis and tetanus
natural passive immunity	Receipt of antibodies from mother in breast milk.	various
artificial passive immunity	Receipt of antibodies made by another living organism.	tetanus

Table 7.1 Types of acquired immunity

The effect is **short-lived** since these antibodies only persist for a short time. However it is often a life-saving procedure since the person would not have produced a sufficient number of antibodies by natural means in time to fight off the disease.

The four categories of acquired immunity are summarised in table 7.1.

Testing your knowledge

1 **a)** Briefly explain the difference between innate and acquired immunity? (2)

   b) **(i)** Give the meaning of each of the following terms: *phagocytosis*, *macrophage*, *lysosome*.

      (ii) Arrange the following steps into the correct sequence in which they occur during phagocytosis. (4)
      A Bacterium digested by enzymes.
      B Bacterium engulfed.
      C Lysosomes fuse with vacuole.
      D Phagocyte meets bacterium.

2 **a)** Which type of blood cell produces antibodies? (1)

   b) Using a diagram to illustrate your answer, explain what is meant by the specificity between an antigen and an antibody. (2)

3 Distinguish between the following pairs:

   a) humoral and cell-mediated response; (2)

   b) primary and secondary response; (2)

   c) active and passive immunity. (2)

Allergy

The immune system responds to a vast variety of agents which are molecularly foreign to it. This enables it to launch attacks on bacteria, fungi, viruses, worms and so on. However sometimes it **over-reacts** and responds to a **harmless** substance such as pollen, dust or feathers, or even a helpful substance such as the antibiotic penicillin.

Such hypersensitivity is called an **allergic reaction**. Pollen, for example, acts as an allergen by causing certain B cells to release antibodies. These become attached to specialised cells in connective tissue which produce a protective substance called **histamine**. When stimulated in this way the cells secrete excessive quantities of histamine which produces the symptoms typical of hay fever: nasal congestion, running nose and constriction of bronchioles. The condition can be relieved by antihistamine drugs.

The sequence of events leading to an allergic reaction are summarised in figure 7.6.

Self and non-self

A remarkable feature of the human body is its ability to recognise its own cells ('**self**') and those which do not belong to it ('**non-self**'). Cells bearing non-self antigens are attacked by antibodies and killer T cells.

ABO blood group system

Four types of blood group exist amongst human beings. These are A, B, AB and O.

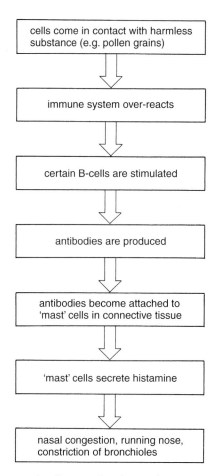

Figure 7.6 Events leading to allergic reaction

Antigens

On the surfaces of their red blood cells, people with blood group A have A antigens, people with blood group B have B antigens, people with blood group AB have both A and B antigens and people with blood group O have neither A nor B antigens (see figure 7.7).

Antibodies

In their plasma, people with blood group A have anti-B antibodies, people with blood group B have anti-A antibodies, people with blood group AB have neither anti-A nor anti-B antibodies and people with blood group O have both anti-A and anti-B antibodies.

Agglutination of blood

Certain combinations of different blood types are non-compatible. If, for example, a person with group A blood were to be given a transfusion of group B blood then anti-B antibodies in his plasma would combine with the B antigens on the surfaces of the donated red blood cells. This would result in clumping (**agglutination**) of red blood cells (see figure 7.8) which would cause major problems by blocking small blood vessels.

Although the blood given in the above transfusion would also contain anti-A antibodies, these would be so diluted relative to the person's own red cells that they would have no significant effect. It is incompatibility between the donor's cells and the recipient's plasma which results in agglutination.

Certain combinations of blood group types are perfectly compatible. For example a person with blood group B can receive blood of type O without risk of agglutination. Possible donors and recipients are given in figure 7.7.

Antigen signature

Other body cells also possess antigens on their plasma membranes. These are different from the red blood cell antigens and make up the **HLA (human leukocyte antigen)** system. This is controlled by four genes each with many alleles coding for many different antigens. This makes it possible to have up to eight different antigens on the surface of a cell. As a result a huge number of different combinations of these antigens exists. Each person's cells have an '**antigen signature**' that is unique in that the chance of it being repeated exactly in someone else's cells is very remote indeed. An exception to this rule is the antigen signature of monozygotic twins.

The body's immune system normally recognises its own antigen signature as meaning 'self' and 'safe' and resists attacking it. Cells lacking this signature are recognised as non-self and attacked.

Rejection of transplanted tissues

When living tissue is transplanted from one individual to another, the T-lymphocytes of the recipient's immune system regard the new tissue as a collection of foreign antigens and attempt to destroy them. This destruction process is called **tissue rejection** and always occurs unless donor and recipient are genetically identical twins.

Successful transplants of tissues and organs (e.g. liver, kidney etc.) are made possible by choosing a donor and a recipient whose antigen signatures are as similar as possible. This is done by careful **typing** and **matching** of tissues beforehand.

In addition doses of **immunosuppressor drugs** are administered to the recipient of the transplant. Unfortunately these drugs greatly inhibit the recipient's immune system and make the person susceptible to serious diseases such as pneumonia. Drugs are now being developed which prevent the activation of killer T cells while at the same time leaving the humoral immune response intact. Scientists are also working on agents which will induce immunological tolerance in advance of the tissue transplant.

blood group	antigen(s) on red blood cell	antibodies in plasma	can donate blood to groups:-	can receive blood from groups:-	percentage of Scottish population
A	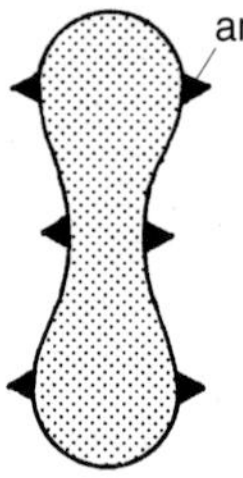 antigen A	 anti-B antibody	A and AB	A and O	35
B	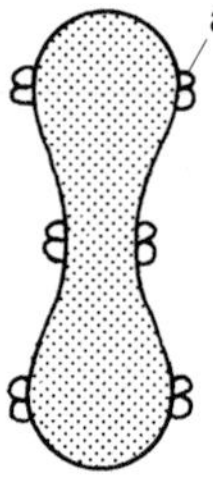 antigen B	 anti-A antibody	B and AB	B and O	11
AB	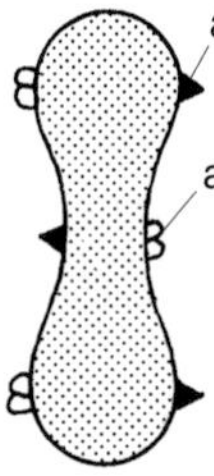 antigen A antigen B	neither anti-A nor anti-B antibodies present	AB	A, B, AB and O	3
O	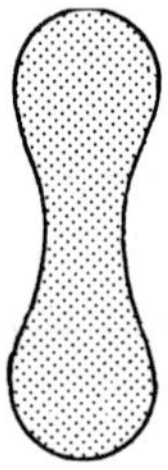 neither antigen A nor antigen B present	 anti-A and anti-B antibodies present	A, B, AB and O	O	51

Figure 7.7 ABO blood group system

Autoimmunity

Normally the immune system does not attack its own cells. Under exceptional circumstances the body's immune system fails to tolerate the antigens making up the 'self' message and launches an attack on its own cells. This is called **autoimmunity**.

Rheumatoid arthritis is an example of an autoimmune disease. The immune system attacks and erodes the cartilage at a joint. It is replaced by fibrous tissue which joins the two bones together making the joint immovable.

In multiple sclerosis, another autoimmune disease, the immune system attacks the myelin sheath surrounding the nerve cells. These can no longer transmit nerve impulses efficiently and the person suffers major disabilities.

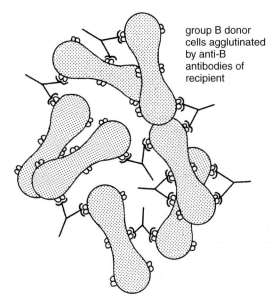

group B donor cells agglutinated by anti-B antibodies of recipient

Figure 7.8 Agglutination of red blood cells

Testing your knowledge

1 Briefly describe the series of events that leads to the body exhibiting an allergic reaction. (3)

2 Rewrite the following sentences giving only the correct answer from each underlined choice. (6)

 a) The four types of blood group that exist amongst human beings are A, B, AB and <u>CD/O</u>.

 b) People with blood group B have antigen <u>A/B</u> on the surface of their red blood cells.

 c) People with blood group A would recognise red blood cells bearing antigen B as <u>self/non-self</u> cells.

 d) People with blood group AB have <u>both/neither</u> anti-A <u>and/nor</u> anti-B antibodies in their plasma.

 e) People with blood group O can donate blood to people with blood group <u>A, B, AB and O/O only</u>.

 f) People with blood group AB can receive blood from people with blood group <u>A, B, AB and O/AB only</u>.

3 a) Why must immunosuppressor drugs normally be administered to patients undergoing kidney transplant surgery? (2)

 b) (i) What problem may arise from their use?
 (ii) Explain why. (2)

4 a) What is meant by the term *autoimmunity*? (2)

 b) Give an example of an autoimmune disease. (1)

Applying your knowledge

1 The 'split' cell in figure 7.9 represents part of a phagocyte and part of a lymphocyte in action.

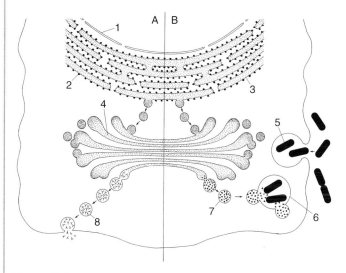

Figure 7.9

 a) Match letters A and B with the two types of white blood cell. (1)

 b) Name structures 1–8. (4)

 c) Compare the contents of structures 7 and 8. (2)

 d) Suggest how a phagocyte avoids self-digestion during the process of phagocytosis. (1)

2 Table 7.2 refers to four types of immunity.

The following list gives several examples of ways in which immunity may be acquired:

	active	passive
natural	W	X
artificial	Y	Z

Table 7.2

 1) by receiving materials across the placenta;
 2) by suffering and surviving measles;
 3) by receiving an injection of molecules made by a horse to prevent diphtheria;
 4) by being vaccinated against diphtheria.

 a) Match 1–4 with W, X, Y and Z in the table. (4)

 b) (i) In the long-term, which is the better way to acquire immunity against diphtheria, method 3 or 4?
 (ii) Explain why. (2)

 c) Which letters in the table represent types of immunity where acquisition depends on receipt of
 (i) antigens;
 (ii) antibodies? (2)

 d) The cornea of the eye has no blood circulation. Explain why it can be transplanted with little risk of rejection. (1)

3 a) A person's blood group can be determined by adding a drop of blood to serum containing anti-A antibodies and a second drop of blood to serum containing anti-B antibodies on a slide (see figure 7.10).

Continued ➤

Applying your knowledge

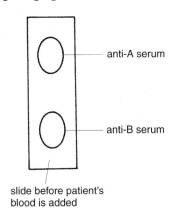

Figure 7.10

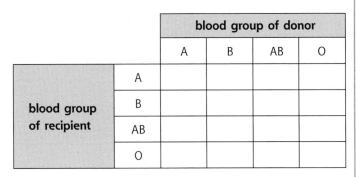

blood group of recipient	blood group of donor			
	A	B	AB	O
A				
B				
AB				
O				

Table 7.3 + = agglutination   – = no agglutination

The results of testing blood from persons Q, R, S and T are shown in figure 7.11. State each person's blood group. (4)

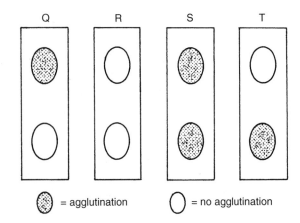

Figure 7.11

b) (i) Copy and complete table 7.3 using the symbols shown to indicate when agglutination would occur and when it would not between potential donors and recipients.

   (ii) Which blood group is described as the universal donor? Why?

   (iii) Which blood group is described as the universal recipient? Why? (12)

4 Table 7.4 refers to antibody proteins called immunoglobulins found in human blood. The graph in figure 7.12 refers to the sequence of events which occurs in response to two separate injections of a type of antigen into a small mammal.

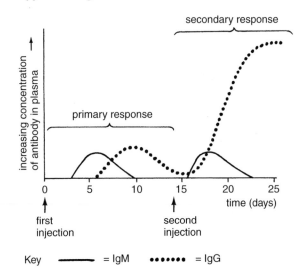

Figure 7.12

a) (i) Which immunoglobulin in the table would be found in the blood of an unborn baby?

   (ii) Suggest why these antibodies are only needed by the baby for a few months after birth. (2)

	immunoglobulin (Ig)				
	IgA	IgD	IgE	IgG	IgM
molecular weight	170 000	184 000	188 100	150 000	960 000
normal serum concentration	1.4–4.0 g/l	0.1–0.4 g/l	0.1–1.3 mg/l	8.0–16.0 g/l	0.5–2.0 g/l
ability to cross placenta	no	no	no	yes	no

Table 7.4

Applying your knowledge

b) Of the five types of immunoglobulin molecules, which is the
   (i) largest
   (ii) rarest? (2)

c) State the normal serum concentration of IgA in mg/ml. (1)

d) With reference to IgM and IgG, state ONE feature common to both the primary and secondary response shown in the graph. (1)

e) With reference to IgG, state THREE differences between the primary and the secondary response. (3)

f) Antibodies such as IgG are now known to be produced by the activity of long-lived lymphocytes. With reference to the graph, suggest why the latter are called 'memory cells'. (1)

5 Give an account of phagocytosis. (10)

(8) Viruses

Most pathogenic organisms (e.g. fungi, protozoa and bacteria) exhibit all the characteristics of **living** things such as nutrition, respiration, excretion, reproduction, growth and sensitivity.

Viruses are unusual micro-organisms in that **reproduction** is the only true characteristic of living things that they exhibit. Other features such as the ability to form a crystalline structure are typical of non-living substances.

Obligate parasites

Since viruses can only reproduce within the living cells of another organism (the **host**), they are described as **obligate parasites**. Animals, plants and bacteria are all susceptible to invasion by viruses. Since the host cell is subsequently damaged or destroyed, viruses are always associated with **diseases**. These range from the common cold to deadly Lassa fever; further examples are given in table 8.1.

Specificity

Viruses are often specific with respect to their chosen type of host cell. The poliomyelitis virus, for example, attacks nerve cells; the hepatitis virus targets liver cells.

Size

Viruses are much smaller than bacteria. They range in size from about 20 to 300 nanometres (nm). (1 nm = 1×10^{-9} m.) Viruses can only be seen with the aid of an electron microscope.

disease (or syndrome) caused by virus	host organism	effect
poliomyelitis	human	Inflammation of spinal cord followed by paralysis.
AIDS	human	Destruction of immune system.
hepatitis	human	Inflammation of liver cells and jaundice.
foot and mouth	farm animals	Development of lesions in mouth.
rabies	mammals	Muscle spasms or paralysis.
bushy stunt	tomato plant	Stunted growth.
leaf mosaic	potato plant	Malformation of leaves.

Table 8.1 Viral diseases

Spread of viruses

Coughing and sneezing spread the viruses that cause respiratory infections such as pneumonia. The poliomyelitis virus is excreted in faeces and can be passed to food by flies. The rabies virus is unusual in that it can affect several different mammals. Its usual mode of transmission to humans is via the bite of a rabid dog. Human immunodeficiency virus (HIV) which causes acquired immune deficiency syndrome (AIDS) is transmitted by blood and sexual contact.

Viruses which attack plants are normally spread by insects such as greenfly. Seeds, bulbs and cuttings can also carry viruses.

Viral Structure

A virus is not a cell. It consists of one type of nucleic acid (either DNA or RNA) surrounded by a protective coat (**capsid**) normally made of protein. Its genetic material carries the information necessary for viral multiplication but lacks the biochemical machinery to carry this out on its own.

A wide variety of viruses exist. Figure 8.1 shows a herpes virus which attacks human skin cells and causes cold sores on the lips. Figure 8.1 also shows a type of virus called a bacteriophage which attacks bacteria. This virus' DNA thread is contained inside a head from which a tail projects. Most viral particles do not have a tail.

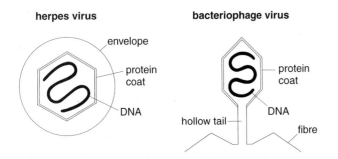

Figure 8.1 Structure of two viruses

Invasion of a cell by a virus

A virus can lie dormant and lifeless for many years until it comes in contact with a suitable host cell which it then invades.

The virus becomes attached to the host cell by binding with certain molecules on the surface of the host cell. Different viruses employ different methods of introducing their nucleic acid into the host cell. In some cases, such as herpes virus, the whole virus enters the cell; in other cases, such as bacteriophage, the viral DNA is

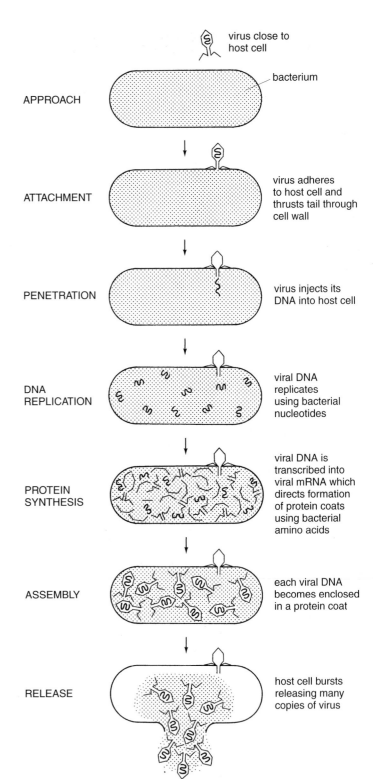

Figure 8.2 Multiplication of a virus

injected via the hollow tail. Figure 8.2 shows the invasion of a bacterium (the host) by a bacteriophage.

Alteration of cell instructions

Although completely inactive outside the host cell, once inside, the virus assumes control of the cell's biochemical machinery. It depends on the host cell for both energy (from **ATP**) and a supply of **nucleotides** and **amino acids** to build new viral particles.

The viral DNA (or RNA) first suppresses the cell's normal nucleic acid replication and protein synthesis. It then uses the host's nucleotides and amino acids to produce many **identical copies** of the viral nucleic acid and an appropriate number of protein coats.

In some cases the whole virus enters the host cell but the final outcome is the same: the release of many copies of the virus capable of infecting new host cells and causing disease. In some cases the release is achieved by viral nucleic acid directing the synthesis of enzymes that cause bursting (**lysis**) of the host cell membrane. In other cases **buds** containing the virus are formed (see HIV p 64).

Some viruses infect a cell and remain dormant for an indefinite period before undergoing reproduction and release.

Testing your knowledge

1 **a)** Under what circumstances could a virus be:
   (i)   active;
   (ii) inactive? (2)

   b) Why are viruses described as obligate parasites? (1)

   c) **(i)** Name TWO viral diseases of plants and TWO viral diseases that affect human beings.
   (ii) In addition to plants and animals, what third group of living things can play host to viruses? (5)

2 Viruses are too small to be seen under a light microscope. How do we know what they look like? (1)

3 **a)** **(i)** Name TWO structural features possessed by all viruses.
   (ii) Which of these enters the host cell and alters the cell's metabolism? (3)

   b) Name TWO substances supplied by the host cell during viral replication. (2)

   c) What is *lysis* and how is it brought about? (2)

History and prevention of viral diseases

Humans are known to have been plagued by viruses since the beginning of recorded time. An ancient Egyptian relic from about 1500 BC shows a priest with a shrivelled leg thought to have resulted from poliomyelitis. The conquest of the Mexican Aztec nation in the 1500s by a small force of Spaniards is thought to have been due in part to the unwitting transfer of smallpox virus from the Europeans to the Mexicans leading to a lethal epidemic.

Smallpox

Up until the end of the eighteenth century **smallpox** was widespread in Britain. This infectious disease caused severe fever and was fatal in about one out of every five cases. Survivors were left permanently scarred.

It was known at that time that smallpox could sometimes be prevented by deliberately inoculating people with pus from a pustule of a person sufferering a mild form of the disease. However this method of immunisation was not reliable and often produced the fatal form of the disease.

In 1796, a British doctor called Edward Jenner decided to act on observations that milkmaids who had suffered **cowpox** (a similar but milder, non-fatal disease) were immune to smallpox. He inoculated a healthy boy with cowpox. Once the boy had recovered, Jenner inoculated him with what would normally have been a deadly strain of smallpox virus. Fortunately for everyone concerned the boy did not contract smallpox, showing that he was immune. The science of artificially acquired active immunity had begun.

Safe vaccines

The first **vaccine** used to induce immunity against the poliomyelitis virus contained dead virus. This was followed by an improved vaccine containing virus which had been **attenuated**. This means that its nucleic acid has been rendered harmless by chemical or heat treatment but that the antigenic properties of its protein coat remain unaltered.

Use of this vaccine has resulted in the almost total eradication of polio in developed countries where vast vaccination campaigns have been mounted. This success has been repeated to a lesser extent for many other diseases (see also chapter 39).

The situation remained much bleaker in most developing countries which lacked nationwide immunisation services until the 1970s. In recent years the situation has improved significantly in many, but not all, developing countries.

Retrovirus

If a virus contains RNA it is called a **retrovirus**. Since it lacks DNA to transcribe into mRNA, it adopts a different strategy. Along with its RNA it injects an enzyme called **reverse transcriptase** into the host cell. This enzyme brings about a reverse version of normal transcription and produces viral DNA from viral RNA. Armed with this DNA, the virus is able to replicate itself many times, escape from the host cell and infect other cells.

Acquired immune deficiency syndrome (AIDS)

AIDS is caused by a retrovirus called **human immunodeficiency virus (HIV)**, as shown in figure 8.3. HIV attacks helper T-lymphocytes. It becomes attached by glycoprotein on its surface to specific receptors on the helper T cell surface (see figure 8.4).

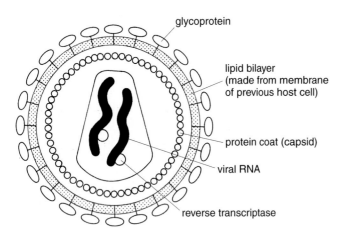

Figure 8.3 Human immunodefiency virus (HIV)

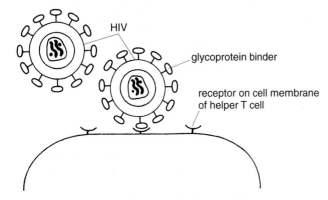

Figure 8.4 Attachment of HIV to a helper T cell

The envelope surrounding the HIV particle fuses with the membrane of the helper T cell and the virus enters the host cell. The events described above involving reverse transcriptase take place. Viral DNA becomes incorporated into the host cell's DNA where it can remain dormant for many years.

Eventually viral mRNA is transcribed and it then directs synthesis of new viral particles inside the host cells. These escape from the infected helper T cell by budding

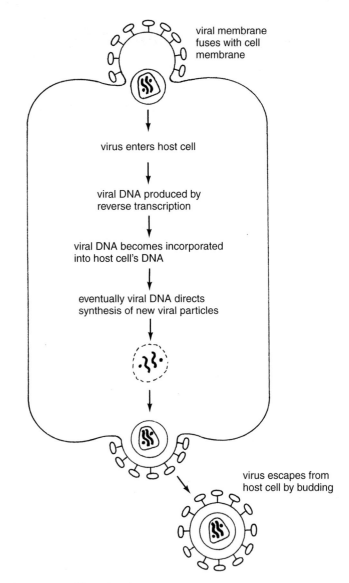

Figure 8.5 Life cycle of HIV

(see figure 8.5) and move off to infect other cells. The original T cell's membrane is left perforated which causes destruction of the cell.

Helper T cells are of critical importance to the immune system since they activate B cells and killer T cells. As the number of helper T cells gradually drops, the body's immunological activity decreases, leaving the person susceptible to serious **opportunistic infections** such as pneumonia and rare forms of cancer.

Certain drugs can inhibit the activity of the enzyme reverse transcriptase and slow down the onset of AIDS but do not cure it. B cells make antibodies in response to HIV but these are ineffective against viral particles 'hiding' inside the helper T cells. Production of successful vaccine has so far eluded scientists because the genetic material in HIV mutates frequently forming many new variants with different antigenic properties.

Testing your knowledge

1 a) (i) Which is the more serious viral disease, cowpox or smallpox?
   (ii) Why does infection by and recovery from one of these diseases give protection against the other? (3)

   b) (i) What is an *attenuated* virus?
   (ii) Why might it be suitable for use in a vaccine? (2)

   c) Name a disease that has been almost eradicated from developed countries as a result of vaccination programmes. (1)

2 a) (i) Which nucleic acid does a retrovirus lack?
   (ii) How does a retrovirus produce this nucleic acid in order to replicate itself? (3)

   b) By what means does HIV
   (i) enter
   (ii) leave its host cell? (2)

   c) Why is the deaths of an AIDS sufferer normally caused by an opportunistic infection such as pneumonia? (1)

Applying your knowledge

1 In the absence of a suitable host cell, a virus exhibits none of the characteristics of living things and may adopt a crystalline form.

   a) Why then do scientists consider viruses to be living things? (1)

   b) Scientists do not, however, classify a virus particle as a cell. Suggest why. (1)

2 Figure 8.6 shows the size of three viruses in relation to a red blood cell and a cell of the bacterium *Escherichia coli*.

   a) Construct a table which shows the given dimension of each of these life forms expressed in nanometres (nm), micrometres (μm), millimetres (mm) and metres (m). (4)

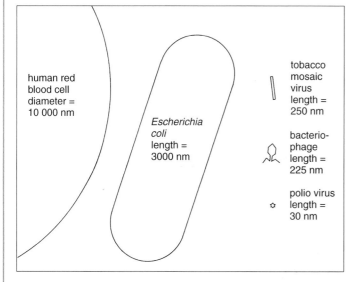

Figure 8.6

   b) (i) By how many times is the length of a cell of *E. coli* greater than that of a polio virus?
   (ii) By how many times is the diameter of a red blood cell greater than the length of a tobacco mosaic virus? (2)

3 Figure 8.7 shows a disease-causing virus (V) and an attenuated version of it (W).

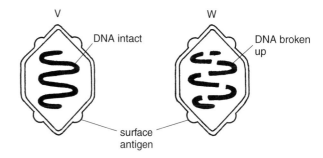

Figure 8.7

   a) Suggest why receiving a vaccine containing W gives immunity against attacks in the future by V. (2)

   b) (i) Would such immunity be described as naturally or artificially acquired?
   (ii) Would the acquisition of such immunity be described as active or passive? (2)

   c) (i) Why has it so far proved impossible to make people immune to HIV by this method?
   (ii) A person who is HIV positive has antibodies against the virus in his blood. Why do these not prevent AIDS from developing? (2)

Continued ➤

Applying your knowledge

4 Figure 8.8 shows the replication cycle of the herpes virus which causes cold sores on the mouth.

a) Is herpes a retrovirus? Explain your answer. (1)

b) Match boxes X, Y, and Z with the terms viral RNA, viral protein and viral DNA. (3)

c) **(i)** What name is given to the method by which herpes leaves the host cell?
(ii) Predict the fate of the cell. (2)

d) Compared with figure 8.2, state ONE way in which figure 8.8 is an oversimplification of the process of viral multiplication. (1)

5 Give an account of the events that occur during the invasion of a host cell by a DNA virus. (10)

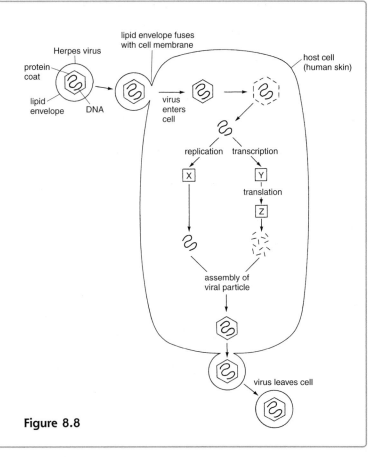

Figure 8.8

What you should know
(Chapters 6–8)

(See table 8.2 for word bank.)

1 The plasma _____ surrounding a cell is composed of protein and phospholipid molecules. These are thought to be arranged as in the fluid _____ model.

2 The bilayer of _____ molecules provides the cell with a stable boundary. The _____ molecules vary in function. Some give support, some contain _____ allowing passive transport of small molecules, others act as _____ and actively transport molecules into or out of the cell.

3 The membranes surrounding cell _____ have the same basic structure as the plasma membrane.

4 A constant environment is maintained within a cell by the membrane acting as a _____ barrier and regulating the entry and _____ of materials.

5 Small molecules may enter or leave the cell by moving passively by _____ (or osmosis) along a concentration _____ from high to low concentration.

6 Molecules or ions may enter or leave a cell by being _____ transported across the membrane _____ a concentration gradient from low to high concentration. This requires _____ .

7 Endocytosis is the process by which the cell membrane _____ relatively large particles in a vesicle. _____ is the process by which a vesicle formed in the cell fuses with the membrane and expels its contents to the exterior.

8 Immunity to disease-causing organisms can be innate or acquired. _____ immunity is inborn; _____ immunity is gained during the person's lifetime.

Continued ➤

What you should know
(Chapters 6–8)

9 _____ is a type of innate immunity by which cells such as _____ engulf bacteria and destroy them using enzymes in _____ .

10 Antibody production is a type of acquired immunity. It is the response made by cells called _____ to the presence in the body of alien molecules called _____ . An _____ possesses receptor sites which bind to one particular type of antigen and render it harmless.

11 B-lymphocytes produce free (_____) antibodies to deal with antigens; T-lymphocytes employ direct contact (_____ response) to destroy cells infected with antigens.

12 Natural _____ is acquired by a person who suffers and survives a disease by producing appropriate antibodies. Some B- and T-lymphocytes remain as _____ cells. _____ immunity is acquired by a person who receives a harmless form of the antigen and responds by producing T and B cells and antibodies.

13 Active immunity is gained by a person's _____ system responding to an antigen and producing it's own antibodies; _____ immunity is gained by a person receiving antibodies made by another person or animal.

14 An over-reaction to a harmless substance by the immune system is called an _____ reaction.

15 Each person's cells have an antigen _____ which is recognised by the immune system as 'self'. This normally guarantees the cells' safety. However under exceptional circumstances, _____ occurs and the immune system attacks 'self' cells.

16 Viruses are very tiny micro-organisms which are unusual in that _____ is the only true characteristic of living things that they exhibit.

17 A virus consists of DNA or _____ surrounded by a coat of protein. It depends on the host cell for energy and building materials.

18 Once inside the host cell, a virus alters the cell's biochemistry, enabling mass _____ of viral nucleic acid to occur. Many copies of the virus are produced and released by _____ of the host cell.

19 Some viral diseases can be prevented using vaccines containing _____ virus to induce immunity.

20 Human Immunodeficiency Virus disrupts the immune system by slowly destroying _____ T cells. Attempts to produce a vaccine have so far failed.

acquired	engulfs	memory
actively	exit	mosaic
against	exocytosis	organelles
allergic	gradient	passive
antibody	helper	phagocytosis
antigens	humoral	phospholipid
artificial	immune	protein
attenuated	immunity	replication
autoimmunity	innate	reproduction
carriers	lymphocytes	RNA
cell-mediated	lysis	selective
channels	lysosomes	signature
diffusion	macrophages	
energy	membrane	

Table 8.2 Word bank for chapters 6–8

9 Chromosomes and DNA replication

Gene

A **gene** is a unit of heredity, which controls a genetically inherited characteristic (e.g. hair colour, blood group etc.). Each gene occupies a specific site on a **chromosome**. Each chromosome is a thread-like structure containing **DNA** (see figure 9.1).

A gene is a region of chromosomal DNA. Genes vary in size but on average a gene consists of about a thousand **nucleotides** with their bases arranged in a particular sequence.

Each gene acts as a discrete functional unit by coding (via mRNA) for one polypeptide (or protein); the order of the amino acids in the polypeptide (or protein) is determined by the sequence of the bases in the gene's DNA (see chapter 3). Chromosomes consist of many genes and are described as vehicles of inheritance.

Chromosome complement

Each species has a characteristic number of chromosomes called the **chromosome complement** present in the nucleus of each of its cells. The appearance of the chromosome complement, showing the size, form and number of the chromosomes, is called the **karyotype**.

The normal chromosome complement present in a human body cell consists of 46 chromosomes. These can be arranged into 23 **homologous pairs** as shown in figure 9.2. The members of a pair of homologous chromosomes match one another gene for gene (though they may each possess different forms of a gene).

Autosomes and sex chromosomes

In the human chromosome complement twenty-two pairs of homologous chromosomes are called **autosomes** and

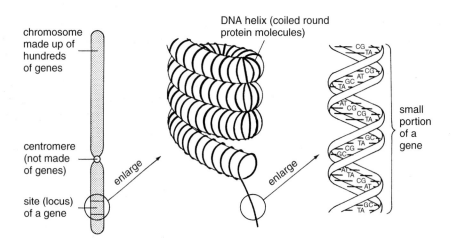

Figure 9.1 A simplified version of gene structure

Figure 9.2 Normal male and female karyotypes

play no part in sex determination. One pair are called the **sex chromosomes** and these determine the sex of the individual.

A human female has two X chromosomes which are fully homologous to one another. A male has one X chromosome and a much smaller Y chromosome which is homologous to only part of the X.

Haploid and diploid

Every normal human body cell (and zygote) contains 46 chromosomes (i.e. 23 pairs). Such a cell, which possesses a double set of chromosomes, is said to be **diploid (2n)**.

Every normal human sex cell (gamete) contains 23 chromosomes (i.e. one unpaired member of each type). Such a cell, which possesses a single set of chromosomes, is said to be **haploid (n)**.

Types of nuclear division

Mitosis is the process by which the nucleus of a normal body cell (or zygote) divides into 2 daughter nuclei. Each of these receives exactly the same number of chromosomes as were present in the original nucleus. (Mitosis is followed by division of the cytoplasm to form 2 daughter cells and sometimes the entire process of cell division is loosely referred to as mitosis.)

Meiosis is the process by which the nucleus of a diploid gamete mother cell divides into 4 daughter nuclei. Each of these receives half the number of chromosomes present in the original nucleus. (Meiosis is followed by

division of the cytoplasm to form 4 sex cells and sometimes the entire process of gamete formation is loosely referred to as meiosis.)

Human life cycle

During sexual reproduction, fertilisation occurs when the nucleus of a haploid sperm (containing 23 chromosomes) fuses with the nucleus of a haploid egg (also with 23 chromosomes). This results in the formation of a diploid zygote (with 46 chromosomes) which divides repeatedly by mitosis to form a human being consisting of millions of diploid cells.

At sexual maturity a few of these cells, called the gamete mother cells, each divide by meiosis to form 4 haploid gametes. This is followed by fertilisation and the whole cycle is repeated generation after generation.

Figure 9.3 summarises the human **life cycle** where the number enclosed in each circle represents the chromosomal complement of the cell. Close inspection of this diagram shows that mitotic nuclear division results in the production of 2 cells each with 46 chromosomes from one nucleus with 46 chromosomes, and that meiotic nuclear division results in the production of 4 gametes each with 23 chromosomes from one nucleus with 46 chromosomes.

In each case a cell preparing to undergo division must double its quantity of genetic material to provide enough to supply the products of the particular type of nuclear division involved. This doubling of genetic material is brought about by replication of DNA.

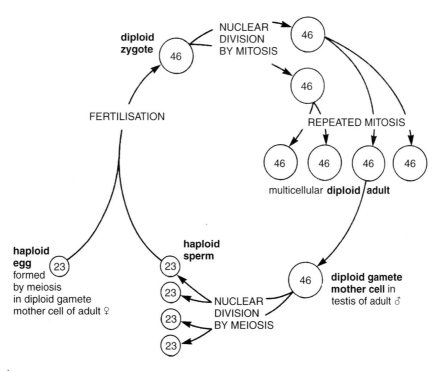

Figure 9.3 Human life cycle

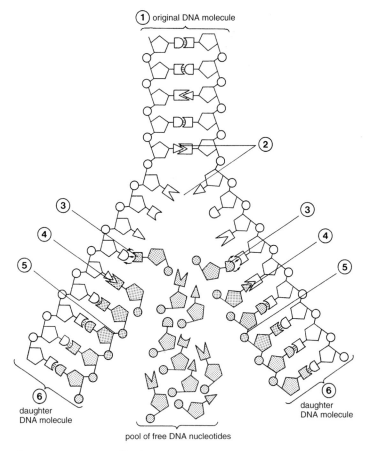

Figure 9.4 DNA replication

Replication of DNA

DNA is a unique molecule because it is able to reproduce itself exactly. This process is called **replication**. It is illustrated in figure 9.4.

Stage 1 shows a region of the original DNA molecule after it has just become unwound. Stage 2 is a little further ahead of stage 1 in the process. Here weak hydrogen bonds between two bases are breaking and causing the two component strands of DNA to separate ('unzip') and expose their bases.

At stage 3, pairing of two bases enables a free DNA nucleotide to find and align with its complementary nucleotide on the open chain. At stage 4, weak hydrogen bonds are forming between complementary base pairs.

At stage 5, slightly ahead of stage 4, a strong chemical bond is forming between the sugar of one nucleotide and the phosphate of the next one in the chain giving each strand its sugar-phosphate 'backbone'. This linking of nucleotides into a chain is controlled by an enzyme called **DNA polymerase**.

Each stage 6 shows a newly formed daughter molecule of DNA about to wind up into a double helix. Daughter molecules have a base sequence identical to one another and to the original DNA molecule.

For DNA replication to occur the nucleus must contain:

◆ **DNA** (to act as a template for the new molecule);

◆ a supply of the four types of DNA **nucleotide**;

◆ the appropriate **enzymes** (e.g. DNA polymerase);

◆ a supply of **ATP** to provide energy.

Semi-conservative replication

DNA replication results in the formation of two new molecules, each of which contains one strand of the original parent molecule. It is therefore said to be **semi-conservative** (see figure 9.5).

Maximum quantity of DNA

DNA replication is the means by which new genetic material is produced in the nucleus of a cell during interphase. The two identical daughter DNA molecules formed from each chromosome coil up and become two **identical chromatids** held together by a centromere (see figure 9.5).

The quantity of genetic material has doubled without changing the cell's chromosome number. It is at this time, following DNA replication but immediately before

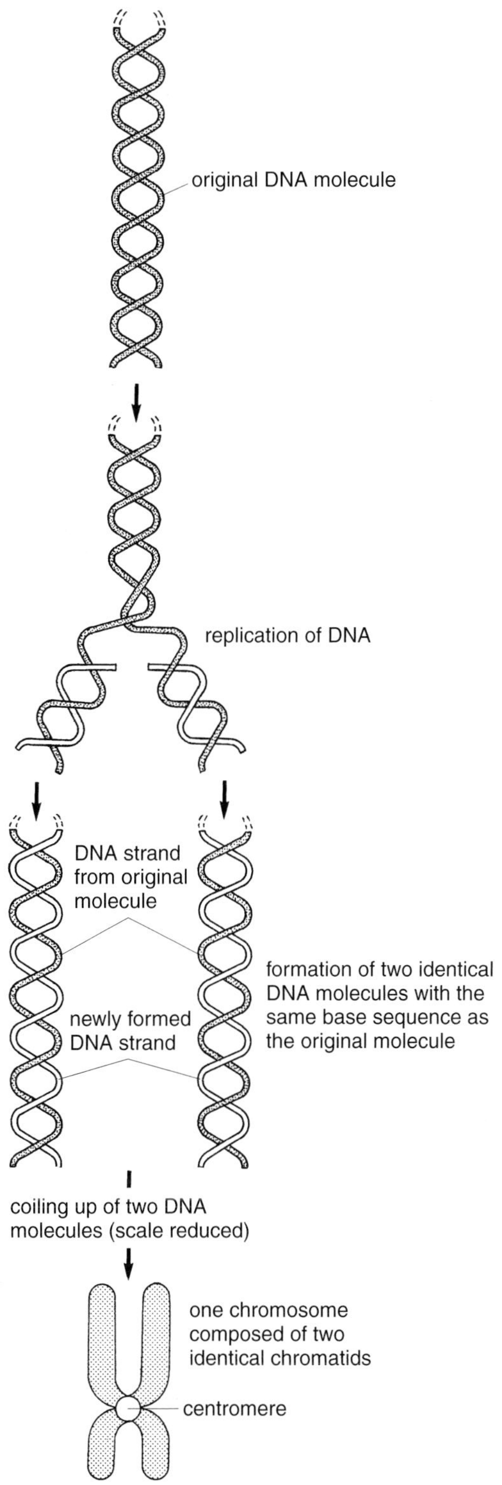

- original DNA molecule
- replication of DNA
- DNA strand from original molecule
- newly formed DNA strand
- formation of two identical DNA molecules with the same base sequence as the original molecule
- coiling up of two DNA molecules (scale reduced)
- one chromosome composed of two identical chromatids
- centromere

Figure 9.5 Semi-conservative replication and chromatid formation

nuclear division (mitosis or meiosis), that the cell's DNA content is at its **maximum**.

Importance of DNA replication

DNA replication ensures that an **exact copy** of the species' genetic information is passed from cell to cell during growth and from generation to generation during sexual reproduction.

If DNA failed to replicate itself, the processes of mitosis and meiosis would not occur and the cycle shown in figure 9.3 would come to a halt. DNA replication is therefore essential for the **continuation of life**.

Testing your knowledge

1 What is a molecule of DNA able to do that makes it unique compared to other chemical molecules? (1)

2 Study figure 9.4 carefully and then answer the following questions.

   a) At which numbered stage has the DNA molecule been involved in the replication process for the shortest time? (1)

   b) (i) What type of bond is breaking at stage 2?
      (ii) What effect does this have on the two compoment strands of the DNA molecule? (2)

   c) At which stage is base-pairing seen to be occurring between the original DNA molecule and free DNA nucleotides? (1)

   d) Name the type of bond formed and the types of molecule involved during:
      (i) stage 4;
      (ii) stage 5. (2)

3 Name FOUR substances that must be present in a nucleus for DNA replication to occur. (4)

4 Why is DNA replication important? (2)

Applying your knowledge

1 Figure 9.6 shows a cell's genetic material.

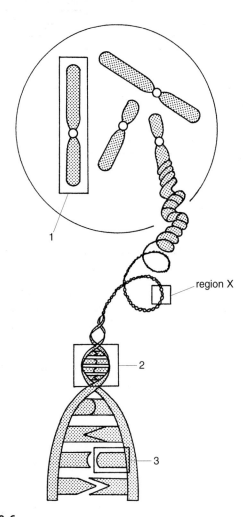

Figure 9.6

a) Name the parts enclosed in boxes 1, 2 and 3. (3)

b) Which of these boxed structures contains nucleic acid and consists of many different genes? (1)

c) Which of these structures is one of four basic units whose order determines the information held in a gene? (1)

d) In what way does region X in the diagram fail to represent one gene adequately? (1)

2 Figure 9.7 represents the human life cycle.

a) Identify processes X, Y and Z. (3)

b) Identify cell types A and B. (2)

c) Explain fully the difference in meaning between the symbols n and 2n. (2)

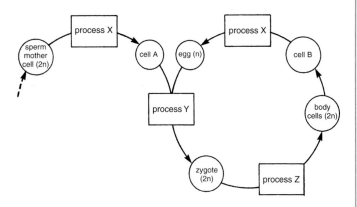

Figure 9.7

3 Figure 9.8 shows a molecule of DNA undergoing replication.

a) What process brings about the change in the DNA molecule's appearance between regions A and B in the diagram? (1)

b) What must happen to the DNA in region B before replication can proceed? (1)

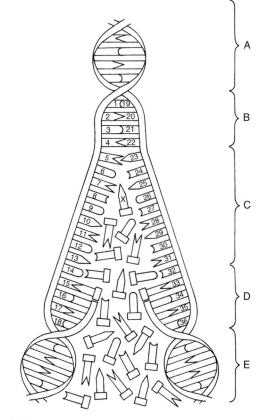

Figure 9.8

Continued ➤

Applying your knowledge

c) (i) Name FOUR numbered base molecules to which nucleotide X could become attached as the diagram stands at present.

(ii) Name TWO additional numbered bases to which nucleotide X could become attached if it were still free as the process of replication continued.

(iii) How many of the free nucleotides in the pool are complementary to site 27? (4)

d) DNA polymerase is an enzyme which catalyses the assembly of nucleotides into DNA by promoting the formation of the sugar-phosphate 'backbone'. In which lettered region of the diagram would this process be taking place? (1)

e) Which lettered stage in the diagram shows the rewinding of daughter DNA molecules? (1)

4 Table 9.1 gives the relative amounts of DNA present in some cell types from four different animals.

a) Account for the fact that the DNA content of human red blood cells is zero. (1)

	DNA content (units)		
	sperm	red blood cell	kidney
carp	1.6	3.5	3.3
chicken	1.3	2.3	2.4
cow	3.3	0	6.4
human	3.3	0	6.6

Table 9.1

b) Based on the data, suggest a structural difference that exists between the red blood cells of a cow and a chicken. (1)

c) Make a generalisation about the DNA content of sperm compared with kidney cells. (1)

d) A scientist who had grown a culture of kidney cells from a young animal found that some of the cells contained twice the normal DNA content. Explain why. (2)

5 Describe the main processes that occur during the replication of a molecule of DNA. (10)

10 Meiosis

Need for reduction division

Sexual reproduction provides the opportunity for genetic material from one individual to meet that of another at fertilisation and form a **diploid zygote**. For this process to be possible, the **sex cells** must be **haploid**. Their formation requires a diploid gamete mother cell to undergo **reduction division** (i.e. division into four cells accompanied by a reduction in chromosome number from the diploid to the haploid complement).

Meiosis is the form of nuclear division that results in this production of four haploid (n) gametes from one diploid (2n) gamete mother cell. It occurs at specific sites in the human body (see table 10.1).

Process of meiosis

Meiosis involves two consecutive nuclear divisions (followed by cell divisions). The gamete mother cell divides

site of meiosis	diploid gamete mother cell	haploid gametes formed
testis	sperm mother cell	sperm
ovary	egg mother cell	eggs (ova)

Table 10.1 Sites of meiosis

into two cells and these then divide again. Figure 10.1 refers to a gamete mother cell containing four chromosomes (two of 'paternal' and two of 'maternal' origin).

During interphase, each chromosome replicates forming two identical chromatids (see p 71). Therefore when the nuclear material becomes visible (on staining), each chromosome is seen to consist of two chromatids attached at a centromere.

Homologous chromosomes pair up and come to lie alongside one another so that their centromeres and genes

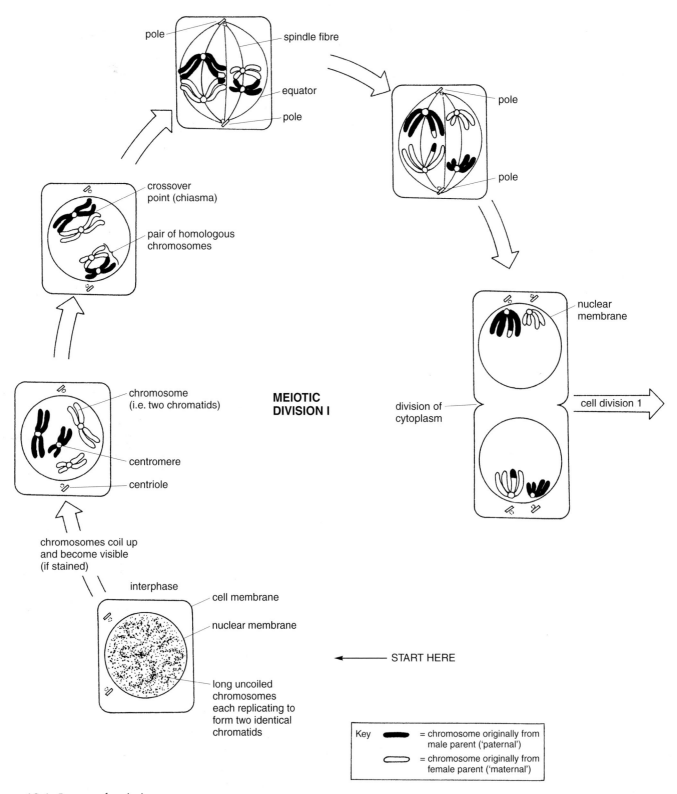

pole
spindle fibre
equator
pole

crossover
point (chiasma)

pair of homologous
chromosomes

pole
pole

nuclear
membrane

MEIOTIC
DIVISION I

chromosome
(i.e. two chromatids)

centromere

centriole

division of
cytoplasm

cell division 1

chromosomes coil up
and become visible
(if stained)

interphase

cell membrane

nuclear membrane

START HERE

long uncoiled
chromosomes
each replicating to
form two identical
chromatids

Key   = chromosome originally from
           male parent ('paternal')

           = chromosome originally from
           female parent ('maternal')

Figure 10.1 Process of meiosis

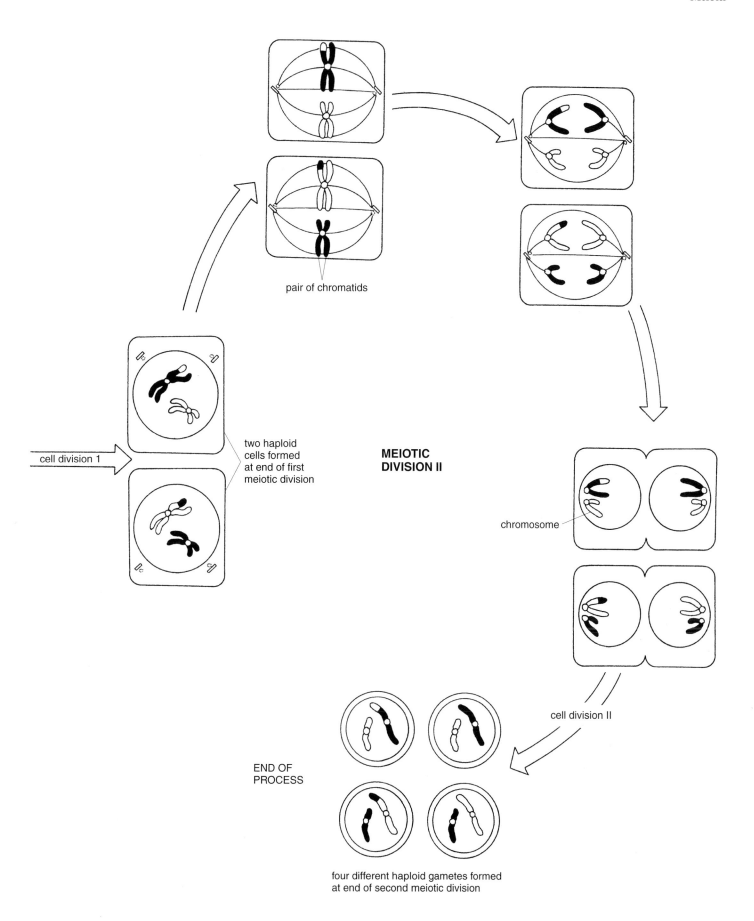

pair of chromatids

MEIOTIC
DIVISION II

cell division 1

two haploid
cells formed
at end of first
meiotic division

chromosome

cell division II

END OF
PROCESS

four different haploid gametes formed
at end of second meiotic division

match exactly. While in this paired state, the chromosomes become even shorter and thicker by coiling up.

Next the members of each homologous pair begin to repel one another and move apart except at points called **chiasmata** (singular = chiasma) where they remain joined together. It is here that exchange of genetic material occurs by two chromatids twisting around one another and 'swapping' portions. This exchange is called **crossing over**.

Next the nuclear membrane disappears, spindle fibres form and homologous pairs become arranged on the equator of the cell. The arrangement of each pair relative to any other is **random**.

On contraction of the spindle fibres, one chromosome of each pair moves to one pole and its homologous partner moves to the opposite pole.

This is followed by a nuclear membrane forming round each group of chromosomes and then by division of the cytoplasm resulting in the formation of two haploid cells.

Each of these haploid cells now undergoes the second meiotic division as shown in figure 10.1. Single chromosomes (each made of two chromatids) line up at each equator. On separation from its partner, each chromatid is regarded as a chromosome.

Each of the four gametes formed contains half the number of chromosomes present in the original gamete mother cell.

Variation

Much of the **variation** that exists amongst the members of a species is inherited and determined by alleles of genes. During meiosis new combinations of existing alleles arise by **independent assortment** and **crossing over**.

Independent assortment of chromosomes

When homologous pairs of chromosomes line up at the equator during the first meiotic division, the final position of any one pair is **random** relative to any other pair.

Figure 10.2 shows a simple example of a gamete mother cell in a pea plant (where only two homologous pairs have been drawn). There are two ways in which the pairs can become arranged. Subsequent meiotic divisions bring about independent (random) assortment of chromosomes. This gives rise to 2^2 (i.e. 4) different genetic combinations in the gametes. This may lead to the formation of new phenotypes.

The larger the number of chromosomes present, the greater the number of possible combinations. For example, a human egg mother cell with 23 homologous pairs has the potential to produce 2^{23} (i.e. 8 388 608) different combinations.

Crossing over and separation of linked genes

Two genes situated on the same chromosome are said to be **linked**. When a chromosome (consisting of two chromatids) is aligned with its homologous partner prior to the first meiotic division, portions of chromatid may be exchanged at points called **chiasmata**.

The process of **crossing over** involves chromatids becoming broken and the broken end of one joining with that of another. By this means, alleles of linked genes can become separated. This can result in the formation of new combinations of alleles and give four genetically different chromatids each of which ends up in a different gamete.

A simple example is shown in figure 10.3 which refers to one homologous pair of chromosomes in a gamete mother cell of a fruit fly. Consider a human gamete mother cell with 23 homologous pairs all capable of undergoing crossing over at one or more chiasmata. The potential for increased variation by this method is enormous.

Sexual reproduction

During sexual reproduction, two haploid gametes (each carrying a unique version of the species' genetic blueprint) meet at fertilisation. This **mixing** of part of one parent's genotype with that of another produces a new individual who is **genetically different** from both parents and from

---

Testing your knowledge

1 a) Define the term *meiosis*. (2)

   b) Identify the sites where meiosis occurs in men and women. (2)

2 a) What name is given to the two identical structures which make up each chromosome prior to meiosis? (1)

   b) (i) What name is given to points of direct contact between adjacent chromatids during the first meiotic division?

      (ii) What may happen at these points of contact? (2)

3 a) Are the products of the first meiotic division haploid or diploid? (1)

   b) Are the products of second meiotic division haploid or diploid? (1)

   c) Compare the chromosome number of a human gamete mother cell with that of each of the four gametes formed. (1)

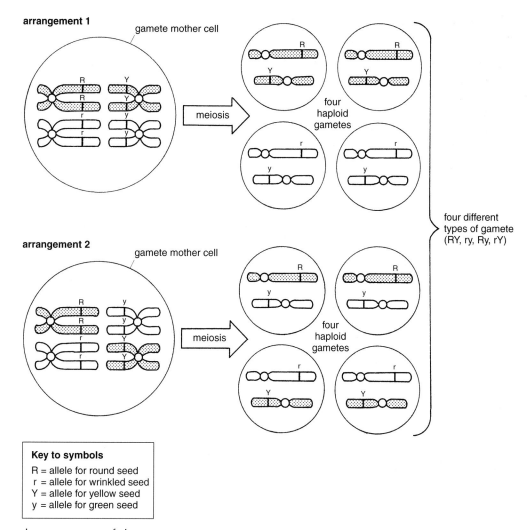

Figure 10.2 Independent assortment of chromosomes

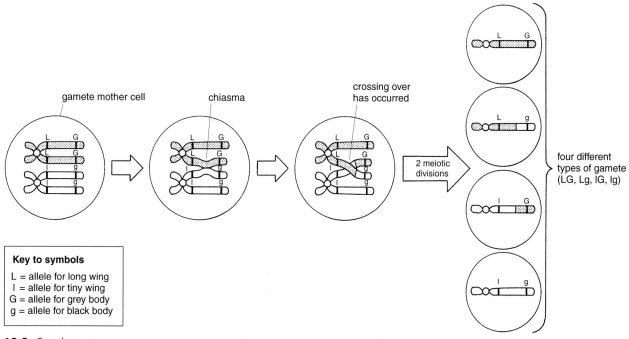

Figure 10.3 Crossing over

all other members of the species. Thus the human population consists of billions of individuals who are genetically unique (unless they have a monozygotic twin).

Such variation is of great importance because it helps the species to adapt to a changing environment. Imagine, for example, that a new disease appears. If great genetic variation exists amongst the members of the species, then there is a good chance that some of them will be resistant and survive. If they were all identical and susceptible to the disease, the whole species would be wiped out.

Genetic fingerprinting

The single haploid set of chromosomes typical of a species is called its **genome**. It has been discovered that some of the DNA in the human genome contains many short, non-coding sequences of bases that are repeated many times. What makes these sequences of particular interest is the fact that they vary in length and number of repeats from person to person.

Following extraction and separation of DNA by special techniques, a pattern of bands is formed. This is referred to as a **genetic 'fingerprint'** since it is unique to the person unless he or she is one of monozygotic twins.

Since each person inherits 50% of their DNA from each parent, every band in their genetic fingerprint must match one in their father's print or one in that of their mother. The fact that each person has 50% of their bands in common with each of their parents (see figure 10.4), enables genetic fingerprinting to be used as a tool to settle paternity disputes. In addition it can be employed to identify criminals who have left cells (e.g. in semen or blood) at the scene of the crime.

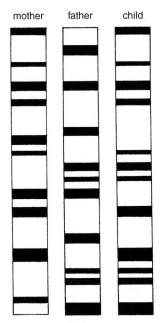

Figure 10.4 Genetic fingerprints

Testing your knowledge

1 Identify the TWO ways in which new combinations of existing alleles may arise during meiosis. (2)

2 Explain why the variation that exists amongst the members of the human species is of survival value. (2)

3 **a)** What is meant by the terms *genome* and *genetic fingerprinting*? (2)

   b) Give a practical use to which genetic fingerprinting can be put. (1)

Applying your knowledge

1 The following statements refer to various stages that occur during meiosis. With reference only to their letters, arrange the statements into the correct sequence. (1)

   A Homologous chromosomes become arranged on the equator of the cell.

   B Homologous chromosomes pair up and their centromeres and genes become aligned.

   C Homologous chromosomes become separated as each is pulled to an opposite pole of the cell.

   D Homologous chromosomes begin to repel one another but remain joined at points called chiasmata.

2 With reference to the cell in figure 10.5, state the number of:

   a) chromatids present; (1)

   b) centromeres present; (1)

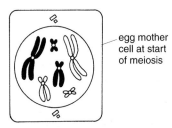

egg mother cell at start of meiosis

Figure 10.5

Continued ➤

Applying your knowledge

	mitosis	meiosis
site of division	occurs all over body of growing animal	
pairing and movement of chromosomes		Homologous chromosomes form pairs; chromosomes line up in pairs on equator
exchange of genetic material	chiasmata not formed and no crossing over occurs	
number of divisions		double division of nucleus
number and type of cells produced	following cell division, two identical daughter cells formed	
effect on chromosome number		chromosome number halved
effect on variation	does not increase variation within a population	

Table 10.2

c) chromosomes present; (1)

d) pairs of homologous chromosomes present; (1)

e) chromosomes that would be present in each gamete produced. (1)

f) **(i)** Draw diagrams to show TWO different ways in which the homologous pairs of chromosomes could become arranged at the equator during the first meiotic division.
   (ii) Give the gametes that would result from each arrangement (if no crossing over occurred). (4)

3 Figure 10.6 shows a pair of homologous chromosomes during meiosis.

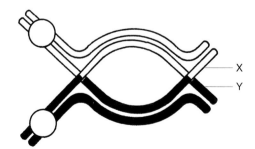

Figure 10.6

a) How many chiasmata occur between chromatids X and Y? (1)

b) Draw a diagram showing the appearance of these chromosomes at the end of the first meiotic division. (2)

4 Copy and complete table 10.2 which compares the processes of mitosis and meiosis. (7)

5 Figure 10.7 shows the genetic fingerprints of seven people.

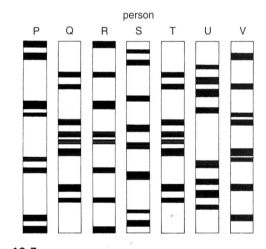

person

P   Q   R   S   T   U   V

Figure 10.7

a) Identify the parents of person P. (1)

b) Identify the monozygotic twins. (1)

c) **(i)** Could person P be the twins' brother?
   (ii) Explain your answer. (2)

d) **(i)** Could the remaining two people in the diagram have the same parents as P?
   (ii) Explain your answer. (2)

What you should know
(Chapters 9–10)

(See table 10.3 for word bank.)

1 A _____ is a unit of heredity which controls a characteristic. It consists of a region of _____ on a chromosome.

2 A species' chromosome _____ is the characteristic number of chromosomes that it possesses (46 in a human). These _____ can be arranged into _____ pairs which match one another gene for gene.

3 In a human, one pair of chromosomes determines the _____ of the individual and are called the sex chromosomes. The other 22 pairs are called _____ .

4 A cell containing 46 chromosomes as 23 pairs is _____ ; a cell containing 23 _____ chromosomes is haploid.

5 _____ is the process by which the nucleus of a diploid gamete mother cell divides into four, resulting in the formation of four _____ .

6 Prior to nuclear _____ , the amount of chromosomal material doubles by DNA undergoing _____ and reproducing itself exactly.

7 DNA replication allows genetic information to be passed on from cell to cell and from generation to _____ .

8 Meiosis involves two consecutive _____ divisions and produces _____ gametes in preparation for sexual reproduction.

9 During meiosis, new combinations of existing alleles arise by independent _____ and _____ between homologous chromosomes.

10 The meeting of two haploid gametes at fertilisation allows mixing of part of one person's _____ with that of another. By producing diploid individuals who are genetically different from their parents, this process produces _____ amongst the members of the human species.

assortment	DNA	meiosis
autosomes	gametes	nuclear
chromosomes	gene	replication
complement	generation	sex
crossing over	genotype	unpaired
diploid	haploid	variation
division	homologous	

Table 10.3 Word bank for chapters 9–10

11 Monohybrid inheritance

Monohybrid cross

A cross between two parents who possess different forms (alleles) of a gene is referred to as **monohybrid inheritance**.

Gregor Mendel (1822–1884), an Austrian monk, carried out early monohybrid crosses using varieties of pea plant. By appreciating the importance of working with **large numbers** of plants, studying **one characteristic** at a time and **counting** the number of offspring produced, Mendel was the first to put genetics on a firm scientific basis.

Pea plant cross

In the experiment shown in figure 11.1, Mendel crossed pea plants which were true-breeding for production of round seeds with pea plants true-breeding for wrinkled seeds. All the seeds produced in the **first filial generation**

(F_1) were round. Once these seeds had grown into plants, they were self-pollinated. The resultant **second filial generation** (F_2) consisted of 7324 seeds (5474 round and 1850 wrinkled). This is a ratio of 2.96:1. When these figures are analysed statistically they are found to represent a ratio of 3 round:1 wrinkled.

Since wrinkled seed, absent in the F_1, reappears in the F_2, 'something' has been transmitted undetected in the gametes from generation to generation. Mendel called this a **factor**. Today we call it a **gene**. In this case it is the gene for seed shape, which has two **alleles**, round and wrinkled.

Since the presence of the round allele masks the presence of the wrinkled allele, round is said to be **dominant** and wrinkled **recessive**.

Genotype and phenotype

An organism's **genotype** is its genetic constitution (i.e. alleles of genes) that it has inherited from its parents. An organism's **phenotype** is its appearance resulting from this inherited genetic information.

Symbols

Using the symbols 'R' for round and 'r' for wrinkled, Mendel's cross can be summarised as follows:

original cross	RR ×	rr
gametes	all R ↓	all r
F_1 **genotype**	all Rr	
phenotype	all round	
second cross	Rr ×	Rr (self-pollinated)
gametes	R and r ↓	R and r
		pollen

F_2 **genotypes (in Punnett square)** ovules

	R	r
R	RR	Rr
r	rR	rr

F_2 **phenotypic ratio** — 3 round:1 wrinkled

Principle of segregation

From the results of many monohybrid experiments involving pea plants, Mendel formulated the **principle of segregation**. Expressed in modern terms this states that: *the alleles of a gene exist in pairs but when gametes are formed, the members of each pair pass into different gametes. Thus each gamete contains only one allele of each gene.*

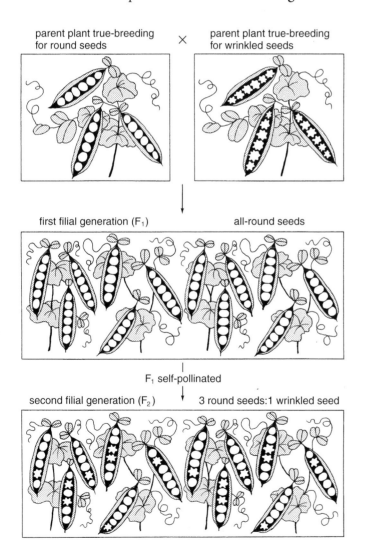

Figure 11.1 Monohybrid cross in pea plants

Homozygous and heterozygous

When an individual possesses two similar alleles of a gene (e.g. R and R or r and r), its genotype is said to be **homozygous** (true-breeding) and all of its gametes are identical with respect to that characteristic.

When an individual possesses two different alleles of a gene (e.g. R and r), its genotype is said to be **heterozygous**. It produces two different types of gamete with respect to that characteristic.

Investigating the phenotypes arising from a monohybrid cross

Use of the fruit fly *(Drosophila)* in breeding experiments

Two features of the reproduction of the fruit fly that make it suitable for the study of genetics are the **shortness of its life cycle** (about 10 days) and the **vast number of offspring** produced (allowing valid statistical analysis of the results).

Inheritance of wing type in the fruit fly

In the following cross, true-breeding long-winged males are crossed with true-breeding short-winged females. (The use of long-winged females and short-winged males would be a genetically identical cross.)

Figure 11.2 shows the procedure used to set up a cross. Table 11.1 lists the reasons for adopting certain techniques or precautions during this investigation.

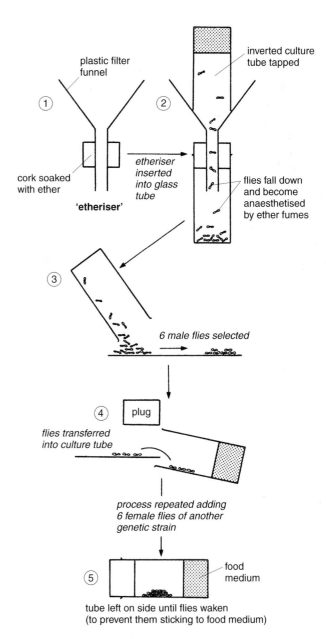

Figure 11.2 Setting up a fruit fly cross

design feature or precaution	reason
Use of several culture tubes.	To produce large number of progeny and make results reliable and statistically valid.
Use of several males and females in each tube.	To allow for infertility or non-recovery from anaesthetic by individual flies.
Use of virgin females.	To ensure that eggs have not been fertilised in advance by male flies of unknown genotype.
Removal of parents after egg-laying.	To ensure that the parents are not confused with the next generation when they emerge.
Experiment repeated several times.	To check that the results can be successfully repeated and were reliable and not the outcome of a lucky chance.

Table 11.1 Design features

Results

Once the F_1 generation has emerged, its members are anaesthetised and examined. All of them are found to be long-winged in appearance showing that the allele for long wing is dominant to the allele for short wing. Some F_1 males and females are then used as the parents of the second cross. When the F_2 generation emerges, it is anaesthetised and the number of each type of fly counted.

Table 11.2 shows a typical set of results for one culture tube from each cross. When the F_2 results are analysed statistically they are found to represent a 3:1 ratio. It is concluded that the inheritance of wing type in the fruit fly obeys Mendel's **principle of segregation** of alleles.

Using the symbols 'L' for long wing and 'l' for short wing, the cross can be summarised as follows:

original cross	LL × ll
gametes	all L ↓ all l
F_1 **genotype**	all Ll
phenotype	all long-winged
second cross	Ll × Ll (F_1 selfed)
gametes	L and l ↓ L and l

F_2 **genotypes (in Punnett square)**

eggs

	sperm	
	L	**l**
L	LL	Ll
l	lL	ll

F_2 **phenotypic ratio** 3 long-winged:1 short-winged

	long-winged	short-winged
parents of F_1	6	6
F_1	198	0
parents of F_2	6♂ and 6♀ from F_1	
F_2	147	52

Table 11.2 Typical results from monohybrid cross

Law of probability

The information in the Punnett square represents only **probabilities** since fertilisation is a **random** process involving an element of **chance**.

Suppose that a box contains one white and three yellow marbles. If a marble is selected at random, there is a 75% (3 in 4) chance that it will be a yellow one. However, although the chance is only 25% (1 in 4), the white one could be selected. If this procedure is repeated 200 times, the law of probability is such that the results would be (but probably not exactly) 150 yellow and 50 white. The more often that this is repeated the closer the combined results will approach the predicted ratio of 3:1.

Equal probability every time

The probability of a particular outcome is always the same regardless of the result that came before it. In the above example every time a marble is selected there is a 25% (1 in 4) chance of selecting the white one regardless of whether or not white was selected the previous time. Lack of understanding of this principle or unwillingness to believe it, is called the **gambler's fallacy**.

● Testing your knowledge ●

1 What term is used to describe a cross between two true-breeding parents that differ from one another in one way only? (1)

2 Give THREE examples of good scientific practice employed by Mendel in his experiments with pea plants. (3)

3 a) Using symbols, represent the genotype of:
   (i)   a pea plant that is true-breeding for production of round seeds;
   (ii) a pea plant that is true-breeding for production of wrinkled seeds;
   (iii) the F_1 offspring that result from crossing **(i)** with **(ii)**. (3)

   b) State the phenotype of the F_1 offspring. (1)

   c) (i)   When these F_1 offspring are self-pollinated, what F_2 phenotypic ratio is produced?
       (ii) Draw a Punnett square to show how this ratio arises. (3)

4 Distinguish between the following pairs:

   a) gene and allele; (2)

   b) genotype and phenotype; (2)

   c) homozygous and heterozygous. (2)

Monohybrid inheritance in humans

Unlike pea plants and fruit flies, human beings are not useful for genetics investigations. Humans do not breed to suit the geneticist. In addition they produce too few offspring to allow meaningful statistical analysis to be carried out. Nevertheless the laws of genetics still apply to humans and particular traits can be traced through several generations of a family by constructing a **family tree (pedigree)**.

Tongue rolling

Some people are able to **roll** their **tongue** whereas others are not. The ability to roll the tongue is inherited as a simple Mendelian dominant trait. The alleles can be represented by the symbols 'R' for roller and 'r' for non-roller.

If a person (e.g. Michelle in figure 11.3) is a non-roller and both of her parents are rollers, then it can be concluded that this person must have the homozygous genotype rr and that both of her parents must have the heterozygous genotype Rr. Piecing together such information for several generations of a family gives a family tree as shown in figure 11.3.

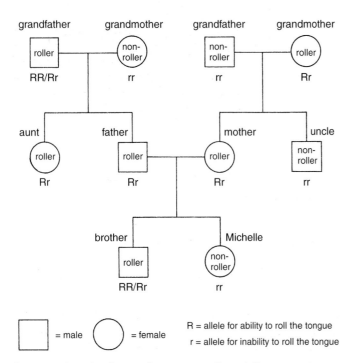

R = allele for ability to roll the tongue
r = allele for inability to roll the tongue
= male
= female

Figure 11.3 A family tree for tongue-rolling ability

Rhesus D-antigen

In addition to the ABO system of antigens, most people have a further antigen on the surface of their red blood cells. This is called **antigen D** and people who possess it are said to be **Rhesus positive (Rh+)**.

A minority of people are described as being **Rhesus negative (Rh−)** because they lack antigen D but react to its presence by forming **anti-D antibodies**. Transfusion of Rh+ red blood cells to a Rh− person must be avoided because the recipient's immune system would respond and produce anti-D antibodies which would persist, leaving the person 'sensitised'. Any subsequent transfusion of Rh+ red blood cells would be liable to cause the sensitised Rh− person to suffer severe or even fatal **agglutination**.

Antigen D is genetically determined by a dominant allele (D); lack of antigen D by a recessive allele (d). Thus Rh+ individuals have genotype DD or Dd; Rh− individuals have genotype dd.

If a Rh− woman (dd) marries a Rh+ man (DD) each of their children will be Rh+ (Dd). If a Rh− woman (dd) marries a Rh+ man (Dd) there is a 50% chance that each of their children will be Rh+ (Dd) as shown in figure 11.4. The biochemical consequences of a Rh− mother carrying a Rh+ baby are discussed in chapter 17.

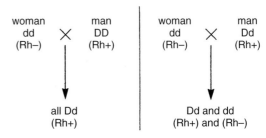

Figure 11.4 Inheritance of Rhesus D-antigen

Albinism

A person affected by **albinism** is unable to make **melanin**, the pigment which gives skin, eye irises and hair their colour (see also p 95).

Albinism is inherited as a simple Mendelian recessive trait. The alleles are often represented by A for normal melanin production and a for albinism. If an albino person marries a heterozygous person with normal pigmentation and they produce four children one of whom is an albino, then a family tree can be constructed as shown in figure 11.5.

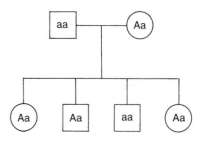

Figure 11.5 A family tree for albinism

Every time that this couple have a child the chance of the child being an albino is 50% (1 in 2). It just happens that only 1 in 4 of their children (so far) is albino owing to the random nature of fertilisation.

Cystic fibrosis

Cystic fibrosis is a disorder of the mucus-secreting glands which causes most sufferers to die at an early age (see also p 95). Like albinism it is inherited as a simple Mendelian recessive trait.

Phenylketonuria

Phenylketonuria (PKU) is a disorder resulting from an inborn error of metabolism (see p 95). It is also inherited as a simple Mendelian recessive trait.

Huntington's chorea

Huntington's chorea is a disorder characterised by degeneration of the nervous system which leads eventually to premature death. Unlike albinism and cystic fibrosis, which are recessive traits, Huntington's chorea is determined by an allele which is **dominant** to the normal allele. It is also exceptional in that it is not expressed in the phenotype until the person is aged, on average, 38 years. By this time the sufferer will probably have had a family and passed the trait on.

This creates a potentially tragic situation (see figure 11.6) where each child of a parent with Huntington's chorea knows that they have a 1 in 2 chance of inheriting the disorder. However they do not find out until they reach their mid-thirties. This begs the further question: should he or she risk having children? This dilemma is further discussed in chapter 14. Huntington's chorea occurs with a frequency of about 1 in 20 000 of the population.

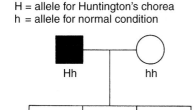

H = allele for Huntington's chorea
h = allele for normal condition

? = person not yet old enough to know if he/she has inherited Huntington's chorea

Figure 11.6 A family tree for Huntington's chorea

Incomplete dominance and co-dominance

In the above examples each allele is either completely dominant or completely recessive to the other allele. As a result the heterozygote (e.g. Rr, Dd, etc.) has the same phenotype as the dominant homozygote (e.g. RR, DD, etc.).

However there are exceptions to this rule. Sometimes the heterozygote exhibits a phenotype which is **different** from both of the homozygotes, as in the following examples.

Incomplete dominance and sickle cell anaemia

Sometimes one allele of a gene is **not completely** dominant over the other allele. For example, when one of the genes that codes for haemoglobin undergoes a certain type of mutation (see p 96), it directs the synthesis of an unusual type of haemoglobin called **haemoglobin S**. Although this differs from normal haemoglobin by only one amino acid, the tiny alteration leads to profound changes in the folding and ultimate shape of the haemoglobin S molecule making it a very inefficient carrier of oxygen.

People who are **homozygous** for the mutant allele suffer drastic consequences. In addition to all of their haemoglobin being type S which fails to perform the normal function properly, sufferers also possess distorted, sickle-shaped red blood cells (see figure 11.7). These are less flexible than the normal type and tend to stick together and interfere with blood circulation. The result of these problems is severe shortage of oxygen followed by damage to vital organs and, in many cases, death. This genetically transmitted condition is called **sickle cell anaemia**.

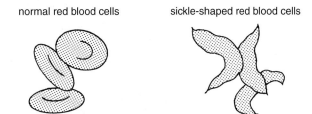

normal red blood cells   sickle-shaped red blood cells

Figure 11.7 Two types of red blood cell

Sickle cell trait

People who are **heterozygous** for the mutant allele do not suffer sickle cell anaemia. Instead they are found to have a milder condition called **sickle cell trait**. Their red blood cells contain both forms of haemoglobin but do not show sickling. The slight anaemia that they tend to suffer does not prevent moderate activity.

This 'in-between' situation where the mutant allele is **partially expressed**, arises because neither allele is completely dominant over the other. Such alleles are said to be **incompletely dominant**. In all cases, the heterozygote is found to exhibit a phenotype which is **intermediate** between those of the two homozygotes.

Symbols

Since neither allele is completely dominant, each is represented by a different upper case letter. For example H is used to represent the allele for normal haemoglobin and S the allele for haemoglobin S.

Resistance to malaria

Allele S is rare in most populations. However, in some parts of Africa up to 40% of the population have the heterozygous genotype HS. This is because sickle cell trait sufferers are **resistant to malaria** (the parasite cannot make use of the red blood cells containing haemoglobin S). People with the homozygous genotype HH have all normal haemoglobin. They are susceptible to malaria and may die during serious outbreaks, as shown in table 11.3.

Co-dominance in the MN blood group system

Blood groups are determined by the presence of antigens on the surfaces of red blood cells. In addition to the ABO and Rhesus D-antigen systems, a further example is the MN blood group system. This is controlled by two alleles M and N which are **co-dominant**. This means that **both** alleles are expressed in the phenotype of the heterozygote. Each allele is represented by a different upper case letter.

People with the homozygous genotype MM have blood group M and bear M antigens on their red blood cells; similarly people with the homozygous genotype NN have blood group N and bear N antigens on their red blood cells.

However, people with the heterozygous genotype MN have blood group MN and possess **both** M and N antigens. They exhibit a phenotype with the characteristics of both the homozygotes.

Since no natural antibodies exist against M and N no problems arise during blood transfusions.

	cross		
	HH × HH	**HH × HS**	**HS × HS**
possible result in non-malarial region	HH, HH, HH, HH (100% of offspring survive)	HH, HH, HS, HS (100% of offspring survive)	HH, HS, HS, S̶S̶ (75% of offspring survive)
possible result in malarial region affected by severe outbreak of disease	H̶H̶, H̶H̶, H̶H̶, H̶H̶ (0% of offspring survive)	H̶H̶, H̶H̶, HS, HS (50% of offspring survive)	H̶H̶, HS, HS, S̶S̶ (50% of offspring survive)

Table 11.3 Survival value of sickle cell trait

Multiple alleles

Each of the genes considered so far has two alleles (which display complete, incomplete or co-dominance). However, some genes are found to possess **three or more** different alleles for a certain characteristic. Such a gene is said to have **multiple alleles**.

Say, for example, three alleles of a certain gene exist. Since each diploid individual possesses a maximum of two of these alleles, there are six possible genotypic combinations of alleles. The number of different phenotypes depends on whether the alleles show complete, incomplete or co-dominance, as shown in the following example.

ABO blood group system

The phenotypic expression of the **ABO system** takes the form of **antigens** on the surface of red blood cells (see p 56). The antigens are coded for by a gene which has three alleles. For the sake of simplicity these are represented by the letters A, B and O.

The A allele produces A antigens, the B allele B antigens and the O allele neither A nor B antigens. Alleles A and B are **co-dominant** to one another and each is completely dominant over allele O. The six different genotypes therefore give rise to four different phenotypes, as shown in table 11.4.

genotype	phenotype	
	blood group	antigens made
AA	A	A only
AO	A	A only
BB	B	B only
BO	B	B only
AB	AB	A and B
OO	O	neither A nor B

Table 11.4 Multiple alleles for ABO blood group system

Testing your knowledge

1 a) Using the symbols H and S, draw a table to compare a person with all normal haemoglobin, a sufferer of sickle cell trait and a sufferer of sickle cell anaemia with reference to their genotype and phenotype. (6)

   b) Why are the alleles H and S described as being incompletely dominant to one another? (1)

2 (i) What is meant by the term *co-dominance* of alleles?

   (ii) Briefly describe an example to illustrate your answer. (3)

3 a) What is meant when a gene is described as having *multiple* alleles? (1)

   b) With reference to the ABO blood group system, identify:
   (i) a phenotype that can result from either of two different genotypes;
   (ii) a phenotype that can only result from one genotype. (3)

Applying your knowledge

1 In fruit flies, grey body colour (G) is dominant to ebony (g). Table 11.5 shows the results of an investigation carried out to examine the phenotypes arising from monohybrid crosses involving the body colour gene.

   a) Present the information in the table in the diagrammatic form used on p 83 for the monohybrid cross based on the wing type. (4)

   b) Why are no ebony-bodied flies produced in the F_1 generation? (1)

   c) (i) What is the expected ratio of grey to ebony in the F_2 generation?

	grey body	ebony body
parents of F_1	6 true-breeding males	6 true-breeding females
F_1	172 flies of both sexes	0
parents of F_2	6 males from F_1	6 true-breeding females
F_2	82 flies of both sexes	88 flies of both sexes

Table 11.5

Continued ➤

Applying your knowledge

(ii) Why do the actual results vary slightly from the expected ones? (2)

d) Explain why each of the following practices is adopted during this investigation.
  (i) Several parental flies of each sex are used per culture tube.
  (ii) Only virgin female flies are used.
  (iii) Parental flies are removed a few days after the eggs have been laid. (3)

2 Albinism is determined by a recessive allele (a). A woman with normal skin pigmentation, whose father was an albino, marries an albino man.

a) What is the chance of each of their children
  (i) being albino
  (ii) having normal skin pigmentation? (2)

b) Which of the following terms refers to the relationship that exists between the two alleles of this gene?
  (i) co-dominance;
  (ii) complete dominance;
  (iii) incomplete dominance. (1)

3 In humans the allele for normal haemoglobin (H) is incompletely dominant to the allele for haemoglobin S (S).

a) Show in diagrammatic form the expected outcome of the following crosses.
  (i) HH × HS
  (ii) HS × HS. (4)

b) In each case state the phenotypes (normal, sickle cell trait or sickle cell anaemia) of the offspring and the ratios in which they would be expected to occur. (4)

4 a) Copy and complete table 11.6 which refers to the MN blood group system. (3)

genotype	blood group	type(s) of antigen on red blood cells
		M only
NN	N	
MN		

Table 11.6

b) Using a Punnett square format, predict the outcome of each of the following crosses.
  (i) MM × NN
  (ii) MN × MN. (4)

c) **(i)** If couple MN × MN have a child, what is the chance of it being
  (1) MM
  (2) MN
  (3) NN?
  (ii) If couple MN × MN have a second child, what is the chance of it being MM? (4)

d) What term is used to refer to this type of relationship between two alleles where both are fully expressed in the phenotype of the heterozygote? (1)

5 In the family tree shown in figure 11.8, a circle represents a woman and a square a man. The upper half of each circle or square contains the person's blood group phenotype and the lower half the person's blood group genotype. Some letters have been omitted.

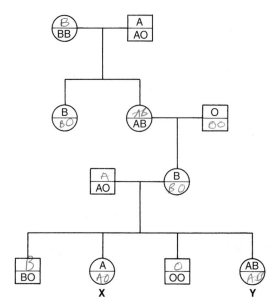

Figure 11.8

a) Copy and complete figure 11.8. (5)

b) If woman X had a child fathered by a man of blood group O, what is the chance of the child having genotype OO? (1)

c) If woman Y had a child fathered by a man of blood group O, what is the chance of the child having blood group O? (1)

Applying your knowledge

6 The presence of antigen D on red blood cells is determined by a dominant allele (D), its absence by a recessive allele (d). A family tree involving this inherited characteristic is shown in figure 11.9.

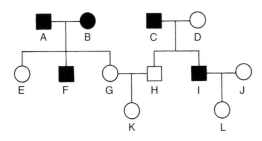

- ■ ♂ possessing antigen D
- □ ♂ lacking antigen D
- ● ♀ possessing antigen D
- ○ ♀ lacking antigen D

Figure 11.9

a) Give the genotype and phenotype of
  (i)   person A;
  (ii) person K. (2)

b) Identify the person whose genotype cannot be worked out from the information given. Explain why. (2)

c) Identify
  (i)   a man who is rhesus negative;
  (ii) a woman who is rhesus positive. (2)

d) If person L marries a man with the same genotype as her father, what is the chance that each of their children will be
  (i)   rhesus positive;
  (ii) rhesus negative? (2)

e) Predict with reasons the outcome of
  (i)   person J receiving a blood transfusion from person B;
  (ii) person B receiving a blood transfusion from person J. (2)

7 With reference to one named example, give an account of monohybrid inheritance in humans. (10)

---

12 Sex-linked and polygenic inheritance

Sex chromosomes

In the nucleus of every normal human body cell there are 46 chromosomes. These exist as 22 homologous pairs of autosomes and one pair of **sex chromosomes** (see also p 68). In the female, the sex chromosomes make up a fully homologous pair, the **X** chromosomes. In the male, the sex chromosomes make up a pair consisting of an X chromosome and a much smaller **Y** chromosome which is homologous to only part of the X chromosome.

Sex-linked genes

The X and Y chromosomes behave as a homologous pair at meiosis. However, the X chromosome differs from the Y chromosome in that the larger X carries many genes not present on the smaller Y. These genes are said to be **sex-linked** (see figure 12.1).

When an X chromosome meets a Y chromosome at fertilisation, each sex-linked gene on the X chromosome (whether dominant or recessive) becomes expressed in the phenotype of the human male produced. This is because

his Y chromosome does not possess alleles of any of these sex-linked genes and cannot offer dominance to them.

Symbols

In crosses and family trees involving sex-linked genes, the sex chromosomes are represented by the symbols X and Y and the alleles of the sex-linked gene by appropriate **superscripts**.

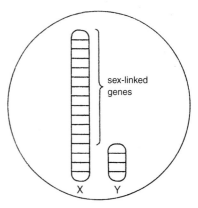

Figure 12.1 Sex-linked genes

Red-green colour blindness

In humans, normal colour vision (C) is completely dominant to **red-green colour blindness** (c). These are alleles of a sex-linked gene on the X chromosome. The five possible genotypes and phenotypes for normal colour vision and red-green colour blindness are given in table 12.1.

genotype	phenotype
$X^C X^C$	Female with normal colour vision.
$X^C X^c$	Female (carrier) with normal colour vision.
$X^c X^c$	Female with colour blindness (very rare e.g. 0.5% of European population).
$X^C Y$	Male with normal colour vision.
$X^c Y$	Male with colour blindness (more common e.g. 8% of European population).

Table 12.1 Red-green colour blindness in humans

Heterozygous females are called **carriers**. Although unaffected themselves, there is a 1 in 2 (50%) chance that they will pass the allele on to each of their offspring. On average therefore, 50% of a carrier female's sons are colour blind. This pattern of inheritance is shown in figure 12.2.

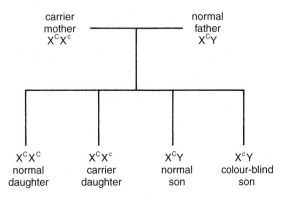

Figure 12.2 Colour blindness cross using superscript symbols

Red-green colour blindness is rare in females since two recessive alleles must be inherited. It is more common in males where only one is needed.

Haemophilia

Clotting of blood is the result of a complex series of biochemical reactions involving many essential chemicals. One of these blood-clotting agents is a protein called **factor VIII**. In humans the genetic information for factor VIII is coded for by a gene carried on the X chromosome.

However, an inferior version of the factor VIII protein is formed if the gene is changed by a mutation (see chapter 13). A person who inherits the altered genetic material suffers a condition called **haemophilia**. The sufferer's

blood takes a very long time (or even fails) to clot resulting in prolonged bleeding from even the tiniest wound. Internal bleeding may occur and continue unchecked leading to serious consequences.

Since haemophilia is caused by a recessive allele carried on the X but not the Y chromosome, it is a **sex-linked** condition. The genotypes of individuals in crosses involving haemophilia are normally represented by the following symbols: X^H (normal blood clotting allele), X^h (haemophilia) and Y (no allele for this gene).

A cross between a carrier female and a normal male would give the same pattern of inheritance as colour blindness in figure 12.2. Figure 12.3 shows the possible outcome of a cross between a normal woman and a man suffering haemophilia. Figure 12.4 shows a cross between a carrier woman and a haemophiliac man using a different style of symbol.

The frequency of haemophilia is approximately 1 in 5000 live births in Britain. Haemophilia amongst females is even rarer than colour blindness. Blood clotting factors

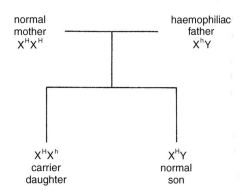

Figure 12.3 Haemophilia cross using superscript symbols

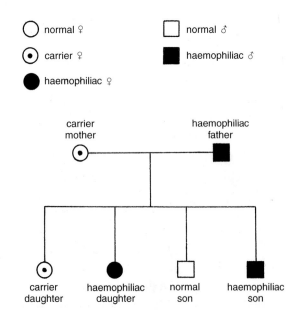

Figure 12.4 Haemophilia cross using alternative symbols

are now available for use to treat this condition and allow haemophiliacs to lead a relatively normal life.

Muscular dystrophy

Duchenne muscular dystrophy is the most common form of this muscle-wasting disease. Skeletal muscles lose their normal structure and fibrous tissue develops in their place. Like the above two examples, this condition is caused by a recessive allele carried on the X chromosome and is sex-linked.

Duchenne muscular dystrophy is found to be almost entirely restricted to males. The sufferers are severely disabled from an early age and normally die without passing the allele on to the next generation. Figure 12.5 shows a family tree where the allele survives by being passed from carrier female to carrier female. The estimated frequency of this inherited disease is 1 in 3000 male infants.

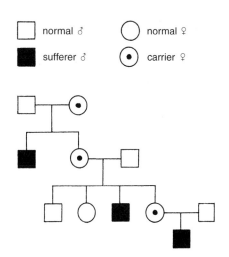

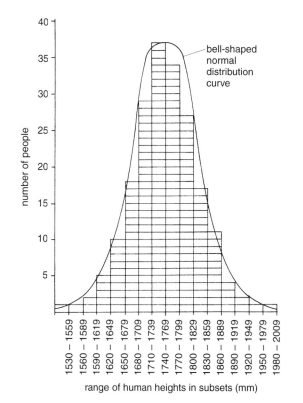

Figure 12.5 A family tree for Duchenne muscular dystrophy

---

presented as a bar chart. A characteristic showing discontinuous variation is normally controlled by the alleles of a single gene.

Continuous variation

A characteristic shows **continuous variation** when it varies amongst the members of the species in a smooth continuous way from one extreme to another and does not fall into distinct groups. For example, human body height varies continuously from very small to very tall. Such information is often presented as a histogram as shown in figure 12.6 which is based on the heights of 200 adults.

Figure 12.6 Histogram of human height

Testing your knowledge

1 a) Which of the human sex chromosomes is the larger one? (1)

b) What term is used to refer to genes that are present on the X chromosome but absent from the Y chromosome? (1)

c) If a human male inherits the recessive allele of a sex-linked gene, it is always expressed in his phenotype. Explain why. (1)

2 Represent symbolically the genotype(s) of:
(i) a colour-blind male;
(ii) a human female with normal vision who is a carrier;
(iii) the offspring that could be produced if **(i)** and **(ii)** were their parents. (3)

3 a) Name a sex-linked condition that involves defective blood clotting in humans. (1)

b) Why are sex-linked conditions expressed much less frequently in the phenotype of females compared with males? (1)

Polygenic inheritance

Discontinuous variation

A characteristic shows **discontinuous variation** if it can be used to divide up the members of a species into two or more distinct groups. For example, humans can be divided into two separate groups based on the ability or inability to roll the tongue. Such information is often

Since the majority of people have heights close to the centre of the range, with fewer at the extremities, a curve drawn round the histogram gives a bell-shaped **normal distribution**.

A characteristic showing continuous variation is controlled by the alleles of more than one gene and is said to show **polygenic inheritance**. The more genes that are involved, the greater the number of intermediate phenotypes that can be produced.

Additive effect

The genes involved in polygenic inheritance are transmitted from generation to generation via meiosis in the normal way. What makes them different from other genes is that their effects are **additive**. This means that each dominant allele of each gene adds a contribution towards the characteristic controlled by the genes.

Example of polygenic inheritance

Grain colour in a certain type of cereal can be explained on the basis that it is determined by two genes (located

on different chromosomes) each with two alleles, as shown in table 12.2.

	dominant allele	recessive allele
gene 1	R^1 (Codes for red colour.)	r^1 (Does not code for red colour.)
gene 2	R^2 (Codes for red colour.)	r^2 (Does not code for red colour.)

Table 12.2 Genes for cereal grain colour

Each dominant allele codes for a quantity of red colour equal to 25% of the maximum amount that can occur in this type of cereal. Thus a strain with the genotype $R^1 R^1 R^2 R^2$ would possess the maximum amount of pigment and be 100% red, strain $R^1 R^1 R^2 r^2$ would be 75% red, and so on to strain $r^1 r^1 r^2 r^2$ which would be white.

Figure 12.7 shows how a cross between a 100% red strain and a white strain gives a 50% red strain in the F_1

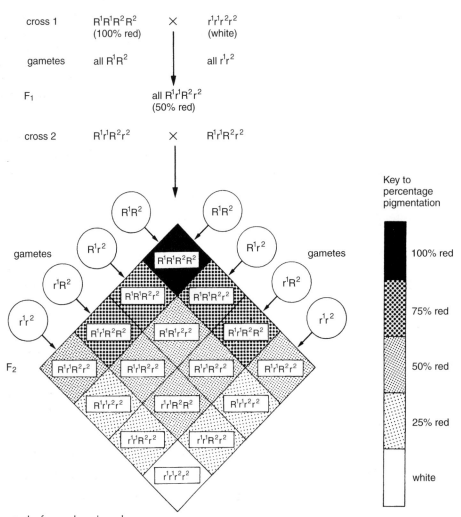

Figure 12.7 Genetic control of cereal grain colour

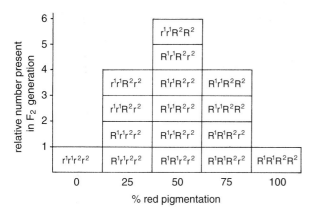

Figure 12.8 Histogram of F$_2$ generation of cereal grains

generation. Self-pollination of the F$_1$ generation produces an F$_2$ whose members display a range of colour types. When these are presented as a histogram (see figure 12.8), the additive effects give a display approaching that typical of continuous variation.

Polygenic inheritance in humans

Many human characteristics such as height, weight, skin colour, hand span, foot size, etc. show a pattern of polygenic inheritance. Since there are many more than five different expressions of height, weight, etc., each of these characteristics must be controlled by more than two genes. Detailed studies suggest that **three or more genes** are probably involved in each case, with every dominant allele making an individual contribution to the characteristic.

Environment

Whereas characteristics which show discontinuous variation (e.g. tongue rolling, ABO blood group, etc.) are usually unaffected by environmental factors, many characteristics which show continuous variation (e.g. height, foot size, etc.) are influenced by the **environment**. They are dependent on favourable environmental conditions for their full phenotypic expression. For example, regardless of how many dominant alleles for height that a person inherits, he or she will not reach their full potential height without consuming an adequate diet during childhood and adolescence.

Thus polygenic inheritance, often combined with environmental factors, produces a phenotypic characteristic which shows a wide range of continuous variation and a normal pattern of distribution.

Testing your knowledge

1 (i) Explain the meaning of the terms *continuous* and *discontinuous* variation giving an example of each in your answer.
   (ii) Which of these forms of variation is controlled by alleles of more than one gene?
   (iii) What term is used to refer to this type of inheritance?
   (iv) What relationship exists between the number of genes involved and the number of intermediate phenotypes that can be produced? (7)

2 Apart from genetic factors, what other type of factors influence the wide range of phenotypic expression shown by some characteristics? (1)

Applying your knowledge

1 Using the same format as figure 12.2, show the possible results of a cross between a colour-blind male and a carrier female. (6)

2 Haemophilia occurs in the family tree shown in figure 12.9.

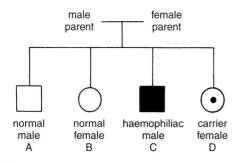

Figure 12.9

a) Using the convention X^H (normal allele), X^h (haemophilia allele) and Y (no allele), give the genotypes of the offspring A, B, C and D. (4)

b) Give the genotype and phenotype of each parent. (4)

c) If C marries a normal female, what proportion of their sons are likely to be haemophiliacs? (1)

3 Decide whether each of the following statements is true or false, and then use T or F to indicate your choice. (5)

a) A man can pass on a sex-linked gene to his sons.

b) In humans, haemophilia is rarer in the female than in the male.

Continued ➤

Applying your knowledge

c) Females heterozygous for a sex-linked gene are called carriers.

d) The sex-linked gene for colour blindness is present on the Y but not the X chromosome.

e) A woman can pass on a sex-linked gene to her daughters.

4 For the sake of simplicity, assume that human height is determined by two genes H^1/h^1 and H^2/h^2 (located on different chromosomes but not on the sex chromosomes).

a) Show in diagrammatic form the genotypes of all the possible offspring that could result from a cross between $H^1 H^1 H^2 h^2$ and $H^1 H^1 H^2 h^2$. (4)

b) State each offspring's phenotype using the scale: very tall, tall, medium, small, very small. (4)

c) Genetically speaking, in what way is this treatment an over-simplification of the true situation? (1)

d) What other factors could affect the heights of the offspring in the cross? (1)

5 Grain colour in wheat is an example of polygenic inheritance. It can be explained on the basis that it is controlled by three genes whose dominant alleles code for red pigment and have an additive effect.

The genotypes of plants that make grain with 100% red pigment and those that make grain with 0% pigmentation (white) are represented in figure 12.10, which also shows the outcome of crossing these two true-breeding plants.

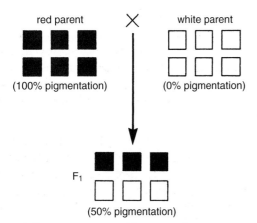

Figure 12.10

	pollen							
ovules	▪▪▪	▪▪□	▪□▪	□▪▪	▪□□	□▪□	□□▪	□□□
▪▪▪								
▪▪□				4				
▪□▪					3			
□▪▪	5							
▪□□								
□▪□								
□□▪							1	
□□□		2						

Figure 12.11

Figure 12.11 shows a Punnett square which represents selfing the F_1 generation. It gives the eight types of pollen and ovules that would be involved.

a) Copy figure 12.11 and complete it by inserting the number of red alleles that would be present in each zygote following fertilisation. (A few have been done for you.) (2)

b) Draw a histogram of the 64 zygotes. (3)

c) (i) Assuming that each red allele contributes one unit of red pigment to the wheat grain's phenotype, state how many different shades of red would be present in the F_2 generation. (1)

(ii) Which shade of red is most common? (1)

(iii) Which shade of red is least common? (1)

(iv) What percentage of grains in an F_2 generation would be expected to have the shade of red determined by one red allele? (1)

d) From the data, express as a ratio the number of F_2 grains whose red colour is determined by 3 alleles to those whose red colour is controlled by 2 alleles. (1)

6 Outline the mechanism of sex-linked inheritance in humans by naming a sex-linked characteristic and showing how it is transmitted from one generation to the next. (10)

(13) Mutations and chromosomal abnormalities

Mutation

A **mutation** is a change in the structure or amount of an organism's genetic material. It varies in form from a tiny change in the DNA structure of a gene to a large scale alteration in chromosome structure or number. When such a change in genotype produces a change in phenotype, the individual affected is called a **mutant**.

Alteration of base type or sequence

This type of mutation (called **gene mutation**) involves a change in one or more of the **nucleotides** in a strand of DNA.

Four examples of gene mutation are shown in figure 13.1. In each case one or more codons for one or more particular amino acids have become altered leading to a change in the protein that is synthesised.

For a protein to work properly it must have the correct sequence of amino acids. **Substitution** and **inversion** are called '**point**' mutations. They bring about only a minor change (i.e. one different amino acid) and sometimes the organism is affected only slightly or not at all. However if the substituted amino acid occurs at a critical position in the protein then a major defect may arise (e.g. formation of haemoglobin S and sickle cell anaemia – see also p 85).

Insertion and **deletion** are called '**frameshift**' mutations. Each leads to a major change since it causes a large portion of the gene's DNA to be misread. The protein produced differs from the normal protein by many amino acids and it is usually non-functional. If such a protein is an enzyme which catalyses an essential step in a metabolic pathway (see p 14), then the pathway becomes disrupted. An intermediate metabolite may accumulate and cause problems, as in the following example.

Phenylketonuria

Phenylalanine and **tyrosine** are two amino acids that humans obtain from protein in their diet. During normal metabolism, excess phenylalanine is acted on by an enzyme (phenylalanine hydroxylase) as shown in the pathway in figure 13.2.

Phenylketonuria (PKU) is a hereditary disorder caused by a genetic defect which disrupts this metabolic pathway. An affected person lacks the normal allele of the gene required to make enzyme 1. Owing to this **inborn error of metabolism**, phenylalanine is no longer converted to tyrosine. Instead it undergoes alternative metabolic pathways producing toxins which affect the metabolism of brain cells and severely limit mental development.

In Britain, new-born babies are screened for PKU (see p 105) and sufferers are put on a diet containing minimum phenylalanine. As a result the worst effects of PKU have been reduced to a minimum.

Albinism

Albinism results from a mutation which prevents the formation of enzyme 3 (melanocyte tyrosinase) in the pathway shown in figure 13.2. Albinos fail to synthesise **melanin**. Complete lack of this pigment causes an albino to have very pale skin (which fails to tan) and white hair. Albinos are perfectly normal in every other way and suffer no medical problems provided that they avoid exposure to ultraviolet radiation.

Cystic fibrosis

Mucus is the slimy substance secreted by the inner lining of the windpipe and intestine. Mucus is composed of a particular type of **glycoprotein** which makes it thick and slimy and perfectly suited to its roles of protection and lubrication. The genetic information for coding this glycoprotein is contained in a gene carried on chromosome 7 in humans.

However, this information can become altered by a gene mutation. People who are homozygous for the mutant allele make abnormally thick, sticky mucus which leads to lung congestion and blockage of the pancreatic duct. This condition is called **cystic fibrosis**. It occurs with a frequency of about 1 in 2500 live births in Britain. 1 in 25 people are heterozygous and therefore carry the mutant allele masked in their genotype.

Frequency of mutation

In the absence of outside influences, gene mutations arise **spontaneously** and at **random** but only occur **rarely**. The mutation rate of a gene is expressed as the number of mutations that occur at that gene site (locus) per million gametes. Mutation rate varies from gene to gene and species to species.

The vast majority of mutant alleles are recessive. Therefore a newly formed mutant allele fails to be expressed phenotypically until two of these recessive alleles meet as a pair in some future generation. However, a few mutant alleles are expressed by the first generation to inherit them because they are either dominant (e.g. Huntington's chorea) or sex-linked (e.g. haemophilia).

Mutagenic agents

Mutation rate can be increased by exposure to mutagenic agents. These include certain chemicals (e.g. mustard gas)

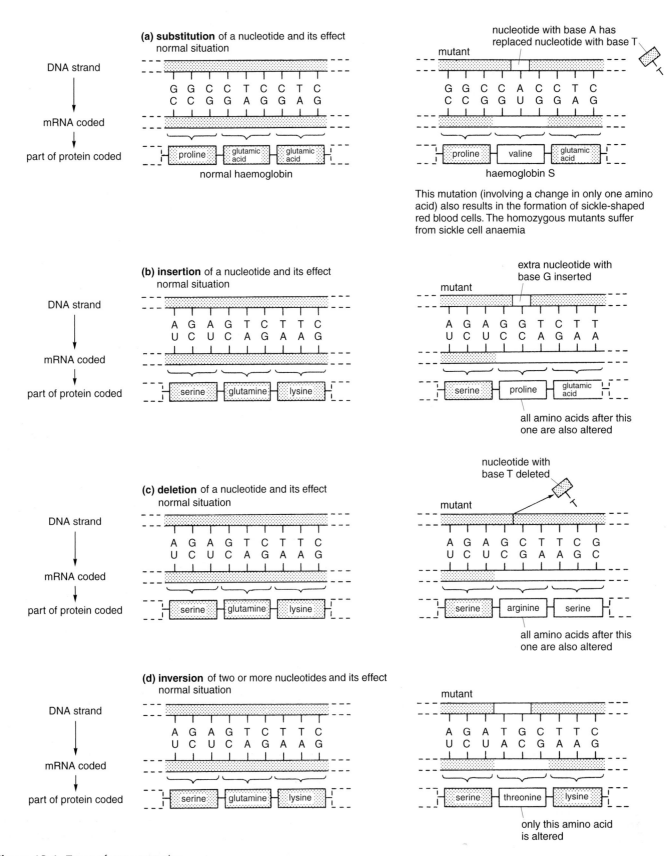

Figure 13.1 Types of gene mutation

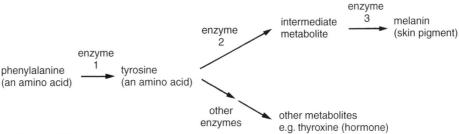

Figure 13.2 Normal fate of phenylalanine

and various types of radiation (e.g. gamma rays, X-rays and UV light).

Chromosomal abnormalities

Chromosomes can be affected by mutations which bring about large scale changes to the genetic material. One type of abnormality arises during meiosis in humans when unusual gametes are formed which contain 22 or 24 chromosomes instead of the normal haploid complement of 23. This leads to the formation of zygotes with **abnormal chromosome complements**. These abnormal gametes are formed as a result of non-disjunction.

Non-disjunction during meiosis

When a spindle fibre fails during meiosis and the members of one pair of homologous chromosomes fail to become separated, this is called **non-disjunction**. Normal meiosis and non-disjunction are compared in figure 13.3 where 3 pairs instead of 23 pairs of homologous chromosomes are shown.

In this example of non-disjunction (where spindle failure occurs during the first meiotic division), two of the gametes receive an extra copy of the affected chromosome and two gametes lack that chromosome.

On the other hand, if non-disjunction occurs during the second meiotic division and only affects one of the two cells, this results in the production of two normal gametes and two abnormal gametes. One of the abnormal gametes receives an extra copy of the affected chromosome and the other lacks that chromosome.

Down's syndrome

If non-disjunction of **chromosome pair 21** occurs in a human egg mother cell, then one or more abnormal eggs (n = 24) may be formed. If one of these is fertilised by a normal sperm (n = 23), this results in the formation of an abnormal zygote (2n = 47). The extra copy of chromosome 21 can be seen in the karyotype (see figure 13.4).

The affected individual suffers **Down's syndrome** which is characterised by mental retardation and distinctive physical features.

Nearly 80% of the non-disjunctions that lead to Down's syndrome are of maternal origin with frequency being related to maternal age (see figure 13.5). Since egg mother cells of older women seem to be more prone to non-disjunction at meiosis, pregnant women over the age of thirty-five are routinely offered a fetal chromosome analysis.

Non-disjunction of sex chromosomes

If human sex chromosomes are affected by non-disjunction during meiosis, then unusual gametes are formed as shown in figure 13.6 on page 99.

Turner's syndrome

If a gamete which possesses no sex chromosomes meets and fuses with a normal X gamete, the zygote formed has the chromosome complement 2n = 45 (44 + XO where O represents the lack of a second sex chromosome). Figure 13.7 on page 99 shows the karyotype.

An individual with this unusual chromosome complement suffers a condition known as **Turner's syndrome**. Such individuals are always female and short

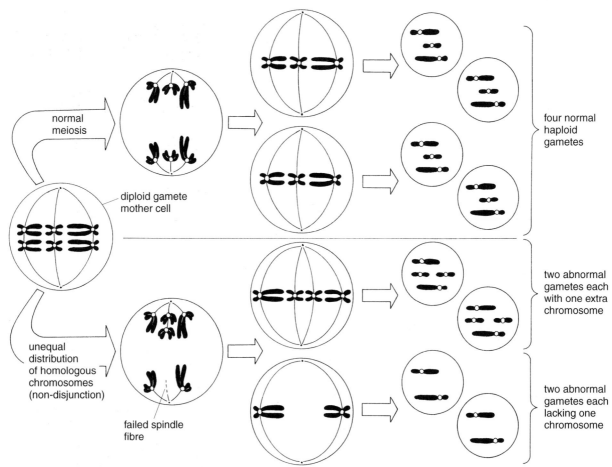

Figure 13.3 Non-disjunction

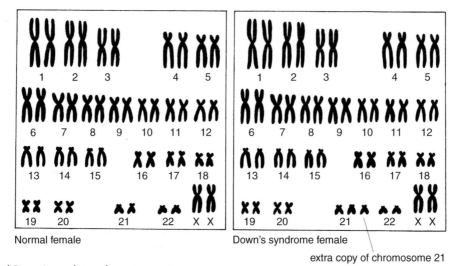

Normal female

Down's syndrome female

extra copy of chromosome 21

Figure 13.4 Normal and Down's syndrome karyotypes

in stature. Since their ovaries do not develop, they are infertile and fail to develop secondary sexual characteristics (e.g. breast development, menstruation, etc.) at puberty.

Turner's syndrome occurs with a frequency of about 1 in 2500 female live births.

Klinefelter's syndrome

If an XX egg (see figure 13.6) is fertilised by a normal Y sperm or a normal X egg is fertilised by an XY sperm then the zygote formed has the chromosome complement 2n = 47 (44 + XXY). Figure 13.8 shows the karyotype.

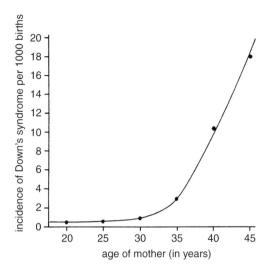

Figure 13.5 Down's syndrome and age of mother

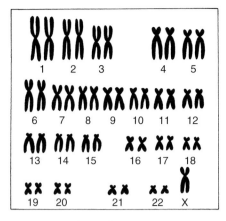

Figure 13.7 Turner's syndrome karyotype

An individual with this unusual chromosome complement suffers a condition known as **Klinefelter's syndrome**. Such individuals are always male and possess male sex organs. However they are infertile since their testes only develop to about half the normal size and fail to produce sperm. The small testes also fail to produce normal levels of testosterone (the male sex hormone) and as a result, male secondary sexual characteristics (e.g. growth of facial hair, deepening of voice, etc.) are only weakly expressed. Some sufferers tend to develop small breasts.

Klinefelter's syndrome occurs with a frequency of about 1 in 1000 male live births.

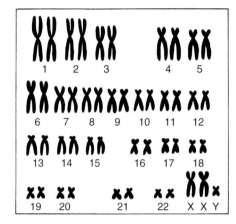

Figure 13.8 Klinefelter's syndrome karyotype

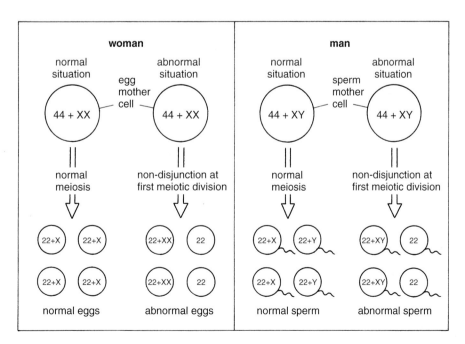

Figure 13.6 Non-disjunction of sex chromosomes

Testing your knowledge

1 a) What name is given to the process by which a spindle fibre fails during meiosis and one or more of the gametes produced receives an extra chromosome? (1)

b) How many gametes (out of four) will receive an extra chromosome if the spindle failure occurs during the first meiotic division? (1)

2 a) If a normal human sperm fertilises an egg containing an extra copy of chromosome 21, what is the diploid number of the zygote formed? (1)

b) (i) What name is given to the condition suffered by a person who develops from an abnormal zygote of this type?

(ii) What relationship exists between age of mother and incidence of this condition? (2)

3 Rewrite the following sentences choosing the correct alternative from each bracketed choice.

The sex of a person with Klinefelter's syndrome is (male/female). Such a person began life as a zygote containing the sex chromosomes (XXX/XXY) which could have resulted from an unusual (XX/XY) egg being fertilised by a normal (X/Y) sperm. (3)

Applying your knowledge

1 In the following four sentences, a small error alters the sense of the message. To which type of gene mutation is each of these equivalent? (4)

a) Intended: She ordered boiled rice.
Actual: She ordered boiled ice.

b) Intended: He walked to the post box.
Actual: He talked to the post box.

c) Intended: She untied the two ropes.
Actual: She united the two ropes.

d) Intended: He put a quid in his pocket.
Actual: He put a squid in his pocket.

2 Figure 13.9 shows part of a metabolic pathway that occurs in humans. Each stage is controlled by an enzyme. Some of the stages have been given a letter.

a) Explain how a gene mutation can lead to a blockage in such a pathway. (2)

b) Identify the letter that represents the point of blockage that leads to each of the following disorders.
(i) phenylketonuria;
(ii) albinism;
(iii) alcaptonuria (characterised by an accumulation of homogentisic acid which is excreted in urine and turns black in light). (3)

c) The graph in figure 13.10 shows the effect of a phenylalanine meal on a normal person and on a sufferer of phenylketonuria (PKU).
(i) Explain the initial rise in level of tyrosine in the normal person.

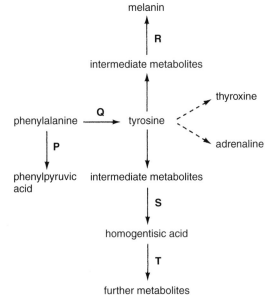

Figure 13.9

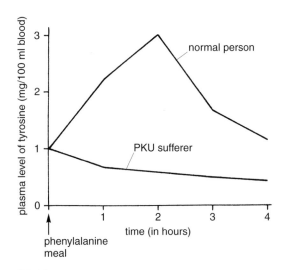

Figure 13.10

Continued ➤

Applying your knowledge

(ii) Why does the PKU sufferer not show a similar increase?

(iii) Why does the level of tyrosine in the normal person fall after two hours? (3)

3 Achondroplasia (a form of dwarfism in humans) is controlled by a dominant mutant allele (A). All achondroplastic dwarfs are heterozygous (Aa) since the homozygous condition is lethal. Imagine that each of the following sets of parents produce a dwarf child.

    A   Aa × Aa
    B   Aa × aa
    C   aa × aa.

a) In which family must a gene mutation definitely have occurred? (1)

b) From such studies it is now known that the mutation rate of this gene is 14 per million gametes. Express this figure as a 1 in _____ chance of a new mutation occurring. (1)

4 a) Refer to the graph in figure 13.5 and estimate the chance of mothers of each of the following ages giving birth to a Down's syndrome baby.
    (i)   20 years
    (ii) 30 years
    (iii) 40 years.

b) Account for this trend. (4)

5 Figure 13.11 shows meiosis in a sperm mother cell. Although the first meiotic division is normal, one of the products is affected by non-disjunction during the second division.

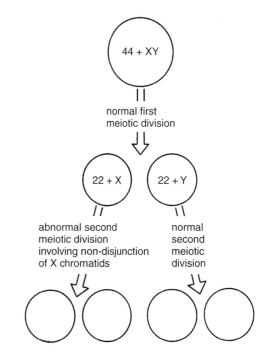

Figure 13.11

a) Using only numbers and letters as required, represent the four sperm that would be formed. (4)

b) Using the same convention, represent the zygote that would be formed if each of these sperm successfully fertilised a normal egg. (4)

c) What percentage of the zygotes in your answer to **b)** would develop into sufferers of Turner's syndrome? (1)

6 Describe the main types of gene mutation and their effects on amino acid sequences. (10)

Use of family histories

A pattern of human inheritance can be revealed by collecting information about a particular characteristic from the members of a family and then using it to construct a **family tree (pedigree)**. Once the phenotypes are known, most of the genotypes can be deduced.

Such construction of a family tree is carried out by a genetic counsellor when information and advice are required by a couple who are worried about the possibility of passing a **genetic disorder** (known to exist in their family) on to their children.

Types of pedigree
Autosomal recessive inheritance

Figure 14.1 shows a family with a history of **cystic fibrosis**. The geneticist recognises that such a trait shows a typical **autosomal recessive** pattern of inheritance because:

◆ the trait is expressed relatively rarely;

◆ the trait tends to skip generations;

◆ the trait is expressed in some of the offspring of a consanguineous marriage (in this case cousins);

◆ males and females are affected in approximately equal numbers.

The geneticist can therefore add genotypes to the family tree by applying the following rules governing any characteristic showing autosomal recessive inheritance:

◆ all sufferers of the trait are homozygous recessive (e.g. cc);

◆ non-sufferers are homozygous dominant (e.g. CC) or heterozygous (e.g. Cc) and most of these genotypes can

be deduced by referring to other closely related members of the tree.

The outcome of the cystic fibrosis example is shown in figure 14.2.

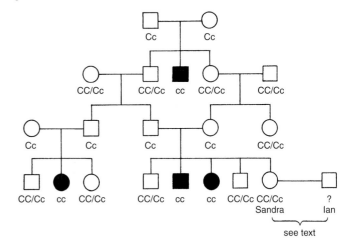

Figure 14.2 Genotypes for autosomal recessive example

Autosomal dominant inheritance

Figure 14.3 shows a family with a history of **Huntington's chorea**. The geneticist recognises that such a trait shows a typical **autosomal dominant** pattern of inheritance because:

◆ the trait appears in every generation;

◆ each sufferer of the trait has an affected parent;

◆ when a branch of the family does not express the trait, it fails to reappear in future generations of that branch;

◆ males and females are affected in approximately equal numbers.

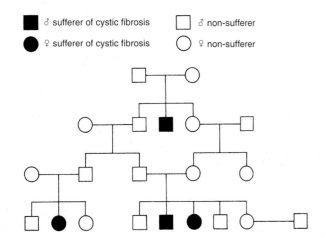

Figure 14.1 Autosomal recessive inheritance

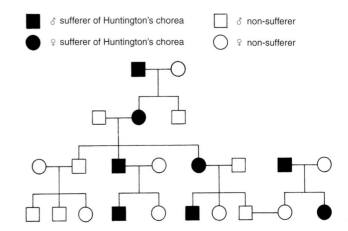

Figure 14.3 Autosomal dominant inheritance

The geneticist can therefore add genotypes to the family tree by applying the following rules governing any characteristic showing autosomal dominant inheritance:

◆ all non-sufferers are homozygous recessive (e.g. hh);

◆ sufferers are homozygous dominant (e.g. HH) or heterozygous (e.g. Hh) and most of these genotypes can be deduced by referring to other closely related members of the tree.

The outcome of the Huntington's chorea example is shown in figure 14.4.

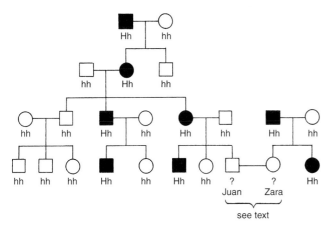

Figure 14.4 Genotypes for autosomal dominant inheritance

Sex-linked recessive trait

Figure 14.5 shows a family with a history of **haemophilia**. The geneticist recognises that such a trait shows a typical **sex-linked recessive** pattern of inheritance because:

◆ many more males have been affected than females (if any);

◆ none of the sons of an affected male show the trait;

◆ some grandsons of affected males show the trait.

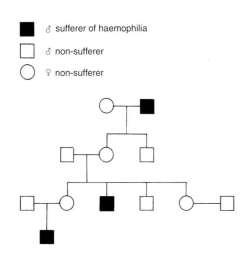

Figure 14.5 Sex-linked recessive inheritance

The geneticist can therefore add genotypes to the family tree by applying the following rules which govern any characteristic showing sex-linked recessive inheritance:

◆ all sufferers of the trait are 'homozygous' recessive (normally male e.g. $X^h Y$ and very rarely female e.g. $X^h X^h$);

◆ non-sufferers are 'homozygous' dominant (e.g $X^H Y$, $X^H X^H$) or heterozygous carrier females (e.g $X^H X^h$) and most or all of these genotypes can be deduced by referring to other closely related members of the tree.

The outcome of the haemophilia example is shown in figure 14.6.

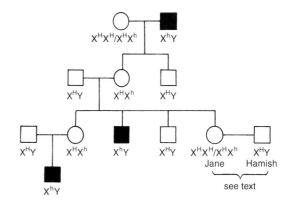

Figure 14.6 Genotypes of sex-linked recessive example

Assessing the risk

Once the genetic counsellor has constructed the family tree(s) and established as many genotypes as possible, he or she is in a position to assess **risk** and state **probabilities**.

Autosomal recessive

Returning to the cystic fibrosis example shown in figure 14.2, consider the situation Sandra and Ian find themselves in. Cystic fibrosis is known to exist in Sandra's family but not in that of Ian. The genetic counsellor would work out from the tree that Sandra has a 2 in 3 chance of being a carrier.

The counsellor would already know that the frequency amongst the British population of an individual being heterozygous for the cystic fibrosis allele is 1 in 25, and would therefore regard this as the risk of Ian being a carrier. Combining all these probabilities, he or she would conclude that the risk of Sandra and Ian having a child with cystic fibrosis is fairly low.

Autosomal dominant

Returning to the Huntington's chorea example shown in figure 14.4, consider the situation that Juan and Zara find themselves in. Unlike their siblings, both are still too young to know whether they have received the harmful allele from an affected parent. At present it is a 1 in 2 chance that each is heterozygous for the condition and destined to develop it later in life.

From the information presently available, the genetic counsellor would conclude that there is a high risk that each of their children would suffer this debilitating disease. For example, if either Juan or Zara turns out to be Hh, then the chance of each child being affected would be 1 in 2; if both Juan and Zara turn out to be Hh then 3 in 4 of their children on average would suffer Huntington's chorea.

Sex-linked recessive

Returning to the haemophilia example shown in figure 14.6, consider the situation that Jane and Hamish find themselves in. Jane is anxious to know if she could pass the trait on to her sons. There is no history of the disorder in Hamish's family.

From the information in the family pedigree, the genetic counsellor would note that Jane's brother and nephew have developed this sex-linked disorder. This shows that Jane's mother and sister are carriers. He or she would therefore conclude that there is a 1 in 2 chance of Jane being a carrier. If she does turn out to be a carrier, then each of her sons (but none of her daughters) would stand a 1 in 2 chance of developing haemophilia. However, from the information presently available the counsellor would assess the risk of each son being a haemophiliac at a 1 in 4 chance.

Genetic counselling based on pedigree analysis

The aim of genetic counselling is to help people to make well **informed decisions** for themselves based on the information available. Analysis of a family tree allows the expert to chart the pattern of the disorder but it is of limited value in that, at best, all that it can offer is an assessment of risk.

Pre-natal (before birth) screening

If a couple decide to go ahead and have a baby, various methods of **pre-natal screening** can be employed in an attempt to identify potential problems before the baby is born.

Use of these techniques is normally restricted to individuals at risk e.g. members of a family with a history of a genetic disorder (e.g. cystic fibrosis) or pregnant women over the age of thirty-five who are more likely to have a Down's syndrome baby than younger mothers.

Use of karyotypes

Two methods of pre-natal screening depend on fetal material being obtained to allow **karyotypes** to be examined.

Amniocentesis

Amniocentesis is carried out at about the eighteenth week of pregnancy. It involves the withdrawal of a little amniotic fluid containing fetal cells. These are cultured, stained and examined under the microscope. A full chromosome complement is photographed, karyotyping is carried out and the chromosomes are arranged into pairs as shown in figure 13.4 (see p 98).

This technique, which takes about two weeks, allows chromosomal abnormalities to be detected. An extra copy of chromosome 21, for example, indicates Down's syndrome. The parents may then elect to have the pregnancy terminated. Amniocentesis slightly increases the risk of a miscarriage.

Chorionic villus sampling

Chorionic villus sampling (**CVS**) involves taking a tiny sample of placental cells using a fine tube inserted into the mother's reproductive tract (see figure 14.7). The cells are then used for karyotyping as before.

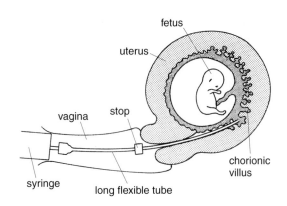

Figure 14.7 Chorionic villus sampling

One benefit of CVS is that it can be carried out as early as eight weeks into the pregnancy. The prospect of a termination at this stage is much less traumatic for many would-be parents than at 20 or more weeks following amniocentesis. However, CVS causes a higher incidence of miscarriage than amniocentesis.

Risk evaluation in polygenic inheritance

When a trait such as cystic fibrosis shows an autosomal recessive pattern of inheritance involving only one gene, a straightforward assessment of risk can be made based on the family tree.

disorder	incidence per (100)	risk of normal parents having a second affected child (per 100)	risk of affected parent having:	
			an affected child (per 100)	a second affected child (per 100)
asthma	4	10	26	*
cleft palate	0.1	2	7	15
congenital heart disease	0.5	1–4	1–4	10
epilepsy	0.5	5	5	10
manic-depressive psychosis	0.4	10–15	10–15	*
schizophrenia	1	10	16	*

Table 14.1 Empirical risks for polygenic disorders   * = data unavailable

However, when a genetic defect or disorder shows a polygenic pattern of inheritance, an evaluation of risk is much more difficult to make with any degree of accuracy. This is because the polygenic condition is normally determined partly by several genes and partly by environmental influences.

Risk evaluation in such cases is usually **empirical** (i.e. derived from data based on many real case histories rather than on genetic theory). A few examples are shown in table 14.1.

Post-natal (after birth) screening

At present almost none of the inherited disorders can be successfully treated. An exception is **phenylketonuria (PKU)**. This disease occurs with a frequency of about 1 in 10 000 in Britain. It results from an inborn error of metabolism (also see p 95).

If PKU is not detected soon after birth, the baby's mental development is affected adversely. In Britain all new-born babies are routinely **screened** for PKU by having their blood tested for the presence of **excess phenylalanine** within the first few days of life. PKU sufferers are then fed a special diet containing the minimum quantity of phenylalanine needed for normal growth.

Excess phenylalanine in an untreated sufferer of PKU is converted to phenylpyruvic acid which is excreted in urine. Early methods of diagnosing the disorder were based on the fact that this acid can be detected in the urine of a PKU baby a few weeks after birth. However, the blood test is more satisfactory since it allows earlier diagnosis and reduces the risk of brain damage occurring.

Provided that PKU sufferers continue to consume a diet low in phenylalanine, especially during childhood when the brain is still developing, mental deficiency is prevented and other adverse effects are kept to a minimum.

Future

As **recombinant DNA technology** (genetic engineering) continues to advance, it enables scientists to devise techniques that make carrier detection and pre-natal diagnosis possible for many traits. For example, the use of modern techniques such as gene probes allows experts to detect an ever-increasing number of single gene disorders including cystic fibrosis, phenylketonuria and Duchenne muscular dystrophy.

Similarly a test can be used to establish if the son or daughter of a sufferer of Huntington's chorea has inherited the abnormal allele. But if the news is bad, the person is left with immense problems to face. He or she must consider questions such as, whether or not to have children, how best to use the remaining disease-free years of their life, and how to prepare for the onset of the disease. Understandably some people do not want to know if they are carrying the harmful allele.

Hopefully in the future, detection of single gene disorders will also provide insight into possible methods of treatment that are more effective and acceptable than simply assessing risk and making fetal termination available.

Testing your knowledge

1 **a)** **(i)** Name TWO characteristics of a family tree that would enable a geneticist to recognise that it showed a pattern of *autosomal recessive inheritance*.
(ii) Give ONE rule that the geneticist would apply when adding genotypes to such a family tree. (3)

b) **(i)** Name TWO characteristics of a family tree that would enable a geneticist to recognise that it showed a pattern of *sex-linked recessive inheritance*.
(ii) Give ONE rule that the geneticist would apply when adding genotypes to such a family. (3)

2 **a)** Why is Huntington's chorea described as an autosomal dominant trait? (1)

b) Why is it not possible for the geneticist to add the genotypes of the younger members of a family tree showing Huntington's chorea? (1)

3 **a)** Briefly explain why, unlike that of a single gene disorder, it is not possible to assess the risk of inheriting a polygenic disorder by pedigree analysis. (2)

b) What alternative method of risk evaluation is employed? (1)

c) What is the difference between genetic counselling and genetic screening? (2)

d) **(i)** Name a genetic disorder that can be detected by pre-natal screening.
(ii) Name an inherited disorder that can be detected by post-natal screening. (2)

Applying your knowledge

1 Figure 14.8 shows a family tree for the inherited trait of deaf-mute.

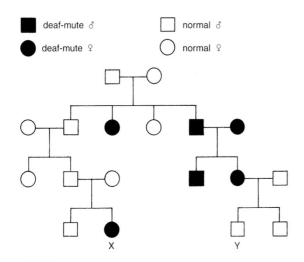

Figure 14.8

a) Which of the following patterns of inheritance is shown by this trait?
(i) autosomal recessive;
(ii) autosomal dominant;
(iii) sex-linked recessive. (1)

b) **(i)** Give ONE reason to support your choice.
(ii) Give ONE reason for deciding against each of the other choices. (3)

c) Copy the family tree and, using symbols of your choice, attempt to supply the genotype of each person (giving both possibilities in uncertain cases). (9)

d) If X marries a man who is homozygous for the normal allele, what is the percentage chance of each child of this union being
(i) a deaf-mute;
(ii) a carrier of the deaf-mute allele? (2)

e) If Y marries a woman who is homozygous for the normal allele, what is the chance of each child of this union being
(i) a deaf-mute;
(ii) a carrier of the deaf-mute allele? (2)

f) If X marries Y, what is the chance of each child being
(i) a deaf-mute;
(ii) a carrier of the deaf-mute allele? (2)

2 Huntington's chorea is an inherited disorder of the human body which has a debilitating effect on the nervous system. It is caused by a dominant allele which normally remains unexpressed until the person is over 30. Figure 14.9 shows two family trees involving this trait.

a) State the genotype of
(i) Maria;
(ii) Carmen's mother (who is aged 45). (2)

Continued ➤

106

Applying your knowledge

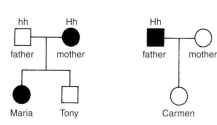

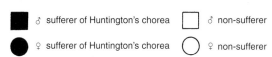

Figure 14.9

b) Carmen and Tony, both aged 21, intend to marry so they seek the advice of the genetic counsellor. He advises them that, depending on their genotypes, their children would be the result of one of the four situations shown in table 14.2.

possible situation	Carmen	Tony
(i)	Hh	Hh
(ii)	Hh	hh
(iii)	hh	Hh
(iv)	hh	hh

Table 14.2

(i) Why is the counsellor unable to state which of the four situations would arise?

(ii) State the chance of a child from each of the four situations inheriting Huntington's chorea. (5)

3 Figure 14.10 shows a pedigree for Duchenne muscular dystrophy.

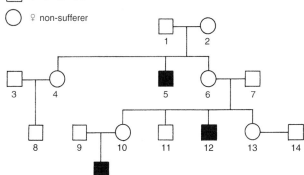

Figure 14.10

a) Which females are definitely carriers of the trait? (1)

b) What is the probability that person 13 is heterozygous for the trait? (1)

c) **(i)** If couple 13 and 14 have a son, what is the chance, going on the information so far available, that he will suffer Duchenne muscular dystrophy?

(ii) If couple 13 and 14 produce a son with Duchenne muscular dystrophy, what is the chance of their next son also being affected? (2)

4 Give an account of pre-natal and post-natal screening for conditions that have a genetic basis. (10)

What you should know
(Chapters 11–14)

(See table 14.3 for word bank.)

1 A _____ cross is one that involves two parents who differ in one way with respect to a particular characteristic.

2 One member of a pair of alleles of a gene exhibits _____ dominance if it completely _____ the expression of the other allele in the phenotype resulting from the heterozygote.

3 The members of a pair of alleles show _____ dominance if the heterozygote results in a phenotype _____ between those of the two homozygotes.

4 The members of a pair of alleles show _____ if the heterozygote produces a phenotype where both alleles are _____ expressed.

5 If three or more alleles of a gene exist, it is said to have _____ alleles.

Continued ➤

107

What you should know
(Chapters 11–14)

6 Human females possess a pair of homologous sex chromosomes called X chromosomes; human males have one X and a _____ Y chromosome which is _____ to part of the X chromosome.

7 Genes present on an X chromosome but not on a Y chromosome are said to be _____.

8 A characteristic which shows _____ variation is controlled by alleles of more than one gene and is said to show _____ inheritance.

9 Mutations are changes in the _____ which involve an alteration of _____ type or sequence in DNA or a change in _____ of chromosomes.

10 Substitution and _____ bring about minor changes and are called point mutations; insertion and _____ lead to major changes and are called frameshift mutations.

11 Mutations occur rarely and at _____. Their frequency can be increased by _____ agents.

12 _____ occurs when a spindle fibre fails during meiosis and the members of a pair of homologous chromosomes fail to separate. This results in some gametes receiving one chromosome too many or one chromosome too few and leads to the formation of individuals suffering chromosomal _____.

13 A pattern of inheritance amongst the members of a family can be established by constructing a

_____. Analysis of a family tree relating to a genetic disorder enables a genetic _____ to help people make decisions about parenthood based on assessment of _____.

14 A _____ is a display of a complement of chromosomes showing their form, size and number.

15 _____ and chorionic villus sampling enable _____ material to be karyotyped and inspected for chromosomal abnormalities.

16 Risk evaluation in cases of polygenic inheritance is usually _____.

17 Post-natal _____ is done to identify babies suffering phenylketonuria.

abnormalities	fetal	multiple
amniocentesis	fully	mutagenic
base	genotype	non-disjunction
co-dominance	homologous	number
complete	incomplete	polygenic
continuous	intermediate	random
counsellor	inversion	risk
deletion	karyotype	screening
empirical	masks	sex-linked
family tree	monohybrid	smaller

Table 14.3 Word bank for chapters 11–14

(15) Sex organs and hormonal control

Testes

The reproductive system of the human male is shown in figure 15.1. The **testes** are the site of **sperm** production and the manufacture of the male sex hormone **testosterone**.

Sperm (full name spermatozoa) are formed by meiosis in tiny tubes called **seminiferous tubules**. These tubules unite to form coiled tubes which connect to the **sperm duct**. It is by the sperm duct that free-swimming sperm leave the testis.

Testosterone is produced by **interstitial cells** located in the tissue between the seminiferous tubules. Testosterone passes directly into the bloodstream.

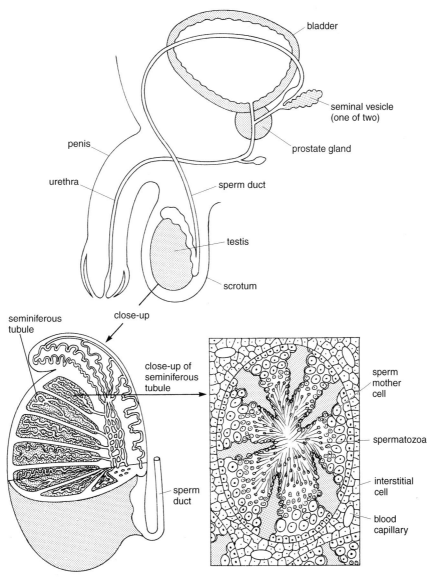

Figure 15.1 Male reproductive system

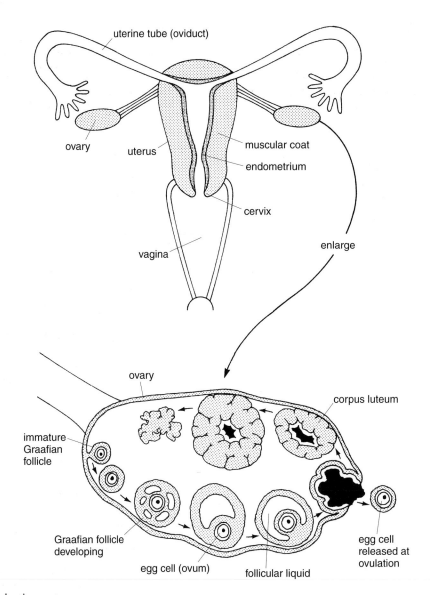

Figure 15.2 Female reproductive system

Sperm are **motile**. On being released during sexual intercourse inside the female body, they move through the uterus and along the oviducts where they may meet an egg. The process of fertilisation is dependent upon the motility of sperm which brings the two gametes together. Such motility requires a fluid medium and a source of energy.

Accessory glands

The **seminal vesicles** (see figure 15.1) secrete a viscous liquid rich in **fructose** and **prostaglandins**. Fructose is a sugar which provides sperm with the energy needed for motility following their release by the male at ejaculation.

Prostaglandins are hormone-like compounds which stimulate contractions of the female reproductive tract. These movements help the sperm to reach the oviduct at a much faster rate than could be achieved by swimming alone.

The **prostate gland** (see figure 15.1) secretes a thin lubricating liquid containing **enzymes** whose action maintains the fluid medium at the optimum viscosity for sperm motility.

Semen is the collective name given to the milky liquid released by the male which contains sperm from the testes and the fluid secretions from the seminal vesicles and prostate gland.

Ovaries

The reproductive system of the human female is shown in figure 15.2. **Eggs** are formed by meiotic division in the **ovaries**. Each egg (ovum) is contained by a developing **Graafian follicle** which secretes the hormone **oestrogen**. Following ovulation (release of an egg), the Graafian follicle develops into a **corpus luteum** (see figure 15.2) which secretes the hormone **progesterone**.

Hormonal control

Hormones are chemical messengers produced by an animal's **endocrine** (ductless) glands and secreted directly into the bloodstream. When a hormone reaches a certain target tissue, it brings about a specific effect.

Pituitary gland

The **pituitary gland** (see figure 15.3) is an endocrine gland which produces many hormones. Two of these are called **gonadotrophic** hormones because their target organs are the gonads (reproductive organs).

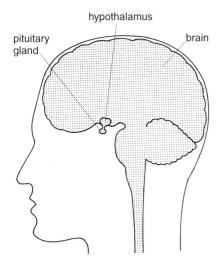

Figure 15.3 Pituitary gland

One gonadotrophic hormone is known as **FSH** (follicle-stimulating hormone); the other is known as **ICSH** (interstitial cell-stimulating hormone) in men and as **LH** (luteinising hormone) in women. The anterior pituitary begins to release these hormones at puberty.

Influence of pituitary hormones on testes

The two functions of a testis are regulated by the pituitary hormones. When FSH arrives in the bloodstream, it promotes **sperm production** in the seminiferous tubules. When ICSH arrives, it stimulates interstitial cells to produce the male sex hormone **testosterone**.

Influence of testosterone

Testosterone stimulates **sperm production** in the seminiferous tubules. It also activates the prostate gland and seminal vesicles to produce their secretions.

Self-regulation of testosterone

As the concentration of testosterone builds up in the bloodstream, it reaches a level where it **inhibits** the secretion of FSH and ICSH by the anterior pituitary

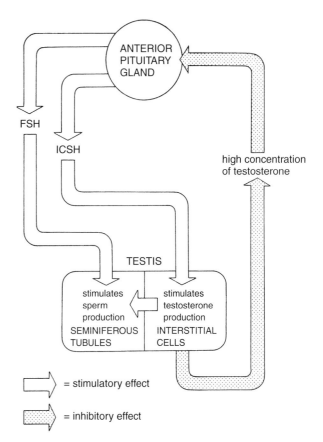

Figure 15.4 Self-regulation of testosterone

(see figure 15.4). Since this leads in turn to a decrease in testosterone concentration, it is soon followed by a resumption of activity by the anterior pituitary which makes the gonadotrophic hormones again, and so on.

This type of **self-regulating** mechanism is called **negative feedback control** (see also chapter 24 for further examples).

Influence of pituitary hormones on ovaries

FSH and LH from the anterior pituitary affect the ovaries in several ways. FSH stimulates the development and maturation of each **Graafian follicle** (see figure 15.5). It also stimulates ovary tissue to secrete the sex hormone **oestrogen**.

LH triggers **ovulation**. It also brings about the development of the **corpus luteum** from the follicle and then stimulates the corpus luteum to secrete the sex hormone **progesterone**. Oestrogen and progesterone are known as the **ovarian** hormones.

Influence of ovarian hormones on uterus and pituitary gland

Oestrogen

Oestrogen stimulates **proliferation** (cell division) of the inner layer of the uterus, called the **endometrium**, thereby effecting its repair following menstruation. This

111

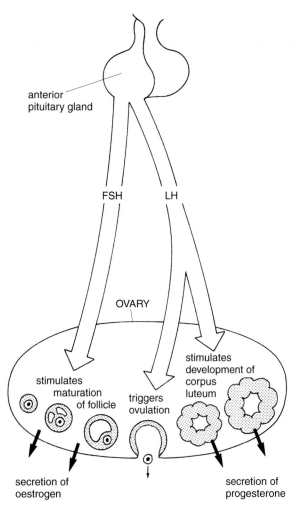

Figure 15.5 Effect of pituitary hormones on ovary

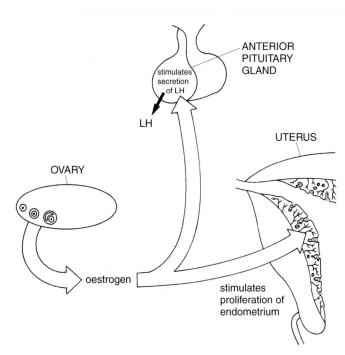

Figure 15.6 Effect of oestrogen on uterus and pituitary

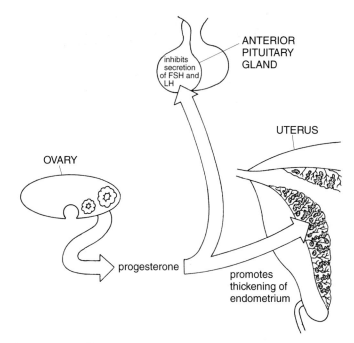

Figure 15.7 Effect of progesterone on uterus and pituitary

ovarian hormone also stimulates the secretion of **LH** by the anterior pituitary (see figure 15.6).

Progesterone

Progesterone promotes the **thickening** of the **endometrium** into a spongy layer rich in blood vessels. Progesterone also **inhibits** the secretion of **FSH** and **LH** by the anterior pituitary (see figure 15.7)

The menstrual cycle

The above events, under hormonal control in the human female, fit together as interacting parts of a synchronised system – the **menstrual cycle**.

A cycle lasts for about 28 days though this can vary from woman to woman. Each cycle is continuous with the one that went before and the one about to follow. For convenience the first day of menstruation (as indicated by menstrual blood flow) is regarded as 'day one' of the cycle. The menstrual cycle is summarised in figure 15.8. It is made up of two phases.

Follicular phase

During this first half of the cycle, FSH from the anterior pituitary stimulates the development and maturation of a Graafian follicle and the production of oestrogen by the ovarian tissues.

As the concentration of oestrogen builds up, it brings about the repair and proliferation of the endometrium. Eventually the high concentration of oestrogen triggers a surge in production of LH (and FSH) by the anterior pituitary at about day 14.

Testing your knowledge

1 a) (i) Where in a testis are sperm produced?
       (ii) Which hormone is produced by interstitial cells? (2)

   b) (i) Which accessory glands secrete a liquid rich in prostaglandins?
       (ii) Describe the contribution to fertilisation made by prostaglandins. (2)

2 a) (i) Name the structure that surrounds an egg in an ovary.
       (ii) What does this structure develop into, following ovulation? (2)

3 a) Name a gonadotrophic hormone in men and name its target. (2)

   b) Copy and complete table 15.1 which refers to four hormones in the female body. (8)

hormone	site of production	one function of the hormone
		stimulates the development and maturation of each Graafian follicle
		brings about development of the corpus luteum
		stimulates secretion of LH by the pituitary gland
		promotes thickening of the endometrium

Table 15.1

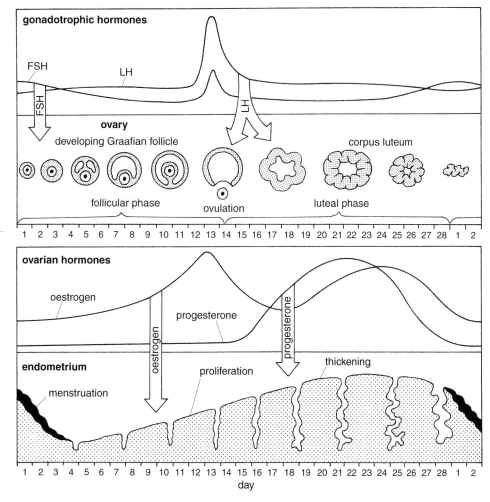

Figure 15.8 Menstrual cycle

This **surge of LH** is the direct cause of **ovulation** since it makes the blister-like wall of the Graafian follicle rupture and release the egg. The egg is then moved slowly along the oviduct. During a short period of about 3 to 4 days, **fertilisation** may occur if the egg meets a sperm.

Luteal phase

During this second half of the cycle (following ovulation), LH stimulates the Graafian follicle to become the corpus luteum. This gland-like structure secretes progesterone and oestrogen. The subsequent rise in progesterone concentration stimulates further development of the endometrium. It becomes thick, vascular and spongy, ready to accept and nourish an embryo if fertilisation takes place and the embryo becomes implanted.

The combined high levels of oestrogen and progesterone during this luteal phase also trigger an inhibitory effect on the anterior pituitary. Concentrations of FSH and LH drop as a result and no new follicles develop at this time. This is a further example of negative feedback control.

However, **lack of LH** leads in turn to the **degeneration** of the corpus luteum by about day 22 in the cycle. This is followed by a rapid **drop in progesterone** (and oestrogen). By day 28 in the cycle, these ovarian hormones are at such a low level that the endometrium can no longer be maintained and **menstruation** begins. This involves the loss of the inner layer of the endometrium accompanied by a small volume of blood. This stage continues for a few days.

Fertilisation

If fertilisation occurs, the fertilised egg secretes a hormone called **human chorionic gonadotrophin (HCG)** which has the same effect as LH. HCG maintains the corpus luteum which continues to secrete progesterone and prevent menstruation from taking place. After about six weeks the placenta takes on the job of secreting progesterone.

The presence of HCG in urine is the basis of pregnancy testing.

Role of cervix in fertility

The cells lining the cervix at the neck of the uterus (see figure 15.2), secrete **mucus** which lubricates the vagina. These cells are stimulated by high levels of oestrogen to secrete watery mucus easily penetrated by sperm. Since the highest concentration of oestrogen immediately precedes ovulation, the secretion of thin mucus at this time increases the chance of fertilisation by facilitating the entry of sperm into the female reproductive tract.

In addition, the sperm point in the correct direction by lining up parallel to the long chain molecules present in the mucus. They are then ready for their passage through the female reproductive tract. This is further assisted by **muscular contractions** of the uterus and oviduct induced by prostaglandins present in the seminal fluid.

High levels of progesterone cause the cervical mucus to become viscous and in the event of pregnancy change into a semi-solid 'plug'. This protects the fertilised egg from possible infection.

Changes in body temperature

Body temperature rises by about 0.5°C at ovulation and remains at a high level during the luteal phase of the cycle. Changes in body temperature and viscosity of cervical mucus are used by some people as indicators upon which to base the rhythm method of birth control (see p 118).

Continuous versus cyclical fertility

The negative feedback effect of testosterone (see figure 15.4) maintains a relatively constant level of the gonatotrophic hormones (FSH and ICSH) in the bloodstream of men. This results in a fairly steady quantity of testosterone being secreted and sperm being produced. Men are therefore **continuously** fertile.

This contrasts markedly with the **cyclical** fertility of women. The delicate interplay of gonadotrophic and ovarian hormones normally results in the period of fertility being restricted to the 3 to 4 days immediately following ovulation.

Testing your knowledge

1 Decide whether each of the following statements is true or false and then use T or F to indicate your choice. Where a statement is false, give the word that should have been used in place of the word in bold print. (6)

a) The menstrual cycle consists of the **endometrial** phase and the luteal phase.

b) FSH stimulates ovary tissue to secrete **oestrogen**.

c) Oestrogen stimulates the **proliferation** of the endometrium.

d) LH triggers the process of **menstruation**.

e) Progesterone inhibits secretion of FSH and LH by the **ovaries**.

f) Lack of LH leads to **degeneration** of the corpus luteum.

2 a) (i) What effect do high concentrations of oestrogen have on the viscosity of the mucus secreted by cervix cells?
  (ii) How does this increase the chance of fertilisation? (2)

b) In what way are sperm assisted in their passage through the female reproductive tract? (1)

c) What change in body temperature occurs during the luteal phase of the menstrual cycle? (1)

Applying your knowledge

letter in figure 15.9 indicating accessory gland	name of this accessory gland	example of substance secreted by accessory gland which contributes to fertilisation	way in which named substance contributes to fertilisation

Table 15.2

1 The male reproductive system is shown in figure 15.9.

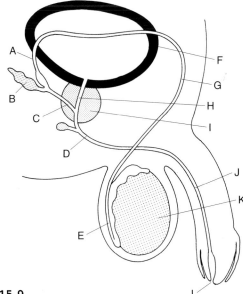

Figure 15.9

a) Using only the appropriate letters, indicate the route taken by sperm from site of production to point of exit from the male body. (1)

b) Copy and complete table 15.2. (8)

2 Figure 15.10 shows a small part of an ovary and some of the stages that occur during the maturation of a follicle.

a) Arrange stages A–E into the correct order starting with D. (1)

b) (i) Which of these stages are controlled by FSH?
  (ii) What name is given to the process that occurs at C?
  (iii) Which hormone triggers this process?
  (iv) Which endocrine gland secretes the hormone that you gave as your answer to **(iii)**? (4)

Continued ➤

Applying your knowledge

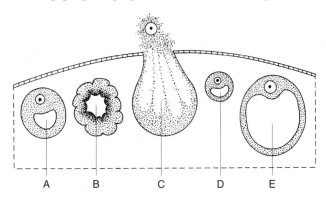

Figure 15.10

c) **(i)** Name structure B.
(ii) Name the hormones that it produces.
(iii) Are these hormones ovarian or gonadotrophic? Explain your answer.
(iv) State ONE effect of these hormones on the pituitary gland. (6)

3 Figure 15.11 shows a graph of thickness of the endometrium during a menstrual cycle.

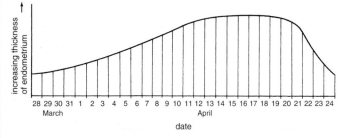

Figure 15.11

a) State the date in April when menstrual flow began. (1)

b) Predict the date in April when ovulation occurred. (1)

c) Answer HIGH or LOW in each of the following statements:
   (i) The relative concentration of oestrogen on April 6 would be _____.

(ii) The relative concentration of FSH on April 15 would be _____.
(iii) The relative concentration of progesterone on April 15 would be _____.
(iv) The relative concentration of LH on April 22 would be _____. (4)

4 A tiny part of the human testis is shown in microscopic detail in figure 15.12.

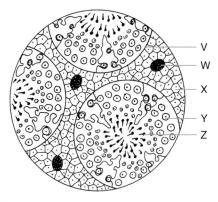

Figure 15.12

a) Name the parts labelled V, W, X, Y and Z. (5)

b) Which of these secretes testosterone? (1)

c) Which hormone from the pituitary stimulates these structures to produce testosterone? (1)

d) By what means is excessive production of testosterone prevented? (2)

e) Explain the meaning of the terms 'continuous fertility' and 'cyclical fertility' with reference to human beings. (2)

5 Give an account of the hormonal control of a menstrual cycle that does not involve fertilisation under the headings:

(i) follicular phase; (5)
(ii) luteal phase. (5)

16 Intervention in fertility

Causes of infertility

Several common causes of **infertility** are given in table 16.1. The cause of infertility varies and may be the result of one or more underlying factors. Treatment often takes the form of an attempt to restore to normal a disturbed or deficient secretion of hormones.

In vitro fertilisation (IVF)

This method of treatment attempts to solve the problem of infertility by bringing about fertilisation outside the bodies of the would-be parents in a glass dish (not a test tube!). Figure 16.1 shows some of the steps involved in this procedure.

At stage 1, the woman is given hormonal treatment to stimulate multiple ovulation. At stage 2, several of these eggs are removed from her abdominal cavity using a special piece of equipment similar to a syringe.

At stage 3, the eggs are placed in a dish of nutrient medium containing sperm to allow fertilisation to occur. The latest treatment involves the injection of a sperm directly into an egg (ovum). At stage 4, the fertilised eggs are incubated in the nutrient medium to allow cell division to occur.

At stage 5, two or three of the embryos are chosen and inserted via the vagina into the mother's uterus (already enriched and ready for implantation). Stage 6 involves

cause of infertility	possible underlying factors	treatments
failure to ovulate	May be due to hormonal imbalance caused by: ◆ failure of pituitary to secrete adequate FSH or LH; ◆ prolonged use of contraceptive pill; ◆ emotional stress; ◆ poor health caused by smoking, excessive alcohol consumption, drugs and/or obesity.	◆ Fertility drugs which stimulate secretion of FSH and LH. ◆ Use of chemical equivalent of LH extracted from placentas of fertile women. ◆ Use of FSH extracted from blood and urine of menopausal women
blockage of uterine tubes (oviducts)	May be due to: ◆ tissue growths (e.g. cyst or tumour); ◆ infection; ◆ spasms in tube caused by emotional stress.	◆ Laser treatment to clear blockage. ◆ *In vitro* fertilisation (see text for details). ◆ Use of antispasmodic agents to prevent involuntary contraction of tube.
failure of implantation	May be due to: ◆ hormonal imbalance caused by failure of ovaries to secrete adequate quantities of ovarian hormones (leaving uterus unenriched and unprepared to receive embryo).	◆ Fertility drugs to restore the normal cycle of synchronised events.
low sperm count	May be due to: ◆ hormonal deficiency caused by failure of pituitary to secrete adequate quantities of gonadotrophic hormones; ◆ emotional stress; ◆ poor health caused by smoking, excessive alcohol consumption, drugs and/or obesity	◆ Use of carefully controlled amounts of testosterone. ◆ *In vitro* fertilisation. ◆ Artificial insemination (see text for details).

Table 16.1 Causes of infertility

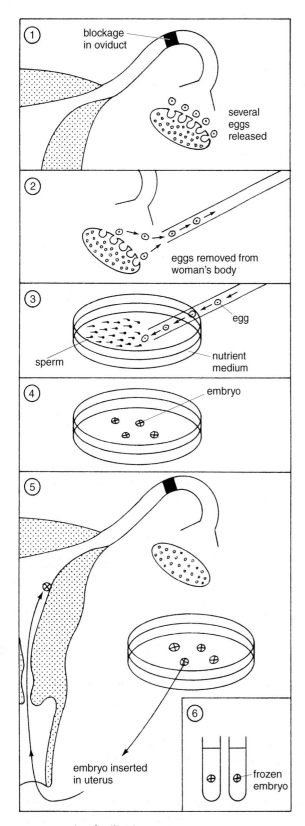

Figure 16.1 *In vitro* fertilisation

freezing the remaining embryos in case a second attempt at implantation is required.

Artificial insemination

Insemination is the introduction of semen into the female reproductive tract. It occurs naturally as a result of sexual intercourse.

Artificial insemination is the insertion of semen into the female system by some means other than sexual intercourse. Artificial insemination may be employed as a method of treating infertility. If a man has a **low sperm count**, several samples of his semen can be collected over a period of time and each preserved by freezing until required. They are then defrosted and released together into his partner's cervix region at the time when she is most likely to be fertile.

Artificial insemination can also be used to insert semen of a donor who has a normal sperm count into the cervix region of a woman whose partner is sterile.

Biological basis of contraception

Contraception is the intentional prevention of conception by natural or artificial means.

Calculation of the fertile period

Temperature

Within the menstrual cycle, the alternating processes of menstruation and ovulation are separated by intervals of about two weeks. Approximately one day after the LH surge which triggers ovulation, the woman's **body temperature** rises by about 0.2–0.5°C under the action of progesterone. It remains at this elevated level for the duration of the luteal phase of the cycle (see figure 16.2).

The **period of fertility** lasts for about 3 or 4 days. The infertile phase is resumed, on average, after the third daily recording of the higher temperature by which time the unfertilised egg has disintegrated.

Mucus

The **cervical mucus** secreted into the vagina during the fertile period is thin and watery to allow sperm easy access to the female reproductive system. However, after ovulation, the mucus gradually increases in viscosity under the action of progesterone showing that the system has returned to the **infertile** phase.

Rhythm methods

The above indicators can be used by the woman to try to calculate her fertile period. This knowledge is useful to a

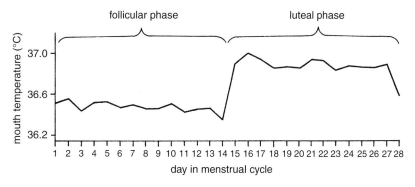

Figure 16.2 Rise in temperature during luteal phase

couple who wish to have a child and want to know when sexual intercourse will be most likely to achieve successful fertilisation.

It is also of use to a couple who do not wish to have a child and therefore want to know when to abstain from sexual intercourse. Such attempts to avoid fertilisation based on temperature and mucus indicators are called **rhythm methods** of contraception. Unfortunately they tend to be unreliable since the cycle can vary in length from month to month.

Hormonal methods of contraception

Oral contraceptive pills normally contain synthetic **progesterone** sometimes combined with synthetic **oestrogen**. One common method involves taking a pill daily for three weeks from the final day of the previous menstrual period. As a result the concentration of progesterone and oestrogen in the bloodstream is increased and this exerts negative feedback control. Secretion of gonadotrophic hormones by the pituitary is therefore inhibited. Since little or no FSH is secreted, follicle maturation remains inhibited and ovulation fails to occur. Sometimes, dummy (placebo) pills are taken during the fourth week to allow the levels of oestrogen and progesterone to drop and menstruation to occur.

Some hormonal methods of contraception involve **injections** or **implants** instead of pills. However they all operate on the same principle of altering the normal sequence of events in the menstrual cycle in order to **prevent ovulation**.

When women discontinue the contraceptive pill after lengthy use, they experience a period of delay before their bodies readjust and return to a normal fertile state.

Testing your knowledge

1 Decide whether each of the following statements is true or false and then use T or F to indicate your choice. Where a statement is false, give the word(s) that should have been used in place of the words in bold print.

  a) (i) Infertility caused by failure to ovulate may be treated using **luteinising hormone**.
     (ii) LH can be extracted from the **corpus luteum** released by fertile women after giving birth. (2)

  b) (i) A further cause of infertility in women is blockage of the **ureter** by tissue growth.
     (ii) **Laser** treatment is often used to try to clear such a blockage. (2)

  c) (i) Infertility in women can also be due to failure of the embryo to become implanted in the **oviduct** wall.
     (ii) This condition is treated using **fertility drugs** to restore the normal cycle. (2)

  d) (i) Infertility in men can be due to inadequate secretion of gonadotrophic hormones by the **prostate gland**.
     (ii) Carefully controlled quantities of **testosterone** may be given as treatment for this condition. (2)

2 Describe what is meant by the terms *in vitro fertilisation* and *artificial insemination*. (2)

3 (i) For how long does a woman's period of fertility last during each menstrual cycle, on average?
  (ii) Describe TWO signs that given an approximate indication of when this time occurs. (3)

Applying your knowledge

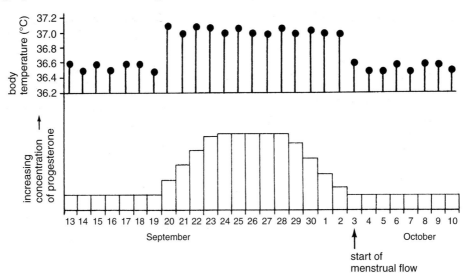

Figure 16.3

1 a) The following list gives the steps in the procedure employed during *in vitro* fertilisation. Arrange them into the correct order. (1)

    A Incubation of fertilised eggs in nutrient medium.

    B Deep freezing of unused fertilised eggs.

    C Stimulation of ovaries to bring about multiple ovulation.

    D Mixing of eggs with sperm in a dish.

    E Insertion of 2 or 3 fertilised eggs into uterus.

    F Removal of eggs from mother's body.

b) What treatment is used in step **C**? (1)

c) What is the purpose of carrying out steps **A** and **B**? (2)

2 Figure 16.3 represents some of the events that occurred during a woman's menstrual cycle.

a) (i) On which dates would sexual intercourse have been most likely to have caused fertilisation in this woman?

    (ii) Give TWO reasons to explain how you arrived at your answer. (3)

b) Give a further physical sign unrelated to the graph that might have helped the woman to identify her most fertile time. (1)

c) What evidence from the graph tells you that fertilisation did not occur during the cycle shown? (1)

d) (i) Assuming that the cycle remains the same length, on which dates in October will sexual intercourse be *most* likely to lead to conception in this woman?

(ii) If fertilisation were to occur, in what way would the progesterone curve differ from the one in figure 16.3? (2)

e) (i) Instead of trying to avoid the fertile phase, the woman decided to use a hormonal method of contraception containing progesterone. Explain how this prevents fertilisation.

(ii) Why does a woman 'on the pill' take pills lacking sex hormones one week in every four? (3)

3 Figure 16.4 shows a simplified version of the male reproductive system following a vasectomy.

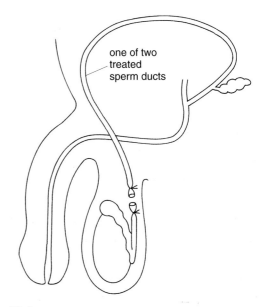

one of two
treated
sperm ducts

Figure 16.4

Continued ➤

Applying your knowledge

a) Explain how this works as a method of contraception. (1)

b) Suggest why vasectomy is more popular amongst middle-aged men than amongst men in their twenties. (2)

4 *In vitro* fertilisation often results in extra unused fertilised eggs being kept in frozen storage. The very existence of these eggs raises many controversial issues. Briefly give your opinions on the following:

a) Should the extra eggs be destroyed after the mother has successfully given birth to one or more healthy babies?

b) Should the extra eggs be kept in storage in case the woman wishes to have more children?

c) (i) Should the extra eggs be offered (with permission) to other women who are suffering fertility problems?

(ii) If so, who in your opinion are the legal parents of the children produced?

d) Should the extra eggs be made available for scientific research?

e) Should a fertilised egg in a deep frozen state, with the potential to develop into a human being, be regarded as an actual human being with rights to protection by law?

5 Describe the principal causes and treatment of infertility in humans. (10)

What you should know
(Chapters 15–16)

(See table 16.2 for word bank.)

1 The _____ of the human male produce sperm and the hormone _____. The _____ vesicles secrete a liquid containing sugar and prostaglandins. The _____ gland makes lubricating liquid.

2 The _____ of the human female produce eggs and the ovarian hormones _____ and progesterone.

3 The pituitary gland produces the following gonadotrophic hormones: follicle-stimulating hormone (FSH) and _____ cell-stimulating hormone (ICSH) in men and _____ hormone (LH) in women.

4 In men, _____ promotes sperm production and ICSH stimulates testosterone production.

5 In women, FSH stimulates the maturation of Graafian _____ containing eggs and the secretion of oestrogen. _____ triggers ovulation and brings about the development of the corpus luteum which secretes _____.

6 In women, oestrogen stimulates proliferation of the _____ and progesterone promotes its development into a spongy layer rich in blood.

7 The regular sequence of events under hormonal control in a female makes up the _____ cycle which has a duration of about 28 days.

8 Fertility in men is _____; fertility in women is _____ being restricted to the 3–4 days following ovulation in each monthly cycle.

9 Infertility may be caused by failure to _____, blockage of _____ tubes or failure of implantation in women, and low _____ counts in men.

10 Methods of treatment of infertility include the use of fertility drugs, *in* _____ fertilisation and artificial _____.

11 Some methods of contraception are based on biological knowledge of the menstrual cycle. By monitoring changes in body _____, thickness of cervical _____ and time of previous menstruation, the approximate time of the fertile period can be calculated and sexual intercourse avoided.

12 Hormonal methods of contraception prevent follicles from being _____ and eggs from being released.

continuous	**luteinising**	**seminal**
cyclical	**menstrual**	**sperm**
endometrium	**mucus**	**stimulated**
follicles	**oestrogen**	**temperature**
FSH	**ovaries**	**testes**
insemination	**ovulate**	**testosterone**
interstitial	**progesterone**	**uterine**
LH	**prostate**	***vitro***

Table 16.2 Word bank for chapters 15–16

17 Pre-natal development

Cleavage

About 36 hours after fertilisation, the zygote undergoes **cleavage**. This means that it divides into two smaller cells and becomes an **embryo**. As the embryo is moved towards the uterus by cilia and movements of the uterine tubes, the process of cleavage continues as shown in figure 17.1.

The number of cells doubles at each mitotic division and soon a solid ball of cells is formed. This develops into a hollow ball with a fluid-filled interior. The group of cells to one side of the fluid interior will become the fetus and is referred to at this stage as the **embryonic area**. The fluid-filled ball is surrounded by a thin outer layer of cells in the form of a membrane called the **chorion**.

Implantation

Implantation occurs about one week after fertilisation. This is the process by which the embryo becomes attached to the uterus wall with the side containing the embryonic area lying against the endometrium (see figure 17.2).

The cells in the embryo's thin outer layer make a space for the embryo in the uterus wall by secreting **enzymes** which digest away part of the endometrium. The embryo grows rapidly amongst the maternal tissues forming finger-like **projections** which eventually become part of the placenta.

As these projections burrow more deeply into the uterine wall, the embryo is drawn into the endometrium and eventually becomes surrounded by it. Once this process is complete, the embryo has become successfully **implanted**. It receives food and oxygen from the surrounding endometrial cells until the placenta develops.

Differentiation

The cells in the embryonic area continue to divide by mitosis forming a multi-layered mass of cells which

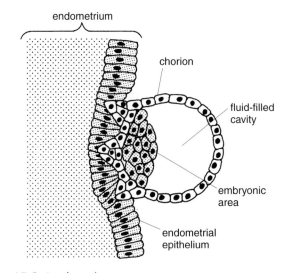

Figure 17.2 Implantation

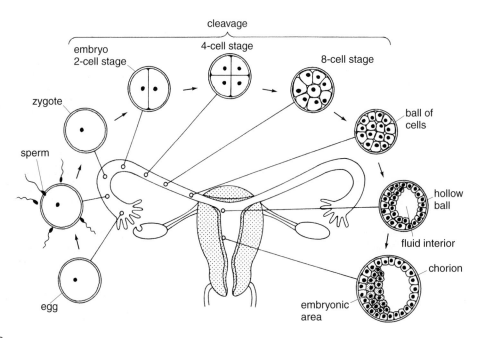

Figure 17.1 Cleavage

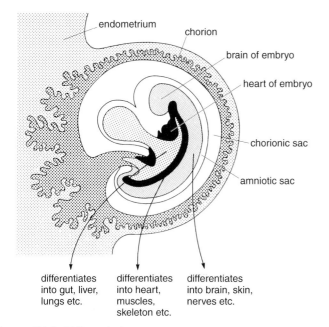

Figure 17.3 Differentiation

undergoes **differentiation**. This is the process by which unspecialised cells become altered and adapted to perform specific functions as part of permanent tissues.

All the cells present in the embryo are derived by mitotic division from the original zygote and all contain exactly the same genes. During differentiation certain genes in different cells become 'switched on' or 'switched off'. By this means many different types of **specialised cells** are formed from the common embryonic tissue (see figure 17.3).

Twins

There are two types of twins. **Monozygotic** twins are 'identical'; **dizygotic** twins are 'non-identical'.

Monozygotic twins both originate from the same single egg fertilised by a single sperm. During cell division, the developing embryo divides to form two separate embryonic areas within the one fluid-filled ball, as shown in figure 17.4. As development continues, monozygotic twins are found to possess separate amnions (water sacs) but to share a common chorion and placenta. They are **genetically identical** to each other since they are derived from the same zygote.

Dizygotic twins are formed when two eggs are released from the ovary at the same time and each is fertilised by a different sperm. Each embryo undergoes independent development and possesses its own amnion, chorion and placenta as shown in figure 17.5. Dizygotic twins may be of the same sex or different sexes. Since they have originated from separate gametes, they are as **genetically**

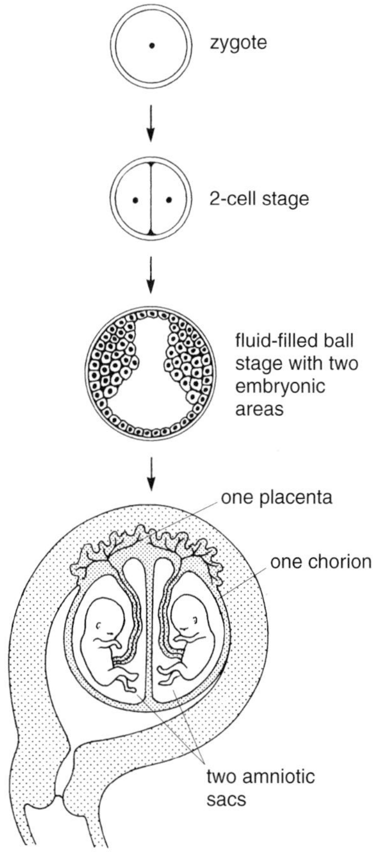

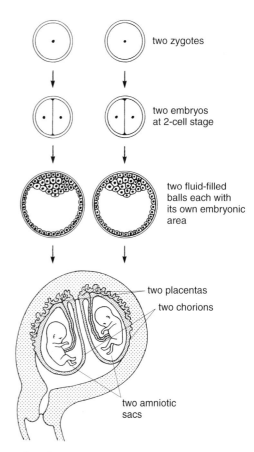

Figure 17.4 Monozygotic twins

Figure 17.5 Dizygotic twins

dissimilar to one another as are any two siblings of the same parents.

Exchanges between maternal and fetal circulation

Useful transfer

During gestation the **placenta** develops into a large disc bearing many finger-like villi. These project into the inner layer of the uterus wall which is richly supplied with maternal blood (see figure 17.6).

Each placental villus contains blood vessels continuous with fetal circulation. Maternal and fetal blood are therefore brought very close together. The two do not become mixed since they are separated by a thin membranous barrier. However, certain molecules can be freely exchanged between mother and fetus across this region.

Carbon dioxide diffuses from the fetal to the maternal bloodstream; **oxygen** diffuses in the opposite direction. **Glucose** moves from mother to fetus by *active transport*; **maternal antibodies** pass through the membrane and gain access to the baby's bloodstream by *pinocytosis* (see p 49). By this means the baby acquires passive immunity to many diseases until its own immune system develops a few months after birth.

Harmful transfer

The close proximity of the maternal and fetal circulations also allows harmful substances and pathogens to pass from mother to baby.

Thalidomide

In the 1950s the drug **thalidomide** was developed and prescribed to pregnant women in order to counteract the feelings of nausea (morning sickness) which many experience. If it was taken during a certain critical period in very early pregnancy then the **limbs** of the fetus failed to develop properly.

As a result, the baby's hands developed attached to the shoulders and the feet to the hip joints. In addition malformation of eyes, ears and heart occurred in some cases together with mental disability and epilepsy.

This tragedy demonstrated the danger of taking drugs during pregnancy. Thalidomide has now been withdrawn from use by pregnant women.

Alcohol

A higher incidence of spontaneous abortion is found to occur amongst women who drink **alcohol** in excess during pregnancy. In those women who do not suffer a miscarriage but who do continue to drink heavily, some of the alcohol crosses the placenta and causes blood vessels in the umbilical cord to collapse temporarily. During these periods the fetus fails to receive an adequate **oxygen supply** vital for the proper development of growing tissues such as the brain.

In addition alcohol interferes with the normal absorption from the mother's gut of nutrients such as vitamin B_6 and zinc which are essential for the health of both the mother and the developing embryo.

In extreme cases of alcohol abuse the fetus suffers several harmful effects known collectively as the **fetal alcohol syndrome**. These include:

◆ pre- and post-natal growth retardation;

◆ facial abnormalities;

◆ heart defects;

◆ development of abnormal joints and limbs;

◆ mental retardation.

To eliminate the possibility of even the mildest form of damage being caused to the fetus, women are advised to avoid drinking alcohol during pregnancy.

Nicotine

Nicotine is a drug present in tobacco plants which stimulates the central nervous system and increases pulse rate and blood pressure. In addition to nicotine, tobacco smoke contains **carbon monoxide** (CO) and **tar** (which has been shown to contain up to 30 different harmful substances). A higher incidence of lung cancer and coronary artery disease is found to occur amongst heavy smokers.

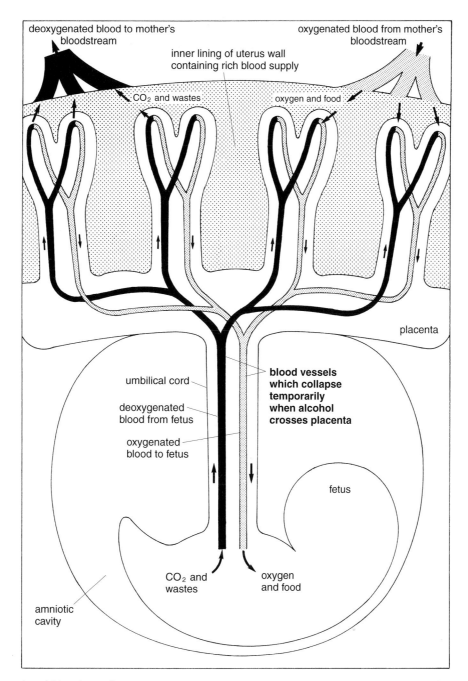

deoxygenated blood to mother's bloodstream

oxygenated blood from mother's bloodstream

inner lining of uterus wall containing rich blood supply

CO_2 and wastes

oxygen and food

placenta

umbilical cord

deoxygenated blood from fetus

oxygenated blood to fetus

blood vessels which collapse temporarily when alcohol crosses placenta

fetus

CO_2 and wastes

oxygen and food

amniotic cavity

Figure 17.6 Umbilical cord and blood vessels

Smoking during pregnancy has been shown to retard the growth of unborn children. CO reduces the amount of **oxygen** that the blood can carry and nicotine in the bloodstream prevents adequate **glucose** reaching fetal tissues including brain cells.

Evidence suggests that babies born to heavy smokers are smaller than average and that they do not develop intellectually at the same rate as children of non-smokers.

Heroin

Heroin is a narcotic drug which induces a temporary sense of relaxed detachment from pain and anxiety. It slows down bodily processes and makes the person feel contented and sleepy. Regular use soon leads to physical and psychological dependency. The addict craves the drug just to feel normal and suffers unpleasant, painful withdrawal symptoms in its absence.

When the addict is a pregnant woman and heroin crosses the placenta on a regular basis, the fetus also becomes addicted and its **vital processes** slow down. In addition, the mother is often found to be eating poorly in order to finance her habit. By neglecting her own health, she further adversely affects the baby's physical and mental development.

If the baby survives, it is found to be weak and undersized at birth and to be exhibiting **withdrawal symptoms** such as muscle tremors, excessive perspiration and insomnia. The baby needs to begin a programme of gradual withdrawal from the drug under medical supervision.

Rubella

Rubella (German measles) is a fairly mild but contagious viral infection similar to measles. It is characterised by a cough, sore throat and skin rash. However, if it is contracted during the first three months of pregnancy, it may have serious effects on the fetus. It can cause the baby to be born with **congenital** (non-hereditary) **defects** affecting the eyes, ears and heart. It is for this reason that British school children are vaccinated against rubella between the ages of 10 and 14.

Human immunodeficiency virus (HIV)

HIV gradually destroys the immune system leaving the body open to fatal attack by **opportunist infections** (see p 64). The process often takes several years and during this time the carrier of the virus is described as being HIV positive.

If a woman who is HIV positive becomes pregnant, the virus is able to cross the placenta and infect the developing fetus. This is found to happen in about 30% of cases. The vast majority of babies that are born HIV positive go on to develop **AIDS** and die at an early age. There is no cure so far and many women whose unborn babies, on being tested, are found to be HIV positive choose to terminate the pregnancy.

Placental hormones

Throughout gestation, the endometrial layer of the uterus wall is maintained by the hormones **oestrogen** and **progesterone**. During the first two to three months, the chorionic cells on the outside of the embryo secrete a hormone which has the same effect as LH and stimulates the corpus luteum to secrete progesterone and oestrogen.

After about two months, the **placenta** takes over this secretory function and the corpus luteum degenerates. Oestrogen and progesterone continue to exert negative feedback control and inhibit the processes of ovulation and menstruation during pregnancy.

Mammary glands

Oestrogen and progesterone also stimulate the proliferation of the milk-secreting tissues of the mammary glands causing the breasts to increase in size and become **prepared for lactation** (milk production).

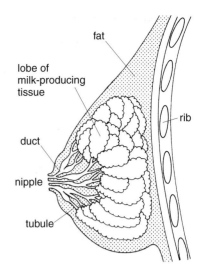

Figure 17.7 Mammary gland

Each mammary gland is composed of lobes that secrete milk into sacs connected by ducts to the nipple as shown in figure 17.7. However, lactation is inhibited during pregnancy since it requires the activity of **prolactin**.

Prolactin

This hormone is secreted by the anterior pituitary gland. It becomes active following the birth of the baby, the expulsion of the placenta and the drop in oestrogen level that occurs at this time. Prolactin **stimulates lactation** and milk is secreted into the sacs and tubules of the breast ready for release (see p 130).

Rhesus factor

The genetics of **Rhesus D-antigen** are discussed in chapter 11 (p 84). Under certain circumstances a Rh− mother has a Rh+ fetus developing inside her body (see figure 17.8). The baby has antigen D on its red blood cells which is regarded as foreign by the mother's immune system.

Normally the placenta prevents maternal and fetal bloodstreams from coming into direct contact. As a result only a very tiny number of fetal blood cells (if any at all) reach the maternal circulation. Therefore the mother's immune system normally remains 'unaware' of the presence of the 'foreign' fetus during the first pregnancy and does not attempt to reject it.

However, at the time of birth (or during a miscarriage) a small quantity of fetal blood does often become mixed with the mother's blood. When this happens the mother's immune system responds by producing anti-D **antibodies** and she is said to have become **sensitised**. If, during subsequent pregnancies, the fetus is Rh+,

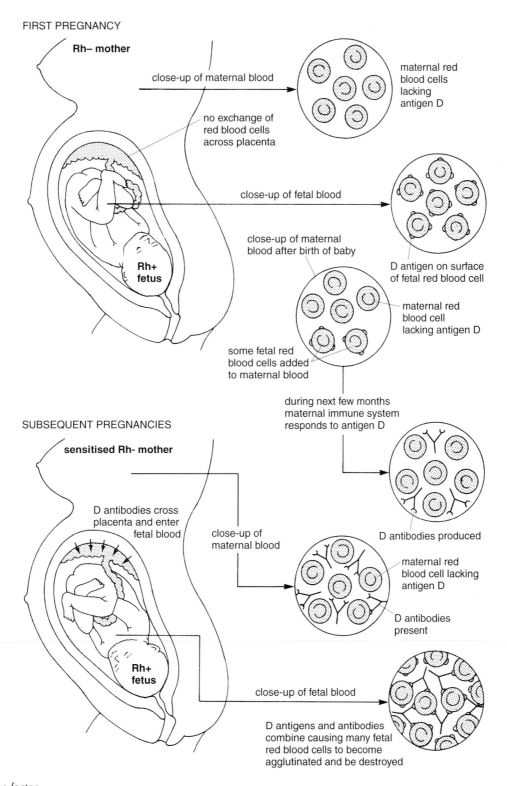

FIRST PREGNANCY

Rh– mother

close-up of maternal blood

maternal red blood cells lacking antigen D

no exchange of red blood cells across placenta

Rh+ fetus

close-up of fetal blood

close-up of maternal blood after birth of baby

D antigen on surface of fetal red blood cell

maternal red blood cell lacking antigen D

some fetal red blood cells added to maternal blood

during next few months maternal immune system responds to antigen D

D antibodies produced

SUBSEQUENT PREGNANCIES

sensitised Rh- mother

D antibodies cross placenta and enter fetal blood

close-up of maternal blood

maternal red blood cell lacking antigen D

D antibodies present

Rh+ fetus

close-up of fetal blood

D antigens and antibodies combine causing many fetal red blood cells to become agglutinated and be destroyed

Figure 17.8 Rhesus factor

antibodies against antigen D cross the placenta and attack and destroy fetal red blood cells. The resulting condition is called **haemolytic disease of the new-born** (HDNB).

It can be **treated** by giving the baby massive **transfusions** of blood. It can be **prevented** by injecting the mother with **anti-D immunoglobulins** soon after the birth of each Rh+ baby. These antibodies destroy any D antigens from the fetus before the mother's immune system has time to respond to them.

Testing your knowledge

1 a) Useful exchanges between maternal and fetal circulation involve movement of dissolved gases, glucose and antibodies. Match each of these with one of the following means of molecular transport: *active transport, pinocytosis, diffusion.* (2)

b) List X below gives four harmful agents that are able to cross the placenta. List Y gives the possible adverse effects on the developing embryo. Match the items in the two lists. (4)

List X	List Y
1) heroin	A) congenital defects of eyes and ears
2) HIV	B) failure of limbs to develop properly
3) rubella	C) painful post-natal withdrawal symptoms
4) thalidomide	D) development of AIDS at an early age

2 a) Identify ONE important role played by progesterone during gestation. (1)

b) (i) Which gland secretes the hormone prolactin?
(ii) Give the function of prolactin. (2)

3 a) Why is a Rh+ fetus regarded as foreign by the immune system of a Rh− mother? (2)

b) (i) What series of events leads to a Rh− mother becoming *sensitised*?
(ii) In the absence of any form of treatment, why will future Rh+ embryos borne by this sensitised Rh− mother be at risk? (2)

Applying your knowledge

1 Figure 17.9 shows a human embryo.

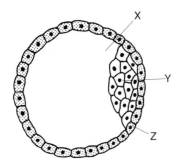

Figure 17.9

a) Name parts X, Y and Z. (3)

b) Where in the female reproductive tract would an embryo at this stage of its development be found? (1)

c) (i) What is meant by the term *differentiation*?
(ii) Which lettered part in the diagram will continue to grow and differentiate for many years to come? (2)

2 Figure 17.10 shows monozygotic twins during gestation.

a) How many gametes were involved in the formation of their genotype? (1)

b) (i) Name TWO structures shown in the diagram that are essential for development and are shared by the twins.

(ii) Which of these would be shared by dizygotic twins? (3)

c) How many gametes are involved in the formation of dizygotic twins' genotypes? (1)

d) Conjoined (Siamese) twins are born joined together at some point. Sometimes they can be successfully separated. Are such twins monozygotic or dizygotic? Explain your answer. (2)

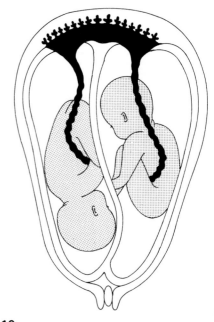

Figure 17.10

Continued ➤

Applying your knowledge

3 The hormonal control of the development of the mammary glands in a pregnant woman is shown in figure 17.11.

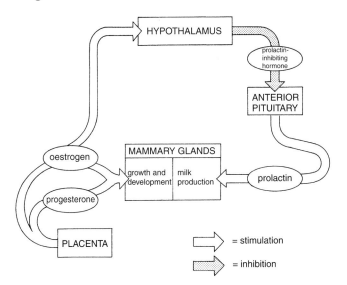

Figure 17.11

a) Which hormones are required for growth and development of the mammary glands? (1)

b) Which hormone is required for milk production by the mammary glands? (1)

c) (i) Which hormone prevents excessive milk production occurring before the birth of the baby?

  (ii) Describe the mechanism that brings this inhibitory effect to a halt when the baby is born. (3)

d) If a woman does not wish to breast-feed her baby, she may take 'milk suppression' tablets which contain synthetic oestrogen. Explain how this preventative mechanism works. (2)

4 A Rhesus negative woman and her Rhesus positive husband produced four children, as shown in figure 17.12.

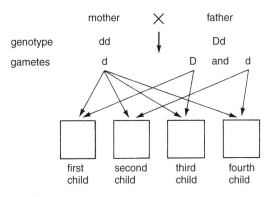

Figure 17.12

a) State
  (i) the genotypes;
  (ii) the phenotypes of the four children with respect to the Rhesus factor. (4)

b) (i) Which child would be most likely to suffer haemolytic disease of the new-born (HDNB)?

  (ii) Explain why you chose this child and not the other one with the same genotype.

  (iii) What treatment could the mother have received to prevent future babies from suffering HDNB?

  (iv) If she had not received this treatment, what could be done to try to save the life of a new-born baby suffering HDNB? (4)

5 Give an account of the effects on the developing embryo of **four** named harmful agents. (10).

18 Birth and post-natal development

Birth

A human fetus is described as 'full-term' after 38 weeks of gestation. At around this time, gentle contractions of the uterus gradually move the fetus into a position with its head close to the cervix ready for birth (parturition).

A series of events called labour then begins. Involuntary rhythmic contractions of the uterine wall start at the top of the uterus and travel downwards in waves. Early in labour the amniotic sac bursts and the cervix gradually dilates. The contractions increase in power and frequency until eventually the baby is expelled from the uterus and delivered through the vagina (see figure 18.1).

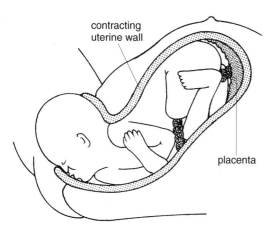

Figure 18.1 Birth

The uterine contractions which occur during labour are brought about mainly by the hormone **oxytocin** secreted by the mother's posterior pituitary gland.

Induction

Birth can be artificially **induced** by gradually injecting oxytocin (or a synthetic hormone which mimics its effect) into the mother's bloodstream.

Nutrition of new-born

Prior to the birth of the baby, the mother's mammary glands become enlarged, ready to produce milk. Following parturition, the hormone **prolactin** stimulates lactation (milk production). However, the milk is not released from the breasts until **oxytocin** is present. This hormone stimulates contraction of muscle tissue in the mammary glands which results in the ejection of milk.

Colostrum

The first milk produced is called **colostrum**. It is a watery yellowish nutrient fluid which is especially rich in **maternal antibodies**. These give the baby passive immunity against a variety of diseases.

After a few days normal breast milk begins to flow. It contains fewer antibodies than colostrum but is richer in **lactose** sugar and **fat** as shown in table 18.1.

component (units per 100ml)	colostrum	breast milk	cows' milk
total protein (g)	2.7	1.2	3.3
antibodies (mg)	720	315	0
fat (g)	2.9	3.8	3.6
lactose (g)	5.3	6.9	4.8
calcium (mg)	31	33	128
Vitamin C (mg)	4.4	4.3	1.6
Vitamin A (μg)	89	53	34

Table 18.1 Comparison of three types of milk

Powdered cow's milk which is used for bottle-feeding is also rich in the nutrients needed by infants, especially protein and minerals. However, it lacks the maternal antibodies that give the baby protection until its own immune system begins to operate.

An infant does not receive an adequate supply of **iron** in milk. Until this chemical element becomes available later in its diet, the infant makes use of iron stored during gestation.

Organochlorines

Organochlorines are non-biodegradable chemicals used as **pesticides** on crops. They increase in concentration along food chains and severely affect final consumers such as large fish and birds of prey (see also p 321).

Some organochlorines (e.g. DDT) have made their way along food chains and into the human body (e.g. following the consumption of contaminated fish). Since these stable molecules are **fat-soluble**, they are stored in the person's fatty tissue including breast milk in women. The release of breast milk is the main 'excretory' route of organochlorines from women.

Research has shown that in some cases the concentration of organochlorines in breast milk is so high that it exceeds by several times the legal limit allowed for commercially produced foodstuffs such as meat and dairy products.

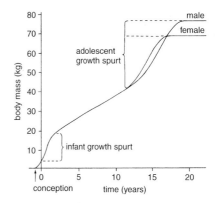

Figure 18.2 Human growth curves

Testing your knowledge

1 **a)** Rewrite the following sentences choosing only the correct terms from the underlined choice.

During labour leading to normal parturition, the amniotic sac bursts releasing watery <u>fluid/blood</u> and the cervix of the womb becomes <u>constricted/dilated</u>. Contractions of the uterine wall start at the <u>top/bottom</u> of the womb and travel <u>downwards/upwards</u> in waves. The contractions gradually <u>increase/decrease</u> in power and frequency until the baby is expelled from the <u>vagina/uterus</u> and delivered through the <u>uterus/vagina</u>. (2)

b) (i) What is *oxytocin* and which gland secretes it?
(ii) By what means can birth be induced artificially? (3)

2 **a) (i)** What is *colostrum*?
(ii) Why is it important that the baby receives colostrum for several days following birth? (2)

b) (i) Identify TWO components of breast milk that give it a higher energy content than colostrum.
(ii) Why is breast milk regarded as being superior to cows' milk as a food source for babies? (3)

c) (i) With what harmful fat-soluble chemical might some breast milk be contaminated?
(ii) How could this be possible? (2)

Pattern of growth after birth
Overall growth

Growth can be measured in different ways. Increasing overall body weight or height can be measured against time. When graphed, these give a **growth curve** (see figure 18.2) with two phases of rapid growth called **growth spurts**. The first occurs during the two years following birth; the second takes place at puberty. On average males reach puberty later and attain a larger adult size than females.

Change in body proportions

Figure 18.3 shows the **relative proportions** of the parts of the body as it grows from an embryo into an adult. The head of a new-born baby makes up about 25% of the total

body length whereas the head in an adult accounts for only about 13%. On the other hand, the new-born baby's lower limbs account for about 33% of the total body length whereas those of the adult make up about 50%.

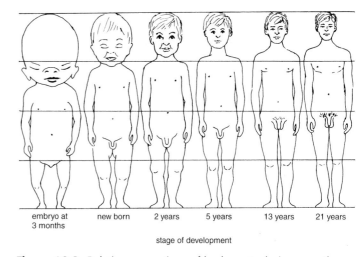

Figure 18.3 Relative proportions of body parts during growth

Figure 18.4 illustrates the different growth rates of various parts of the body. The brain normally approaches adult size by the fifth year; the sex organs remain dormant until adolescence.

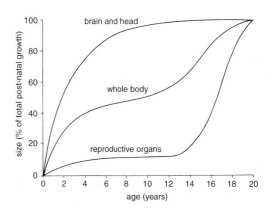

Figure 18.4 Different growth rates of body parts

131

Role of growth hormone

The anterior pituitary (under the control of the hypothalamus) secretes human **growth hormone (somatotrophin)**. This hormone promotes growth by accelerating the transport of amino acids into the cells of soft tissues and bones and by stimulating the breakdown of fats for energy release. This allows rapid synthesis of tissue proteins to occur. In particular it promotes increase in length of long bones during the growing years.

Figure 18.5 shows the effect of over-production and under-production of human growth hormone during adolescence, and the effect of over-production during adulthood.

Production of somatotrophin is controlled by a gene. Genetic engineering has enabled scientists to transfer this gene into a bacterium which then produces human growth hormone. The hormone is extracted and used to treat children who show early signs of pituitary dwarfism. The graph in figure 18.6 shows the effect of treatment on a typical patient.

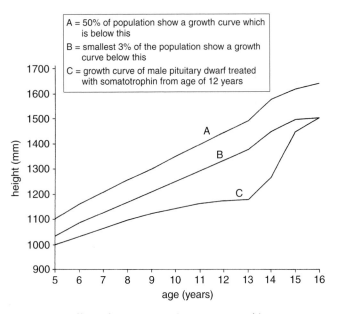

Figure 18.6 Effect of treatment using somatotrophin

Changes in the body at puberty

Puberty is the stage of human development during which the reproductive organs become functional and a child changes into an adult. Puberty is accompanied by several bodily changes as summarised in table 18.2. These are called **secondary sexual characteristics**. (Primary sexual characteristics, such as possession of male or female genitals, are present at birth.)

Hormonal changes at puberty

Hypothalamus

The **hypothalamus** (see figure 18.7) is a region of the brain connected to the anterior part of the pituitary gland by tiny blood vessels. The hypothalamus contains secretory cells which make **releaser hormone**.

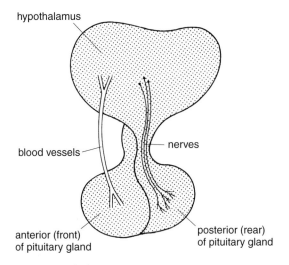

Figure 18.7 Hypothalamus

Pituitary

At puberty, releaser hormone is transported in the bloodstream to the **anterior pituitary** gland which becomes stimulated and starts to release **FSH** and **LH** or **ICSH**. These gonadotrophic hormones are transported round the body in the bloodstream to their target organs, the **gonads**.

female	male
Growth and development of uterus, oviduct, vagina and breasts.	Growth and development of testes and penis.
Onset of menstrual cycle involving ovulation and menstruation.	Production and release of sperm.
Increase in height and weight (largely due to growth of skeleton and muscles).	Increase in height and weight (largely due to growth of skeleton and muscles).
Growth of pubic and other adult body hair.	Growth of facial, pubic and other adult body hair.
Widening of hips.	Deepening of voice following development of larynx.

Table 18.2 Secondary sexual characteristics

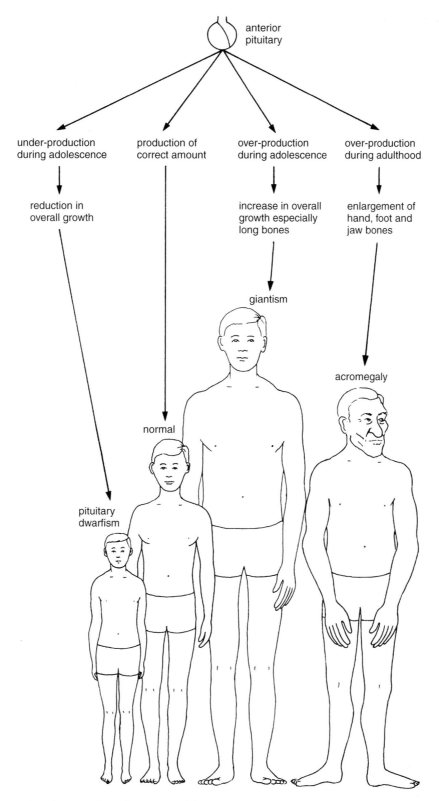

Figure 18.5 Effects of over- and under-secretion of somatotrophin

Gonads

The gonads (ovaries or testes) respond to the gonadotrophic hormones by producing the **sex hormones**. The ovaries make oestrogen and progesterone and the testes produce testosterone.

The sex hormones are **steroid** hormones. This means that they are fat-soluble lipids able to pass through cell membranes and influence some of the target cell's genes (e.g. switch them on). In this way, sex hormones promote the development of secondary sexual characteristics and control the menstrual cycle (see chapter 15).

The sequence of events under hormonal control is summarised in figure 18.8.

Anabolic steroids in sport

The term **anabolic steroids** refers to male sex hormones (e.g. testosterone) and their derivatives produced pharmaceutically. When taken into the body as pills or by injection, these hormones increase the **muscle mass** and **strength** of people who exercise intensively and consume a high protein diet.

This effect had obvious attractions for competitors in sports such as weight-lifting and athletics where extra muscle bulk was found to provide the extra strength or turn of speed needed to win.

However, anabolic steroids were found to have serious side effects. Excessive use by women leads to **masculinisation** (i.e. growth of facial hair, deepening of the voice and development of a masculine physique). Excessive use by men leads to shrinkage of the testes and reduction in sperm production often accompanied by **temporary sterility**. The man's body is affected in this way because high levels of testosterone-like substances cause inhibition of ICSH and FSH secretion by the pituitary gland (see figure 15.4, p 111).

In addition, large doses of anabolic steroids increase the risk of damage to the liver and disease of the heart and kidneys. They also tend to make the person feel aggressive, antisocial and depressed and may even cause serious psychological changes.

Despite all of these adverse effects and the fact that anabolic steroids have been banned by the International Olympic Committee since 1976, their illicit use still continues. Some over-ambitious competitors are willing to risk permanent damage to their bodies, and international disgrace if found to fail the drugs test, in their desperate bid to be 'winners'.

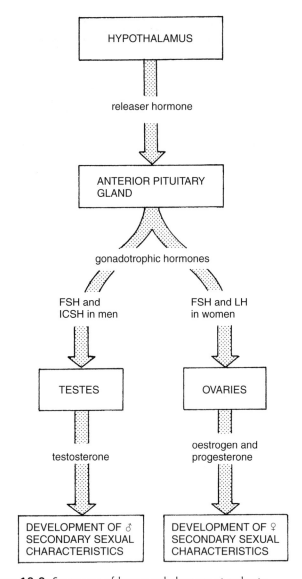

Figure 18.8 Summary of hormonal changes at puberty

Testing your knowledge

1 a) (i) What is a *growth spurt*?
   (ii) When do the two growth spurts that affect humans occur? (3)

b) Draw a table to compare the relative size of the head and lower limbs (as a percentage of total body length) of a newborn baby and an adult. (2)

2 a) Describe TWO ways in which somatotrophin promotes growth. (2)

b) By what means is growth hormone obtained for use in treating children who show early signs of pituitary dwarfism? (1)

3 Major changes to the body occur in males and females at puberty. List THREE for each sex. (3)

4 a) Name THREE natural steroid hormones. (3)

b) (i) What are anabolic steroids?
   (ii) Why do some healthy people choose to take these?
   (iii) Give ONE possible harmful side effect of anabolic steroids to each sex. (4)

Applying your knowledge

1 a) (i) Briefly describe the part played by oxytocin during labour.
   (ii) One of the world's largest pharmaceutical companies is attempting to produce a drug that will prevent pregnant women from going into premature labour. Suggest how the drug would work. (2)

b) The pathway in figure 18.9, which shows a second role played by oxytocin, represents a neuroendocrine reflex action. Identify the
   (i) stimulus;
   (ii) receptor;
   (iii) response;
   (iv) effector, in this reflex action. (4)

c) In what way is this type of reflex action different in its mode of action from the reflex one which brings about limb withdrawal? (1)

d) By what means is oxytocin transported from the posterior pituitary to the breasts? (1)

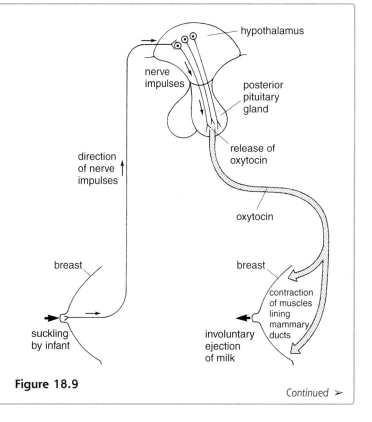

Figure 18.9

Continued ➤

Applying your knowledge

2 a) Copy and complete table 18.3 which refers to use of energy and increase in mass by a human female. (2)

age (years)	percentage energy in food used to build tissues	total mass (kg)	annual increase in mass (kg)
0 (birth)	40	3.40	
1	25	9.75	
2	20	12.30	
3	10	14.43	
4	10	16.43	
5	10	18.59	
6	10	21.10	
7	10	23.69	
8	10	26.36	
9	10	29.22	
10	11	32.17	
11	12	36.02	
12	15	40.02	
13	15	45.23	
14	10	49.45	
15	8	51.76	
16	4	53.35	
17	4	54.30	
18	4	54.67	

Table 18.3

b) Draw a line graph of annual increase in mass with age. (2)

c) (i) Compare the girl's growth rate at ages 9 and 13 years.
(ii) Account for this difference.
(iii) During which year of her life did the girl gain most mass? (3)

d) (i) Make a generalisation about the effect of age on the percentage energy in food used to build tissues.
(ii) Suggest why this should be the case. (2)

3 The histograms in figure 18.10 show the growth rates of two boys A and B.

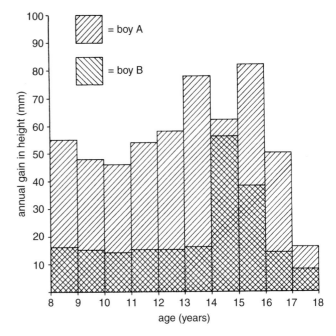

Figure 18.10

a) By how many millimetres did boy A increase in height at age
(i) 8–9
(ii) 13–14
(iii) 15–16? (1)

b) By how many millimetres did boy B increase in height at age
(i) 8–9
(ii) 13–14
(iii) 15–16? (1)

c) (i) Which of the two boys was a potential pituitary dwarf?
(ii) Suggest the treatment that the boy was given to prevent him remaining a dwarf and state the earliest age at which the treatment started to take effect. (3)

4 a) Using only the information in figure 18.11, draw up a table to clearly show the two hormones, the endocrine glands that secrete them, and the target tissues that they act on. (3)

b) Name a further target tissue of testosterone. (1)

c) With reference to the diagram, explain how, in a normal healthy adult male, it is not possible for testosterone to build up by natural means to an excessively high level. (2)

Continued ➤

Applying your knowledge

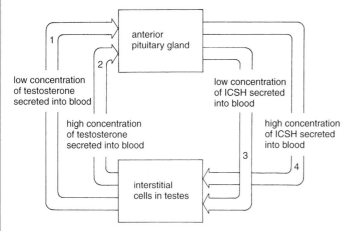

Figure 18.11

(i) reproductive organs;
(ii) whole body;
(iii) brain? (1)

b) At age 10 years, what is the percentage of total post-natal growth shown by the
(i) reproductive organs;
(ii) whole body;
(iii) brain? (1)

c) Which body part shows
(i) most;
(ii) least development during childhood? (1)
(iii) Suggest why it is of survival value to humans to have this growth pattern rather than one where all the organs develop at the same rate, as shown by many other mammals. (2)

d) **(i)** Is the data graphed in figure 18.12 based on averages for human males or females?
(ii) Explain your choice of answer. (2)

e) During which 2-year period did general body growth occur at the fastest rate? (1)

f) At what age in years was each of the following body parts found to be at 50% of its post-natal final size?
(i) Reproductive organs;
(ii) whole body;
(iii) brain. (1)

g) If the size of the cranium had been graphed, as percentage of post-natal growth, which curve would it most closely resemble? Why? (1)

d) Suggest how ingestion of excessive quantities of anabolic steroids may disturb the above pathway. (2)

e) If consumption of excessive anabolic steroids continues, the male body eventually compensates by converting these molecules to female sex hormones in the liver. Predict the effect that this will have on the man's breast tissue. (1)

f) Consumption of anabolic steroids in women brings about masculinisation. Name TWO masculine features that the woman would develop and explain why. (2)

5 Figure 18.12 shows the average growth rates of the human body and two types of organ.

a) At age 2 years, what is the percentage of total post-natal growth shown by the

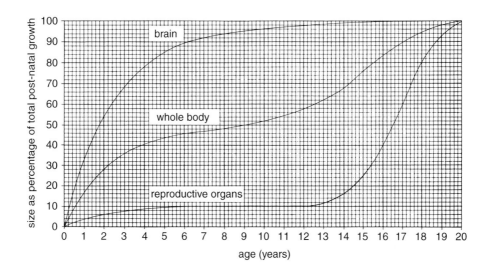

Figure 18.12

What you should know
(Chapters 17–18)

(See table 18.4 for word bank.)

1 Cleavage is the process of cell _____ by which a zygote becomes an _____ and an embryo develops into a ball of cells. _____ is the attachment of the embryo to the uterus wall. Differentiation is the process by which _____ cells become altered to perform specific functions.

2 _____ twins are 'identical'; _____ twins are non-identical.

3 During _____ useful transfer of materials occurs continuously between maternal and _____ circulations. Harmful substances and _____ can also be transferred from the mother and affect the fetus adversely.

4 During gestation, _____ and oestrogen secreted by the corpus luteum, and later by the placenta, maintain the endometrium, inhibit release of new _____ and stimulate milk-secreting tissues in the _____ glands. The hormone _____ from the anterior pituitary stimulates milk production.

5 A Rhesus positive fetus developing inside a _____ negative mother is regarded as foreign by the mother's _____ system. The mother makes antibodies which destroy the fetal _____ cells.

6 The hormone oxytocin brings about the contractions of the uterus which lead to the _____ of the baby. Synthetic oxytocin can be used to _____ birth artificially.

7 _____ brings about release of milk from the mother's breasts. _____, the first milk, is watery and rich in _____. Normal breast milk contains fewer antibodies but is richer in lactose and _____.

8 Two _____ in overall growth occur in humans: the first during the two years following birth; the second at _____. Changes in body _____ also occur during growth.

9 The anterior pituitary secretes the hormone somatotrophin which promotes _____. Over or under-production in adolescence leads to giantism or _____ respectively.

10 At puberty male and female _____ organs mature and begin to function. This process is accompanied by changes in the body which lead to the development of _____ sexual characteristics. These are controlled by _____ hormones.

antibodies	gestation	prolactin
birth	growth	proportions
colostrum	immune	puberty
division	implantation	red blood
dizygotic	induce	reproductive
dwarfism	mammary	Rhesus
eggs	monozygotic	secondary
embryo	oxytocin	sex
fat	pathogens	spurts
fetal	progesterone	unspecialised

Table 18.4 Word bank for chapters 17–18

19 Need for transport system

Exchange of materials

The cells of a living organism need to receive a supply of nutrients and oxygen and have wastes such as carbon dioxide removed. The exchange of materials between an organism and its external environment is brought about by processes such as diffusion and active transport (see chapter 6). Efficient exchange of materials depends on the organism possessing a **large surface area** in relation to its volume.

Surface area to volume ratios

Table 19.1 shows how a small object has a large surface area in relation to its volume and that as the volume increases, the **relative surface area** decreases. For example a 'one centimetre cube' has a surface area to volume ratio of 6:1, a 'two centimetre cube' has a surface area to volume ratio of 3:1 and a 'six centimetre cube' has a surface area to volume ratio of 1:1.

In effect this means that a small organism has nearly all of its body tissue close to the outside surface (see figure 19.1). A large organism, on the other hand, has much less of its inner tissue close to the outside surface; most of it is buried in the body core.

Comparing ratios of surface area to volume for two mammals

The approximate surface area of a small mammal can be determined by measuring the area of a suitable paper cylinder as shown in figure 19.2. An estimate of its volume can be made using the method shown in figure 19.3.

The surface area of a human can be estimated using a **nomogram** (see figure 19.4). The straight line connecting the person's weight and height indicates their surface

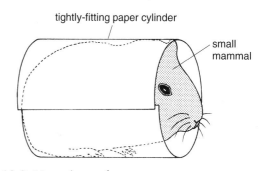

Figure 19.2 Measuring surface area

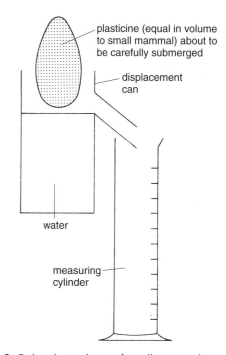

Figure 19.3 Estimating volume of small mammal

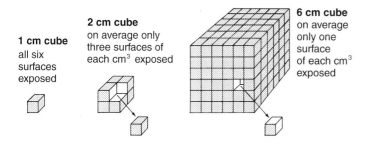

Figure 19.1 Relative surface areas

length of side of cube (cm)	surface area of one side (cm²)	total surface area (cm²) (SA)	volume (cm³) (VOL)	SA/VOL	ratio (SA:VOL)
1	1	6	1	6	6:1
2	4	24	8	3	3:1
3	9	54	27	2	2:1
6	36	216	216	1	1:1

Table 19.1 Size and relative surface area

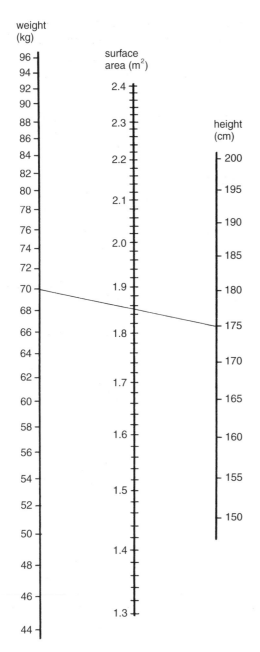

Figure 19.4 Nomogram

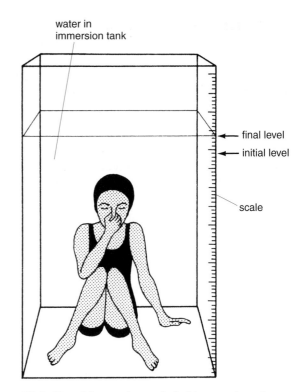

Figure 19.5 Use of immersion tank (ladder not shown)

area. For example, an adult who weighs 70 kg and is 175 cm in height would have a surface area of approximately 1.85 m².

The volume of a human can be measured using an immersion tank (see figure 19.5) and calculating the difference between the initial and final levels of water.

When the surface area to volume ratios are calculated, the small mammal is found to have a much larger surface area to volume ratio than the human.

Absorbing surfaces

A tiny unicellular animal (e.g. *Amoeba*) has a very large surface area to volume ratio. As a result it is able to absorb sufficient quantities of essential materials from its external environment through its cell membrane.

Since a large multicellular animal has a small surface area to volume ratio, it needs **additional absorbing surfaces** to take in oxygen and food. In humans, for example, alveoli in the lungs and villi in the small intestine greatly increase the surface area available for absorption of essential materials.

Need for a transport system

Once essential substances have entered a living organism, they must spread through its body since all of its living parts need oxygen and food. In tiny *Amoeba* only very short distances are involved and the passive process of diffusion is adequate to transport materials to all parts of the cell.

However, diffusion is too slow for larger organisms where the absorbing organs are located at a considerable distance from most of the metabolising cells in need of food and oxygen. Larger organisms need a specialised **transport system** to deliver essential materials to living cells at a rate which is rapid enough to keep pace with their continuous demands.

Circulatory system

In large, advanced animals such as humans where a division of labour exists amongst the internal parts, the tissues and organs are found to be both highly specialised and interdependent. As a result, materials need to be exchanged continuously between the different structures that make up the body's internal environment in addition to the exchanges made between the organism as a whole and the external environment.

These requirements are met by having a **closed circulatory system** containing a special fluid (**blood**) which is confined to tubes (**vessels**). The smallest of these are called exchange vessels (**capillaries**). They transport materials to within diffusion distance of every living cell. A muscular pump (**heart**) continuously circulates blood round the system (approximately 60 000 miles of vessels in a human adult!).

Such a closed circulatory system is especially beneficial to the organism because the distribution of blood is under efficient control at all times and can be finely adjusted to meet the changing demands of different tissues (see p 190). This enables the circulatory system to work in close harmony with the digestive, respiratory, excretory, locomotor and endocrine systems.

Arteries and veins

Arteries are vessels which carry blood away from the heart. Each possesses a thick muscular layer in its wall (see figure 19.6) which is able to withstand the high pressure of blood coming from the heart. Arteries pulsate (expand and contract with a rhythmical beat) due to the pumping action of the heart.

Veins carry blood back to the heart. The muscular layer in the wall of this type of vessel is thin since blood flows along a vein at low pressure. Compared with an artery, the **lumen** (cavity in the centre of the vessel) of a vein is wide. This reduces resistance to flow of blood to a minimum.

Valves are present in veins to prevent backflow of blood. Their presence can be demonstrated by the method shown in figure 19.7 on page 142.

Smaller vessels

Blood is transported from arteries to veins through a series of smaller blood vessels. Each artery branches into smaller and smaller vessels called **arterioles**. Each vein, on the other hand, is formed from the convergence of many tiny **venules**. Blood passes from arterioles to venules via a dense network of tiny microscopic vessels called **capillaries** (see figure 19.8).

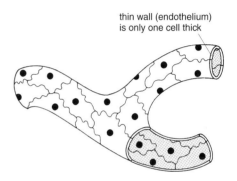

Figure 19.8 Capillary

Capillaries are the most numerous type of blood vessel in the body. They are referred to as the exchange vessels since all exchanges of materials between blood and living tissues take place through their thin walls (only one cell thick). The relationship between blood vessels and the direction of blood flow in the circulatory system is summarised in figure 19.9.

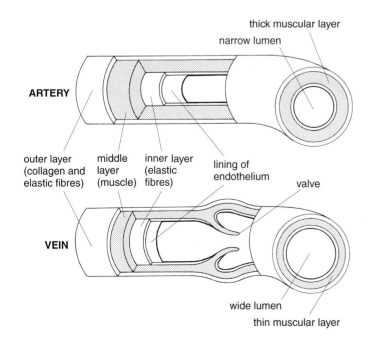

Figure 19.6 Comparison of structure of an artery and a vein

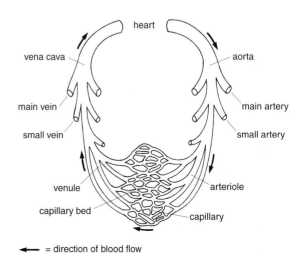

Figure 19.9 Relationship of blood vessels

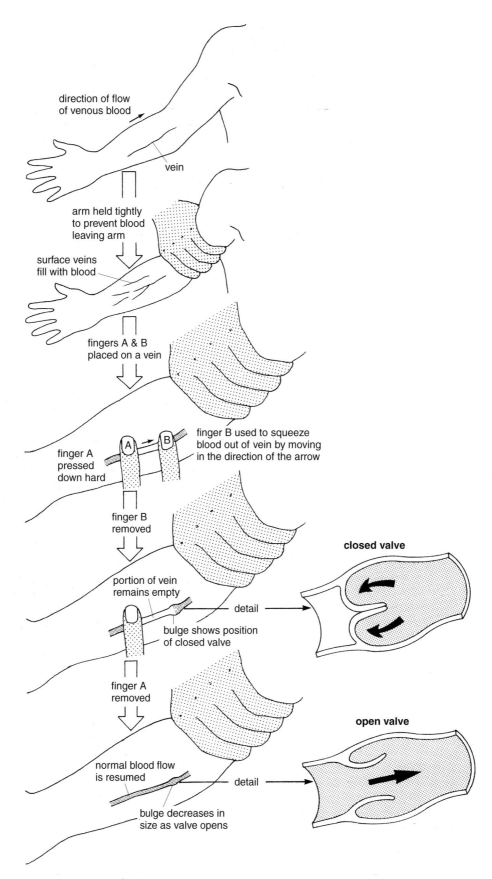

direction of flow
of venous blood

vein

arm held tightly
to prevent blood
leaving arm

surface veins
fill with blood

fingers A & B
placed on a vein

finger A
pressed
down hard

finger B used to squeeze
blood out of vein by moving
in the direction of the arrow

finger B
removed

portion of vein
remains empty

bulge shows position
of closed valve

detail

closed valve

finger A
removed

normal blood flow
is resumed

detail

bulge decreases in
size as valve opens

open valve

Figure 19.7 Demonstrating the presence of valves

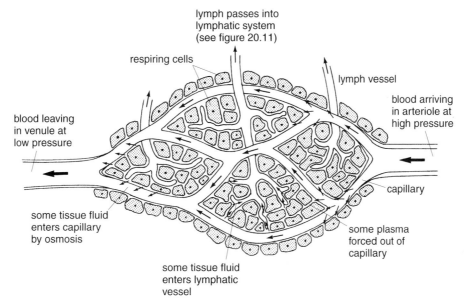

Figure 19.10 Exchange of materials in a capillary bed

Tissue fluid

Blood consists of red blood cells, white cells and platelets bathed in **plasma**. Plasma is a watery yellow fluid which contains many dissolved substances such as glucose, amino acids, respiratory gases, plasma proteins and useful ions.

Blood arriving at the arteriole side of a capillary bed (see figure 19.10) is at a higher pressure than blood in the capillaries. As blood is forced into these narrow exchange vessels, it undergoes a form of **pressure filtration** and much of the plasma (containing small dissolved molecules) is squeezed out through the thin walls. This liquid is called **tissue fluid**. It differs from blood plasma in that it contains little or no protein.

Exchange of materials

The network of capillaries in a bed is so dense that every living cell in the body is located close to a blood capillary and is constantly bathed in tissue fluid. Since tissue fluid contains a high concentration of soluble food molecules, dissolved oxygen and useful ions, these diffuse down a concentration gradient into nearby cells supplying them with their requirements. At the same time carbon dioxide and other metabolic wastes diffuse out of the cells into the tissue fluid.

Osmotic return of tissue fluid

Much of the tissue fluid returns to the capillaries at the venule side of the capillary bed. This process is brought about by **osmosis** (see p 46) with water passing from a region of higher water concentration (tissue fluid lacking plasma proteins) to a region of lower water concentration (blood plasma rich in soluble proteins) down a water concentration gradient. Carbon dioxide and metabolic wastes enter the bloodstream by diffusion.

Lymphatic return of tissue fluid

Some of the tissue fluid does not return to the blood in the capillaries. Instead it enters tiny thin-walled **lymphatic vessels** which have blind ends and are located in the connective tissue amongst the living cells (see figure 19.10).

Once in a lymphatic vessel, the tissue fluid is called **lymph**. The lymphatic system (see p 154) collects lymph from all parts of the body and eventually returns it to the blood circulatory system.

Need to circulate blood

Blood must be continuously circulated round the body to allow exchanges of materials between the bloodstream and:

◆ the **external environment** (e.g. absorption of oxygen and release of carbon dioxide at alveoli);

◆ the **internal environment** (e.g. release of oxygen and removal of carbon dioxide at living cells).

To maintain this regular flow of blood, the circulatory system employs a powerful muscular pump, the heart.

Heart

This organ is divided into four chambers, two **atria** and two **ventricles** (see figure 19.11). The right atrium receives deoxygenated blood from all parts of the body via two main veins called the superior and inferior **venae cavae**. This deoxygenated blood passes into the right ventricle and then leaves the heart by the **pulmonary artery** which divides into two branches each leading to a lung.

Following oxygenation in the lungs, blood returns to the heart by the **pulmonary veins** and enters the left atrium.

It flows from the left atrium into the left ventricle and leaves the heart by the **aorta**, the largest artery in the body.

Thickness of ventricle walls

The wall of the left ventricle is particularly thick and muscular since it is required to pump blood all round the body. The wall of the right ventricle is less thick since it only pumps blood to the lungs.

Valves

Figure 19.11 shows the four heart valves. Two of these, situated between the atria and the ventricles, are called the **atrio-ventricular (AV) valves**. The AV valve between the right atrium and ventricle has three flaps and is called the tricuspid valve. The one between the left atrium and ventricle has two flaps and is called the bicuspid (mitral) valve. The AV valves allow blood to flow from atria to ventricles but prevent backflow from ventricles to atria.

The other two heart valves, situated at the origins of the pulmonary artery and aorta, are called the **semi-lunar (SL) valves**. The one on the right side is also called the pulmonary valve and the one on the left the aortic valve. These valves open during ventricular contraction allowing blood to flow into the arteries. When arterial pressure exceeds ventricular pressure, they close, preventing backflow. The presence of the valves ensures that blood is only able to flow in **one direction** through the heart.

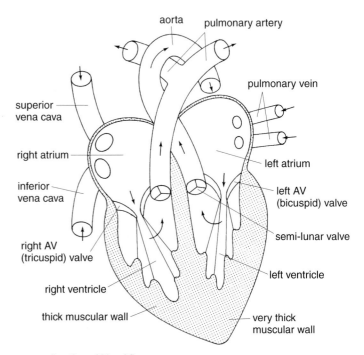

→ = direction of blood flow

Figure 19.11 Human heart

Double circulation

Pulmonary system

This is the name given to the route by which blood is circulated from the heart to the lungs and back to the heart (see figure 19.12). It should be noted that as a rule arteries carry oxygenated blood and veins carry deoxygenated blood. However the pulmonary system is exceptional in that the artery carries deoxygenated and the vein carries oxygenated blood.

Systemic system

This is the name given to the route taken by blood as it passes from the heart to a region of the body and then back to the heart. In this system arterial branches of the aorta supply oxygenated blood to all parts of the body. Figure 19.12 shows a simplified version of the human circulatory system which includes the main organs. Deoxygenated blood leaves the organs in veins. These unite to form the venae cavae which return blood to the heart.

Hepatic portal vein

Whereas veins normally carry blood from a capillary bed in an organ directly back to the heart, the hepatic portal vein is exceptional in that it carries blood from the capillary bed of one organ (the intestine) to the capillary bed of a second organ (the liver). This means that the liver has **three** blood vessels associated with it (see also p 170).

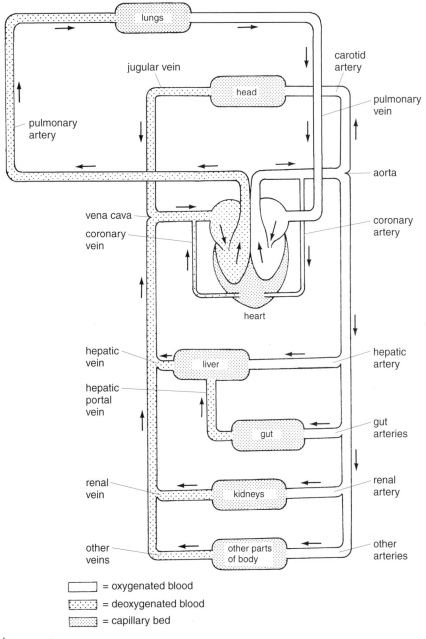

Figure 19.12 Human circulatory system

145

Coronary artery

The first two branches of the aorta are the left and right **coronary arteries** (see figure 19.13). These vessels spread out over the surface of the heart and divide into an enormous number of tiny branches leading to a dense network of capillary beds in the muscular wall of the heart itself.

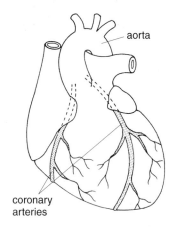

Figure 19.13 Coronary arteries

Each cardiac muscle cell is within $10\,\mu m$ of a capillary compared with the average distance of 60–$80\,\mu m$ in other organs. This close proximity to exchange vessels allows very rapid diffusion of oxygen and food into actively respiring cardiac muscle cells.

Coronary veins return deoxygenated blood from the heart wall to the vena cava.

Coronary heart disease

This general term refers to any disease which results in restriction or blockage of the coronary blood supply to part of the heart's muscular wall. It is the most common form of premature death in many developed countries (see figure 19.14).

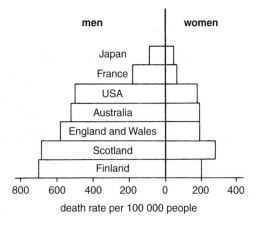

Figure 19.14 Deaths from coronary heart disease

The restriction or blockage causes partial or complete deprivation of oxygen to the affected part and may result in death of muscle cells. Sudden irreversible damage of this kind is called **myocardial infarction**. If a large part of the heart is affected, the person may die instantly; if a small region is affected, the person may make a satisfactory recovery.

Atherosclerosis

This is the term used to refer to the most common form of hardening of the arteries. It begins with plaques of fatty material called **atheromas** developing in the inner coat of the vessel wall (see figure 19.15).

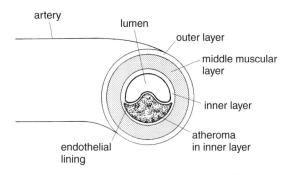

Figure 19.15 Atheroma in an artery

As the years go by, these atheromas become enlarged by the addition of lipid and cholesterol molecules from the blood and become hardened by deposits of calcium. The larger these plaques become, the more their presence restricts flow of blood to an organ (e.g. blood flow through a coronary artery to cardiac muscle in the heart wall).

Angina

This term refers to the crushing pain in the centre of the chest which tends to radiate out into the left arm and up to the neck and jaws. It is suffered by people whose coronary arteries have become narrowed by atherosclerosis. Coronary arteries obstructed in this way allow sufficient blood to flow to the cardiac muscle only when the person is at rest.

During exercise or stress, the heart beats faster and the demand for oxygen by cardiac muscle cells increases accordingly. However, this cannot be met by the reduced blood flow through the narrowed coronary arteries and so **angina** results.

Coronary thrombosis

Atheromas on the inside lining of an artery make the surface uneven and disturb the smooth flow of blood. Each of these hard protrusions provides a site upon which a blood clot (thrombus) can slowly develop and further block the affected artery (see figure 19.16).

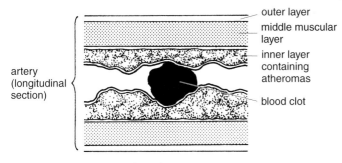

Figure 19.16 Coronary thrombosis

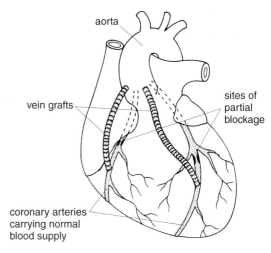

Figure 19.17 Double bypass of blocked coronary arteries

When a clot breaks loose, it is carried along by the blood until it blocks some narrow vessel and causes blood flow to be restricted or even brought to a complete halt in that vessel. Blockage of a coronary artery by a blood clot is called **coronary thrombosis**. It deprives part of the heart muscle of oxygen and leads to a myocardial infarction ('heart attack').

Detection and treatment

Partial blockage of a coronary artery can be detected by selective arteriography. If the coronary angiogram produced indicates that the partial blockage is advanced, a **coronary bypass** operation may be performed. This is done by connecting the aorta to the coronary artery using a length of vein taken from the patient's leg (see figure 19.17).

Reducing risk

The chance of coronary artery disease is kept to a minimum by avoiding the main risk factors:

◆ cigarette smoking;

◆ very stressful lifestyle;

◆ consumption of diet containing excessive quantities of cholesterol and saturated fat;

◆ being overweight;

◆ lack of regular exercise.

● **Testing your knowledge** ●

1 a) Construct a table that names the four chambers of the human heart, the type of blood (oxygenated/deoxygenated) that it contains, where this blood has come from and where this blood is going to. (8)

b) Compare the location and function of an atrio-ventricular valve with those of a semi-lunar valve. (2)

2 Decide whether each of the following statements is true or false and then use T or F to indicate your choice. Where a statement is false, give the word that should have been used in place of the word in bold print. (6)

a) The **carotid** vein returns deoxygenated blood from the head to the vena cava.

b) The **renal** artery carries blood to the kidneys to be purified.

c) The pulmonary **vein** carries deoxygenated blood from the heart to the lungs.

d) The **left** atrium receives deoxygenated blood from all parts of the body.

e) The **right** ventricle pumps blood round to the lungs for oxygenation.

f) The **coronary** vein carries oxygenated blood from the lungs to the left atrium.

3 a) Give the meaning of the terms *atheroma*, *angina* and *coronary thrombosis*. (3)

b) Identify THREE risk factors that increase the chance of coronary artery disease. (3)

Applying your knowledge

1 a) Calculate the total surface area and the total volume of the cube shown in figure 19.18
(i) before it was sawn up
(ii) after it was sawn up. (4)

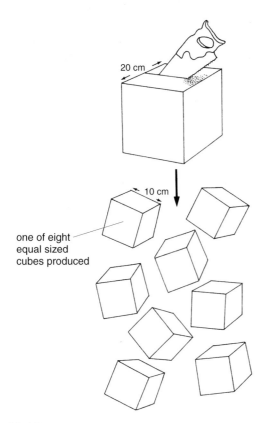

20 cm

10 cm

one of eight equal sized cubes produced

Figure 19.18

b) Calculate the surface area to volume ratio of
(i) the original large cube
(ii) one of the smaller cubes produced after cutting. (2)

c) Imagine that each size of cube represents a living organism. Which size would have the greater difficulty exchanging essential materials with its surroundings by diffusion through its surface. Explain why. (2)

d) In relation to one another, most of the cells in the human body are stationary. How then are they able to obtain essential raw materials for growth and dispose of their wastes? (1)

2 Figure 19.19 shows a transverse section of part of a vein and the outline for the equivalent part of an artery.

a) Copy or trace the diagram and name parts A, B, C and D. (4)

vein   artery

A
B
C

D

wide lumen

Figure 19.19

b) Complete the diagram to show the structure of an artery and then label the parts. (4)

c) (i) State a further structural difference between the two types of vessel that is not shown in this diagram.
(ii) With the aid of simple diagrams, describe the role played by these structures. (2)

3 *Arteriole, artery, capillary, vein* and *venule* are five types of blood vessel. Using only these terms (but as often as you require), construct a flow chart to indicate the route taken by a red blood cell as it travels from a capillary bed in the body via the heart, lungs and heart again before returning to a capillary bed in the body. (4)

4 Figure 19.20 shows part of the human circulatory system and the details of exchange of materials in a capillary bed.

a) Name the different types of blood vessel numbered 1–5. (5)

b) In what way does blood pressure differ between points W and X in the diagram of the close-up? (1)

c) (i) Name the liquid present in space Y.
(ii) Describe how it is formed.
(iii) Explain why the presence of this liquid is of importance to nearby cells.
(iv) State ONE way in which the liquid differs from blood plasma. (4)

d) Identify structure Z and state its function. (2)

e) Which of arrows A–D represents the osmotic return of tissue fluid? (1)

Continued ➤

Applying your knowledge

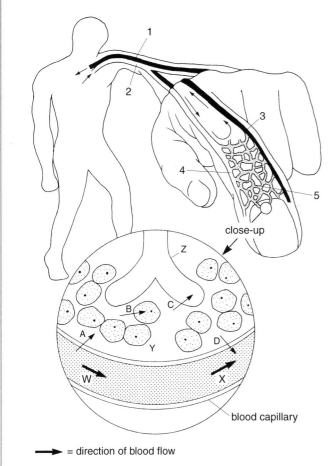

close-up

blood capillary

⟶ = direction of blood flow

Figure 19.20

5 Fish, fruit and olive oil are the major components of the traditional diet of the people living in Mediterranean countries such as Italy and Greece. However in recent years, local people have developed a taste for hamburgers, chips and butter which have become readily available to satisfy the demands of tourists. The incidence of heart disease in these countries has soared in the last 20 years. Suggest why, with reference to possible

   (i) dietary and
   (ii) non-dietary factors. (2)

6 Describe in detail the route taken by:

   a) an oxygen molecule absorbed into the blood at an alveolus and transported to a kidney cell; (5)

   b) a carbon dioxide molecule formed in a respiring brain cell and transported to an alveolus for removal. (5)

(20) Transport mechanisms

Cardiac cycle

The term **cardiac cycle** refers to the pattern of contraction (**systole**) and relaxation (**diastole**) shown by the heart during one complete heartbeat. On average the length of one cardiac cycle is 0.8 seconds, as shown in figure 20.1, which is based on a heart rate of 75 beats per minute.

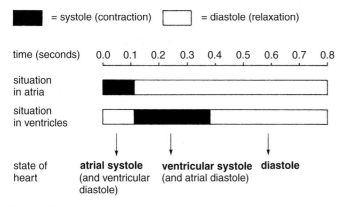

Figure 20.1 One cardiac cycle

During **atrial** systole (see figure 20.2), the two atria contract simultaneously and send blood down into the ventricles through the open AV valves. The ventricles (still in the relaxed state of ventricular diastole) fill up with blood and the SL valves remain closed.

Atrial systole is followed about 0.1 seconds later by **ventricular** systole. This stage involves the contraction of the ventricles and the closure of the AV valves. The pressure exerted on the blood in the ventricles (as the cardiac muscle contracts) soon exceeds the blood pressure in the arteries. The SL valves are pushed open and blood is ejected from the heart.

During diastole, the return of blood via the venae cavae and pulmonary veins to the atria causes the volume of blood in the atria to increase. Eventually atrial pressure exceeds that in the ventricles, the AV valves are pushed open and blood starts to enter the ventricles. This is soon followed by atrial systole and a repeat of the cardiac cycle.

Valves and heart sounds

Figure 20.3 refers to some of the changes that occur during the cardiac cycle in a mammal.

At point W in the graph (which refers to the left side of the heart only), ventricular pressure exceeds atrial pressure forcing the AV (bicuspid) valve to close. This produces the first heart sound ('**lubb**') which can be heard using a **stethoscope**. It can also be detected as a pattern shown on a **phonocardiogram** (see figure 20.3).

At point X, ventricular pressure exceeds aortic pressure forcing open the SL (aortic) valve.

At point Y, ventricular pressure falls below aortic pressure causing the SL valve to close. This produces the second heart sound ('**dupp**') heard through a stethoscope.

At point Z, ventricular pressure falls below atrial pressure and the AV (bicuspid) valve opens.

(A mnemonic to aid memory of this sequence of closed, open, closed, open is COCO.)

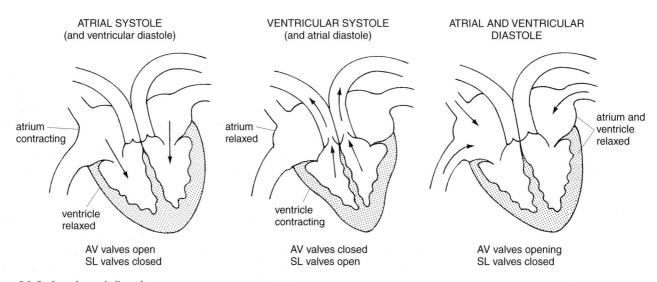

Figure 20.2 Systole and diastole

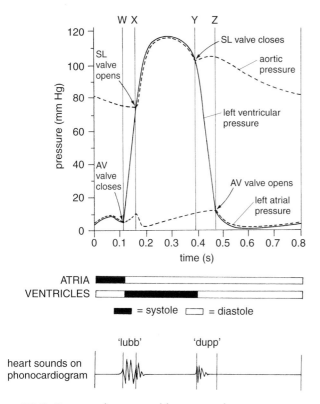

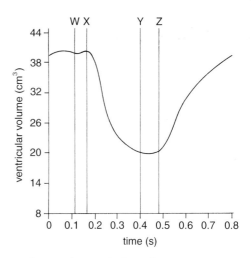

Figure 20.4 Changes in ventricular volume

Figure 20.3 Pressure changes and heart sounds

The heart sound 'lubb' is heard at the start of ventricular systole and 'dupp' at the start of ventricular diastole. Abnormal heart sounds produced by abnormal patterns of cardiac blood flow are called **heart murmurs**. These are often caused by defective valves which fail to open or close fully. This type of condition may be inherited or result from diseases such as rheumatic fever.

Figure 20.4 shows the changes in ventricular volume that occur during the cardiac cycle.

Conducting system of the heart

The sequence of events which occurs during each heartbeat is brought about by the activity of the **pacemaker** and the **conducting system** of the heart (see figure 20.5).

The pacemaker, also known as the **sino-atrial node (SAN)**, is located in the wall of the right atrium close to the entrance of the superior vena cava. It is a small region of specialised tissue which exhibits **spontaneous excitation**. This means that it initiates electrical impulses which make heart muscle cells contract at a certain rate. This rate can then be regulated by other factors to suit the body's requirements (see also p 187).

The pacemaker works automatically and would continue to function even in the absence of nerve connections from the rest of the body.

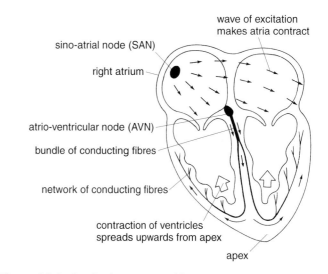

Figure 20.5 Conducting system of heart

A wave of excitation originating in the SAN spreads through the muscle cells in the walls of the two atria making them contract (i.e. atrial systole). The impulse is then picked up by the **atrio-ventricular node (AVN)** located centrally near the base of the atria.

The impulse passes from the AVN into a bundle of **conducting fibres** which divides into left and right branches. Each of these is continuous with a dense network of conducting fibres in the ventricular walls. Stimulation of these fibres causes simultaneous contraction of the two ventricles (i.e. ventricular systole) starting from the heart apex and spreading upwards.

Such coordination of heartbeat ensures that each type of systole receives the combined effect of many muscle cells contracting and that ventricular systole occurs slightly later than atrial systole allowing time for the ventricles to fill completely before they contract.

151

Electrocardiogram

The electrical activity of the heart can be picked up by electrodes placed on the skin surface. The electrical signals, once amplified and displayed on an oscilloscope screen, produce a pattern called an **electrocardiogram** (**ECG**).

The normal ECG pattern is shown in figure 20.6. It consists of three distinct waves normally referred to as P, QRS and T.

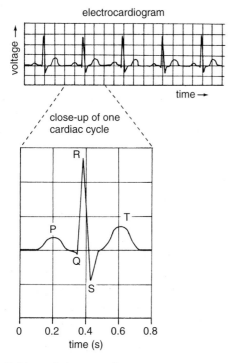

Figure 20.6 Normal electrocardiogram

The **P wave** corresponds to the wave of electrical excitation spreading over the atria from the SAN. The **QRS complex** represents the wave of excitation passing through the ventricles. The **T wave** corresponds to the electrical recovery of the ventricles occurring towards the end of ventricular systole.

Abnormal ECGs

Abnormal heart rhythms and some forms of heart disease can be detected and diagnosed using ECGs since these produce unusual but identifiable patterns. Some examples are shown in figure 20.7.

When extremely rapid rates of electrical excitation occur, these lead to an increase in rate of contraction of either atria or ventricles.

In an **atrial flutter** the contractions occur much more rapidly than normal but do remain coordinated. The example shown in the diagram shows four P waves for every one QRS complex.

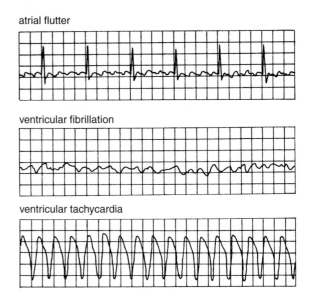

Figure 20.7 Abnormal ECGs

In a **fibrillation**, contractions of different groups of heart muscle cells occur at different times making it impossible for coordinated pumping of the heart chambers to take place. Ventricular fibrillation, for example, produces an ECG with an irregular pattern. This condition is lethal if it is not corrected.

During **ventricular tachycardia**, abnormal cells in the ventricle walls act like pacemakers and make these chambers beat rapidly and independently of the atria. The P (atrial) waves are absent and the wide QRS waves are abnormal.

Relief for some sufferers of abnormal heart rhythms can be provided by fitting them with an **artificial pacemaker**. This stimulator sends out small electric impulses to the heart making it beat in a normal, regular manner.

Blood pressure

The pressure of blood as it flows through the circulatory system is generated initially by the contraction of the ventricles. As the heart goes through systole and diastole, the arterial pressure rises and falls.

During ventricular systole, the pressure of blood in the aorta rises to a maximum (e.g. 120 mm Hg); during ventricular diastole, it drops to a minimum (e.g. 80 mm Hg). Figure 20.8 shows the blood pressure trace for a normal 18-year-old at rest.

Measurement of blood pressure

Systolic and diastolic pressures can be measured using a **sphygmomanometer**. Blood pressure is found to vary from person to person over a fairly wide range of normal values.

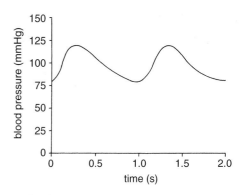

Figure 20.8 Blood pressure trace

Testing your knowledge

1 a) Distinguish between the terms *systole* and *diastole*. (2)

   b) Construct a table to compare atrial systole and ventricular systole with reference to state of atrial wall, state of ventricular wall, state of AV valves and state of SL valves. (4)

2 a) What causes the heart sounds 'lubb' and 'dupp' to be produced? (1)

   b) At what point in the cardiac cycle does each heart sound occur? (2)

   c) What is a heart murmur? (1)

3 a) (i) By what other name is the heart's pacemaker known?

      (ii) Briefly describe the function performed by the pacemaker. (2)

   b) (i) What heart structure is represented by the letters AVN?

      (ii) This structure passes impulses on to the conducting fibres. In which region of the heart are these fibres located?

      (iii) Which stage of the cardiac cycle occurs as a direct result of the conducting fibres passing on the impulses? (3)

4 a) What is an *electrocardiogram*? (1)

   b) (i) Of how many waves does a normal ECG consist?

      (ii) How many of these represent waves of electrical excitation affecting regions of the heart? (2)

Role of elastic walls

Although the ventricles do not contract during diastole, the blood pressure in the aorta does not drop to a low level. This maintenance of pressure is made possible by the fact that the walls of the aorta (and the large conducting arteries near the heart) are **elastic** enabling them to stretch during ventricular systole. During ventricular diastole (with the SL valve closed), the elastic walls **recoil** (see figure 20.9) and continue to propel blood through the vessels. A similar series of events occurs in the pulmonary artery.

Decreasing blood pressure

Although the pumping action of the heart causes fluctuations in **aortic blood pressure** (e.g systolic 120 mm Hg and diastolic 80 mm Hg), the average pressure in the aorta remains fairly constant (e.g. 100 mm Hg).

Figure 20.10 shows how a progressive decrease in pressure occurs as blood travels round the circulatory system dropping to almost zero by the time it reaches the right atrium again.

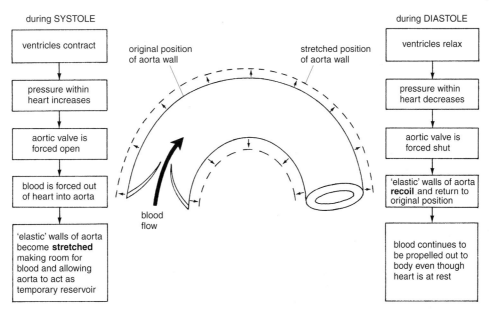

Figure 20.9 Elastic artery

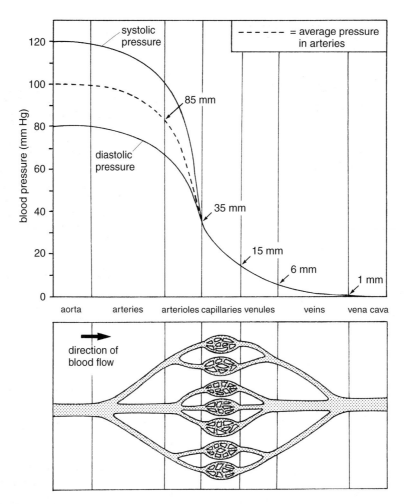

Figure 20.10 Decrease in blood pressure

Peripheral resistance

Peripheral resistance means the resistance to blood flow caused by friction between the blood and the walls of the vessels. This friction occurs because blood is fairly sticky and the arterioles and capillaries through which it passes are narrower in diameter and present a large surface area of wall in contact with blood.

The **arterioles** present the greatest resistance to blood flow and bring about the largest drop in pressure (i.e. around 50 mm Hg) as shown in figure 20.10.

Changes in blood pressure

Blood pressure is also directly related to the **volume** of blood present in the arteries. An increase in arterial volume leads to an increase in arterial pressure. In addition any factor that increases the **rate** and **force** of contraction of the heart tends to increase arterial blood pressure. High levels of sustained stress and intake of excessive amounts of salt appear to act together in the development of high blood pressure.

Dangers

Prolonged high blood pressure is dangerous because it:

◆ requires the ventricles to work harder (in order to eject blood into the arteries);

◆ makes arterial walls more prone to atherosclerosis;

◆ may damage blood vessels (e.g. in cerebrum leading to a 'stroke').

Lymphatic system

Lymph circulation

The walls of the tiny **lymphatic vessels** (see p 143) are porous enabling them to absorb the excess tissue fluid filtered out of the bloodstream in capillary beds. This fluid, called **lymph**, is collected by a vast network of lymph capillaries which unite to form larger lymphatic vessels, a very few of which are shown in figure 20.11.

Flow of lymph through the system is brought about mainly by the vessels being periodically compressed

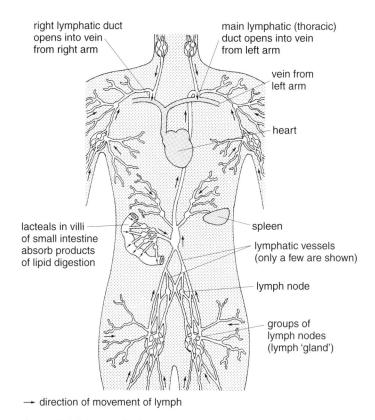

Figure 20.11 Lymphatic system

→ direction of movement of lymph

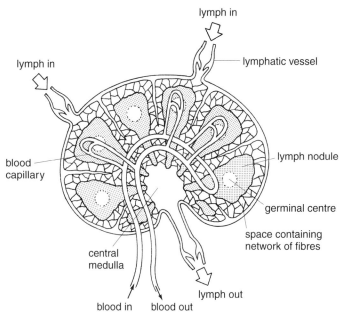

Figure 20.12 Lymph node

when muscles contract during breathing, locomotion and other body movements. Backflow of lymph is prevented by the presence of valves in the larger lymphatics. These vessels eventually return their contents to the bloodstream via two **lymphatic ducts** which enter the veins coming from the arms (see figure 20.11). By this means, tissue fluid which was once part of blood plasma is returned to the blood circulatory system.

The lymphatic system is regarded as a specialised part of the circulatory system since it consists of lymph fluid derived from blood and a system of vessels that returns lymph to the bloodstream.

Absorption of lipids

Each finger-like villus in the small intestine possesses a tiny lymphatic vessel called a **lacteal**. The products of fat digestion are absorbed by the epithelial cells on the surface of a villus (see p 169). Droplets of lipid then enter the lacteals and pass into the lymphatic system where they become a component of lymph. The entry of lipids into the bloodstream is therefore an indirect one via the lymphatic system.

Lymph nodes

Lymph nodes are oval or bean-shaped structures of various sizes found throughout the lymphatic system and especially at the junctions of several lymphatic vessels, as shown in figure 20.11. Most lymph nodes occur in groups ('glands') in certain areas of the body e.g. neck, armpit and groin.

Each lymph node consists of a layer of **lymph nodules** surrounding a **central medulla** (see figure 20.12). In the middle of each lymph nodule there is a **germinal centre** which is the site of **lymphocyte** production.

Around each lymph nodule is found a space containing a network of fibres. Lymph enters a node by several lymphatic vessels and percolates slowly through the network of fibres in the spaces between the nodules. This gives the **macrophage** cells that line these channels an opportunity to remove any micro-organisms (and other unwanted material) present in the lymph, by phagocytosis (see p 52). The lymph drains into the medulla and makes its exit by a lymphatic vessel.

Sometimes, during illness, so many micro-organisms enter the nodes that they swell up and may even become infected themselves if their phagocytic cells become overworked. Healthy lymph nodes are of critical importance to the body's well being since they engulf microbes by phagocytosis, filter unwanted debris and toxins from lymph and produce lymphocytes which make antibodies.

Oedema

This is the name given to the condition where tissue fluid accumulates in the spaces between cells and blood capillaries causing tissues to swell up. **Oedema** can be caused by several factors as follows.

Blood pressure

High blood pressure may result in tissue fluid being produced at a rate faster than it is drained away by the lymphatic system.

Malnutrition

A low level of plasma protein in blood caused by prolonged malnutrition results in the blood's water concentration being similar to that of tissue fluid. Little or no tissue fluid is returned osmotically to the blood. The lymphatic system is unable to remove the extra volume which tends to gather in the abdominal region. This is a symptom of **kwashiorkor** (see p 299).

Parasite

The tiny larvae of the filarial worm are transmitted by mosquitoes. Once inside the body they invade the lymphatic system and mature into adult worms which block the vessels especially those in the legs. This obstruction along with excessive growth of tissue in the infected area results in **elephantiasis**, an enormous enlargement of the affected extremity.

Testing your knowledge

1 a) (i) Is the pressure of blood in the aorta at its maximum during ventricular systole or ventricular diastole?
       (ii) Explain your answer. (2)

   b) What name is given to an instrument used to measure blood pressure? (1)

   c) Why is it important that the walls of the aorta are elastic and able to recoil during ventricular diastole (1).

2 a) (i) Give ONE reason why blood pressure decreases as blood is circulated round the body.
       (ii) Name the TWO types of blood vessel in which the greatest decrease in blood pressure occurs. (3)

   b) Give TWO reasons why prolonged high blood pressure is dangerous. (2)

3 a) (i) Describe the means by which lymph in a lymph vessel is forced along through the lymphatic system.
       (ii) What structures prevent backflow of lymph?
       (iii) Which structures allow lymph to return to the blood circulatory system? (3)

   b) Which type of food is absorbed into the body via the lymphatic system? (1)

   c) (i) Which type of white blood cell is produced in the germinal centre of lymph nodes?
       (ii) Which type of white blood cell removes micro-organisms from lymph as it passes through the spaces in a lymph node? (2)

Applying your knowledge

1 Figure 20.13 represents the repeated series of events that occurs during the human heartbeat.

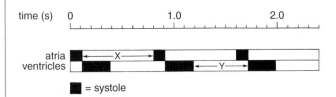

Figure 20.13

   a) (i) Which lasts longer, atrial or ventricular systole?
       (ii) Explain why this difference is necessary. (2)

   b) (i) Name the stages of the cardiac cycle represented by X and Y.
       (ii) In what state is cardiac muscle in the atria during stage X? (3)

   c) (i) How many complete heartbeats are represented by the diagram?
       (ii) Express the person's pulse rate in beats per minute. (2)

   d) Redraw part of the diagram to represent one complete heartbeat and then add the letters L and D and arrows to indicate when the two heart sounds would be heard. (3)

2 a) Figure 20.14 shows a normal electrocardiogram containing waves X, Y and Z. Which of these waves is produced during

Continued ➤

Applying your knowledge

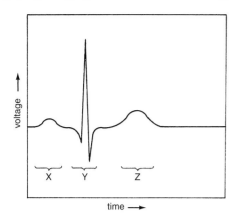

Figure 20.14

(i) electrical recovery of the ventricles;
(ii) spread of electrical impulses across the atria;
(iii) spread of electrical signals through the ventricles? (3)

b) Figure 20.15 shows two abnormal ECGs. Which of these indicates
(i) an abnormally slow heart rate
(ii) atrial fibrillation?
(iii) Briefly explain your choice in each case. (4)

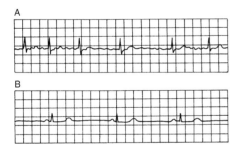

Figure 20.15

3 **a)** **(i)** Copy table 20.1 and complete the left hand column using the terms *capillaries, large arteries, left ventricle, small arteries, venae cavae and venules.*
   (ii) Complete the other two columns. (8)

b) **(i)** In which TWO parts of the system do the greatest drops in pressure occur?
   (ii) With reference to these parts only, state the total drop in pressure that occurs.
   (iii) Account for this drop in pressure. (3)

4 The data in table 20.2 refer to normal systolic blood pressures found in humans at different ages.

a) Present the data as a two-tone bar chart. (4)

part of circulatory system	range of blood pressure (mm Hg)	drop in pressure in this part of system (mm Hg)
	100	
aorta		
	95–100	
	85–95	
arterioles		
	15–35	
	6–15	
small veins		
large veins	1–2	
	0–1	

Table 20.1

age (years)	male	female
0–4	93	93
5–9	97	97
10–14	106	106
15–19	119	116
20–24	123	116
25–29	125	117
30–34	126	120
35–39	127	124
40–44	129	127
45–49	130	131
50–54	135	137
55–59	138	139
60–64	142	144
65–69	143	154
70–74	145	159
75–79	146	158

Table 20.2

Continued ➤

Applying your knowledge

b) (i) Make a generalisation about the effect of age on blood pressure.

   (ii) Give a possible explanation related to diet to account for this trend. (2)

c) It has been suggested that female sex hormones may in some way offer protection against high blood pressure. What information from the table seems to support this theory? (1)

5 Figure 20.16 shows a simplified version of the human circulatory system.

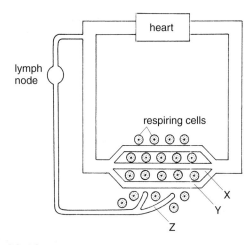

Figure 20.16

a) (i) Copy or trace the diagram and label it using the terms *artery, capillary, lymphatic vessel, lymphatic duct* and *vein*.

   (ii) Add at least five arrows to your diagram to show the direction of flow of the liquids in the vessels. (6)

b) Which letter in the diagram indicates the presence of
   (i) blood plasma;
   (ii) lymph;
   (iii) tissue fluid? (3)

c) State ONE difference in composition between
   (i) blood plasma and tissue fluid;
   (ii) tissue fluid and lymph. (2)

d) State TWO functions of a lymph node. (2)

6 The graphs in figure 20.17 show the pressure changes that occur in the heart and associated blood vessels.

a) (i) State the highest pressure exerted by each ventricle during the cycle.

   (ii) With reference to the structure of the heart,

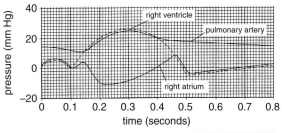

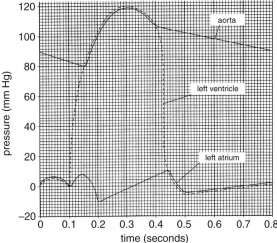

Figure 20.17

explain the marked difference between these two pressures. (2)

b) State the pressure at which the following valve movements occurred:
   (i) The right AV (tricuspid) valve closed.
   (ii) The SL (aortic) valve opened.
   (iii) The SL (pulmonary) valve closed.
   (iv) The left AV (bicuspid) valve opened. (4)

c) At what time in the cycle did ventricular systole begin? (1)

d) Between which TWO times in the cycle did ventricular pressure exceed aortic pressure? (1)

e) State the effect of diastole on the pressure of blood in the pulmonary artery. (1)

f) Make a simple line graph to indicate the state of ventricular volume during the same 0.8 second period. (1)

7 Give an account of the heart under the following headings:
   (i) the cardiac cycle; (6)
   (ii) the conducting system. (4)

8 Give an account of the structure and functions of the lymphatic system. (10)

What you should know
(Chapters 19–20)

(See table 20.3 on page 160 for word bank.)

1 A small object has a large _____ relative to its volume; as volume increases, relative surface area _____.

2 In large organisms the organs which absorb materials are situated at a distance from many of the cells in need of these essentials. A _____ system is required to deliver materials to cells at a rate faster than _____.

3 _____ are thick-walled vessels which carry blood away from the heart; veins are thinner-walled vessels with _____ which carry blood back to the _____.

4 Arteries divide into smaller vessels called arterioles; veins are formed by a convergence of smaller vessels called _____. Blood passes from arterioles to venules through tiny exchange vessels called _____.

5 When blood is forced through a capillary bed, some plasma passes out through the vessel walls. This liquid which bathes the cells is called _____. It differs from plasma in that it contains little or no _____.

6 Some tissue fluid returns to blood capillaries by _____; the remainder enters tiny lymphatic vessels and becomes _____.

7 The heart has two upper chambers called _____ and two lower chambers called _____. Deoxygenated blood returns to the heart from the body by the _____; it is pumped by the heart to the lungs via the _____. Oxygenated blood returns to the heart from the lungs by the _____; it is pumped by the heart to the body via the _____.

8 The aorta divides into arteries which supply oxygenated blood to all parts of the body. The _____ artery supplies cardiac muscle, the _____ arteries take blood to the head, the _____ artery supplies the liver, the _____ arteries transport blood to the kidneys. Similarly veins from each of these organs return deoxygenated blood to the vena cava.

9 The hepatic _____ vein is exceptional in that it connects one capillary bed (the gut) to another (the liver).

10 Coronary heart disease involves the restriction or blockage of the coronary blood supply to the heart wall. This may be caused by fatty deposits called _____ or blood clots.

11 The risk of heart disease is increased by cigarette smoking, _____, a diet rich in fatty foods, _____ and lack of exercise.

12 A cardiac cycle consists of a period of contraction called _____ and a period of relaxation called _____.

13 During a cardiac cycle two separate heart _____ are heard; each indicates the closing of a set of valves.

14 A cardiac cycle is initiated in the heart itself by the _____ (sino-atrial node). Its messages are picked up by the _____ node and passed via conducting _____ to the ventricular walls which respond by contracting.

15 The electrical activity of the heart can be displayed on a screen as an _____.

16 Blood pressure can be measured using a _____.

17 Blood pressure shows a progressive decrease as it travels round the circulatory system; the greatest drop occurs in the _____ and capillaries which offer the greatest _____ to flow.

18 The _____ system transports lymph in lymphatic vessels; lymph is returned to the bloodstream via two _____ which enter veins from the arms.

19 The products of _____ digestion are transported from gut to bloodstream via the lymphatic system.

20 Lymph _____ are the sites of _____ formation and phagocytic removal of microbes.

Continued ➤

What you should know
(Chapters 19–20)

aorta	carotid	fat	nodes	pulmonary vein	systole
arteries	coronary	fibres	osmosis	renal	tissue fluid
arterioles	decreases	heart	overweight	resistance	transport
atheromas	diastole	hepatic	pacemaker	sounds	valves
atria	diffusion	lymph	portal	sphygmomanometer	vena cava
atrio-ventricular	ducts	lymphatic	protein	stress	ventricles
capillaries	electrocardiogram	lymphocyte	pulmonary artery	surface area	venules

Table 20.3 Word bank for chapters 19–20

21 Delivery of oxygen to cells

Human cells are bathed in tissue fluid. Delivery of essential materials to within **diffusion distance** of cells is brought about by the circulatory system. Since blood plasma consists of water and dissolved solutes, it would seem reasonable to expect that materials to be transported would need to be highly soluble in water. However this is not the case with oxygen.

Since oxygen is only slightly soluble in water, the quantity that could be carried dissolved in plasma would be inadequate to satisfy the needs of respiring cells. This problem is overcome by the presence of **haemoglobin** (a respiratory pigment) which combines with oxygen and significantly increases the oxygen-carrying capacity of the blood.

Haemoglobin consists of haem (a compound containing iron) and globin (a protein made of several polypeptide chains). A molecule of human haemoglobin (see figure 21.1) contains four haem groups each able to carry a molecule of oxygen.

Association and dissociation

To be effective a respiratory pigment must be able to combine readily (**associate**) with oxygen on those occasions when the oxygen concentration in the surroundings is high, and rapidly release (**dissociate** from) oxygen when the surrounding oxygen concentration is low.

Haemoglobin meets these requirements exactly by having a **high affinity** for oxygen when the oxygen concentration in the surrounding environment is high (e.g. at the respiratory surface of the lungs) and a **low affinity** for oxygen when the oxygen concentration is low

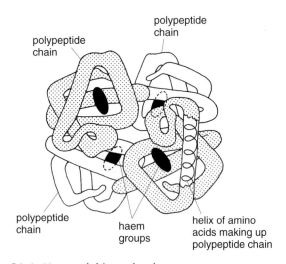

Figure 21.1 Haemoglobin molecule

(e.g. in actively respiring cells). (Affinity means tendency to combine with a substance.)

When haemoglobin combines with oxygen it forms **oxyhaemoglobin**. This reversible chemical reaction is summarised by the equation:

$$\text{haemoglobin} + \text{oxygen} \underset{\substack{\text{dissociation}\\\text{(in tissues)}}}{\overset{\substack{\text{association}\\\text{(in lungs)}}}{\rightleftharpoons}} \text{oxyhaemoglobin}$$

Oxygen tension

The partial pressure (tension) of oxygen is a measure of its concentration and is expressed in kilopascals (kPa).

The oxygen tension of inhaled alveolar air, for example, is about 13 kPa.

Oxygen dissociation curve

Percentage saturation of haemoglobin with oxygen decreases with decreasing oxygen tension of the surroundings. However, the relationship between the two is not a linear one; when graphed it gives an S-shaped curve (see figure 21.2) called the **oxygen dissociation curve**.

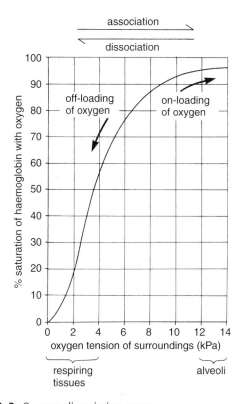

Figure 21.2 Oxygen dissociation curve

At the extreme right hand side of the curve, the oxygen tension in the environment (e.g. alveoli) is high and haemoglobin's level of saturation with oxygen is close to 100%.

Moving gradually to the left along the graph, the oxygen concentration of the surroundings is found to decrease yet haemoglobin still remains loaded up with oxygen to levels of over 85% saturation even when the oxygen tension of the surroundings has dropped to 8 kPa. This is due to the fact that haemoglobin has a high affinity for oxygen.

Moving further to the left, the oxygen tension of the surroundings drops to below 6 kPa and the percentage saturation of haemoglobin with oxygen drops rapidly. This is because haemoglobin's affinity for oxygen decreases rapidly in surroundings of low oxygen concentration. As a result it unloads its oxygen. This process is represented by the steep part of the S-shaped dissociation curve.

Respiring cells

Actively respiring cells (e.g. working muscles and liver) consume much oxygen and their oxygen tension is found to be low, at around 2.7 kPa or less. At the other extreme the oxygen tension of alveolar air is high at about 13 kPa.

When haemoglobin from respiring cells returns to the lungs, it becomes loaded up with oxygen which moves along the diffusion gradient from alveoli to blood. This process of association continues as before until haemoglobin is almost 100% saturated.

When this haemoglobin is transported to actively respiring cells with an oxygen tension of 2.7 kPa, haemoglobin's percentage saturation with oxygen drops to a low level (about 35%). This is because haemoglobin rapidly dissociates from its oxygen and unloads it. As a result oxygen becomes available to satisfy the demands of the actively respiring cells.

Resting cells

Cells at rest do not consume as much oxygen as actively respiring cells. The oxygen tension of cells at rest is therefore found to be higher at around 5.3 kPa. When blood with an oxygen tension of 13 kPa from the lungs arrives at resting cells, its oxygen tension drops to 5.3 kPa. Haemoglobin now unloads its oxygen by dissociation until its percentage saturation has dropped to about 75% (see figure 21.2).

Blood with an oxygen tension of 5.3 kPa and haemoglobin which is still 75% saturated with oxygen then returns to the lungs and loads up again by association to almost 100%, and so on.

Effectiveness of haemoglobin

The oxygen dissociation curve is especially steep between oxygen tensions of 6 and 2 kPa. This means that any slight drop in oxygen tension of body cells within this range results in a rapid release of oxygen by haemoglobin to these cells.

So effective is haemoglobin at this loading up (association) and unloading (dissociation) of oxygen, that it is responsible for the transport of 97% of the oxygen carried in the bloodstream.

Temperature

As the temperature of blood increases, haemoglobin's affinity for oxygen decreases (see figure 21.3). This means that at higher temperatures, haemoglobin (initially loaded up with oxygen to almost 100% saturation) starts to unload its oxygen sooner than it does at lower temperatures.

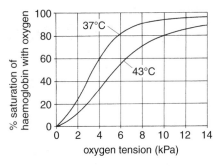

Figure 21.3 Effect of temperature

It can be seen, for example, from figure 21.3 that at an oxygen tension of 8 kPa and a temperature of 37°C, the percentage saturation of haemoglobin with oxygen is still up at around 90% whereas at the same oxygen tension but at a temperature of 43°C, the percentage saturation of haemoglobin with oxygen has dropped to about 70%. The haemoglobin at 43°C has released more of its oxygen.

Significance

Large quantities of energy are generated by respiring muscle cells and inflamed tissues suffering microbial infection. The rise in temperature that occurs locally in these tissues triggers the release of extra oxygen from haemoglobin. This is beneficial since these cells are exactly where extra oxygen is required for aerobic respiration.

Fetal haemoglobin

Fetal haemoglobin (see figure 21.4) has an oxygen dissociation curve to the left of adult haemoglobin since it releases its oxygen less readily (i.e. at a lower range of oxygen tension values) than adult haemoglobin.

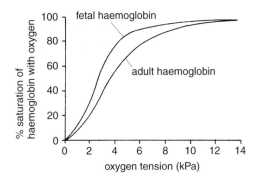

Figure 21.4 Fetal haemoglobin dissociation curve

This difference is essential to enable fetal haemoglobin to function effectively. By having a higher affinity for oxygen, it is able to draw oxygen from the mother's bloodstream across the placenta and deliver it to the growing embryo's cells.

Red blood cells

Structure

Each red blood cell (**erythrocyte**) is shaped like a **biconcave disc** (see figure 21.5). It contains cytoplasm rich in **haemoglobin** (about 28 million molecules per cell) but lacks a nucleus. The cell membrane contains many different proteins and bears **antigens** on its surface (see p 57).

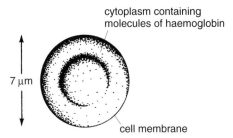

Figure 21.5 Red blood cell

A red blood cell's biconcave shape gives it a **larger surface area** in relation to its volume than it would have if it were a sphere (see figure 21.6). This increases its ability to absorb oxygen since it exposes a larger surface area of haemoglobin molecules to the surrounding environment. (The total surface area of all the red blood cells in an adult's body provides an area larger than a football pitch for the uptake of oxygen!)

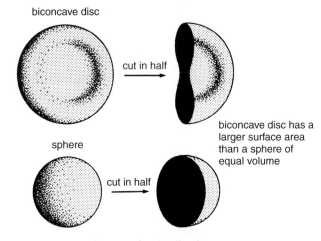

Figure 21.6 Significance of red cell's shape

Since red blood cells are **tiny** in size and **flexible** in shape they are able to squeeze through the narrowest of blood capillaries and deliver oxygen to nearby body cells.

Production of red blood cells

Red blood cell production takes place in the **red bone marrow**. This tissue is distributed throughout the skeleton in children. In adults it is confined to certain bones (e.g. sternum, ribs, vertebrae and long bones in the arms and legs).

Red marrow contains undifferentiated cells known as **stem cells**. At any given moment some of these are dividing by mitosis. Of the daughter cells produced, some remain as stem cells and others undergo differentiation into red blood cells. This involves several stages of development including transcription of the mRNA needed for haemoglobin formation. Once haemoglobin has been produced, the cell's nuclear material disintegrates. Immature red cells enter the bloodstream and become fully differentiated erythrocytes after a few hours.

Nutritional factors

Vitamin B$_{12}$ is required for the development of red blood cells in the bone marrow. **Iron** is required for haemoglobin formation. Deficiency in either of these nutrients prevents production of red blood cells and leads to **anaemia** (lowering of the blood's capacity to carry oxygen).

Vitamin B$_{12}$ can only be absorbed from the gut if a chemical called **intrinsic factor** is present. Intrinsic factor is secreted by the stomach. Failure by the stomach to produce it leads to pernicious anaemia.

Destruction of red blood cells

The life span of a red blood cell is about 120 days. Since it lacks a nucleus and ribosomes, a red blood cell cannot synthesise proteins and is incapable of growth and repair. Instead it begins to undergo fragmentation in the capillaries after completing four months of oxygen transport.

Worn out red blood cells are removed by the liver, bone marrow and spleen. The spleen is an organ on the left side of the abdomen above the kidney (see figure 20.11, on p 155). The liver, bone marrow and spleen contain **macrophage** cells which destroy old red blood cells by phagocytosis.

Haemoglobin molecules are broken down and the iron stored in the liver for future use. The haem groups minus iron are converted to **bilirubin** which is excreted as bile pigment (see p 175).

Testing your knowledge

1 a) Within a molecule of haemoglobin, what is the difference between *haem* and *globin*? (2)

   b) Distinguish clearly between the terms *association* and *dissociation*. (2)

   c) (i) Under what conditions of oxygen concentration in the surrounding environment does haemoglobin have a high affinity for oxygen?
       (ii) identify a region of the body where this occurs. (2)

   d) (i) Under what conditions of oxygen concentration in the surrounding environment does haemoglobin have a low affinity for oxygen?
       (ii) Identify a region of the body where this occurs. (2)

   e) What effect does increase in temperature have on haemoglobin's affinity for oxygen? (1)

2 a) Name THREE structural differences between a red blood cell and a cheek epithelial cell. (3)

   b) Explain why an erythrocyte is a good example of a cell whose structure is related to its function. (2)

3 a) Where in the body are red blood cells produced? (1)

   b) Which vitamin is essential for red blood cell production? (1)

   c) What is anaemia? (1)

   d) How long is the average life span of an erythrocyte? (1)

   e) Name TWO organs that remove old red blood cells from the bloodstream. (2)

Applying your knowledge

1 a) Describe the effect that increasing partial pressure of oxygen has on percentage saturation of haemoglobin as shown by the two curves in figure 21.7. (1)

   b) State the partial pressure of oxygen at which
       (i) adult haemoglobin;
       (ii) fetal haemoglobin shows 60% saturation. (2)

   c) State the percentage saturation of
       (i) adult haemoglobin;
       (ii) fetal haemoglobin with oxygen when the partial pressure is 5.5 kPa (2)

Continued ➤

Applying your knowledge

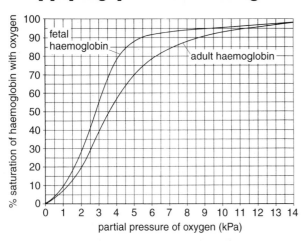

Figure 21.7

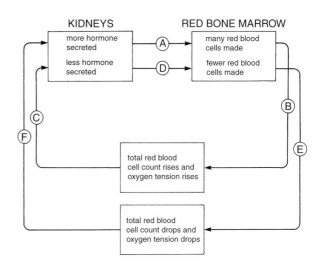

Figure 21.8

d) (i) What important difference between fetal and adult haemoglobin is highlighted by the fact that the curve for fetal haemoglobin is to the left of that for adult haemoglobin?
(ii) Suggest why this difference is of survival value to the fetus. (2)

e) State the approximate range of partial pressure of oxygen (in kPa) over which there would be maximum transfer of oxygen from adult to fetal haemoglobin. (1)

2 a) Construct a simple flow chart to show the main steps that occur during the process of red blood cell production. (3)

b) Pernicious anaemia is a condition caused by lack of vitamin B_{12} needed for red blood cell maturation in the bone marrow.
(i) Suggest why a person who consumes a diet rich in vitamin B_{12} but who has undergone a gastrectomy (surgical removal of the stomach) suffers pernicious anaemia.
(ii) Suggest how this type of anaemia is treated. (2)

3 Figure 21.8 shows how the process of red blood cell production is regulated by a hormone released by the kidneys. The quantity of this hormone (which stimulates red blood cell formation) is increased in response to a drop in the oxygen tension of the blood. The reverse occurs when blood tension rises.

a) Identify
(i) the receptor;
(ii) the effector in this pathway. (2)

b) With reference to the diagram explain how the total red blood cell count remains fairly constant under normal circumstances. (2)

c) Which letter in the pathway would be equivalent to giving a blood donation? (1)

d) Which letter corresponds to a blood transfusion being received by a dishonest athlete who has not suffered blood loss? (1)

e) Starting at the kidney, give the next TWO letters in the pathway that would occur if a lowland person took up residence at a high altitude for two months. (1)

4) Graph 1 in figure 21.9 shows the relationship between partial pressure of oxygen and percentage saturation of haemoglobin with oxygen under normal conditions. Graph 2 shows the same relationship at two different pH values.

a) (i) With reference to graph 1, compare the percentage oxygen saturation of haemoglobin that occurs at partial pressure of 110 units with that at 60 units. (1)
(ii) Explain therefore the advantage of possessing haemoglobin when breathing for a long period in an extremely poorly ventilated room. (1)

b) (i) What process occurring in body tissues maintains their partial pressure at the low value range of 5–30 units? (1)

Continued ➤

Applying your knowledge

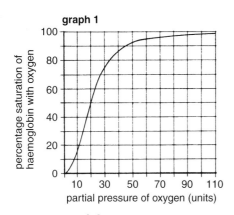

graph 1

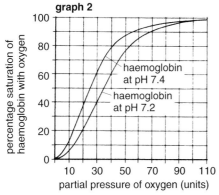

graph 2

Figure 21.9

(ii) Why is it ideal that the steep part of haemoglobin's dissociation curve in graph 1 corresponds to this range of partial pressure values? (1)

c) The pH of body tissues may decrease from 7.4 to 7.2 following especially high rates of tissue respiration. Account for this change. (1)

d) (i) With reference to graph 2, state the percentage saturation of haemoglobin with oxygen at partial pressure 30 units for pH 7.4 and pH 7.2. (1)

(ii) If the haemoglobin began at 97% oxygen saturation, calculate the percentage of oxygen released by the haemoglobin at partial pressure 30 units for both of these pH values. (1)

(iii) Does a drop in pH increase or decrease haemoglobin's affinity for oxygen? (1)

(iv) Why is this effect on haemoglobin's affinity for oxygen of benefit to the body? (1)

(v) Name a second abiotic factor which has a similar effect on haemoglobin's affinity for oxygen. (1)

5) Give an account of the production and breakdown of red blood cells. (10)

22 Delivery of nutrients to cells

Preparation for nutrient absorption

As food is moved along the alimentary canal from mouth to small intestine by peristalsis, a series of **digestive enzymes** promotes the breakdown of large insoluble molecules to small soluble molecules in preparation for their **absorption**, directly or indirectly, into the bloodstream.

Small intestine

The small intestine is structurally suited to the function of food absorption in several ways as follows:

◆ By being long and having a folded inner lining which bears thousands of finger-like villi, it presents a **large absorbing surface area** to digested food. This effect is further increased by the membranes of the epithelial cells which line the villi being folded into **microvilli** (see figure 22.1).

◆ The lining (epithelium) covering each villus is only **one cell thick** allowing nutrient molecules to pass through it easily.

◆ A **blood capillary** network and a central **lacteal** (tiny lymphatic vessel) are present in each villus ready to provide efficient means of transport to absorbed molecules.

Absorption of nutrients

Glucose and **amino acids**, the soluble end products of carbohydrate and protein digestion, are absorbed into the epithelial cells from where they pass directly into the blood capillaries.

The products of **lipid** digestion also pass into the epithelial cells but enter the central lacteal (not the blood capillary) as described later in this chapter.

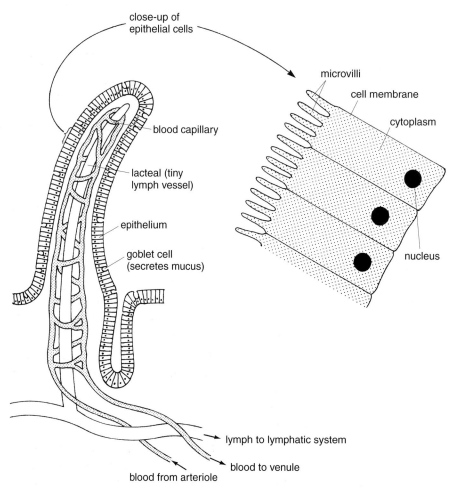

Figure 22.1 Villus and microvilli

166

Nutrients requiring no digestion by enzymes are also absorbed by the lining of the small intestine. These include **calcium**, **iron** and many **vitamins**. Vitamin B_{12} can only be absorbed if intrinsic factor (a polypeptide made by the stomach) is present to stimulate endocytosis (see p 49) by the membrane of the epithelial cells.

Investigating the effect of bile salts as an emulsifier

A lipid (e.g. olive oil) is insoluble in, and less dense than, water. When the two come into contact, lipid floats as a layer above water as shown in figure 22.2.

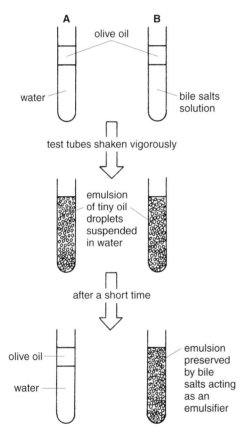

Figure 22.2 Emulsifying effect of bile salts

In test tube A, when the layers are shaken vigorously, they become mixed forming an **emulsion** of tiny oil droplets suspended in water. However this state is short-lived. The lipid droplets soon float to the surface and reform as a layer separate from the water.

In test tube B, when the lipid is vigorously shaken with bile salts solution, an emulsion of tiny oil droplets is again formed. However, in this case the emulsion does not quickly revert to two separate layers.

An **emulsifier** is an agent which preserves an emulsion. From this experiment, it is concluded that **bile salts** act as an emulsifier.

Mode of action of bile salts

One end of a bile salt molecule (the 'tail') is lipid-soluble and hydrophobic ('water-hating'). The other end (the 'head') is water-soluble, hydrophilic ('water-loving') and negatively charged.

During vigorous shaking, bile salt molecules become attached to the outside of each tiny droplet of lipid with their lipid-soluble tails to its inside and their water-soluble heads to its outside, as shown in figure 22.3.

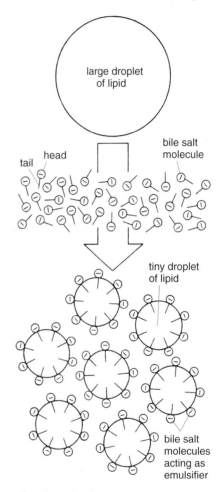

Figure 22.3 Bile salt molecules in action

The lipid droplets fail to rejoin because their negatively charged surfaces repel one another. This preservation of the emulsion by the action of bile salts is called **emulsification**.

Bile salts are made in the liver and stored in the gall bladder. They pass into the small intestine through the bile duct.

Lipase

Lipase is a digestive enzyme made in the pancreas. It is active in the small intestine where it catalyses the breakdown of lipid molecules by cleaving off the first and third fatty acid molecules, as shown in figure 22.4.

167

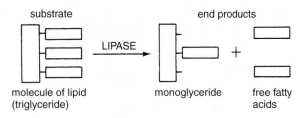

Figure 22.4 Action of lipase

Investigating the effect of bile salts on the action of lipase

In the experiment shown in figure 22.5, the lipid substrate being used is olive oil. After 30 minutes the contents of tubes A and B are found to show a drop in pH indicating the presence of acidic conditions. It is therefore concluded that lipase has promoted the breakdown of lipid to fatty acids in tubes A and B.

Since no change in pH is found to occur in tube C, it is concluded that lipase is required to catalyse the digestion of lipid and that bile salts alone are unable to bring about the digestive reaction illustrated in figure 22.4.

Comparison of tubes A and B shows that A has undergone a greater drop in pH than B. It is therefore concluded that more digestion of lipid to fatty acids occurs when bile salts are present.

Explanation

Bile salt molecules maintain an emulsion of small droplets of lipid (see figure 22.3) by preventing them from reuniting as large droplets. This process of emulsification significantly increases the **relative surface area** of lipid exposed to the action of lipase.

Thus bile salts promote lipid digestion by increasing the number of substrate molecules available for action by the enzyme lipase.

Absorption of end products of lipid digestion

Following digestion by lipase, the end products (monoglycerides and fatty acids) combine with bile salts to form minute water-soluble particles called **micelles** (see figure 22.6).

The micelles move to the surface of the intestinal epithelium which consists of microvilli. Molecules of monoglyceride and fatty acid leave the micelles and diffuse through the cell membrane into the epithelium (see figure 22.7).

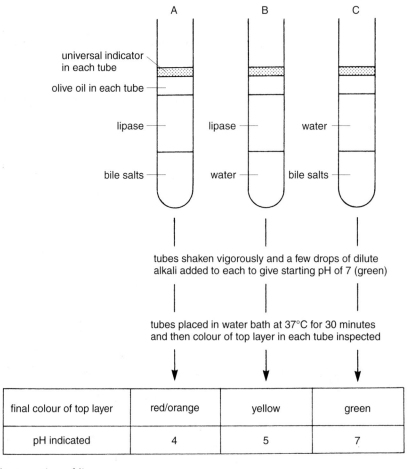

Figure 22.5 Effect of bile salts on action of lipase

The monoglycerides and fatty acids pass into the cell's smooth endoplasmic reticulum where they are built back up into molecules of **lipid** (triglyceride). These are coated with **lipoprotein** and passed out of the cell by exocytosis. They are then absorbed by the lacteals which transport them into the **lymphatic system** from where lipids, as components of lymph, pass into the bloodstream.

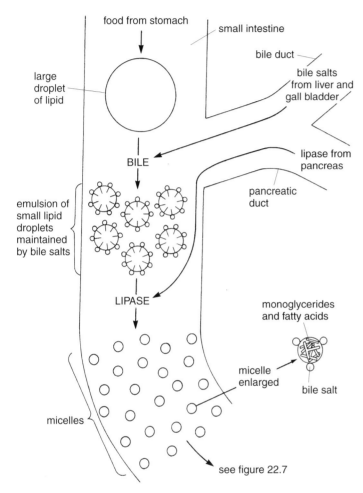

Figure 22.6 Formation of micelles

Dual supply of blood to the liver

Oxygenated blood is carried to the liver by the **hepatic artery** (a branch of the aorta); deoxygenated blood is carried away from the liver by the **hepatic vein** (which leads to the vena cava).

The liver is unusual in that in addition to its arterial supply it receives blood from a second source, via the **hepatic portal vein**. This vessel carries deoxygenated blood to the liver directly from the gut.

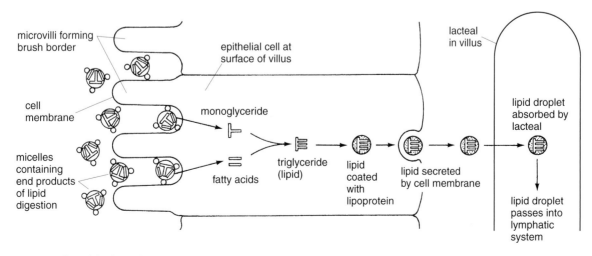

Figure 22.7 Uptake of lipid by lacteal

Portal system

This term refers to the unique pattern of circulation where blood in a capillary bed (e.g. gut) passes through a vein (e.g. hepatic portal vein) and into a second capillary bed (e.g. liver) before returning to general circulation.

The presence of such a portal system in the human body prevents the end products of digestion from entering general circulation directly. Instead they must first pass through the liver where its cells can exert a regulatory effect as described later in this chapter.

Composition of plasma

Figure 22.8 shows in a simple way the relative concentrations of three solutes present in the plasma of the hepatic blood vessels some time after a meal has been consumed and digested.

The hepatic artery (in common with all other branches of the aorta) contains blood plasma with normal concentrations of essential nutrients. It also contains the normal concentration of urea found in general circulation.

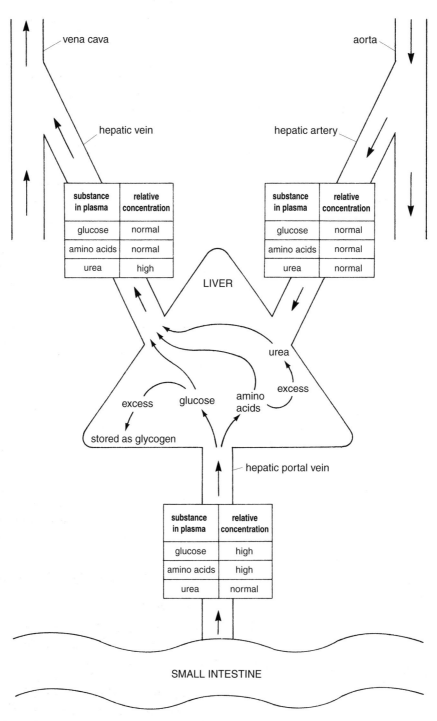

Figure 22.8 Hepatic blood supply

The hepatic portal vein contains blood plasma with high concentrations of the end products of digestion from the gut and the normal concentration of urea found in general circulation.

The hepatic vein contains blood plasma concentrations of glucose and amino acids which have been returned to normal by the regulatory action of the liver. Excess glucose has been stored as glycogen and excess amino acids have been converted to urea and passed out of the liver thereby increasing the concentration of urea in the plasma of the hepatic vein.

Role of liver in metabolism

Carbohydrate metabolism

The liver plays a major role in the regulation of the body's blood glucose concentration by removing glucose from, or adding glucose to, the blood as required.

After a carbohydrate-rich meal, blood entering the liver by the hepatic portal vein contains a concentration of **glucose** in excess of the body's immediate requirements. In response to the hormone **insulin** from the pancreas (see p 192), an enzyme in the liver becomes active and promotes the conversion of glucose to **glycogen** (see figure 22.9).

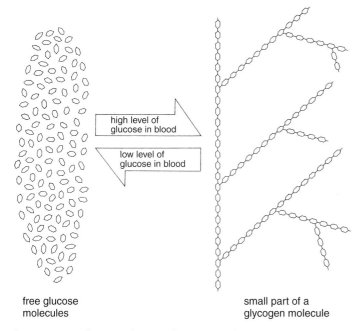

free glucose molecules

small part of a glycogen molecule

Figure 22.9 Glucose–glycogen interconversions

Glycogen molecules are large and insoluble in water. Up to about 100 g of glycogen can be stored in the liver. Beyond this limit, excess glucose is converted to lipid and deposited in one of the body's fat reserves.

When the blood's sugar level is low, a different hormone called **glucagon** is secreted by the pancreas. This activates

a different enzyme in the liver which promotes the conversion of glycogen to glucose. Glucose is then released into the bloodstream for use by living cells.

Lipid metabolism

Liver cells remove certain **lipid** molecules from the bloodstream and modify them as required to manufacture other lipids and lipid-related substances. For example, **cholesterol**, which is present in cell membranes and is essential for the manufacture of some steroid hormones, is synthesised in the liver when dietary intake is inadequate. The liver is also responsible for the excretion of excess cholesterol which is passed out of the body in bile.

Various types of **lipoprotein**, including those required to coat lipid molecules in preparation for their absorption into lacteals from gut cells, are formed in the liver. Liver cells also store fat-soluble vitamins (A, D, E and K).

Protein metabolism

The liver is the site of synthesis of three types of **plasma protein** (see table 22.1). The amino acids required for this synthesis and the formation of other cell proteins are absorbed from the bloodstream by liver cells.

type of plasma protein	function
albumins	Bring about osmotic return of water from tissue fluid in capillary beds.
globulins	Bring about transport of lipids and fat-soluble vitamins.
fibrinogen	Plays an essential role in clotting of blood.

Table 22.1 Types of plasma protein synthesised in liver

Liver cells also contains several **transaminase** enzymes which enable them to convert one amino acid to another as required. A wide range of amino acids can therefore be produced by liver cells despite a limited dietary intake.

Fate of absorbed materials

Carbohydrate

Blood leaving the liver contains a normal concentration of glucose (e.g. 5 millimoles per litre). It is transported to within diffusion distance of all living cells by the blood circulatory system. Much of this glucose is used by cells to obtain **energy** which is released during aerobic respiration (see chapter 5). Excess glucose is stored as glycogen in the liver and muscle cells, and as fat in fatty tissues.

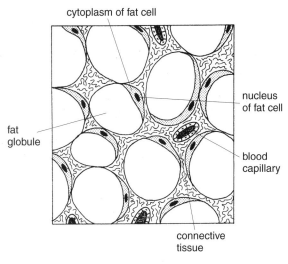

cytoplasm of fat cell

nucleus
of fat cell

fat
globule

blood
capillary

connective
tissue

Figure 22.10 Fat cells

Lipids

As molecules of lipid (triglyceride) enveloped in lipoprotein are transported round the body in the blood plasma, the triglyceride component is removed and digested by an enzyme attached to the lining of blood vessels. This makes the molecules of fatty acids and glycerol become available for use by cells as a source of **energy**. Fatty acids, for example, are broken down to acetyl CoA which then enters the Krebs' cycle (see p 39).

Excess fatty acids and glycerol are converted back to lipid and stored in fatty (**adipose**) tissue. This connective tissue consists of fat cells each of which is occupied almost entirely by a fat globule (see figure 22.10). A fat globule can be broken down to fatty acids and glycerol when energy is required.

Protein

Blood leaving the liver contains the normal concentration of amino acids dissolved in its plasma. Blood is transported to within diffusion distance of all living cells. On entering the cells, many of the amino acid molecules are used for **protein synthesis** (see chapter 3). The proteins formed play a wide variety of roles e.g. as enzymes, hormones, antibodies and structural proteins.

Excess amino acids cannot be stored. Some are used as an energy source by cells following **deamination** in the liver (see p 175).

Vitamins and minerals

Some vitamins and minerals absorbed from food play a key role in enzyme reactions. Metal ions such as zinc, iron, copper and magnesium act as enzyme activators.

Such substances are called **co-factors** (see p 14). Iron, for example, is the co-factor responsible for activating the enzyme catalase.

Sometimes the co-factor is a small non-protein molecule composed of an organic substance (e.g. a vitamin). Then it is called a co-enzyme. Vitamin B is an essential component of the co-enzymes which act as the hydrogen carriers during aerobic respiration.

● Testing your knowledge ●

1   Rewrite the following sentences to include only the correct word from each underlined choice.

   a)   The hepatic artery carries blood <u>to/from</u> the liver <u>to/from</u> the aorta. (1)

   b)   The hepatic vein carries blood <u>to/from</u> the liver <u>to/from</u> the vena cava. (1)

   c)   The hepatic portal vein carries blood <u>to/from</u> the liver <u>to/from</u> the gut. (1)

2   Briefly describe the importance of the hepatic portal system to the human body. (2)

3   a)   (i)   How does the liver deal with concentrations of glucose in the blood that are in excess of the body's requirements?

        (ii)   Which hormone is required to activate the enzyme involved in this metabolic process? (2)

    b)   (i)   Identify the lipid, essential for the production of some steroid hormones, that is made in the liver.

        (ii)   Give TWO examples of fat-soluble vitamins stored in the liver. (3)

    c)   Name ONE type of plasma protein and briefly describe the role that it plays in the human body. (2)

4   a)   Name an end product of digestion that is a carbohydrate and is used by body cells to obtain energy. (1)

    b)   What is the fate of excess fatty acids and glycerol absorbed into the bloodstream via the lymphatic system? (1)

    c)   Give ONE possible fate of an amino acid molecule leaving the liver and passing into the blood circulatory system. (1)

    d)   Name TWO examples of absorbed materials that act as co-factors in enzyme-controlled reactions. (2)

Applying your knowledge

1 Table 22.2 gives details of four test tubes that were set up by a pupil to investigate the effect of bile salts and boiling on the activity of the enzyme lipase.

	test tube			
	A	**B**	**C**	**D**
water	✓		✓	
bile salts		✓		✓
lipase	✓	✓		
boiled lipase			✓	✓
full cream milk	✓	✓	✓	✓
Universal Indicator	✓	✓	✓	✓
initial colour	green	green	green	green
initial pH	7	7	7	7

Table 22.2

a) Predict the final colour and pH of the contents of each tube after one hour. (4)

b) Which tubes should be compared to draw a conclusion about
   (i) the effect of bile salts;
   (ii) the effect of boiling on the activity of lipase? (2)

c) Which tube need not have been included in the experiment? Explain why. (2)

d) After one hour the contents of one of the tubes had turned orange-red (pH 4) and the pupil concluded that lipase had digested the fat in milk to fatty acids. However, his partner insisted that lipase must have digested the protein in milk to amino acids. How could the experiment be improved to establish who was correct? (2)

2 Table 22.3 refers to the concentrations of lipid molecules in two body fluids.

body fluid	concentration of lipid (mg/cm³)	
	before meal	**after meal**
lymph	220	6400
blood plasma	380	800

Table 22.3

a) Suggest why there is less lipid in lymph than in blood plasma before the meal. (1)

b) Account for the unequal distribution of lipids in the two body fluids after the meal. (1)

c) Why is the total concentration of lipids for both body fluids much lower before the meal than after it? (1)

3 Figure 22.11 shows two blood vessels associated with the liver and the results of analysing their plasma for glucose and urea.

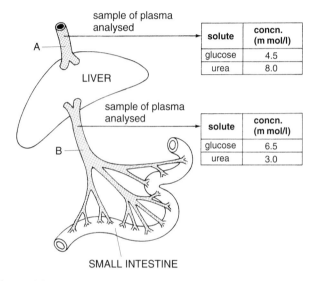

solute	concn. (m mol/l)
glucose	4.5
urea	8.0

solute	concn. (m mol/l)
glucose	6.5
urea	3.0

Figure 22.11

a) Name vessels A and B. (2)

b) Account for the change in
   (i) glucose concentration;
   (ii) urea concentration that occurs as blood passes through the liver. (2)

c) (i) Name the third blood vessel (not shown in the diagram) that is associated with the liver.
   (ii) Predict the concentrations of glucose and urea present in the plasma of this third vessel. (3)

4 Figure 22.12 represents some of the metabolic processes involving glucose that occur in the human body, in relation to increasing blood glucose concentration.

a) Match boxes X, Y and Z with the following answers. (3)
   A Stored as fat in adipose tissue.
   B Store of glycogen broken down.
   C Excreted in urine.

Continued ➤

Applying your knowledge

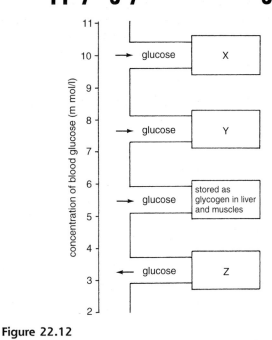

Figure 22.12

b) Suggest an optimum range of blood glucose concentration. (1)

5 Give an account of the role played by the liver in carbohydrate, lipid and protein metabolism. (10)

㉓ Removal of materials from blood

Role of lungs

Carbon dioxide produced by living cells during respiration is transported to the lungs by the circulatory system. The pulmonary artery (carrying deoxygenated blood rich in carbon dioxide to the lungs) branches into smaller and smaller vessels which lead to pulmonary capillaries. These are in intimate contact with the air sacs (alveoli) of the lungs.

Most carbon dioxide is carried in blood plasma in the form of bicarbonate ions (HCO_3^-). As blood flows through the pulmonary circulation, bicarbonate ions enter the red blood cells and combine with hydrogen ions (H^+) to form carbonic acid (H_2CO_3). An enzyme then promotes the reaction:

$$H_2CO_3 \xrightarrow{\text{enzyme}} H_2O + CO_2$$

Since the concentration of carbon dioxide in the blood plasma is now much higher than that in the air in the alveoli, carbon dioxide diffuses out of the blood into the lungs down a concentration gradient (see figure 23.1).

This gradient is maintained by breathing movements that exhale air rich in carbon dioxide.

Excretion

Excretion is the elimination of the waste products of metabolism. Since carbon dioxide is unwanted waste produced during respiration, its removal from the blood by the lungs is an example of excretion.

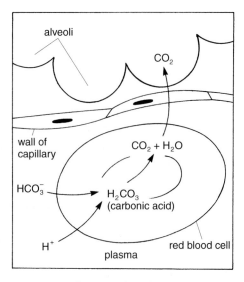

Figure 23.1 Removal of carbon dioxide

Role of liver
Conservation of useful substances

By regulating the level of **glucose** present in the bloodstream and storing the excess as glycogen, the liver conserves the balance of this essential nutrient and ensures that supplies are readily available to all living cells for energy release.

Blood contains three types of **plasma protein**. While some molecules of these proteins are undergoing deamination in the liver, new molecules are also being synthesised. By this means the liver maintains a stable pool of plasma proteins needed to perform the functions outlined in table 22.1.

By regulating the concentrations of important components of blood plasma, the liver helps to maintain a stable internal environment within the body and to provide living cells with optimum conditions for growth and development.

Detoxification of toxic materials

Certain substances which gain access to the body or are produced by the body itself as a result of metabolic reactions are potentially **toxic**. They would do the body harm if left unaltered. These substances are **detoxified** by liver cells in one or more of the following ways.

Chemical alteration

Biologically active molecules (e.g. drugs) are rendered inactive by being **chemically altered** in the liver. The products are then excreted in bile or released into the bloodstream and removed by the kidneys.

Chemical breakdown

Hydrogen peroxide is a highly toxic by-product of metabolism. The liver is rich in the enzyme **catalase** which promotes the breakdown of hydrogen peroxide to harmless substances as in the equation:

$$\text{hydrogen peroxide} \xrightarrow{\text{catalase}} \text{water} + \text{oxygen}$$
$$(2H_2O_2) \qquad\qquad (2H_2O) \quad (O_2)$$

Alcohol (ethanol) is converted in liver cells by a series of enzyme-controlled steps to acetyl CoA which acts as a respiratory substrate (see p 32).

However, there is a limit to the concentration of alcohol that the liver can tolerate without its cells becoming damaged. When alcohol is consumed to excess on a regular basis, the process of detoxification occurs but eventually the liver cells become permanently damaged. This leads to a chronic progressive disease of the liver known as **cirrhosis** which is often fatal.

Chemical attachment (conjugation)

Some unwanted substances (e.g. certain types of food preservative) become attached by liver cells to the amino acid glycine. This acts as a **molecular label** which is recognised as a waste by the kidneys and excreted.

Uptake by macrophages

Foreign particles are removed by **macrophages** (phagocytic cells) which line the liver's blood vessels. If, for example, an animal is injected intravenously with a suspension of carbon particles, samples of liver obtained only minutes later show numerous carbon-laden macrophage cells.

Removal and excretion of bilirubin

When red blood cells reach the end of their 120-day life span, they are destroyed by macrophage cells in the liver, bone marrow and spleen. Haemoglobin is broken down by these cells into a yellow pigment called **bilirubin** which is released into the blood giving plasma its faint yellow colour.

Cells in the liver continuously remove free bilirubin molecules from blood plasma and, with the aid of an enzyme, attach them to molecules of a second substance. It is in this conjugated form that bilirubin is added to bile and becomes **bile pigment.**

When bile passes into the small intestine, **bile salts** aid digestion by emulsifying lipids. However, bile **pigment** (conjugated bilirubin) does *not* perform a useful role in digestion. Its release in bile is a form of excretion. In the gut, bilirubin is converted by bacteria to the brown pigment that gives faeces their characteristic colour. The sequence of events involving bilirubin is summarised in figure 23.2.

Jaundice

Bilirubin accumulates in the bloodstream if:

◆ the liver suffers a disease such as hepatitis which prevents its cells absorbing bilirubin;

◆ the bile duct becomes blocked preventing the release of bile (and bilirubin) into the intestine;

◆ an excessively high rate of red blood cell destruction occurs.

As the concentration of bilirubin builds up, the skin and the whites of the eyes become yellow in appearance and the person is said to be suffering from **jaundice**.

Production of urea

Unlike carbohydrate and lipid, protein is not stored in the body. Excess **amino acids** absorbed from the gut undergo **deamination** in liver cells. During this process,

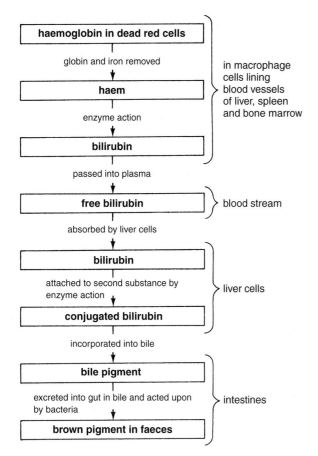

Figure 23.2 Removal of bilirubin

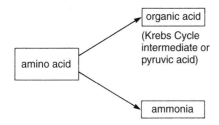

Figure 23.3 Deamination of an amino acid

the amino acid is broken down to form **ammonia** and an **organic acid** (see figure 23.3).

Depending on which amino acid has been deaminated, the organic acid may be pyruvic acid or one of the Krebs Cycle intermediates. It can then enter the respiratory pathway and be used for energy release (see p 40).

Since the ammonia formed during deamination of an amino acid is highly toxic, it is immediately passed on into the **ornithine cycle** (see figure 23.4) which is controlled by enzymes in the liver cells. During this cycle, ammonia reacts with carbon dioxide to form less toxic **urea**, as in the equation:

$$\text{ammonia} + \text{carbon dioxide} \longrightarrow \text{urea} + \text{water}$$
(very toxic)   (less toxic)

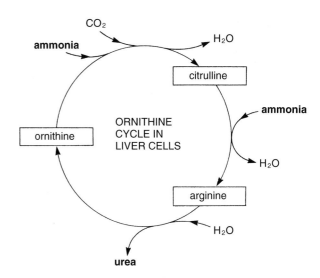

Figure 23.4 Production of urea from ammonia

Urea is then passed into the bloodstream and leaves the liver by the hepatic vein. It is removed from blood by the kidneys.

Determining the quantity of urea in 'urine' samples

Background information

The enzyme urease catalyses the following reaction:

$$\text{urea} + \text{water} \xrightarrow{\text{urease}} \text{ammonium carbonate}$$
(an alkali)

The quantity of alkali formed during this reaction is directly related to the quantity of urea present in the original solution. The relative quantity of alkali (and therefore urea) present in a solution is indicated by the volume of acid needed to neutralise it.

Methyl orange is an indicator which shows when the solution changes from an alkaline to an acidic state by going from orange to red.

Using urea solutions of known concentration to plot a calibration graph

Four solutions of known urea concentration are made up as shown in figure 23.5. Following enzyme activity at 37°C, each solution is titrated against hydrochloric acid. The volume of acid needed to neutralise the alkali in each solution is indicated by the methyl orange changing colour.

Repeat titrations are done for all of the urea concentrations, the results pooled and averages calculated. The results (see table 23.1) are then plotted to give a **calibration graph** (see figure 23.6).

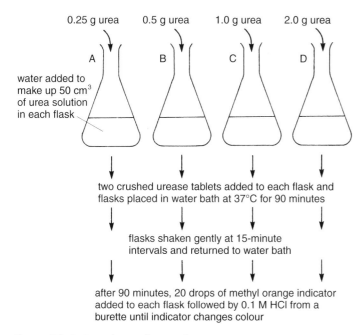

Figure 23.5 Experimental procedure

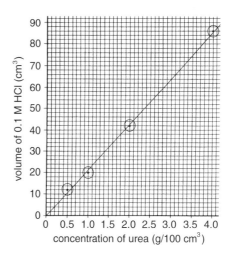

Figure 23.6 Calibration graph

Urea content of unknown samples

Solution X represents a sample of normal urine taken from a person eating a protein-rich diet. Solution Y represents a sample of urine from the same person 30 minutes after drinking a litre of water.

Two urease tablets are added to each of several 50 cm³ samples of both solutions and the above procedure

repeated. Averages are calculated and the calibration graph used to determine the quantity of urea present in each of the unknown 'urine' samples.

Say, for example, that solution X needs 64 cm³ of acid to neutralise it and that solution Y needs 16 cm³, then reference to the graph shows that the concentration of urea in solution X is 3 g/100 cm³ and in solution Y is 0.75 g/100 cm³. These results would show that drinking a litre of water had temporarily diluted the urea concentration of the person's urine by four times.

Table 23.2 gives some of the design features included in this experiment and the reasons for adopting them.

flask	A	B	C	D
mass of urea in 50 cm³ solution	0.25	0.5	1.0	2.0
concentration of urea (g/100 cm³)	0.5	1.0	2.0	4.0
average volume of 0.1M HCl needed for neutralisation (cm³)	12	20	42	86

Table 23.1 Results for calibration graph

design feature or precaution	reason
Urease tablets crushed.	To increase the surface area of tablet (and enzyme) in contact with the substrate.
Flasks gently shaken at regular intervals.	To promote thorough mixing of enzyme with substrate.
Several titrations done for each urea solution.	To obtain a more reliable result for each solution.
Flasks placed in water bath at 37 °C.	To provide optimum temperature for enzyme activity.
All aspects of experiment kept identical except concentration of urea solution.	To prevent a second variable factor being introduced into the investigation.

Table 23.2 Design features

● Testing your knowledge ●

1 **a)** Name the blood vessel that carries deoxygenated blood to the lungs. (1)

b) **(i)** In what form is most of the carbon dioxide carried in blood plasma?

(ii) Describe the chemical reactions that must occur to enable free molecules of carbon dioxide to diffuse from the bloodstream to the alveoli. (3)

2 **a)** By what means does the liver maintain a stable pool of blood plasma proteins? (1)

b) Briefly describe TWO ways in which the liver detoxifies named toxic materials. (2)

c) By what means is conjugated bilirubin removed from the body? (4)

3 **(i)** Which end products of digestion, if absorbed in excess, are broken down into ammonia and organic acids by the liver?

(ii) What term is used to refer to this breakdown?

(iii) How does the body deal with the very toxic ammonia that is formed? (4)

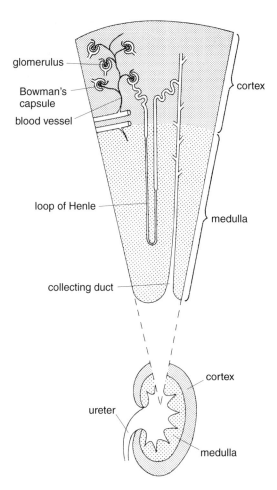

Figure 23.7 Internal structure of kidney

Role of kidneys

Structure

Each **kidney** (see figure 23.7) contains about a million microscopic functional units called **nephrons**. Each nephron is composed of several parts. A **glomerulus** (knot of blood vessels) is enclosed in a cup-shaped **Bowman's capsule** which leads into a long kidney **tubule** surrounded by a dense network of blood capillaries.

Two regions of the tubule possess several twists and turns (see figure 23.8) and are therefore described as **convoluted**. The **proximal convoluted tubule** is the twisted region in closer proximity to the Bowman's capsule; the **distal convoluted tubule** is the twisted region at the greater distance from the Bowman's capsule.

The long, U-shaped stretch of tubule between the convoluted regions is called the **loop of Henle**. Each kidney tubule leads to a communal collecting duct.

Function

The kidneys remove waste materials from the blood and excrete them in **urine**. The production of urine involves the **ultrafiltration** of blood and the **reabsorption** of useful materials from the filtrate.

Ultrafiltration

Blood containing waste products enters the kidney by the renal artery which divides into about a million branches each supplying a **glomerulus**. Each glomerulus consists of a coiled knot of blood capillaries. This arrangement enables a large surface area of blood vessel to be in contact with the inner lining of the **Bowman's capsule**. It is at this interface that ultrafiltration takes place.

Basement membrane filter

The layer of cells which makes up the capillary wall of a glomerulus differs from that of a normal blood capillary. The glomerular wall possesses **pores** which are large enough to let all of the constituents of plasma pass through. This porous layer is attached to a thin layer of highly permeable non-living material called the **basement membrane** which lacks the large pores (see figure 23.9 on p 180).

The basement membrane acts as a filter by allowing the very rapid passage of small molecules (e.g. glucose, water, salts and urea) but preventing large molecules of plasma protein from leaving the bloodstream.

The cells which form the lining of the Bowman's capsule are located on the other side of the basement membrane.

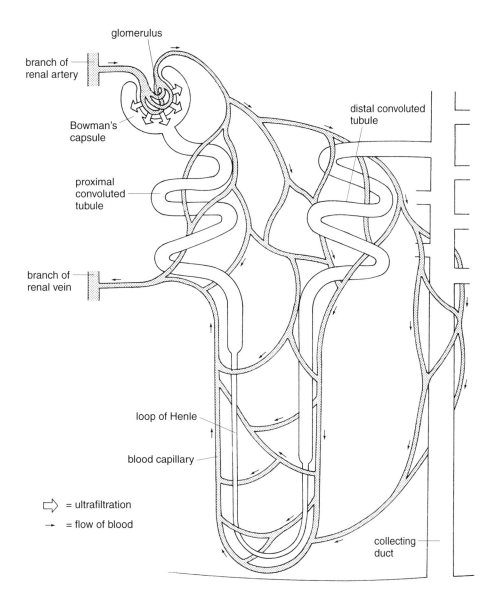

Figure 23.8 Nephron

These cells are unusual in that they do not form a flat continuous sheet but instead make up a **loose irregular network**. This is raised off the basement membrane by **cytoplasmic projections**, leaving large spaces which allow the rapid passage of filtrate into the lumen of the Bowman's capsule.

Blood pressure

Plasma proteins which remain in the blood plasma tend to draw water back from the filtrate in the capsule by osmosis. In addition, filtrate already present in the capsule tends to resist the delivery of further filtrate into the capsule.

Successful ultrafiltration of blood depends therefore on the blood in the glomeruli being at a high enough pressure to overcome both of these factors and force filtrate out of the blood plasma.

High blood pressure in glomeruli is maintained as a direct result of the following two factors:

◆ each vessel supplying a glomerulus is a branch of the **renal artery**, itself a branch of the aorta which carries blood at high pressure directly from the heart;

◆ each vessel entering a glomerulus is **wider** than the vessel leaving it, which creates a 'bottle-neck' effect and causes the blood in a glomerulus to be squeezed.

Rate of production of filtrate and urine

A human adult's body contains about 4.5 litres of blood. During its continuous circulation round the body, blood repeatedly enters the kidneys and undergoes filtration. Each day a human adult's kidneys filter a total volume of around 1500 litres of blood and produce about 180 litres of glomerular filtrate. However, the daily production of urine is only about 1–2 litres.

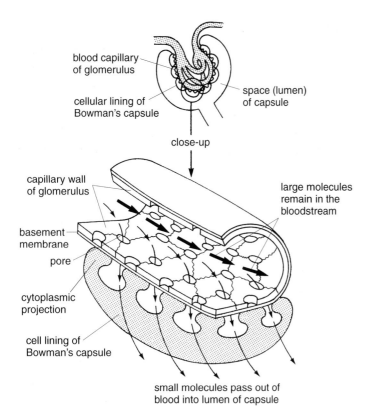

blood capillary
of glomerulus

space (lumen)
of capsule

cellular lining of
Bowman's capsule

close-up

capillary wall
of glomerulus

large molecules
remain in the
bloodstream

basement
membrane

pore

cytoplasmic
projection

cell lining of
Bowman's capsule

small molecules pass out of
blood into lumen of capsule

Figure 23.9 Basement membrane filter

Reabsorption

The difference between the volumes of glomerular filtrate and urine produced daily is accounted for by the fact that about 99% of the water in glomerular filtrate is **reabsorbed** back into the bloodstream.

Table 23.3 gives a comparison of the average quantities of water and solutes present in **blood plasma**, **glomerular filtrate** and **urine**. Apart from plasma proteins, the chemical compositions of blood plasma and glomerular filtrate are very similar. This is because almost every type of constituent of blood plasma except the larger protein

molecules passes through the basement membrane during ultrafiltration to become part of the glomerular filtrate.

Comparison of glomerular filtrate and urine shows these fluids to be different in chemical composition. This is because glomerular filtrate undergoes considerable modification as it passes through the kidney tubules. Essential molecules are reabsorbed from the tubules into the blood in nearby capillaries; otherwise these valuable substances would be excreted from the body and be lost permanently.

Reabsorption from proximal convoluted tubules
Glucose

Essential nutrients such as **glucose** (and amino acids) in glomerular filtrate are actively absorbed by the **epithelial cells** lining the inner surface of the **proximal convoluted tubules**. These cells (see figure 23.10) are structurally suited to this function as follows:

◆ the region of the cell membrane facing the inside of the tubule is folded into numerous **microvilli** which increase the surface area in contact with glomerular filtrate;

◆ the cells possess numerous **mitochondria** which provide the energy needed during active transport of molecules against a concentration gradient;

◆ specific **carrier molecules** are present which carry glucose across the cell membranes.

The glucose molecules then pass across the cells of the capillary wall into the bloodstream. Normally all glucose is reabsorbed in this way from the proximal convoluted tubule. However, in the case of a sufferer of untreated diabetes mellitus (see p 192), blood plasma contains so much glucose that once it is in the glomerular filtrate, the epithelial cells are unable to reabsorb it all. Much glucose passes on down the tubule and is excreted in urine.

substance	quantity in 180 litres of renal blood plasma	quantity in glomerular filtrate/day	quantity in urine/day	quantity returning to blood/day
water (l)	180	180	1–2	178–179
glucose (g)	180	180	0	180
plasma proteins (g)	7000–9000	10–20	0	10–20
sodium ions (g)	540	540	3	537
chloride ions (g)	630	630	5	625
amino acids (g)	48	48	0.6	47.4
urea (g)	53	53	25	28

Table 23.3 Typical chemical composition of three renal fluids

Salt (sodium chloride)

About 90% of the **sodium** ions in glomerular filtrate are also actively absorbed from the **proximal convoluted tubule**. The positively charged sodium (Na$^+$) ions are actively pumped across the tubule's epithelial cells into the bloodstream and this causes an equivalent number of negatively charged **chloride** (Cl$^-$) ions to pass into the blood.

Water

The active transport of glucose, sodium ions (and other solutes such as amino acids) into the bloodstream reduces the blood plasma's water concentration relative to that of glomerular filtrate. **Water** therefore passes into the blood by osmosis. This movement of water is a form of passive transport and does not require an energy supply. About 85% of water is reabsorbed from the proximal convoluted tubule.

Reabsorption from loop of Henle

Each U-shaped **loop of Henle** lies in the medulla of the kidney (see figure 23.7). It consists of a **descending limb** and an **ascending limb**. As glomerular filtrate passes down the descending limb and round the U-bend, **water** continues to be reabsorbed from it by osmosis. However, salt (sodium chloride) is not pumped out from this region of the tubule (see figure 23.11).

The way in which the glomerular filtrate is modified changes significantly as it passes up the **ascending limb**. The basic function of this region of the tubule is to produce a low water (high solute) concentration in the tissue fluid in the surrounding medulla. This is achieved by **sodium** and **chloride** ions from the glomerular filtrate in the thick ascending limb being actively pumped out into the tissue fluid. However, water does not follow by osmosis from this region of the tubule because the wall of the thick ascending limb is almost completely impermeable to water.

Reabsorption from distal convoluted tubule

Sodium chloride is reabsorbed from the **distal convoluted tubule** by being actively transported into the bloodstream as before but in much smaller quantities. **Water** also passes from the distal convoluted tubule into the bloodstream.

Reabsorption from collecting duct

The creation of a low water (high solute) concentration of the kidney's medullary tissue fluid by the activities of the ascending loop of Henle enables the kidney tissues to reabsorb large quantities of **water** by osmosis from the **collecting ducts** when required (see figure 23.12).

The exact volume of water needed to restore the blood's water concentration to normal is reabsorbed from passing filtrate. This process is under the control of the hormone **ADH** (as described below). The remainder of the filtrate is allowed to pass out in urine.

Since urine contains the nitrogenous waste urea, the kidneys are described as organs of **nitrogenous excretion**.

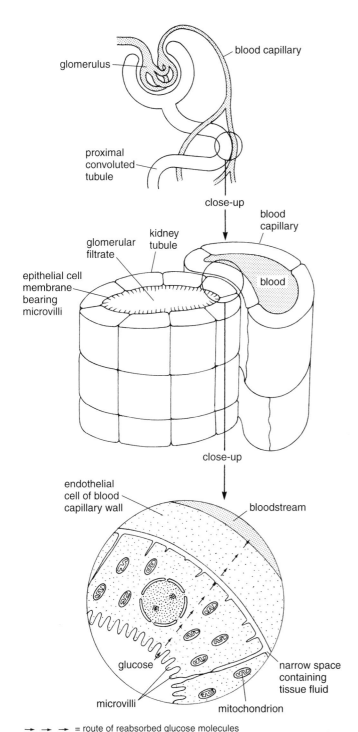

glomerulus

blood capillary

proximal convoluted tubule

close-up

glomerular filtrate

kidney tubule

blood capillary

blood

epithelial cell membrane bearing microvilli

close-up

endothelial cell of blood capillary wall

bloodstream

glucose

microvilli

mitochondrion

narrow space containing tissue fluid

→ → → = route of reabsorbed glucose molecules

Figure 23.10 Reabsorption from proximal convoluted tubule

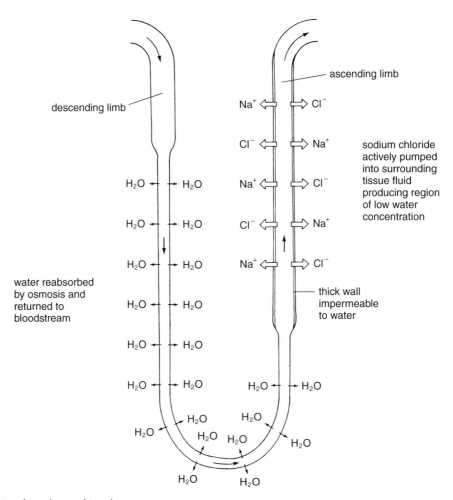

descending limb

ascending limb

sodium chloride actively pumped into surrounding tissue fluid producing region of low water concentration

thick wall impermeable to water

water reabsorbed by osmosis and returned to bloodstream

Figure 23.11 Reabsorption from loop of Henle

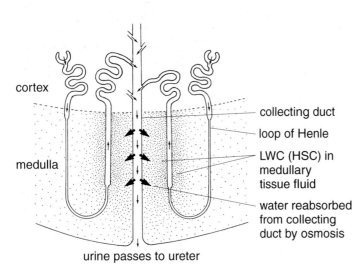

cortex

medulla

collecting duct

loop of Henle

LWC (HSC) in medullary tissue fluid

water reabsorbed from collecting duct by osmosis

urine passes to ureter

Figure 23.12 Reabsorption from collecting duct

Anti-diuretic hormone and osmoregulation

The volume of water reabsorbed from the distal convoluted tubules and collecting ducts varies markedly. It is regulated by the concentration of **anti-diuretic hormone (ADH)** present in the bloodstream.

ADH acts by increasing the **permeability** to water of the distal convoluted tubules and collecting ducts. When the water concentration of blood is high, very little ADH is released into the bloodstream from the pituitary gland (see figure 23.13). The distal convoluted tubules and collecting ducts remain practically impermeable to water and almost none is reabsorbed from these regions of tubule. A large volume of dilute urine is therefore produced.

When the water concentration of blood is low the situation is reversed and a small volume of **concentrated** urine is produced.

This mechanism allows the kidneys to play an osmoregulatory role in the maintenance of the body's internal steady state (see also chapter 24).

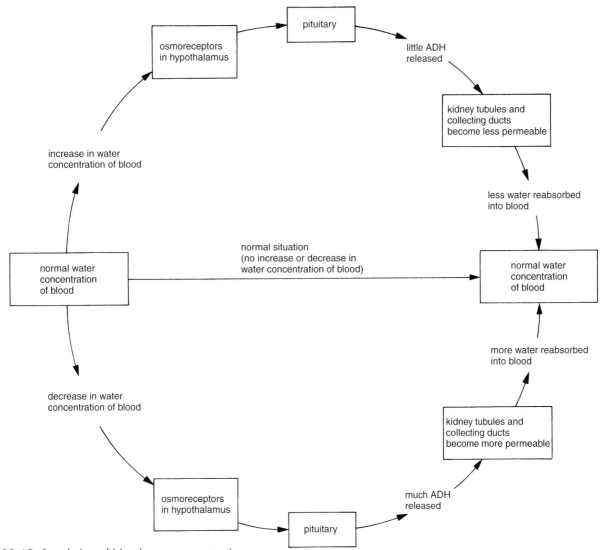

Figure 23.13 Regulation of blood water concentration

Testing your knowledge

1 a) Describe the structure of a nephron and distinguish between the terms *proximal* and *distal* convoluted tubule. (5)

b) Where in a nephron does ultrafiltration take place? (1)

2 Copy and complete table 23.4 which refers to reabsorption in a nephron. (7)

3 a) (i) Name in full the hormone that regulates the volume of water reabsorbed from kidney tubules.
(ii) Which gland releases this hormone into the bloodstream? (2)

b) Outline the sequence of events that occurs when the water concentration of the blood is very low and a high concentration of the hormone has been released. (2)

structure involved in reabsorption process	type of reabsorption (active or passive transport)	substance reabsorbed
proximal convoluted tubule	active	
		water
	passive	water
ascending limb of loop of Henle		sodium and chloride ions
	active	
	passive	water

Table 23.4

Applying your knowledge

1 The relative concentrations (in units) of carbon dioxide in the air in an alveolus and in the blood in a pulmonary capillary are shown in figure 23.14.

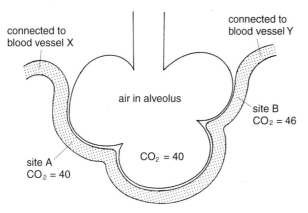

Figure 23.14

  a) At which site is the blood
  (i) deoxygenated;
  (ii) oxygenated?
  (iii) Explain your choice. (2)

  b) Match X and Y with the two main vessels that connect the lungs with the heart. (2)

  c) **(i)** What is meant by the term *excretion*?
  (ii) Explain why the lungs are regarded as organs of excretion. (2)

2 a) What is bilirubin? (1)

  b) **(i)** In what way is bilirubin altered by enzyme action in the human liver to make it suitable for excretion?
  (ii) Suggest why there is no need for this enzyme-controlled reaction to occur in a fetus in order to excrete bilirubin. (2)

  c) In the first few days after birth, rapid destruction of red blood cells occurs while the baby's fetal haemoglobin is broken down to be replaced by normal haemoglobin. Suggest why many babies suffer 'physiological jaundice' at this time. (2)

3 Figure 23.15 refers to the fate of nitrogen contained in excess amino acids. Copy the diagram and use the following words to complete the blanks: *ammonia, intestine, kidney, liver, ornithine, protein, urea.* (7)

4 Figure 23.16 shows a nephron from a human kidney.

  a) State the TWO factors that make the blood pressure at A higher than that at B. (2)

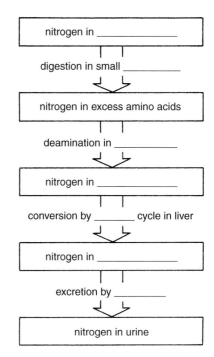

Figure 23.15

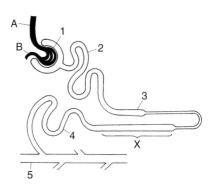

Figure 23.16

  b) Name structures 1–5 and state ONE function of each. (5)

  c) **(i)** At which numbered point in figure 23.16 would a microscopic close-up have the appearance shown in figure 23.17?
  (ii) Name parts P, Q, R and S.
  (iii) With reference to figure 23.17, explain how loss of protein from the kidney is prevented under normal circumstances. (6)

  d) The water concentration of glomerular filtrate is found to increase as the fluid passes through region X in figure 23.16. Give ONE reason why. (1)

Continued ➤

Applying your knowledge

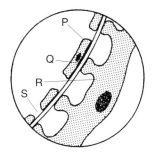

Figure 23.17

a) Name TWO substances that are completely reabsorbed back into the bloodstream. (2)

b) (i) Which TWO substances became concentrated in urine?
(ii) For each of these, state the concentration factor. (4)

c) A man produces a total of 180 litres of glomerular filtrate in one day. Calculate his GFR (volume of glomerular filtrate in millilitres produced per minute by both kidneys). (1)

d) If the man produces 1.8 litres of urine per day,
(i) what percentage of glomerular filtrate is passed as urine?
(ii) What happened to the rest of the glomerular filtrate? (2)

e) (i) Describe the state of the bloodstream's water concentration that leads to an increased quantity of anti-diuretic hormone (ADH) being released by the pituitary.
(ii) In what way are structures 4 and 5 in figure 23.16 affected by an increase in concentration of ADH in the bloodstream?
(iii) Relate this change to the control of the blood's water concentration. (3)

6 Describe the mechanisms of kidney function under the headings:
(i) ultrafiltration; (4)
(ii) reabsorption. (6)

5 Table 23.5 gives the results of an investigation into the composition of three types of renal fluid in an adult male.

		type of renal fluid		
		plasma	**glomerular filtrate**	**urine**
solute concentration (g/100 cm³)	urea	0.03	0.03	2.10
	glucose	0.10	0.10	0
	proteins	8.00	0	0
	salts	0.72	0.72	1.44
	amino acids	0.05	0.05	0

Table 23.5

What you should know
(Chapters 21–23)

(See table 23.6 for word bank.)

1 The blood's oxygen-carrying capacity is significantly increased by the presence of the respiratory pigment _____.

2 Haemoglobin has a high _____ for, and loads up with, oxygen when the concentration in its surroundings is high. Haemoglobin has a low affinity for, and releases _____ when the concentration in the surroundings is low.

3 The _____ disc shape of red blood cells presents a relatively large _____ of haemoglobin molecules to the surrounding environment for oxygen uptake and release. Their tiny size and _____ enable them to pass through capillaries easily.

Continued ➢

What you should know
(Chapters 21–23)

4 The production of red blood cells takes place in _____ and requires a supply of iron and _____ .

5 Red blood cells live for about 120 days and then undergo breakdown in the liver, bone marrow and _____ . _____ from haemoglobin is stored and the remaining haem molecules are converted to _____ .

6 _____ and amino acids are absorbed directly into the bloodstream from the small intestine. Vitamin B_{12} needs _____ in order to be absorbed.

7 Bile salts act as an _____ . By maintaining an emulsion of tiny _____ droplets, bile salts increase the relative surface area of lipid exposed to the enzyme _____ and therefore promote the action of lipase.

8 Lipid is absorbed into _____ in villi and transported through the body in the _____ system.

9 Three blood vessels are associated with the liver. Comparison of their contents after a meal shows the hepatic portal vein's plasma to be rich in _____ and glucose, the hepatic vein's plasma to be rich in _____ and the hepatic artery's plasma to be normal compared with arterial blood in other parts of the body.

10 Glucose is transported in the bloodstream to living cells to provide them with a source of _____ .

11 Amino acids are used by cells to synthesise various types of _____ .

12 Lipid molecules act as a further source of energy. Excess are stored as fat in _____ tissues.

13 Certain vitamins and minerals are needed to act as _____ in enzyme reactions.

14 Blood sugar concentration is conserved at optimum level by excess glucose being converted to _____ and stored in the liver.

15 Poisonous materials undergo _____ in the liver.

16 Bilirubin from the breakdown of haemoglobin is removed from the bloodstream by the _____ , converted to bile pigments and excreted in _____ .

17 Excess amino acids are _____ in the liver to form urea.

18 _____ of blood in kidneys forces filtrate out of each _____ into a Bowman's capsule and on through a proximal _____ tubule, loop of _____ and _____ convoluted tubule before reaching a collecting duct. During this journey, various substances are _____ from the filtrate, leaving _____ which is removed from the body.

19 The _____ are organs of excretion and _____ . The water content of the blood is controlled by _____ .

20 Since excretion means the elimination of the waste products of metabolism, the _____ are also excretory organs since they remove carbon dioxide from the body.

adipose	emulsifier	liver
affinity	energy	lungs
amino acids	flexibility	lymphatic
anti-diuretic hormone	glomerulus	osmoregulation
biconcave	glucose	oxygen
bile	glycogen	protein
bilirubin	haemoglobin	reabsorbed
bone marrow	Henle	spleen
co-factors	intrinsic factor	surface area
convoluted	iron	ultrafiltration
deaminated	kidneys	urea
detoxification	lacteals	urine
distal	lipase	vitamin B_{12}

Table 23.6 Word bank for chapters 21–23

24 Regulating mechanisms

Internal environment

A human being is a multicellular organism; the body consists of a community of cells. Since each type of cell is specialised to perform a particular function, the different parts of the body are dependent upon one another for survival. The millions of cells that make up the community and the tissue fluid that bathes them are collectively known as the **internal environment**.

Need for control

For the human body to function efficiently and work as an integrated whole, the state of the internal environment must be maintained within tolerable limits. For example, the **water concentration** of the blood (see chapter 23) must be regulated at a fairly constant level or problems would be caused by osmotic imbalances.

Blood **sugar level** must be kept within a certain range of concentration to provide the energy needed by cells to perform energy-demanding jobs.

The **temperature** of the internal environment must be kept at around 37°C to provide optimum conditions for the many enzyme-controlled reactions of metabolism to proceed efficiently. In addition, a steady flow of blood must be maintained to provide the internal environment with a constant supply of essential substances and to remove metabolic wastes.

Homeostasis

Homeostasis is the maintenance of the body's internal environment within certain tolerable limits despite changes in the body's external environment (or changes in the body's rate of activity).

Principle of negative feedback control

When some factor affecting the body's internal environment deviates from its normal optimum level (called the **norm** or **set point**), this change in the factor is detected by **receptors**. These send out nerve or hormonal messages which are received by **effectors**.

The effectors then bring about certain responses which counteract the original deviation from the norm and return the system to its set point. This corrective homeostatic mechanism is called **negative feedback control** (see figure 24.1). It provides the stable environmental conditions needed by the body's community of living cells to function efficiently and survive.

Control of heart rate

Pacemaker

The **pacemaker** tissue (see p 151) initiates each heartbeat. However, the rate at which the heart beats is not set at a fixed pace. It can be altered by **nervous** and **hormonal** activity both of which exert control over rate (though not initiation) of heartbeat.

Autonomic nervous control

The heart is supplied with branches of the two opposing parts of the **autonomic nervous system** (see chapter 26). Control centres located in the medulla of the brain

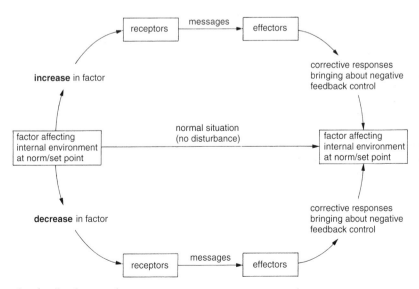

Figure 24.1 Principle of negative feedback control

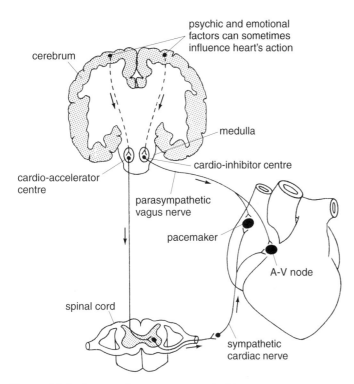

Figure 24.2 Autonomic nervous control of heart rate

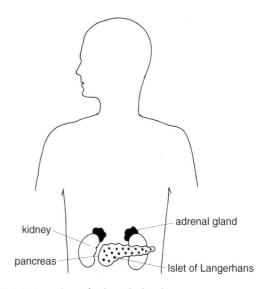

Figure 24.3 Location of adrenal glands

regulate heart rate (see figure 24.2). The **cardio-accelerator** centre sends its nerve impulses via the sympathetic cardiac nerves to the heart; the **cardio-inhibitor** centre sends its information via the parasympathetic vagus nerve.

The two pathways are **antagonistic** to one another in that they have opposite effects on heart rate. An increase in the relative number of nerve impulses conducted to the pacemaker by the **sympathetic** nerve results in an **increase** in heart rate.

On the other hand, an increase in the relative number of impulses conducted to the pacemaker by the **parasympathetic** nerve results in a **decrease** in heart rate. The rate at which the heart beats is determined by the antagonist which exerts the greater influence over the heart at any given moment.

Hormonal control

The hormone **adrenaline** secreted by adrenal glands (see figure 24.3) also affects heart rate. Under certain conditions (e.g. exercise or stress), the sympathetic nervous system acts on the adrenal gland making it release adrenaline into the bloodstream. On reaching the pacemaker, this hormone makes it generate cardiac impulses at a higher rate and bring about an **increase** in heart rate.

Exercise

Vigorous exercise results in profound changes occurring in the body's internal environment. **Metabolic rate** rises

in those skeletal muscles that are hard at work. They demand more oxygen (and glucose) and produce more carbon dioxide than they would if they were at rest. Certain adjustments in various bodily functions take place to meet these demands and return the body to its steady state as quickly as possible.

Effect of exercise on respiratory system

Rate and **depth** of breathing increase during exercise. This results in increased ventilation of the lungs which promotes the uptake of oxygen and the removal of carbon dioxide.

Carbon dioxide as the stimulus

The graph in figure 24.4 shows the results from an experiment to compare the effect on breathing rate of inhaling normal air, 'abnormal' air type 1 and 'abnormal' air type 2.

Only the 'abnormal' air type 2 is found to cause breathing rate to increase sharply. It is concluded that it is the high level of **carbon dioxide** in the 'abnormal' air type 2 (and not the low level of oxygen in 'abnormal' air type 1) that acts as the **stimulus** triggering increased rate of breathing.

Further experiments show that the depth of breathing also increases in response to inhalation of air rich in carbon dioxide. Similarly in the body of a person undergoing vigorous exercise, it is the increased level of carbon dioxide in the bloodstream that acts as the main stimulus bringing about an increase in rate and depth of breathing. However, severe lack of oxygen eventually also causes increased rate and depth of breathing.

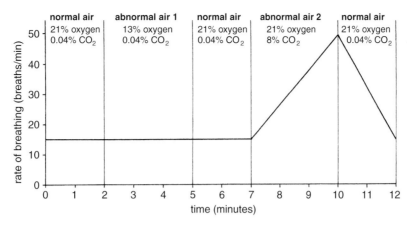

Figure 24.4 Effect of gases on breathing rate

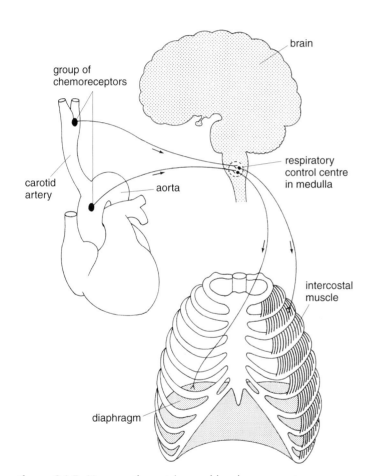

Figure 24.5 Nerve pathway triggered by chemoreceptors

Homeostatic control

Chemoreceptors in the carotid arteries and aorta (see figure 24.5) are sensitive to the concentration of carbon dioxide present in the bloodstream. A rise in carbon dioxide level during vigorous exercise causes these sensory cells to send an increased number of nerve impulses to the **respiratory control centre** in the **medulla**.

This region of the brain responds by sending a greater number of nerve impulses to the **intercostal muscles** and **diaphragm**. The subsequent increased activity of these structures brings about an increase in rate and depth of breathing. Excess carbon dioxide is removed and the internal environment is kept within tolerable limits. This homeostatic pathway is summarised in figure 24.6.

Effect of exercise on cardiovascular system

Heart rate (pulse) is the number of cardiac cycles (heartbeats) that occurs per minute.

Stroke volume is the volume of blood expelled by each ventricle on contraction. The stronger the contraction, the greater the stroke volume.

Cardiac output is the volume of blood pumped out of a ventricle per minute. Thus cardiac output = heart rate × stroke volume.

Table 24.1 shows the effect of **exercise** on cardiac output for an average adult human. The cardio-accelerator centre

state of body	heart rate (beats/min)	stroke volume (ml)	cardiac output by each ventricle (l/min)
at rest	60	60	3.6
during exercise	120	70	8.4
during strenuous exercise	180	80	14.4

Table 24.1 Effect of exercise on cardiac output

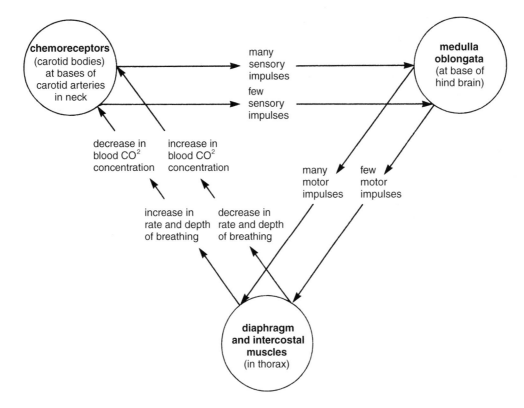

Figure 24.6 Homeostatic control of CO$_2$ concentration of blood

in the medulla sends impulses via the sympathetic nerves to the heart making it beat more often and more powerfully.

This increase in both heart rate and stroke volume brings about the increase in total cardiac output needed to boost the delivery of oxygenated blood to respiring tissues and to return deoxygenated blood to the lungs.

During very **strenuous exercise** (i.e. approaching maximum exertion), the cardiac output of an average person can increase by about five times. This is mainly due to increase in **heart rate**. In very well trained athletes whose cardiac muscle is especially well developed and powerful, a significant increase in **stroke volume** also occurs. This enables some athletes to achieve a cardiac output of around seven times their resting value.

Distribution of blood to tissues during exercise

All parts of the body need an adequate supply of blood in order to function efficiently. However the demands made by the different parts are neither equal nor constant.

When the body is at **rest**, its 'vegetative' functions (e.g. digestion, urine production, etc.) are promoted. Much blood is diverted to organs such as the small intestine (to absorb the end products of digestion) and the kidneys (to be purified).

When the body undergoes strenuous **physical activity**, much blood is diverted to the skeletal muscles where it is needed to provide additional supplies of oxygen and glucose for energy release.

The bar graph in figure 24.7 shows the **rate of blood flow** in various parts of the body when it is in different states of activity. Table 24.2 explains the main differences highlighted by the graph.

Control of local distribution of blood

During the early stages of exercise, the cardio-accelerator centre in the medulla receives nerve impulses from chemoreceptors that have detected an increase in concentration of carbon dioxide in the bloodstream. This centre responds by sending nerve impulses to the body's **arterioles**.

The vessels leading to the abdominal organs (and many other regions) undergo **vasoconstriction** (see figure 24.8). This reduces blood flow to these parts during exercise.

At the same time the arterioles leading to the working muscles respond to nerve impulses by becoming **dilated** (see figure 24.8). This has the effect of increasing the flow of blood to the skeletal muscles involved in the vigorous activity.

These effects of exercise on the cardiovascular and respiratory systems are examples of negative feedback control.

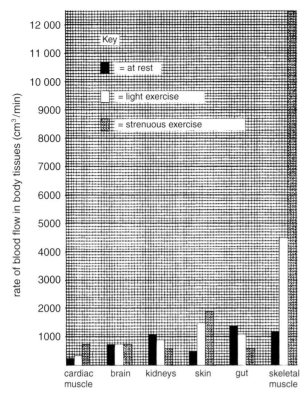

Figure 24.7 Rates of blood flow with varying levels of activity

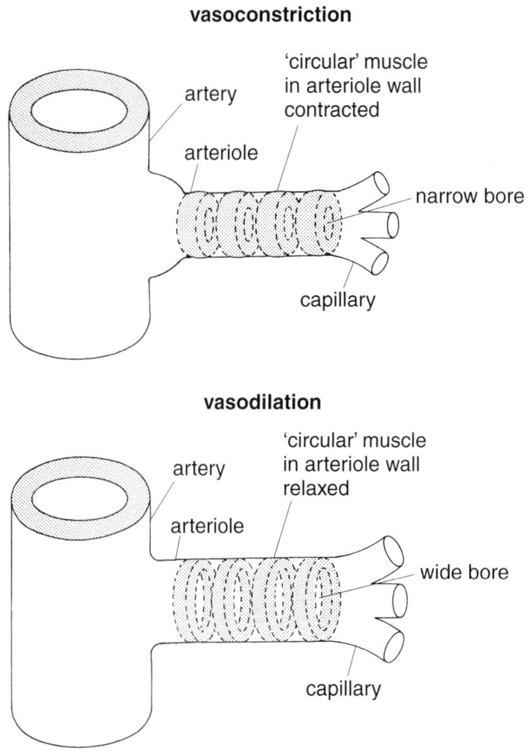

vasoconstriction

artery

'circular' muscle in arteriole wall contracted

arteriole

narrow bore

capillary

vasodilation

artery

'circular' muscle in arteriole wall relaxed

arteriole

wide bore

capillary

Figure 24.8 Simplified version of vasoconstriction and vasodilation

body tissue	effect of exercise on rate of blood flow in this tissue	explanation
heart (cardiac) muscle	increase	Extra blood needed to satisfy increasing energy demands of muscle cells.
brain	no change	Basic energy demands of cells continue to be met but remain unaffected by exercise.
kidneys	decrease	Much blood diverted away from kidneys to muscles since purification of blood can be largely postponed until after exercise.
skin	increase	Extra blood sent to skin surfaces to liberate excess heat generated during exercise.
gut, liver, etc.	decrease	Much blood diverted away from gut to muscles since absorption of end products of digestion can be postponed.
skeletal muscles	increase	Vast redistribution of blood occurs to supply increasing energy demands of working muscles.

Table 24.2 Distribution of blood to tissues during exercise

● Testing your knowledge ●

1 a) Identify the TWO components of the human body's internal environment. (2)

   b) What is meant by the term *homeostasis*? (2)

   c) With reference to the roles played by receptors and effectors, describe the mechanism of negative feedback control. (4)

2 a) (i) Which structure initiates each heartbeat?
          (ii) Where are the centres that control heart rate located? (2)

   b) (i) What effect does an increase in the number of nerve impulses conducted to the heart by the parasympathetic nerve have on heart rate?
          (ii) What effect does an increased concentration of adrenaline have on heart rate? (2)

3 a) State TWO effects of excercise on breathing. (2)

   b) (i) Define the terms *stroke volume* and *cardiac output*.
          (ii) What effect does exercise have on cardiac output? (3)

Control of blood sugar level

All living cells in the human body need a continuous supply of energy. Most of this energy is released by the oxidation of glucose. Cells are therefore constantly using up the glucose present in the bloodstream (i.e. **blood sugar**).

However, the body obtains supplies of glucose only on those occasions when food is eaten. To guarantee that a regular supply of glucose is available for use by cells regardless of when and how often food is consumed, the body employs a homeostatic mechanism.

Liver as a storehouse

About one hundred grams of glucose are stored as **glycogen** in the liver. Glucose can be added to or removed from this reservoir of stored carbohydrate depending on shifts of supply and demand.

Insulin and glucagon

A rise in blood sugar level to above its set point (e.g. following a meal) is detected by cells in regions of the **pancreas** called the **Islets of Langerhans** (see figure 24.3). These receptor cells produce **insulin**. This hormone is transported in the bloodstream to the

liver where it activates an enzyme which catalyses the reaction:

$$\text{glucose} \longrightarrow \text{glycogen}$$

This brings the blood sugar concentration down to around its normal level.

If the blood sugar level drops below its set point (e.g. between meals or during the night), different cells in the Islets of Langerhans detect this change and release **glucagon**. This second hormone is transported to the liver and activates a different enzyme which catalyses the reaction:

$$\text{glycogen} \longrightarrow \text{glucose}$$

The blood sugar concentration therefore rises to around its normal level. Figure 24.9 gives a summary of this homeostatic system and shows how insulin and glucagon act antagonistically.

Adrenaline

During an **emergency** when the body needs additional supplies of glucose to provide energy quickly for 'fight or flight', the **adrenal glands** (see figure 24.3) secrete an increased amount of the hormone **adrenaline** into the bloodstream.

Adrenaline overrides the normal homeostatic control of blood sugar level by inhibiting the secretion of insulin and promoting the breakdown of glycogen to glucose.

Once the crisis is over, secretion of adrenaline is reduced to a minimum and blood sugar level is returned to normal by the appropriate corrective mechanism involving insulin or glucagon.

Alternative diagram

Every factor under homeostatic control can be represented by the type of diagram shown in figure 24.1. However it must be kept in mind that when a factor deviates from its norm and is then returned to this set point by negative feedback control, it often overshoots the mark thereby triggering the reverse set of corrective mechanisms.

To illustrate that a factor which is in a state of dynamic equilibrium is **constantly wavering on either side of its set point**, homeostasis is often represented as two interrelated circuits (see figure 24.10).

Diabetes mellitus

Some people suffer a disorder known as **diabetes mellitus** because some (or all) of their insulin-secreting pancreas cells are non-functional. Since sufferers produce insufficient (or no) insulin, the concentration of glucose

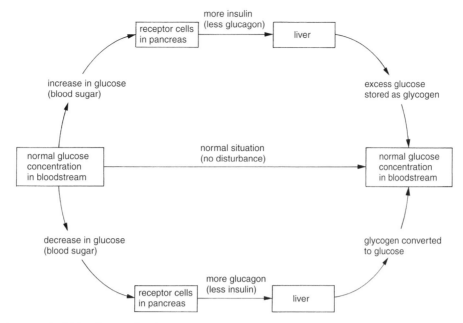

Figure 24.9 Homeostatic control of blood sugar level

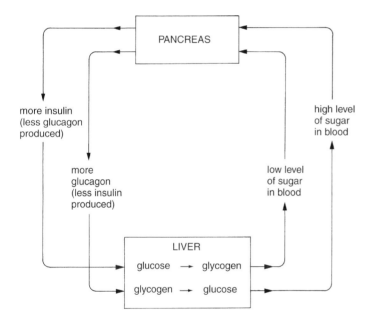

Figure 24.10 Alternative diagram of blood sugar control

in their blood rises to 10–30 millimoles per litre compared with the normal concentration of around 5 millimoles per litre.

The glomerular filtrate formed in the kidneys of a diabetic is so rich in glucose that much of it is not reabsorbed into the bloodstream but is instead excreted in urine.

In the absence of insulin, cells are unable to use glucose efficiently and fat stores become depleted leading to loss in weight and wasting of tissues. Whereas diabetes mellitus used to be a fatal disorder, it is now successfully treated by regular injections of insulin and a controlled diet.

Glucose tolerance test

Glucose tolerance is the capacity of the body to deal with ingested glucose. This depends on the body being able to produce adequate quantities of insulin. Measurement of glucose tolerance is a clinical test used to find out by indirect means if insulin production is normal.

After fasting for 8 hours, a person has their blood glucose level measured and then consumes a known mass of glucose to give a glucose load. Their blood glucose level is monitored over a period of 2½ hours and the results plotted to give a **glucose tolerance curve**.

Analysis of glucose tolerance curves (figure 24.11)

Curve 1

The person's glucose concentration rises to a maximum at around 30 minutes and then quickly drops to its initial low level well within the 2½ hour period. This indicates that insulin production is normal. The increase in blood glucose concentration has triggered the sequence of events shown in figure 24.9 and has been brought back to normal by negative feedback control.

This process may be so effective that the blood glucose level dips below the initial fasting level for a short time.

Curve 2

The person's blood glucose concentration begins at normal fasting level but continues to rise to a maximum at around 60 minutes (or even later) before beginning to decrease. This delay in insulin response to glucose load indicates **mild** diabetes mellitus. This condition may respond to a careful diet and not require administration of insulin.

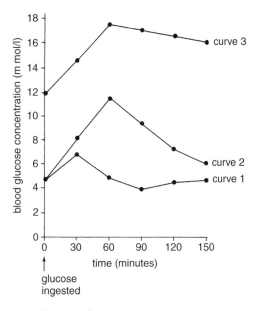

Figure 24.11 Glucose tolerance curves

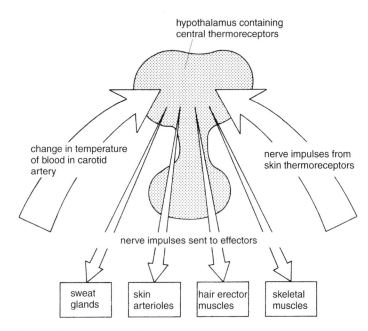

Figure 24.12 Hypothalamus as temperature-monitoring centre

Curve 3

After fasting the person's blood glucose concentration is still at an abnormally high level. After ingestion of glucose it continues to rise for 60 minutes (or more) and then shows a slight decrease but fails to drop even to its initial (high) level. This sequence of events indicates **severe** diabetes mellitus. The person is producing little or no insulin and is incapable of making a normal insulin response to glucose load. Regular injections of insulin and a carefully controlled diet are required.

Control of body temperature

Figure 15.3 (see p 111) shows the location of the **hypothalamus**. In addition to playing many other roles, the hypothalamus is the body's temperature-monitoring centre. It acts as a **thermostat** and is sensitive to nerve impulses that it receives from heat and cold **thermoreceptors** in the skin. These convey information to it about the surface temperature of the body.

In addition, the hypothalamus itself possesses **central thermoreceptors** (see figure 24.12). These are sensitive to changes in temperature of blood which in turn reflects changes in the temperature of the **body core** (see figure 24.13).

The thermo-regulatory centre in the hypothalamus responds to this information by sending appropriate nerve impulses to **effectors**. These trigger corrective feedback mechanisms and return the body temperature to its normal level (set point).

Role of skin

The **skin** plays a leading role in temperature regulation. In response to nerve impulses from the hypothalamus,

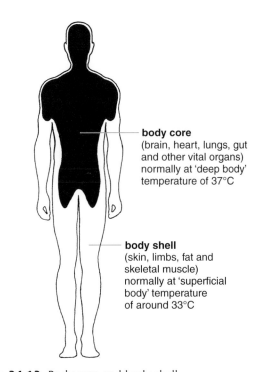

Figure 24.13 Body core and body shell

the skin acts as an effector. It helps to correct overheating of the body by employing the following mechanisms which promote heat loss.

(i) Increase in rate of sweating

Heat energy from the body is used to convert the water in sweat to **water vapour** and by this means brings about a lowering of body temperature.

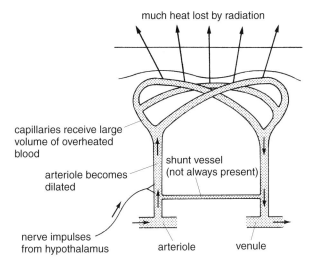

Figure 24.14 Vasodilation in skin

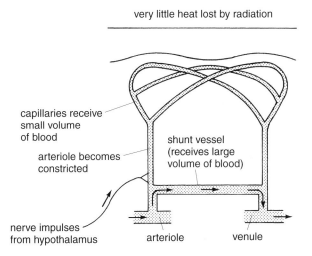

Figure 24.15 Vasoconstriction in skin

(ii) Vasodilation

Arterioles leading to skin become **dilated** (see figure 24.14). This allows a large volume of blood to flow through the capillaries near the skin surface from where it is able to lose heat by **radiation**.

The skin helps to correct overcooling of the body by employing the following mechanisms which reduce heat loss.

(i) Decrease in rate of sweating

Since sweating is reduced to a minimum, heat is conserved.

(ii) Vasoconstriction

Arterioles leading to the skin become **constricted** (see figure 24.15). This allows only a small volume of blood to flow to the surface capillaries. Little heat is therefore lost by radiation.

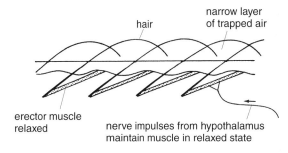

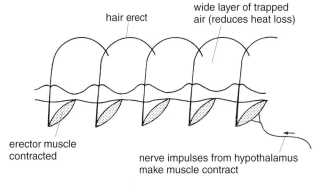

Figure 24.16 Action of hair erector muscles

(iii) Contraction of erector muscles

This process (see figure 24.16) is more effective in furry animals than in human beings. It results in hairs being raised up from the skin, and a wide layer of air (which is a poor conductor of heat) being trapped between the animal's body and the external environment. This layer of **insulation** reduces heat loss.

Investigating response to sudden heat loss (using a thermistor)

A **thermistor** is a device which responds to tiny changes in temperature. In this investigation the thermistor is taped between two fingers of one hand, as shown in figure 24.17, and the initial temperature of the skin recorded from the digital meter. (Alternatively the thermistor can be connected up to interface with a computer.)

The other hand is plunged into a container of icy water to cause a sudden heat loss.

Temperature readings are taken every 30 seconds for five minutes; the skin temperature of the hand attached to the thermistor is found to drop by around 1 °C. A second thermistor positioned in the armpit during the experiment shows that the temperature of the body core remains constant.

It is therefore concluded that when heat is lost from one extremity (e.g. hand in icy water), a **compensatory**

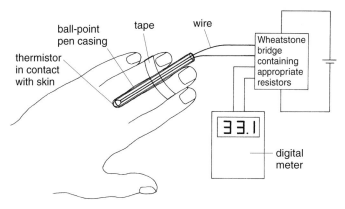

Figure 24.17 Use of thermistor

reduction in temperature occurs in the other extremity but not in the temperature of the body core.

This reduction in temperature is brought about by the following homeostatic mechanism: thermoreceptors in the skin in icy water send nerve impulses to the hypothalamus, which in turn sends impulses to the other hand causing **vasoconstriction** which reduces heat loss.

This response by the body's extremities helps to conserve heat when the body is exposed to extremes of temperature. The temperature of the body's extremities is therefore found to fluctuate more than that of the body core.

Role of other effectors

In addition to skin, the body possesses other effectors which play an important part in temperature regulation by generating heat energy when necessary.

Shivering by skeletal muscles

When the hypothalamus detects a drop in body temperature, nerve impulses to skeletal muscles cause them to undergo brief repeated contractions. This process, called **shivering,** generates heat energy and helps to return body temperature to its normal level.

Liver

The high **metabolic rate** that occurs in active organs such as the liver produces heat and helps to maintain body temperature at its set point. When the hypothalamus detects a rise in body temperature, shivering ceases and metabolic rate is reduced.

Hormones

Sudden exposure of the body to cold is followed by the release of the hormone **adrenaline** from the adrenal glands. This results in an increase in metabolic rate. Increased activity of the thyroid gland (see appendix 1) brings about the release of the hormone **thyroxin**. This

also increases rate of metabolism and raises the temperature of the body.

However these hormones are not thought to play a significant role in the day to day control of body temperature but rather to affect metabolic rate during long-term acclimatisation (e.g. settling in a cold climate after having lived in a warm one).

Voluntary responses

The mechanisms of temperature regulation summarised in figure 24.18 are all **involuntary** and controlled at a subconscious level by the hypothalamus.

However, when body temperature drops below normal, nerve impulses transmit this information to the cerebrum (thinking part of the brain). This makes the person 'feel cold' and become aware of the problem. He or she then takes an appropriate course of action (e.g. puts on extra clothing, turns up the heating, exercises vigorously, consumes a hot drink, etc.) and by doing so helps to return the body to its normal temperature.

When the body temperature rises above tolerable limits, a reverse set of behavioural responses is made. This ability to make appropriate **voluntary responses** is an important part of control of body temperature.

Temperature regulation in infants

The exposed surface area of a small animal relative to its volume is greater than that of a larger animal of similar shape (see also p 139). It follows therefore that the **relative surface area** of a baby is greater than that of an adult. If the two were placed in a cold environment and all other factors were equal, the baby would suffer more rapid loss of body heat than the adult. The smaller the baby the greater the relative heat loss.

A newborn baby's involuntary thermoregulatory mechanisms are less well developed (see p 218) and therefore less efficient than those of an adult. In addition, a baby is incapable of avoiding cold by making useful voluntary responses.

Brown fat

A baby responds involuntarily to a drop in body temperature by vasoconstriction of its skin blood vessels. This is accompanied by an increase in metabolic rate in the cells of its **brown fat (adipose) tissue** (see figure 24.19).

Unlike normal white subcutaneous (under-the-skin) fat which acts as a passive layer of insulation, brown fat (which is well supplied with blood vessels) actively generates heat. It therefore plays a major role in the temperature regulation of an infant. The quantity of

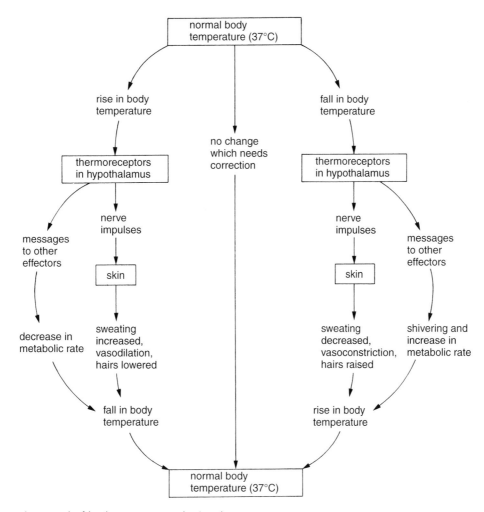

Figure 24.18 Homeostatic control of body temperature by involuntary means

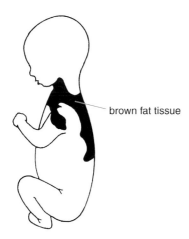

brown fat tissue

Figure 24.19 Brown fat in infant

brown fat present in adults varies and is much less important as a means of temperature control.

Critical temperature

As external temperature drops to about 27°C, a point is reached when a naked adult's mechanisms of temperature regulation (e.g. vasoconstriction) can only just manage to maintain normal body temperature. The external temperature at which this situation occurs is called the **lower critical temperature**. Any further reduction in external temperature to below this critical level requires heat energy to be generated by **metabolic means** to keep the body at 37°C.

Since a baby's relative surface area is larger than that of an adult and its temperature control mechanisms are not fully developed, a baby's lower critical temperature is found to be above that of an adult. Therefore the baby needs to begin to employ metabolic means of temperature regulation at a higher external temperature than an adult.

A newborn baby possesses a limited store of food to sustain it during the first few days after birth until it receives adequate nourishment from milk. If the newborn baby is subjected to below its critical temperature for extended periods, the subsequent increase in metabolic rate that occurs uses up the baby's food reserves. If these are consumed too quickly, the baby will lack sufficient

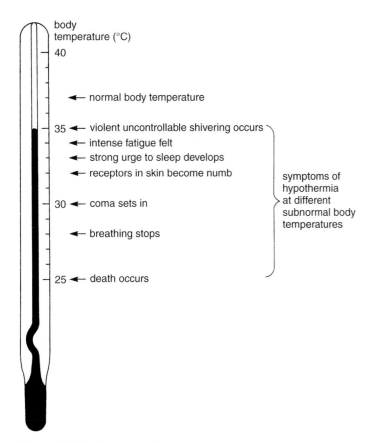

body temperature (°C)

40

← normal body temperature

35 ← violent uncontrollable shivering occurs
← intense fatigue felt
← strong urge to sleep develops
← receptors in skin become numb

symptoms of hypothermia at different subnormal body temperatures

30 ← coma sets in

← breathing stops

25 ← death occurs

Figure 24.20 Hypothermia

energy and its body core temperature will begin to drop rapidly.

Hypothermia

This term refers to the condition suffered by a person whose body temperature is at a subnormal level (see figure 24.20).

Hypothermia in infants

Failure to appreciate the differences between the temperature regulation mechanisms of adults and babies can leave normal full term babies at risk of **hypothermia** and even death. Environmental conditions which are uncomfortably cold (but tolerable) to adults may be intolerable to babies since their physiological mechanisms of temperature regulation are not yet sufficiently developed to cope. It was for this reason that during an especially cold winter in Scotland in the 1960s, many babies were admitted to hospital suffering from hypothermia with an average core body temperature of 32°C.

Preterm babies

Preterm (premature) babies are even more likely to be unable to maintain body temperature for the following reasons:

◆ their mechanisms of temperature regulation are even less well developed than normal;

◆ they are small in size and therefore have an even larger relative surface area from which heat energy can be lost;

◆ their critical temperature is even higher than normal and they burn up their reserves at a higher external temperature;

◆ they begin with a smaller than normal food reserve to cover the first few days after birth and this runs out quickly.

To avoid the risk of hypothermia, preterm babies are normally kept in an **incubator** for some time and their progress carefully monitored.

Hypothermia in the elderly

As people grow older they become more susceptible to hypothermia for a variety of reasons.

Their mechanisms of temperature regulation become less efficient. For example, when elderly people are exposed to a cold environment, the blood vessels in the skin may fail to undergo the normal level of vasoconstriction. Blood continues to circulate through the **body shell** (see figure 24.13) and lose heat. Furthermore, old people often fail to shiver when cold.

The elderly also tend to have a slower rate of metabolism which fails to generate adequate heat energy to keep the body warm. They are generally less active than younger people and their bodies therefore fail to be warmed naturally by heat energy released from working muscles. Their body temperature drops when they sit for long periods in a cold room which might be tolerable to a more active, younger person.

Breakdown of homeostasis

Homeostatic systems only work within certain limits. If a person is exposed to any extremely adverse condition in the external environment for a prolonged period of time, the appropriate system of negative feedback control eventually breaks down.

Old people, for example, can gradually become extremely cold and suffer hypothermia. They fail to realise what is happening to them in time to take **corrective action** and make suitable voluntary responses. Their homeostatic control has broken down and they are no longer able to bring about their own recovery. Old people suffering in this way require urgent medical attention.

Testing your knowledge

1 a) (i) Which hormone promotes the conversion of glucose to glycogen?
(ii) Which hormone promotes the conversion of glycogen to glucose?
(iii) Where in the body are these hormones produced? (3)

b) (i) What is meant by the term *glucose tolerance*?
(ii) Under what circumstances would a person be given a glucose tolerance test? (2)

2 a) (i) Distinguish between the terms *body core* and *body shell*.
(ii) By what means does the hypothalamus detect changes in temperature affecting the 1) body shell and 2) body core. (4)

b) Give TWO examples of mechanisms employed by the skin to correct overheating and for each explain how it works. (4)

3 a) (i) Compare the surface area to volume ratio of a baby with that of an adult.
(ii) Which would suffer more rapid loss of body heat if exposed to a very cold environment? (2)

b) (i) Define *hypothermia*.
(ii) Give TWO reasons why pre-term babies are more susceptible to hypothermia than full term babies.
(iii) Give TWO physiological reasons why elderly people are more susceptible to hypothermia than teenagers. (Note: The term *physiological* refers to the workings of the body.) (5)

Applying your knowledge

1 a) (i) Copy and complete figure 24.21 which represents part of the system by which breathing is controlled in the human body.
(ii) With reference to this diagram as it would relate to a person exercising vigorously and then having a rest, describe the principle of negative feedback control.
(iii) Why is such control of benefit to a human being? (10)

b) The data in table 24.3 refer to the results from an investigation into breathing.

% carbon dioxide in inspired air	average depth of breathing (cm³)	average number of breaths per minute
0.04	673	14
0.79	739	14
1.52	794	15
2.28	911	15
3.11	1232	15
5.48	1845	16
6.02	2104	27

Table 24.3

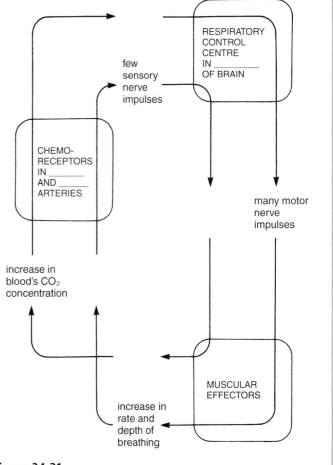

Figure 24.21

Continued ➤

199

Applying your knowledge

(i) Plot the data to give two line graphs on the same sheet of graph paper.

(ii) What variable factor was studied in this investigation?

(iii) Make a generalisation about the effect of the variable factor on breathing.

(iv) Which was affected first, rate or depth of breathing? (7)

c) During forced breathing, a person who has been at rest deliberately breathes rapidly and deeply for several minutes.

(i) Predict the effect that this procedure will have on the concentration of carbon dioxide in the person's lungs and arterial blood.

(ii) When the forced breathing is brought to a halt, the person sometimes finds that their breathing rate stops for a short period. Account for this effect with reference to figure 24.21. (4)

d) (i) State the effect of holding the breath on the carbon dioxide concentration of arterial blood.

(ii) With reference to figure 24.21, explain why the breath can only be held for a short time. (2)

2 a) (i) State TWO means by which the heart's pacemaker can be stimulated bringing about an increase in heart rate.

(ii) Give ONE example of a situation in which this increase would occur. (3)

b) Show by means of an equation the relationship between heart rate (HR), cardiac output (CO) and stroke volume (SV). (2)

c) Calculate

(i) CO when HR = 72 beats/min and SV = 80 ml;

(ii) HR when SV = 85 ml and CO = 8.5 l/min;

(iii) SV when HR = 150 beats/min and CO = 15 l/min;

(iv) SV when HR = 125 beats/min and CO = 15 l/min. (4)

d) If situations (iii) and (iv) in c) refer to monozygotic twins doing the same exercise, which one is fitter? Explain your answer. (2)

3 Table 24.4 shows the rate of blood flow in various parts of a person's body under differing conditions of exercise.

	rate of blood flow (cm³/min)		
	at rest	light exercise	strenuous exercise
skeletal muscle	1200	4500	12 500
gut	1400	1100	600
skin	500	1500	1900
kidneys	1100	900	600
brain	750	750	750
heart muscle	250	350	750

Table 24.4

a) What effect does increasingly strenuous exercise have on blood flow

(i) in skeletal muscle;

(ii) to the gut?

(iii) Suggest the reason for the difference in each case. (4)

b) Which other body part(s) show the same trend in response to increase in exercise as

(i) skeletal muscle;

(ii) gut? (2)

c) (i) Which body part's rate of blood flow remains unaffected by exercise?

(ii) Suggest why. (2)

d) (i) In what way would the appearance of facial skin change as a result of strenuous exercise?

(ii) Explain your answer. (2)

e) Briefly describe the mechanism by which blood vessels control distribution of blood to different parts of the body. (2)

4 Figure 24.22 shows the effect of consuming 50 g of glucose (after a period of fasting) on the concentrations of fatty acids, glucose and insulin in the bloodstream.

a) (i) During which period of time was the person's blood sugar concentration at a steady level?

(ii) By what means is this steady level maintained? (2)

Continued ➤

Applying your knowledge

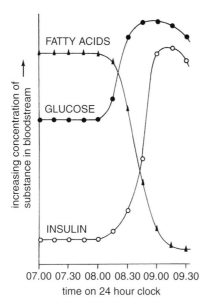

Figure 24.22

b) (i) At what time was the glucose consumed?

(ii) What initial effect did the intake of glucose have on blood sugar level and concentration of insulin in the blood?

(iii) Why was there a short time lag between these two effects? (4)

c) What evidence is there from the graph that insulin suppresses the breakdown of stored fat? (1)

d) Redraw the axes and extend the time scale to 11.00 hours. Draw the glucose curve to show the concentration from 07.00 to 11.00 hours. (2)

e) State TWO ways in which the glucose tolerance curve for a sufferer of diabetes mellitus would differ from the one that you have drawn. (2)

f) Suggest why the average birth weight of babies born to diabetic mothers is significantly higher than that of non-diabetic mothers. (Do not attempt to give a genetic explanation in your answer.) (1)

5 Hormones are chemical messengers released directly into the bloodstream by endocrine glands.

a) Copy table 24.5 and complete the central column. (5)

b) Complete the right hand column in the table by using a selection of one or more answers from the following list:
A promotess conversion of excess glucose to glycogen;
B increases permeability of kidney collecting ducts;
C promotes conversion of glycogen to glucose;
D decreases blood sugar level;
E prepares the body to cope with an emergency;
F brings about an increase in metabolic rate. (8)

6 Figure 24.23 represents a section through human skin.

a) Name the part of the brain to which heat and cold receptors relay information about the external environment. (1)

b) By what means does the thermoregulatory centre of the brain communicate information to structures X and Y in order to effect control of body temperature? (1)

c) (i) In what way would structure X respond following a drop in body temperature?

(ii) Explain how this response would help to conserve heat. (1)

hormone	endocrine gland from which hormone originates	letter(s) indicating effect(s) of hormone
adrenaline		
insulin		
ADH		
glucagon		
thyroxin		

Table 24.5

Continued ➤

Applying your knowledge

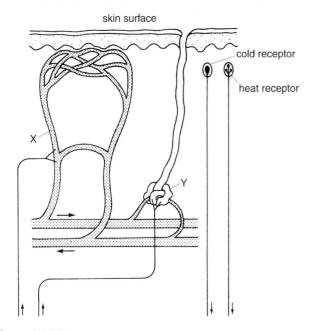

Figure 24.23

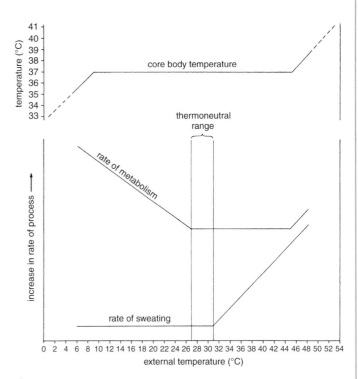

Figure 24.24

d) (i) In what way would structure Y respond to an increase in body temperature?

(ii) Explain how this response would help to promote heat loss.

7 The graph in figure 24.24 shows the results from an investigation into the effect of varying external temperature on the rates of sweating and metabolism of a naked man in air of normal humidity.

The thermoneutral range of external temperature is the range within which the heat generated by the man's metabolism was lost to the surroundings at the same rate as it was produced.

a) (i) Identify the lowest external temperature at which the man's mechanisms of temperature regulation alone were able to maintain his body temperature at 37 °C without increasing his rate of metabolism.

(ii) Name ONE of these mechanisms. (2)

b) What effect did a decrease in external temperature to below the thermoneutral range have on metabolic rate? Relate this response by the man's body to survival. (2)

c) In what way did the man's body respond to an increase in external temperature to above the thermoneutral range? Relate this response by the body to survival. (2)

d) (i) The higher critical temperature is the external one at which the body's ability to regulate its own temperature breaks down after lengthy exposure to this temperature. Identify the higher critical temperature in this investigation.

(ii) What effect did an increase in external temperature to beyond higher critical temperature have on the man's metabolic rate? Account for this effect. (2)

e) Suggest why a broken line has been used to draw each end of the line graph of core body temperature. (1)

8 Describe the principle of negative feedback control as illustrated by the control of blood sugar level. (10)

What you should know
(Chapter 24)

(See table 24.6 for word bank.)

1 To function efficiently, many aspects of the human body's _____ must be maintained within tolerable limits.

2 Physiological _____ is the name given to this maintenance of the internal environment despite changes in the _____.

3 Homeostasis operates on the principle of negative _____. By this means, a change in the internal environment is detected by _____ which send messages to _____. These trigger responses which negate the deviation from the norm and return the internal environment to its _____.

4 Although the _____ initiates each heartbeat, the rate at which the heart beats is controlled by the action of the _____ nervous system and the hormone adrenaline.

5 Rate and _____ of breathing increase during exercise. The main stimulus for these changes is an increase in _____ concentration of blood. This is detected by _____ which send messages via the medulla to the muscular effectors.

6 During strenuous exercise, the cardiac _____ increases significantly. In addition blood is diverted to _____ and cardiac muscles and away from digestive organs. Local distribution of blood is effected by some arterioles undergoing _____ and others becoming vasoconstricted.

7 Receptor cells in the pancreas detect a rise in blood sugar level and produce _____. This hormone activates an enzyme in the liver which promotes the conversion of _____ to glycogen.

8 Other receptor cells in the _____ detect a drop in blood sugar level and produce _____. This hormone activates an enzyme in the liver which promotes the breakdown of glycogen to glucose.

9 In an emergency, _____ inhibits the secretion of insulin and promotes the breakdown of glycogen to glucose.

10 _____ is the condition suffered by people whose insulin secreting cells are partly or completely non-functional. Diabetic people fail to make a normal response to the glucose _____ test.

11 The _____ is the body's temperature-monitoring centre. It possesses _____ and communicates with effectors by sending out nerve impulses.

12 The skin acts as an effector in the control of body _____ by bringing about several _____ responses which exert negative feedback.

13 _____ responses are also important in the regulation of body temperature.

14 Infants are less efficient at controlling body temperature because their involuntary response mechanisms are not fully _____ and they cannot employ voluntary means to warm up or cool down.

15 The elderly are often less efficient at controlling body temperature because their involuntary mechanisms are _____. If body temperature drops to a subnormal level, the person suffers _____.

adrenaline	feedback control	pacemaker
autonomic	glucagon	pancreas
carbon dioxide	glucose	receptors
chemoreceptors	homeostasis	set point
depth	hypothalamus	skeletal
developed	hypothermia	slow-acting
diabetes	insulin	temperature
mellitus	internal	thermoreceptors
effectors	environment	tolerance
external	involuntary	vasodilation
environment	output	voluntary

Table 24.6 Word bank for chapter 24

BEHAVIOUR, POPULATIONS AND ENVIRONMENT

The **brain** is a large organ composed of billions of nerve cells (neurones). Compared with other animals, the human brain is disproportionately large, relative to body size (also see question 1 on p 211).

Fossils

Fossil evidence indicates that a rapid **increase** in human **brain capacity** (volume of skull occupied by brain) has occurred over a fairly recent evolutionary timescale.

Figure 25.1 depicts in a simple way the possible evolutionary relationship that exists between modern humans and two extinct groups of human-like primates with whom we are thought to have shared a common ancestor.

Apes

When compared with the brains of modern apes, the human brain is found to be approximately **three** times

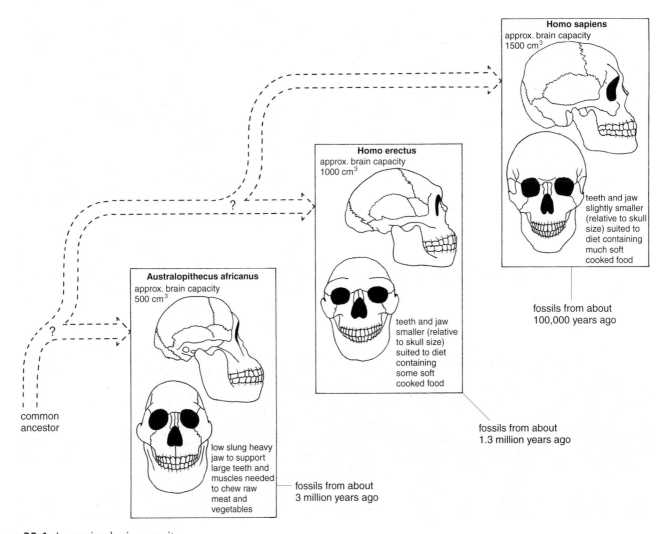

Figure 25.1 Increasing brain capacity

larger. It is interesting to note that this increase in volume does not take the form of a straightforward enlargement of each region in proportion to all of the others. Much of the extra space is occupied by certain parts which are greatly enlarged relative to the other parts. These enlarged areas are found to include the **centres** responsible for **higher mental faculties** such as intelligence, speech, hearing and sight.

In an ape's brain the areas controlling speech are so small and poorly developed that it is impossible to teach an ape to speak like a human, however patient and ingenious the trainer. The ape's brain is simply not equipped to handle the subtleties of human speech.

Dominant species

Compared with many other forms of life, humans are quite feeble creatures physically. It is due to the **large size** of their brain and its complex level of **internal development** and **organisation** that humans have become the dominant animal species on Earth.

Cerebrum

The **cerebrum** is the largest part of the human brain. It is split by a deep **cleft** into two halves called **cerebral hemispheres**. The left hemisphere controls the right side of the body and vice versa. The two hemispheres are not completely separated but are connected by a large bundle of nerve fibres called the **corpus callosum** (see figure 25.2). This fibrous link between the two hemispheres is important to allow information to be transferred from one to the other. Whatever happens in one side of the brain is quickly communicated to the other side, thereby co-ordinating brain functions.

Grey and white matter

The surface of the cerebrum consists of **grey** matter whereas its inner tissue is mainly **white** matter. Grey matter is composed of nerve **cell bodies**; white matter is made of nerve **fibres** (see chapter 26).

Convoluted surface

The surface of the cerebrum is extensively **convoluted** (folded in on itself). This arrangement greatly increases

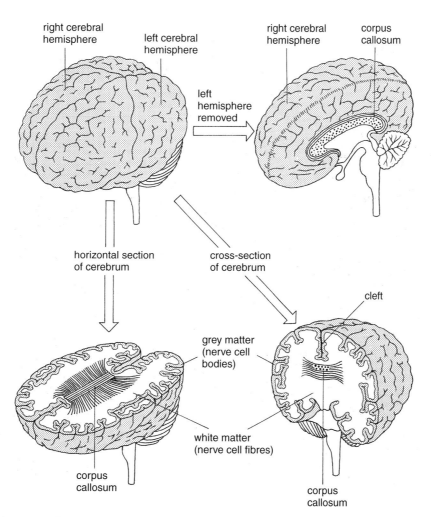

Figure 25.2 Cerebrum and corpus callosum

its **surface area** allowing many more cell bodies to be located together at the surface than would be possible if it were smooth and non-folded. The convoluted nature of the cerebral surface therefore maximises the potential for interconnections to occur and messages to be transmitted between neighbouring neurones.

Testing your knowledge

1 By approximately how many times has human brain capacity increased in the last 3 million years? (1)

2 Humans are not the fastest, largest or strongest animals yet they claim to be the dominant species on Earth. Briefly justify this claim. (2)

3 **(i)** What is the *corpus callosum*?
(ii) State its function. (2)

4 **a)** With reference to the human cerebrum, explain what is meant by the term *convoluted*. (1)

b) Why is the possession of a convoluted cerebrum of advantage to humans? (2)

Discrete functional areas of cerebrum

The cerebrum can be divided into three types of functional area: **sensory**, **association** and **motor**. These areas are **discrete**. This means that each performs its own particular function distinct from the others.

The sensory areas **receive information** as sensory impulses from the body's receptors (e.g. touch receptors in the skin and thermoreceptors in the hypothalamus). The association areas **analyse** and **interpret** these impulses, 'make sense' of them and 'take decisions' if necessary. The motor areas receive information from association areas and 'carry out orders' by **sending motor impulses** to the appropriate effectors (e.g. muscles).

As a simple example, imagine that you are blindfolded and a very large ice cube is placed in your hand. Sensory areas in your cerebrum receive information from touch, pressure and cold receptors in your skin. By analysing and interpreting these impulses, association centres in your cerebrum gain an impression of the size, shape, weight, texture and temperature of the 'mystery object'. When they put all of this information together, it results in you experiencing the sensation of holding a very large ice cube.

As the ice cube becomes uncomfortably cold and heavy, you reach a decision to let it go. The appropriate motor centre carries out orders by sending impulses to the muscles which operate the hand causing your grip on the ice cube to relax.

Localisation of function

A cerebral hemisphere consists of several **distinct regions**, as shown in figure 25.3 which refers to the left side of the cerebrum. Each of these areas has a particular function to perform as described in table 25.1.

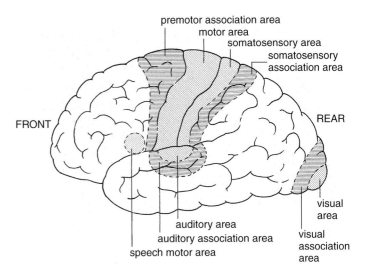

Figure 25.3 Detail of left cerebral hemisphere

Every area shown in figure 25.3 is **duplicated** (in mirror image) in the right cerebral hemisphere with the exception of the speech motor area. Each person has only one such region; it is situated on the left cerebral hemisphere in 90% of the population.

Of particular importance for normal sensations are the **somatosensory**, **visual** and **auditory** areas. These localised regions receive separate sets of sensory impulses and register sensations which are evaluated in their association centres.

However, no part of the brain works in complete isolation. **Interconnections** in the form of tiny nerve fibres link up the different areas and messages are constantly passing between them from sensory areas to motor areas via association areas. This allows for **sophisticated perception** of a situation involving several types of sensory impulse e.g. recognising a favourite musician performing a familiar piece of music on television while 'flicking' across the channels.

Further exchanges of impulses between different cerebral areas then allow a **sophisticated response** to be made involving several integrated activities e.g. singing and dancing to familiar music.

The large uncharted areas of the cerebrum in figure 25.3 are thought to be concerned with **higher mental processes** such as memory (chapters 28 and 29), intelligence, creativity, imagination, conscience, etc.

area of cerebral hemisphere	function
somatosensory	Receives impulses from receptors in skin, organs and muscles.
somatosensory association	Receives impulses from somatosensory area which it analyses, interprets and may 'act on'; also stores memories of previous experiences.
visual	Receives impulses from retina and interprets these as images involving shape, colour, and so on.
visual association	Receives impulses from visual area and brings about recognition of observed objects by referring to memory of previous visual experiences.
auditory	Receives impulses from cochlea and interprets these as sounds involving pitch, volume, and so on.
auditory association	Receives impulses from auditory area and brings about conversion of sounds into recognisable patterns which can be understood depending on previous experience.
premotor association	Receives messages from other association areas and stores memories of past motor experiences, enabling it to plan and control complex sequences of motor activities such as writing, running down stairs, and so on, in the light of past experience.
motor	Receives messages from other areas e.g. premotor association and obeys orders by sending motor impulses to appropriate skeletal muscles.
speech motor	Receives messages from other parts of cerebrum; translates thoughts into speech by sending impulses to the appropriate parts of motor area which in turn send motor impulses to muscles controlling lips, tongue and vocal chords.

Table 25.1 Functions of cerebral areas

Motor area

The **motor area** is one of the largest regions of each cerebral hemisphere. Each motor area consists of motor neurones which send out impulses to bring about voluntary movement of skeletal muscles.

However, the size of the part of the motor area devoted to any one part of the body operated by skeletal muscles is not in proportion to the actual size of the body part. Instead the amount of motor area allocated to a particular body part is found to be in proportion to the **relative number** of **motor endings** present in that body part.

Figure 25.4 shows the extent of motor area given over to each body part capable of movement. The larger the region of motor area, the more mobile the part.

Motor homunculus

Figure 25.5 shows an imaginary human figure ('motor homunculus') whose body parts have been drawn in proportion to their **mobility** and fine motor control as opposed to their actual size.

It is interesting to note the large amount of the motor area devoted to the mobility of the **lips** and **hands**. The fingers in particular are capable of fine motor control enabling humans to perform an incredible variety of complex manual skills which even the most advanced robot is (so far) incapable of emulating.

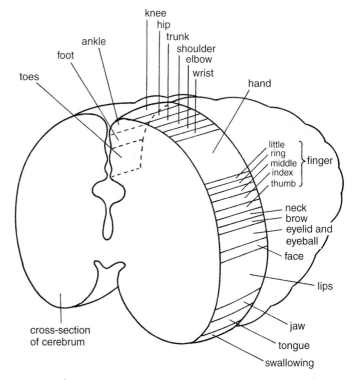

Figure 25.4 Motor area of cerebrum

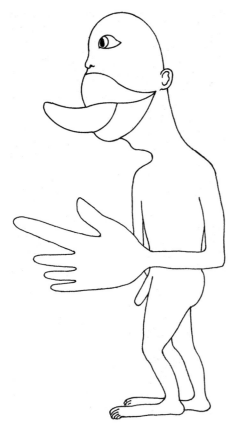

Figure 25.5 Motor homunculus

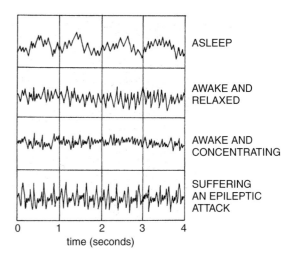

Figure 25.6 EEG wave patterns

Methods of studying the brain

Electroencephalograms (EEGs)

An **EEG** is a record of the cerebrum's **electrical activity**. It is made using information from impulses picked up by electrodes placed on different regions of the scalp. Different **brain wave patterns** indicate different levels of mental activity, as shown in figure 25.6.

Compare the long rolling wave pattern typical of sleep with the concentrated non-rolling pattern obtained when the subject is awake and concentrating. The more densely packed the 'spikes' in the pattern, the higher the level of electrical activity present in the brain. An extreme version of this is seen in the EEG of the person suffering an epileptic attack. Patients who suffer personality problems accompanied by extreme changes of behaviour usually produce **abnormal EEGs**.

EEGs are useful but not very precise since they reflect the simultaneous activity of many cells all over the brain. Although an EEG may show an abnormal pattern indicating a possible problem, it fails to pinpoint the particular region of the brain responsible.

Brain scans

Brain scans allow medical experts to obtain clear visual images of inside the brain without surgery being required.

Certain brain scans provide pictures which indicate areas of high **metabolic activity**. Although designed primarily to diagnose abnormalities, scans can also be used to identify those parts of the brain which show highest metabolic activity during particular actions and emotions.

For example a scan will show which area of the brain is most active when the person is, say, listening to music or stroking a furry object or suddenly feeling angry, etc. These findings provide convincing evidence for the localisation of brain functions.

The process of speech is found to involve several specific regions of the brain. These different 'language' areas also show up on brain scans as regions of high metabolic activity (see figure 25.7). When the information from several scans is put together, it gives a map of the brain's language areas as shown in figure 25.8.

Split-brain studies

Each cerebral hemisphere controls the **opposite side** of the body. Thus damage to the motor area of the left cerebral hemisphere during a stroke results in partial loss of the motor functions of body parts such as arm and leg on the right side.

Visual pathways

Normal situation

When the two eyes are looking at a two-tone field of view, each eye receives light from both sides of the field of view as shown in figure 25.9. However, each cerebral hemisphere only receives information about **half** of this visual field. Everything to the left of the central line (the dotted region in the diagram) is represented in the visual area of the right cerebral hemisphere; everything to the right of the central line (the striped region in the diagram) is represented in the left cerebral hemisphere.

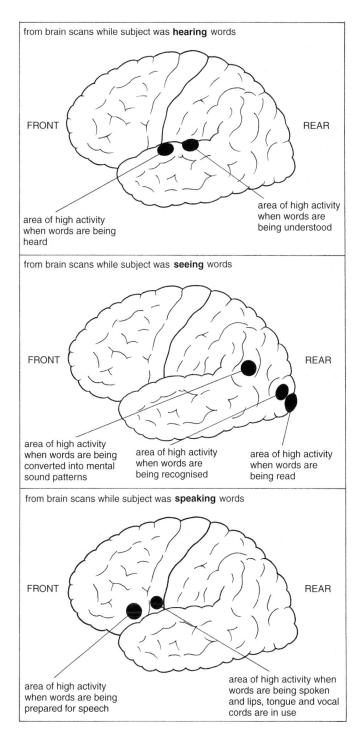

from brain scans while subject was **hearing** words

FRONT   REAR

area of high activity when words are being heard

area of high activity when words are being understood

from brain scans while subject was **seeing** words

FRONT   REAR

area of high activity when words are being converted into mental sound patterns

area of high activity when words are being recognised

area of high activity when words are being read

from brain scans while subject was **speaking** words

FRONT   REAR

area of high activity when words are being prepared for speech

area of high activity when words are being spoken and lips, tongue and vocal cords are in use

Figure 25.7 Language areas from brain scans

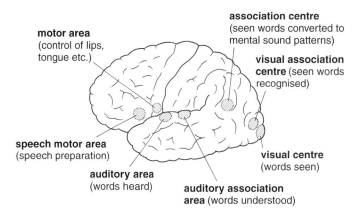

motor area (control of lips, tongue etc.)

association centre (seen words converted to mental sound patterns)

visual association centre (seen words recognised)

speech motor area (speech preparation)

visual centre (words seen)

auditory area (words heard)

auditory association area (words understood)

Figure 25.8 Map of brain's language areas

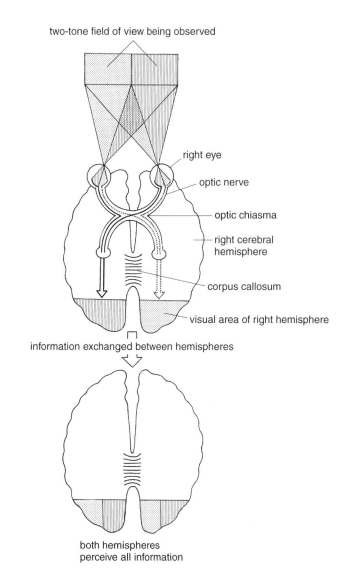

two-tone field of view being observed

right eye

optic nerve

optic chiasma

right cerebral hemisphere

corpus callosum

visual area of right hemisphere

information exchanged between hemispheres

both hemispheres perceive all information

Figure 25.9 Normal visual pathway

This occurs because half of the nerve fibres in each optic nerve **cross over** to the opposite side of the brain at the optic chiasma. Normally each side of the cerebrum quickly communicates its share of the information with the other side via the **corpus callosum**. As a result both hemispheres perceive the whole field of view.

Abnormal situation

A person whose corpus callosum has been cut (e.g. during an operation to try to relieve intractable epilepsy)

is described as a '**split-brain**' patient. In such a person the exchange of information between the cerebral hemispheres as described above cannot take place and each hemisphere receives only half of the information about the field of view (see figure 25.10).

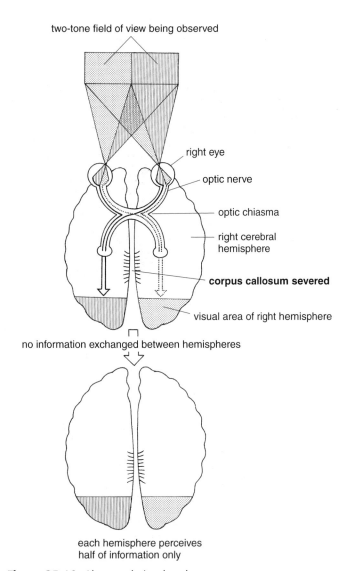

two-tone field of view being observed

right eye

optic nerve

optic chiasma

right cerebral hemisphere

corpus callosum severed

visual area of right hemisphere

no information exchanged between hemispheres

each hemisphere perceives half of information only

Figure 25.10 Abnormal visual pathway

When asked to **say** what he or she sees, the split-brain patient describes a field of view corresponding to the striped region in figure 25.9. (Remember that the motor speech area is in the left cerebral hemisphere only and this is the left side of the brain that is 'talking'.)

However, when asked to **point with the left hand** to what he or she saw from a selection of possible fields of view, the person chooses a field of view corresponding to the dotted region in figure 25.9, since the left hand is controlled by the right side of the brain which is now indicating its version of the events.

Evidence from brain injuries

Some forms of tumour and disease may injure certain areas of the brain. Similarly, specific regions of the brain may be damaged by accidents. Careful study of the effects of such **injuries** sometimes allows experts to infer the role played by a particular part of the brain.

Damaged frontal lobe

In 1848, an accident led to an inch-thick rod being driven into the head of a young American railroad worker. The rod entered beneath his left eye and exited through the top of his head. Amazingly the man survived and was able to speak, think, remember and eventually return to work.

However, he had changed. From having been mild-mannered and dependable, he had become ill-tempered, unreliable and no longer able to stick to a plan. This case and others involving damage to the **frontal lobes** of the brain show that they are involved in planning, goal setting and personality.

Wife or hat?

In another case, a musician of great ability developed a problem in later life. He no longer recognised people or objects and failed to remember the past visually. He would chat to pieces of furniture thinking that they were people. On one occasion he reached out, took hold of his wife's head and tried to lift it to put it on, thinking that it was his hat! The problem was due to damage to his **visual association centres**.

Shrapnel wounds

Experts have studied soldiers blinded or paralysed as a result of shrapnel wounds received during warfare. Their findings provided early evidence that the rear of the cerebrum is responsible for vision and that the region we now call the **motor area** controls movement.

Lesions

Lesions are small regions of damage. The location of the brain's **language areas** is verified by the fact that lesions in these regions give rise to speech defects. For example, damage to the speech motor area results in the person being unable to articulate words despite the fact that they fully understand the words that they hear.

Strokes

Nerve cells in the human brain show a high rate of metabolic activity and depend on the bloodstream for the delivery of a constant supply of oxygen. A **stroke** may occur when a blockage in a blood vessel disrupts the flow of blood to some region of the brain. This leads to the death of some brain cells and the loss (temporary or permanent) of some faculty. By matching the affected area of the brain with the lost faculty, scientists are able to identify which region of the brain is responsible for controlling a particular bodily function.

Testing your knowledge

1. **(i)** Name THREE different types of functional area into which the cerebrum can be divided.
   (ii) Briefly describe the function carried out by each of these different types of areas. (6)

2. State the relationship that exists between the degree of mobility of a body part and the share of the motor area in the cerebrum devoted to its operation. (1)

3. **a)** **(i)** What do the letters EEG stand for?
   (ii) How is such a record of the brain's electrical activity made? (2)
   b) Give ONE difference between an EEG for a person asleep and that of the same person awake. (1)

4. Give TWO pieces of evidence from studies of people with brain injuries that allow experts to attribute certain functions to certain discrete areas of the brain. (4)

Applying your knowledge

1. **a)** Copy and complete table 25.2. (3)

	average brain weight (kg)	average body weight (kg)	ratio (brain weight/body weight)
elephant	6.00	1500	
human	1.36	68	
gorilla	0.50	200	

Table 25.2

   b) **(i)** Which of the three animals has the largest brain relative to its body size?
   (ii) Which of the three animals has the smallest brain relative to its body size? (2)

2. Imagine that you are at home when the door bell rings. You respond by heading towards the door. Identify FOUR areas of the cerebrum (shown in figure 25.3) that are in use during this entire operation and for each briefly describe the role that it plays in the process. (4)

3. This question refers to 'motor homunculus' shown in figure 25.5.
   a) Identify TWO especially mobile parts of the body. (2)
   b) Which third part of the body is sufficiently mobile to be used, with much practice, to operate a pencil or paint brush? (1)
   c) With reference only to the pinna (ear flap), predict how 'motor homunculus' would differ if a rabbit had been drawn. Explain your answer. (2)

4. Figure 25.11 shows a map of the brain's language areas in the left cerebral hemisphere.

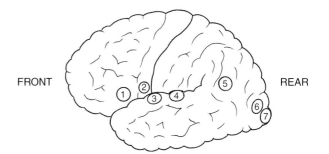

FRONT   REAR

Figure 25.11

   a) Which TWO areas would show highest activity while the person was listening to and understanding a play on the radio? (2)
   b) Suggest what the person is doing when a high level of activity is registered in the following language areas in the order
   (i) 7, 6, 5, 4;
   (ii) 7, 6, 5, 4, 1, 2. (2)
   c) Identify the areas involved and state their correct sequence of involvement when a spoken message is heard and then repeated out loud. (1)
   d) Suggest what effect severe damage to region 1 in figure 25.11 would have on the ability to
   (i) understand language;
   (ii) speak language. (2)

5. Figure 25.12 is a composite picture which was shown to several split-brain patients. A little later the patients were asked to study the four pictures shown in figure 25.13.

Continued ➤

Applying your knowledge

Figure 25.12

State with reasons which picture all of the patients chose when asked to
  (i)   say what they had seen;
  (ii) point with their left hand to what they had seen. (2)

6 Give an account of the discrete areas of the cerebrum that control specific functions (10).

Figure 25.13

26 Organisation of the nervous system

Structural division

Based on **structure** and **location** of component parts, the nervous system can be divided as shown in figure 26.1. Figure 26.2 shows in a simple way where these parts are located in the human body.

Sensory and motor pathways

Many of the peripheral nerves contain a **sensory pathway** consisting of sensory nerve cells and/or a **motor pathway** consisting of motor nerve cells.

Sensory pathways carry nerve impulses to the CNS from **receptors**. Some receptors are located in external sense organs (e.g. skin, eye retina and ear cochlea); others are found in internal sense organs (e.g. CO_2 receptors in carotid arteries and thermoreceptors in the hypothalamus). Sensory pathways keep the brain in touch with what is going on in the body's external and internal environments.

The brain analyses, interprets, processes and stores some of this constant stream of information which is based on **stimuli** such as sounds, sights, colours, tastes,

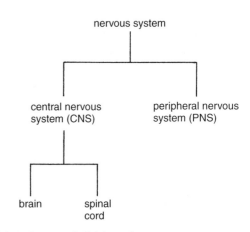

Figure 26.1 Structural division of nervous system

temperature of skin and blood, CO_2 and water concentration of blood, etc.

The brain's association centres (see p 206) may act on this information by sending nerve impulses via the motor pathways to **effectors** (e.g. muscles and glands). These then bring about the appropriate **response** such as muscular contraction, enzyme secretion, etc. This relationship is summarised in figure 26.3.

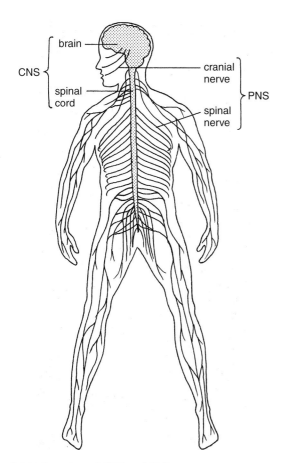

Figure 26.2 Location of CNS and PNS

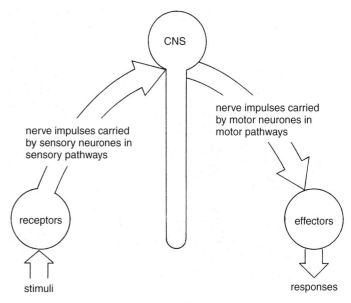

Figure 26.3 Flow of information through nervous system

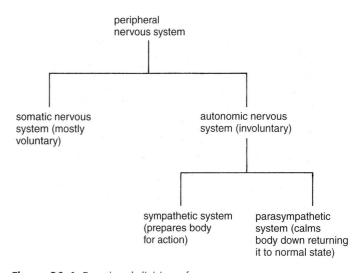

Figure 26.4 Functional division of nervous system

Functional division

A further method of dividing up the nervous system is based on the **different functions** performed by the two separate branches of the peripheral nervous system as shown in figure 26.4.

Somatic nervous system

The **somatic** nervous system (which includes the spinal nerves) controls the body's skeletal muscles. This involves sensory and motor pathways as outlined in figure 26.3.

The somatic nervous system is responsible for bringing about certain involuntary reflex actions (e.g. limb withdrawal) but most of the control that it exerts is over **voluntary** actions.

Imagine, for example, that you are invited to select your four favourite chocolates from a large box of a familiar make. The displayed chocolates act as visual stimuli. Nerve impulses pass from each retina via sensory nerve cells in the optic nerve to the brain. There, association centres process the information and compare it with previous experiences. Decisions are taken and nerve impulses pass to the brain's motor area. This in turn

sends impulses via motor nerve cells to the appropriate skeletal muscles of the arm and hand allowing the voluntary responses needed to pick out the four sweets. This series of events involves the somatic nervous system.

Autonomic nervous system

The **autonomic nervous system** (see figure 26.5) regulates internal structures and organs such as the heart, blood vessels, bronchial tubes, alimentary canal and sweat glands. It normally works **automatically** without the person's conscious control being involved (although under exceptional circumstances, some people may be able to heighten or suppress certain autonomic responses intentionally).

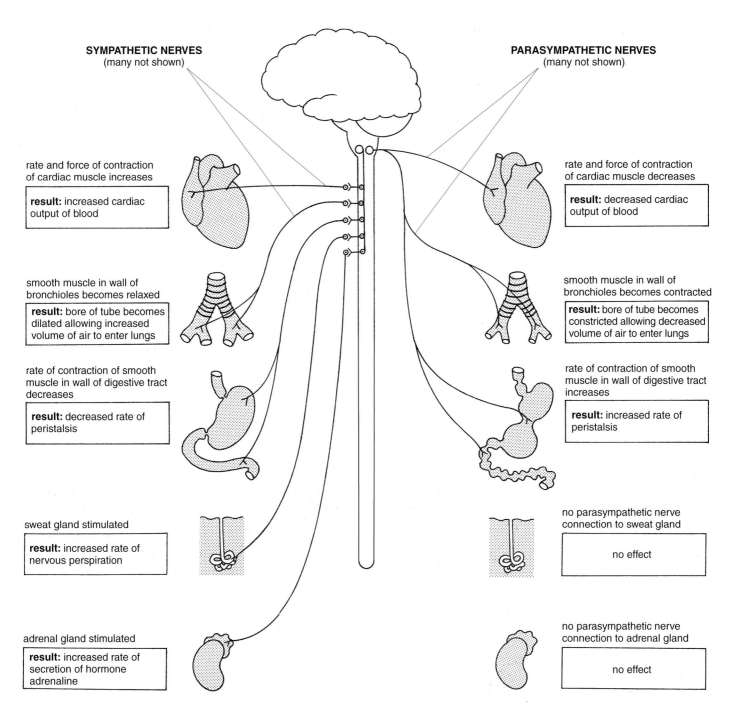

SYMPATHETIC NERVES
(many not shown)

PARASYMPATHETIC NERVES
(many not shown)

rate and force of contraction
of cardiac muscle increases

result: increased cardiac
output of blood

rate and force of contraction
of cardiac muscle decreases

result: decreased cardiac
output of blood

smooth muscle in wall of
bronchioles becomes relaxed

result: bore of tube becomes
dilated allowing increased
volume of air to enter lungs

smooth muscle in wall of
bronchioles becomes contracted

result: bore of tube becomes
constricted allowing decreased
volume of air to enter lungs

rate of contraction of smooth
muscle in wall of digestive tract
decreases

result: decreased rate of
peristalsis

rate of contraction of smooth
muscle in wall of digestive tract
increases

result: increased rate of
peristalsis

sweat gland stimulated

result: increased rate of
nervous perspiration

no parasympathetic nerve
connection to sweat gland

no effect

adrenal gland stimulated

result: increased rate of
secretion of hormone
adrenaline

no parasympathetic nerve
connection to adrenal gland

no effect

Figure 26.5 Autonomic nervous system

The nerves which comprise the autonomic nervous system arise from nerve cells in the brain and emerge at various points down the spinal cord to reach the organs that they stimulate with nerve impulses.

Antagonistic nature of autonomic nervous system

The **sympathetic** and **parasympathetic** systems which make up the autonomic nervous system are described as being **antagonistic**. This means that they affect many of the same body structures but exert opposite effects on them. Figure 26.5 shows only a few of the many tissues and organs controlled in this way.

Harmonious balance

The autonomic nervous system is concerned with maintaining a **stable internal environment** by playing its part in the process of homeostasis (see p 187). Under normal circumstances the sympathetic and parasympathetic systems are constantly working in an equal but opposite manner with neither gaining the upper hand. The activity of a tissue or organ under their control is the result of the two **opposing influences**. It is therefore normally in a state midway between the extremes of hyper and hypoactivity.

Finely tuned control

The stimulation of an effector by both sympathetic and parasympathetic nerves provides a fine degree of control over the effector. The system works like a vehicle equipped with both an **accelerator** and a **brake**. If the car had an accelerator but no brake then the process of reducing speed would depend solely on decreasing the pressure on the accelerator. This method would require too much time to elapse before the car responded and slowed down.

Use of a brake which can be applied in addition to decreasing the pressure on the accelerator, allows for a much more rapid and effective means of regulating the car's speed.

There are exceptions to the rule of dual innervation of an effector by both parasympathetic and sympathetic nerves. For example, the adrenal gland which secretes the hormone adrenaline receives a supply of sympathetic nerves only (see figure 26.5).

Fight or flight

On being stimulated and briefly gaining the upper hand, the **sympathetic** system arouses the body in preparation for action and the expenditure of energy (e.g. 'fight or flight').

The heart rate and blood pressure increase. Blood supplies are **diverted** to the skeletal muscles (in great need of an increased supply of oxygen) and away from the gut and skin (which require minimal servicing during the crisis). Rate of perspiration also increases. Hence a thudding heart, a face white with fear and a clammy sensation in localised areas of the body that are in a 'cold sweat' (e.g. armpits and palms of hands) are all characteristic responses to a crisis.

The hormone **adrenaline** helps to sustain the arousal effects until the emergency is dealt with. This might involve taking a determined and defensive stand perhaps involving a fight or cutting your losses and running away. In either case the vast amount of extra energy required by the skeletal muscles is supplied by their increased blood flow.

Calming down

When the excitement is over, the **parasympathetic** system takes over for a brief spell, calming the body down and returning it to normal.

Heart rate and blood pressure drop to normal. Rate of peristaltic contractions in the digestive tract increases. Blood is diverted to the intestines where it can resume its job of absorbing the end products of digestion now that the crisis is over.

The effects brought about by the parasympathetic nerves help the body to **conserve resources** and **store energy.**

Testing your knowledge

1 a) Name the TWO components of the central nervous system (CNS). (2)

   b) What collective name is given to all the nerves excluding the central nervous system (1)

2 Differentiate between the following pairs of terms:

   a) *sensory* and *motor pathways*; (2)

   b) *receptors* and *effectors*. (2)

3 a) Name the TWO branches of the autonomic nervous system. (2)

   b) State the effect of each branch of the autonomic nervous system on:
      (i) cardiac output;
      (ii) width of bore of the bronchioles. (4)

4 Rewrite the following sentences choosing only the correct word at each underlined choice.
   The body becomes aroused ready for 'fight or flight' by the action of the sympathetic/parasympathetic nerves. As a result, rate of blood flow to the skin increases/decreases, rate of blood flow to the gut increases/decreases and rate of perspiration increases/decreases. (4)

Applying your knowledge

1 Copy and complete figure 26.6 which shows two ways of classifying the parts of the human nervous system. (5)

2 Imagine a person taking a carefree stroll through a field on a summer's day. Suddenly a bull appears from behind a hedge and charges towards the person. She runs for her life and just manages to escape in time.

a) With reference to BOTH parts of the autonomic nervous system, briefly describe the events occurring in the person's body during and immediately after this crisis. (4)

b) Predict the possible outcome to a person if the parasympathetic system took control of the body on a permanent basis. (1)

Continued ➤

● Applying your knowledge ●

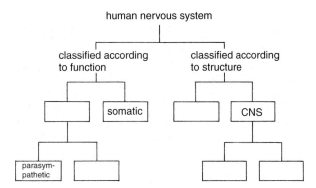

Figure 26.6

3 Figure 26.7 shows a simplified version of the sympathetic nerve supply to two parts of the body containing smooth involuntary muscle.

a) (i) Predict the effect of nerve impulses on the smooth muscle of the arteriole supplying blood to the gut.

(ii) What effect will this have on the bore of the tube?

(iii) Why is this response of survival value to the body during a crisis? (3)

b) (i) Predict the effect of sympathetic nerve impulses on the muscle making up the stomach's sphincter valves.

(ii) By what means could the reverse effect be brought about?

(iii) Under what circumstances would this reverse effect be of advantage to the body? Explain why. (4)

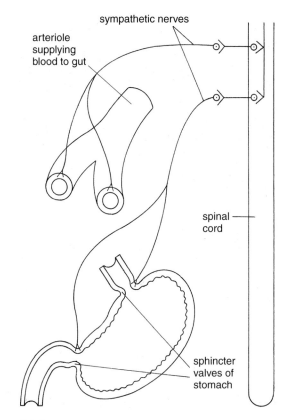

Figure 26.7

4 Describe the antagonistic nature of the autonomic nervous system and compare the effect of its two branches on heart beat, blood distribution and perspiration. (10)

27 Neurones and neural pathways

Neurones

The nervous sytem consists of a complex network of nerve cells called **neurones**. Neurones conduct nerve impulses and provide the body with rapid means of communication and control. There are three types of neurone – **sensory**, **association** and **motor**, as shown in figure 27.1.

Although these appear to be very different, they all share the same basic structures. Each consists of a **cell body** and associated processes: one **axon** and several **dendrites**.

These thread-like extensions of the cytoplasm are often referred to as **nerve fibres**.

Dendrites

Dendrites are nerve fibres which receive nerve impulses and pass them **towards** a cell body. A sensory neurone's dendrites gather into one elongated fibre which transmits information from **receptors** (in contact with the environment) and sends it to the cell body.

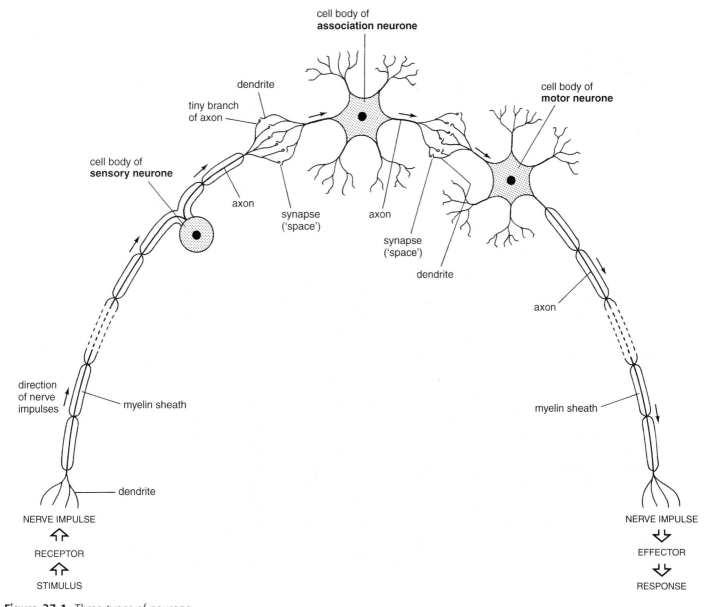

Figure 27.1 Three types of neurone

Association and motor neurones have several short dendrites which collect messages from other neurones and send them to their respective cell bodies.

Cell body

The cell body of a neurone contains the **nucleus** and most of the **cytoplasm**. It is the **control centre** of the cell's metabolism and contains clusters of ribosomes. These are required to make various proteins including the enzymes needed for the synthesis of neurotransmitters.

The cell bodies of association neurones are situated in the central nervous sytem.

Axon

An axon is a single nerve fibre which carries nerve impulses **away from** a cell body and, in the case of sensory and association neurones, on to the next neurone in the sequence.

The axons of motor neurones are extremely long. For example, those that connect with distant parts of the body (e.g. toes) can be more than a metre in length! Each axon from a motor neurone carries a message from the cell body to an effector.

The direction in which a nerve impulse travels is always:

$$\text{dendrites} \longrightarrow \text{cell body} \longrightarrow \text{axon}$$

At the two points in figure 27.1 where information passes from the axon of one neurone to the dendrites of the next, there is great potential for successful transmission because in reality one neurone ends in many tiny axon 'branches' and the next neurone normally begins as many tiny dendrite 'branches'.

Myelin sheath

This sheath of **fatty material** forms an insulating jacket around a nerve fibre. It is composed of tightly packed double layers of plasma membrane derived from special cells which lay it down as a spiral around the nerve fibre (see figure 27.2).

A nerve fibre lacking myelin is described as **unmyelinated**.

Speed of transmission of impulse

The presence of the myelin sheath greatly **increases the speed** at which impulses can be transmitted along the axon of a neurone. In unmyelinated fibres, the axon is exposed to the surrounding medium and the velocity at which impulses are conducted is greatly reduced.

Myelination

Myelination, the development of myelin round axon fibres of individual neurones, takes time and is not complete at birth but continues during postnatal development.

Infants

The **hypothalamus** is not fully myelinated until about six months of age. For this reason a very young baby does not have a fully effective 'thermostat' able to bring about finely tuned control of body temperature.

Similarly, an infant is unable to control fully the lower body because the neurones in the spinal cord which transmit impulses from the brain to the lower body are not fully myelinated until the child is about two years old.

Multiple sclerosis

Multiple sclerosis is a disorder involving the breakdown of the myelin sheaths. Such demyelinated nerve fibres are no longer able to transmit nerve impulses efficiently. The sufferer gradually develops a variety of symptoms (e.g. numbness, walking difficulties and impaired vision) as the ability to control muscles is lost.

Chemical transmission at a synapse

A **synapse** (see figure 27.3) is a tiny region of functional contact between an axon ending (**synaptic knob**) of one neurone and the membrane of a dendrite (or sometimes the cell body) of the next neurone.

The nerve cell before the synapse is called the **presynaptic** neurone; the one after the synapse the **postsynaptic** neurone. The similar region of contact between a motor neurone and an effector is called a **neuro-effector junction**.

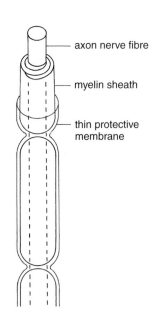

— axon nerve fibre

— myelin sheath

— thin protective membrane

Figure 27.2 Myelin sheath

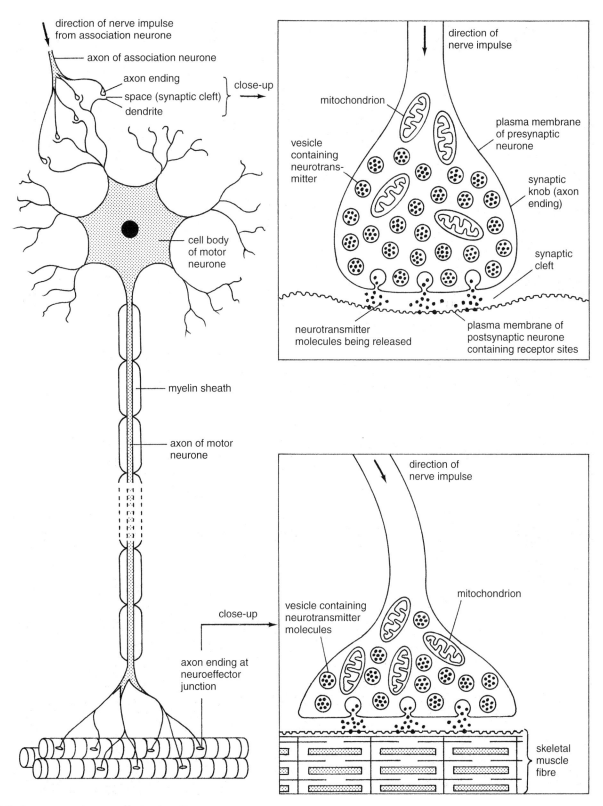

Figure 27.3 Synapse and neuroeffector junction

It is at a synapse that information is passed on by means of a chemical called a **neurotransmitter**. Two examples of the many neurotransmitters now known to exist are **acetylcholine** and **noradrenaline**.

The plasma membranes of the two neurones at a synapse are situated very close to one another and separated only by a narrow space called a **synaptic cleft**. A synaptic knob contains a rich supply of **vesicles** full of one type of neurotransmitter.

When a nerve impulse passes through the presynaptic neurone and reaches the synaptic knob, it stimulates several vesicles. These simultaneously move to the knob's surface, fuse with its membrane, form openings and discharge their contents (about 10 000 molecules of neurotransmitter per vesicle) into the synaptic cleft.

Once in the cleft, the neurotransmitter molecules briefly combine with **receptor molecules** at sites on the membrane of the postsynaptic dendrite. This process alters the membrane's electrical state enabling it to transmit the nerve impulse on through the system.

Threshold

A nerve impulse is only transmitted across a synapse and on through the postsynaptic neurone if it first brings about the release of a certain **minimum number** of neurotransmitter molecules. This critical number is needed to affect a sufficient number of receptor sites on the membrane of the postsynaptic neurone. Achievement of this is called reaching the membrane's **threshold**.

Weak stimuli which fail to do so are called **subthreshold** stimuli. They are filtered out by the synapse acting as an unbridgeable gap.

Direction of impulses

Since vesicles containing neurotransmitter occur on one side only of a synapse, this ensures that nerve impulses are transmitted in **one direction** only.

Fate of neurotransmitter after transmission of impulse

To ensure precise control of the system and allow for the successful transmission of each short-lived impulse, the postsynaptic membrane must remain excited for only the brief moment required to pass on that impulse. This is achieved by the neurotransmitter being **rapidly removed** as soon as the impulse has been transmitted.

Acetylcholine is broken down into non-active products by an enzyme present on the postsynaptic membrane, as in the following equation:

$$\text{acetylcholine} \xrightarrow{\text{acetylcholinesterase}} \text{non-active products}$$

The non-active products are **reabsorbed** by the presynaptic neurone and **resynthesised** into active neurotransmitter which is stored in vesicles ready for reuse. The energy required is supplied by the **mitochondria** present in the presynaptic knob.

Noradrenaline, on the other hand, is **reabsorbed** by the presynaptic membrane which secreted it and stored in vesicles ready for reuse.

Frequency of impulses

Each nerve impulse transmitted by the postsynaptic membrane is equal in size. So how then is information about the intensity of an environmental stimulus (e.g. volume of noise) conveyed?

The number of impulses transmitted per second (i.e. the **frequency** of impulses) depends on the **intensity** of the original environmental stimulus at the start of the pathway. For example, loud music causes more impulses

Testing your knowledge

1 a) Draw a simple diagram of a motor neurone and label the parts: cell body, dendrite and axon. (3)

   b) State the function of each of the labelled parts in your diagram. (3)

2 a) What effect does the presence of a myelin sheath around a nerve fibre have on the speed at which the fibre can transmit a nerve impulse? (1)

   b) Why are children unable to exert full control of their lower body before the age of two years? (1)

3 Decide whether each of the following statements is true or false and then use T or F to indicate your choice. Where a statement is false, give the word that should have been used in place of the word in bold print. (5)

   a) The nerve cell before a synapse is called the **postsynaptic** neurone.

   b) An example of a neurotransmitter is **noradrenaline**.

   c) The membranes of the two neurones at a synapse are separated by a space called a **synaptic cleft**.

   d) A synaptic knob contains mitochondria full of neurotransmitter.

   e) Following the transmission of an impulse, **acetylcholine** is reabsorbed by the membrane that secreted it.

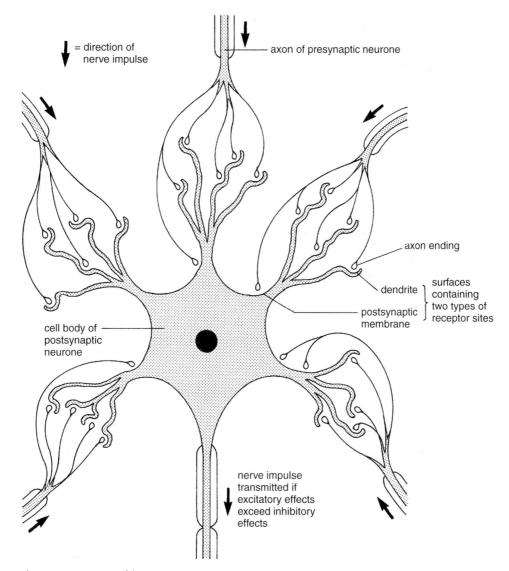

Figure 27.4 Postsynaptic neurone as neural integrator

per second to be sent through the auditory nerve's chain of neurones than soft music. This allows an impression of high intensity (many impulses passed) or low intensity (few impulses passed) to be conveyed.

Need for removal of neurotransmitter

If the neurotransmitter were not removed quickly between impulses then only a **limited number** of impulses would be able to pass in a given time. Say this low frequency of impulses was equivalent to a noise of low volume, the 'low volume' would be the maximum that the system would be capable of communicating. As a result we would be unable to differentiate between soft and loud music and similarly between mild and severe pain, etc.

However, removal of the neurotransmitter substance after an impulse has crossed the synapse is so rapid and efficient that a neurone can send **many separate impulses** per second across a neural cleft, if required to do so.

Excitatory and inhibitory signals

The examples given so far have referred mainly to simple arrangements of neurones in the peripheral nervous system. Deep in the central nervous system (CNS) the situation is much more complex. One postsynaptic neurone normally forms synapses with **many** presynaptic axons from several different neurones as shown in figure 27.4.

At some of these synapses the receptor sites in the postsynaptic membrane respond to the arrival of neurotransmitter (e.g. acetylcholine) by having an **excitatory** effect which increases the membrane's chance of reaching threshold and transmitting a nerve impulse.

At other synapses, the receptor sites respond to the neurotransmitter (e.g. acetylcholine) by having an **inhibitory** effect which reduces the membrane's chance of reaching threshold and transmitting a nerve impulse.

Overall effect

When the sum of the excitatory effects from the synaptic connections affecting the postsynaptic membrane is greater than the sum of the inhibitory effects and threshold is reached, a nerve impulse is transmitted.

When the inhibitory effects are in excess, no signal is fired. By this means a postsynaptic neurone acts as a **neural integrator**, reflecting the overall balance between the two types of synaptic input arriving from many other nerve cells.

Parasympathetic nerves

Figure 27.5 shows how the release of the same neurotransmitter at parasympathetic nerve endings results in two **different** effects.

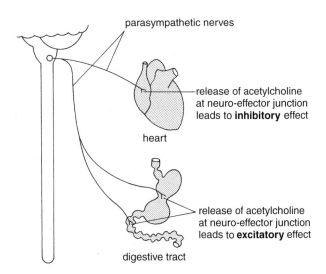

Figure 27.5 Two effects of acetylcholine

Acetylcholine released at a parasympathetic nerve's neuro-effector junction with the heart, combines with receptor sites of the type that pass a signal which causes the heart's activity to be **inhibited**. As a result the rate and force of contraction of cardiac muscle decreases.

Acetylcholine released at a parasympathetic nerve's neuro-effector junction with the digestive tract's muscle, combines with receptor sites of the type that pass on an **excitatory** signal. As a result, the rate of peristaltic contractions increases.

Thus the nature of the signal which is transmitted depends on the type of **receptor site** present in the postsynaptic membrane with which the neurotransmitter combines.

Complex neural pathways

Neurones are found to be connected to one another in many different ways in the CNS. The various combinations allow many types of complicated interaction to occur between neurones. This enables the nervous system to carry out its many complex functions. Two examples of neural pathways are as follows.

Diverging neural pathway

To **diverge** means to branch out from a common point. In a diverging neural pathway, the route along which an impulse is travelling divides. This allows information from the original single source to be transmitted to several destinations. Figure 27.6 shows a simplified version of this principle.

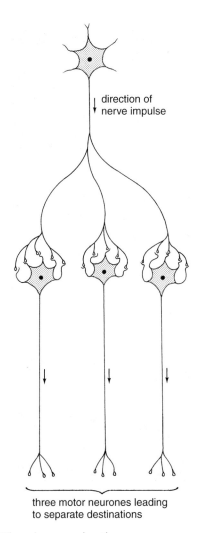

Figure 27.6 Diverging neural pathway

Fine motor control

Movement of those parts of the body operated by skeletal muscles is controlled by the motor area of the cerebrum (see figure 25.3 on p 206).

The cerebrum communicates with the muscles by sending impulses via motor neurones in neural pathways.

Divergence of these pathways from a common starting point allows impulses to be simultaneously transmitted to different muscles of the hand, for example. This brings about fine motor control of the fingers and thumb by allowing them to operate in unison when required to do so.

Temperature control

Similarly, a neural pathway which begins in the **hypothalamus** is found to diverge into branches which lead to sweat glands, skin arterioles and skeletal muscles.

This enables the hypothalamus to exert **co-ordinated control** over the structures involved in temperature regulation. For example, vasoconstriction, shivering and decreased rate of sweating can all be initiated simultaneously if the body temperature begins to drop.

Converging neural pathway

To **converge** means to come together and meet at a common point. In a convergent neural pathway, impulses from several sources are channelled towards and meet at a common destination as shown in figure 27.7.

Rods and cones

Rods and **cones** are visual receptors present in the retina of the eye. They contain pigments which break down in the presence of light. In each case, this breakdown forms

a chemical which triggers off nerve impulses along a pathway of neurones.

The pigment present in cones is not very sensitive to light. Bright light (e.g. daylight) is needed to break it down and trigger off the transmission of nerve impulses.

The pigment in rods, on the other hand, is so sensitive to light that it even reacts in very **dim light** and fires off impulses. It is quickly rendered temporarily inactive in bright light.

Convergence of signals from rods

As the intensity of light entering the eye decreases, cones cease to respond and rods take over. Unlike cones, several rods form synapses with the next neurone in the pathway as shown in figure 27.8.

The nerve impulse transmitted by one rod in dim light is weak. On its own it would be unable to bring about the

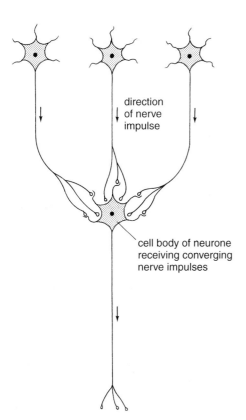

Figure 27.7 Converging neural pathway

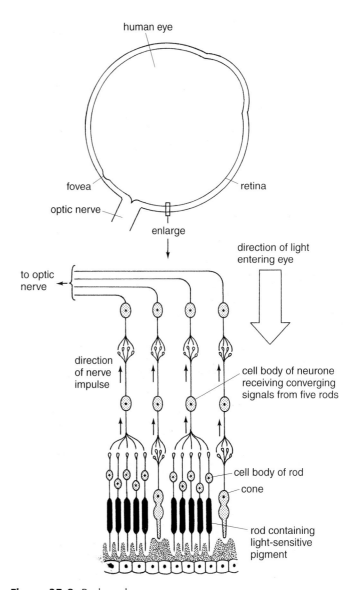

Figure 27.8 Rods and cones

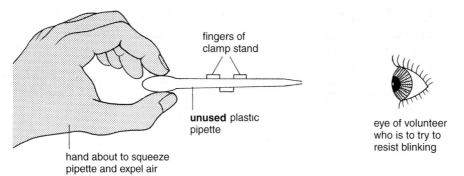

fingers of
clamp stand

unused plastic
pipette

eye of volunteer
who is to try to
resist blinking

hand about to squeeze
pipette and expel air

Figure 27.9 Resisting blinking

release at the synapse of enough neurotransmitter to raise the postsynaptic membrane to threshold.

However, the **convergent arrangement** of several rods allows several impulses to be transmitted simultaneously and have the combined effect of releasing enough neurotransmitter. The postsynaptic membrane now reaches **threshold** and transmits the nerve impulse on through the neural pathway of the optic nerve to the brain.

This process increases the human eye's sensitivity to low levels of illumination and allows vision in conditions of almost total darkness. Furthermore, we gain a reasonably comprehensive view of the surroundings since the rods are thoroughly distributed throughout the retina (except for the fovea).

Plasticity of response of the nervous system

People who have suffered certain types of irreparable brain damage are found to be severely affected. They may, for example be unable to speak or unable to move one or more of their limbs. However, within a few months some sufferers are found to regain normal speech or regain the use of the limb.

The damaged region of the brain has not regenerated. What has happened is that other versatile regions of the brain which escaped damage have taken on these jobs in addition to their own.

This remarkable flexibility of the brain is called **plasticity**. Plastic in this biological sense means able to be influenced or changed. The above example demonstrates **major** plasticity. In the following experiments, examples of **minor** plasticity are investigated.

Investigating the brain's capacity to suppress the blinking reflex

A **reflex action** is a rapid, automatic, involuntary response to a stimulus. Blinking the eye by contraction of

the eyelid muscle in response to a real or imaginary danger is a reflex action.

In the experiment shown in figure 27.9, ten attempts are made to make the volunteer blink using their right eyelid. An interval of ten seconds is allowed between each trial to allow the volunteer to compose themself and summon maximum willpower. The eye is held at the same distance from the pipette at each trial.

It is found that some people are very good at suppressing this reflex action whilst others cannot resist blinking however hard they try.

Investigating the ability of the brain to suppress sensory impulses

The person being tested is given two minutes to attempt a task which requires a reasonable amount of concentration (e.g. to correctly solve as many simple arithmetical problems as possible from a long list).

The first trial is conducted in optimum conditions (e.g. silence, good lighting, etc.). The second trial using a fresh list of problems of equal difficulty to the first is carried out under conditions of **auditory distraction** (e.g. sound of a car alarm). The final trial is performed under conditions of **visual distraction** (e.g. flashing light).

Some people are found to be very good at suppressing the sensory impulses from the distractions and perform very well each time. Other people find it very difficult to concentrate when distracted and fail to block out the sensory impulses.

Discussion

From the above two investigations, it can be concluded that responses shown by a normal healthy person's nervous system are not necessarily fixed and unchangeable. Sometimes the brain can be persuaded to temporarily suppress a reflex action or block out certain sensory impulses. This demonstrates **plasticity of response** of the nervous system.

Plasticity is thought to occur in the following way. Since the nervous system consists of many interconnecting nerve cells, two conflicting types of message (one type 'saying' Blink!; the other type 'saying' Resist blinking!) meet in a convergent pathway. If the overall effect at the synapses affected is **excitatory** then a nerve impulse is fired and the blinking response occurs. If the overall effect is **inhibitory** then no impulse is fired and blinking fails to occur.

Thus some people cannot resist blinking whilst others can successfully 'stare out' the stimulus.

Testing your knowledge

1   a)   What is a *synapse*? (1)

   b)   A signal arriving at a synapse may be excitatory or inhibitory. Is the state of the signal determined by the type of neurotransmitter released at the synapse or the type of receptor sites present on the postsynaptic membrane? (1)

   c)   What is the overall effect in a postsynaptic neurone acting as a neural integrator when
      (i)   the inhibitory signals exceed the excitatory ones?
      (ii)   the excitatory signals exceed the inhibitory ones? (2)

2   a)   Explain what is meant by the expression *diverging* neural pathway. (1)

   b)   Describe how such a pathway allows fine motor control of the fingers. (2)

3   a)   Explain what is meant by the expression *converging* neural pathway. (1)

   b)   Under what conditions of light intensity do
      (i)   cones
      (ii)   rods work most effectively? (2)

   c)   With reference to convergence of nerve signals, explain how rods enable us to see even in conditions of almost total darkness. (3)

4   Give an example of
   (i)   major
   (ii)   minor plasticity of response of the neural system. (2)

Applying your knowledge

1   Copy and complete figure 27.10 which shows a simplified version of a reflex arc involving three neurones. (5)

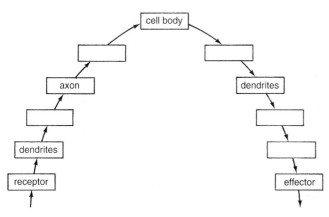

Figure 27.10

2   Figure 27.11 shows the reflex arc involved in the withdrawal of the arm when the hand touches a naked flame.

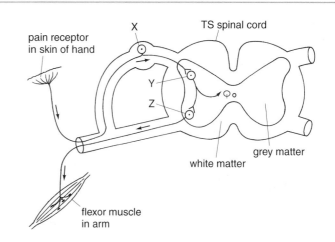

Figure 27.11

   a)   Identify neurone types X, Y and Z. (3)

   b)   Rewrite the following sentence to include only the correct word at each choice: When the reflex action of limb withdrawal occurs, this involves the somatic/autonomic nervous system and the type of response is described as voluntary/involuntary. (2)

Continued ➤

Applying your knowledge

c) Give ONE structural difference between grey and white matter. (1)

d) Suggest where the impulse passing along route Q could be going to. (1)

3 Figure 27.12 shows a synapse.

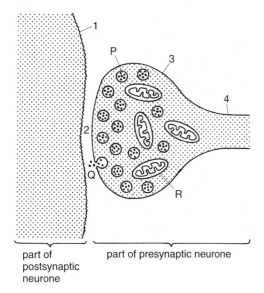

part of postsynaptic neurone

part of presynaptic neurone

Figure 27.12

a) Match numbered parts 1–4 with the following terms: *synaptic cleft, axon, synaptic knob, membrane of dendrite*. (4)

b) (i)   Identify structure P.
   (ii)   Give the name of a neurotransmitter that could be released at Q.
   (iii) To what structures would these neurotransmitter molecules briefly combine?
   (iv)   In which direction would the nerve impulse pass in this diagram?
   (v)   State the fate of the neurotransmitter that you gave as your answer to part (ii) once the nerve impulse has been transmitted.
   (vi)   Identify structure R and state its function. (7)

4 a) Why is it important that the neurotransmitter molecule is removed from the synaptic cleft as soon as the nerve impulse has passed through? (1)

   b) The drug curare combines with the acetylcholine receptor sites on the membranes of muscle fibres at neuro-effector junctions. Predict with reasons the overall effect of a dose of curare on a human being. (2)

c) The drug strychnine prevents cholinesterase from playing its role. Administration of small quantities of strychnine to neuro-effector junctions causes twitching of skeletal muscles. Suggest why. (2)

5 Figure 27.13 shows a small portion of the retina of a human eye.

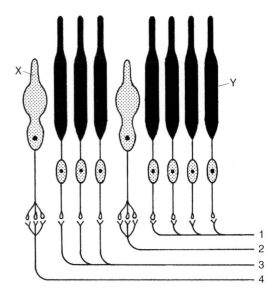

Figure 27.13

a) Identify the receptors X and Y. (2)

b) Which TWO of the numbered nerve fibres will transmit an impulse when light of very low intensity reaches the retina? (1)

c) Give a reason for your answer to question b). (1)

6 In an experiment to investigate plasticity of response of the nervous system, six students were each given two minutes to correctly solve as many mathematical problems as possible under three different sets of conditions. The results are shown in table 27.1.

a) Identify the
   (i)   auditory;
   (ii)   visual distraction used. (2)

b) (i)   Which student(s) demonstrated plasticity of response of the nervous system?
   (ii)   Explain how you arrived at your answer. (2)

c) Briefly explain how such plasticity is thought to occur. (4)

d) (i)   Why are the two types of distraction investigated separately rather than simultaneously?

Continued ➢

Applying your knowledge

student	number of problems solved in 2 min.		
	silence + uninterrupted lighting	car alarm + uninterrupted lighting	silence + flashing light
A	20	18	21
B	12	12	11
C	14	3	5
D	18	5	7
E	22	23	21
F	25	8	6

Table 27.1

(ii) Why is a fresh set of problems needed for each trial?

(iii) Identify a possible source of error in this experiment.

(iv) Suggest TWO ways in which the reliability of the experiment could be improved. (5)

7 Write notes on the transmission of nerve impulses under the following headings:
(i) the synapse; (6)
(ii) diverging pathways; (2)
(iii) converging pathways. (2)

What you should know
(Chapters 25–27)

(See table 27.2 for word bank.)

1 The human _____ is large relative to body size.

2 The _____ is the largest part of the human brain. It is made up of two halves called _____ which are connected by the _____ callosum. This enables information to be transferred from one half to the other.

3 The _____ nature of the cerebrum's surface allows a large number of nerve cell bodies to be located close together, increasing the potential for exchange of information between them.

4 The cerebrum possesses three types of functional area: _____ areas which receive information from receptors, association areas which analyse the information and _____ areas which send out information to effectors.

5 Different functions are localised in discrete areas of the cerebrum e.g. auditory, _____ and motor areas.

6 The size of the region of motor area devoted to part of the body is in proportion to the relative _____ of the body part and not to its actual size.

7 Evidence for the localisation of different brain functions comes from studies of EEGs, brain _____, split-brain patients and observations of people suffering brain injuries and _____.

8 The human nervous system can be divided on a structural basis into the _____ and peripheral nervous systems.

9 The human nervous system can be divided on a _____ basis into the somatic and _____ systems.

10 Most of the control exerted by the somatic system is over _____ actions.

11 The autonomic system works automatically without involving the person's conscious thought.

12 The autonomic system is made of the _____ and parasympathetic systems which are often _____.

13 The sympathetic system arouses the body in preparation for _____; the parasympathetic helps the body to conserve _____.

14 The nervous system is composed of sensory, association and motor nerve cells (_____).

Continued ➤

What you should know
(Chapters 25–27)

15 Each neurone consists of a cell body and associated nerve fibres: one _____ and several dendrites.

16 A nerve fibre is surrounded by a _____ sheath whose presence greatly increases the _____ at which nerve impulses can be transmitted through the fibre.

17 A _____ is a tiny space between two neurones. Information is transmitted at a synapse by _____ being released by the presynaptic neurone. This chemical combines with _____ sites in the postsynaptic membrane.

18 Some receptor sites respond by having an _____ effect on the postsynaptic membrane; others have an inhibitory effect.

19 In a _____ neural pathway, the route along which a nerve impulse travels divides allowing information to pass to several destinations; in a _____ neural pathway, nerve impulses from several sources are channelled towards and meet at a common destination.

20 Sometimes the brain can suppress a reflex action or block out certain sensory impulses, thereby demonstrating _____ of response.

action	diverging	plasticity
antagonistic	excitatory	receptor
autonomic	functional	resources
axon	hemispheres	scans
brain	lesions	sensory
central	mobility	speed
cerebrum	motor	sympathetic
convoluted	myelin	synapse
converging	neurones	visual
corpus	neurotransmitter	voluntary

Table 27.2 Word bank for chapters 25–27

(28) Localisation of memory

Memory is one of our major mental faculties. It is the capacity of the brain to **retain** information and **retrieve** it when required. Memory is so **versatile** that it can capture images of sights, sounds, smells, tactile sensations and emotions all experienced at the one time. For example, a child receiving a present of a new puppy remembers various details of the experience vividly for a very long time.

Memory has such an amazingly **large capacity** that it is able to store the experiences of a lifetime. In the absence of memory we would be helpless, unable to manage even the simplest task without having to first relearn it. The future of each individual and of society in general is shaped by memories of past experiences.

Location of areas responsible for memory

Different types of memory exist, as shown in figure 28.1. These are associated with particular areas of the brain although evidence suggests that there is a degree of overlap. Close communication certainly exists between the different parts involved in memory.

Declarative memories ('remembering that...')

Declarative memories (facts and episodes) are needed and drawn upon when performing mental **recall** operations such as identifying a familiar object (without a key) or recalling a past experience. Successful formation

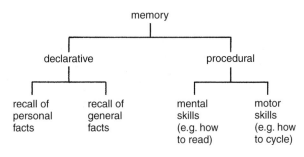

Figure 28.1 Different types of memory

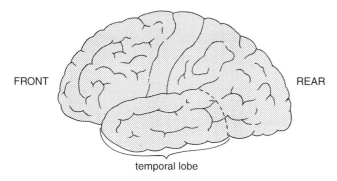

Figure 28.2 Temporal lobe of left cerebral hemisphere

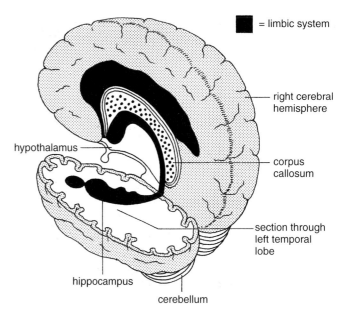

Figure 28.3 Limbic system

of declarative memories is closely associated with areas of the **temporal lobes** at the sides of the cerebrum (see figure 28.2) and parts of the **limbic system**.

The limbic system (see figure 28.3) is a composite region of the brain which surrounds and connects with the hypothalamus. On each side it possesses a structure called the **hippocampus** which projects into the temporal lobe.

Procedural memories ('remembering how to...')

Procedural memories (skills and habits) are needed and drawn upon in order to perform **mental** skills such as remembering how to read, how to play chess, etc., and **motor** skills such as swimming, cycling and knitting. The **cerebellum** is found to be vital for many of these skills especially the ones involving muscular co-ordination.

Evidence for localisation of memory

Amnesia is the partial or complete loss of memory. It takes several forms and can result from an injury, disease or stroke which affects the brain; or from surgery or electric shocks applied to the brain.

A case history

In order to relieve life-threatening epilepsy, much of the limbic system (including both hippocampi) was removed from the brain of a patient. As a result he was found to have lost his ability to recall new factual information for any longer than a few minutes. Doctors had to reintroduce themselves to him at every visit.

However, the patient could still retrieve old declarative memories stored before the operation. He also retained procedural skills such as tying his shoe laces. Although he could remember how to read, he was satisfied with the same magazine every day since he failed to retain any of the information that he had read.

He was able to learn some new problem-solving skills (e.g. mirror-drawing – see p 267) and new motor skills

(e.g. how to play a sport). He retained these as procedural memories but could not recall the actual coaching sessions.

Drawing tentative conclusions

This case study provides evidence to support the view that parts of the **limbic system** (the hippocampi in particular) are essential for the **formation** and **transfer** of new declarative memories but are not the storage sites.

Such **declarative** memories are thought to be **stored** in the **temporal lobes**. (The above patient, whose temporal lobes remained undamaged, was able to recall old declarative memories but not deposit any new ones there.)

Procedural memories are thought to involve the **cerebellum** and parts of the **cerebrum** other than the limbic system. (The patient was able to form and store new procedural memories and retrieve old ones.)

Evidence from other patients suffering similar brain damage and memory loss supports these tentative conclusions. Experimental work done on monkeys with lesions in the hippocampus show the same pattern of memory loss.

Personal versus general memories

Some people suffering amnesia forget the details of their personal history but remember general facts such as the meaning of the words of the language that they speak, the buying power of the country's currency, and so on. This suggests that **personal** and **general** declarative memories may occupy different areas of the brain.

Left or right temporal lobe

Patients who have had their left temporal lobe removed are found to have great difficulty remembering unfamiliar words and associations between pairs of words.

Patients who have undergone a right temporal lobectomy have great difficulty remembering unfamiliar geometrical figures, new faces and musical sequences. These findings suggest that memories of **different categories** of general facts are stored in different sides of the brain.

Electrical stimulation

Electrical stimulation of the temporal lobes of patients undergoing brain surgery (to relieve epilepsy) resulted in them recalling, in minute detail, events (and even songs) from their distant past. This suggests that the **temporal lobes** were the site of at least some of their **personal fact** (declarative) memory. Research using monkeys supports this view. A monkey's temporal lobes show increased electrical activity when it is viewing a picture of its own hand.

However great care must be taken when attempting to draw conclusions about the exact locations of the different types of memory since the many brain circuits involved are **intimately interconnected** and constantly exchanging information. Damage to one part may have a knock-on effect on another. Most investigators believe that many different regions of the brain are involved in memory with some regions playing a larger role than others.

Memory at neuronal level

Most procedural skills, once learned, are not easily forgotten. Once a person has learned to swim, drive a car, ice-skate, etc. he or she retains these skills, almost indefinitely even if they are not put to use for many years.

Many declarative memories are similarly retained on a long-term or even permanent basis. Most people are able to recite the words of at least one nursery rhyme from childhood, recall the address of the house that they lived in when they began school at the age of five, and so on.

In the above examples, it would seem that memory is the result of a **long-term change** in some part of the brain, presumably affecting **neurones**.

Synaptic transmission

The vast majority of experts support the view that the formation of each specific memory involves **synaptic transmission**. It is thought that each memory is held by a group of neurones arranged or adapted in a particular way to form a specific '**memory circuit**'.

It is proposed that the brain contains a neural representation of each remembered fact, event, skill, etc. and that these collectively make up billions of possible neuronal memory circuits.

It is thought that each memory can be retrieved by a nerve impulse being transmitted through its particular memory circuit and **reactivating** it. (This would be rather like operating an electrical appliance by passing electricity through its circuit.)

Some kind of interchange of nerve impulses would also have to occur between certain memory circuits to account for the fact that an experience of one kind often awakens a memory of a different kind. For example hearing a familiar voice on the telephone produces a visual image of the caller in the 'mind's eye'.

Molecular basis of memory

Although the mechanism of memory remains unknown, it seems certain that it has a **molecular basis** and requires chemical changes to occur at neurone level. It seems highly likely that specific assemblies of neurones are involved and that the system is dependent upon the release of certain **neurotransmitters** at synapses to allow impulses to flow through 'memory circuits'.

It is possible that the more often an impulse passes through a circuit, the better preserved the neural pattern becomes and the greater the likelihood of the memory becoming long-lasting.

Evidence

Failing to retrieve an old memory

The molecular basis of memory is supported by findings from studies of patients suffering **Alzheimer's disease**. This condition is characterised by the presence of numerous abnormal tangles of brain neurones, the death of many brain cells and the irreversible loss of parts of the memory.

Progression of this condition is found to be accompanied by continuous loss of acetylcholine-producing cells in the limbic system. Since secretion of this neurotransmitter normally enables impulses to flow through a neural pathway, this suggests that **acetylcholine** may play an important role in linking the neurones that normally allow certain memory circuits to be activated and memories to be retrieved.

Experiments using monkeys show that their visual recognition memory becomes impaired when they are given a drug which blocks the action of acetylcholine. It is greatly improved, on the other hand, when they are given a drug which enhances the action of acetylcholine.

Evidence also links Alzheimer's disease in humans with disturbance and breakdown of the NMDA receptor system described below.

Forming a new memory

Research using rats and mice shows that the development of a new memory (in this case learning and remembering the way through a water maze by referring to spatial clues) is dependent on the possession of the **hippocampus** region of the brain's limbic system.

Study of synaptic transmission between neurones of the hippocampus reveals that the neurotransmitter released by the presynaptic membrane is **glutamic acid** (an amino acid). The sites on the postsynaptic membrane receptive to glutamic acid are found to consist of **NMDA receptor** (so-called because it is also receptive to N-methyl-D-aspartic acid). These receptor molecules alter the electrical state of the membrane, allowing the nerve impulse to be transmitted (see figure 28.4). Inhibitors of NMDA receptor are found to produce amnesia in rats.

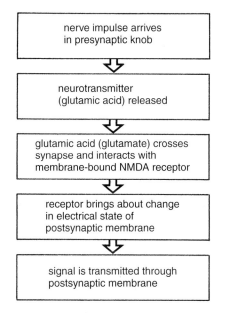

Figure 28.4 Nerve impulse transmission in memory formation

The neurones in the limbic system of normal healthy humans are found to be rich in NMDA receptor and it is therefore thought that it may also play a major role in memory formation in humans.

Alteration of neurones

For a memory to be laid down the neurones involved must become altered in some way on a long-term basis. Research using chickens shows that neurones present in the region of the brain involved in the formation of a new memory (learning to avoid an unpleasant taste) respond to the arrival of the nerve impulse by undergoing a series of biochemical events (see figure 28.5).

This leads to the synthesis of certain **protein** molecules which are essential for formation of the memory. Inhibitors which prevent their synthesis produce amnesia.

These proteins become incorporated into the postsynaptic membrane altering its **size** and **shape**. They also become built into **new dendrites**. These changes increase the cell's synapse number and its **long-term sensitivity** to future nerve impulses. The more receptive the cell becomes, the stronger the memory laid down.

Although clear evidence exists of these modifications to the structure of the neurones involved in the formation of memory, scientists are so far unable to explain why neurones altered in this way allow the animal (and presumably humans also) to remember a past experience.

Testing your knowledge

1 a) Differentiate between *procedural* and *declarative* memories including TWO examples of each in your answer. (6)

b) Which of these memory types involves skills which show marked improvement with practice? (1)

2 (i) Identify TWO regions of the cerebrum closely associated with declarative memories.
(ii) Which of these is thought to be an important storage site for declarative memories? (3)

3 Which non-cerebral region of the brain is closely associated with the storage of procedural memories? (1)

4 Decide whether each of the following statements is true or false and then use T or F to indicate your choice. Where a statement is false, give the word that should have been used in place of the word in bold print. (6)

a) Personal facts and general facts are two categories of **procedural** memory.

b) Memories involving muscular co-ordination are thought to be stored in the **cerebellum**.

c) Each memory is thought to be held by a group of **neurotransmitters** which form a memory circuit.

d) Neurones in the limbic system are rich in a receptor called **mRNA**.

e) Alzheimer's disease is characterised by loss of **memory**.

f) Sufferers of Alzheimer's disease are found to have lost many of their **noradrenaline**-producing cells.

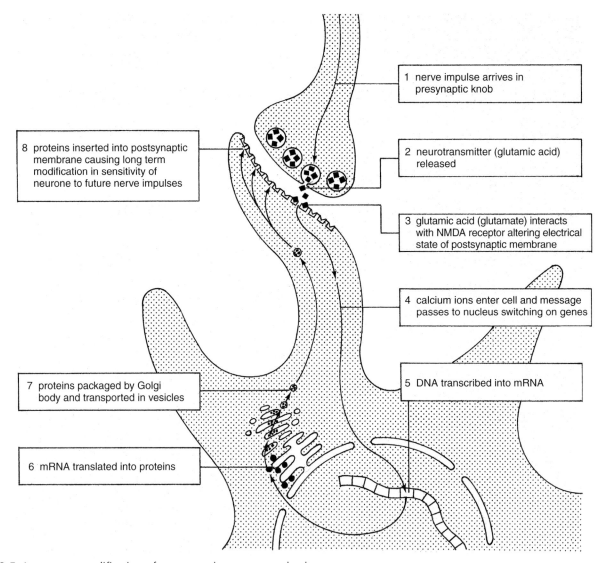

Figure 28.5 Long term modification of a neurone in a memory circuit

The following labels appear in the figure:

1 nerve impulse arrives in presynaptic knob

2 neurotransmitter (glutamic acid) released

3 glutamic acid (glutamate) interacts with NMDA receptor altering electrical state of postsynaptic membrane

4 calcium ions enter cell and message passes to nucleus switching on genes

5 DNA transcribed into mRNA

6 mRNA translated into proteins

7 proteins packaged by Golgi body and transported in vesicles

8 proteins inserted into postsynaptic membrane causing long term modification in sensitivity of neurone to future nerve impulses

● Applying your knowledge ●

1 a) A patient suffering recent brain damage to both hippocampi (parts of the limbic system) was found to lack the ability to recall football highlights seen on TV only minutes before, yet could remember details of a World Cup match that he had seen on TV ten years earlier.

Give a possible explanation for this situation (with reference only to old and new declarative memories). (2)

b) The same patient was able to learn and then remember how to play table tennis but was unable to remember the rules for keeping the score. Give a possible explanation for this situation (with reference only to new procedural and declarative memories). (2)

c) Does the above case history justify the claim that 'the hippocampus is the gateway to all memories'? Explain your answer. (2)

2 Sufferers of Alzheimer's disease are found to remember how to pronounce 'difficult' words such as 'gnat', 'weight', 'pyjamas', etc. but no longer remember the meaning of the words.

a) State TWO characteristics of Alzheimer's disease. (2)

b) 'A human being possesses different types of memory.' Justify this claim with reference to the above information and name the types of memory involved. (2)

Continued ➤

Applying your knowledge

3 Read the following passage and answer the questions.

Drinking water in areas affected by acid rain often contains higher than normal concentrations of aluminium. Aluminium ions have the same electrical charge and are of similar size to iron ions. Once taken into the body (e.g. in drinking water) aluminium ions are mistaken for iron and picked up by transferrin, the protein responsible for the transport of iron ions from the gut to the bone marrow.

Unlike iron, aluminium ions do damage by blocking the transfer of calcium ions across the postsynaptic membranes of nerve cells. This leads to a breakdown in the sequence of events shown in figure 28.5 on page 232.

Scientists have discovered that silicon combines with aluminium to form compounds that are too large to be asorbed into the bloodstream from the gut.

a) What is the normal function of transferrin? (1)

b) Why does transferrin transport aluminium that has been taken into body? (1)

c) **(i)** What effect does aluminium have on nerve cells?

　　(ii) Suggest the specific effect that this will have on the neurones in regions of the brain responsible for storage of memories. (3)

d) Why might the addition of silicon to drinking water help to protect people against Alzheimer's disease? (2)

4 Give an account of the molecular basis of memory. (10)

29 Memory – encoding, storage and retrieval

Selective memory

The receptors in the human sense organs are continuously picking up stimuli and transmitting impulses to the brain. This results in **sensory images** such as visual and acoustic (auditory) impressions being formed in certain areas of the cerebrum.

However, only a fraction of these sensory images become committed to memory because the process is highly **selective**. If this were not the case the mind would become cluttered with useless information such as every phone number ever used, every musical note of every tune ever heard whether liked or disliked, and so on.

Encoding

To become part of the memory, the selected sensory images must first be **encoded**. This requires their conversion into a form that the brain can process and store. Imagine, for example, that you are trying to remember that the Spanish word for *fork* is *tenedor*. You could try to encode this new word by forming a visual image of the 7-lettered word itself (**visual** encoding). You could form an acoustic image of the word by saying

'tenedor' to yourself a few times (**acoustic** encoding). Or you could form a semantic representation of the word 'tenedor' by thinking about its meaning as an implement for lifting food to the mouth (**semantic** encoding).

Some types of information are encoded automatically. Think of the kitchen in your home. Where is the sink in relation to the cooker and the fridge? You can remember their spatial relationship without ever having had to make an effort to encode it.

Some types of information are encoded only with effort. Think of the first chapter in this book (assuming that you have read it!). To memorise its contents for an exam needs effort using techniques such as **rehearsal**, **organisation** and **elaboration** (which will be discussed later in this chapter).

Storage and retrieval

Storage is the retention of information over a period of time. This may last for only a brief spell such as 30 seconds or for a very long period, perhaps a complete lifetime.

Retrieval is the recovery of the stored material. This involves the recall of information which has been committed to either the **short-term** or the **long-term** memory (see p 235). Thus when memory is functioning properly, encoding leads to storage of information which can be retrieved later when required.

Investigating memory span

A person's **short-term memory** span can be measured by finding out the number of individual 'meaningless' items which they can reproduce correctly and in order immediately after seeing or hearing them once.

In the following investigation there is one tester (e.g. the teacher) and many subjects (e.g. all members of the class). The tester reads out the first series of digits (see table 29.1) clearly and at uniform speed. Immediately after reading out the last digit of the first series, the tester signals that all subjects should lift their pencils, write down the series of digits that they have just heard and then lay their pencils down again.

The tester then reads out the next series, and so on until the end of the list. The responses are checked and each subject's memory span for the first list is identified.

The procedure is repeated twice using different lists. Each subject's best overall score is taken to represent his or her memory span. The class results are pooled and graphed. Figure 29.1 charts a typical set of results for a class of 20 pupils. Table 29.2 outlines the design features of this investigation and the reasons for employing them.

From the results in figure 29.1, it is concluded that for this group of pupils, the poorest (minimum) memory span was 5 digits (one pupil), the best (maximum) memory span was 9 digits (one pupil) and that all of the other subjects had a memory span somewhere in between.

series	number of digits in series
741	3
2835	4
46279	5
584153	6
9082637	7
16136209	8
592403517	9
8076148362	10
78501942493	11
512367509308	12
6821496708754	13

Table 29.1 List of series of digits

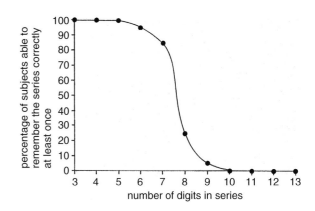

Figure 29.1 Graph of memory span results

design feature or precaution	reason
Series of random numbers used.	To eliminate easily remembered sequences or groups of numbers.
All information read out clearly at uniform speed by the same tester.	To ensure that the only variable factor was the number of digits in the series.
Pencils laid down between responses.	To prevent over-eager subjects starting to write down the series before it has been completely read out.
Each subject given three attempts.	To obtain a more reliable result for each subject's overall best score.
Many pupils tested and the results pooled as a graph.	To further increase the reliability of the results.

Table 29.2 Design features

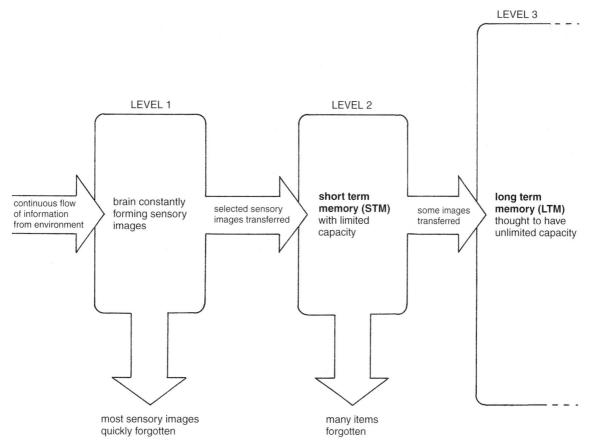

Figure 29.2 Three levels of memory

On average the human short-term memory span is found to be 7 ± 2 digits, though some amazing exceptions have been recorded.

The effect of 'chunking' on memory span

A **chunk** is a meaningful unit of information made up of several smaller units. To most people familiar with the dates of the Second World War, 1945 is one chunk of information not four chunks. However to most people 4951 is four chunks of information (unless it happens to be something significant such as the PIN number of their bank account).

Since short-term memory is only capable of holding about seven new items at one time, **chunking** is a useful method of increasing its memory span. The compilers of all-digit telephone numbers provide users with the means to transfer an 11-digit number from directory to telephone by chunking.

Imagine, for example, that a business woman in Aberdeen wishes to phone an unfamiliar Glasgow number (e.g. 01416293801). If she already knows that Glasgow's national code is 0141 then that chunk reduces her task to remembering 8 items. If in addition she has cause to phone Glasgow fairly regularly and recognises 629 as a district code then this becomes a second chunk.

The job now demands a memory span of 6 items which many people can manage comfortably.

Different levels of memory

Memory is thought to involve three separate **interacting** levels as shown in figure 29.2.

Level 1

Stimuli from the outside world are continuously being perceived as sensory images by the brain. These impressions are very **short-lived** (e.g. 0.5 seconds for visual and 2 seconds for auditory) and only a few are selected and transferred to level 2.

Level 2 – short-term memory (STM)

Most of the information encoded into this second level of the system consists of **visual** and **auditory** images. However, the STM holds only a **limited** amount of information. The investigation into the short-term memory span on p 234, for example, establishes that only about seven items can be held at this level at one time (although this can be increased by chunking).

Not only does the STM have a limited capacity, in addition the items are held for a **short time**

235

(approximately 30 seconds). During this time, retrieval of items is very accurate. Thereafter they are either transferred to level 3 or **displaced and forgotten**.

Level 3 – Long-term memory (LTM)

This third level in the system is thought to be able to hold an **unlimited** amount of information. During encoding the items are organised into **categories** such as facts and episodes (declarative memories) and skills and habits (procedural memories). These are then stored for a long time, perhaps even permanently.

It must be stressed that this multi-level model of memory and how it works is probably an oversimplification. In addition, the three levels of memory should not be thought of as occupying three distinct regions of the brain. Much remains to be discovered about the mysteries of memory and how it actually functions.

Transfer of information between STM and LTM

A hypothetical representation of this process is shown in figure 29.3. Information is constantly being

transferred between the brain's two storage 'depots', the **STM** and the **LTM**. Although information is normally stored in the STM for only 30 seconds or less, it can be retained for longer if conscious effort is made (e.g. when the person is motivated and wants to remember). One way of doing this is by **rehearsal** (see p 237).

If, during its brief stay in the STM, an item is successfully **encoded** then this enables it to be transferred for **storage** in the LTM which has an enormous, perhaps unlimited, capacity. This item may later be **retrieved** from the LTM when required.

Once the item (e.g. the French words for the request 'Two coffees, please.') has been retrieved from the LTM and is back in the STM, it can be recalled into the conscious mind and put to use. In this case nerve impulses would pass to those parts of the brain responsible for language (see p 209). Once certain mental and motor operations had occurred, the words would be spoken to the French waiter patiently awaiting the person's order. (Discussion of the process of retrieval is continued on p 238.)

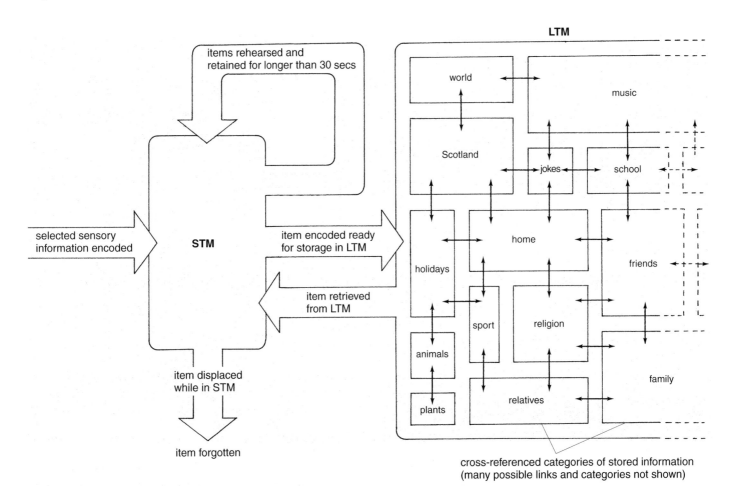

Figure 29.3 Transfer of information

Rehearsal

Rehearsal involves repeating to yourself (either silently or out loud) what you have just learned, over and over again. In addition to extending the length of time for which the information is held in the STM, rehearsal **facilitates its transfer** from STM to LTM.

Research shows that students who regularly stop and rehearse what they are reading (and trying to learn) are much more successful at committing the information to memory than students who read continuously and resist taking rehearsal breaks. Reciting in your own words what you have just read forces your attention (probably starting to wander) back to the material. Several short rehearsal breaks during the learning process are found to be more effective than one long rehearsal at the end of a marathon learning session.

Investigating the serial position effect

In this investigation, the tester informs the subjects that they will be required to memorise 20 fairly similar objects. The tester reveals the first object and allows the subjects to view it for 5 seconds. Object 1 is then removed and object 2 revealed for 5 seconds.

This procedure is repeated for the remaining objects. As soon as the last one has been removed, the subjects are invited to pick up their pencils and write down as many of the objects as they can recall in any order.

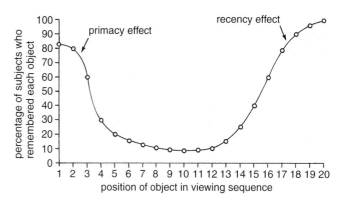

Figure 29.4 Serial position effect

Figure 29.4 shows a graph of a typical set of results for a group of 100 subjects. From these results it can be seen that recall is best for the objects shown at the end (**recency effect**), closely followed by those shown at the start (**primacy effect**). Those in the middle of the viewing sequence gain a very poor score. This memory pattern is called the **serial position effect**.

Explanation of serial position effect

Images of the first few objects can be remembered because during the experiment there has been enough time for them to have been well **rehearsed**. In many cases they have therefore become encoded and **transferred** to the **LTM** from where they can be retrieved at the end of the experiment.

The last 7 or so objects are remembered because images of them are still present in the **STM** and are quickly 'dumped' onto paper by the subjects as soon as they start writing. (If there is a one minute delay and rehearsal is prevented before subjects are allowed to write down the objects that they recall, the recency effect vanishes.)

Images of the objects in the middle of the sequence are not well retained by the vast majority of the subjects because, by the time these images enter the STM, it is already crowded. Many are therefore forgotten before they can be rehearsed, encoded and stored in the LTM.

Organisation

Consider the two lists of words in table 29.3. The words in list 2 are much easier to memorise than those in list 1 because the items have been organised into logical categories. Grouping items of information in an **organised** fashion increases their chance of being successfully encoded and transferred from STM to LTM.

The group headings ('fruit', 'seasons', 'family', etc.) act as **contextual cues** (see p 238) which facilitate the retrieval of the information from LTM to STM at a later stage. Thus organisation of material helps to transfer it in both directions.

list 1	list 2
apple	apple
skirt	orange
autumn	banana
father	pear
pear	spring
iron	summer
brother	autumn
summer	winter
jacket	mother
lead	father
trousers	sister
winter	brother
orange	copper
tin	lead
sister	iron
shirt	tin
spring	jacket
copper	shirt
banana	trousers
mother	skirt

Table 29.3 Effect of organisation

Elaboration of meaning

Elaboration is a further means of aiding the encoding and transfer of information from STM to LTM. It involves analysing the meaning of the item to be memorised and taking note of its various features and properties.

Let us imagine, for example, that you are trying to commit the idea 'cerebral hemisphere' to your LTM. You could try rehearsing 'cerebral hemisphere – important part of the brain' a few times and it might become encoded. However, as it stands, this information is sparse and lacking in interest. Therefore it will probably make little impression and is unlikely to be well retained.

Successful **long term retention** is much more likely if elaboration of meaning is employed, as shown in figure 29.5. By being analysed and elaborated, the idea 'cerebral hemisphere' becomes more interesting and meaningful, enabling it to make a long-lasting impression.

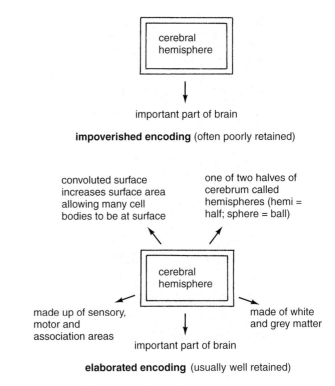

Figure 29.5 Elaboration of meaning

Classification of information in the LTM

The system of storage in the LTM is analogous to a filing cabinet of unlimited capacity, organised into **distinct categories** of information (see figure 29.3). As items are encoded and transferred to the LTM, they are classified and filed in the appropriate section(s).

Retrieval of items from the LTM

The LTM contains a vast and permanent store of remembered experience which is constantly being revised, reorganised and enlarged as new material flows into it.

When a piece of information needs to be called up and retrieved from the LTM, a search is mounted. This is aided by **contextual cues**. (A cue is a signal or reminder; contextual means relating to the conditions or circumstances that were present at the time when the information was encoded and committed to the LTM.) It is thought that a contextual cue somehow triggers off an impulse through a 'memory circuit' (see p 230).

If a memory has been stored under several different categories (e.g. dandelion might feature under 'plants', 'flowers', 'leaves', 'clocks', 'weeds', etc.) then it can be retrieved in various ways. This is because many contextual cues for it exist and lead to the different files relating to it. These can then be checked out to see if one contains the information being sought (e.g. names of common weeds with yellow flowers).

It is more difficult to retrieve a memory which has been filed under a few categories only, since it will have few contextual cues relating to it. Hence the beneficial effects of **organisation** and **elaboration** when trying to memorise information (see p 237 and 238).

A memory whose encoding in the LTM is accompanied by unusual and/or dramatic events (e.g. the person's wedding day) possesses powerful contextual cues. These enable the experience to be retrieved and recalled clearly throughout life.

Lapses in memory

Once information has been transferred to the LTM, it is stored permanently. In theory this means that it is never forgotten! So how can failure to recall some item that was once very well known, be explained?

It is thought that this is due to the fact that the contextual cues needed to lead to the information (and trigger the appropriate 'memory circuits') are **weak** or **incomplete**. Under such circumstances a search of the LTM produces incorrect recall or even draws a complete blank.

Tip-of-the-tongue state

An individual experiencing this frustrating state of affairs lacks sufficient contextual cues to recall the required information immediately. However, the person is armed with an adequate number of cues to narrow down the area of search and retrieve some related information (e.g. several words that are similar in certain ways to the elusive one). The person has the impression that the required information is 'on the tip of the tongue'.

Sometimes the related information leads slowly by a long roundabout route through various marginally related files in the LTM to the required information which suddenly 'flashes' into the conscious mind.

Mnemonic devices

A **mnemonic device** is a trick used to aid memory. Some take the form of easily remembered rhymes (e.g. Thirty days hath September, April, June and November...). Others depend for their success on a simple sentence (e.g. Every good boy deserves favour.) being memorised; the first letter of each word taken together make up the information to be remembered (e.g. E G B D F are the

musical notes on the lines of the treble clef in musical notation).

Some mnemonic devices depend on the formation of a bizarre or nonsensical association between a group of items to be remembered.

Books that claim to improve memory normally base their techniques on elaborate mnemonics. One such method instructs you to take a mental stroll through your home memorising a list of familiar items by making a visual image of each in its particular location. You must then work hard at rehearsing this list of say 30 items until they are firmly encoded in a particular sequence in your LTM. In theory you should then be able to memorise any list of 30 unrelated items by forming bizarre associations between them and the items on your 'mental stroll' list. However, this practice would seem to be especially onerous and wasteful of time unless the ability to memorise 30 items was, for some reason, of particular use.

Psychologists advocate **rehearsal**, **organisation** and **elaboration** as the most reliable methods of improving **encoding** into, and **retrieval** from, long-term memory.

Testing your knowledge

1. a) What is meant by the term *rehearsal* in relation to a piece of information to be memorised? (1)

   b) Suggest why rehearsal aids the transfer of information from the STM to the LTM. (1)

2. a) Explain the reasons for the *primacy* and *recency* effects found to occur during an investigation into the serial position effect. (2)

   b) Why should the 20 objects chosen to investigate the serial position effect be fairly similar? (1)

3. Explain the meaning of the terms *organisation* and *elaboration* in relation to the transfer of information from the STM to the LTM. (4)

4. a) Why is it easier to retrieve information from the LTM if its components were organised and elaborated prior to their transfer to the LTM? (1)

   b) Explain the *tip-of-the-tongue* state. (2)

   c) Give the meaning of the term *mnemonic device* and include an example in your answer. (2)

Applying your knowledge

1 In an investigation into memory span, 40 students were asked to listen to and then attempt to write down each of several series of letters, the first series containing three letters. The results are shown in figure 29.6.

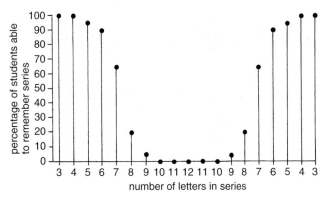

Figure 29.6

a) What relationship exists between the number of letters in a series and the percentage of students able to remember the series? (1)

b) (i) What was the best memory span recorded in this experiment?
   (ii) How many students possessed this memory span? (2)

c) (i) What was the poorest memory span recorded in this experiment?
   (ii) What percentage of students possessed this memory span? (2)

d) (i) Does presenting the series of letters in descending order of length produce a different set of results from presenting them in ascending order of length?
   (ii) Explain how you arrived at your answer to **(i)**. (2)

e) Give a reason for the adoption of each of the following design features in this investigation:
   (i) nonsense groups of letters used to make up the series rather than proper words;
   (ii) each series of letters read out by the same tester at a uniform speed;
   (iii) 40 students invited to take part rather than just a few. (3)

2 The plastic card used to release money from a bank's cash dispensing machine has a PIN (personal identification number) known only to the owner. Suggest why banks decided to give each PIN four digits. (2)

3 01034544423317 is the phone number of a hotel in the city centre of Seville, Spain, when phoned from Britain. Analysis of this series of numbers shows it to comprise:

international code	code for Spain	code for Seville	district of city	hotel number
010	34	54	442	3317

Imagine that this hotel is about to be telephoned from Britain by:

a) a person who has never phoned Spain before;

b) a travel agent who regularly phones Seville's city centre hotels. Predict which person will be faster at placing the call and explain your answer. (2)

4 In an experiment to investigate the effect of lack of rehearsal on memory, some students listened to a group of three unrelated letters being read out.

They were asked to try to recall the letters at three-second intervals but were asked to count backwards in threes from 99 (i.e. 99, 96, 93, etc.) during each of the intervals between recall attempts. Figure 29.7 shows the results.

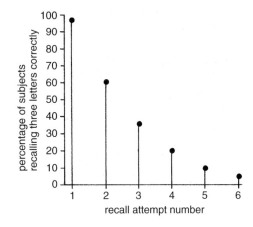

Figure 29.7

a) What was the purpose of asking students to count backwards in threes from 99 between recall attempts? (1)

b) (i) What percentage of students were able to correctly recall the three letters six seconds after attempt number 1?
   (ii) At which recall attempt did 80% of the students fail to recall the correct answer? (2)

Continued ➤

Applying your knowledge

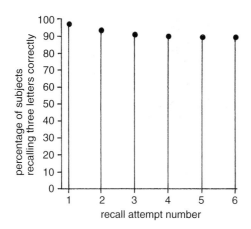

Figure 29.8

c) Figure 29.8 shows a graph of the results from the control experiment. In what way would the instructions given to the control subjects differ from those given to the subjects involved in the original experiment? (1)

d) **(i)** State the factor under investigation in the original experiment.
   (ii) What conclusion can be drawn about the effect of this factor?
   (iii) Suggest why this should be the case. (3)

5 The accompanying list a–h gives eight instructions which, according to experts, aid the processes of memory and learning if put into practice.

Rewrite them and complete the blanks using the following words: *attention, bizarre, groups, long, meaning, overlearn, recreation, repeating, rest, short, visual*. (11)

a) Pay close _____ to the information to be memorised.

b) Organise items to be learned into _____.

c) Rehearse items by _____ them over and over to yourself.

d) Elaborate the _____ of a difficult item.

e) Create a _____ image of a group of unrelated items (the more _____ the image the better).

f) _____ i.e. learn information well beyond the point of bare recall rather than risk underlearning it.

g) Spread the learning process over several _____ sessions rather than one _____ one.

h) Use breaks from study for _____ and _____.

6 Give an account of the factors that promote:

(i) the transfer of information from the STM to the LTM; (7)

(ii) the retrieval of stored information from the LTM. (3)

What you should know
(Chapters 28–29)

(See table 29.4 for word bank.)

1 _____ is the capacity to retain information and retrieve it when required.

2 Different types of memory exist: _____ memories ('facts') and _____ memories ('skills').

3 Evidence suggests that the _____ system of the brain is involved in the transfer of new declarative memories to their storage site in _____ lobes of the cerebrum. Other cerebral areas and the _____ are thought to be the sites responsible for procedural memories.

4 Each memory is thought to be held by a group of neurones which form a memory _____.

5 Evidence supports a molecular basis for memory. _____ disease (characterised by memory loss) is accompanied by the loss of _____-producing cells in the limbic system.

6 Neurones in the limbic system are rich in _____ receptors which allow nerve impulses to be transmitted through neurones thought to form memory circuits.

7 To become part of the memory, selected sensory images are first _____ and then _____. This information is later retrieved when required.

8 The _____ memory (STM) has a capacity limited to about 7 items which it holds for about 30 seconds. Short-term memory span can be increased by _____.

Continued ➤

What you should know
(Chapters 28–29)

9   The _____ memory (LTM) has an unlimited capacity. The information that it holds is organised into _____ and stored permanently.

10 Transfer of information from STM to LTM and its _____ from LTM at a later stage are aided by _____, _____ and organisation during encoding. Contextual _____ aid the retrieval of information from LTM.

acetylcholine	declarative	procedural
Alzheimer's	elaboration	rehearsal
categories	encoded	retrieval
cerebellum	limbic	short term
chunking	long term	stored
circuit	memory	temporal
cues	NMDA	

Table 29.4 Word bank for chapters 28–29

(30) Factors influencing development of behaviour

Maturation
Walking

In humans, **walking** is a natural process that normally begins between the ages of 9 and 15 months. A newly born baby is unable to walk because his or her legs cannot support the weight of his or her body. The activities that an infant can master gradually become more complicated as the nervous system develops and the process of myelination continues (see p 218). As the infant grows, a genetically 'preprogrammed' series of events occurs which leads eventually to the ability to walk. This behaviour pattern takes the form of an orderly sequence as shown in figure 30.1.

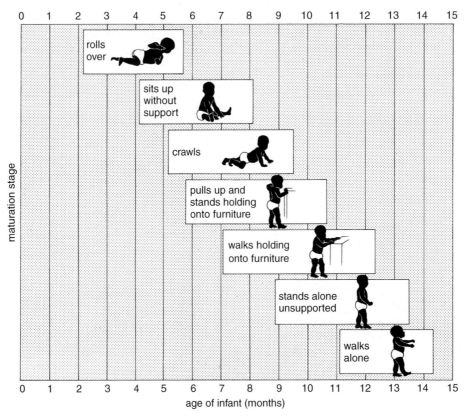

Figure 30.1 Maturation of walking

average age of infant	stage in development of speech
birth–6 months	Phase of crying and cooing.
6–12 months	Phase of babbling sounds (e.g. 'baba').
12–24 months	Production of definite sounds on recognising favourite objects and persons (e.g. 'mama').
2–3 years	Production of 2–3 word combinations (e.g. 'Where dada go?').
3–4 years	Creation of longer, more grammatical sentences (e.g. 'What's it for, Mummy?').
4+ years	Production of words and sentences of greater complexity as child's thinking processes develop.

Table 30.1 Maturation of speech

The diagram gives the results of a survey done on a large number of infants in a baby clinic. Each bar shows the range of age within which 95% of the infants were successfully performing the activity. Progression through such a sequence of inherited developmental stages is called **maturation**.

Further examples

All aspects of human development are influenced by maturation. For example growth of the fetus in the uterus, development of **speech** and acquisition of **cognitive abilities** (e.g. reasoning) are all found to follow a sequential unfolding of genetically controlled stages.

With respect to development of behaviour, maturation is thought to provide periods of optimum '**potential to learn**'. The rate at which the learning occurs is then promoted or limited by the genetic and environmental factors that affect the person.

Speech

Table 30.1 shows the biologically programmed sequence of events involved in the process of **speech development**.

Infants only become able to proceed from one stage to the next as they grow and develop. It is pointless to try to teach or train a child to perform a skill if their natural maturational level for that ability has not yet been reached.

Cognitive abilities

Cognitive abilities are higher mental skills which involve perception, intuition, thinking and reasoning. Table 30.2 lists some examples which illustrate that the acquisition of intellectual abilities of this type is dependent in part upon the process of maturation. For example, the average six-year-old's brain has reached a stage of development which can appreciate the ideas of mass and weight but

approximate age (years)	cognitive ability	explanation
0.5–2	object permanence	Child understands that an object (e.g. toy) continues to exist even if it can no longer be seen or touched.
2–5	egocentric thinking	Child thinks that the environment is an extension of self (e.g. if it rains while the child is out walking, child thinks their walking brings on the rain).
5–7	conservation	Child understands that the physical properties of substances remain the same even when their appearance changes (see figure 30.2 on p 244).
7–11	concrete operations	Child understands principle of reversibility (e.g. $3 \times 6 = 18$ and $18 \div 3 = 6$); child able to classify (e.g. organise objects into groups) and form a sequence (e.g. organise items into an order of increasing size).
11+	formal operations	Young person is able to deal with abstract ideas (e.g. this topic, justice, freedom, law and order, infinity, etc.); young person is able to test an hypothesis (untested idea or theory based on facts).

Table 30.2 Maturation of cognitive abilities

not volume (see figure 30.2). Intellectual development is also affected by **environment** and **inherited** factors.

Inheritance

The development of behaviour is in part influenced by the person's **genotype**. Normal development of the nervous system (and of human behaviour) is dependent upon possession of the appropriate **genes** which code for the **proteins** involved in the production of nerve cells, neurotransmitters and neuroreceptors. Inherited disorders which affect the nervous system also affect behaviour.

Huntington's chorea

Approximately 1 in 20 000 people in Britain suffer from this inherited disorder caused by a single dominant mutant allele. The condition is characterised by **premature death of neurones** in certain regions of the brain and a decreased production of neurotransmitters. As the process of neural degeneration continues it normally leads to:

◆ movement disorder (lack of normal muscular contraction);

◆ behavioural disturbance;

◆ personality change;

◆ mental deterioration (dementia);

◆ decrease in brain weight by 20–30%;

◆ death of sufferer in middle life.

The symptoms of this condition do not appear until the affected person is about 38 years old. This means that the sufferer has often unwittingly passed the mutant allele on to many of his or her offspring before discovering that he or she is affected (see also chapter 14).

Phenylketonuria (PKU)

Approximately 1 in 10 000 people in Britain suffer from this inherited disorder (inborn error of metabolism) caused by a single recessive mutant allele.

The sufferer is unable to make the enzyme which converts the amino acid phenylalanine to tyrosine. This results in **excess phenylalanine** accumulating and some of it being converted to **toxins**. These inhibit one or more of the enzymes which control biochemical pathways in brain cells. The brain fails to develop properly resulting in the person having severe learning difficulties.

Nowadays PKU children are identified at birth and put on a special diet which allows normal development of the brain (see also p 105).

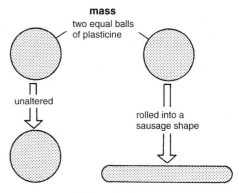

The average 4-year old insists that the sausage contains more plasticine than the ball. The average 5-year old understands that change in shape has not changed amount of matter (mass)

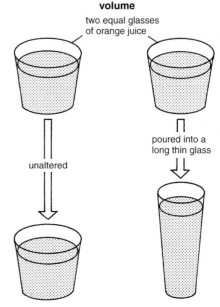

The average 5-year old insists that the sausage will be heavier than the ball. The average 6-year old grasps the idea that change in shape has not changed weight.

The average 6-year old insists that the long thin glass contains more orange juice. The average 7-year old realises that change in shape has not altered volume

Figure 30.2 Conservation of physical properties of a substance

type of intelligence ability	description of skill
linguistic	Understanding and use of language.
logical-mathematical	Manipulation of numbers and solution of mathematical problems.
spatial	Handling of visual relationships and construction of designs.
musical	Appreciation and creation of musical compositions.
bodily-kinesthetic	Movement of body in a controlled way to great athletic or artistic effect.
psychological	Understanding of oneself and possession of insight into other people.

Table 30.3 Intelligence abilities

Intelligence

It is impossible to define intelligence to the satisfaction of everyone. Intelligence can be regarded as the capacity to develop a wide range of intellectual skills. The more highly these can be developed, the more intelligent the person.

It is thought that several **distinct intelligence abilities** exist. Some of these are shown in table 30.3. This list fails to exhaust all of the possibilities. There are many other abilities such as mechanical aptitude, colour sense, social skills, sense of humour, etc. which could also be included.

Every human being possesses a unique combination of these intelligence abilities and has something valuable to contribute to fellow human beings.

Intelligence testing

An intelligence **test** sets out to provide a scientific measurement of a child's intelligence. In theory the test aims to be objective and reliable; in practice these aims are difficult to achieve since intelligence itself cannot be defined objectively.

A standard intelligence test consists of items which are intended to be **culture-free** or **culture-fair**. Figure 30.3 shows an example of a logical-mathematical item which is regarded as being culture-fair in that all children being tested would be equally familiar with the idea of the numbers involved.

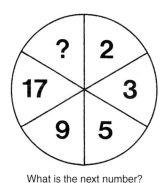

What is the next number?

Figure 30.3 Example from an intelligence test

In the past the result of a test (containing a mixture of items) was taken as an indication of the child's mental age. For example, a 10-year-old child able to complete questions solved by most 12-year-olds would be regarded as having a mental age of 12. Measurement of intelligence was then expressed as an **intelligence quotient (IQ)**. This was calculated using the formula:

$$IQ = \frac{\text{mental age}}{\text{chronological age}} \times 100$$

Thus the child referred to in the above example would have an IQ of 120 (12/10 × 100). A person's IQ is now worked out by matching his or her performance in the test with the appropriate score in the set of performance norms accompanying the test.

Cautious interpretation of results

It must be remembered that an IQ score only represents how well or badly a person has performed in a standard intelligence test compared with others of the same age. In addition, the test normally measures only the first three types of ability listed in table 30.3 and gives no indication of the person's other intellectual qualities. It is important therefore that the results of IQ tests be interpreted with caution since they reflect only in part the person's actual intelligence.

Environment
Twin studies

The development of human behaviour is influenced by **genetic** and **environmental** factors. Both of these factors are largely the same for monozygotic ('identical') twins reared together. However, only the inherited factors remain the same for monozygotic twins reared apart. Such twins provide scientists with an opportunity to investigate the influence of the environment on the development of behaviour.

Correlation

When two things (e.g. factors, theories, objects, etc.) match one another exactly they are said to show **complete correlation**. This is expressed numerically as 1.00. Incomplete correlations are expressed in decimal fractions of 1.00.

Twin studies and intelligence

If intelligence depended solely on inherited factors then identical twins would be expected to be equally intelligent (and show complete correlation of IQ scores) whether raised together in the same environment or apart in different environments.

Figure 30.4 shows a summary of the results from a survey of case studies of IQ correlations for biological relatives. For each category of biological relative a bar representing the actual average correlation is accompanied by a bar representing the correlation expected if heredity alone were responsible for IQ (and environment played no part). Allowing for the reservations stated above, let us assume that IQ scores give a fairly accurate indication of intelligence.

A comparison of groups A and B reveals that the IQs of monozygotic ('identical') twins reared together correlate

more closely than the IQs of monozygotic twins reared apart. Since the **variable factor** in this comparison is **environment** (and not heredity), this suggests that environmental factors do play a part in the development of intelligence. This is further confirmed by a comparison of groups D and E.

A comparison of groups A and C reveals that the IQs of monozygotic twins reared together correlate more closely than the IQs of dizygotic ('non identical') twins reared together. Since the **variable factor** in this comparison is **heredity** (and not environment) this suggests that inherited factors also play a part in the development of intelligence.

However, it is impossible to separate and give accurate weight to the actual contributions made by inheritance and environment on the development of intelligence and human behaviour. Each person inherits a unique hereditary base upon which a set of controlled and uncontrolled environmental factors act. This results in each person being physically, mentally and intellectually different from everyone else.

Abnormal behaviour and twin studies
Alcoholism

Studies amongst monozygotic twins show that where one is an alcoholic, the chance is no greater than 1 in 2 that the other will also become an alcoholic.

Although alcoholism tends to run in families, it is thought that this is due mostly to **imitation** and social learning. This type of behaviour would seem to result

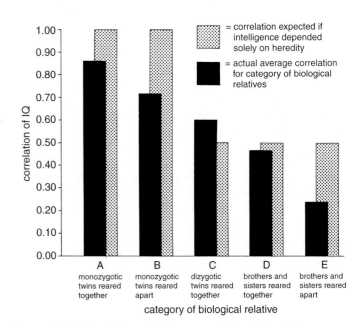

Figure 30.4 Correlation of IQ amongst biological relatives

largely (if not exclusively) from the effect of **environmental** factors.

Schizophrenia

This condition is characterised by severe personality disorders often involving delusions and hallucinations. Amongst dizygotic twins, if one is schizophrenic the chance of the other becoming schizophrenic is slightly greater than amongst unrelated people.

Amongst monozygotic twins the chance is many times higher suggesting a major influence by **genetic** factors in the development of this disorder.

Inter-relationships between factors

All forms of human behaviour are influenced by **inherited**, **maturational** and **environmental** factors which are closely inter-related. The particular set of genes inherited by an individual provides the genetic potential for developmental stages; the environment then interacts with the person's genotype producing his or her phenotype.

The ability to develop **speech**, for example, is biologically preprogrammed (see also p 243) but the actual language learned (e.g. Spanish, Japanese, Urdu, etc.) is determined by the environmental culture in which the child is raised. The proficiency with which the person is eventually able to use the language depends on the interaction of **environmental** influences (e.g. access to educational resources) and **genetic** factors (e.g. inheritance of alleles of genes that result in the development of superior linguistic skills) as indicated in figure 30.5.

Similarly the development of intelligence, behaviour and many other aspects of a person's physical and mental growth are influenced by the close **interaction** between heredity and environment. It is for this reason that growing children need an environment which provides adequate support and stimulation in order to realise the full physical and intellectual potential that they have inherited in their genotype.

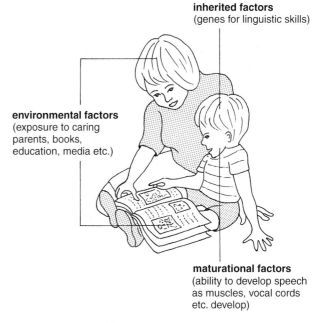

inherited factors (genes for linguistic skills)

environmental factors (exposure to caring parents, books, education, media etc.)

maturational factors (ability to develop speech as muscles, vocal cords etc. develop)

Figure 30.5 Factors affecting language development

Testing your knowledge

1 Identify THREE types of intellectual skill that contribute towards intelligence and give a brief description of each. (6)

2 What is meant by the term *complete correlation*? (1)

3 a) If intelligence depended solely upon inherited factors, what degree of correlation of IQ would be expected to exist for monozygotic twins (regardless of their environment)? (1)

   b) (i) What difference in degree of correlation of IQ is found to exist when a comparison is made of monozygotic twins reared together with others reared apart?

      (ii) What tentative conclusion about the influence of the environment on behaviour can be drawn from these twin studies? (2)

Applying your knowledge

1 a) Arrange the following stages involved in the development of walking by a child into the correct sequence. (1)
   A stands alone unsupported.
   B pulls up and stands holding onto furniture.
   C walks alone.
   D crawls.
   E rolls over.
   F walks holding onto furniture.
   G sits up without support.

   b) (i) What general name is given to progression through this type of preprogrammed sequence of developmental stages?
      (ii) Give TWO further examples of this found in growing children. (3)

Continued ➤

Applying your knowledge

c) State the average age at which a child is able to appreciate the concept of
  (i) mass;
  (ii) weight;
  (iii) volume. (3)

2 An experiment was set up to investigate the effect of training children beyond their natural maturational level for a certain ability using a pair of identical twin girls.

Four-year-old Fiona and Susan were taught separately to memorise and repeat a number of digits spoken slowly by the experimenter. Figure 30.6 shows a graph of the results from the experiment.

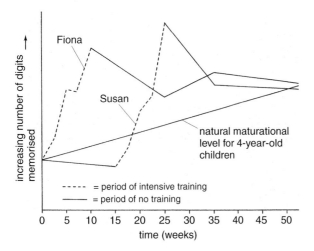

Figure 30.6

a) Which twin received training first? (1)

b) **(i)** Which twin showed more improvement as a result of training?
  (ii) Suggest why. (2)

c) **(i)** What happened to the gains made by both twins when training stopped?

(ii) Give a possible explanation for your answer to **(i)** using the term *natural maturational level* in your answer. (2)

d) Some experts claim that premature training, if frustrating and unrewarding, can do more harm than good to a child. State whether you agree or disagree and justify your choice. (1)

3 Table 30.4 shows the results from four surveys investigating the incidence of schizophrenia amongst twins.

a) What is schizophrenia? (1)

b) Calculate the average percentage of twin pairs affected with schizophrenia when the twins are
  (i) monozygotic;
  (ii) dizygotic. (2)

c) What conclusion about the part played by inherited factors can be drawn from these findings? (1)

d) Why is a study of monozygotic twins reared together *especially* helpful in this type of study? (1)

e) Which survey's data do you consider to be the
  (i) most reliable;
  (ii) least reliable?
  (iii) Explain your choices for **(i)** and **(ii)**. (4)

4 '*Like love, intelligence is highly valued but difficult to define.*' Briefly discuss the truth in this statement. (2)

5 Excess phenylalanine is normally converted to tyrosine by the enzyme phenylalanine hydroxylase in the human body. In the absence of this enzyme the person suffers the disorder phenylketonuria (PKU).

survey	monozygotic twins		dizygotic twins	
	number of twin pairs	% of affected twin pairs	number of twin pairs	% of affected twin pairs
1	21	66.6	60	4.6
2	41	68.3	101	14.9
3	41	76.0	115	14.0
4	268	85.1	685	14.5

Table 30.4

Continued ➤

Applying your knowledge

	test group		
	A	**B**	**C**
dietary details	Minimum supply of normal food containing enzyme inhibitor plus extra phenylalanine.	Minimum supply of normal food containing enzyme inhibitor.	Minimum supply of normal food.

Table 30.5

In an investigation to study PKU under laboratory conditions, scientists used 120 normal, healthy young rats. These were divided into 3 groups and fed the diets indicated in table 30.5. The enzyme inhibitor used on groups A and B acts on the enzyme phenylalanine hydroxylase, thereby creating 'PKU models'. Random samples of 10 rats from each group were tested at 5-day intervals giving the results shown in table 30.6.

a) (i)   State the means by which the scientists overcame the problem that PKU does not occur naturally amongst rats.
    (ii) Explain how their technique was expected to work. (2)

b) (i)   Which group of rats failed to show proper development of brain tissue?
    (ii) Give a possible explanation for this effect.
    (iii) Would it be valid to conclude that this group of rats had undergone a *decrease* in brain mass? Explain your answer. (4)

c) What conclusion can be drawn about the effect of the inhibitor only, on the development of the brain? (1)

d) (i)   Which group of rats gained most overall weight during the experiment?
    (ii) Suggest why the other two groups failed to gain as much weight. (2)

e) Explain why as many as 10 rats are tested at each 5-day interval and why the 10 were chosen at *random*. (1)

6 Give an account of the factors that affect the development of behaviour. (10)

		A		B		C	
		body mass (g)	**brain mass (g)**	**body mass (g)**	**brain mass (g)**	**body mass (g)**	**brain mass (g)**
number of days on diet	0	60.5	1.46	60.6	1.41	60.3	1.43
	5	61.2	1.44	62.3	1.49	85.7	1.51
	10	63.7	1.48	65.8	1.58	122.1	1.57
	15	72.1	1.41	71.9	1.65	151.9	1.64
	20	84.9	1.43	83.7	1.68	180.4	1.67

Table 30.6

What you should know
(Chapter 30)

(See table 30.7 for word bank.)

1 Progression through a genetically preprogrammed sequence of developmental stages which leads to the development of _____, speech, cognitive abilities, etc. is called _____ .

2 Development of behaviour is in part influenced by the person's _____ (certain genes are needed to code for the proteins involved in the production of nerve cells, _____ and neuroreceptors).

3 Development of behaviour is in part influenced by the _____ . Studies of _____ twins reared apart allow scientists to investigate the influence of the environment on _____ .

4 Intelligence can be regarded as the capacity to develop a wide range of _____ skills. Measurement of _____ is attempted using tests, the results of which are expressed as an intelligence _____ (IQ). Studies of monozygotic _____ show that IQ is affected by both _____ and environmental factors.

5 All forms of human behaviour are influenced by inherited, maturational and environmental factors.

development	intellectual	neurotransmitters
environment	intelligence	quotient
genetic	maturation	twins
genotype	monozygotic	walking

Table 30.7 Word bank for chapter 30

(31) Importance of infant attachment

Communication and social behaviour

Humans are **social** animals. The vast majority prefer to live in communities rather than lead a solitary existence. To operate successfully the members of a group must be able to **communicate** with one another. Such social behaviour involves transmitting and receiving information using **signs** and **signals** (e.g. verbal, written and body language). Communication between humans begins at birth and continues throughout life.

Infant attachment

In humans the period of dependency of the infant upon the adult members of the species is a very lengthy one. Under normal circumstances nature provides the newly born infant with a mother (and/or other primary carer) who is able to satisfy the baby's needs.

The newborn baby's activities such as suckling, clinging and crying, help to trigger in the mother a desire to protect and care for the child. As she does, a strong emotional tie develops between the baby and the mother. The tie that binds the baby to the carer is called **infant attachment**.

At first, attachment is **indiscriminate** on the baby's part but as the months go by the baby narrows down its

interest to selected people. **Specific** attachment to the mother (and a few other carers) begins at about 6–7 months. As specific attachment develops, indiscriminate attachment weakens. This is shown in figure 31.1 where attachment is measured as the amount of protest shown by the baby on being separated from the carer.

For many years it was thought that babies became attached to their parents principally because the parents

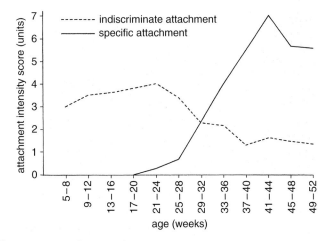

Figure 31.1 Infant attachment

provide **food**. However, in recent years, the additional importance of **contact comfort** has become appreciated.

Contact comfort

This was first demonstrated experimentally using infant monkeys exposed to two types of substitute mother. The first 'mother' was constructed of bare wire; the second 'mother' was made of the same wire covered in thick, soft towelling (see figure 31.2).

Figure 31.2 Contact comfort with cloth 'mother'

In one experiment, only the bare wire mother supplied food. However, once the infant monkeys had finished feeding they spent much more of their time clinging to the cloth mother than the bare one. They always ran to the cloth mother when frightened. Cuddling the cloth mother's soft towelling material calmed the infants down.

These experiments demonstrate a high level need for **close bodily contact** and the sensation of physical well-being and safety. Contact comfort similarly plays a basic role in establishing attachment between a human infant and his or her primary carer.

Importance of infant attachment

The long period of dependency on the parent(s) provides the infant with a **secure base** from which to operate. The child can explore the environment, all the time safe in the knowledge that the parent is present as a haven of safety to be returned to at the merest hint of danger.

During these explorations the infant will come across many opportunities for learning. The number and variety of these and level of stimulation that they provide will depend upon what the environment to which he or she is exposed has to offer. A sense of safety is needed in order that **social skills** and **cognitive abilities** can begin to develop. A feeling of security at this stage is also

especially important to promote the early development of **trust**.

Infant attachment is of fundamental importance because it provides the basis for social, linguistic and intellectual skills to develop and be built upon for the rest of life.

Effects of deprivation

In a variation of the experiment illustrated in figure 31.2, some infant monkeys were denied access to the cloth mother. Such **deprivation** of contact comfort led to the development of disturbed adults. Some were over-aggressive, others withdrawn and uncommunicative and all became inadequate parents. Human infants who receive plenty of food and warmth but are denied contact comfort also exhibit maladjusted behaviour.

Children who suffer **social** deprivation (e.g. isolation caused by separation from loved ones) are prevented from forming social attachments. In the absence of such attachments, the deprived infant misses out on many of the opportunities which should be triggering the development of essential communication skills and abilities.

Strange situation

In order to study infant attachment and determine its type and quality, a method called the 'strange situation' was devised. It involves seven episodes (each lasting three minutes) as follows:

◆ A mother (or primary carer) brings the baby into an unfamiliar room supplied with toys.

◆ A stranger enters the room and after a few moments tries to play with the infant.

◆ The mother leaves the baby with the stranger.

◆ The mother returns and plays with the child while the stranger leaves.

◆ The mother leaves the baby alone.

◆ The stranger returns.

◆ The mother returns.

This series of episodes allows hidden observers to study the behaviour of the baby a) with the mother, b) with the stranger and c) alone. Table 31.1 shows the different categories of children identified by the experts.

Experts are now of the opinion that sensitive, perceptive, responsive mothers create happily attached, **secure** infants. On the other hand, **insecurely** attached infants who are deprived of normal social contact, affection and cuddling, suffer long-lasting **ill effects**.

The period of dependency in humans is so lengthy that some of the problems resulting from early deprivation can be, in part, overcome if tackled in time. Young children who have suffered neglect and isolation as infants do respond, in most cases, to love, care and attention. They do show marked progress in their social development after such an unpromising start.

However, it is debatable whether they ever reach the level of social competence that they would have attained had they been allowed to form a loving and long-lasting attachment to their primary carer during infancy.

		type of attachment		
		secure	insecure	
			detached (avoidant)	resistant
examples of baby's behaviour during the 'strange situation'	response to departure of mother	Displays major distress.	Displays indifference or mild distress.	Displays major distress.
	response to presence of stranger in absence of mother	Resists offers of comfort from stranger.	Accepts comfort from stranger if required.	Resists offers of comfort from stranger.
	response to return of mother	Goes to mother immediately for comfort and then calms down and returns to play.	Ignores mother or approaches her looking away.	Both seeks and resists comfort (e.g. approaches her to be picked up but then struggles to be released again).
psychologists' interpretation from the study of many case histories		Baby is more attached to mother than to stranger. This situation is thought to arise because the mother is capable, demonstrative of her love and sensitive to the baby's needs. (She can often interpret these from the baby's various forms of crying.)	Baby treats mother and stranger equally. This situation is thought to arise because the mother is inept and insensitive to the baby's needs, though not rejecting him or her. (Often the mother lacks perception and does not know how to relieve the baby's distress.)	Baby is more attached to mother but in an erratic way. This situation is thought to arise because the mother tends to be often irritated by the baby. On occasions she is insensitive to the baby's needs and, by expressing controlled anger towards the baby, is rejecting him or her.

Table 31.1 Results of the 'strange situation'

• Testing your knowledge •

1 What is *social behaviour*? (1)

2 a) In general what is meant by the term *infant attachment*? (2)

   b) Give ONE difference between *indiscriminate* and *specific* attachment. (2)

3 a) In addition to food, what other factor, provided by the primary carer, is important in the development of infant attachment? (1)

   b) Give a method of measuring infant attachment. (1)

   c) Suggest TWO possible effects on individuals in later life of social deprivation during infancy. (2)

4 a) Name TWO forms of insecure infant attachment. (2)

   b) Describe briefly the way in which psychologists believe that each of these arises. (4)

Applying your knowledge

1 Figure 31.3 shows a graph of the results from studies of two different types of infant attachment in human infants.

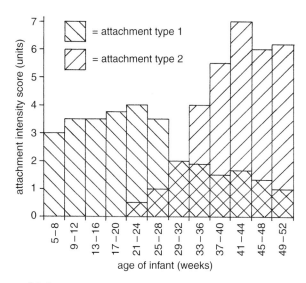

Figure 31.3

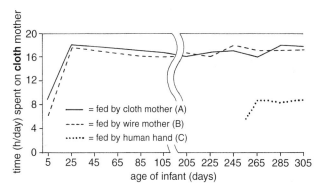

Figure 31.4

a) (i) Identify each type of attachment referred to in the graph.
(ii) State the relationship that exists between them as indicated by the graph. (2)

b) (i) At what age were the two forms of attachment found to be equal in intensity?
(ii) Which form had gained the upper hand four weeks later?
(iii) Predict the intensity score of indiscriminate attachment at age two years.
(iv) Why is specific attachment of survival value to an infant? (4)

2 During the Second World War, there were so many homeless infants in some countries that orphanages became overcrowded. In some the babies received little more than food and basic hygiene; in others the staff managed to find time to hold the babies *every* day and give them a little physical attention. Predict which type of orphanage was found to have the higher infant mortality rate. Suggest why. (2)

3 The accompanying graphs and data refer to experiments involving infant monkeys and cloth and wire 'mothers' as described in the text on p 251.

Figures 31.4 and 31.5 give graphs of the results of experiments comparing time spent by infants on different types of 'mother'.

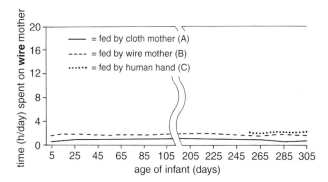

Figure 31.5

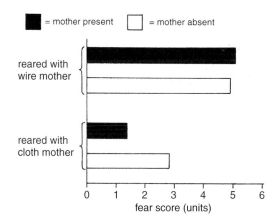

Figure 31.6

Figure 31.6 shows the results from an experiment where the infant monkeys were exposed to a room containing unfamiliar objects. Their fear score was based on activities such as crying, crouching, rocking and thumb-sucking.

A further experiment called the curiosity test made use of young monkeys who had been reared from birth in the presence of both cloth and wire

Continued ➤

Applying your knowledge

'mothers'. Each monkey was kept in a cage which contained a lever. When this was pressed a window opened for 15 seconds to reveal one of the four views listed in table 31.2. The number of lever presses scored by a particular view was taken to represent the interest level of the young monkey (see table 31.2).

a) (i) Study figures 31.4 and 31.5 with respect to the 25-day-old monkeys of group A and state the amount of time per day spent on each type of mother. (1)

   (ii) Make a generalisation about the type of mother and the time spent by infant monkeys in contact with 'her'. (1)

   (iii) Is the behaviour that you described in your answer to **(ii)** affected by the infant monkeys' source of food? Explain how you arrived at your answer. (1)

b) (i) Which group of monkeys had not known a monkey 'mother' during the first eight months of their life? (1)

   (ii) In what way did their behaviour differ from the other groups when they finally met the two types of 'mother'? (1)

view from window	average number of lever presses per 4-hour session
wire 'mother'	602
live adult monkey	855
empty chamber	597
cloth 'mother'	839

Table 31.2

c) (i) Study figure 31.6 and identify the type of 'mother' that offered no comfort to a frightened young monkey. (1)

   (ii) Describe the effect that absence of the cloth 'mother' had on the fear score of an infant exposed to an unfamiliar environment. (1)

   (iii) Compare your answer to **(ii)** with the fear score of an infant reared with a wire 'mother' and suggest a reason for the difference. (1)

d) With reference to all four views listed in table 31.2, draw TWO conclusions from the data about the interest level of young monkeys. (2)

(32) Effect of communication

Communication is the exchange of information, facts, feelings, ideas and opinions between people. Most people spend a large part of their time each day communicating (at various levels) with other people. To do so they make use of **verbal** and **non-verbal** means of contact.

Non-verbal communication in infants

Parent-infant bonding

Bonding is the name given to the strong emotional tie that forms between parents and their newborn baby. (Attachment is the strong emotional tie that the baby feels towards its primary carers – see p 250.)

Figure 32.1 shows the results from a survey in which a large number of mothers of newborn babies were asked to indicate the side on which they normally held their infant. The majority of mothers (whether left- or right-

handed) were found to hold their baby with the left arm, pressing the baby against the heart. It is possible that heart beat offers a **familiar rhythm** and comforts the infant.

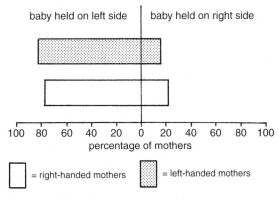

Figure 32.1 Holding the baby to one side

The newborn baby's means of communication, e.g. **crying, clinging** and **suckling**, help to trigger in the mother a desire to protect and provide for the child. When breast-feeding can be established easily it provides a satisfying experience to both mother and infant and strengthens the bond between them. However, if the baby is not a strong suckler or the mother has insufficient milk then the baby's demands may lead to tension and anxiety. Under these circumstances bottle-feeding will satisfy all the baby's nutritional needs.

Smiling in infants

Before long, the baby is capable of taking part in a non-verbal dialogue based on sounds and visual signals such as **smiling**. Smiling occurs long before it can be considered a genuine social activity. At first some internal stimulus creates smiling. Four-week-old babies smile even when no one else is present.

By the second month, smiling occurs in response to various pleasant stimuli from the external environment and indicates a feeling of well-being. At about six months, smiling becomes a **selective social** act normally reserved for the mother (and other close members of the family) whom the baby recognises.

Smiling is important because it makes the baby especially appealing and lovable thereby strengthening the bond between the carers and the baby. This is of **survival value** since it helps to ensure that the baby (who is almost totally helpless at this stage) will receive the food, care and attention that he or she needs.

Sounds

As the infant grows older, an increased 'vocabulary' of sounds (and signals) develops between the baby and the parents. This gradually leads to the development of **speech** (see p 243).

Testing your knowledge

1 a) In general what is meant by the term *communication* in relation to human social behaviour? (1)

   b) Identify the TWO types of communication. (2)

2 a) What is parent-infant *bonding*? (1)

   b) State TWO means by which a newborn infant communicates with its primary carer. (2)

   c) Why is smiling by an infant of survival value? (2)

Non-verbal communication in adults

In addition to communicating verbally, humans transmit a great deal of information to one another through **non-verbal** communication. On some occasions this reinforces the verbal messages; on others it adds to the information being transmitted. It may even send emotional messages that contradict the spoken word. **Non-verbal** communication comes in many forms, some of which are included in the following examples.

Facial expressions

In addition to being an effective means of reinforcing parent-infant bonding, **smiling** is also an important form of non-verbal communication. It often indicates pleasure shared by the people exchanging the smiles.

Many other facial expressions are also used to act as indicators of emotions. A few are shown in figure 32.2. It is interesting to note in particular the varied use to which the eyes and mouth are put to convey these non-verbal messages.

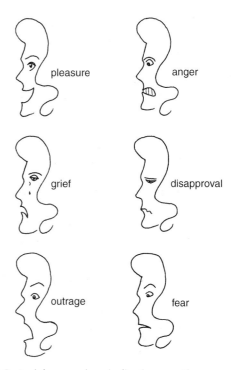

Figure 32.2 Facial expressions indicating emotion

Cartoonists are especially skilful at employing facial expressions to communicate **attitudes** and **emotions** essential to the understanding of a joke (see figure 32.3).

Surveys show that on average women are better than men at correctly recognising the emotion represented by a facial expression.

Figure 32.3 Cartoonist's use of facial expressions

"Don't hurt him!"

Looking as signalling

In addition to various eye movements such as eyes popping, eyes narrowing etc., the eyes are used to convey **signals** by simply looking at another person in a meaningful way. For example **winking** at someone only slightly known to you might indicate friendliness (or overfriendliness!) and the wish to become better acquainted. On the other hand, winking discreetly at a good friend in the company of others, might indicate the mutual enjoyment of a private joke.

When the process of looking normally at another person continues for a period of time beyond that required for routine information-gathering, the signals become loaded with further meaning. Consider an individual (e.g. male person A in figure 32.4) who wants to make contact with another individual (e.g. female person B). One way of indicating this is for A to catch B's eye. If, in return, B wishes to signal that she is not interested in making contact, she will avoid his gaze. Then A will either give up or persist. If he persists, B may then decide to adopt an angry defiant stare to signal rejection.

On the other hand, B may wish to signal that she does want to make contact with A and therefore will allow him to catch her eye. This may lead to a conversation.

During conversation, the participants take turns at speaking. As the speaker (say B) comes to the end of her turn, she will tend to look A in the eye more often than she did while speaking. The speaker, who is probably not conscious of doing this, is looking for confirmation of the listener's interest and is giving him a signal that his turn to speak is about to arrive.

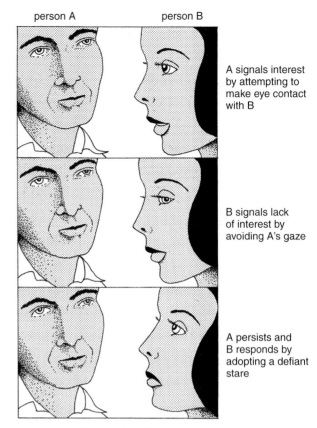

person A   person B

A signals interest by attempting to make eye contact with B

B signals lack of interest by avoiding A's gaze

A persists and B responds by adopting a defiant stare

Figure 32.4 Looking as signalling

Research shows that the more the speaker manages to meet the listener's gaze during the conversation, the more likely the listener will be to warm to the speaker and believe in what is being said. A speaker unable to meet the listener's gaze during a conversation tends to give the impression (rightly or wrongly) that they have something to hide and are not completely trustworthy.

Eye contact

The eyes are also used to communicate information by the length of time that they are allowed to continue making contact with those of another person. This maintenance of gaze between two people is called **eye contact**.

People who are in a close relationship exchange glances and meet one another's direct gaze much more often than people who are strangers. Extended eye contact is one method by which people communicate sexual interest in one another. Therefore strangers (who wish to remain strangers) feel embarrassed if eye contact extends beyond a mere exchange of glances and tend to play safe by avoiding unnecessary eye contact.

Body language

Often people are unaware of the extent to which they use their bodies to communicate with one another

posture	suggested attitude
sprawled back in easy chair with legs spread	relaxed
sitting up stiffly with legs together	tense
standing with feet apart and arms akimbo	confrontational
slumped forward in chair with arms folded	bored or sad
lying curled in 'fetal' position	frightened

Table 32.1 Communication by posture

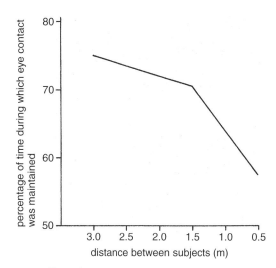

Figure 32.5 Effect of physical proximity on eye contact

non-verbally. Such **body language** is expressed by posture, gestures and certain other activities.

Several examples of **posture** and the possible attitude of the person adopting the bodily position are given in table 32.1.

Some **gestures** have definite meaning. Beckoning someone forward, nodding the head and pointing, all give clear signals. Other gestures indicate emotional states of mind. For example, continuous drumming of the fingers or fidgeting suggests tension or boredom; wringing of the hands indicates anguish; clenched fists signal pent up anger. Under certain circumstances, folding of the arms suggests squaring up in preparation for a verbal confrontation; under other circumstances, it suggests resignation or withdrawal from a situation.

Some people engage in certain activities which give an indication of their state of mind. Nail-biting and hair-chewing are outward signs of nervous tension or stress.

Personal space

Within each culture there is a generally accepted **distance** which two people keep between them while conducting a normal conversation. Increase in this distance may suggest dislike or even repugnance between the two participants; decrease in the distance may indicate sexual attraction or aggression (i.e. invasion of someone's **'personal space'** – the invisible territorial 'bubble' that surrounds each human body).

Effect of physical proximity on eye contact

In an experiment, a group of female volunteers each agreed to take part in three brief interviews with a female stranger who would be sitting at a different distance from the volunteer each time.

The interviewer had been trained to stare continuously at the volunteer during each interview. Each volunteer's

percentage eye contact was measured for each interview. The results are shown as a graph in figure 32.5.

As distance between the two people decreased, the amount of eye contact also decreased. At a distance of 0.5 m the two people were physically and psychologically much **closer** than the generally accepted level for strangers. They were within the region associated with aggression or sexual attraction. In each case the specially trained interviewer continued to stare while talking; the volunteer appeared uncomfortable and embarrassed and tried to avoid making eye contact.

Universal understanding

Each culture has its own 'vocabulary' of non-verbal communication. For example, sticking out the tongue is a sign of rudeness in Europe but is taken to mean an apology in China. However, generally speaking, most people have little difficulty recognising emotions expressed by members of another culture.

Non-verbal communication allows people to convey emotions and attitudes (such as happiness, grief, anger, etc.) which are universally understood. However, the onlooker must be wary of attempting too precise an interpretation. Crying, for example, can mean rage, grief, joy or even a mixture of all three. Interpretations based on several signals are more reliable than those based on one isolated and perhaps exaggerated feature.

Verbal communication

Mode of delivery

Tone, accent, emphasis, speed of delivery and timing of speech are **auditory signals** which depend on spoken language for their existence. They often indicate the person's frame of mind. A monotonous voice suggests fatigue and boredom; loudness can indicate anger; high speed often signals excitement or nervousness.

Language

A **language** is a system that combines basic sounds (in themselves meaningless) into **spoken words** usually also represented by **written symbols**. These sounds and symbols represent information that can then be arranged into simple categories (e.g. words) and more complex hierarchies (e.g. phrases, sentences and paragraphs). Since the sounds and symbols have meaning to the members of the society in question, they enable its members to express thoughts and feelings and convey information to one another. The ability to make sophisticated use of language is one of the distinguishing features which makes much of our behaviour unique and which sets us apart from other animals.

Production and comprehension

The possession of a language enables humans to manipulate and sort out information (represented by symbols) into ordered groupings (e.g. sentences). For the language to remain 'alive', the members of the society must **produce** and **comprehend** it, as shown in the simple example in figure 32.6.

Transfer of information

On a short term basis, language allows humans to convey to one another the information necessary for successful day-to-day living. We are able, for example, to request our basic needs, express feelings about others and handle a variety of interpersonal situations. We soon learn how to employ certain **linguistic strategies** to advantage. For example, adopting a friendly tone of voice, speaking clearly and not too quickly, varying the tone of voice and listening to the other person's point of view, are all techniques employed by good communicators.

On a long term basis, language allows the **transfer** and **receipt** of information. For most people in Britain this occurs during 11 or more years of schooling often followed by several years of further education.

Knowledge possessed and discoveries made by one generation are passed on by **spoken** and **written** word to the next generation without each new generation having to make each discovery for itself. This saves time and enables successive generations to go on and make new discoveries which then become added to the existing body of human knowledge.

Thus language promotes the acceleration of **learning** and the development of **intellect**. It allows us to make detailed plans which in turn affect and benefit future generations by promoting their continued cultural and scientific progress.

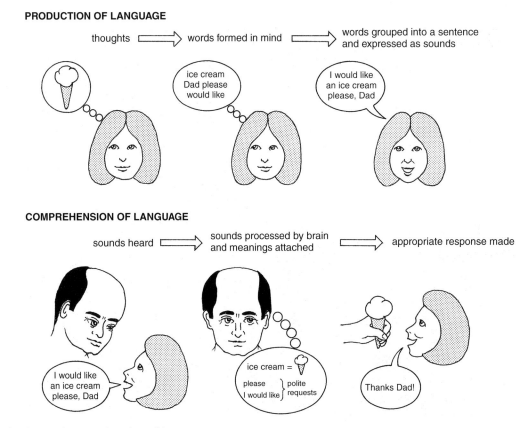

Figure 32.6 Production and comprehension of language

Testing your knowledge

1 **(i)** Give TWO examples of emotions that are often indicated by facial expressions.
 (ii) For each of these expressions, describe the state of the person's mouth and eyes when the facial expression is adopted. (6)

2 Give TWO meanings that could be communicated by winking. (2)

3 Give THREE examples of postures adopted by the body that communicate information about the person's attitude and for each state the attitude suggested. (6)

4 **a)** What is *language*? (2)

 b) Construct a simple flow diagram to show how language is
 (i) produced
 (ii) comprehended. (2)

 c) State TWO methods by which language can be transferred from person to person. (2)

 d) Why is transfer of language from generation to generation important? (2)

Applying your knowledge

1 The bar graph in figure 32.7 shows the results from a survey done on young babies in a large hospital over a period of two days. Group A were exposed night and day to the sound of a normal heartbeat; group B were exposed to irregular sounds.

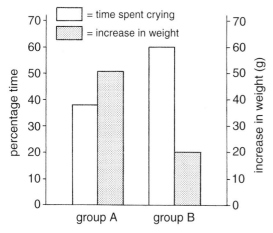

Figure 32.7

 a) Draw TWO conclusions from the graph. (2)

 b) Construct a hypothesis to account for the results. (2)

2 **a)** Why are sales staff trained to engage a potential customer in regular eye contact while extolling the virtues of the product on sale? (1)

 b) (i) State the most common facial expression adopted by sales staff eager for a sale.
 (ii) Give TWO features of vocal delivery employed by persuasive sales staff. (3)

3 Two experiments investigating the *effect* of physical proximity on eye contact were done using male interviewers (trained to stare continuously) first with male volunteers and then later with female volunteers. The results are summarised in the graph in figure 32.8.

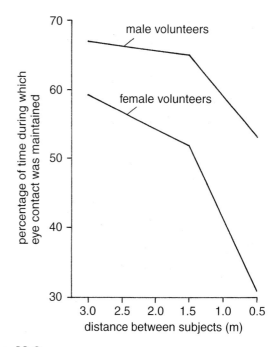

Figure 32.8

 a) (i) State the reduction in the percentage of eye contact time that occurred when distance decreased from 3 to 0.5 metres for male volunteers.

Continued ➤

Applying your knowledge

(ii) By how many more times did the percentage eye contact time decrease for female volunteers over the same distance? (2)

b) (i) Give a possible reason why male volunteers show a decrease in percentage eye contact as distance decreases.

(ii) Give an additional possible reason why female volunteers show an even greater decrease in percentage eye contact time as distance decreases. (2)

4 a) Some people find it more difficult to communicate important information to a stranger by telephone than by talking face to face. Suggest why by referring to THREE examples of ways in which information can be communicated by non-verbal means. (3)

b) Other people are described as having an 'excellent telephone manner'. Suggest THREE possible features of such a person's verbal skills that this might include. (3)

5 A large group of students who had never previously met were divided into same-sex pairs, and invited to chat and become acquainted. While they were in conversation with one another, each person's direction of gaze was recorded on videotape. This was analysed and the percentage of time that each person spent gazing at the other person ('percentage gazing time') was calculated per second. Figure 32.9 shows an extract from the results obtained for one of the pairs (persons A and B).

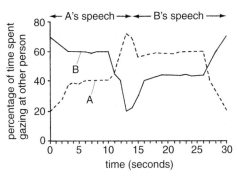

Figure 32.9

a) (i) At what time did A's speech come to an end?

(ii) At what time did A's percentage gazing time begin to alter indicating that A was about to stop speaking?

(iii) In what way did A's percentage gazing time alter at this stage?

(iv) In what way did B's percentage gazing time alter at this stage? (4)

b) Make a generalisation about the difference between the percentage of time spent gazing at the other person while
(i) listening and
(ii) speaking. (2)

6 Discuss the ways in which humans communicate under the headings:
(i) non-verbal communication; (6)
(ii) the use of language. (4)

33 Effect of experience

Effect of practice on motor skills

Once a **motor skill** (e.g. riding a bicycle) has been mastered, repeated use of it promotes the establishment of a motor pathway in the nervous system. Repetition of the skill is thought to result in an increased number of synaptic connections being formed between the neurones in the pathway. This leads to the formation of a '**motor memory**' for the skill. Practice improves performance; lack of practice results in the skill becoming 'rusty' (but not being completely lost).

Investigating learning using a finger maze

The apparatus shown in figure 33.1 is used by a learner, who is blindfolded throughout the experiment. The learner's task is to proceed through the maze from entrance to exit using the tip of their forefinger.

The observer's job is to measure the time taken for each trial by the learner. The procedure is repeated to give a total of ten trials. Table 33.1 lists some design features (and precautions) and the reasons for adopting them in this investigation.

After several trials, the time required to pass through the maze is found to decrease until eventually a minimum is reached. When graphed, the results give a **learning curve** (see figure 33.2). From this investigation it is concluded that practice improves performance of a motor skill.

In the case of the finger maze, a best time is eventually reached and this cannot be improved upon. By trial-and-error learning, the person has formed a picture (cognitive map) of the route through the maze in their 'mind's eye' and a certain minimum amount of time is required to physically run the finger tip through it.

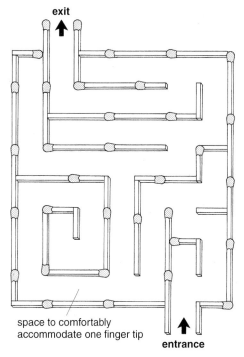

Figure 33.1 Finger maze

space to comfortably accommodate one finger tip

exit

entrance

Types of learning curve

The curve shown in figure 33.2 from the results of a finger maze investigation charts the decrease in time taken as an indication of the effect of practice on learning. Counting the decreasing number of errors made by the learner in successive trials is an alternative method of carrying out this investigation and gives a learning curve of similar shape.

Learning can also be measured as an increase in the number of correct responses achieved per unit time (e.g. the number of three-lettered words that a person

design feature or precaution	reason
Same learner used for each group of ten trials; same finger used each time; same design of maze used each time.	To ensure that no second variable factor is included in the investigation.
Ten trials per learner.	To give learner opportunity to reach best score.
Learner blindfolded throughout all ten trials.	To prevent learner improving their performance artificially.
Path between matchsticks just wide enough to accommodate one finger tip comfortably.	To prevent two fingers being used to explore simultaneously two routes at a junction and establish the correct one more quickly.
Experiment repeated with many learners and learning curves compared.	To obtain a more reliable set of results.

Table 33.1 Design features

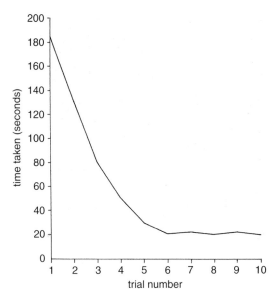

Figure 33.2 Learning curve of typical set of results

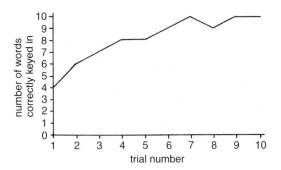

Figure 33.3 Second type of learning curve

unfamiliar with a keyboard can key in in one minute from a long list). When graphed, the results give a second type of learning curve (see figure 33.3).

Again practice is found to improve performance. Eventually, after much practice, a maximum level of performance is reached which cannot be improved upon. However skilled the person, there is a physical limit to the number of words that he or she can key in in one minute.

Imitation

Children learn by observing and **imitating** adults and other older children. This often occurs during play. A child dressing up in adult clothes (see figure 33.4) is imitating the behaviour of adult relatives and friends.

Learning by imitation is not restricted to children. Throughout life, many apects of human behaviour are learned by this means. When faced with a new task (e.g. learning how to operate a word processor/knitting machine/video recorder, etc.), it is much easier and takes less time to learn by watching and then imitating an expert than by reading the manual.

Figure 33.4 Learning by imitation

Imitation is an especially effective method of learning if the expert breaks up the demonstration into several small parts and allows the learner to try to **repeat** what they have seen after each part. Learning by imitation is further promoted if the expert is perceived by the learner as an attractive role model whose status is enhanced by the possession of the skill being demonstrated.

For most people, copying a **demonstration** is the preferred method of learning a new skill. To try to compensate for the lack of a live expert to imitate, instruction manuals often include many diagrams of human models which aid comprehension.

Imitation of social skills

Behaviour acquired by imitation is not restricted to the learning of physical tasks and skills; it is also involved in the learning of **social skills** and **attitudes**. Parents, other adults and perhaps older brothers and sisters, provide children with a variety of possible models to imitate.

Children tend to imitate many aspects of a model's cultural and social behaviour. Once learned, many of these **values** and **traditions** (e.g. being kind and generous to others, belonging to a certain religion, etc.) may be adopted for life. Some may be accepted during childhood (e.g. belief that smoking damages health) but be rejected during adolescence (e.g. smoking made to seem attractive by peer group). However, in adulthood the person may resume the original belief. Most people eventually embrace many of the cultural and social traditions and values held by their parents.

Amongst adults, imitation is an especially effective method of learning certain **social techniques**. For example, tone of voice, sympathetic manner and oral delivery carrying authority cannot be described easily. They need to be experienced to be learned.

Influence of media

People also learn by observing and then imitating behaviour presented by the **media** (e.g. TV and films). Children enthusiastically re-enact in detail recently viewed programmes. Laboratory experiments have demonstrated that many of the children who have seen a film featuring violent scenes tend to become more violent, whereas many of the children shown TV programmes containing 'do-good' themes tend to imitate this behaviour.

However, before a hasty conclusion is drawn from these surveys about the effect of imitation, a word of caution is needed. It must be kept in mind that those children who responded most to the violence may already have been potentially more aggressive for some other reason and did not simply learn it by imitating events on the screen.

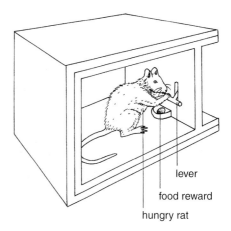

Figure 33.5 Trial and error learning in rats

Motivation

Motivation is the 'inner drive' which makes an animal want to participate in the learning process. Animals are motivated by many factors (e.g. hunger, thirst, sexual drive and curiosity).

The effect of motivation on an animal's ability to learn can be investigated by comparing hungry and well-fed rats which must negotiate a maze before receiving a food reward. From the graph in figure 33.6, it can be seen that the number of errors made per trial by the hungry rats quickly decreased since they were motivated to learn. The performance of the well-fed rats failed to improve because they lacked motivation.

> ## Testing your knowledge
>
> 1 a) Give an example of a motor skill. (1)
>
>   b) State the effect of practice on the performance of motor skills. (1)
>
> 2 a) When using the finger maze shown in figure 33.1, why is the learner blindfolded? (1)
>
>   b) Why is the learner given as many as ten trials? (1)
>
>   c) Why is the pathway between the matches built so that it is a comfortable fit for only one finger? (1)
>
> 3 Make simple labelled diagrams of the TWO forms of learning curve. (4)
>
> 4 a) With reference to the learning of a new skill, what is meant by the term *imitation*? (2)
>
>   b) Give an example of a cultural tradition that a person may learn by imitation from their parents and adopt for life. (1)

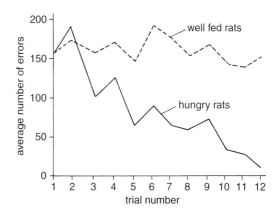

Figure 33.6 Effect of motivation on learning

Trial-and-error learning

If a rat is placed in a specially designed box (see figure 33.5) it responds in various ways (e.g. it explores the box, touches the floor and leans against the sides). Sooner or later the animal pushes the lever and food immediately appears in the food tray. If the rat is only rewarded with food when it presses the lever, it soon learns to associate its own behaviour with the delivery of food.

Reinforcement of behaviour

In the above examples, the behaviour pattern (trial-and-error learning) has positive consequences for the animal (it gets fed). The behaviour is therefore repeated and, as a result, becomes reinforced.

Reinforcement is the process that makes an organism tend to repeat a certain piece of behaviour. During reinforcement, a reinforcing stimulus (the **reinforcer**) strengthens or increases the probability of the response that it follows being repeated.

Reinforcers are roughly equivalent to **rewards**. However, strictly speaking, it is the response that is strengthened and reinforced whereas it is the organism (not the response) that is rewarded.

Positive reinforcement

This occurs when something pleasant or **positive** is received by the organism after a particular response has been made, thereby increasing the chance of the response being repeated. For example, a hungry rat rewarded with food for pressing the lever repeats the operation.

Negative reinforcement

This occurs when something unpleasant or **negative** is brought to a halt when the organism makes a particular response, thereby increasing the chance of the response being repeated. For example, a human discovering that an aspirin cures a headache is likely to use this remedy when pain strikes in the future. (Negative reinforcement should not be confused with punishment which is the application of a penalty or sanction following the wrong response by the learner.)

Continuous and intermittent reinforcement

Behaviour is said to be **continuously** reinforced when the response is **always** reinforced (e.g. the hungry rat receives food every time it presses the lever).

Behaviour is said to be **intermittently** reinforced if the response is reinforced on only **some** of the occasions that it occurs. For example, a child's mother is not always present to reward him or her with praise for following the Green Cross Code. However, the influence of the reinforcements that do occur is (hopefully) strong enough to persist and make the child cross the road safely when on his or her own.

Superstition

People develop a **superstition** as a result of a favourable event (which has occurred merely by chance) apparently occurring in response to some piece of behaviour by the person. The person repeats the behaviour and occasionally the favourable event also occurs thereby reinforcing the probability of the person repeating the behaviour.

The gambler who blows on the dice muttering 'Luck, be a lady tonight,' is rewarded with a win sufficiently often to reinforce the belief that his behaviour is affecting the response.

Shaping of behaviour

Shaping is the process by which a desired pattern of behaviour is eventually obtained from the learner by the

trainer **reinforcing successive approximations** of the desired response. Normally the desired response would have a low probability of occurring spontaneously.

For example, the proper use of a knife and fork by a child has almost no probability of occurring of its own accord. By using shaping, the parents direct the child's behaviour along the desired route by praising (and therefore reinforcing) those responses which are approximations of the required response.

The flow chart in figure 33.7 shows how reinforcement of responses that are successively more and more similar to the final desired response results in the child learning the new skill. Shaping also features in toilet-training, learning to dress oneself, tying shoe laces and many other skills.

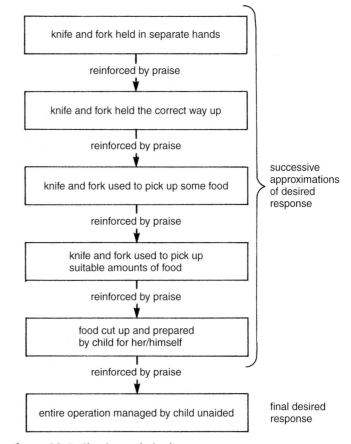

Figure 33.7 Shaping a desired response

Animals

Animal trainers use shaping to teach dolphins to balance balloons on their snouts, pigeons to dance in patterns, and bears to ride bicycles. An especially useful application of shaping is the training of dogs to act as the eyes of the blind (see figure 33.8).

Extinction of behaviour

Extinction is the name given to the eventual disappearance of a behaviour pattern when it is no longer reinforced.

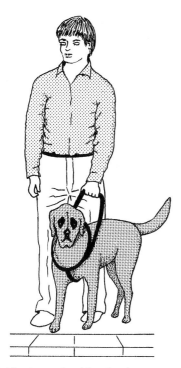

Figure 33.8 Guide dog trained by shaping

Consider the rat in figure 33.5 which has learned that pressing the lever gives food **every time**. If this rat is now put into a situation where pressing the lever fails to give food, the rat is found to press it less and less frequently. Eventually the rat does not press it at all and the earlier behaviour pattern (which had been reinforced continuously and learned quickly) is said to have become **extinct**.

Rats which have learned that pressing the lever **sometimes** gives food (i.e. have been subjected to intermittent reinforcement) take longer to learn the behaviour pattern but also take much longer to give it up completely. They tend to persist in giving the lever an occasional 'hopeful' press. They had learned not to expect food every single time and are not so easily put off by the lack of the reward. Thus intermittent reinforcement is **more resistant** to extinction than continuous reinforcement.

Rewarded and unrewarded behaviour

Responsible parents try to teach their children the difference between acceptable and unacceptable behaviour. They tend to encourage the development of 'good' behaviour by reinforcing it. For example, parents might be of the opinion that being truthful, showing consideration for others and trying hard at school are all forms of desirable behaviour. They would therefore reinforce these behaviour patterns with **rewards** such as attention, praise, outings, birthday presents and pocket money.

Parents also have to deal with their children when their behaviour is unacceptable. In theory, behaviour that goes **unrewarded** should become **extinct**. In some cases unacceptable behaviour (such as a child nagging a parent for sweets every time they arrive at the supermarket checkout) does disappear provided that the parent can summon the patience to ignore it and ensure that the behaviour always goes unrewarded.

However, most parents find that many forms of unacceptable behaviour shown by their children are impossible to ignore (in the hope that they will simply become extinct). In addition, unacceptable behaviour often carries its own rewards and is therefore **reinforced**. For example, a bully extorting money or a thief stealing from members of their peer group is rewarded and encouraged to repeat the process.

Responsible parents normally attempt to modify such unacceptable behaviour on the part of their children by resorting to punishment. This might involve a long talk followed by removal of the rewards stated above, accompanied perhaps by further sanctions such as being 'grounded'.

Some parents, while angry and disappointed, may resort to physical punishment. While an infrequent smack is regarded by some parents as a suitable response on certain occasions, excessive smacking of children now meets with society's total disapproval.

Generalisation

Generalisation is the ability to respond in the same way to many different but related stimuli.

In an experiment, an 11-month-old boy who liked furry animals was put in a room with a tame white rat. He reached out for the rat showing no fear. Each time just as his hand went to touch the animal, a very loud noise was deliberately made using a steel bar. As a result, the child developed an aversion for white rats. It was also discovered that the child had developed a fear for many furry objects that he had not seen before e.g. fur jacket, rabbit, Santa Claus mask (see figure 33.9). The spread of the response (in this case fear) to different but related stimuli is called **generalisation**.

Similarly a child who is hugged and kissed for saying 'Mama' when it sees its mother may respond by calling all adults 'Mama'. If the child does, it is showing a generalised response to different but related stimuli.

Discrimination

Discrimination is the ability to distinguish between different but related stimuli and give different responses.

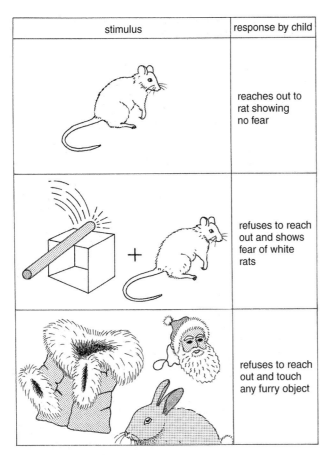

stimulus	response by child
	reaches out to rat showing no fear
	refuses to reach out and shows fear of white rats
	refuses to reach out and touch any furry object

Figure 33.9 Generalisation

Discrimination is taught by reinforcing the desired response (e.g. hugs and kisses for the baby from the mother when addressed as 'Mama') and by not reinforcing the wrong response (e.g. no response from the father when addressed as 'Mama').

The baby is soon able to tell the difference between similar stimuli (e.g. several adults) and determine whether or not the correct stimulus (the mother) is present before saying 'Mama'. It has learned to **discriminate**.

Learning to discrimate is an essential part of a child's preparation for coping with everyday life. It is important for the child to appreciate, for example, that some loud noises (e.g. thunder) do not indicate danger, that some green fruit (e.g. Granny Smith apples) are ripe and ready for eating and that some dogs are unfriendly and might bite.

Testing your knowledge

1 a) Suggest a factor that would motivate the rat in figure 33.5 to learn to operate the lever. (1)

   b) Why do well-fed rats, on average, make far more errors than hungry rats when finding their way through a maze offering a food reward at its end? (1)

2 a) What is meant by the term *reinforcement*? (2)

   b) Briefly compare the meanings of the terms *continuous reinforcement* and *intermittent reinforcement*. (2)

   c) What name is given to the rewarding of behaviour that approximates to the desired behaviour. (1)

3 a) What is meant by the *extinction* of behaviour? (1)

   b) Comparing intermittent reinforcement with continuous reinforcement, which is found to be more resistant to extinction ? Suggest why. (3)

4 a) Define *generalisation* and give an example to illustrate your answer. (3)

   b) Define *discrimination* and give an example to illustrate your answer. (3)

Applying your knowledge

1 Figure 33.10 shows a learner using her normal writing hand to do a mirror drawing. This involves joining up the dots to form a star outline while looking only at the mirror image.

An investigation was set up to study the effect of two types of practice on this learning process. The ten members of group A did 20 trials in one day; the ten members of group B each did one trial daily for twenty days. The graph in figure 33.11 shows the results.

a) Which group was being tested for the effect on learning of
   (i) distributed practice;
   (ii) massed practice? (1)

b) (i) Compare the effect that the two types of practice had on the learning process.
   (ii) Give a possible explanation for this difference. (2)

c) Why were as many as ten learners used in each group? (1)

Continued

266

Applying your knowledge

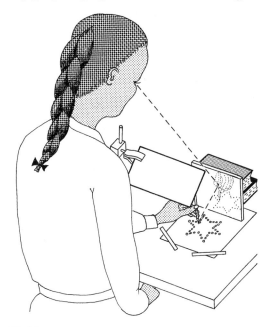

Figure 33.10

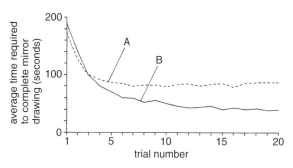

Figure 33.11

d) Why is the size of the star outline kept constant throughout the investigation? (1)

e) How could the investigation be adapted to test the effect of an auditory distraction on this learning process? (2)

2 Identical twins volunteered to learn a new task: how to convert a Hoover Aquamaster from its vacuum-cleaning mode to its carpet-shampooing mode. Twin X was given the instructions booklet; twin Y was given a demonstration by a regular user of the machine.

a) Predict, with reasons, which twin mastered the new task more quickly. (1)

b) Why were identical twins used in this investigation? (1)

3 Imagine that you look after your 5-year-old cousin every Saturday afternoon. One Saturday, annoyed by his failure to persuade you to give him 50p for sweets, he throws a tantrum by screaming and kicking the floor. Some adults might shout at him or even smack him, others might hug and soothe him. You decide to follow the experts' advice and ignore him.

a) Using the words *extinction*, *reinforcement* and *reward* in your answer, explain why this course of action is considered to be the best one (although difficult to maintain). (3)

b) If this behaviour is repeated on future Saturdays, why must you be absolutely consistent and not let him have the 50p sometimes 'for an easy life'? (2)

4 Each of the following paragraphs describes a situation involving some aspect of behaviour. Give a brief explanation for each using one or more of the terms that you have met in chapter 33.

a) Certain animals can be trained to do 'clever' tricks. A group of rats, for example, were taught to cross a drawbridge, climb a ladder, crawl through a tunnel, slide down a chute and press a lever for a food pellet. (2)

b) Many years ago, cigarette smoking was regarded by most people as a harmless habit. A survey taken at the time showed that there was a much higher incidence of smoking amongst people who had grown up in a family of smokers than amongst those raised by non-smoking parents. (1)

c) A girl suffering from anorexia nervosa was admitted to hospital and put in a private room on her own without books, magazines or TV. She was only allowed a visitor, a book, a magazine or a TV programme if she agreed to eat something. She gained 5 kg in ten days. (2)

d) A small girl was bitten by a Scots terrier (a small black dog). She developed a fear of all small black dogs. Her younger brother was bitten by a West Highland terrier (a small white dog). He developed a fear of all dogs. (1)

5 In an investigation, rats learned to select a particular side of a T-maze (see figure 33.12). Members of group X were rewarded with 4 food pellets and those of group Y with 2 food pellets for each correct response made. Figure 33.13 shows a graph of the results where each rat ran 4 trials per day.

Continued ➤

Applying your knowledge

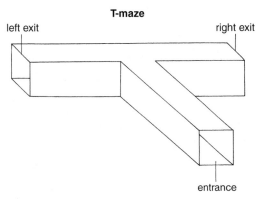

T-maze

left exit   right exit

entrance

Figure 33.12

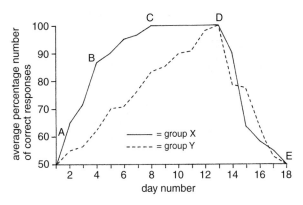

Figure 33.13

a) What name is given to the type of graph indicated by letters A–D? (1)

b) What effect does size of food reward have on the learning process? (1)

c) Suggest why portion C–D of the graph is a straight flat line. (1)

d) Why does each graph begin at 50% and not 0%? (1)

e) Within each test group of rats, half were trained to choose the right exit and half to choose the left exit. Explain why. (1)

f) **(i)** Which lettered region of the graph indicates that extinction of the learned behaviour is taking place?

(ii) Suggest why the behaviour became extinct.

(iii) What conclusion can be drawn about the relationship between resistance to extinction and size of reward during training? (3)

g) In your opinion, was the reinforcement in this investigation continuous or intermittent? Justify your choice of answer with reference to the graph. (2)

6 Give an account of reinforcement and shaping of behaviour as illustrated by trial-and-error learning. (10)

Social groups

Human beings are social animals. A large part of the average person's life is spent **interacting** with other people who act as stimuli and offer responses to the person's behaviour. Almost without exception, people belong to one or more **social groups** of different types and sizes. These could include, for example, the family, the teenage gang, the sports team, the trade union, the army regiment, the cub pack, the football supporters' club, the political party, the religious sect, the school orchestra, and so on.

Social groupings provide people with a feeling of belonging and of being accepted. Many groups are held together by **rules**, written and unwritten, and **symbolism** e.g. a uniform that sets the group apart from the non-members.

Groups provide support for their members especially in times of need. However, the group also affects the behaviour of the individual members by setting standards and even deciding what should be done in certain situations. An individual who accepts these conditions must behave in the same way as the other members of the group.

Social facilitation

One of the factors that motivates many people is the need for **status**. They want to impress and be admired by other members of a social group to which they belong. It is interesting therefore to consider whether or not the presence of other people affects an individual's performance.

Research shows that in competitive situations, subjects do tend to work faster and achieve a higher level of productivity and energy output than they do when working alone.

Figure 34.1 shows the results from a survey done by an athletics club on its members (in the absence of spectators). The presence of other competitors seems to spur the individual on to heights not achieved on their own. This increased performance in a competitive situation is called **social facilitation**.

Even in non-competitive situations where the workers know that the results will not be compared, they are found to achieve more when working in a group than when working in isolation.

Familiarity with the task

Competition is especially effective at improving an individual's performance if he or she is already very

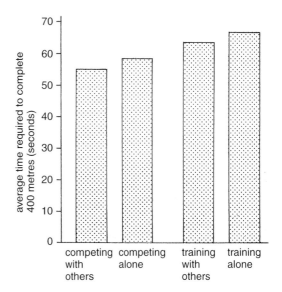

Figure 34.1 Effects of social facilitation

familiar with the task in hand. However, competition tends to interfere with progress when the person is trying to learn something new. They imagine that the others are monitoring their progress, feel stressed and tend to make more mistakes.

Intensity of competition

Intense competition in the workplace leads to anxiety, insecurity and hostility. It affects the health of some of the workforce and results in a drop in productivity.

During games and sports, players and spectators are stimulated by the competitive nature of the activity. The players' performance is increased if the event involves a meeting between two well-matched teams watched by an appreciative and demonstrative crowd of spectators.

However, taken to extremes, such competiton can become devisive and psychologically hazardous to the participants. When winning becomes everything, there is little joy for the losers.

Group pressure

The following experiment was set up to investigate the effect on an individual of **majority opinion** even when it was clearly **contrary** to fact. A group of eight people together in the same room were invited in turn to solve the problem of visual judgement shown in figure 34.2.

Unknown to the eighth member of the group, the other seven were part of the experiment and had agreed in advance to give wrong answer C. When it came to the

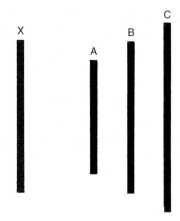

To which line is X equal in length?

Figure 34.2 Visual judgement problem

turn of number eight (the experimental subject), they were placed in the position of having to disagree with the majority or doubt their own judgement sufficiently to conform to group opinion. The experiment was tried out on many subjects and repeated several times with each one. The results are shown in figure 34.3.

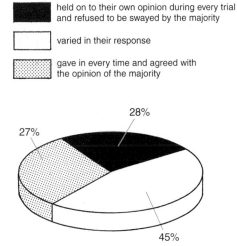

held on to their own opinion during every trial and refused to be swayed by the majority

varied in their response

gave in every time and agreed with the opinion of the majority

28%

27%

45%

Figure 34.3 Results of group pressure experiment

During the discussion sessions that followed the investigation, some interesting points emerged. Many of the subjects who had agreed with the majority had not done so simply to bring the confusing episode to an end. At the time they had expressed genuine respect for the (wrong) judgement of the majority! They had come to the conclusion that there had been something wrong with their own eyesight or that they had been experiencing an optical illusion.

The process of exerting such a strong influence on an individual that they abandon their own views or ideas in favour of those held by the social group, is called **group pressure**.

If susceptible individuals can be pressurised into agreeing to the wrong answer in a straightforward situation like the one above, the possibility of influencing a person's judgement is increased dramatically when the controversial subject is an opinion or an attitude.

Deindividuation

In real life, group pressure is a powerful force. People find it difficult to resist going along with the decisions made by the group. Members of a group conform because they:

◆ **identify** with other group members and want to be like them;

◆ desire the **personal gain** which membership often brings;

◆ want to be **liked** and not be thought of as unpopular.

Once under the influence of group pressure, individuals think and act differently from the way that they would if they were on their own. Decisions and behaviour now depend less on the members' individual personalities and more on the collective influence of the group. This loss by an individual of personal identity when in a group is called **deindividuation** and it can lead to diminished restraints on behaviour.

Deindividuated people feel indistinguishable from others in the group and are more likely to act **mindlessly** and do things that they would never consider doing on their own. This often takes the form of anti-social, aggressive behaviour by a 'faceless' mob whose members have temporarily lost awareness of their own individuality and sense of responsibility (see figure 34.4).

"Which embassy's this?"

Figure 34.4 Deindividuation

Risk-taking

The members of a group will take bigger risks when in the group than when alone. A gang of teenagers will taunt and dare one another into pursuing **extreme activities** (e.g. playing 'chicken' on a railway line, experimenting with drugs, fighting a rival gang, etc.) which they would be unlikely to attempt on their own.

Anonymity

Being an **anonymous** member of a crowd offers the individual protection from punishment. If the members of a mob do not have to worry about being caught breaking the law then they are more likely to pursue their irresponsible activities.

Influences that change beliefs

Internalisation

Internalisation is the process by which an individual incorporates within him or herself an enduring changed set of beliefs, values or attitudes. Radio, television and newspapers subject listeners, viewers and readers to a mass of information which may or may not become internalised.

By attempting to persuade people to change their current beliefs and adopt a different set of beliefs, politicians, government departments and big businesses try to use internalisation to make people do their bidding.

Televised party political broadcast

Politicians regularly use this method to try to persuade viewers to vote for their party. Research shows that viewers are most likely to pay attention if the presenter:

◆ has a pleasant appearance;

◆ has a good vocal delivery including warmth and humour;

◆ presents a two-sided argument but favours one side;

◆ gives convincing reasons for supporting his or her side;

◆ shows him or herself to be an expert on the subject being discussed.

However, it is debatable how many people actually alter their beliefs and vote for the speaker's political party, having been fully convinced that unemployment will plummet, the economy will boom, the national debt will shrink, and so on.

Health warning

Drug education programmes and anti-smoking campaigns often use posters (see figures 34.5 and 34.6) in an attempt to persuade people to alter their behaviour.

Internalisation and advertising

One method of advertising attempts to create a feeling of dissatisfaction with our current situation while at the same time presenting us with the allegedly better alternative. By this means big businesses try to effect internalisation and persuade us that a particular brand is faster, smoother, sexier, cheaper, etc. than the 'inferior' one that we are at present using. Table 34.1 lists a few products and suggests the **altered belief** that the advertiser is hoping to create.

Figure 34.5 Anti-drugs poster

Figure 34.6 Anti-smoking poster

product	altered belief intended by advertiser
foodstuff	Will nourish the family and make the person who serves it a 'good mum or dad'.
soap powder	Will get clothes cleaner and softer than ever before.
item of clothing	Will make the wearer fashionably dressed and the envy of his or her peer group.
toothpaste	Will clean teeth and reduce fillings because it has been proved scientifically.
double-glazing	Will improve the quality of life and make the neighbours envious.
aftershave	Will make a man smell so sexy that women will find him irresistible.
cosmetics	Will make a woman look so beautiful that men will find her irresistible.
motor car	Will offer excitement, freedom and escapism previously only dreamed of.

Table 34.1 The power of advertising

Identification

Identification is the process by which person A deliberately changes his or her beliefs in an attempt to be like person B. Person B exerts a strong influence over person A, since A admires B enormously and makes B the object of hero-worship. In extreme cases, A attempts to enhance his or her self-esteem by behaving, in fantasy and/or in real life, as if he or she actually were person B.

To a greater or lesser extent most people tend to identify with one or more of the personalities who dominate the worlds of entertainment, big business, politics, sport, and so on.

Identification and advertising

One method of advertising sets out to exploit the process of identification by employing a personality with whom an enormous number of potential customers (with disposable income) identify. This 'superstar' is made the focus of a massive, nationwide (or even international) advertising campaign covering all sections of the mass media.

If the superstar is a reasonable actor he or she will be able to endorse the product with apparent sincerity (perhaps combined with humour and other memorable gimmickry). Such endorsement dramatically increases the product's desirability. It is therefore eagerly purchased by the legions of fans who identify with Ms or Mr 'Wonderful' and their achievements, beliefs and lifestyle.

Testing your knowledge

1 a) Give TWO examples of a social group. (2)

b) Give ONE reason why people like being members of a social group. (1)

2 a) Explain what is meant by the term *social facilitation*. (2)

b) Under what circumstances does competition **not** result in increased performance? (1)

3 a) Give TWO reasons why the members of a social group agree to go along with the decisions and rules made by the group. (2)

b) What term is used to refer to the loss by an individual of personal identity when subjected to group pressure? (1)

Applying your knowledge

1 A large number of volunteers were given a short period of intensive training to teach them how to monitor light panels for bulbs that failed to light up in the proper sequence. They were then divided into two groups and allowed to compete at this task.

The members of one group worked individually but within sight of one another and able to follow one another's progress. The members of the other group worked individually and in isolation. Each group was then allowed a rest period before the competition was repeated. The bar graphs in figure 34.7 summarises the results.

a) (i) Make a generalisation about the *effect on performance* of competing with others present compared with competing in isolation.

(ii) Which of the following terms is used to refer to this effect? (2)
   A internalisation
   B deindividuation
   C group pressure
   D social facilitation

Continued ➤

Applying your knowledge

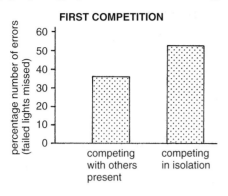

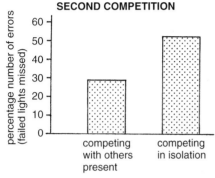

Figure 34.7

b) State the effect on performance of repeating the experiment when
   (i) competing with others;
   (ii) competing in isolation.
   (iii) Give a possible explanation for the effect in each case. (4)

2 'A little healthy competition is a good thing.'

a) State whether you consider this statement to be TRUE or FALSE. (1)

b) Justify your choice of answer with reference to the term *social facilitation*. (1)

3 The Ku Klux Klan is a secret organisation of white American men who perpetrate acts of violence against Black people and other minority groups. The members keep their identities secret and wear robes and hoods to disguise themselves while carrying out their disreputable deeds. Briefly discuss this form of group behaviour including the following terms in your answer: *anonymity, deindividuation, faceless mob, group pressure* and *risk-taking*. (5)

4 The posters shown in figures 34.5 and 34.6 are designed to attempt to change people's beliefs.

a) For each poster, state a possible version of the altered belief. (2)

b) What name is given to this type of social influence? (1)

5 Olympic gold medalists in athletics events are a popular choice by manufacturers of expensive sportswear as models to feature in advertising campaigns. Briefly explain how the advertising campaign is intended to work on potential customers. (2)

6 Give an account of human behaviour under the following headings:
   (i) deindividuation; (5)
   (ii) internalisation; (3)
   (iii) identification. (2)

What you should know
(Chapters 31–34)

(See table 34.2 for word bank.)

1 Humans are social animals and _communi_ with one another throughout life by means of signs and _signals_.

2 The period of _dependency_ of a human infant upon adults is lengthy.

3 The strong emotional tie that binds a baby to the mother is called _attatchment_.

4 Infant attachment provides the basis for the development of social, _linguistic_ and intellectual skills.

5 Insecurely attached infants who are _deprived_ of normal social contact and cuddling tend to suffer long lasting ill effects.

6 People communicate by verbal and _non-verbal_ means.

7 _bonding_ is the name given to the strong emotional tie that forms between parents and their newborn infant. The formation of the bond makes the parents want to _protect_ and provide for the child.

Continued ➤

What you should know
(Chapters 31–34)

8 Adults communicate non-verbally by employing facial expressions, eye _contact_ , postures and _gestures_ to express attitudes and _emotions_

9 Adults communicate _verbally_ by using language which allows information to be transferred from generation to generation, thereby accelerating _learning_ and intellectual development.

10 Once a motor skill has been mastered, _practise_ improves performance.

11 Most people learn a new task more quickly by _imitating_ an expert than by following instructions.

12 During trial-and-error learning, animals are _motivated_ to learn by factors such as hunger and thirst.

13 _reinforcement_ is the process that makes an animal tend to repeat a certain piece of behaviour.

14 _shaping_ is the process by which a desired pattern of behaviour is eventually obtained from the learner by the trainer reinforcing successive approximations of a desired _response_.

15 _extinction_ is the eventual disappearance of a behaviour pattern when it is no longer reinforced.

16 Most people belong to one or more social _groups_ of different types and sizes.

17 In general, individuals are found to perform better in _competitive_ situations than on their own. This process is called social _facillitation_.

18 Group _pressure_ occurs when a social group exerts such an influence over an individual that he or she abandons their own ideas in favour of those of the group. _deindividuation_ occurs when the individual undergoes loss of personal _identity_ and is unable to resist going along with the behaviour of the group regardless of whether it is acceptable or not.

19 _internalisation_ is the process by which an individual incorporates within himself a set of _beliefs_.

20 During _identification_, individuals deliberately change their beliefs to try to be like some other person whom they strongly admire.

attachment	extinction	motivated
beliefs	facilitation	non-verbal
bonding	gestures	practice
communicate	groups	pressure
competitive	identification	protect
contact	identity	reinforcement
deindividuation	imitating	response
dependency	internalisation	shaping
deprived	learning	signals
emotions	linguistic	verbally

Table 34.2 Word bank for chapters 31–34

35 Population change

A **population** is a group of individuals of the same species which makes up part of a community. The number of individuals present per unit area of habitat is called the **population density**.

The **birth rate** of a population is a measure of the number of new individuals produced during a certain interval of time. The **death rate** is a measure of the number of individuals that died during the same interval of time.

Carrying capacity

Each species has an enormous **reproductive potential** (see table 35.1). When a population colonises a new environment its number rapidly increases in **abundance**. However, this increase does not continue indefinitely. It stops when the population reaches a certain size which the available environmental resources can just maintain.

animal	average number of offspring per year
fox	5
red grouse	8
rabbit	24
mouse	30
trout	800
cod	4 000 000
oyster	16 000 000

Table 35.1 Reproductive potential

The maximum size of population that can be supported by a particular environment is called its **carrying capacity**. At this point the population's birth rate and death rate are equal.

Population of rabbits

The period of gestation in rabbits lasts one month. The female produces several young per litter. The young reach sexual maturity at age six months.

If a pair of rabbits were released on a grassy island free from predators then the rabbit population would quickly increase and follow a pattern of growth similar to the one shown in figure 35.1.

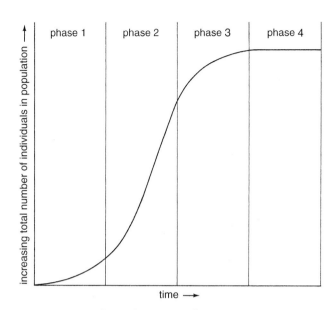

Figure 35.1 Typical population growth curve

Phases of growth curve

During **phase 1** in figure 35.1, the population size increases slowly (and the growth rate of the population gradually increases).

During the **early** stages of **phase 2**, the population size increases rapidly (with the growth rate of the population continuing to increase and then reach its maximum level). Since no limiting factors are present, the conditions are ideal and the increase in population size shows a geometric progression (e.g. $2 \rightarrow 4 \rightarrow 8 \rightarrow 16 \rightarrow 32 \rightarrow 64$ etc.). This pattern of very rapid growth is described as **exponential** growth. The curve in a graph of exponential growth always becomes steeper with time.

During the **later** stages of **phase 2**, the population size continues to increase rapidly (with the growth rate remaining steady at its maximum level).

During **phase 3**, the population size increases slowly (and the growth rate of the population gradually decreases). The population is approaching the carrying capacity of the environment.

During **phase 4**, the population size stops increasing and remains stable since the environment cannot support any additional members of the population. (Now birth rate is equal to death rate and growth rate has dropped to zero.)

Population stability

Figure 35.2 shows the growth curve of the population of sheep following their introduction to the Australian

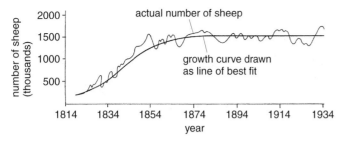

Figure 35.2 Population growth and stability

island of Tasmania in the nineteenth century. Although the numbers varied from one census to another, the population remained fairly stable once it had reached the carrying capacity of the environment in the 1870s. Fluctuations around the average value were caused by irregular droughts which affected the food supply.

Regulation

The carrying capacity of an environment is determined by factors such as amount of food, water, oxygen and space available. Sooner or later one of these factors becomes **limiting** and prevents the population from continuing to increase in size. Such factors exert a **regulatory effect** on the population as shown in figure 35.3.

In a natural ecosystem, the abundance of a population may also be affected by other causes of mortality such as predation, disease and pollution of the environment by the organisms' wastes.

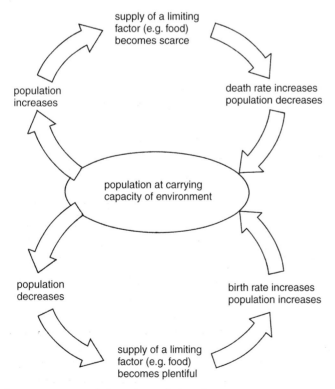

Figure 35.3 Regulation of population size

Human population explosion

Unlike other species, human beings have managed to overcome many of the causes of mortality that normally affect a population in its natural ecosystem.

By employing our exceptional intellect, we have removed the threat of predation, developed vast areas of land for food production and improved public health. As a direct result the carrying capacity of the environment has increased, allowing the human population to continue its phase of exponential growth.

If the population continues to increase in this way, it could eventually exceed the carrying capacity of the environment. The human population would then be affected by regulatory mechanisms as outlined in figure 35.3. Opinions differ on the exact form that these mechanisms of regulation would take if this situation were to arise.

History of population growth

The graph in figure 35.4 shows the changes that have occurred in human population size over the last 100 000 years. (The x-axis has been rescaled at 10 000 BC.)

Fossils and archaeological evidence suggest that the human population was fairly stable at around 5 million individuals until about 10 000 years ago (i.e. 8 000 BC). Then the first major **population 'spurt'** took place. This resulted in the population reaching an estimated 300 million by the time of Christ and 500 million by 1650. At around this time the second major population 'spurt' began. Both of these dramatic increases in population are attributed to **revolutionary changes** in human culture that took place at the time.

Effect of agriculture on human population growth

Up until about 10 000 years ago, humans had depended on **hunting** and **gathering** as methods of obtaining food supplies. When the need arose, the people tried to catch animals and forage for other requirements from the immediate environment. However, there was no guarantee that they would always be successful; in addition there were no means of storing excess food when it was available. As a result the people's existence was precarious especially during seasonal extremes of climate, and the population remained fairly stable at the environment's carrying capacity of about 5 million.

About 10 000 years ago some humans began to practise **agriculture** in the lands around the eastern end of the Mediterranean Sea. In this region, wild wheat and barley grew and wild goats, sheep and cattle roamed free.

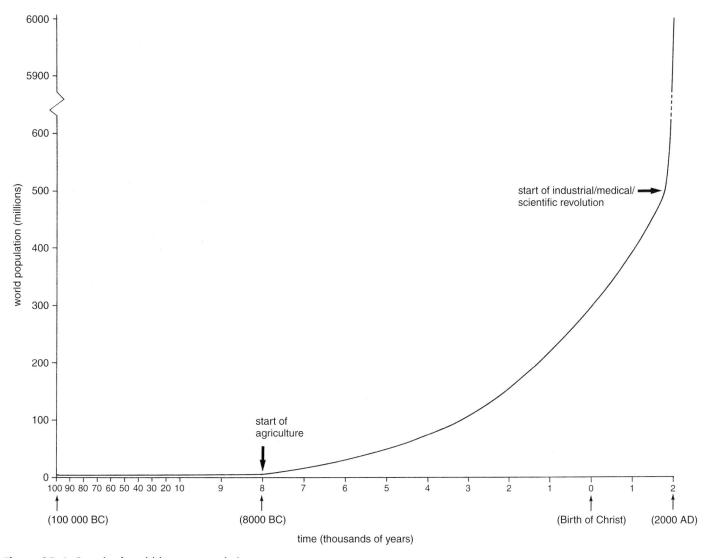

Figure 35.4 Growth of world human population

The people domesticated and bred the animals and planted crops on cleared ground. Permanent settlements developed since the people became tied to the piece of land that they cultivated. Surplus grain was stored for the lean years when food was scarce; regular supplies of meat and dairy products could be depended upon. As a result the carrying capacity of the environment was raised and the human population began its first major 'spurt' (see figure 35.4).

Surviving undeveloped societies

An **undeveloped** society is one in which the members are totally dependent upon their immediate environment for food, water and shelter. They live a 'hand-to-mouth' existence and survive without practising agriculture or employing modern technology.

Hunter-gatherers

In a few regions of the world e.g. the Kalahari Desert, Australian Outback and Arctic Circle, the remnants of

Stone Age-type communities of **hunter-gatherers** survive to this day. They live in **remote locations** where conditions are harsh and the environment's carrying capacity is **low**. The population density of such communities is therefore also low (see figure 35.5).

Bushmen of Kalahari Desert

Thousands of years ago the ancestors of the Bushmen of South-West Africa lived in well-watered grasslands and scrub forest. Over the past 500 years they have been driven into the Kalahari Desert by other human groups.

In this desert ecosystem there is never enough water to grow crops or keep livestock. For this reason the people have never practised agriculture and in many ways lead a life similar to people living in the Stone Age. The women dig up edible roots and tubers and **gather** berries and nuts. The men **hunt** game such as antelope using bows and arrows and spears. All food and possessions are **shared** since it is only through trust and co-operation

277

Figure 35.5 World population densities

that the members of such a group can survive the hardship imposed by the environment.

As civilisation continues to advance and the desert resources become depleted, the number of Bushmen continuing to lead the hunter-gatherer way of life has now dwindled to a few thousand who live in the most remote parts of the desert.

Australian Aborigines

The word aboriginal means 'existing in a place from the earliest known time'. The Aborigines are the original inhabitants of Australia. They lived for many thousands of years with minimum contact with the outside world until Australia was colonised by the British in the eighteenth century.

Many Aborigine tribes lived as **hunter-gatherers** in the bush (semi-desert and scrub land). They used spears, stone axes, boomerangs and traps. They never tilled the soil or domesticated animals (possibly due to the lack of suitable types – a kangaroo, for example, cannot be milked or ridden). Their way of life involved close kinship and sharing of all food and goods. They lacked metal tools and lived in many ways like their Stone Age ancestors had done thousands of years earlier.

Research has shown that in the past the amount of food available in a particular area of the bush and the

population density of the Aborigines living there were directly related to the **quantity of rainfall** that the area received. In other words, the availability of water was the **limiting factor** which determined the carrying capacity of the environment and kept the human population density at a certain stable level.

The British colonists dispossessed the Aborigines of the best land and herded them onto settlements and missions on poor lands. These measures, combined with the arrival of diseases such as smallpox and measles, reduced the Aborigine population from 300 000 to about 45 000 by the mid-twentieth century. Nowadays only a very few isolated tribes remain unaffected by European culture and continue to follow their traditional way of life.

Arctic Inuit

The Inuit (Eskimos) have become adapted to life in an environment dominated by extremely **low temperatures** for most of the year. Food has traditionally been obtained by **hunting** e.g. spearing seals at a blow hole in the ice in winter and tracking caribou in summer.

In early times the human population density remained at a low yet stable level because the environment's carrying capacity was **limited** by the effect of low temperature. All food and goods were **shared** since the members of such a society of hunters depend on being able to count on one another in times of hardship.

Contact with Europeans over the last few hundred years has introduced new tools, new ideas and new diseases to the Eskimos. These have shaken the whole fabric of Inuit society and initially they caused the population to decline rapidly. However, Inuit are no longer in danger of becoming extinct. In most areas the rifle has replaced the harpoon, the snowmobile is used instead of the sled and dogs, and the population is increasing. Very few (if any) groups remain unaffected by modern civilisation and the traditional culture of the Inuit people is rapidly disappearing.

In common with the world's other aboriginal peoples, the main problems facing the Inuit are those of adapting to the **economic** and **social** problems created by contact with outsiders whose cultures have already been advanced by the agricultural and industrial revolutions.

With the advent of modern methods of travel and communication, it is debatable whether any undeveloped society will continue to exist in its truly natural 'hunter-gatherer' state in the future.

Contemporary non-industrial cultures

Subsistence farming

This form of agriculture is common in Latin America, Asia and Africa (see figure 35.6). A typical **subsistence farmer** and his or her family grow crops and rear animals on a small piece of land to meet their own needs. Any surplus products are **stored** for use during times of

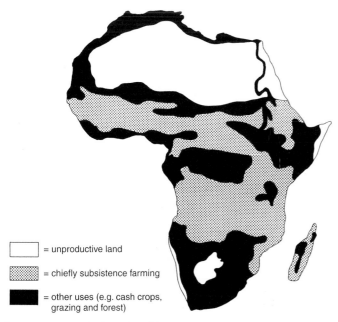

= unproductive land

= chiefly subsistence farming

= other uses (e.g. cash crops, grazing and forest)

Figure 35.6 Agriculture in Africa

shortage. Only rarely does subsistence farming produce crops or animals for sale. It is characterised by the use of **basic farm tools** and simple methods of cultivation employing **family labour**.

The people have a low standard of living often lacking access to electricity and modern sanitation. In many ways their lifestyle resembles that of the first farmers about 10 000 years ago when the **agricultural revolution** began.

Increased food production raises the carrying capacity of the environment. Regions where subsistence farming is practised are therefore found to be more densely populated than those inhabited by hunter-gatherer peoples (see figures 35.5 and 35.6).

Effect of science on human population growth

The second 'spurt' in the human population of the world began at around 1650 AD (see figure 35.4). From this time onwards great advances were made in scientific understanding which were soon followed by major **discoveries** and **inventions**. These gradually led to the **industrial revolution** of the last 200 years which has also been accompanied by significant advances in **medicine**.

Methods of **food production** have become more efficient. A major assault has been launched on deadly diseases such as smallpox and poliomyelitis. This has involved large scale programmes of **immunisation** in many countries and has been accompanied by significant improvements in child care.

In many parts of the world, people have benefited from better housing, piped water, modern sanitation and easy access to antibiotics. These advances achieved by the industrial/scientific revolution have contributed to the current human population boom by largely **removing the limiting factors** that previously regulated the population.

Factors contributing to exponential growth of human population

Overcoming predation

The chance of humans being attacked by large predators had been decreasing over the years and was reduced to a negligible level by the invention of **guns** and other **advanced weaponry**.

Although weapons have also provided the sophisticated means by which human beings are able to kill large numbers of other human beings during warfare, even the millions of people lost in the First and Second World

1 a) Define the terms *population* and *carrying capacity*. (2)

b) State the relationship between a population's birth rate and death rate when its size has reached the environment's carrying capacity. (1)

2 a) What is meant by the term *exponential growth* of a population? (2)

b) Give THREE factors that could exert a regulatory effect on a population of animals living in their natural habitat and prevent exponential growth from continuing indefinitely. (3)

c) In the past, which environmental factor limited population growth of
(i) Bushmen of the Kalahari Desert
(ii) Inuit people of the Arctic Circle? (2)

3 a) (i) Approximately when did the first major 'spurt' in human population size occur?
(ii) Until this time what factor in particular had limited human population growth? (2)

b) (i) Approximately when did the second major 'spurt' in human population size occur?
(ii) What name is given to this time in history when humans began to benefit from scientific discoveries and inventions? (2)

Wars made little impact on the exponential growth pattern of the human population.

Increased food availability

Development of farm **machinery, fertilisers** and **pesticides** have led to production of food on a hitherto undreamed of scale (see chapter 37). Adequate supplies of food have become available to meet the needs of the world population. In most parts of the world availability of food no longer acts as a factor limiting human population growth.

Reduction of child mortality

This has resulted from improved levels of child care, better hygiene and sanitation, and major advances being achieved in medicine. Effective **vaccines** and **antibiotics** are now widely available for use in the prevention and control of diseases which were previously lethal. In addition, improved nutrition has increased children's natural resistance to disease.

Reduction in child mortality has allowed even more people to survive to reproductive age and produce children of their own, thereby contributing to the exponential growth of the human population.

Increased life expectancy

Improved health and standard of living bring about an increase in **life expectancy** (see table 35.2). This in turn extends the period during which people can reproduce, enabling them to have even more children than the previous generation.

period of time	average life expectancy of European male (years)
8000–3000 BC	18.0
800–1600 AD	31.0
1600–1700 AD	33.5
1700–1800 AD	35.3
1800–1900 AD	37.0
around 1910 AD	57.4
around 1950 AD	66.5
around 1990 AD	74.0
2000 AD onwards	?

Table 35.2 Average life expectancies

Increase in female fertility

An increased life expectancy combined with earlier puberty extends the number of years during which women are able to bear children. This therefore leads to a relative increase in **female fertility** (fecundity) compared with the previous generation.

Change in cultural habits

Breast-feeding stimulates secretion of the hormone prolactin which in turn inhibits secretion of luteinising hormone. As a result most mothers do not ovulate during the time they are breast-feeding their baby. This is found to be especially true of women who are surviving on a barely adequate diet.

In many developing countries it has long been the custom for a mother to suckle her infant for a prolonged period. This acts as a **natural method of contraception** by delaying conception of the next baby. However, as cultural habits change and women cut short the period of suckling, they are more likely to conceive the next child sooner than they would have done previously. Births are no longer as spaced out and the birth rate increases.

date (AD)	estimated world population (billions)	time required for this population to double itself (years)
1650	0.5	200
1850	1.0	80
1930	2.0	45
1975	4.0	25
2000	8.0	?

(1 billion = 1000 million)

Table 35.3 Doubling time based on earlier data

date (AD)	estimated world population (billions)	time required for this population to double itself (years)
1650	0.5	200
1850	1.0	80
1930	2.0	45
1975	4.0	53
2028	8.0	?

(1 billion = 1000 million)

Table 35.4 Doubling time based on more recent data

Doubling time

A combination of the above factors has led to the world population changing from a period of relatively slow growth to one that is in the grip of exponential growth. Table 35.3 is based on data assembled during the 1980s. It shows how the length of time required for the world population to **double** (doubling time) was steadily decreasing as the years went by.

Table 35.4 is based on data assembled at the end of the twentieth century. It shows a reverse in the trend of decreasing doubling time.

Whereas the world's population was expected to reach 8 billion in the year 2000, in fact it only reached 6 billion and is not expected to reach 8 billion until 2028. This slowing down of population growth rate is thought to be due mainly to increased use of contraception worldwide, social pressures (for example in China) and the devastating effect of AIDS on the people living in many developing countries (especially some of those in Sub-Saharan Africa).

However the world population is still increasing rapidly and the problem of overpopulation in the future remains as pressing as ever. Even in those countries most severely affected by AIDS, fertility levels are very high and the population is expected to double between 1995 and 2050.

The world's wealth and resources are not distributed equally. Those countries with the highest rates of population growth are often amongst the poorest nations on Earth and least able to cope with the problem. As a result, about half of the world's population still lives in conditions of extreme poverty. This situation is unlikely to improve if the human population continues to increase exponentially.

Testing your knowledge

1 The end of major food shortages and the absence of predators have contributed to the exponential growth of the human population. By what means have humans brought about these important changes? (3)

2 By what means has child mortality been drastically reduced in many countries during the last 300 years? (2)

3 Why do earlier onset of puberty and increase in life expectancy contribute to the exponential growth of the human population? (2)

4 Why does a cultural change such as curtailment of prolonged breast-feeding tend to promote increase in human population numbers? (2)

5 a) What is meant by the term *doubling time* with reference to population studies? (1)

   b) (i) State the trend shown by doubling time between 1650 and 1975. (1)
      (ii) Give ONE possible reason for the change in this trend found at the end of the twentieth century. (2)

Applying your knowledge

1 The graph in figure 35.7 refers to a population of goats introduced to an uninhabited, grassy island.

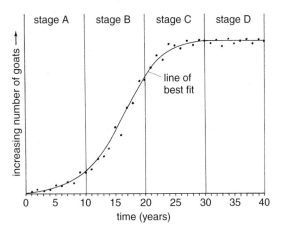

Figure 35.7

a) At which lettered stage was the population
   (i) increasing in number most rapidly;
   (ii) neither increasing nor decreasing in number? (2)

b) At which lettered stage was the population's growth rate
   (i) decreasing gradually;
   (ii) at zero;
   (iii) increasing gradually;
   (iv) at maximum level? (4)

c) Copy and complete table 35.5 (where br means birth rate and dr means death rate). (6)

situation	does this situation occur in the graph? (answer YES or NO)	if YES identify the stage(s)
br = dr		
br > dr		
br < dr		

Table 35.5

d) At which lettered stage had the population reached the environment's carrying capacity? (1)

e) Imagine that predators were introduced to the island at the end of stage D. Predict the form that the next part of the graph would take. (1)

2 Many years ago a scientist carried out a survey to investigate the relationship between water availability and size of territory occupied by each of 120 Australian

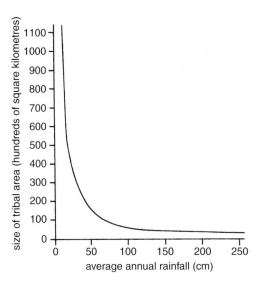

Figure 35.8

Aborigine tribes. He chose tribes which each contained about 500 members and whose only source of water was the rain that fell on their territory. The graph in figure 35.8 summarises his results.

a) Name the TWO sets of data that had to be recorded by the scientist. (2)

b) Which of the two variables was the one being investigated to find out if it affected the size of the other? (1)

c) (i) Why did the scientist study as many as 120 tribes?
   (ii) Why did he choose to study only tribes of similar size? (2)

d) (i) Draw a conclusion from the graph about the apparent effect of one factor on the other.
   (ii) Suggest why this should be the case. (2)

e) State TWO ways in which the lifestyle of the Aborigines considered in this study probably resembled that of the people who lived in the Stone Age. (2)

f) Why would it be impossible to repeat the above survey nowadays? (1)

3 a) What is meant by the term *subsistence farming*? (2)

b) Suggest THREE ways in which an African subsistence farmer of today shares a similar lifestyle to that of one of the earliest farmers of about 10 000 years ago. (3)

Continued ➢

Applying your knowledge

age (years)	number of survivors out of 1000	probable life expectancy (years)
0	1000	71.7
1	982	71.9
2	981	71.1
3	980	70.2
4	979	69.2
5	978	68.2
10	976	63.3
20	973	53.1
30	966	44.0
40	955	34.4
50	921	25.4
60	837	17.4
70	643	10.9
80	338	6.2

Table 35.6

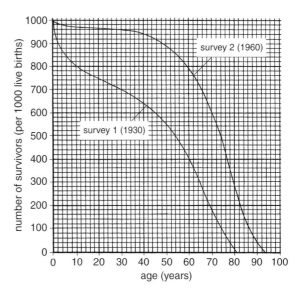

Figure 35.9

4   Table 35.6 shows the life expectancy data for a sample of a thousand people in a developed European country in 1980.

Figure 35.9 gives graphs of the survival rate per thousand live births for the same country. Survey 1 was carried out in 1930; survey 2 in 1960.

a)   Using data from the table, calculate the percentage of the original sample that reached their sixtieth birthday. (1)

b)   From the table,
   (i)   state how many more years a person who has reached her thirtieth birthday can expect to live;
   (ii)   calculate the total age that a person who has reached his fiftieth birthday can expect to reach finally. (1)

c)   The table shows that the life expectancy of babies under the age of one year is less than that of babies between one and two years. Suggest why. (1)

d)   From figure 35.9, draw a general conclusion about the length of life expectancy in 1960 compared with that in 1930. (1)

e)   Unlike the graph of survey 2, the graph of survey 1 declines steadily between 0 and 10 years. Name TWO factors that could account for this difference. (2)

f)   By what age had half of the original population of one thousand people died in the
   (i)   1930 survey;
   (ii)   1960 survey? (1)

g)   (i)   At which of the following ages did the number of survivors differ most between surveys?
   A   35 years
   B   45 years
   C   55 years
   D   65 years
   (ii)   How many more people per thousand survived to age 70 and beyond in 1960 compared with 1930? (2)

h)   Make a simple copy of the graph to include both curves and then add a third curve to represent the survival rate as it could have been for the same country in the year 1600. (1)

5   Give an account of the factors that may explain the exponential growth of the human population of the world. (10)

36 Demographic trends

Demography is the study of human population statistics. A population's size is comparable to the volume of water in a bath. It is affected by several factors as shown in figure 36.1. Any change (**demographic trend**) in a country's population size depends on the four factors listed in table 36.1.

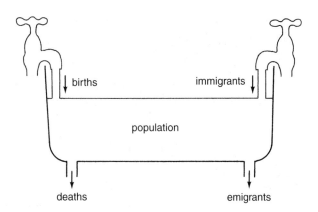

Figure 36.1 Factors affecting population size

Using the abbreviations explained in table 36.1, the formula used to calculate the overall increase (or decrease) in size of a population is

> change in population size = (br + ir) − (dr + er)

This is sometimes given in the simpler form

> change in population size = br − dr + ir − er

For the sake of simplicity it is going to be assumed that ir and er are equal and cancel one another out. Therefore they have been omitted from the following examples.

factor	abbreviation	description
birth rate	br	annual number of births per 1000 population
death rate	dr	annual number of deaths per 1000 population
immigration rate	ir	annual number of immigrants per 1000 population
emigration rate	er	annual number of emigrants per 1000 population

Table 36.1 Factors affecting changes in population size

Comparing a developing and a developed country

The population in each of the countries referred to in figure 36.2 increases by the difference between the birth rate and the death rate as indicated by the shaded areas.

In country A (which is still developing) the death rate is decreasing more rapidly than the birth rate. The difference between the two is therefore **increasing** with time and population growth rate is speeding up.

In country B (which is already developed) the birth rate is decreasing more rapidly than the death rate. The difference between the two is therefore **decreasing** with time and population growth rate is slowing down.

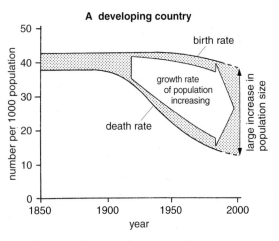

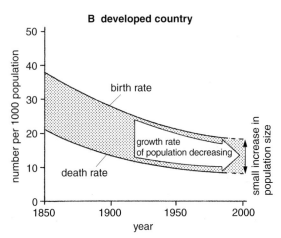

Figure 36.2 Population growth rates of two countries

Demographic transition model

This model (illustrated in figure 36.3) attempts to relate rate of population growth with **cultural development**. It maintains that as a developing country gradually becomes developed (industrialised) it passes through four demographic stages represented by the equations below.

1   **high br + high dr** $\longrightarrow$ **stable population**

Birth and death rates are roughly equal and population growth is slow or non-existent.

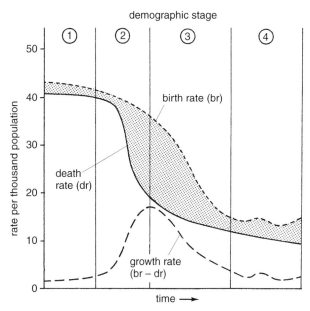

Figure 36.3 Demographic transition model

2   **high br + moderate dr** $\longrightarrow$ **early expanding population**

Since birth rate exceeds death rate, rapid population growth occurs.

3   **moderate br + low dr** $\longrightarrow$ **late expanding population**

Birth rate exceeds death rate but the difference is narrowing. The population continues to grow but at a slower rate than stage 2.

4   **low br + low dr** $\longrightarrow$ **stable population**

Birth and death rates are roughly equal and population growth is slow or non-existent.

Since decrease in death rate occurs before decrease in birth rate, **a large increase in population** occurs during the period of change from developing to developed country.

Population pyramids

A **population pyramid** is a representation of the structure of a population with respect to the **age** and **sex** of its members at one point in time. Figure 36.4 and table 36.2 compare the population pyramid of a developing country with that of a developed one.

Anticipating future needs

In addition to providing information about the state of a country's population at a certain point in time, such

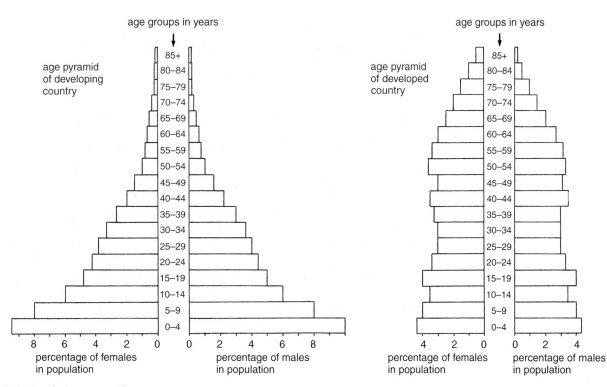

Figure 36.4 Population pyramids

	developing country	developed country
shape of pyramid	broad-based	top-heavy
factors affecting shape of pyramid	high birth rate, relatively short life expectancy, moderate death rate	low birth rate, relatively long life expectancy, low death rate
relative number of people who live to 65+ years	few	many
average age of population (years)	15	35
relative number of people who have most or all of reproductive years ahead of them	much larger	much smaller
population growth rate at present	rapid	very slow
potential for future population growth	enormous	limited

Table 36.2 Comparison of population pyramids

pyramids are especially useful as **predictors** of future population structure and **indicators** of future needs of the populace. These include satisfactory standards of public health facilities, transport, public utilities (e.g. water, electricity, gas, etc.) and education.

The government of a **developing** country could find that 50% or more of the population comprises a **young dependent group** under the age of 16. It would then look ahead and try to invest a large portion of the country's gross national product (GNP) in appropriate medical care, education and employment opportunities for the young. For example, it might embark on a programme of building hospitals and schools and training suitable staff. It would probably also promote family planning and birth control. It would be unlikely to be able to invest significant amounts in care for the elderly minority.

The government of a **developed** country would find itself in a different position. With a smaller proportion of the population made up of younger people, the demand for the construction of new schools would be relatively small. However, the government would have to make preparations to meet the pressing demands of an ever increasing proportion of the population that survive into old age and make up an **elderly dependent group**. Preparing for this large number of older people means investing in areas of specialised medical care and welfare, and financing building programmes which include sheltered housing, old folks' homes and geriatric hospitals.

Gender imbalance

Close inspection of the age pyramid for the developed country in figure 36.4 shows it to be **asymmetrical** for the two sexes beyond the age of 50. The higher death rate amongst middle- to old-aged men is attributed in part to factors such as excessive stress, smoking, excessive alcohol consumption and lack of exercise, though genetic factors may also play a part.

Most recent surveys show that this difference in the pyramid between the two sexes is gradually diminishing. This could be due in part to many men adopting a healthier lifestyle.

Testing your knowledge

1. a) What is meant by the term *demography*? (1)
   b) Define the terms *birth rate* and *death rate*. (2)
   c) Give the full formula used to calculate the change in size of a population. (2)

2. a) During which TWO phases of the demographic transition model is birth rate approximately equal to death rate? (2)
   b) Describe the relationship that exists between birth rate and death rate during the other two stages of the model. (2)

3. a) What is a *population pyramid*? (2)
   b) Give THREE ways in which a population pyramid for a developed country differs from that for a developing country. (3)
   c) Give TWO examples of useful information that a developing country's government may be able to obtain from a pyramid of the country's population. (2)

Population control

The human population is growing exponentially (see figure 35.4 on p 277). Every **minute** it increases by 180 individuals; every **day** by 22 000; every **year** by over 90 million. Although some developed European countries have a zero (or even negative) population growth rate, many developing countries have such high growth rates that already since 1960 they have added more people to the world's population than the present combined population of USA, Europe, Russia and Japan!

If this trend is allowed to continue, a new global **carrying capacity** will be reached. At that point planet Earth will be unable to support any further increase in population since one or more factors essential for life (e.g. food, clean air, clean water, etc.) will become **limiting** and exert a **regulatory effect** by increasing the death rate.

Populations of deer

Studies of populations of other vertebrates (e.g. deer) caught up in a small scale version of this 'runaway' situation show that the population numbers drop, sometimes going into a period of **'free fall'**.

Careful study of figure 36.5 reveals that the deer population goes through the following stages:

1 Small population of deer gains access to an uninhabited grassy island free of predators.

2 Population grows rapidly and approaches the carrying capacity of the environment.

3 Population exceeds the carrying capacity, the environment becomes severely damaged and the death rate of the deer population increases.

4 Population goes into free fall and crashes down until a new carrying capacity is reached.

5 Population stabilises at new lower carrying capacity which the damaged environment can support.

6 Population may increase to a new higher carrying capacity if the environment recovers from damage.

7 On some occasions the deer population crashes to zero for reasons that are not fully understood.

Birth control

It is inevitable that the type of disaster indicated by figure 36.5 will similary affect the human population in the future if it is allowed to continue to increase at its current rate.

In the opinion of experts, the only way to ensure that this does not happen is for the present world population to exert rigorous **population control** without further delay. **Birth control** (the process by which fertilisation or pregnancy is prevented from occurring) is generally regarded as the most humane and realistic option.

However, the world is populated by many diverse groups of people whose ways of life differ in:

◆ **religious beliefs** (some religions oppose birth control and encourage their followers to 'Go forth and multiply');

◆ **standards of medical care** (the higher the rate of child mortality the greater the resistance to birth control since a large family is the only 'guarantee' of some children surviving);

◆ **economic situation** (the greater the degree of poverty in a society the greater the resistance to birth control since children are an essential source of cheap labour needed to support the family);

◆ **cultural and social backgrounds** (birth control is resisted in poor societies where a large family is the only form of old age 'insurance');

◆ **educational opportunities** (increase in number of years of schooling especially for girls results in a decrease in birth rate as women seek career opportunities outside the home);

◆ **degree of status accorded to women** (increased emancipation of women is accompanied by decrease in birth rate since women who have more control over their lives often choose later marriage and make use of contraception).

Moral dilemma

Energy consumption in relation to percentage of world population varies enormously from country to country. For example, the USA possesses 6% of the world's population but consumes 30% of its energy resources. India has 20% of the world's population

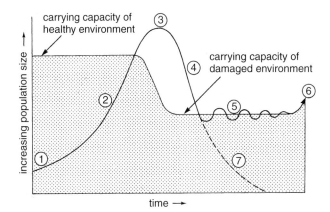

Figure 36.5 Population in 'free fall'

but only uses 2% of its energy. During his or her lifetime an average American consumes about 40 times as much of the planet's resources as their counterpart in Asia.

Many people feel therefore that it is **immoral** of the inhabitants of the more affluent developed countries to try to impose birth control on the people in poorer developing countries without also addressing the problems of unequal use of resources and distribution of wealth.

Present situation in developing countries

Family planning involves helping couples to make a conscious effort to regulate the **number** and **timing** of new births. The governments of most developing countries promote and give financial support to programmes of family planning. However, when these are carried out in isolation they often prove to be ineffective. They are much more likely to succeed if they are accompanied by **social** and **economic** developments which give families security.

The future

Despite the devastating effect of AIDS in some countries and increased use of contraception worldwide, the rapid growth of the human population still remains the single most serious problem facing humankind. An all-nation global solution is urgently required before resources become limiting and the human death rate increases. Figure 36.6 shows the trends that have been predicted for the future if the world population continues to grow at its present rate.

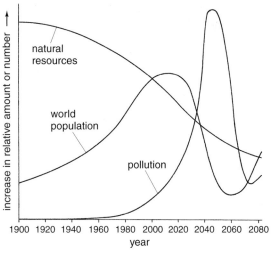

Figure 36.6 Predicted trends

Testing your knowledge

1 Identify THREE factors that could eventually limit further exponential growth of the world's human population. (3)

2 a) Define the term *birth control*. (2)

  b) Give THREE reasons why some people are unwilling to adopt birth control measures. (3)

3 a) Why is the increased emancipation of women in a country normally accompanied by a decrease in that country's birth rate? (2)

  b) Why is family planning more likely to succeed in a country when it is accompanied by economic developments? (1)

Applying your knowledge

1 a) A population of 2 million people was found to produce 400 babies in one year. What was the birth rate that year? (1)

  b) In a country with a population of 25 million, a quarter of a million people died in one year. Calculate the death rate for that year. (1)

  c) One year a country was found to have a birth rate of 25. If the total population comprised 30 million people, calculate the actual number of babies born during that year. (1)

2 The graph in figure 36.7 illustrates the demographic transition theory.

  a) State the main difference between this diagram and figure 36.3. (1)

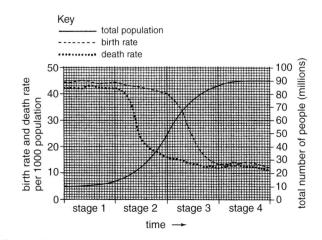

Figure 36.7

Continued ➤

Applying your knowledge

b) At the very end of stage 1 in figure 36.7, what was
  (i) the birth rate;
  (ii) the death rate;
  (iii) the natural increase in the population? (3)

c) At the very end of stage 2, what was
  (i) the birth rate;
  (ii) the death rate;
  (iii) the natural increase in the population? (3)

d) By how many times was the population's natural increase at the end of stage 2 greater than that at the end of stage 1? (1)

e) State the total number of people in the population at
  (i) the start of stage 1;
  (ii) the end of stage 4.
  (iii) State the total number of people by which the population had increased between these two points in time.
  (iv) Express your answer to **(iii)** as a percentage increase. (4)

3 The data in table 36.3 refer to a developing country in Asia.

year	birth rate	death rate
1920	38.1	34.0
1925	37.5	34.5
1930	38.2	35.1
1935	36.8	34.3
1940	38.3	34.5
1945	36.7	27.2
1950	37.6	13.8
1955	37.0	9.0
1960	36.5	6.1
1965	34.1	6.8
1970	29.5	6.3

Table 36.3

a) Present birth rate and death rate as line graphs using shared axes on the same sheet of graph paper. (4)

b) **(i)** Which TWO stages of the demographic transition model are passed through by this country in the course of the timescale covered by the graph? (1)
  (ii) Predict approximate values of birth rate and death rate for this country in the year 2000 and explain your answer. (3)

c) This country has raised the status of women by discouraging arranged marriages and improving the educational opportunities available to schoolgirls. Explain why each of these measures helps to reduce the birth rate in the long run. (2)

d) Suggest TWO factors that may have contributed to decrease in infant mortality in this Asian country in recent years. (2)

e) In almost all developing countries the drop in birth rate only occurs once a significant drop in death rate has become established. With reference to the economic structure of the family unit, suggest why this should be the case. (2)

f) What must happen to the birth rate and death rate of a country's population to keep the population size at a constant level? (1)

4 In the Bible the last book of the New Testament, called Revelation, contains a description of the Apocalypse. It predicts that the world will come to an end by being overpowered by the four Horsemen of the Apocalypse who represent famine, war, plague and death. State TWO things that humans could and should be doing now to try to prevent this prediction from coming true. (2)

5 **(i)** Give an account of the demographic transition model. (6)
  (ii) Describe TWO factors that contribute to the changes to the birth and death rates present in the model. (4)

What you should know
(Chapters 35–36)

(See table 36.4 for word bank.)

1 When a population colonises a favourable new environment, its number increases in _____ .

2 The maximum size of a population that can be supported by a particular environment is called its _____ .

3 The carrying capacity of an environment is determined by limiting factors such as available food supply, _____ and space which exert a _____ effect on the population.

4 Humans have increased the carrying capacity of their environment by producing vast amounts of _____ and improving public _____ which in turn have reduced child _____ and increased life _____ . This has led to the human population changing from a period of stability to one of exponential growth.

5 The first population spurt began about 10 000 years ago when humans began to practise _____ ; the second began around 1650 AD when great advances in scientific understanding led to the _____ revolution.

6 Examples of pre-industrial cultures exist in many developing countries and a few examples of pre-agricultural cultures survive amongst _____ societies.

7 A change in a country's population size is called a _____ trend. It is affected by _____ and death rates, and immigration and _____ rates.

8 The demographic _____ model tries to relate rate of human population growth to cultural development. It suggests that as a developing country becomes _____ it passes through four demographic stages from stable to _____ to late expanding to _____ .

9 A population _____ represents the structure of a population with respect to the age and _____ of its members. It is useful as a predictor of future needs of a population. The population pyramid of a developing country is broad-based whereas that of a developed country is _____ .

10 If the human population continues to increase _____ , a new carrying capacity will be reached and certain factors such as food and clean water will become _____ . Such a disaster may be averted if population _____ through birth rate reduction is adopted worldwide.

abundance	emigration	pyramid
agriculture	expectancy	regulatory
birth	exponentially	sex
carrying capacity	food	stable
control	health	top-heavy
demographic	industrial	transition
developed	limiting	undeveloped
early expanding	mortality	water

Table 36.4 Word bank for chapters 35–36

37 Food supply as a limiting factor

Natural succession

Imagine a sheet of **bare rock** exposed by a landslide and completely uninhabited by living things. If this rock remained undisturbed by human activities for a very long time then the following sequence of events would take place.

The first colonisers (**pioneer community**) of the rock would be **lichens** (see figure 37.1). These plants would retain moisture and survive periods of water shortage. They would produce acids which would break down the rock.

Mosses would follow and as the rock disintegration process continued and dead plants and microbes accumulated, a layer of **soil** would gradually develop. Eventually this would be able to support small **flowering plants** and **grasses**, then **woody shrubs** and finally (after, say, 1000 years) **deciduous trees** (the **climax community**).

This series of changes that occurs during the development of a climax community is called **natural succession**. The form that the climax community takes varies from climate to climate.

Effect of land use on natural succession

As recently as 400 years ago, Britain was covered by such a dense layer of climax community forest that a squirrel would probably have been able to travel from one end of the country to the other without ever having to come down onto the ground.

This would be impossible today because vast areas of natural forest have been cleared for **agricultural use** and **human settlement**. This pattern is also true for most other developed countries. It has resulted in the process of natural succession being brought largely to a halt since useful land is rarely left abandoned to nature for extensive periods of time. Instead, ever-increasing demands are made on the land to supply the growing population with food by intensive crop growing and animal husbandry.

Developing countries

As the human population continues to increase, the demands put on the existing agricultural land in developing countries become untenable. The land is overused and soil fertility drops. It becomes essential to find additional land for food production. Figure 37.2 charts the **rising demand** for agricultural land in tropical

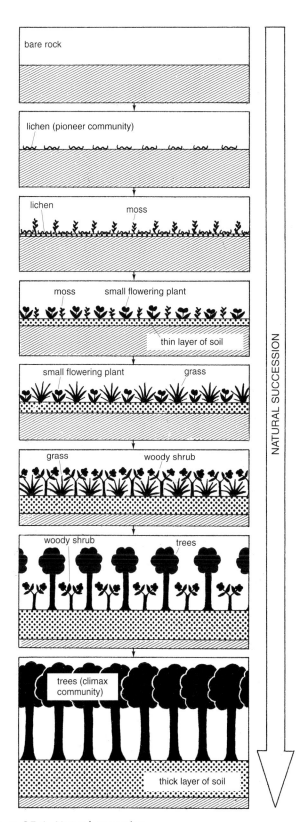

Figure 37.1 Natural succession

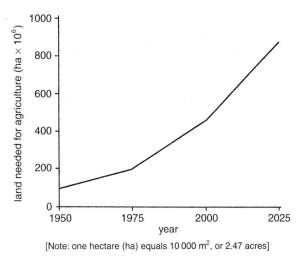

[Note: one hectare (ha) equals 10 000 m^2, or 2.47 acres]

Figure 37.2 Demand for agricultural land

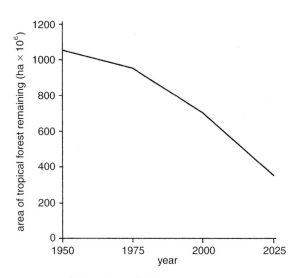

Figure 37.3 Depletion of tropical forest

countries where it is often used for smallholder cultivation, cash crop plantations and cattle ranches.

Deforestation

To satisfy this demand for land, vast areas of forest are cleared and the process of natural succession by which the forest would eventually regenerate itself is prevented from taking place. Figure 37.3 shows the process of **forest depletion** and projects the expected extent of this trend in the future if land is cleared to cope with the needs of the expanding human population.

Each year about ten million hectares of tropical forest (an area roughly twice the size of Scotland) are being eliminated from the face of the Earth. **Deforestation** on this scale amounts to a drastic irreversible loss which the world can ill afford. In 1950, 15% of the world's land mass was covered with tropical forest. By the year 2010 this will have declined to 6% or less if current trends continue.

Cash crops

Instead of using the land made available by clearing tropical forest to grow basic foodstuffs for local consumption, many poor developing countries use it to grow a **cash crop** such as coffee or cocoa. By exporting this commodity to wealthy countries, a developing country attempts to earn the hard cash needed to support its fragile economy.

However, this system is risky because the world price of the commodity may drop, leaving the developing country in debt *and* short of food for its people. This results in more forest having to be cleared to grow a food crop and/or another cash crop. In the meantime the country has to borrow from international banks to buy food, seeds and fertilisers, and sinks more deeply into debt.

Energy

In developed countries fossil fuels and nuclear power are used to provide energy. However, in developing countries many people still depend on wood for fuel. This makes further demands on the ever-shrinking forest. As supplies of wood become scarce, people use **animal dung** and **crop stubble** for fuel. This in turn deprives agricultural land of supplies of natural fertiliser and its fertility decreases.

Far-reaching consequences

If the process of **deforestation** is allowed to continue and tropical forests are not renewed in developing countries then severe consequences will follow. Some of these are discussed in chapter 38 (p 308).

Use of marginal land

Marginal land is located on the edge of cultivated land. It is usually relatively infertile and lacks regular rainfall. However, as people become more and more desperate for land on which to grow crops, attempts are made to cultivate marginal land. These are rarely successful and often accelerate the process of **desertification** (see p 309).

Use of chemicals to increase food production

Monoculture

A **monoculture** is a vast cultivated population of one type of crop plant whose members are normally genetically identical. In order to feed the ever-growing world population, humans have cleared natural ecosystems to accommodate vast monocultures of crops such as wheat, maize, rice and potatoes.

Modern agriculture has become so efficient that the increased level of food production achieved in recent years has kept pace with the 90 million or more new human beings added annually to the world population.

Farming in many developed countries has become remarkably productive. For example, farmers in the USA, who make up only 2% of the population, grow the food consumed by the rest of the population and produce more than half of all the agricultural products exported worldwide. These same farmers produce 46% of the world's maize, 21% of its oats and 15% of its wheat on only 11% of the world's croplands. Britain also has an impressive record. Wheat yields have been raised by 250% since 1945. Such advances in agriculture in recent years have been largely dependent on the use of various chemicals for their success.

Fertiliser

The maintenance of a natural balanced ecosystem depends on the repeated **cycling** of chemical nutrients such as nitrogen. The natural processes of **decay** and **nitrification** in the soil replace nutrients as fast as they are used by plants.

However, when a crop is grown on cleared land and then harvested and removed, the balance is disturbed. The cycles are broken since almost no dead plant material is returned to the soil for breakdown by micro-organisms. Less nitrate is generated by nitrifying bacteria and the soil becomes less fertile.

This problem is tackled by adding **synthetic fertiliser** to the soil. Fertilisers are chemicals rich in **nitrate** and other chemicals (e.g. phosphate and potassium) which are essential for healthy plant growth. Sufficient quantities of fertiliser are added to soil to raise its nutrient supply to the level needed to promote optimum growth of a particular crop.

Used in conjunction with pesticides and herbicides (see p 294), fertilisers continue to play a key role in **boosting crop yields** with more and more being used worldwide every year (see table 37.1).

The graph in figure 37.4 shows the effect of nitrate and potassium on yield of maize plants. It is interesting to note that in this example, yield obtained depends on both the quantity of nitrate and the quantity of potassium added.

In many developed countries the use of fertilisers have eliminated the need for crop rotation since they can be used to support **continuous use** of a piece of land for growth of the same crop.

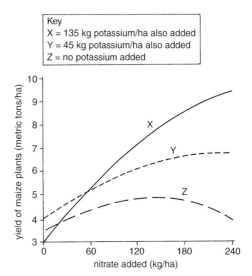

Figure 37.4 Effect of fertiliser on maize yield

year	worldwide annual use (kg × 10⁹)		
	nitrate	**phosphate**	**potassium**
1910	0.51	0.57	0.55
1920	0.97	0.99	1.11
1930	1.58	1.33	1.78
1940	2.78	1.65	2.59
1950	4.33	2.45	3.72
1960	12.67	4.92	7.97
1970	28.68	8.40	13.89
1980	57.16	13.59	23.43

Table 37.1 Increasing use of fertiliser

Disadvantages

Soil structure

Manufactured fertiliser is not a complete substitute for natural fertiliser such as manure since it fails to add humus to the soil and maintain its crumb structure. This leads to poorer aeration of the soil and decreased ability to hold water.

Quality of drinking water

When **nitrate** is applied too liberally to the soil, the excess may be washed (leached) out by rain into rivers and lochs including those which supply us with drinking water (see p 328).

Eutrophication

Eutrophication is the process by which leachate from fertilised fields (or sewage effluent) makes a waterway or loch over-rich in mineral nutrients (e.g. nitrate). This promotes the rapid growth of certain algae and leads to a depletion of the water's oxygen supply (see also p 324).

Herbicides

Competition

Crop plants often have to **compete** with vigorous weeds which may deprive the crop of one or more of many possible factors, such as water, light, mineral nutrients, space to grow, and so on.

Selective weedkiller

In an attempt to control populations of unwanted weeds, farmers often apply **herbicides** (weedkillers). Some of these act **selectively** by stimulating the rate of growth of broad-leaved weeds to such an extent that they exhaust their food reserves and die (see figure 37.5). The narrow-leaved cereal plants absorb little of the chemical and are hardly affected. Sometimes the selective chemical is laid down as a barrier just after the crop has been planted. The cereal crop's shoots (protected by sheaths) are able to grow up through the barrier unaffected. However, the unprotected leafy shoots of the weeds die on making contact with the herbicide barrier.

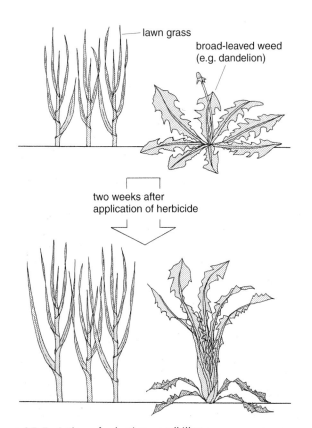

lawn grass

broad-leaved weed (e.g. dandelion)

two weeks after application of herbicide

Figure 37.5 Action of selective weedkiller

Other herbicides (e.g. paraquat) are **non-selective** and have a destructive (but short-lived) effect on *all* green tissue. They can be used to clear an area completely before the crop is sown.

Pesticides

In a natural ecosystem, a **balance** exists between producers and consumers. In addition the members of the plant, animal and microbial communities tend to live in small mixed populations. If the numbers of a certain species of green plant decrease then the numbers of animals and microbes that depend on the plant fall accordingly. This allows the plant species to recover and soon the balance is restored.

However, in a **monoculture** of a crop plant, ideal conditions are presented to **pests** and **parasites** (e.g. fungus) to feed and reproduce repeatedly without ever running out of food (see figure 37.6).

Fungal diseases (e.g. mildew and rust) spread rapidly through cereal monocultures. Invertebrate pests (e.g. nematode worms, slugs and insects) quickly infect and ruin a crop of food plants such as potatoes. Some pests reduce crop yield directly by feeding on the plant part intended for human consumption. Others do damage indirectly by attacking the crop plant's roots or leaves so that the plant fails to grow properly.

Chemicals called **pesticides** are applied liberally to crops in order to control pests. Over 400 different pesticides are approved for use in Britain, each designed to act on a particular type of pest. For example, **fungicides** kill fungi and **insecticides** kill insects. In 1990 the farming industry in UK spent £440 million (6% of its annual budget) treating crops with pesticides.

Use of fungicides

Fungicides are often sprayed onto crop plants prior to fungal attack (see figure 37.7 on p 296) or used to dress cereal grains contaminated with fungal spores. When the fungal spores begin to germinate they absorb the chemical and die. Repeated applications are needed, since rain tends to wash the chemical off and new leaves, on emerging, are unprotected and act as prime targets for fungal attack.

Importance of pesticides

It has been estimated that in the 1960s, 30–35% of the world's crops were lost due to pests, diseases and deterioration during storage. Use of chemicals in recent years has significantly reduced this loss. Without pesticides, cereal crop yield would be reduced by 25% after one year and by 45% after three years. It is unlikely that wholesome, healthy, unblemished food, sufficient in quantity to feed the world's rising

NATURAL ECOSYSTEM

unaffected wild
oat plant

wild oat plant infected
by fungus which
attacks oats

unaffected wild
oat plant

oat plant dies but
parasite is unable to
attack neighbouring
plants

ARTIFICIAL ECOSYSTEM (OAT MONOCULTURE)

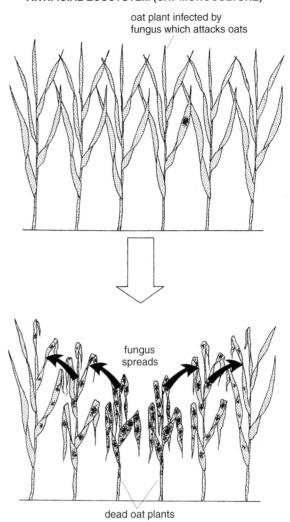

oat plant infected by
fungus which attacks oats

fungus
spreads

dead oat plants

Figure 37.6 Effect of fungal parasite on two ecosystems

population could be produced without the aid of pesticides.

Characteristics of a pesticide

Ideally a pesticide should be **specific** to the pest, **short-lived** in its action and **safe**. It should not persist when released into the environment but instead break down into simple chemicals which are harmless to the host plant, the environment and the human consumer.

Whereas early pesticides failed to meet several of these criteria (see p 321), modern chemicals achieve high levels of specificity and safety.

Pesticides of the future

Pheromones are chemicals released by animals which affect the **behaviour** of other members of the same species (e.g. cause them to become sexually aroused). Scientists are attempting to develop insecticides containing pest pheromones which would be sprayed near but not on the crop and simply attract the pests away from the crop.

Genetic engineers are developing 'new style' pesticides. In one project scientists are working with a type of virus that only infects caterpillars. By inserting into the virus the gene for scorpion toxin, they have produced a new version of the virus which is harmless to humans but which paralyses and kills caterpillars within a few days. Such **genetically engineered** pesticides are expected to be used in the future to protect crops against pests.

Selective plant breeding

The plants that form the basis of the human diet have been derived from wild species by **selective breeding**. Since agriculture first began, people have selected repeatedly from each generation of food plants those individuals possessing **desirable characteristics**. These

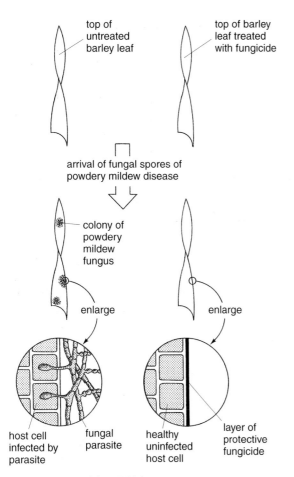

Figure 37.7 Impact of fungicide

have been used as the parents of the next generation, and so on down through the ages. The plants lacking the beneficial characteristics have been prevented from breeding.

Selection over many generations has improved the quality of the plants with respect to their usefulness to humans as food plants. For example, cultivated varieties of wheat, barley and potatoes have been bred which produce **higher yields** and are more **resistant** to disease than their predecessors. In some cases, several varieties have been developed from one original type (see figure 37.8).

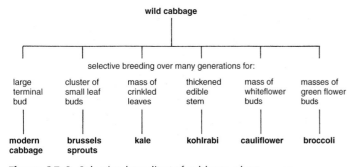

Figure 37.8 Selective breeding of cabbage plant

Testing your knowledge

1 a) What is meant by the term *natural succession*? (2)

   b) What TWO changes in land use in Britain over the last 400 years have brought natural succession to a halt? (2)

   c) Give TWO reasons why deforestation is practised on such an enormous scale in many developing countries. (2)

2 a) What is meant by the term *monoculture*? (1)

   b) When a crop is harvested, the nitrogen cycle is disrupted.
      (i) By what artificial means do some farmers attempt to solve this problem?
      (ii) What advantage is gained by the use of such chemicals?
      (iii) Identify ONE disadvantage that may result if the chemical is used excessively. (3)

3 a) Most cereal crops are narrow-leaved; the weeds that compete with them tend to be broad-leaved.
      (i) What type of chemical could be used in an attempt to destroy only the weeds?
      (ii) Explain how this method works. (3)

   b) (i) What is a *fungicide*?
      (ii) Give TWO reasons why repeated applications of a fungicide to a crop are required? (3)

Two methods of selective breeding

Inbreeding involves crossing closely related members of the same species with one another. In plants this is achieved by employing **self-pollination**. **Outbreeding** involves crossing unrelated members of the same species with one another. This is achieved by employing **cross-pollination**.

Once a strain has been produced which possesses a collection of desirable characteristics, inbreeding is used to try to maintain uniformity in future generations. However, this process often results in the strain eventually suffering reduced vigour (**inbreeding depression**).

Outbreeding is often used to produce new strains by crossing two different parental types and 'mixing' their genetic material. This often produces a strain that shows **hybrid vigour** and is better than either of the parents (see figure 37.9).

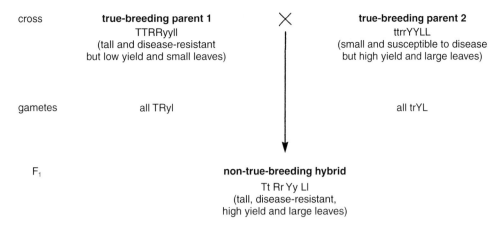

Figure 37.9 Hybridisation

However, the new strain is usually not true-breeding and cannot be depended upon to produce offspring all of which possess the improved characteristics such as increased yield or disease resistance. It is for this reason that the hybridisation process must be repeated every year using the original parental lines.

Green Revolution

By a combination of inbreeding and outbreeding techniques, plant breeders have succeeded in developing new varieties of several staple food plants such as barley, maize and rice. These have been selected for many of the characteristics shown in figure 37.10.

Introduction of these new improved varieties on a massive scale brought about the so-called **Green Revolution**. Record-breaking crops were first grown in the USA in the 1940s followed by Europe in the 1950s and then developing countries in the 1960s.

Using a strain of drought-resistant Mexican high-yield wheat, India increased its harvest in 1965 by 35% and doubled its wheat yield over the following 15 years. From the early 1960s to the mid-1980s world food production grew faster than the population (see figure 37.11) though the average increase in food production achieved during each period of time showed a decreasing trend.

Other side of success story

Although the Green Revolution has achieved a remarkable increase in food production, there is a downside to the story. The tendency towards using **genetically uniform** varieties of high-yielding strains makes them more **vulnerable to attack** by new mutant strains of disease organisms. If the crop has no natural resistance to a pest, the entire crop may be lost unless costly pesticide can be applied in time.

In addition, the new so-called high-yield varieties are in fact 'rapid-response' strains. Two or three crops can be

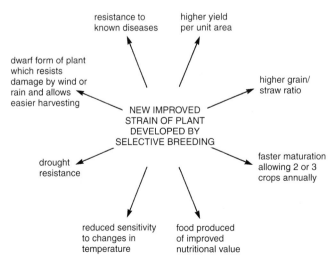

Figure 37.10 Beneficial characteristics of selectively bred strain

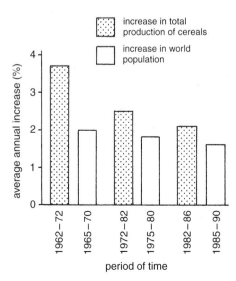

Figure 37.11 Effect of Green Revolution on food production

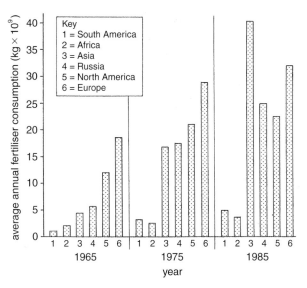

Figure 37.12 Worldwide use of fertiliser

genetically engineered characteristic	potential benefit resulting
Increased efficiency at assimilating fertiliser.	Reduced quantity of fertiliser required.
Ability to fix nitrogen.	Reduced quantity of fertiliser required.
Resistance to pests.	Reduced quantity of pesticide needed.
Resistance to herbicides.	Less damage caused to crop during treatment of weeds.
Increased photosynthetic capacity.	Higher yield of food produced.
Enhanced seed oil production.	Higher yield of oil produced.
Increased resistance to drought and salinity.	Crops suited to marginal environments developed.

Table 37.2 Genes under investigation by genetic engineers

produced per year, but only if massive amounts of fertiliser are added to the ground.

Figure 37.12 shows the annual consumption of fertiliser in major regions of the world. It is interesting to note the rapid increase in use of fertiliser in Asia. However, many farmers in developing Asian countries cannot afford to buy the necessary fertiliser without going into heavy debt. So the system tends to be divisive, with those who can afford fertiliser capitalising on the Green Revolution and those who cannot losing out.

Genetic manipulation and the future

The challenge to agriculture is to continue to boost food production to the levels achieved by the Green Revolution but at the same time reduce the burden put on the environment by the escalating use of fertilisers and pesticides.

Recombinant DNA technology

Sexual reproduction is the conventional means by which DNA from one organism meets and combines with DNA of another. Under natural conditions such DNA recombination can only occur amongst the members of the same species.

Genetic engineering

In the 1970s it was discovered that certain bacterial enzymes could be used to cut and join DNA from different species of living organisms. This technique has enabled scientists to transfer DNA from one species (e.g. gene for human insulin) into the genotype of another species (e.g. the bacterium *Escherichia coli*). Such genetic engineering is called **recombinant DNA technology** and

many applications of it involving plants are now being attempted.

Pea plants possess a gene which codes for a protein called lectin. Although harmless to humans, lectin is poisonous to caterpillars and acts as a **natural insecticide**. A type of soil bacterium has been successfully used by genetic engineers to transfer the lectin gene from pea to potato plant.

So far, recombinant DNA technology has not been successful with most cereal plants. However, it is expected that the problems will be solved in the future and that cereal crops will eventually be engineered genetically to contain genes for useful characteristics such as those shown in table 37.2.

Production of new crop plant by somatic fusion

Two different species cannot interbreed successfully. In some cases this problem can be overcome by **fusion of somatic** (non-sex) **cells**. Unspecialised cells from the two different plant species are selected and their cell walls digested away using enzymes. This leaves naked protoplasts each consisting of the living cell components (nucleus and cytoplasm) surrounded by the cell membrane (see figure 37.13).

In some cases isolated protoplasts from two different species can be induced to fuse and form a **hybrid protoplast** if certain chemicals are added to the culture

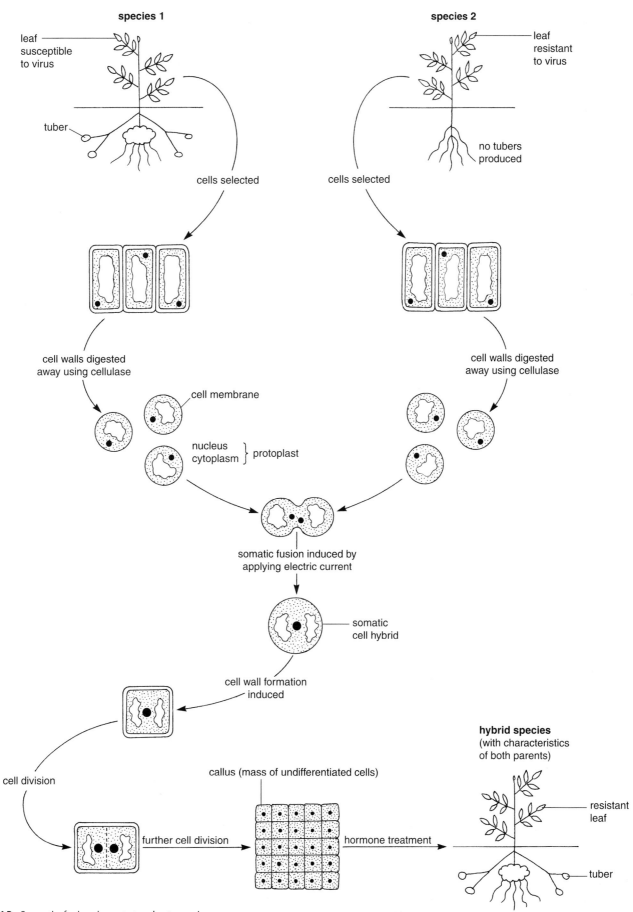

Figure 37.13 Somatic fusion in potato plant species

medium, or the protoplasts are subjected to an electric current.

The hybrid formed by somatic fusion is induced to form a cell wall and divide into an undifferentiated cell mass (callus). In the presence of hormones, calluses develop into hybrid plants containing a mixture of the parents' genetic traits.

Resistance to potato leaf roll

Potato leaf roll is a disease caused by a virus which is spread by aphids. It can severely reduce the yield of a crop of the potato plant (*Solanum tuberosum*). *Solanum brevidens* is a wild non-tuber-bearing species of potato plant which is resistant to potato leaf roll virus.

Scientists have overcome the lack of sexual compatibility between these two species of plant by uniting them by somatic fusion. This has resulted in the production of a new variety of potato plant which is tuber-bearing *and* resistant to potato leaf roll virus.

Testing your knowledge

1 a) Briefly describe the procedure employed during selective breeding in plants. (2)

b) Is a uniform, true-breeding strain of crop plant produced by inbreeding or outbreeding? (1)

c) State ONE advantage and ONE disadvantage to the farmer of producing a crop that is uniform and true-breeding. (2)

2 The *Green Revolution* has resulted from the development of *rapid-response* strains of plant. Give ONE advantage and ONE disadvantage of the use of such plant strains. (2)

3 a) (i) What is meant by the term *recombinant DNA technology*?
(ii) Briefly describe an example of genetic engineering involving crop plants. (4)

b) (i) What is meant by the term *somatic fusion*?
(ii) Briefly describe an example of this process. (4)

Effects of food shortage

Famine

Food supply is one of the factors that limits the population size of non-human vertebrate species living in a natural ecosystem. All through its history, the human population has also been affected periodically by spells of food shortage which have led to local outbreaks of **famine**. During the twentieth century alone, millions of people have died in Russia, Asia and Africa from lack of food.

Balanced diet

A **balanced diet** consists of an adequate supply of each of the main classes of food such as **protein** (for growth and tissue repair), **carbohydrate** and **fat** (for energy), **minerals** (for healthy blood and strong bones) and **vitamins** (to prevent deficiency diseases).

The diet must provide a minimum of around 9500 kilojoules (kJ) per day to supply the energy needs of the average working person.

Starvation

This state results when a person's diet is so inadequate that it continuously fails to meet the requirements of the body.

Undernutrition

Undernutrition describes the condition suffered by a person who fails to receive enough food. The person receives neither an adequate quantity of protein to build new cells nor a sufficient number of kilojoules to meet their energy requirements. Over an extended period this situation results in wasting away of body tissues, emaciation and eventually death.

Malnutrition

Malnutrition describes the condition suffered by a person who fails to receive a balanced diet. The lack of one or more essential foodstuffs in the diet leads to a **deficiency disease**.

Figure 37.14 compares two children both of whom are receiving an adequate supply of energy. However, the African child is suffering from a form of malnutrition called **kwashiorkor** caused by shortage of protein in the diet.

An unbalanced diet (especially one low in protein) leaves people more susceptible to disease. Children deprived of adequate protein are likely to suffer permanent **mental** and **physical retardation**.

Unequal distribution of food

Sufficient food is produced each year to feed the entire world population. However, the food is not shared out equally (see figure 37.15). Every year at least 40 million people in developing countries die of starvation or hunger-related diseases. Many millions more suffer malnutrition which makes them less able to work and support their families, and so the vicious circle continues.

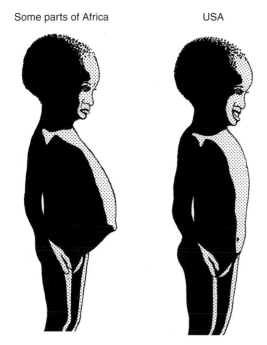

Figure 37.14 Kwashiorkor

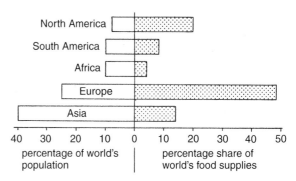

Figure 37.15 Unequal distribution of world food supplies

Food production versus population growth

The world's percentage annual increase in food production is greater than the percentage annual increase in population, as shown by graph A in figure 37.16. Although graph B shows an overall picture of food production outpacing population growth in developing countries, graph C reveals that the figures vary significantly from region to region. For example, during the period of time covered by the data, East Africa had the largest percentage annual increase in population but the smallest percentage annual increase in food production.

Lack of distribution

Many developed countries produce enormous **surpluses** of food. To prevent a surplus depressing the market price, the food is stored as a 'mountain' or 'lake' for future use. This keeps the price high but makes it too expensive for many poorer developing countries to purchase without incurring further heavy debt.

The lack of fair distribution of food at global level is one of the main contributing factors leading to starvation. The affected people become helpless and are forced to depend on **emergency aid** from developed countries for survival.

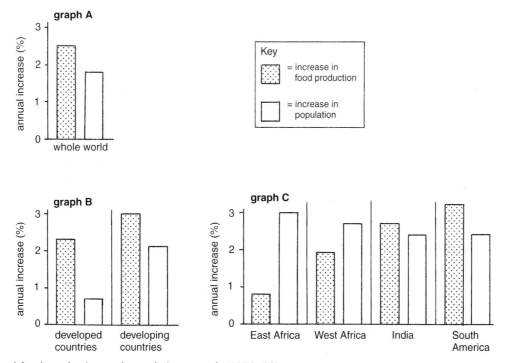

Figure 37.16 Annual food production and population growth (1970–82)

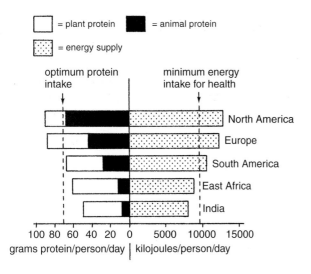

Figure 37.17 Comparative average protein and energy intakes

In some developing countries adequate food supplies do exist but unequal distribution at a local level results in a privileged minority consuming excess and the majority of the population going hungry.

Overeating and long food chains

In developed countries many people **overeat**. In the USA, one in three people over the age of forty is obese. On average a person in a developed country consumes about 1.5 times as many kilojoules and twice as much protein as a person in a developing country (see figure 37.17). Of this protein the component derived

from animals is approximately 5 times greater in the diet of the person from the developed country.

Energy is **lost** at each link in a food chain. A certain quantity of grain can support many people directly by providing them with cereal products (e.g. bread) or it can support far fewer people indirectly by first feeding it to livestock and then providing humans with meat and milk products. A reduction in consumption of meat in developed countries would make more food become available for people in developing countries.

Testing your knowledge

1 Construct a table to show the 5 main classes of food present in a balanced diet and the reason why each food type is required. (5)

2 Distinguish between the terms *undernutrition* and *malnutrition*. (2)

3 Sufficient food is produced annually to feed the entire world population, yet millions of people starve every year. Explain why. (2)

4 a) Why are shorter food chains preferable to longer ones when attempting to feed a population as economically as possible? (2)

   b) What simple change in eating habits by people in developed countries would immediately reduce the length of many food chains? (1)

Applying your knowledge

1 Each complete pie chart in figure 37.18 represents the world's total land mass.

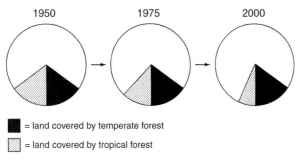

= land covered by temperate forest

= land covered by tropical forest

Figure 37.18

   a) Draw TWO conclusions from the data using the terms *deforestation* and *reforestation* in your answer. (2)

   b) (i) Give TWO reasons why the trend relating to tropical forest is especially pronounced in many developing countries.

      (ii) Predict ONE consequence for a developing country if this trend continues in the 21st century. (3)

2 Table 37.3 summarises the results from an investigation into the effect of fertilisers on a species of pasture grass used for animal feed. The growth rate of the grass was measured in kilograms of dry mass per hectare per day (kgDM/ha/day).

   a) Present the data as FIVE line graphs sharing common axes on the same sheet of graph paper. (4)

Continued ➤

Applying your knowledge

		growth rate of grass (kgDM/ha/day)						
		concentration of nitrate fertiliser applied (kg/ha)						
		0	40	80	120	160	200	240
no lime or phosphate added to soil		123	234	275	318	323	320	305
lime added to change soil pH from 5.4 to 5.9		105	242	271	318	325	318	307
concentration of phosphate fertiliser applied (kg/ha)	40	120	240	279	316	323	323	300
	80	110	305	347	360	360	339	308
	160	139	200	231	222	201	213	190

Table 37.3

b) (i) Describe the effect of increasing concentration of nitrate fertiliser only, on growth rate of the pasture grass.

(ii) What additional effect did liming the soil prior to application of each concentration of nitrate have on growth? (2)

c) Describe in turn the effect of each concentration of phosphate when used in combination with nitrate fertiliser. (3)

d) From the data, state the minimum concentrations of nitrate and phosphate that should be used to promote optimum growth of this grass. (2)

3 The cultivated variety of tomato plant develops excellent fruit but is susceptible to eelworm. A wild variety of tomato plant from South America is resistant to eelworm but produces small sour fruit.

a) Assume that both varieties belong to the same species. Briefly describe how scientists could attempt to produce a variety of tomato plant better than either of these two types. (2)

b) Assume that the two varieties belong to different species. Briefly describe how scientists could attempt to combine their genetic material without using recombinant DNA technology. (4)

4 Study figure 37.17 on p 302 of the text.

a) State THREE ways in which the protein intake of an average Indian differs from that of an average North American. (3)

b) (i) In which region of the world is the daily intake of kilojoules closest to the minimum number required for health?

(ii) Does the average person in this region receive an adequate number of kilojoules per day? (2)

5 Translated literally, the term *kwashiorkor* means 'the sickness that the old baby suffers when the new baby comes'.

a) (i) What causes kwashiorkor?

(ii) Suggest why the 'old' baby but not the 'new' baby suffers in this way.

(iii) Strictly speaking, why is kwashiorkor described as a form of malnutrition rather than starvation? (4)

b) Kwashiorkor is normally cured by the regular inclusion of soya bean or lean red meat in the diet. Which of these two foodstuffs is always the more expensive? Explain why. (2)

6 A wide variety of fungi attack crop plants. A few are listed in table 37.4.

Such fungal attack can often be prevented by spraying the surface of a potential host plant with fungicide. This reduces the number of fungal spores which germinate. A chemical company set out to investigate the effectiveness of two new fungicides (A and B). Petri dishes of nutrient agar containing fungicide were inoculated with fungal spores. Table 37.5 shows the results. Table 37.6 gives further information about the two fungicides.

Continued ➤

Applying your knowledge

scientific name of fungus	symbol for easy reference	disease caused	host plant affected
Erysiphe graminis	W	mildew	wheat and barley
Urcinula necator	X	mildew	grapevine
Puccinia graminis	Y	black rust	wheat
Phytophthora infestans	Z	blight	potato

Table 37.4

a) Give the scientific names of TWO fungal pathogens to which wheat can play host. (1)

b) Why was each condition of the experiment set up in triplicate? (1)

c) Summarise, in turn, the effect of fungicides A and B on fungus Z. (1)

d) Summarise, in turn, the effect of fungicides A and B on fungus Y. (1)

e) Which fungicide had the greater overall effect on
   (i) fungus W;
   (ii) fungus X?

	concentration of fungicide (ppm)	plate	% germination of fungal spores			
			fungus W	fungus X	fungus Y	fungus Z
control	0	1	100	97	77	44
		2	99	100	74	41
		3	100	100	76	43
fungicide A	5	1	20	5	76	45
		2	23	9	75	41
		3	22	7	76	43
	50	1	0	0	49	44
		2	0	0	48	42
		3	0	0	49	43
fungicide B	5	1	100	60	76	43
		2	97	62	76	42
		3	100	61	77	44
	50	1	18	5	76	42
		2	17	7	78	43
		3	19	6	74	44

Table 37.5   (ppm = parts per million)

	fungicide A		fungicide B	
concentration (ppm)	5	50	5	50
toxic effect on wildlife	none	very slight	very slight	slight
effect on host plant (% reduction in yield)	0	3	0	1
projected cost of spray	cheap	fairly cheap	very cheap	cheap
biodegradable?	Yes		Yes	

Table 37.6

Continued ➤

Applying your knowledge

(iii) Which concentration of which fungicide prevented all of fungus W's spores from germinating? (2)

f) (i) State the average percentage germination of spores from fungus X under control conditions.

(ii) Calculate the reduction in percentage germination of spores caused by applying 5 ppm of fungicide B to fungus X. (2)

g) Experts claim that fungicides A and B tend to show a degree of specificity in their action. Justify this claim with reference to the data. (1)

h) The chemical company running the trials found that they could only afford to continue with one of the fungicides. Suggest TWO reasons why they chose A in preference to B. (2)

7 Give an account of the various methods that have been employed by humans to increase food production since agriculture began. (10)

(38) Water as a limiting factor

When the Earth is viewed from space, its predominant colour is **blue**. This represents the world's **water** supply. However, 97.4% of the Earth's water is salty and found in seas and oceans (see figure 38.1). Of the 2.6% of water that is fresh, most is not readily available to humans because it is in the form of polar ice caps or glaciers or it has seeped deep into the soil and become ground water.

Only about 0.014% of the total global water supply is available for use by human beings and other life forms. Fortunately this supply is replenished continuously by **recycling**.

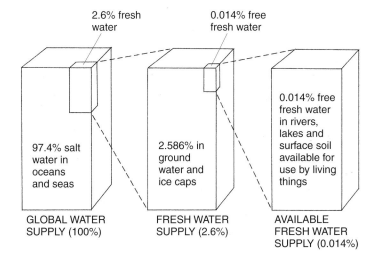

Figure 38.1 World's water supply

Water cycle

The **water cycle** involves the processes of **evaporation** and **precipitation** (as rain or snow) as shown in figure 38.2. Energy from the sun causes about 430 000 cubic kilometres (km^3) of water to evaporate annually as pure water vapour from the world's oceans. Most of this (about 390 000 km^3) condenses and returns to the oceans as rain.

However, about 40 000 km^3 is blown inland where it joins a further 70 000 km^3 of water vapour which has evaporated from lakes and rivers or has been given off by plants during transpiration. This 110 000 km^3 condenses as clouds and falls as rain or snow. About 70 000 km^3 is recycled by transpiration and evaporation and only about 40 000 km^3 finds its way back to the sea as free-flowing water.

Of this 40 000 km^3, about 30 000 returns directly to the sea without humans managing to gain useful access to it. The remaining 10 000 km^3 is put to use by humans in various ways as it makes its way to the sea.

This volume of readily available water is one of the Earth's most precious resources. Human beings are dependent upon it for their existence. Although it is renewable in that it is being recycled constantly, it is a finite resource. Already total global water use amounts to about 4 000 km^3 per year. It has been estimated that 10 000 km^3 of water is sufficient to support about 20 billion people. The water supply therefore has the

305

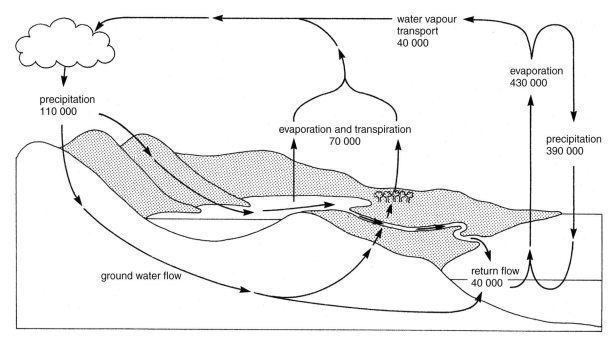

Figure 38.2 Water cycle

potential to act as a **limiting factor** on human population growth.

Increasing demand for water

The uses to which water is put vary from country to country. Figure 38.3 shows average use on a global basis. 73% is used for **agriculture**, since about 3 million km^2 of land needs to be irrigated (and this total is increasing by 8% annually). **Industry** accounts for a further 22% and demand continues to increase as technology advances and requires more and more water to act as a solvent, cleanser, coolant, and so on. **Domestic usage** amounts to 5%.

It has been estimated that each person needs about 80 litres of water per day to enjoy a reasonable quality of life. In reality consumption is found to vary considerably from less than 10 litres/day in the poorest developing countries to 500 litres/day in the USA (see figure 38.4).

Meeting the increased demand

As the population of the world increases, the demand for water increases in both developed and developing countries. Since the supply of freely available fresh water is not an infinite resource, water management programmes now concentrate on ways of **increasing efficiency** of water consumption rather than trying to increase the water supply.

With careful management, up to 90% of water used for domestic and industrial purposes can be returned to waterways and reused. However, irrigation is a very inefficient use of water. Only about 35% of all water that

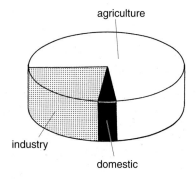

Figure 38.3 Global uses of water

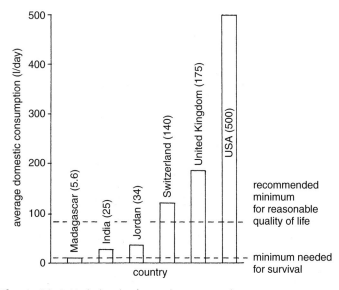

Figure 38.4 Variation in domestic consumption

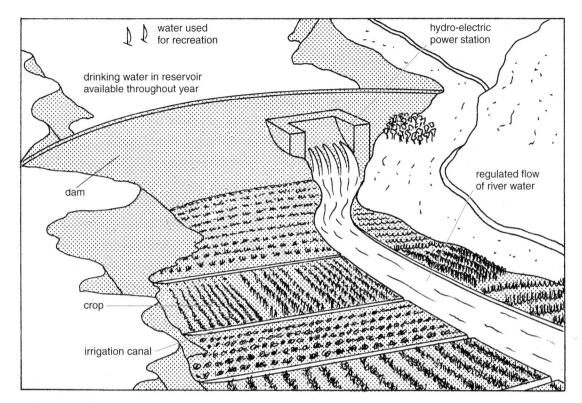

Figure 38.5 Multi-purpose dam

passes along irrigation channels is absorbed by the plants.

Micro-irrigation

A new technique using perforated pipes which deliver small quantities of water directly to the crop plants at regular intervals has been successfully employed in the USA and Israel. By ensuring that the minimum quantity of water is targeted to exactly where it is needed, this **drip-feed** method of irrigation is expected to save water on a massive scale in the future.

Dam

The local water supply of a region can be further managed by the building of a **dam** (see figure 38.5) in order to exert a degree of control over the water cycle. Such a multi-purpose scheme provides water for drinking, industry, irrigation, hydroelectric power and recreation. It also regulates the flow of the river thereby preventing seasonal flooding of farmlands.

However, there may be disadvantages to the use of dams:

◆ Silt from the uplands which previously fertilised the downstream fields may **clog up** the dam. In addition, expensive fertiliser may be needed to restore fertility in the affected fields.

◆ Irrigation channels may carry **parasites** which are harmful or even lethal to the local community (see p 316).

◆ Shallow water at the edge of a hydroelectric power reservoir may provide the conditions for malaria-carrying **mosquitoes** to breed.

◆ Habitat destruction of the lands upstream from the dam may leave communities **homeless** and in need of resettlement.

Testing your knowledge

1 a) Name TWO of the processes that make water move round the water cycle. (2)

  b) (i) Of the water flowing round the water cycle, what is the estimated volume readily available for use by humans?

     (ii) Explain how this volume of water could act as a factor limiting growth of the human population in the future. (2)

2 a) Give TWO reasons why the demand for water continues to increase with time. (2)

  b) Explain why micro-irrigaton is regarded as an important method of water management. (1)

  c) Give THREE advantages and THREE disadvantages of building a dam to manage water supply. (6)

Unpredictability of supply

In most developed countries, the majority of households receive a continuous supply of **clean piped water** and have a **mains sanitation** system for the disposal of sewage. Only rarely does such a shortage occur that water has to be rationed and use needs to be made of standpipes in the street.

In many developing countries the people are unable to depend on a reliable supply of safe drinking water being available. Figure 38.6 shows how the world's water supply is **unevenly distributed**. In some regions the problem is one of permanent shortage; in others the rainfall is seasonal and found to vary erratically from year to year.

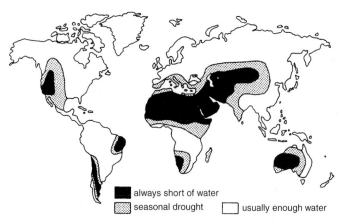

Figure 38.6 Unequal water supply

Climate

Climate refers to the long term prevalent weather conditions of a region. The climate that affects a region is the result of complex interactions between the **atmosphere**, the **land mass**, the **oceans** and the **geographical location** of the region. Over very lengthy periods (thousands or millions of years) the climate gradually changes. For example, it may go from one extreme which causes an ice age to the other extreme which leads to a warm phase of global climate.

In addition, short-lived extreme changes in climate occur periodically. Whether widespread or local, the effects of these can be devastating to the regions affected.

El Nino

In 1982–3, for example, a rapid warming of part of the Pacific Ocean produced an extreme version of the warm ocean current known as 'El Nino'. This contributed to the temporary breakdown of normal weather patterns and many regions of the world suffered freak weather conditions. India and Bangladesh suffered severe flooding while many parts of Africa and Indonesia were hit by prolonged drought. Crops failed, livestock had to be slaughtered and the people suffered lack of drinking water and famine.

Erosion

Erosion is the loss of the fertile top soil by the action of **water** or **wind** on the land. It rarely occurs in areas well covered by vegetation such as forest slopes (see figure 38.7). This is because the leaf canopy reduces the force of falling rain and the soil litter acts as a sponge, reducing violent run-off of water. In addition, roots both open up soil (thus increasing its porosity) and bind the soil particles together.

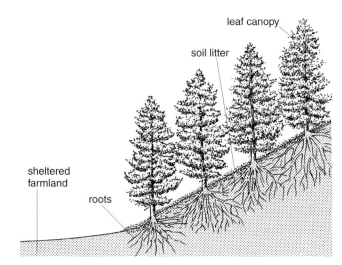

Figure 38.7 Ecosystem free from erosion

Erosion is prevented on farmland by employing good management practices such as constructing **terraces** for rice-growing on steep hillsides and ploughing sloping fields round the **contours** of the hill rather than up and down it (see figure 38.8).

However, erosion does occur where the land has been misused, especially if this is accompanied by extreme climatic conditions.

Deforestation

This term is used to refer to the complete clearing away of vast tracts of natural forest and the failure to plant new forest in their place.

Many disastrous consequences for the water supply cycle can result from **intensive deforestation**. Table 38.1 and figure 38.9 give some examples of the possible far-reaching consequences of this form of environmental mismanagement. Many of these have already occurred in various regions of the world.

effect of deforestation	consequence
Loss of forest's retentive 'sponge' effect (especially during rainy season); flow of water to rivers no longer regulated.	Rivers fail to provide regular supplies of water needed for human consumption and irrigation of crops.
Rapid rather than gradual run-off of rain water from hillsides.	Flooding of low-lying downstream areas which are often cultivated and inhabited.
Erosion of fertile top soil from hillsides by fast-moving water.	Soil fertility of hillsides reduced; rivers, lakes, irrigation channels and dams become blocked with silt; water becomes muddy and undrinkable.
Less water vapour returned to the atmosphere by evaporation and transpiration.	Reduction in rainfall making local climate become drier.
More CO_2 produced during burning of forest; less CO_2 absorbed from atmosphere in absence of photosynthesising forest.	Extra CO_2 in the atmosphere may contribute to 'green-house effect' (see chapter 40).

Table 38.1 Possible consequences of deforestation

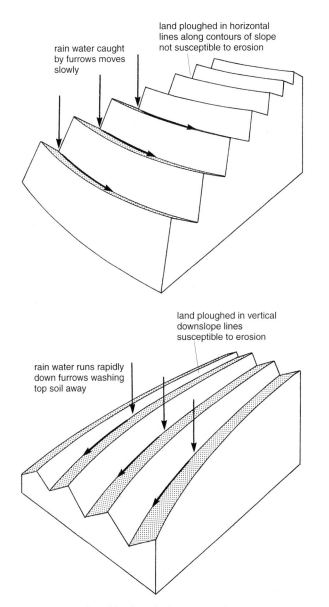

Figure 38.8 Good and bad agricultural practice

rain water caught by furrows moves slowly

land ploughed in horizontal lines along contours of slope not susceptible to erosion

land ploughed in vertical downslope lines susceptible to erosion

rain water runs rapidly down furrows washing top soil away

Desertification

In some dry parts of the world, the area of land covered by **desert** is increasing. When this process is largely the result of human activities it is called **desertification**.

The top part of figure 38.10 shows a typical scene at the edge of a desert as it was in the 1960s. The rainfall is erratic but adequate to sustain the plants and maintain the water table. **Marginal land** (i.e. territory on the edge of a cultivated zone) and **forests** hold soil and form a **windbreak**. Some land is used for grazing. Traditional agricultural practices are employed on cropland. For example, crops are **rotated**, allowing each piece of land in turn to lie **fallow** for a spell and recover its fertility.

Factors accelerating desertification

◆ The growing human population puts ever-increasing pressure on the land to produce more food.

◆ Traditional farming methods are abandoned and croplands are no longer allowed fallow periods to recover. Reduced fertility leads to decrease in yield so more land is needed.

◆ Marginal land (see figure 38.10) is pressed into service. First it is cleared of any plants that can be used for firewood or animal feed. Then it is dug up and deeply rooted, drought-resistant plants discarded. Next crops are planted but these normally fail during the first drought. Finally the soil dries out to dust.

◆ The forest is cleared giving a temporary supply of firewood and building materials. This results in the removal of a further population of deeply rooted plants that previously retained soil particles and held soil water. Again the soil dries to dust.

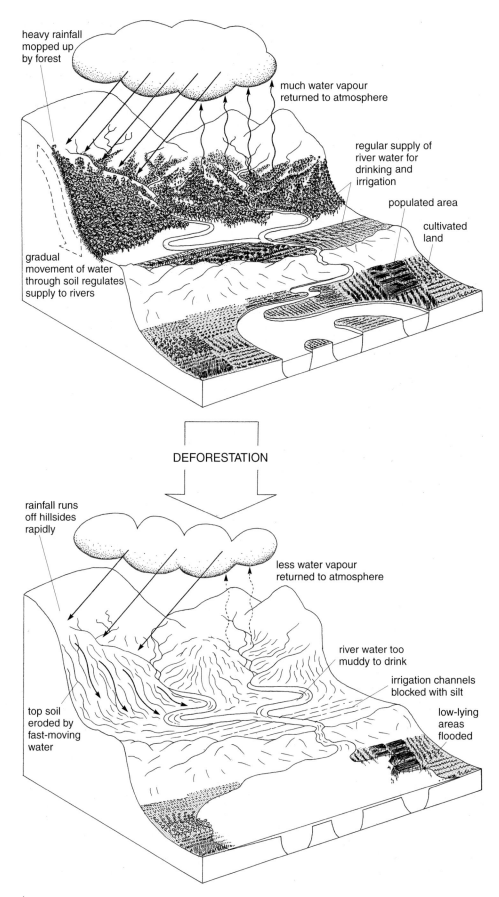

heavy rainfall
mopped up
by forest

much water vapour
returned to atmosphere

regular supply of
river water for
drinking and
irrigation

populated area

cultivated
land

gradual
movement of water
through soil regulates
supply to rivers

DEFORESTATION

rainfall runs
off hillsides
rapidly

less water vapour
returned to atmosphere

river water too
muddy to drink

irrigation channels
blocked with silt

top soil
eroded by
fast-moving
water

low-lying
areas
flooded

Figure 38.9 Deforestation

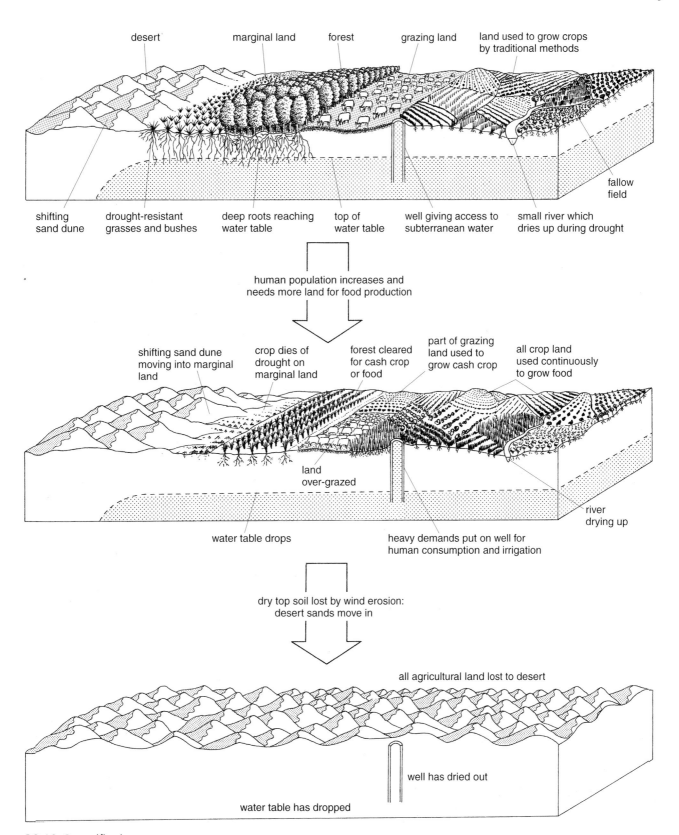

desert   marginal land   forest   grazing land   land used to grow crops by traditional methods

shifting sand dune   drought-resistant grasses and bushes   deep roots reaching water table   top of water table   well giving access to subterranean water   small river which dries up during drought

fallow field

human population increases and needs more land for food production

shifting sand dune moving into marginal land   crop dies of drought on marginal land   forest cleared for cash crop or food   part of grazing land used to grow cash crop   all crop land used continuously to grow food

land over-grazed

water table drops   heavy demands put on well for human consumption and irrigation

river drying up

dry top soil lost by wind erosion: desert sands move in

all agricultural land lost to desert

well has dried out

water table has dropped

Figure 38.10 Desertification

◆ Some grazing land is cultivated for crop-growing (often a cash crop). The remainder becomes overgrazed and the grass plants die. Water is no longer retained by the soil and it turns to dust.

◆ Dry top soil suffers wind erosion and is blown away. The land becomes invaded by sand from the desert.

◆ Severe drought causes the water table to drop leading to overall crop failure.

The bottom part of figure 38.10 shows the situation in the 1990s. The land has been lost to the desert and there is little chance of such land being returned to cultivation. The people can no longer feed themselves and their supply of drinking water has dried up. Out of desperation they may try to cultivate other areas of marginal land which in turn accelerates the process of desertification.

Testing your knowledge

1 a) With reference to climate, explain why the people in many developing countries cannot depend on a reliable supply of water. (2)

  b) (i) Identify TWO agents of soil erosion.
      (ii) Briefly describe TWO management practices that are effective at preventing soil erosion. (4)

2 a) What is meant by the term *deforestation*? (1)

  b) State TWO effects of intensive deforestation on an ecosystem. (2)

3 a) Define the term *desertification*. (1)

  b) What is *marginal* land? (1)

  c) Why do humans pursue activities that lead, in the end, to desertification? (2)

Applying your knowledge

1 Copy and complete figure 38.11 which shows a simplified version of the water cycle.
(All units are in $km^3 \times 10^3$) (5)

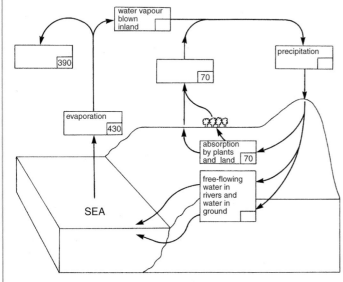

Figure 38.11

2 The bar graph in figure 38.12 refers to the flow of river water affecting the farmland immediately below a dam in a developing country.

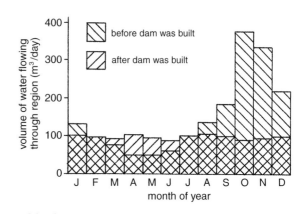

Figure 38.12

  a) When more than $110\,m^3$ of water flows daily, the river bursts its banks and floods the local farmland. On how many months of the year did this occur before the dam was built? (1)

  b) (i) Identify the month when the local people were most likely to suffer shortage of drinking water before the dam was built.
      (ii) Suggest what caused the variation in water flow before the dam was built. (2)

  c) Make a generalisation about the effect of the dam on volume of water flow. (1)

Continued ➤

Applying your knowledge

procedure adopted	reason why land becomes susceptible to erosion	agent of erosion	possible consequence
	Top soil no longer bound to roots of forest plants.		Silting up of rivers and dams; flooding of low-lying land.
overgrazing of grassland		wind	
cultivation of marginal land	Crop dies and soil dries out.		

Table 38.2

3 Copy and complete table 38.2 which refers to certain procedures adopted by humans in order to gain more land for food production. (6)

4 Give an account of the factors that accelerate the process of desertification. (10)

(39) Effect of disease

Disease is an impairment of the normal functioning of part (or all) of the body. Diseases are caused by many factors such as pathogenic (disease-causing) micro-organisms, deficient diet and stress. In extreme cases, some diseases result in death.

Regulatory effect of disease on a population

In the absence of environmental resistance, a population increases in size until it reaches a certain density. Its growth rate is then affected by factors such as disease which have a **regulatory effect**. Compared with a sparse population, a dense population is more prone to widespread attack by a disease-causing organism and more likely to suffer relatively high losses if the disease is fatal. By this means, disease acts as a **limiting factor** which keeps the population in check (see figure 39.1).

Effect of disease on human population

Throughout history, certain diseases have had a regulatory effect on the human population. For example, **bubonic plague** (the 'Black Death') which is caused by a pathogenic bacterium, occurred throughout most of Europe from the thirteenth to the nineteenth century. One epidemic in the fourteenth century alone wiped out about 25% of the European population. Fortunately the incidence of bubonic plague has now decreased to a very low level.

Within the last 300 years or so, life expectancy has steadily increased (especially in developed countries) as a result of increased food supply, improved hygiene and reduction of disease. However, many diseases (see figure 39.2) continue to rage on in developing countries and cause many millions of deaths annually. In

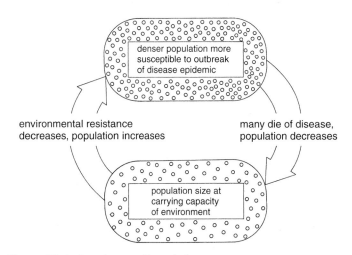

Figure 39.1 Regulatory effect of disease

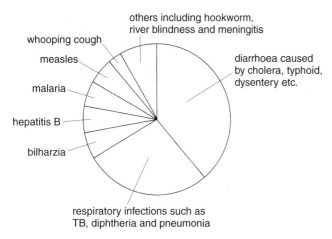

Figure 39.2 Estimated mortality due to disease in developing countries

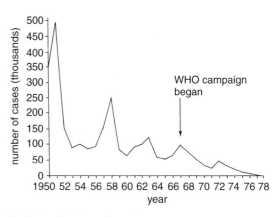

Figure 39.3 Eradication of smallpox

addition, the prospect of **HIV** (AIDS virus) exerting a major regulatory effect on the human population in the near future is a very real one as long as the development of an effective vaccine continues to elude scientists.

Use of vaccines

Immunisation and vaccination

Immunisation is the process by which a person's ability to resist a disease-causing organism is increased. **Vaccination** is a method of immunisation which deliberately introduces a weakened or altered form of the pathogen into the body so that the body will make antibodies against the antigen and develop immunity to it (see also chapter 7).

Smallpox

In 1796, Edward Jenner successfully immunised a boy against **smallpox** using **cowpox** virus as the 'vaccine' (see chapter 8). In those days no one understood how vaccination worked and many years elapsed before scientists learned how to produce specific vaccines for different diseases.

Eradication of smallpox

Free vaccination against smallpox became available in Britain in the 1840s and was made compulsory for babies ten years later. In Britain and other developed countries the death rate gradually decreased to a low level.

However, it was not until many years later that one of the greatest triumphs in medical history was achieved. This was the **complete eradication** of smallpox. It was brought about by a World Health Organisation (WHO) programme begun in 1967. It involved vaccinating as many people as possible shortly after birth and quickly homing in on fresh outbreaks of the disease and then

vaccinating all known and suspected contacts. This **surveillance-containment** campaign was so successful that the last recorded case of smallpox occurred in Somalia in 1977 (see figure 39.3).

Inspiration and frustration

The successful eradication of smallpox inspired the launch of many other campaigns against diseases. However, it must be kept in mind that elimination of smallpox was only possible for the following reasons:

◆ The infection spreads directly from human to human. No other animal can act as a reservoir of the virus and play the role of secondary host.

◆ The immunity resulting from vaccination persists for a very long time.

◆ The smallpox virus acts as a single antigen making the production of a vaccine a relatively straightforward procedure.

Vaccines for many diseases have been successfully developed, especially in cases where the pathogen resembles smallpox in the above three ways.

However, there are many other deadly diseases where success continues to elude scientists because the pathogen does not meet the above criteria. For example, the unicellular organism which causes **malaria** requires both a human and a mosquito host in its life cycle. Furthermore it changes from one form to another giving three phases in all. A vaccine that protects against one form of the pathogen normally fails against another. Even if three separate vaccines could be developed, many strains of the pathogenic organism exist which differ in the composition of the antigenic proteins on their surfaces.

It is for these reasons that malaria and several other diseases continue to resist eradication and, to a certain extent, exert a **regulatory effect** on the population of some developing countries.

314

Control of childhood diseases

Developed countries

Six diseases – **measles, whooping cough, diphtheria, tetanus, polio** and **tuberculosis** – were common causes of death amongst young children in Britain as recently as 150 years ago.

In developed countries these diseases have now been successfully brought under control and their incidence kept to a very low level. This has been achieved mainly as a result of higher standards of living, and vaccination programmes.

The graphs in figure 39.4 show how the death rates in England and Wales from measles and whooping cough have been dramatically reduced within the last century.

Vaccination targets

In the UK, Health Departments have set a **minimum target** of 95% of children to be vaccinated against the common infectious diseases. Table 39.1 shows the **immunisation schedule** recommended for children in Britain. Similar vaccination programmes operate in other developed countries.

By the year 2000, great progress had been made in the European area towards meeting the WHO's declared aim of eradicating polio, tetanus, diphtheria and measles by the end of the twentieth century. Although the WHO's target was not met in full, these diseases continue to become rarer and rarer in most European countries. However this trend will only continue in the future if a high uptake of the vaccination programme is maintained. An uptake of at least 95% is required to provide protection for the population as a whole.

Developing countries

In many poor developing countries, the picture is much more gloomy. Child mortality from vaccine-preventable diseases is still very high. In 1974 the WHO launched

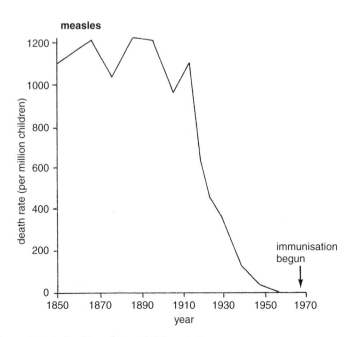

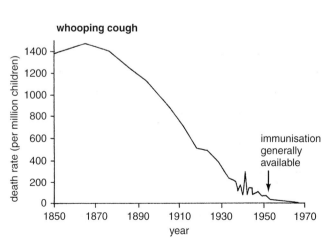

Figure 39.4 Decline of two childhood diseases

age	vaccine	notes
during first year of life	polio, tetanus, diphtheria, whooping cough and meningitis	1st dose at 2 mths, 2nd dose at 3 mths, 3rd dose at 4 mths
during second year of life	measles, mumps and rubella, or measles only	single dose
4–5 years	polio, tetanus and diphtheria	booster dose
10–14 years	tuberculosis (BCG)	single dose
10–14 years	rubella	girls *and* boys
15–19 years	polio and tetanus	booster dose

Table 39.1 Recommended vaccinations for children in the UK

EPI (Expanded Programme of Immunisation) in developing countries in order to increase the level of vaccination of children against the six diseases stated above.

However, lack of information, understanding and financial means often results in parents failing to bring children to health centres for vaccination. Of those children that are brought in for the first dose, many fail to return for the second or third dose needed for full protection. The majority of these children therefore remain **susceptible** and millions die of diseases which have become rare in developed countries.

Improved hygiene, sanitation and living conditions

Developed countries

Close examination of the graphs in figure 39.4 reveals that the death rate in England and Wales for measles and whooping cough had already dropped sharply to a low level **before** immunisation programmes were begun. This early decline in mortality in developed countries is attributed not to medical intervention but to changing **social** and **economic** factors which resulted in improved living conditions for the vast majority of the population.

Compared with previous generations who lived in the nineteenth and early twentieth century, most people living in a developed country today enjoy far higher standards of **hygiene**, **waste disposal** and **nutrition**. All of these factors contribute directly or indirectly to the development of increased **resistance** to disease with vaccination and health care programmes playing preventative roles.

In the distant past, a major epidemic of a fatal disease (e.g. bubonic plague) could sweep through a population leaving millions dead, especially amongst poor people living in damp, overcrowded conditions lacking proper sanitation.

Nowadays an epidemic (e.g. influenza) only occurs on a relatively small scale. In a developed country it is prevented from escalating by advance warnings, availability of vaccine for the vulnerable (e.g. the elderly) and a generally healthier population with a higher level of resistance. If a minor outbreak of a serious, life-threatening disease such as cholera does occur, it is quickly contained and dealt with in a specialised unit of a hospital (with WHO assistance if necessary).

Developing countries

In more than 50% of developing countries, the majority of the population have neither a reliable source of **clean drinking water** nor proper facilities for sewage disposal. Water for drinking is often drawn from a river which may also have served as launderette or public toilet further upstream.

Water contaminated by sewage normally contains the **pathogens** which cause several diseases (e.g. cholera and dysentery). It is estimated that 80% of the diseases that affect people in poor countries are **water-related** (see table 39.2). Of these, **diarrhoea** which is caused by several different diseases is the most serious. It is responsible for about half of all the deaths involving children under the age of five.

Many people in developing countries are caught up in a vicious circle of debilitating factors. Only provision of clean drinking water, mains sanitation, adequate diet and comprehensive vaccination programmmes will significantly reduce the number of people (estimated at 18 million) who die each year of these deadly diseases.

disease	role played by water	estimated number of cases per year (millions)	estimated number of deaths per year (millions)
diarrhoea (caused by cholera, dysentery, typhoid, etc.)	Water used for drinking and washing is contaminated with pathogens.	1500	7
malaria	Water acts as breeding ground for mosquito larvae.	110	1
bilharzia	Water in irrigation canals provides habitat for snail that carries pathogen.	200	1

Table 39.2 Water-related diseases

Testing your knowledge

1 a) Name THREE diseases that were common causes of death amongst children in developed countries 150 years ago. (3)

b) In recent years, these diseases have been brought under control in Britain. Briefly describe the health care programme that has brought this about. (2)

c) Death rates of common childhood diseases had dropped sharply before vaccination programmes were introduced. Identify TWO of the factors responsible and for each describe how it contributed to the decline in incidence of the disease. (4)

2 a) Give TWO reasons why immunisation programmes often have only limited success in poor developing countries. (2)

b) Why would a reliable source of clean drinking water available to all people in the world lead to a dramatic rise in world health? (1)

3 Decide whether each of the following statements is true or false and then use T or F to indicate your choice. Where a statement is false, give the word that should have been used in place of the word in bold print. (6)

a) A potentially fatal disease caused by a bacterium often present in water contaminated by sewage is **cholera**.

b) A viral disease that has been completely eradicated by a WHO immunisation campaign is **bubonic plague**.

c) A disease caused by a unicellular animal carried by mosquitoes that kills millions of humans annually is **malaria**.

d) A viral disease that attacks the immune system and for which there is no vaccine is **rubella**.

e) A major childhood disease caused by a virus and successfully controlled by vaccination is **measles**.

f) A fairly mild viral infection that may have serious effects on the growing fetus if contracted by the mother during the first three months of pregnancy is **smallpox**.

Applying your knowledge

1 Each graph in figure 39.5 shows the number of reported cases of smallpox in a particular country over a period of time.

a) Which country is
   (i) developing;
   (ii) developed?
   (iii) Give a reason for your choice of answer. (3)

b) At the start of the vaccination campaign in each country, medical experts suspected that the system of reporting had been inadequate and that many cases had previously gone unreported. In what way do the data in the graphs provide evidence to support this view? (1)

Continued ➤

Applying your knowledge

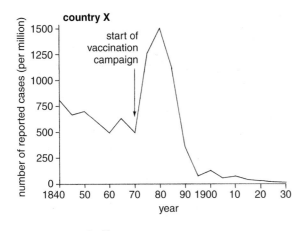

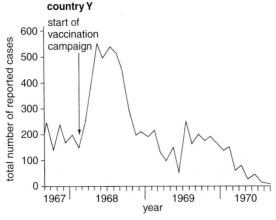

Figure 39.5

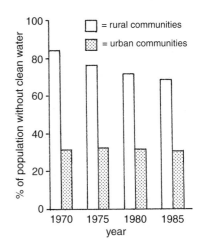

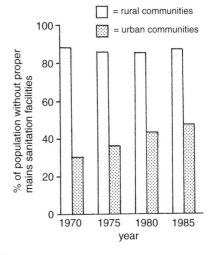

Figure 39.6

c) **(i)** What was the long-term effect of the vaccination campaign in each case?
   (ii) Give TWO reasons why scientists have been unable, so far, to repeat this success story with a vaccine for malaria. (3)

2 The bar graphs in figure 39.6 refer to a developing country in Asia.

a) With respect to access to both clean water and proper mains sanitation, which type of community is worse off? (1)

b) Using the symbols indicated, copy and complete table 39.3 to show the changing level of access to each facility with time, for each type of community. (4)

c) Name TWO water-borne diseases likely to be common amongst the poorest people of this country. (2)

d) It has been claimed that 'The number of taps supplying clean piped water per 1000 people in a population is a better indication of the nation's health than the number of hospital beds available per 1000'. Do you agree? Justify your answer. (2)

type of community	changing level of access to facility with time	
	clean water	proper sanitation
urban		
rural		

✓ = increasing   0 = unchanged   ✗ = decreasing

Table 39.3

Continued ➢

Applying your knowledge

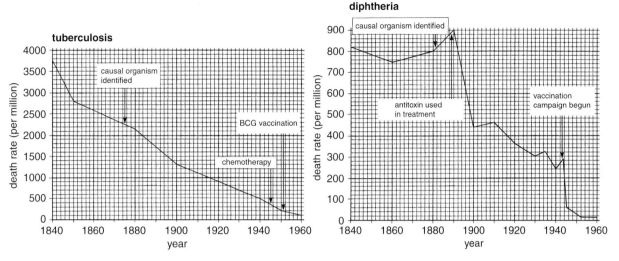

Figure 39.7

3 The graphs in figure 39.7 show the death rates in a European country for two diseases.

  a) For which disease did an early drop in death rate occur
   (i) as a result of medical intervention?
   (ii) in the absence of medical intervention?
   (iii) Name THREE factors that could account for the decline in death rate from a disease in the absence of medical intervention. (5)

  b) **(i)** By how many times was the death rate from tuberculosis greater in 1850 than in 1930?
   (ii) Compared with the death rate from diphtheria in 1890, what percentage reduction had occurred by 1920?

  (iii) In which year did 2 people per 1000 die of tuberculosis?
  (iv) How many people per 1000 died of diphtheria in 1880? (4)

  c) A rise in the number of cases of tuberculosis was recorded during 1994 amongst homeless people in Britain. Suggest why. (1)

4 Discuss the level of success achieved by mankind in the eradication of disease in developed and developing countries under the headings:

  (i) improved hygiene and sanitation; (4)

  (ii) use of vaccines. (6)

What you should know
(Chapters 37–39)

(See table 39.4 for word bank.)

1 The process of natural _____ leading to formation of forests has been brought largely to a halt in developed countries as a result of the ever-increasing demand for _____ land to feed the human population.

2 Extensive deforestation is carried out in developing countries to provide land for crop-growing and timber for _____ .

3 The increased level of food production achieved in recent years has been in part due to the use of _____, herbicides and _____ although their use also carries disadvantages.

4 A significant increase in food production has been achieved by using _____ varieties of plants developed by _____ breeding, although these plants need high concentrations of fertiliser.

5 Future _____ manipulation of plants by recombinant _____ is expected to produce high-yield crops requiring little or no fertiliser or pesticide.

Continued ➤

What you should know
(Chapters 37–39)

6 _____ is the condition suffered by a person who fails to receive an adequate quantity of food. _____ is the condition suffered by a person who fails to receive a balanced diet. Lack of an essential foodstuff in the diet leads to a _____ disease.

7 Water is renewable in that it is constantly _____. However, fresh water is a _____ resource which could act as a limiting factor on the increase of the human population.

8 The demand for water is always increasing and it is therefore important to find ways of making more efficient use and reuse of it, such as constructing _____ and _____ schemes.

9 Supplies of water in some parts of the world are unpredictable due to _____ changes.

10 _____, erosion and _____ all lead to environmental degradation and disturb or eliminate the effects of the water supply cycle.

11 A disease can have a _____ effect on a population and keep it in check. This natural check is removed when a _____ is found for the disease.

12 _____ and antibiotics have been used successfully against many diseases and have contributed to the increase in human _____.

13 _____ and childhood diseases still account for millions of deaths amongst children in developing countries every year.

14 Improved _____, mains sanitation and quality of living conditions promote development of good health and natural _____ to disease and contribute to population increase.

agricultural	finite	rapid-response
climatic	fuel	recycled
cure	genetic	regulatory
dams	hygiene	resistance
deficiency	malaria	selective
deforestation	malnutrition	succession
desertification	micro-irrigation	undernutrition
DNA technology	pesticides	vaccines
fertilisers	population	

Table 39.4 Word bank for chapters 37–39

(40) Human population effects on environment

Food web

Only green plants can photosynthesise the energy-rich carbohydrates which act as the starting point in all **food chains**. Animals depend directly or indirectly on plants for their energy as it passes along food chains.

Under natural conditions an ecosystem contains several interconnecting food chains which make up a **food web**. This more complex relationship has normally evolved over a very long period of time and is in a finely balanced state, in equilibrium with the environment.

Disruption of food webs

If a factor affects one type of organism in a food web, this is likely to have a knock-on effect which disrupts the lives of several other species in the food web.

Effects of chemicals on wildlife

Every year massive quantities of chemicals are used in agriculture and forestry. For example, **fertilisers** are added to improve soil fertility; **pesticides** are used to limit damage done to crops by pests (also see chapter 37). In addition to having the desired effect, some of these chemicals also affect other populations in the ecosystem. The extent of these disruptive 'side effects' depends on various factors relating to the chemical. These factors are highlighted by posing the following questions.

◆ Is the chemical **specific** in its action or is it poisonous to a wide variety of organisms?

◆ Is it **biodegradable** or is its molecular structure so stable that it persists for a very long time in the environment?

◆ Is its concentration (and its frequency of application) kept to a **minimum** or is it used in excess?

In the past people often failed to address these issues, with unexpected and sometimes disastrous consequences for wildlife, as shown by the following examples.

Increase in concentration of chemical

The insecticide **DDT**, which is both **persistent** and very **toxic**, was widely used during the 1950s and 1960s. It was found to pass easily through food chains and webs and become more and more **concentrated** at each level.

Consider the example shown in figure 40.1. The producers (green leaves of various plant species) become contaminated with a very low concentration of chemical pesticide blown off neighbouring farmland during spraying of crops. The concentration increases, however, as much plant material is eaten by the primary consumers (many species of herbivorous invertebrates), and persists in their cells.

Progression on up the pyramid of numbers (and biomass) leads to ever-increasing concentrations of the chemical accumulating in living cells. Finally the few large tertiary consumers (sparrowhawks) at the very top suffer severe poisoning.

Thin egg shells

The female birds at the top of an affected pyramid suffer an upset in the balance of the hormones which control the manufacture of strong egg shells. As a result they lay eggs with **thin shells** which often break during incubation leading to a significant decrease in reproductive success.

The graph in figure 40.2 shows that as few as 25 parts per million of pesticide can reduce the shell's thickness by as much as 15%. Once the shell is more than 23% thinner than normal, it breaks with disastrous results.

Aquatic ecosytems

Pesticide sprays are also washed off farmlands into local waterways where they similarly increase in concentration amongst the members of the fresh-water ecosystem's community.

So persistent is DDT that it has found its way into marine ecosystems despite the dilution effect of the sea on polluted river water. Traces of DDT have even been found in the fatty tissue of penguins living in the Antarctic.

Resistance to chemical

DDT has also been widely used to kill several types of insect associated with diseases that affect humans. Initially great success was achieved against mosquitoes (which carry malaria and yellow fever), tse-tse flies (which transmit sleeping sickness) and many other pests.

However, within a few years of use, **mutant** forms of these insects which were **resistant** to DDT emerged. In the absence of competition the resistant strains multiplied (see figure 40.3) and the incidence of the diseases that they carry returned to the original high levels.

It is for these reasons of **persistence** and **resistance** that stable non-biodegradable pesticides such as DDT (which

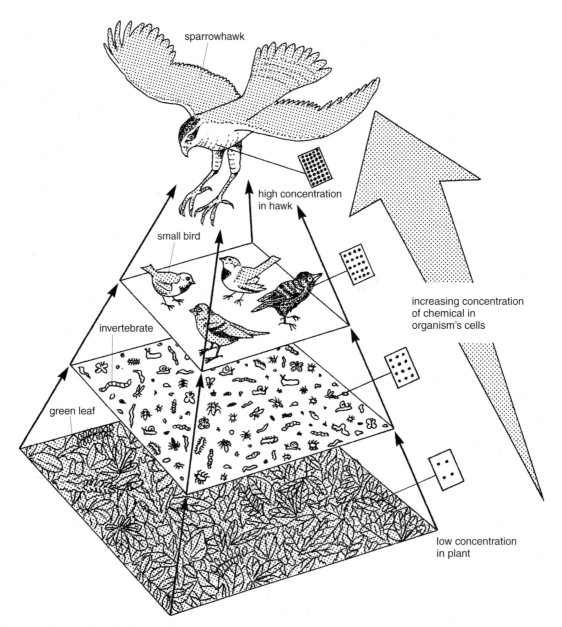

Figure 40.1 Accumulation of chemical in food pyramid

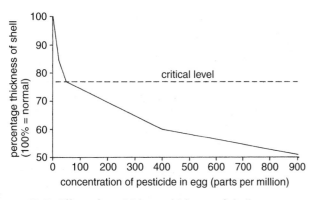

Figure 40.2 Effect of pesticide on thickness of shell

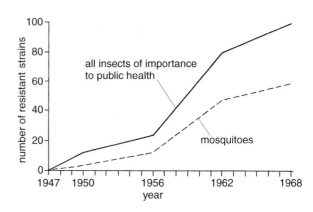

Figure 40.3 Increase in resistant species

neither decompose in the organism nor in the environment) have been **banned** in most countries since the early 1980s. In developed countries all pesticides have become subject to strict control measures in recent years.

However, in many developing countries fewer regulations exist and persistent toxic chemicals are still in use. It is critical that this situation is reversed and that persistent pesticides are replaced by chemicals that break down to harmless products after killing the pest.

Disturbing the balance

Banana plantation

In temperate climates, agricultural systems benefit from the natural 'pest-control' effect of the **cold winter** season. In tropical climates the system depends instead on natural controls such as **predatory insects** to limit the damage done to crops by pests. Indiscriminate application of pesticide spray tends to disrupt the system by killing the predators which normally exert **natural control**.

Banana plantations sprayed with insecticide in the 1960s, for example, were found to suffer more damage from leaf-eating insect larvae than plantations left untreated. It was discovered that the chemical was especially harmful to a type of predatory wasp. The wasps do not eat the larvae directly but lay their eggs inside them. As the wasp eggs develop they feed on the plant-eating larvae and eventually kill them. Although the banana plants suffered some damage, this was much less than that caused by the larvae in the absence of the wasps.

Stimulatory effect of chemicals

When excess fertiliser runs off agricultural land into waterways it can promote excessive growth of the producers in the food web. The subsequent rapid growth of algae leads to an **algal bloom** and the food web becomes disrupted (see p 326).

Interdependence of community members

A natural ecosystem consists of a community of plants ('producers'), animals ('consumers') and micro-organisms ('decomposers') living together in one or more habitats.

The members of the community are **interdependent**. Animals and micro-organisms depend on plants directly or indirectly for food and oxygen. Plants and animals depend on micro-organisms to decompose wastes and release chemical elements into the ecosystem for reuse.

Animals may depend on plants for shelter and camouflage. Plants may need animals to bring about pollination or seed dispersal.

Thus a natural ecosystem is a **delicately balanced** biological unit of interdependent living things in a state of dynamic equilibrium. The more easily it is able to recover from a disturbance the more **ecologically stable** it is said to be.

Loss of complexity leading to instability

Whenever one or more plant or animal species is removed from an ecosystem by pesticide spraying, herbicide application, deforestation, etc., the ecosystem becomes altered and impoverished. The more drastic the effect, the more unlikely it is that the ecosystem will be able to recover its stability.

For every species that is eradicated through human activity, several others that were dependent upon it are also threatened. The greater the loss of complexity in an ecosystem by human intervention, the greater the likelihood of **ecological instability** and collapse. Human beings put this strain on the world's ecosystems in order to support the ever-growing human population.

Testing your knowledge

1. a) What overall benefit is gained by the use of chemicals such as fertilisers and pesticides in agriculture? (1)

   b) Identify TWO features that would be possessed by an ideal pesticide. (2)

2. a) Although applied in low concentrations, some pesticides are found to exist in high concentrations in the bodies of tertiary consumers. Explain why. (2)

   b) Give TWO reasons why the use of DDT has been banned in most countries. (2)

3. a) *The members of a community are interdependent.* Explain the meaning of this statement with reference to plants, animals and micro-organisms. (3)

   b) If one species is destroyed by a pesticide, what is the possible effect of this on the other species that make up the interdependent community. (1)

   c) How can an ecosystem's degree of ecological stability be assessed? (1)

Nitrogen cycle

It is recommended that Standard grade notes on the nitrogen cycle be revised at this point. Question 6 parts a), b) and c) at the end of this chapter should be attempted before the next section of text is studied.

Disruption of nitrogen cycle

Algae

Algae are simple photosynthetic plants which lack roots, stems and leaves. The vast majority live in water and many are microscopic (e.g. phytoplankton).

The rate at which algae grow depends on the availability of adequate light energy, carbon dioxide, warmth and mineral nutrients (e.g. nitrate and phosphate). If one or more of these factors is limiting, algal growth is held in check.

Algal bloom

If none of the above factors is in short supply, algae are able to multiply rapidly and form an **algal bloom**. Water affected in this way is often so densely populated with algal cells that it resembles thick pea soup.

Some algal blooms occur naturally. Scanners fitted to weather satellites reveal that enormous numbers of phytoplankton occur in the oceans at certain times of the year. For example, explosive blooms appear in the North Atlantic in spring when **warmth** and **increasing daylengths** coincide with rich supplies of **nutrients** stirred up from the deep by winter storms (see figure 40.4). Smaller autumn blooms occur if the level of nutrients rises again in late summer. The algal blooms decline again as winter approaches and daylengths decrease.

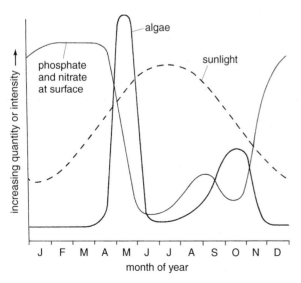

Figure 40.4 Algal blooms in North Atlantic

Eutrophication

Eutrophication is the enrichment of an aquatic environment by nutrients such as **nitrate** and **phosphate**. This is a natural process which normally occurs at a very slow rate. For example, the water in a loch gradually becomes enriched (eutrophic) as rivers deposit sediment into it.

Levels of eutrophication have significantly increased in many freshwater and marine ecosystems in recent years for the following reasons.

◆ Intensive crop-growing uses ever-increasing quantities of **fertilisers** containing nitrate and phosphate, much of which may be washed into rivers and lochs by rain.

◆ Intensive livestock farming produces vast amounts of animal **sewage**, some of which finds its way into waterways adding phosphate and nitrate.

◆ **Effluent** from sewage treatment works containing nitrate and phosphate is discharged into rivers and canals.

◆ Some forms of **detergent** are rich in phosphate which is not removed by sewage treatment and ends up in rivers and canals.

When sunshine and warm temperatures coincide with an **artifically high level** of **eutrophication**, the affected environment is suddenly able to support an enormous number of algae. These tiny plants reproduce prolifically, forming an **algal bloom**. A river or canal with slow-moving water is more prone to an algal bloom since the excess nutrients are not as well diluted as in fast-flowing water.

Investigating the effect of increasing concentration of nitrate on algal growth

Different masses of nitrate fertiliser are added to five flasks containing a solution of complete medium, as shown in figure 40.5. A further flask receives no fertiliser and acts as the control.

A sample of unicellular algae from a pond or fish tank is shaken up vigorously in $20\,cm^3$ of complete medium solution and then a $3\,cm^3$ inoculum of algal suspension is added to each flask using a syringe. The flasks are kept in constant illumination in a warm room. Distilled water is added as required to compensate for loss by evaporation and to maintain the solution in each flask at its starting level.

After four weeks the appearance of the plant population in each flask is noted and then the contents are filtered. Each filter paper is dried in a warm oven to constant mass and the dry mass of algae from each flask calculated by subtracting the weight of an unused filter paper. The experiment is repeated several times and the class results pooled to allow averages to be calculated.

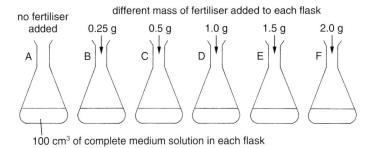

Figure 40.5 Investigating the effect of eutrophication

Table 40.1 summarises the reasons for adopting certain design features during the investigation. Table 40.2 gives a specimen set of results. The effect of increasing concentration of nitrate fertiliser on dry mass of algae is represented by a graph of the results in figure 40.6, which shows the line of best fit.

Discussion of results

At the end of the investigation the population of algae in the control flask is found to be the smallest (as indicated by dry mass) and least healthy (as indicated by colour). It is concluded that the low concentration of nitrate present in complete medium solution acts as the **limiting factor** and prevents a population explosion in flask A.

In the other flasks increasing **eutrophication** of the solution by nitrate promotes algal growth and the population increases (as indicated by dry mass). The cells are also healthier (as indicated by their dark colour). The population does not show uncontrolled growth, however. At the higher concentrations of nitrate, the graph levels off showing that some other factor has become limiting.

design feature	reason
Use of complete medium solution.	To supply plants with a small quantity of all the chemical nutrients required for healthy growth.
Use of control flask A.	To check that the one variable factor under investigation is responsible for the results.
Algal sample shaken vigorously before taking each inoculum.	To disperse algae evenly so that each inoculum is similar in density and variety of algae.
Light intensity, temperature and volume of liquid kept equal for all flasks.	To ensure that only one variable factor is being investigated.
Experiment repeated, results pooled and averages calculated.	To obtain a more reliable result for each concentration of nitrate.

Table 40.1 Design features

flask	mass of nitrate fertiliser added (g)	colour of solution in flask		dry weight of algae (g)
		at start	after 4 weeks	
A	0.0	faint green	yellow-green	0.04
B	0.25	faint green	dark green	0.09
C	0.5	faint green	dark green	0.14
D	1.0	faint green	very dark green	0.16
E	1.5	faint green	very dark green	0.18
F	2.0	faint green	very dark green	0.18

Table 40.2 Algal growth results

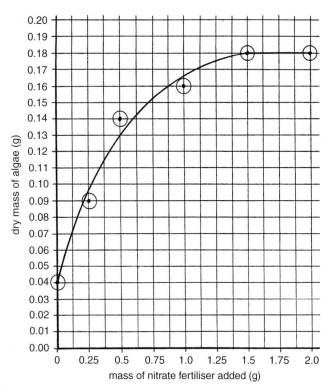

Figure 40.6 Graph of algal growth results

Marine ecosystems

Many rivers eventually discharge their contents into the sea. So great is the quantity of nutrient-rich material being passed into parts of the North Sea that the material is no longer being diluted to a harmless level.

High concentrations of **nitrate** are found to occur in offshore water especially near the mouths of the main European rivers. Algae thrive in these waters (see question 5 at the end of this chapter). The Baltic and Mediterranean Seas are also suffering excessive eutrophication and algal blooms.

Effect of algal blooms

Decrease in level of dissolved oxygen

Since extra algae provide consumers with more food, a minor algal bloom may be beneficial to an aquatic ecosystem. However, a major algal bloom causes a disturbance in the ecosystem's balance (see figure 40.7).

The algae become so numerous that they are no longer held in check by the primary consumers. When the algae die, they are decomposed by aerobic bacteria which in turn undergo a population explosion. This results in the supply of dissolved **oxygen** in the water

being **depleted**. The river or loch's capacity to support animal life is dramatically reduced. Fish and many other freshwater organisms are deprived of oxygen and suffocate. Fish may also die as a result of their gills becoming coated with algae which prevents them from breathing.

Reduction in light

Sometimes an algal bloom forms a **scummy layer** at the surface which is so thick that it prevents light from reaching water plants at the bottom of the river or shallow loch. These die, decompose and cause a further reduction in the water's oxygen concentration.

Poisons

Some freshwater algae are toxic and produce **poisons**. If they develop into an algal bloom, the quantity of poison in the water increases, killing fish and other animals. Some marine algae produce toxins which are absorbed by shellfish making them poisonous to humans.

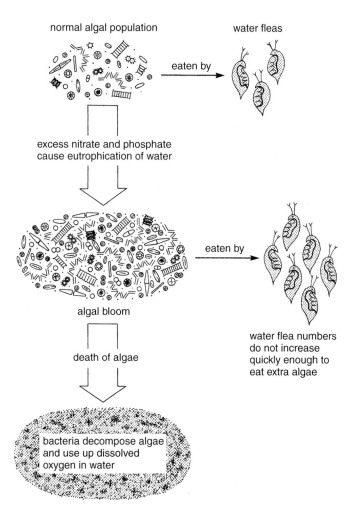

Figure 40.7 Effect of algal bloom on oxygen supply

Inadequate sewage treatment

Raw sewage contains many different organic chemicals such as **protein** and **urea** which are rich in **nitrogen**. In developed countries, several different species of bacteria are used during the treatment of sewage. These convert protein to ammonium compounds which are then oxidised to nitrites and nitrates by nitrifying bacteria. This is basically an intensification of the natural processes that take place during the **nitrogen cycle**.

Overloaded sewage works

If a sewage treatment works becomes overloaded, raw or inadequately treated sewage may be discharged into a river, with the effects shown by the graphs in figure 40.8.

Graph 1 shows how decomposition of organic matter by bacteria is accompanied by a sharp drop in the river's **oxygen** concentration. This occurs because the bacteria use up the oxygen during respiration. Nitrogen-containing organic waste in the sewage is first converted to ammonium compounds whose concentration rises to a

maximum and then declines again on being converted to nitrates.

Graph 2 shows the fates of three types of **micro-organism**. The population of bacteria (responsible for decomposition of organic matter) quickly reaches a maximum and then goes into gradual decline as the sewage food runs out. The population of sewage fungus also increases steadily while food supplies last and then dies out.

The presence of large amounts of sewage and millions of bacteria causes the water to become cloudy (turbid). In such conditions of **poor illumination**, photosynthesis is reduced and the number of algae decreases.

However, their numbers begin to pick up again as the water becomes enriched with nitrates and the illumination improves with decline in the population of bacteria. With continuing eutrophication of the water, the algae form a **bloom** which leads to the events described on page 326.

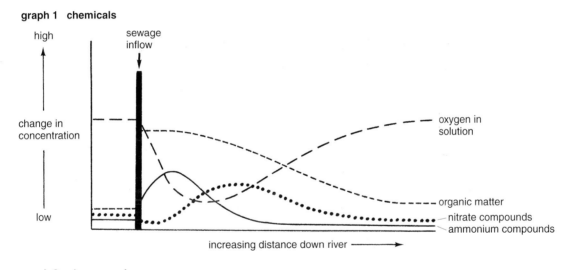

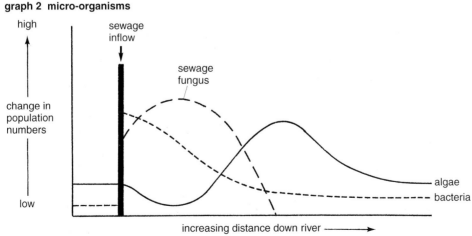

Figure 40.8 Effect of raw sewage on river ecosystem

The changes shown in graph 1 also affect the river's animal life. Stonefly and mayfly nymphs are the first to disappear in the polluted water followed by most species of fish. These indicator organisms eventually reappear if the river's oxygen concentration returns to normal and the river makes a full recovery, as shown in this example.

Problem of sewage disposal

As the human population increases so too does the volume of **sewage** that needs to be disposed of. This is a particularly serious problem in densely populated countries. Disposal of raw sewage into rivers creates the environmental degradation outlined above. Even adequately treated sewage released as large quantities of 'harmless' effluent can adversely affect rivers by increasing the level of eutrophication and promoting algal blooms.

In recent years much of Britain's sewage sludge has been disposed of in the North Sea. However, even this vast volume of water is becoming badly polluted, especially in coastal waters and estuaries. Britain has therefore agreed to stop dumping sewage sludge in the North Sea. This leaves land-fill sites as the alternative solution to the problem of dealing with wastes generated by the ever-increasing human population.

Sanitation in developing countries

In many poor, developing countries, the majority of people do not have access to proper mains sanitation. Often removal of wastes relies on **open sewers** in the streets which in turn contaminate the local rivers and lakes. This inadequate disposal of sewage is the cause of many lethal diseases (see chapter 39).

Contamination of drinking water by nitrates and nitrites

Nitrate is very soluble in water and does not bind to soil particles. When excessive or ill-timed use is made of fertiliser on farmland, some of the nitrate may be leached (washed) out into ground water and eventually reach **water supplies** intended for human consumption. In areas of low rainfall, the concentration of nitrate ions in the water is higher because the effect of dilution by rain is reduced.

According to medical experts, nitrate is harmless to adult humans. It is claimed that levels as high as 100 ppm in drinking water pose no threat to health. However, when nitrate is reduced to **nitrite** by enzyme action in the gut of babies, the nitrite combines with haemoglobin and reduces the oxygen-carrying capacity of the baby's blood. High levels of nitrite are therefore potentially dangerous to young babies. High nitrite levels have been implicated in **blue-baby syndrome** (bluish tinge to the skin due to

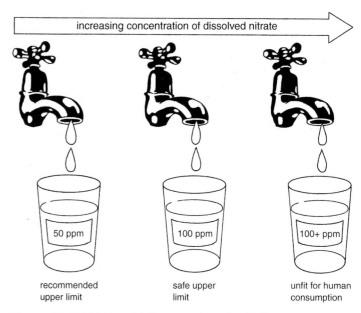

Figure 40.9 WHO's guidelines on nitrate in drinking water

shortage of oxygen in blood) though much controversy still surrounds this issue.

WHO guidelines

The WHO recommendation of a **50 ppm limit** of nitrate in drinking water (see figure 40.9) has been adopted by the European Community. However, water in a few parts of the UK still contains concentrations of nitrate in excess of this since it is drawn from deep wells into which nitrate is leached.

The WHO has deemed water containing more than 100 ppm of nitrate unfit for human consumption. In the UK it is the responsibility of water companies to monitor nitrate levels and ensure that they remain within safe limits.

In some parts of the world, levels are found to be well above 100 ppm. Excessively high concentrations of nitrate in drinking water have been linked with gastric ulcers in adults and abnormalities in fetal development. Laboratory animals given very high levels of nitrate are found to be prone to gastric cancer.

Carbon dioxide and the carbon cycle

It is recommended that Standard Grade notes on the carbon cycle be revised at this point. Question 8 a) at the end of this chapter should be attempted before the next section of text is studied.

Carbon dioxide makes up only a very small part of the world's atmosphere. Prior to the industrial revolution this tended to remain fairly constant due to the activities of the **carbon cycle**. The volume of CO_2 released by the

during photosynthesis, and burning the felled trees adds still more CO_2 to the air. The concentration of CO_2 in the world's atmosphere is now increasing at a rate of about 0.4% of its current level per year (see figure 40.10).

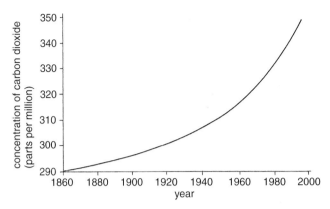

Figure 40.10 Increase in CO_2 concentration in atmosphere

processes of **respiration** and **combustion** was absorbed by green plants during **photosynthesis**. It is thought that any slight imbalances that occurred were corrected by the oceans acting as a **reservoir** ('sink') of dissolved CO_2 and absorbing or releasing it as required, thereby maintaining an equilibrium.

Global increase in carbon dioxide level

As the human population continues to increase, this results in a greater total number of people needing **energy**. As technology advances and more countries become developed and industrialised, the average amount of energy consumed per person per year increases. This rising demand for energy is met largely by the combustion of **fossil fuels**, which adds about 5 billion tons of CO_2 to the atmosphere annually.

Disruption of carbon cycle

Green plants and the ocean reservoir are unable to absorb all of this extra CO_2 and the carbon cycle becomes disrupted as a result. The problem is aggravated by **deforestation** of tropical rain forest in two further ways. Fewer trees are left to absorb CO_2 from the atmosphere

Global increase in methane level

Methane (CH_4) is the principal component of natural gas and a minor component of the Earth's atmosphere. Methane production is a natural process which occurs when plant or animal remains decay in the absence of oxygen. Methane is sometimes referred to as 'marsh gas' because it is released from swamps and marshy wetlands.

Rice paddies and ruminants

It is estimated that at least 120 million tons of methane are produced annually by the activity of **anaerobic bacteria** in the mud of rice paddy fields. A further 78 million tons are released during flatulence by cattle and other ruminants. The guts of these herbivorous mammals contain anaerobic micro-organisms which aid the digestion of plants and produce methane gas.

As rice-growing and animal husbandry continue to increase in the future to feed the growing world population, so too will the volume of methane released into the atmosphere.

Further sources of methane

The burning of **tropical biomass** (e.g. forests cleared to create pastureland) adds a further 50 million tons of methane to the atmosphere annually. Methane is also released from **land-fill rubbish dumps** and during recovery of coal, oil and natural gas. The concentration of methane is increasing now at a rate of just over 1% of its current level per year.

Chlorofluorocarbons

Chlorofluorocarbons (CFCs) are gases which were absent from the world's atmosphere prior to industrialisation. They are used as aerosol propellants, refrigerator coolants

gas	estimated atmospheric concentration (ppm)			current rate of increase (% per year)	average time molecules persist in atmosphere (years)
	before 1800	1995	2030		
CO_2	280	350	400–550	0.4	100
CH_4	0.65	1.7	2.2–2.5	1.0	10
CFCs	0	0.0004	0.0004–0.0006	4.0	60–100

Table 40.3 Summary of changes to atmospheric level of three gases

and blowing agents in foam production. Their relative lack of chemical reactivity prevents them from breaking down easily. Their concentration in the atmosphere continues to increase.

Summary of changes

Table 40.3 summarises the changes in atmospheric levels of the above three carbon-containing gases which have occurred largely as a result of human activities.

Greenhouse effect – a case study

Greenhouse gases

Carbon dioxide, methane and chlorofluorocarbons are often referred to as 'greenhouse' gases. This is because they trap infra-red radiation (heat) coming from the Earth's surface and reflect it back to Earth, keeping the planet **warm** (see figure 40.11).

This **greenhouse effect** (so-called because the gases play a role similar to the panes of glass in a greenhouse), causes global warming which is *essential* to life on Earth. Without it the world would be too cold to support life.

Excessive global warming

As concentrations of CO_2, CH_4 and CFCs build up in the atmosphere and form an ever denser layer, a corresponding increase in the greenhouse effect is expected to occur. This would result in global warming well in excess of the present desirable levels.

Evidence suggests that this additional global warming may have already begun.

◆ There has been a slight increase in mean world temperature over the last 130 years (see figure 40.12).

◆ By 1990, seven of the eight warmest years in the 130 years since records began had all occurred within the previous decade.

◆ In 1994 scientists found grasses and other flowering plants growing in regions of Antarctica previously covered permanently with ice and too cold to support life.

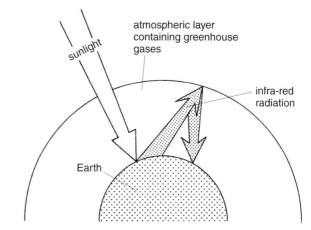

Figure 40.11 Greenhouse effect

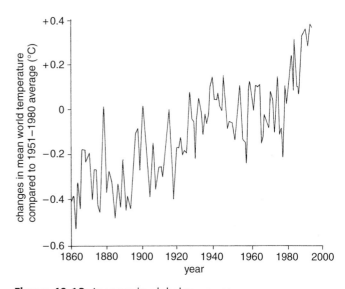

Figure 40.12 Increase in global temperature

However, it is debatable whether these effects are due solely to an increase in the greenhouse effect. The situation is complicated by many other factors such as atmospheric pollution and holes in the ozone layer.

The future

Greenhouse gases

The gases responsible for the greenhouse effect are not equally effective at absorbing infra-red radiation (see table 40.4). Molecule for molecule, methane is thirty times better at trapping infra-red rays than CO_2 and the concentration of methane is expected to go on increasing.

gas	relative efficiency at absorbing infra-red radiation	approximate contribution at present to green-house effect (%)
CO_2	1	50
CH_4	30	18
CFCs	10 000–20 000	14
other non-carbon-containing gases	200–2000	18

Table 40.4 Heat-trapping efficiency of gases

The present concentration of CFCs in the atmosphere is very low (see table 40.3). However, CFCs are such effective greenhouse gases that even a small rise in their concentration would result in a significant increase in the greenhouse effect and a major contribution to further global warming.

Temperature

Experts predict that an increase in **global temperature** of 4–5°C could occur by the year 2050. It is interesting to note that the average global temperature during the last ice age was only about 4–5°C cooler than it is at present. So a change of a few degrees can make an enormous difference to climatic conditions worldwide.

Rise in sea level

If a significant rise in global temperature does occur in the future, this could cause partial melting of the polar ice caps, releasing extra water into the world's oceans. The inevitable result would be a substantial **rise in sea level**, estimated at about 1.5 metres over the next 50 years. If this happens, many population centres would be destroyed by **flooding** since 65% of the world's cities are situated at sea level. Low-lying coastal regions, many at present cultivated and used for growing food, would also become permanently submerged.

Although developed countries such as the UK may be able to build some sort of protection (e.g. the Thames flood barrier in London), developing countries such as low-lying Bangladesh would suffer disastrous consequences.

Changes in climate

A rise in temperature of a few degrees Celsius would cause a **global shift** in climate and rainfall patterns. Less rain would fall in subtropical regions (near the equator) and more rain would fall in northerly (and southerly) latitudes. Already unprecedented drought conditions in parts of Africa in recent years have led to widespread famine. It is too soon to tell whether this is the start of the predicted trend or due to a combination of other factors.

Agriculture

If equatorial regions were to become even hotter and drier, there would be a shift of the **thermal limits** of agriculture towards the poles. 'Breadbasket' regions such as the American mid-west would suffer a major reduction in soil water and be unable to produce the vast quantities of maize and wheat with which they supply the world at present. This would affect food supplies on a global scale unless intensive agricultural practices could be established in more northerly (or southerly) latitudes (see figure 40.13).

Success would depend largely on the existing soils in these regions (at present supporting forests and cooler-climate crops) being able to meet the demands of vast monocultures of rapid-response cereals.

Even if this did prove to be possible, it is unlikely that there would be a net gain in food production if agriculture in other parts of America, Southern Asia and Australia were to break down.

Excessive global warming is likely to lead to a decrease in forestation, an increase in desertification and a worsening of conditions for the rural poor of the world scraping a living in marginal farming regions.

Wildlife

Global warming by a few degrees Celsius would bring about dramatic changes to many natural ecosystems. It is estimated that climatic zones would move toward the poles at a rate of about 100 km per decade over the next 50 years if this temperature increase were to occur.

Many plants and animal species, especially those living in the **wild**, would be unable to adapt to this pace of change. A few might be able to move with the **climatic shift** but most would be unable to move quickly enough or adapt in time. Especially at risk would be those plants and animals that are highly specialised to suit life in one **specific ecosystem** (e.g. an island). It seems certain therefore that many forms of wildlife would become **extinct**.

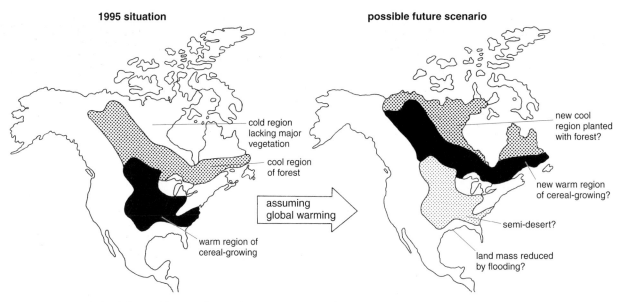

1995 situation

possible future scenario

cold region
lacking major
vegetation

cool region
of forest

assuming
global warming

warm region of
cereal-growing

new cool
region planted
with forest?

new warm region
of cereal-growing?

semi-desert?

land mass reduced
by flooding?

Figure 40.13 Poleward shift of thermal limits of agriculture in N. Hemisphere

Uncertainty

Knowledge of the behaviour of the greenhouse gases is incomplete. Scientists can only speculate, for example, about the actual volume of carbon dioxide that enters and leaves the ocean reservoir (a complex system which is not yet fully understood). Since CO_2 is more soluble in cold than in hot water, it is even possible that excess global warming could lead to the release of further CO_2 from the ocean which would in turn add to the greenhouse effect!

An increase in global temperature would increase the rate of evaporation of water from oceans. This would probably lead to greater precipitation, as the water condensed. If much of this fell on polar regions and froze, it could make these increase in size and cause a decrease in sea level!

Long-term climate and day-to-day weather both result from the complex interaction of many variable factors including the atmosphere, oceans, land surfaces, vegetation and polar ice. It is therefore impossible to make accurate predictions about climate and weather.

Some people insist that scientists are not justified in relating recent unusual climatic effects to global warming. They claim that the variations are due to other unknown factors and point out that the temperature in Europe is known to have varied from the mean by at least two degrees Celsius over the last thousand years. However, the vast majority of experts are of the opinion that **excessive global warming is inevitable** if humans continue to pursue activities that increase the concentrations of the greenhouse gases in the atmosphere.

Possible courses of action

It is unlikely that an increase in global temperature can be completely prevented. However, it is estimated that it could be reduced from a rate of increase of 0.5°C to about 0.05°C per decade by a massive reduction in the release of greenhouse gases.

Emission of carbon dioxide could be cut by promoting more **efficient use** of energy and reducing our reliance on the combustion of fossil fuels by developing **alternative sources** of energy.

Reduction in methane (and CO_2) output could be achieved by discouraging both deforestation and the burning of tropical biomass. Destruction of tropical forest could be reduced by offering **financial incentives** (such as relief of debt burden) to the developing countries that possess the forests, in exchange for guarantees of **conservation**. Well designed **land-fill dumps**, which allow methane to be collected and put to use instead of escaping into the atmosphere, would also be beneficial.

A significant decrease in the volume of CFCs released into the atmosphere could be brought about by exerting **strict control** over their use and phasing them out completely as soon as **harmless substitutes** are found.

Excessive global warming (the greenhouse effect) is a major environmental problem that can only be tackled successfully by **international co-operation**. If we ignore the warning signs and remain short-sighted, will future generations ever forgive us?

Testing your knowledge

1 Copy and complete table 40.5. (9)

2 a) (i) What is meant by the *greenhouse effect*?
       (ii) Why, in moderation, is it essential to our
             continued existence on Earth? (3)

   b) Predict ONE effect of excessive global warming
       on each of the following:
       (i) sea levels around the world;
       (ii) climate in northerly latitudes;
       (iii) agriculture in temperate regions;
       (iv) wildlife adapted to an island ecosystem. (4)

	'greenhouse' gas		
	CO_2	CH_4	CFCs
One major natural source of the gas which does not involve human activity.			
Two major sources of the gas resulting from human activity.			
One way in which release of this gas could be reduced in future.			

Table 40.5

Applying your knowledge

1 The graph in figure 40.14 shows the results of an
   experiment in which two pesticides (X and Y) were
   sprayed onto separate sample areas of a cereal crop.
   The concentration of each residue remaining on the
   crop after spraying was measured over a period of
   60 days.

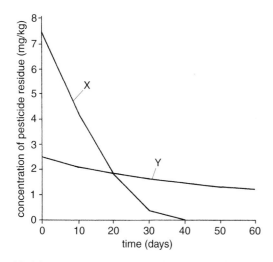

Figure 40.14

   a) By how many times was the concentration of
       pesticide X greater than that of Y immediately
       after spraying? (1)

   b) Which pesticide was biodegradable? Explain your
       answer. (2)

   c) Suggest which pesticide was DDT. Justify your
       choice. (2)

2 The spider mite feeds on green leaves, making them
   turn yellow and fall off the plant. This tiny creature
   belongs to the food web shown in figure 40.15
   where * indicates organisms that are sensitive to a
   certain type of pesticide spray.

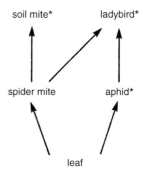

Figure 40.15

   One year a farmer sprayed his crop with the
   pesticide and found that only a little of the crop was
   lost. The next year he found his crop to be plagued
   with a pest so he sprayed again. However, he lost
   most of the crop.

   a) Under natural conditions, which animals keep the
       numbers of plant-eating pests in check? (2)

   b) Why was any of the crop lost following the first
       application of pesticide? (1)

   c) Why was damage to the crop so severe the
       second year? (1)

Continued ➤

Applying your knowledge

d) Rewrite the following sentence to include only the correct word from each choice.

This example shows how the removal of the primary/secondary consumers from a food chain/web enables a primary/secondary consumer to undergo a population increase/decrease and destroy most of the decomposer/producer. (5)

3 Dieldrin is a type of pesticide which was used in Britain in the 1950s to dress wheat grains against attack by insects. During each year of its use, thousands of seed-eating birds were found to be poisoned.

In the 1960s a severe decline in number of peregrine falcons occurred (see figure 40.16) and many of the survivors were found to have high concentrations of dieldrin in their bodies.

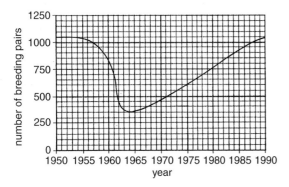

Figure 40.16

a) Construct a food chain to include the organisms named above. (1)

b) Low concentrations of dieldrin were used to dress the grain, yet high concentrations were found in the falcons' bodies. Explain fully how this difference arose. (2)

c) During which of the following intervals of time did the number of breeding pairs decrease at the fastest rate? (1)
A 1956–58
B 1958–60
C 1960–62
D 1962–64

d) Calculate the percentage decrease in breeding pairs that occurred between 1957 and 1964. (1)

e) Why does production of thinner egg shells lead to a reduction in number of future breeding pairs? (1)

f) Account for the trend shown by the graph from 1965 onwards. (1)

4 This question refers to algal blooms in temperate seas as illustrated by the graph in figure 40.4 on p 324.

a) Give a possible explanation for the increase in concentration of phosphates and nitrates at the surface during winter. (1)

b) Name TWO factors which limited algal growth during the winter. (2)

c) (i) During which month did the algal bloom reach its highest peak?
(ii) Which factor became limiting and led to a decline in algal numbers? (2)

d) (i) Suggest the source of the nitrate that supplied the autumn algal bloom.
(ii) Why was the autumn algal bloom smaller than the one that occurred in the spring? (2)

5 The map in figure 40.17 shows the pollution of shallow and coastal waters of the North sea by nitrate.

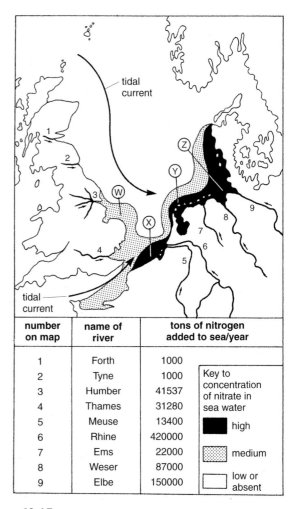

number on map	name of river	tons of nitrogen added to sea/year	
1	Forth	1000	
2	Tyne	1000	Key to concentration of nitrate in sea water
3	Humber	41537	
4	Thames	31280	
5	Meuse	13400	■ high
6	Rhine	420000	
7	Ems	22000	▒ medium
8	Weser	87000	
9	Elbe	150000	□ low or absent

Figure 40.17

Continued ➤

Applying your knowledge

a) Which agricultural practice, if performed irresponsibly, burdens the environment with excessive concentrations of nitrate? (1)

b) By what means does much of this nitrate find its way into the North Sea? (1)

c) (i) Which of the four lettered sites in the map would be least likely to suffer an algal bloom?
   (ii) Explain your choice fully. (3)

d) Briefly describe, in turn, the chain of events occurring in a region affected by an algal bloom that could lead to
   (i) the death of fish;
   (ii) the poisoning of the local human community. (2)

6 Figure 40.18 shows part of the nitrogen cycle.

a) Copy the diagram and complete the blanks using the terms: *ammonium, animal, nitrites, nitrogen, protein* and *waste*. (6)

b) Which type of bacteria bring about the process indicated by arrow G? (1)

c) Which arrow(s) represents the activity of
   (i) nitrogen-fixing bacteria;
   (ii) nitrifying bacteria? (2)

d) Effluent from adequately treated sewage, when discharged into a river, may lead to an algal bloom.
   (i) Which arrow in the diagram represents the stage in the cycle at which this process would occur?
   (ii) In which chemical form is most of the nitrogen in such effluent? (2)

e) Untreated sewage may be discharged into a river.
   (i) What process brings about the conversion of substances in this sewage to ammonium compounds?
   (ii) Which arrow in the diagram represents this process?
   (iii) What effect do the micro-organisms that bring about this process have on the river's oxygen content? Explain why. (4)

7 The graph in figure 40.19 refers to the quantity of nitrogen released from the soil and the quantity required by a crop planted in October.

a) (i) Identify the months of the year during which the two peaks of natural release of nitrogen occur.

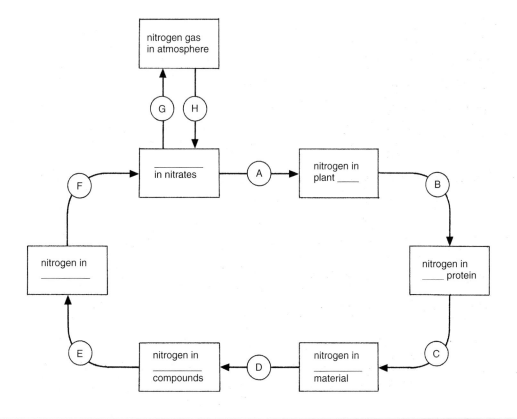

Figure 40.18

Continued ➤

Applying your knowledge

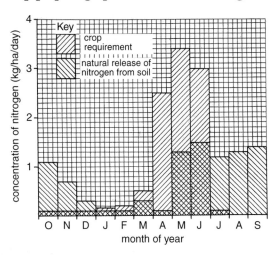

Figure 40.19

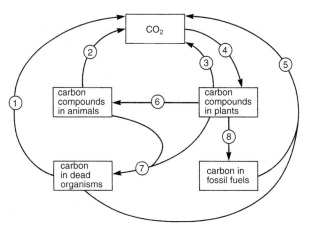

Figure 40.20

(ii) Which of these peaks occurs at a time when no demand for nitrogen is being made by the crop?

(iii) Which of these peaks fails to fully support the nitrogen requirement of the crop? (4)

b) (i) During which ONE of the following months would application of fertiliser be most likely to lead to leaching of nitrate from this farmland into the local supply of drinking water?

    A March
    B May
    C June
    D August

(ii) Explain your choice of answer to **(i)**. (2)

c) To reduce the chance of nitrate being leached out of a soil the farmer should apply nitrogen fertiliser:

    A when the cereal crop is actively growing.
    B in early autumn before the ground freezes over.
    C in one large dose rather than several smaller ones.
    D when the soil is bare and fallow in the winter.

    (i) Choose ONE correct answer only.
    (ii) Explain why each of the others is wrong. (4)

8 Figure 40.20 shows an incomplete version of the carbon cycle.

a) Copy the diagram and complete the numbered blanks using the following words and phrases: *animal nutrition, combustion, death, fossilisation, photosynthesis, respiration by decay microbes, respiration by animals, respiration by plants*. (8)

b) Which of the numbered processes in the diagram represents an activity pursued by humans that is disrupting the carbon cycle and contributing to the greenhouse effect? (1)

9 Analysis of gases contained in tiny air bubbles trapped in ice crystals of different ages indicates the concentrations of methane present in the atmosphere over the last 10 000 years. The results of this survey are shown in the scatter graph in figure 40.21.

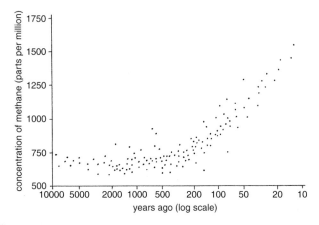

Figure 40.21

Continued ➤

Applying your knowledge

a) Trace the axes and then draw a line of best fit. (1)

b) **(i)** Estimate the average global concentration of methane 2000 years ago.
(ii) From your graph, estimate when the concentration of methane began to rise.
(iii) Relate your answer to **(ii)** with the graph in figure 35.4 on p 277. (3)

c) Why is methane referred to as one of the 'greenhouse' gases? (1)

d) A small emission of methane can contribute as much to global warming as a large emission of CO_2. Explain why. (1)

10 Describe how human activities disrupt the nitrogen cycle, under the following headings:

(i) algal blooms; (4)
(ii) inadequate treatment of sewage; (3)
(iii) contamination of drinking water. (3)

What you should know
(Chapter 40)

(See table 40.6 for word bank.)

1 Various types of _____ are employed to promote the growth of crop plants needed to feed the ever-increasing human population. Some of these chemicals have disruptive side-effects on food _____ .

2 If a pesticide is non-biodegradable it tends to increase in _____ along a food chain and affect the final _____ seriously or even fatally.

3 Repeated use of a pesticide often leads to the emergence of _____ strains of the pest that cause as much damage as before.

4 Destruction by a chemical of one or more members of an ecosystem's interdependent community results in loss of _____ and leads to _____ within that ecosystem.

5 _____ is the enrichment of an aquatic environment by nutrients such as nitrate and _____ . It is increased to unnaturally high levels by excess fertiliser or sewage passing into waterways and disturbing the _____ cycle.

6 Algal _____ occur in _____ ecosystems when excessive quantities of nitrate become available. Death of the _____ cells and their decomposition by _____ causes environmental degradation.

7 Disposal of inadequately treated sewage into a waterway leads to serious _____ problems. _____ which has been adequately treated still presents human society with the problem of finding a suitable site for its safe _____ especially if the community is densely populated.

8 Supplies of drinking water may be contaminated by _____ from excessive or ill-timed use of _____ on farmland.

9 The rising demand for energy by the increasing human population (especially in industrialised societies) is met largely by the combustion of _____ . This is causing the concentration of carbon dioxide in the Earth's atmosphere to increase.

10 Human activities are also causing the concentrations of _____ and CFCs in the atmosphere to increase.

11 Carbon dioxide, methane and CFCs are called _____ gases because they trap heat coming from the Earth's surface and keep the planet warm. This _____ effect is essential to life.

12 Evidence suggests that global warming may increase in the future to well in excess of desirable levels. It is thought that this could lead to a rise in _____ , disturbance of world _____ , disruption of agriculture and _____ of many forms of wildlife.

algal	disposal	nitrate
aquatic	eutrophication	nitrogen
bacteria	extinction	pollution
blooms	fertiliser	phosphate
chemical	fossil fuels	resistant
climate	global warming	sea level
complexity	greenhouse	sewage
concentration	instability	webs
consumer	methane	

Table 40.6 Word bank for chapter 40

Appendix 1 ■■■■■■■■■■■■■■■■■

Endocrine glands

Figure Ap1 shows the sites of the main **endocrine glands** in the human body. Endocrine glands secrete one or more hormones directly into the bloodstream.

Hormones are chemical messengers that are transported in the bloodstream to target sites in the body where they exert specific effects.

endocrine gland	hormone	role of hormone	primary target site(s)
pituitary	follicle-stimulating hormone (FSH)	stimulates development and maturation of Graafian follicles	ovary
	luteinising hormone (LH)	triggers ovulation and brings about development of corpus luteum	ovary
	interstitial cell-stimulating hormone (ICSH)	stimulates production of testosterone	interstitial cells in testes
	prolactin	stimulates lactation and secretion of milk into breast tubules	mammary glands
	oxytocin	stimulates contractions of uterus during labour and causes ejection of milk from lactating breasts	uterus and mammary glands
	somatotrophin (growth hormone)	promotes growth of body	bones and many soft tissues
	anti-diuretic hormone (ADH)	regulates blood water concentration by promoting water retention	distal tubules and collecting ducts in kidneys
thyroid	thyroxin	increases metabolic rate	most body tissues
adrenal	adrenaline	stimulates body in preparation for 'fight or flight'	heart, bronchioles and blood vessels
pancreas (Islets of Langerhans)	insulin	promotes conversion of glucose to glycogen	liver
	glucagon	promotes conversion of glycogen to glucose	liver
ovary (female)	oestrogen	stimulates proliferation of endometrium and promotes development of female secondary sexual characteristics	uterus
	progesterone	promotes thickening of endometrium and development of female secondary sexual characteristics	uterus
testis (male)	testosterone	stimulates sperm production, activates prostate gland and seminal vesicles and promotes development of male secondary sexual characteristics	testes, prostate gland and seminal vesicles

Figure Ap1 Endocrine glands

Appendix 2

The Genetic Code

		second letter of triplet			
		A	G	T	C	
first letter of triplet	A	AAA AAG AAT AAC	AGA AGG AGT AGC	ATA ATG ATT ATC	ACA ACG ACT ACC	A G T C
	G	GAA GAG GAT GAC	GGA GGG GGT GGC	GTA GTG GTT GTC	GCA GCG GCT GCC	A G T C
	T	TAA TAG TAT TAC	TGA TGG TGT TGC	TTA TTG TTT TTC	TCA TCG TCT TCC	A G T C
	C	CAA CAG CAT CAC	CGA CGG CGT CGC	CTA CTG CTT CTC	CCA CCG CCT CCC	A G T C	third letter of triplet

(A = adenine,　G = guanine,　T = thymine,　C = cytosine)

Table Ap 2.1 DNA's bases grouped into 64 (4 × 4 × 4) triplets

abbreviation	amino acid	abbreviation	amino acid
ala	alanine	lys	lysine
arg	arginine	met	methionine
asp	aspartic acid	phe	phenylalanine
aspn	asparagine	pro	proline
cys	cysteine	ser	serine
glu	glutamic acid	thr	threonine
glun	glutamine	tryp	tryptophan
gly	glycine	tyr	tyrosine
his	histidine	val	valine
ileu	isoleucine	◆	chain terminator
leu	leucine		

Table Ap 2.3 Key to amino acids

codon	anti-codon	amino acid	codon	anti-codon	amino acid	codon	anti-codon	amino acid	codon	anti-codon	amino acid
UUU	AAA	phe	UCU	AGA	ser	UAU	AUA	tyr	UGU	ACA	cys
UUC	AAG	phe	UCC	AGG	ser	UAC	AUG	tyr	UGC	ACG	cys
UUA	AAU	leu	UCA	AGU	ser	UAA	AUU	◆	UGA	ACU	◆
UUG	AAC	leu	UCG	AGC	ser	UAG	AUC	◆	UGG	ACC	tryp
CUU	GAA	leu	CCU	GGA	pro	CAU	GUA	his	CGU	GCA	arg
CUC	GAG	leu	CCC	GGG	pro	CAC	GUG	his	CGC	GCG	arg
CUA	GAU	leu	CCA	GGU	pro	CAA	GUU	glun	CGA	GCU	arg
CUG	GAC	leu	CCG	GGC	pro	CAG	GUC	glun	CGG	GCC	arg
AUU	UAA	ileu	ACU	UGA	thr	AAU	UUA	aspn	AGU	UCA	ser
AUC	UAG	ileu	ACC	UGG	thr	AAC	UUG	aspn	AGC	UCG	ser
AUA	UAU	ileu	ACA	UGU	thr	AAA	UUU	lys	AGA	UCU	arg
AUG	UAC	met	ACG	UGC	thr	AAG	UUC	lys	AGG	UCC	arg
GUU	CAA	val	GCU	CGA	ala	GAU	CUA	asp	GGU	CCA	gly
GUC	CAG	val	GCC	CGG	ala	GAC	CUG	asp	GGC	CCG	gly
GUA	CAU	val	GCA	CGU	ala	GAA	CUU	glu	GGA	CCU	gly
GUG	CAC	val	GCG	CGC	ala	GAG	CUC	glu	GGG	CCC	gly

Table Ap 2.2 mRNA's 64 codons, tRNA's anticodons and amino acids coded　　　　　　(U = uracil)

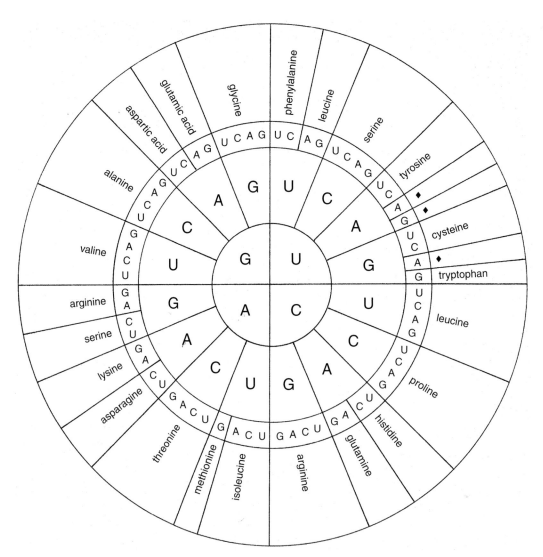

Figure Ap2 Alternative presentation of mRNA's 64 codons and the amino acids coded

Index

Answers

1 Structure and variety of proteins

1 See figure A1.1.

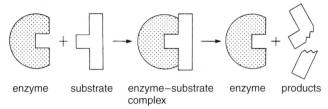

enzyme   substrate   enzyme–substrate   enzyme   products
                        complex

Figure A1.1

2 **a)** **(i)** C.

    (ii) A.

    (iii) B.

    (iv) A.

  b) **(i)** B.

    (ii) Collagen consists of strong fibres as shown by B.

    (iii) Its fibres are strong and inelastic which makes them perfectly suited to the function of attachment as part of a tendon.

  c) **(i)** A.

    (ii) It contains a non-protein part called a haem group.

    (iii) The possession of a haem group enables it to pick up and transport oxygen

  d) **(i)** C.

    (ii) It has an active site allowing it to fit its substrate like a key fits a lock.

3 **a)** Casein contains them all. Group 2 rats gained weight throughout the experiment. Zein lacks two essential amino acids. Group 1 rats lost weight throughout the experiment.

  b) **(i)** Zein.

    (ii) Their diet could have been changed to casein or to zein supplemented with the two essential amino acids that it lacks.

  c) 35 g.

  d) 20%.

4 Many types of fibrous protein exist and each possesses a structure suited to its function. Elastin, for example, is strong and elastic and gives artery walls flexible support. Collagen is strong and inelastic to serve as a component of bones, tendons and ligaments. Actin and myosin are contractile to suit their role as components of muscle tissue.

Globular proteins play a variety of roles. Some are hormones (chemical messengers) that are transported in the bloodstream to target tissues where they exert an effect. Insulin, for example, is made in the pancreas and promotes the conversion of excess glucose to glycogen in the liver.

Some globular proteins support the cell membrane; others act as antibodies and defend the body against antigens (e.g. viruses). Enzymes are globular proteins which act as biological catalysts needed to speed up chemical reactions.

Conjugated proteins also carry out several different functions. Mucus, for example, lubricates and protects parts of the body. Haemoglobin combines with oxygen in the lungs and delivers it to respiring cells.

The healthy functioning of the body therefore depends on many different types of protein each performing its particular function efficiently.

2 Role of enzymes

1 **a)** Enzyme–substrate complex.

  b) **(i)** Y, Z, X.

    (ii) X, Z, Y.

2 **a)** See figure A2.1.

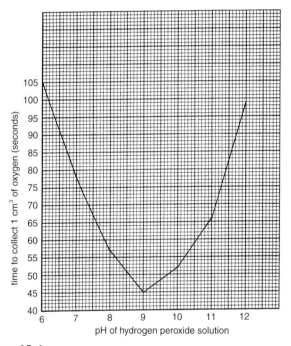

Figure A2.1

  b) **(i)** 9.

    (ii) 6.

  c) 9.

  d) Use a more detailed range of pH values between 8 and 10 (e.g. 8.5 and 9.5).

3 **a)** Important enzymes are becoming denatured and are no longer able to promote those biochemical reactions that are essential for life to continue.

  b) Most enzymes including those made by micro-organisms are unable to function in acidic conditions. Decomposers are therefore unable to act in conditions of low pH.

  c) Enzymes including those made by a fungal mould work much better at room temperature than at the low temperature found in a fridge so the fungus digests the cheese and grows more rapidly at the warmer temperature.

347

experimental set-up	enzyme concentration	substrate concentration	enzyme–substrate complex	number of molecules of product produced per unit time

1

unused substrate

2

unused substrate

3

4

unused enzyme

Figure A2.2

4 a) (i) Concentration of substrate.

(ii) As the concentration of substrate increased, the rate of reaction increased.

b) Concentration of enzyme.

c) (i) A.

(ii) C.

(iii) B.

d) Increase the concentration of enzyme.

5 a) See figure A2.2.

b) (i) Enzyme concentration.

(ii) Substrate concentration.

c) (i) Number of molecules of product produced per unit time.

(ii) It brought about an increase in reaction rate.

d) Substrate concentration.

6 a) (i) P.

(ii) Q.

b) (i) Q.

(ii) R.

c) The concentration of P will remain unaltered, that of Q will decrease and that of R will increase.

d) The concentration of P will be normal, that of Q will be very high and that of R very low or non-existent.

7 An enzyme molecule combines with its substrate to form an enzyme–substrate complex. This exists for a brief moment and then the end products are released. The enzyme's active site becomes free to repeat the process.

An increase in concentration of enzyme (i.e. an increase in number of enzyme molecules) results in an increase in enzyme activity (and rate of reaction) since more substrate molecules are being acted upon. For this increase to continue, the concentration of substrate must be in excess. If substrate concentration is limited, the reaction rate levels off.

An increase in concentration of substrate results in an increase in enzyme activity provided that a sufficient number of enzyme

molecules are available. Once all of the active sites on the available enzymes are in use, the reaction rate levels off. Further increase in concentration of substrate fails to bring about an increase in reaction rate until it is accompanied by an increase in concentration of enzyme.

An inhibitor is a substance that decreases the rate of an enzyme-controlled reaction and may bring it to a halt.

A molecule of competitive inhibitor is similar in structure to that of the substrate. Molecules of competitive inhibitor compete with substrate molecules for the active sites on the enzyme molecules. Active sites blocked by inhibitor are non-functional and result in a decrease in enzyme activity. The extent of this decrease is affected by both the concentration of the inhibitor and the concentration of the substrate.

A molecule of non-competitive inhibitor alters the enzyme's active site indirectly by combining with the enzyme molecule at some other site. Since the substrate molecules are no longer able to combine with the enzyme, enzyme activity decreases. The extent of this decrease is dependent on the concentration of the inhibitor only.

3 Nucleic acids and protein synthesis

1 a) Nucleotide.

b) X = phosphate, Y = deoxyribose sugar, Z = cytosine.

c) See figure A3.1.

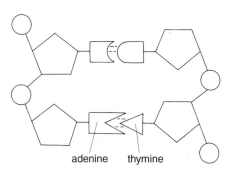

adenine   thymine

Figure A3.1

d) (i) 2.

   (ii) 1.

e) That it takes the form of a double helix.

2 a) 30%.

 b) 2000.

3 E, C, A, G, B, D, F.

4 a) A = cell membrane, B = vesicle, C = Golgi apparatus,
D = pore in nuclear membrane, E = nuclear membrane,
F = chromosome, G = nucleolus, H = ribosome,
I = rough endoplasmic reticulum.

 b) (i) Protein.

   (ii) H.

 c) C – processes and packages protein,
G – controls synthesis of RNA needed to build ribosomes,
I – acts as pathway for transport of newly synthesised protein.

5 a) 1 = C, 2 = T, 3 = T, 4 = A, 5 = U, 6 = A, 7 = G, 8 = C, 9 = G.

 b) P = transcription and release of mRNA,
Q = translation of mRNA into protein.

 c) See table A3.1

amino acid	codon	anticodon
alanine	GCG	CGC
arginine	CGC	GCG
cysteine	UGU	ACA
glutamic acid	GAA	CUU
glutamine	CAA	GUU
glycine	GGC	CCG
isoleucine	AUA	UAU
leucine	CUU	GAA
proline	CCG	GGC
threonine	ACA	UGU
tyrosine	UAU	AUA
valine	GUU	CAA

Table A3.1

d) CAA.

e) U = proline, V = glutamine, W = glutamic acid, X = cysteine,
Y = arginine, Z = isoleucine.

f) (i) ACACUUGCGGGC.

   (ii) TGTGAACGCCCG.

6 *Transcription*

The sequence of bases along part of a DNA strand (one gene)
contains the instructions for determining the sequence of amino
acids in a particular protein. This information is carried from the
nucleus to ribosomes in the cytoplasm by messenger RNA
(mRNA).

Transcription is the process by which mRNA is formed from the
appropriate part of a DNA strand. The DNA molecule uncoils
and part of it opens up by weak bonds between its bases breaking.

Free RNA nucleotides become attached to their complementary
DNA nucleotides on one of the open strands by their bases.
Adenine on DNA, for example, pairs with uracil on RNA;
guanine pairs with cytosine.

In the presence of the enzyme RNA polymerase and ATP (for
energy), strong chemical bonds form between adjacent nucleotides
giving the single-stranded mRNA its sugar-phosphate 'backbone'.
The weak bonds between DNA and mRNA break and mRNA is
released.

Translation

Molecules of transfer RNA (tRNA) are present in the cytoplasm.
Many different types exist and each has a single triplet of bases
exposed. This is called an anticodon and it corresponds to an
amino acid. Each type of amino acid molecule becomes attached
to its tRNA and is transported to a ribosome.

The ribosome becomes associated with one end of the mRNA
molecule and two molecules of tRNA enter the ribosome and
become attached by their anticodons to the complementary
codons (triplets of bases) on the mRNA. A strong peptide bond
forms between the two adjacent amino acid molecules.

As the ribosome moves along the mRNA, the process continues
with further tRNA molecules entering in turn and their amino
acids being added to the growing polypeptide chain. By this
means mRNA's genetic code of triplets (codons) is translated into
protein. The tRNA and mRNA molecules are normally reused
several times.

4 ATP and energy transfer

1 a) See figure A4.1.

 b) (i) Between minutes 3 and 4.

   (ii) Between minutes 5 and 6.

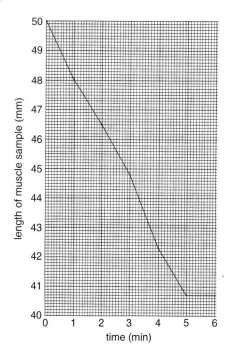

Figure A4.1

c) ATP → ADP + Pi + energy

d) Run a control without ATP.

2 a) and b) See figure A4.2.

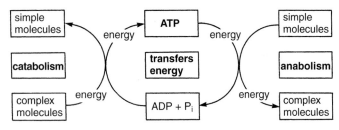

Figure A4.2

3 a) Q = 3, R = 3, S = 6, T = 1, U = 4, V = 4.

b) Q = pyruvic acid, R = lactic acid, S = citric acid, T = carbon dioxide, W = water.

c) (i) H.

(ii) A.

(iii) A.

(iv) B, C, D, E, F and G.

4 The concentrations of lactic acid and carbon dioxide increase. Since both of these are acidic, they depress the pH.

5 Sources of energy

1 See table A5.1.

test	heat or no heat	result when test is positive	carbohydrate present
solubility in water	no heat	soluble	mono/ disaccharide
Benedict's reagent	heat	brick–red ppte	reducing sugar
acid hydrolysis + Benedict's reagent	heat	brick–red ppte	sucrose
Barfoed's reagent	heat	brick–red ppte	glucose/ fructose/ maltose
Clinistix	no heat	purple–blue	glucose
iodine solution	no heat	blue–black	starch
	no heat	purple–red	glycogen

Table A5.1

2 a) (i) Glycogen.

(ii) Maltose.

b) Once the powder has passed the solubility test, a sample of the solution is tested with Benedict's reagent. This should give a positive result. A fresh sample of the solution is then tested with Barfoed's solution. This should also give a positive result. Finally when a fresh sample of the solution is tested with clinistix, a positive result is not obtained within 10 seconds showing that fructose is present.

3 a) 1 = protein, 2 = fat (triglyceride), 3 = amino acids, 4 = glycerol, 5 = acetyl CoA.

b) Protein.

c) Lipid.

d) Lipid.

e) The person uses up their reserves. Glycogen stored in the liver is broken down into glucose and fat stored in the adipose tissues is broken down into fatty acids and glycerol. These products can supply the body with energy for many days.

4 a) Triglyceride = 60 hours; glycogen (liver) = 15 minutes; glycogen (muscle) = 56 minutes; glucose = 1 minute.

b) (i) Triglyceride.

(ii) Time is required for triglyceride to release its energy and the body depends on muscle glycogen to release energy during the early stages of the race.

5 See pages 39–40.

6 Cell membrane and transport of materials

1 a) Fluid mosaic.

b) A = phospholipid, B = protein.

c) (i) C and D.

(ii) To allow small molecules to pass through the membrane.

2 a) (i) X = diffusion, Y = active transport.

(ii) Y.

(iii) X.

b) (i) It will decrease.

(ii) It requires energy from respiration but respiratory enzymes do not work well at low temperatures.

3 AECBFD.

4 a) (i) Outside the cell.

(ii) Inside the cell.

(iii) Inside the cell.

(iv) Outside the cell.

(v) They are maintained by active transport of ions across the membrane against a concentration gradient.

b) 55.

c) Chloride. It is the smallest.

d) Although the concentrations of sodium and chloride ions inside the cell are fairly similar, the concentrations outside are very different, supporting the idea that the membrane selects more chloride than sodium ions for expulsion by active transport.

e) (i) It brings about an increase in rate of ion uptake.

(ii) Beyond 30% oxygen, some other factor (e.g. sugar concentration) has become the limiting factor.

(iii) An inverse relationship. Sugar is used up to generate the energy needed for the active transport of the ions into the cell.

5 See pages 44–45.

7 Cellular response in defence

1 **a)** A = lymphocyte, B = phagocyte.

b) 1 = nuclear membrane, 2 = ribosome, 3 = endoplasmic reticulum, 4 = Golgi apparatus, 5 = bacterium, 6 = vacuole, 7 = lysosome, 8 = vesicle.

c) 7 contains digestive enzymes, 8 contains antibodies.

d) The enzymes are kept enclosed inside lysosomes and vacuoles.

2 **a)** W = 2, X = 1, Y = 4, Z = 3.

b) **(i)** Method 4.

(ii) The body responds by making antibodies and remembers how to do so in the future. Method 3 leaves the body unprotected when the horse's antibodies disappear.

c) **(i)** W and Y.

(ii) X and Z.

d) Since it lacks a blood supply, no antibodies can reach and 'attack' the antigens in the transplanted cornea.

3 **a)** Q = A, R = O, S = AB, T = B.

b) **(i)** See table A7.1

		blood group of donor			
		A	B	AB	O
blood group of recipient	A	−	+	+	−
	B	+	−	+	−
	AB	−	−	−	−
	O	+	+	+	−

Table A7.1

(ii) O because it does not contain antigens A or B and therefore will not cause agglutination if the recipient's blood contains anti-A or anti-B antibodies.

(iii) AB because it contains neither anti-A nor anti-B antibodies and will not agglutinate in the presence of antigens A or B.

4 **a)** **(i)** IgG.

(ii) The baby's own immune system makes antibodies after a few months.

b) **(i)** IgM.

(ii) IgE.

c) 1.4–4.0 mg/ml.

d) The concentration of IgM increases before that of IgG in both the primary and the secondary response.

e) During the primary response, the concentration of IgG takes a longer time to begin to rise than during the secondary response. The highest concentration of IgG reached during the primary response is less than that reached during the secondary response. The concentration of IgG decreases after reaching its maximum level in the primary response but remains level at its highest concentration in the secondary response.

f) Since the response to the second injection was faster than that to the first, this suggests that certain lymphocytes already 'knew what to do' from the previous time.

5 See pages 52–53. Use should be made of the information in figure 7.1.

8 Viruses

1 **a)** They are able to reproduce themselves.

b) It lacks a cell membrane and normal organelles such as mitochondria and ribosomes.

2 **a)** See table A8.1.

life form	nm	μm	mm	m
human red blood cell	10 000	10	1×10^{-2}	1×10^{-5}
Escherichia coli	3000	3	3×10^{-3}	3×10^{-6}
tobacco mosaic virus	250	0.25	2.5×10^{-4}	2.5×10^{-7}
bacteriophage	225	0.225	2.25×10^{-4}	2.25×10^{-7}
polio virus	30	0.03	3×10^{-5}	3×10^{-8}

Table A8.1

b) **(i)** 100 times.

(ii) 40 times.

3 **a)** In response to the antigen (even in a damaged state) lymphocytes make antibodies which give immunity. In addition some of these lymphocytes act as memory cells allowing a rapid response to the antigen if invasion occurs in the future.

b) **(i)** Artificially.

(ii) Active.

c) **(i)** The genetic material in HIV mutates frequently forming many new variants with different antigenic properties.

(ii) The HIV particles are 'hidden' inside the helper T cells where they remain unaffected by the antibodies.

4 **a)** No. Retroviruses contain RNA not DNA.

b) X = viral DNA. Y = viral RNA. Z = protein.

c) **(i)** Budding.

(ii) Death.

d) Figure 8.8 shows the production of only one viral particle. In reality, many copies of the virus would be produced.

5 See pages 62–63. Use should be made of the information in figure 8.2.

9 Chromosomes and DNA replication

1 **a)** 1 = chromosome, 2 = DNA, 3 = base.

b) 1.

c) 3.

d) It is too short.

2 **a)** X = meiosis, Y = fertilisation, Z = mitosis.

b) A = haploid sperm, B = diploid egg mother cell.

c) The symbol n means the cell is haploid and contains one set of chromosomes; the symbol 2n means the cell is diploid and contains two sets of chromosomes.

3 a) Unwinding of the double helix.

b) It must open up by weak hydrogen bonds between base pairs breaking.

c) **(i)** 7, 11, 28, 31.

(ii) 4, 20.

(iii) Four.

d) D.

e) E.

4 a) A human red blood cell lacks a nucleus.

b) That of a chicken does have a nucleus but that of a cow does not.

c) For each type of animal, the DNA content of its sperm is half that of its kidney cells.

d) The chromosomes in these cells had undergone DNA replication in preparation for nuclear and cell division but had been caught at the stage before nuclear division had occurred.

5 See page 70. Use should be made of the information in figure 9.4.

10 Meiosis

1 B, D, A, C.

2 a) 12.

b) 6.

c) 6.

d) 3.

e) 3.

f) **(i)** See figure A10.1.

arrangement 1

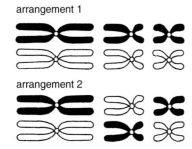

arrangement 2

Figure A10.1

(ii) See figure A10.2.

3 a) 2.

b) See figure A10.3.

4 See table A10.1.

5 a) R and V.

b) Q and T.

c) **(i)** Yes.

(ii) They have 50% of their bands in common with the parents of P.

gametes from arrangement 1

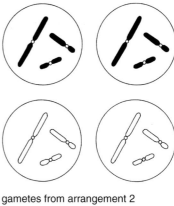

gametes from arrangement 2

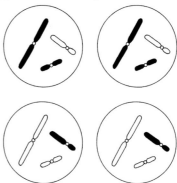

Figure A10.2

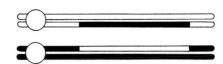

Figure A10.3

d) **(i)** No.

(ii) They have no bands in common with R and V.

11 Monohybrid inheritance

1 a)

original cross	GG × gg
gametes	all G ↓ all g
F₁ genotype	all Gg
F₁ phenotype	all grey body

second cross	Gg × gg
gametes	G and g ↓ all g
F₂ genotypes	Gg and gg
F₂ phenotypic ratio	1 grey body : 1 ebony body

b) All members of the F₁ possess the genotype Gg where G (grey body allele) is dominant to g (ebony allele) preventing the latter from being expressed.

c) **(i)** 1 grey body : 1 ebony body.

(ii) Fertilisation is a random process and involves an element of chance.

	mitosis	meiosis
site of division	occurs all over body of growing animal	occurs only in gamete mother cells in sex organs
pairing and movement of chromosomes	homologous chromosomes do not form pairs; chromosomes line up singly on equator	homologous chromosomes form pairs; chromosomes line up in pairs on equator
exchange of genetic material	chiasmata not formed and no crossing over occurs	chiasmata may be formed and crossing over may occur
number of divisions	single division of nucleus	double division of nucleus
number and type of cells produced	following cell division, two identical daughter cells formed	following cell division, four genetically different gametes formed
effect on chromosome number	chromosome number unaltered	chromosome number halved
effect on variation	does not increase variation within a population	increases variation by providing opportunity for independent assortment and crossing over to occur

Table A10.1

d) (i) To allow for the possibility that some may be infertile or not recover from the anaesthetic.

(ii) To make sure that eggs have not been fertilised already by a male fly of unknown genotype.

(iii) To ensure that the parents are not confused with the members of the next generation when they emerge.

2 a) (i) 1 in 2.

(ii) 1 in 2.

b) Complete dominance.

3 a) (i) **original cross**   HH × HS

gametes   all H ↓ H and S

F$_1$ **generation**   HH and HS

(ii) **original cross**   HS × HS

gametes   H and S ↓ H and S

F$_1$ **generation**   HH, HS, HS, SS

b) (i) phenotypes: HH = normal

HS = sickle cell trait

ratio = 1 normal : 1 sickle cell trait

(ii) phenotypes: HH = normal

HS = sickle cell trait

SS = sickle cell anaemia

ratio = 1 normal : 2 sickle cell trait : 1 sickle cell anaemia.

4 a) See table A11.1.

genotype	blood group	type(s) of antigen on red blood cells
MM	M	M only
NN	N	N only
MN	NM	M and N

Table A11.1

b) (i)

		sperm	
		M	**M**
eggs	**N**	MN	MN
	N	MN	MN

all blood group MN

(ii)

		sperm	
		M	**N**
eggs	**M**	MM	MN
	N	MN	NN

1 blood group M, 2 blood group MN and 1 blood group N

c) (i) (1) 1 in 4 chance

(2) 1 in 2 chance

(3) 1 in 4 chance.

(ii) 1 in 4 chance.

d) Co-dominance.

5 a) See figure A11.1.

b) 1 in 2 chance.

c) No chance.

6 a) (i) A = Dd (rhesus positive).

(ii) K = dd (rhesus negative).

b) F. Genotype could be DD or Dd.

c) (i) H.

(ii) B.

d) (i) 1 in 2.

(ii) 1 in 2.

e) (i) Person J's immune system would respond and produce anti-D antibodies which would persist leaving J sensitised. If more blood containing antigen D were given to J, she would suffer severe or even fatal agglutination.

(ii) This transfusion would be successful because B's immune system would not respond to the presence of J's blood.

Answers

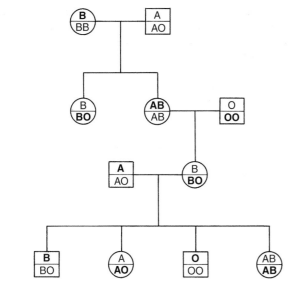

Figure A11.1

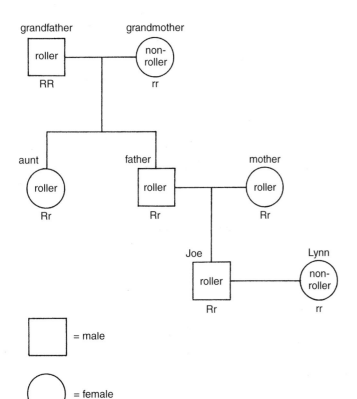

= male

= female

Figure A11.2

7 A cross between two parents who possess different alleles of one gene is called monohybrid inheritance. An example of a characteristic possessed by humans that shows a monohybrid pattern of inheritance is the ability or inability to roll the tongue. Two alleles of this gene exist. These are the dominant allele for tongue-rolling ability (normally represented by the symbol R) and the recessive allele for inability to roll the tongue (normally represented by the symbol r).

Such an inherited trait can be traced through the generations of a family by constructing a family tree as shown in figure A11.2. In

this example, Joe's paternal grandparents have the homozygous genotypes RR and rr. As a result all of their offspring (e.g. Joe's father) must have the genotype Rr (having received one of each type of allele from each parent) and the phenotype tongue-rolling ability.

Since both of Joe's parents have the genotype Rr, each time they have a child there is a 1 in 4 chance that the child will be a tongue-roller (RR), a 1 in 2 chance that it will be a tongue-roller (Rr) and a 1 in 4 chance that it will be a non-roller (rr).

In this case Joe happens to have the genotype Rr. If he marries Lynn with genotype rr, each time they have a child, there is a 1 in 2 chance that the child will be a tongue-roller (Rr) and a 1 in 2 chance that it will be a non-roller (rr).

12 Sex-linked and polygenic inheritance

1 See figure A12.1.

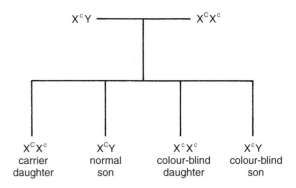

Figure A12.1

2 a) $A = X^H Y$, $B = X^H X^H$, $C = X^h Y$, $D = X^H X^h$.

  b) Male $= X^H Y$ (normal), female $= X^H X^h$ (carrier)

  c) None.

3 a) F.

  b) T.

  c) T.

  d) F.

  e) T.

4 a) See table A12.1.

		male gametes	
		$H^1 H^2$	$H^1 h^2$
female gametes	$H^1 H^2$	$H^1 H^1 H^2 H^2$	$H^1 H^1 H^2 h^2$
	$H^1 h^2$	$H^1 H^1 H^2 h^2$	$H^1 H^1 h^2 h^2$

Table A12.1

  b) $H^1 H^1 H^2 H^2 = $ very tall, $H^1 H^1 H^2 h^2 = $ tall, $H^1 H^1 h^2 h^2 = $ medium.

  c) It is very likely that more than two genes contribute to height in humans.

  d) Environmental factors such as diet and quality of housing.

5 a) See figure A12.2 on page 355.

  b) See figure A12.3 on page 355.

  c) (i) Six shades of red (+white).

  (ii) Shade 3 (3 red alleles).

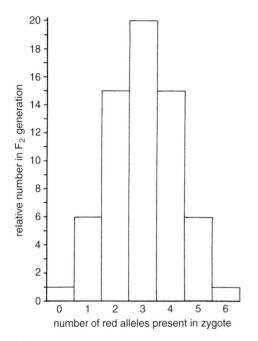

Figure A12.2

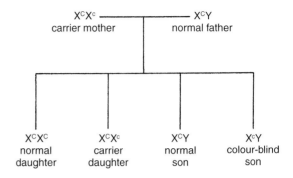

Figure A12.3

(iii) Shade 6 (6 red alleles).

(iv) 9.38.

d) 4:3.

6 In humans, the female possesses a pair of fully homologous sex chromosomes called X chromosomes. The male possesses one X chromosome and a much smaller Y chromosome which is homologous to only part of the X chromosome. A sex-linked gene is one that is present on the X but not on the Y chromosome. An example of a sex-linked characteristic in humans is red-green colour blindness. The two alleles of this gene are normal colour vision (often represented by the symbol C) and red-green colour blindness (often represented by the symbol c).

When an X and Y chromosome meet at fertilisation, the allele present on the X chromosome (whether C or c) is expressed in the phenotype of the male produced since the Y chromosome has no allele to offer dominance. In the example shown in figure A12.4,

the parents are a carrier mother and a normal father. The mother produces two types of egg, X^C and X^c. The father produces two types of sperm, X^C and Y. The cross can be represented by a Punnett square.

Figure A12.4

		sperm	
		X^C	**Y**
eggs	**X^C**	X^CX^C	X^CY
	X^c	X^CX^c	X^cY

Every time this couple produce a child, there is a 1 in 4 chance of the child being a normal daughter, a 1 in 4 chance of it being a carrier daughter, a 1 in 4 chance of it being a normal son and a 1 in 4 chance of it being a colour-blind son. Such a colour-blind son would only be able to pass allele c on to future generations via his daughters.

13 Mutations and chromosomal abnormalities

1 **a)** Deletion.

b) Substitution.

c) Inversion.

d) Insertion.

2 **a)** The gene will no longer be able to code the correct message for the production of its particular enzyme. Lack of the enzyme will prevent the pathway from proceeding normally.

b) **(i)** Q.

(ii) R.

(iii) T.

c) **(i)** All the excess phenylalanine has been converted to tyrosine.

(ii) The PKU sufferer is unable to make the enzyme needed to convert phenylalanine to tyrosine.

(iii) The tyrosine has been converted to other metabolites.

3 **a)** Family C.

b) 1 in 71428.6.

4 **a)** **(i)** 0.5 in 1000 = 1 in 2000.

(ii) 1 in 1000.

(iii) 10 in 1000 = 1 in 100.

b) The egg mother cells of older women are more prone to non-disjunction at meiosis.

5 a) 22 + XX, 22, 22 + Y, 22 + Y.

b) 44 + XXX, 44 + X, 44 + XY, 44 + XY.

c) 25.

6 A gene mutation involves a change in one or more nucleotides in a DNA strand. There are four types of gene mutation.

During substitution, one nucleotide drops out of the DNA chain and is replaced by another possessing a different base. This may result in the production of a triplet of bases (a codon) which corresponds to a different amino acid from before. Following transcription and translation a protein molecule will be formed with one 'wrong' amino acid in its chain.

During inversion, two or more nucleotides become disconnected from the chain and then join up again but in reverse order. This may result in the production of one (or two) different codons from normal and ultimately a protein with one (or two) 'wrong' amino acids in its chain.

Substitution and inversion are called point mutations since they bring about only minor changes (e.g. a change in one amino acid in the chain). Often the organism is hardly affected.

During deletion, a nucleotide is lost permanently from the DNA chain. During insertion, a nucleotide is added to the DNA chain. These two changes are called frameshift mutations. Each leads to a major change since it causes a large proportion of DNA to be misread (from where the mutation occurs, all the way along to the end of the gene). This involves many different codons and an equally large number of 'wrong' amino acids.

The protein formed following deletion or insertion is so different from the normal protein that it is non-functional. Since most proteins are essential to an organism, a mutant lacking a functional version of one of its proteins often fails to survive and the mutation is described as being lethal.

14 Genetic screening and counselling

1 a) (i) Autosomal recessive.

b) (i) The trait is expressed relatively rarely.

(ii) If the trait had been autosomal dominant then the two normal parents would not have been able to have children who are sufferers. If the trait had been sex-linked recessive then there would be far fewer or no female sufferers.

c) See figure A14.1.

d) (i) 0%.

(ii) 100%.

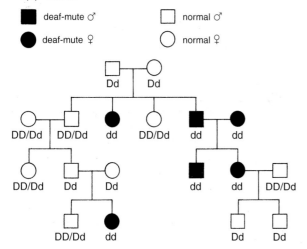

Figure A14.1

e) (i) No chance.

(ii) 1 in 2 chance.

f) (i) 1 in 2 chance.

(ii) 1 in 2 chance.

2 a) (i) Hh.

(ii) hh.

b) (i) Neither is old enough yet to show a phenotypic expression of the disorder which would indicate the presence of the H allele in their genotype.

(ii) 3 in 4, 1 in 2, 1 in 2, no chance.

3 a) 2, 6 and 10.

b) 1 in 2 chance.

c) (i) 1 in 4.

(ii) 1 in 2.

4 Pre-natal (before birth) screening involves examining genetic material obtained from the fetus. One technique, called amniocentesis, involves the withdrawal of amniotic fluid containing fetal cells. These are cultured to allow the full chromosome complement of the fetus to be examined for abnormalities. Amniocentesis is carried out at about week 18 of the pregnancy. It increases slightly the risk of a miscarriage.

A second technique, called chorionic villus sampling (CVS), involves taking a sample of placental cells and culturing them as before. CVS can be carried out at week 8 of the pregnancy when the prospect of a termination is less traumatic. However it carries a higher risk of a miscarriage than amniocentesis.

Both of these techniques allow the karyotype of the fetus to be examined and checked for Down's syndrome (indicated by the presence of an extra copy of chromosome 21). These forms of screening are normally restricted to individuals at high risk such as pregnant women over the age of 35.

In Britain, all babies undergo post-natal (after birth) screening for phenylketonuria (PKU). This is one of the few inherited disorders that can be successfully treated.

A sufferer of PKU is unable to convert the amino acid phenylalanine to tyrosine due to an inborn error of metabolism. This results in the production of poisonous chemicals which adversely affect the development of the child's brain.

Excess phenylalanine in the blood of very young babies is detected by screening. Potential sufferers of PKU are put on a special diet low in phenylalanine and develop normally.

15 Sex organs and hormonal control

1 a) K, E, A, C, D, J, L.

b) See table A15.1.

2 a) D, A, E, C, B.

b) (i) D, A and E.

(ii) Ovulation.

(iii) LH.

(iv) Anterior pituitary gland.

c) (i) Corpus luteum.

(ii) Progesterone and oestrogen.

(iii) Ovarian. They are produced by ovarian tissue.

(iv) Inhibitory.

letter in figure 15.9 indicating accessory gland	name of this accessory gland	example of substance secreted by accessory gland which contributes to fertilisation	way in which named substance contributes to fertilisation
B	seminal vesicle	prostaglandin	stimulates contractions of uterus which help sperm to reach oviduct and meet egg
I	prostate gland	enzymes	maintain lubricating fluid at optimum viscosity for sperm motility

Table A15.1

3 **a)** 21 April.
   b) 7 April.
   c) **(i)** High.
      (ii) Low.
      (iii) High.
      (iv) Low.

4 **a)** V = seminiferous tubule.
      W = blood capillary.
      X = interstitial cell.
      Y = sperm mother cell.
      Z = spermatozoa.
   b) X.
   c) ICSH (interstitial cell-stimulating hormone).
   d) By negative feedback control. As the concentration of testosterone builds up in the bloodstream, it reaches a level where it inhibits the secretion of FSH and ICSH by the anterior pituitary which leads in turn to a decrease in testosterone concentration. This is followed by resumption of activity of the pituitary and so on.
   e) Continuous fertility occurs in men since a fairly steady concentration of testosterone is maintained and this results in continuous sperm production.
      Cyclical fertility occurs in women because the delicate interplay of gonadotrophic and ovarian hormones results in the period of fertility being restricted to the 3 or 4 days following ovulation each month.

5 See pages 112–114.

16 Intervention in fertility

1 **a)** C, F, D, A, E, B.
   b) The woman is given hormonal treatment.
   c) A = The eggs are placed in a dish of nutrient medium to allow cell division to occur. B = The unused embryos are frozen in case a second attempt at implantation is required.

2 **a)** **(i)** 19–22 September approximately.
      (ii) At this time her body temperature rises by 0.5 °C showing that she is entering the luteal phase of the cycle that follows ovulation. In addition this time is approximately 2 weeks before the start of menstruation which alternates fortnightly with ovulation.
   b) Her mucus would be thin and watery at this time.
   c) Menstruation occurred 2 weeks later.
   d) **(i)** 17–20 approximately.
      (ii) The concentration of progesterone would remain at a high level so the graph would not drop from the 29th September onwards.
   e) **(i)** The increased concentration of progesterone exerts negative feedback control. Secretion of gonadotrophic hormones by the pituitary is inhibited. In the absence of FSH no new follicles mature and ovulation fails to occur.
      (ii) Placebo pills are taken during the fourth week to allow levels of progesterone and oestrogen to drop and menstruation to occur.

3 **a)** Sperm are unable to leave the man's body since both of his sperm ducts have been cut and tied.
   b) Compared with younger men, middle-aged men are more likely to already have a family and not wish to father any more children

4 These questions are intended to stimulate debate. There are no 'correct' answers.

5 See page 117 and convert the contents of table 16.1 into four paragraphs.

17 Pre-natal development

1 **a)** X = fluid interior
      Y = embryonic area
      Z = chorion
   b) Endometrium.
   c) **(i)** Differentiation is the process by which unspecialised cells become altered and adapted to perform specific functions as part of permanent tissues.
      (ii) Y.

2 **a)** 2.
   b) **(i)** Placenta and chorion.
      (ii) Neither.
   c) 4.
   d) Monozygotic. They have both developed from the same zygote.

3 **a)** Oestrogen and progesterone.
   b) Prolactin.
   c) **(i)** Prolactin-inhibiting hormone.
      (ii) After birth, oestrogen levels drop due to loss of the placenta. Therefore the hypothalamus stops secreting prolactin-inhibiting hormone. Prolactin is now secreted and brings about milk production.
   d) The increased level of oestrogen stimulates the hypothalamus to produce prolactin-inhibiting hormone.

4 **a)** **(i)** and
      (ii) First child = Dd (Rh+), second child = dd (Rh−), third child = Dd (Rh+), fourth child = dd (Rh−).
   b) **(i)** Third child.
      (ii) Following the birth of the first child, the mother

produces anti-D antibodies and is said to be sensitised. Therefore when she is carrying the third child her anti-D antibodies will combine with the baby's D antigens causing agglutination of many fetal red blood cells.

(iii) She could have been given anti-D immunoglobulins soon after the birth of the first Rh+ baby to destroy any D antigens before her immune system responded.

(iv) The baby could be given a massive transfusion of blood.

5 Rubella (German measles) is a fairly mild infection caused by a virus. However if it is contracted by the mother during the first three months of a pregnancy, it can cause the baby to be born with congenital defects affecting the eyes, ears and heart.

Thalidomide is a drug that was prescribed in the 1950s to pregnant women to quell early morning sickness. If taken at a critical time in very early pregnancy, it affected the development of the baby's limbs. The baby was born with its hands attached to its shoulders and its feet attached to its hips. In some cases the babies also suffered malformation of eyes, ears and heart and mental disability.

Alcohol is a depressant drug. If consumed in large quantities by a pregnant woman, it crosses the placenta and causes the blood vessels in the cord to temporarily collapse. The fetus receives an inadequate supply of oxygen and certain nutrients essential for normal development of growing tissues such as the brain. In extreme cases, fetal alcohol syndrome occurs. This includes harmful effects such as growth retardation, physical abnormalities and mental retardation.

Heroin is a habit-forming drug to which an addict becomes physically and psychologically dependent. In the body of an addicted pregnant woman, heroin crosses the placenta and affects the fetus. The baby's vital processes slow down and it also becomes addicted. If it survives, it is found to be weak and undersized at birth. It also shows withdrawal symptoms such as muscle tremors and excessive sweating.

18 Birth and post-natal development

1 a) (i) Oxytocin brings about involuntary rhythmic contractions of the uterus.

(ii) The drug would suppress the secretion of oxytocin until the fetus had reached full-term.

b) (i) Suckling by infant.

(ii) Nipple of breast.

(iii) Ejection of milk.

(iv) Muscles lining mammary ducts.

c) In this case a hormone transmits the message to the effector; in the limb withdrawal reflex a motor neurone plays this role.

d) In the bloodstream.

2 a) See table A18.1.

b) See figure A18.1.

c) (i) She was growing faster at age 13 than at age 9 years.

(ii) At age 13 she was undergoing her adolescent growth spurt.

(iii) Her first year.

d) (i) As age increases, percentage energy in food used to build tissues decreases.

(ii) Most growth (irreversible increase in body mass) occurs in the early years of a person's life. In later life the person is not growing irreversibly, however some energy is needed to replace lost or damaged tissues.

age (years)	percentage energy in food used to build tissues	total mass (kg)	annual increase in mass (kg)
0 (birth)	40	3.40	0.0
1	25	9.75	6.35
2	20	12.30	2.55
3	10	14.43	2.13
4	10	16.43	2.00
5	10	18.59	2.16
6	10	21.10	2.51
7	10	23.69	2.59
8	10	26.36	2.67
9	10	29.22	2.86
10	11	32.17	2.95
11	12	36.02	3.85
12	15	40.02	4.00
13	15	45.23	5.21
14	10	49.45	4.22
15	8	51.76	2.31
16	4	53.35	1.59
17	4	54.30	0.95
18	4	54.67	0.37

Table A18.1

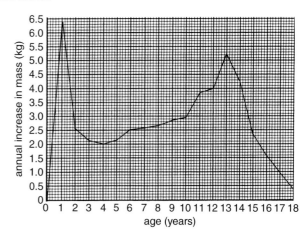

Figure A18.1

3 a) (i) 55.

(ii) 79.

(iii) 82. (All approximate.)

b) (i) 16.
(ii) 16.
(iii) 38. (All approximate.)
c) (i) B.
(ii) He was given somatotrophin. 14 years.

4 a) See table A18.2.

hormone	endocrine gland	target tissue
ICSH	anterior pituitary	interstitial cells in testes
testosterone	interstitial cells in testes	anterior pituitary

Table A18.2

b) Seminiferous tubules.

c) An increase in concentration of testosterone is detected by the anterior pituitary gland. It responds by releasing a lower concentration of ICSH. The interstitial cells in the testes respond by secreting less testosterone and so on.

d) Anabolic steroids are the chemical equivalents of testosterone. Their ingestion will result in a low concentration of ICSH being secreted by the anterior pituitary. This will lead to reduced sperm production.

e) The man's breast tissue will become enlarged.

f) Growth of facial hair and deepening of the voice. Steroids are chemically equivalent to testosterone, the hormone which promotes the development of male secondary sexual characteristics.

5 a) (i) 6.
(ii) 28.
(iii) 54.
b) (i) 10.
(ii) 52.
(iii) 96.
c) (i) Brain.
(ii) Reproductive organs.
(iii) It allows plenty of time during a lengthy childhood for humans to learn useful survival skills from their parents before becoming adults and parents themselves.
d) (i) Males.
(ii) The reproductive organs remain dormant until 12–13 years which is typical of males and later than females.
e) 0–2 years.
f) (i) 16.5.
(ii) 9.
(iii) 1.8.
g) The brain curve. The skull protects the brain and must therefore develop at the same rate.

19 Need for transport system

1 a) (i) 2400 cm², 8000 cm³.
(ii) 4800 cm², 8000 cm³.
b) (i) 0.3 : 1.
(ii) 0.6 : 1.

c) The original large cube because it has a smaller surface area in relation to its volume.

d) By means of a specialised transport system.

2 a) and b) See figure A19.1.

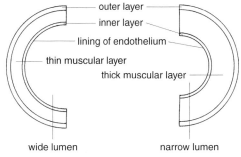

Figure A19.1

c) (i) Veins possess valves whereas arteries do not.
(ii) They prevent backflow of blood. See figure A19.2.

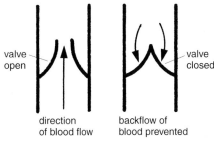

Figure A19.2

3 Capillary → venule → vein → artery → arteriole → capillary → venule → vein → artery → arteriole → capillary.

4 a) 1 = vein
2 = artery
3 = venule
4 = arteriole
5 = capillary

b) Higher at W, lower at X.

c) (i) Tissue fluid.
(ii) When blood arrives in a capillary bed it undergoes pressure filtration and plasma is squeezed out of the vessels. This liquid bathing the cells is called tissue fluid.
(iii) It supplies them with dissolved oxygen, useful ions and soluble food molecules.
(iv) Tissue fluid contains little or no protein.

d) Z = lymphatic vessel. It collects tissue fluid (now called lymph) and returns it to the blood circulatory system via the lymphatic system.

e) D.

5 (i) Hamburgers, chips and butter are rich in lipids and cholesterol. These build up inside blood vessels and tend to block them. Coronary arteries affected in this way can cause heart disease.

(ii) Catering for the tourist industry may have altered their lifestyle by making it more stressful and leaving them less time to relax and take regular exercise.

6 The oxygen molecule is picked up by a red blood cell in a capillary closely associated with an alveolus. This capillary carries oxygenated blood to a pulmonary venule and then to the pulmonary vein.

The blood (carrying the oxygen molecule) then enters the left atrium of the heart and passes down into the left ventricle. It is then pumped out via the aorta. One of the branches of the aorta, the renal artery, delivers oxygenated blood to the kidney. The renal artery divides into many smaller branches and ultimately capillaries. The oxygen molecule diffuses from a capillary into a respiring kidney cell.

A carbon dioxide molecule diffuses from a respiring brain cell into a nearby capillary. This capillary carries deoxygenated blood to a venule and then to the jugular vein and vena cava.

The blood (carrying the carbon dioxide molecule) then enters the right atrium of the heart and flows down into the right ventricle. It is then pumped out via the pulmonary artery which transports it to one of the lungs. There the pulmonary artery divides into many smaller branches and finally capillaries. The carbon dioxide molecule diffuses from a capillary into an alveolus.

20 Transport mechanisms

1. a) (i) Ventricular systole.
   - (ii) The atria only have to pump blood a short distance to the ventricles but the ventricles have to pump blood to the lungs and body.
   b) (i) X = atrial diastole.
   - Y = ventricular diastole.
   - (ii) Relaxed.
   c) (i) 3.
   - (ii) 75 beats per minute.
   d) See figure A20.1.

atria
ventricles

L   D

Figure A20.1

2. a) (i) Z.
   - (ii) X.
   - (iii) Y.
   b) (i) B.
   - (ii) A.
   - (iii) B's waves are further apart than normal but remain coordinated whereas A's waves are uncoordinated.

3. a) (i) and
   - (ii) See table A20.1.
   b) (i) Arterioles and capillaries.
   - (ii) 70 mm Hg.
   - (iii) The arterioles and capillaries are narrow in diameter and present a large surface area of wall in contact with blood. This offers peripheral resistance to blood flow causing the drop in pressure.

4. a) See figure A20.2.
   b) (i) Blood pressure rises with increase in age.
   - (ii) It is possible that increase in age is accompanied by increased level of stress in lifestyle (and possibly increased intake of unnecessary salt).
   c) When females reach adolescence their blood pressure remains lower than that of males but after menopause it catches up again.

part of circulatory system	range of blood pressure (mm Hg)	drop in pressure in this part of system (mm Hg)
left ventricle	100	0
aorta	100	0
large arteries	95–100	5
small arteries	85–95	10
arterioles	35–85	50
capillaries	15–35	20
venules	6–15	9
small veins	2–6	4
large veins	1–2	1
venae cavae	0–1	1

Table A20.1

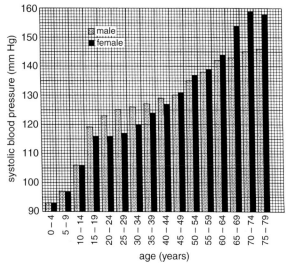

Figure A20.2

5. a) (i) and
   - (ii) See figure A20.3 on p 361.
   b) (i) Y.
   - (ii) Z.
   - (iii) X.
   c) (i) Unlike blood plasma, tissue fluid contains little or no protein.
   - (ii) Unlike tissue fluid, lymph is rich in lipid (absorbed by lacteals in small intestine).
   d) It produces lymphocytes capable of making antibodies against antigens. It contains macrophages capable of engulfing microbes by phagocytosis.

6. a) (i) right = 26 mm Hg, left = 120 mm Hg.
   - (ii) The wall of the left ventricle is thicker than that of the right ventricle. This enables the left ventricle to exert the higher pressure needed to pump blood all round the body.

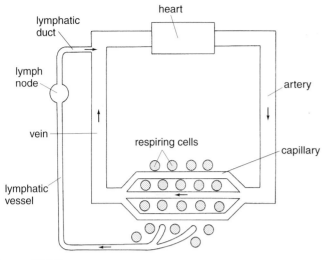

Figure A20.3

b) (i) 0 mm Hg.
   (ii) 80 mm Hg.
   (iii) 20 mm Hg.
   (iv) 10 mm Hg.
c) 0.1 s.
d) 0.15–0.4 s.
e) During diastole the pressure of blood in the pulmonary artery returns to 16 mm Hg where it started.
f) See figure A20.4.

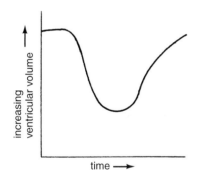

Figure A20.4

7 (i) See page 150.
  (ii) See page 151.

8 The lymphatic system consists of a network of vessels. These begin as tiny blind-ending lymph capillaries (embedded in all of the body's tissues) which unite to form larger and larger lymphatic vessels. These join up with the blood transport system at two lymphatic ducts in the upper chest region of the body. The main duct opens into the vein from the left arm; the right duct into the vein from the right arm.

Lymph nodes are oval-shaped structures found throughout the lymphatic system especially at the junctions of several lymph vessels.

The lymphatic system performs several functions. Porous lymphatic capillaries absorb excess tissue fluid from capillary beds and return it via the larger lymphatic vessels and ducts to the bloodstream. Flow of lymph is brought about mainly be the vessels being squeezed during body movements. Valves prevent backflow.

Tiny lymphatic vessels called lacteals in the villi of the small intestine absorb lipids from digested food and enable their indirect entry into the bloodstream via the lymphatic system.

Lymph nodes help to defend the body against infection. Each lymph node consists of several smaller lymph nodules surrounded by a continuous network of spaces lined with macrophage cells. As lymph passes through these spaces, macrophages remove microbes and destroy them by phagocytosis.

The centre of each lymph nodule is a site of lymphocyte production. These white blood cells defend the body by making antibodies in response to antigens.

21 Delivery of oxygen to cells

1 a) For both types of haemoglobin, increase in partial pressure results in an increase in percentage saturation of haemoglobin with oxygen.
  b) (i) 4.25.
     (ii) 3.2.
  c) (i) 75.
     (ii) 90.
  d) (i) Fetal haemoglobin has a higher affinity for oxygen than adult haemoglobin.
     (ii) Only by having a higher affinity is fetal haemoglobin able to draw oxygen across the placenta from the mother's haemoglobin.
  e) 4–6.

2 a) See figure A21.1.
  b) (i) Since they lack a stomach, they are unable to produce intrinsic factor which is needed to absorb vitamin B_{12}.
     (ii) They are given intrinsic factor.

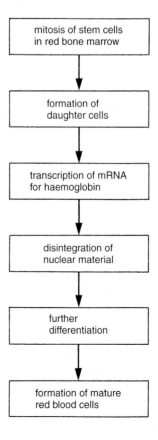

Figure A21.1

3 a) (i) Kidney.

(ii) Red bone marrow.

b) When the red blood cell count rises, less hormone is secreted and fewer red blood cells are made; when the cell count drops, more hormone is made and more cells are made. The system is therefore self-regulating and the red cell count remains fairly constant.

c) E.

d) B.

e) A and B.

4 a) (i) 110 = 98% whereas 60 = 95%.

(ii) The haemoglobin still has a strong affinity for oxygen even at oxygen concentrations as low as 60 units (e.g. a poorly ventilated room).

b) (i) Aerobic respiration.

(ii) It releases lots of oxygen which is needed to satisfy the demands of the respiring cells.

c) Build-up of carbon dioxide and lactic acid from anaerobic respiration would lower the pH.

d) (i) pH 7.4 = 60%, pH 7.2 = 40%.

(ii) pH 7.4 = 37%. pH 7.2 = 57%.

(iii) Decrease.

(iv) When anaerobic respiration occurs, acidic conditions follow and this leads to the haemoglobin releasing its oxygen in actively respiring tissues, exactly where it is needed.

(v) Temperature.

5 See pages 162–163.

22 Delivery of nutrients to cells

1 a) A = yellow, pH 5. B = orange, pH 4. C = green, pH 7. D = green, pH 7.

b) (i) A and B.

(ii) B and D (or A and C).

c) C. It differs from tube B (the experiment) in two ways and is therefore not comparable to it.

d) Use a lipid lacking protein such as olive oil in place of the creamy milk and see if acidic conditions were still produced.

2 a) Most of the digested lipid absorbed by the lymphatic system following the previous meal has had time to enter the bloodstream.

b) Digested lipid has been absorbed by the lacteals and entered the lymphatic system. Very little has had time to enter the bloodstream at this stage.

c) Lipids have been used up for energy release or stored in adipose tissues.

3 a) A = hepatic vein, B = hepatic portal vein.

b) (i) Glucose concentration decreases as blood passes through the liver because excess glucose is converted to glycogen.

(ii) Urea concentration increases as blood passes through the liver because the blood picks up urea formed in the liver during the breakdown of excess amino acids.

c) (i) Hepatic artery.

(ii) Glucose = 4.5 mmol/l, urea = 3 mmol/l.

4 a) X = C, Y = A, Z = B.

b) 4–7 mmol/l.

5 See page 171.

23 Removal of materials from blood

1 a) (i) B.

(ii) A.

(iii) The CO_2 concentration at B is greater than at A. The CO_2 concentration at A is equal to that of alveolar air.

b) X = pulmonary vein, Y = pulmonary artery.

c) (i) The elimination of the waste products of metabolism.

(ii) They remove CO_2 which is a waste product of metabolism.

2 a) A yellow pigment resulting from the breakdown of haemoglobin.

b) (i) It becomes conjugated by becoming attached to a second substance. This enables it to be added to bile as bile pigment.

(ii) Like other fetal waste products, bilirubin crosses the placenta and is excreted by the mother.

c) They do not have enough of the enzyme needed to deal with the bilirubin that is produced from the breakdown of haemoglobin. The bilirubin accumulates causing jaundice for a few days until sufficient quantities of the necessary enzyme are produced.

3 See figure A23.1.

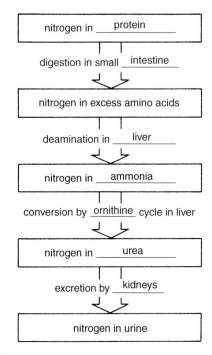

nitrogen in ____protein____

digestion in small ____intestine____

nitrogen in excess amino acids

deamination in ____liver____

nitrogen in ____ammonia____

conversion by ____ornithine____ cycle in liver

nitrogen in ____urea____

excretion by ____kidneys____

nitrogen in urine

Figure A23.1

4 a) The blood is in a branch of the renal artery which carries blood at high pressure from the heart. The vessel entering a glomerulus is wider than the vessel leaving so a 'bottle-neck' effect is produced.

b) 1 = basement membrane (of Bowman's capsule) for ultrafiltration of blood,

2 = proximal convoluted tubule for reabsorption of glucose,

3 = loop of Henle for reabsorption of water,

4 = distal convoluted tubule for reabsorption of water,

5 = collecting duct for reabsorption of water.

c) **(i)** 1.

(ii) P = capillary wall of glomerulus,

Q = basement membrane,

R = cell lining of Bowman's capsule,

S = pore.

(iii) It is prevented by the basement membrane which only allows small molecules to pass through.

d) Water concentration increases because water is not being reabsorbed but salt is being actively pumped out of the tubule.

e) **(i)** Low water concentration of blood.

(ii) They become more permeable.

(iii) More water is reabsorbed into the bloodstream thereby returning the blood's water concentration to normal.

5 a) Glucose and amino acids.

b) **(i)** Urea and salts.

(ii) Urea = 70 times, salts = 2 times.

c) 125 ml

d) **(i)** 1.

(ii) It is reabsorbed.

6 *Ultrafiltration*

Blood from a branch of the renal artery enters the glomerulus (knot of blood capillaries) present in each of the kidneys' many nephrons through a vessel that is wider than the one leaving the glomerulus. Blood in a glomerulus is therefore under pressure. This promotes the ultrafiltration of blood which takes place at the interface between the walls of the glomerulus and the inner lining of a Bowman's capsule.

The glomerulus wall is porous. However it is attached to a non-living layer, the basement membrane, which lacks pores but allows the rapid passage through it of small molecules (e.g. water, glucose, urea and salts). Large molecules (e.g. blood proteins) remain in the bloodstream.

The ultrafiltration process is further promoted by the presence of large spaces amongst the cells that make up the lining of the Bowman's capsule.

Reabsorption

As glomerular filtrate passes through each kidney tubule it undergoes many changes. In the proximal convoluted tubule glucose is actively reabsorbed by the cells lining the tubules and returned to the blood capillaries. This process requires energy from ATP. In the same region of the tubule, positively charged sodium ions are actively reabsorbed and this causes an equivalent number of negatively charged chloride ions to pass into the bloodstream. Water is reabsorbed passively by osmosis.

In the descending limb of each loop of Henle, water continues to be reabsorbed by osmosis. In the ascending limb, sodium and chloride ions are actively pumped out into the surrounding tissue creating a region of low water concentration in the medulla region of each kidney.

In the distal convoluted tubule, sodium chloride continues to be actively transported into the bloodstream and water is reabsorbed by osmosis. As glomerular filtrate from several tubules flows through each collecting duct, further water passes by osmosis into the surrounding tissues which have a lower water concentration.

Reabsorption results in essential substances (e.g. glucose) being retained by the body and waste substances (e.g. urea) being excreted.

24 Regulating mechanisms

1 a) **(i)** See figure A24.1.

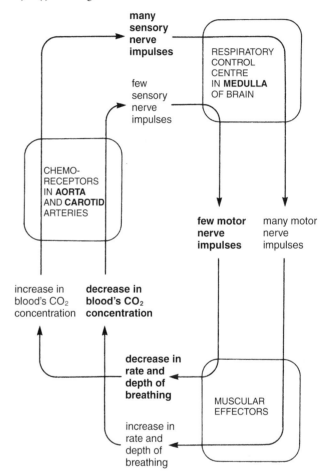

Figure A24.1

(ii) Vigorous exercise increases the blood's CO_2 concentration making it rise above its set point. This deviation is sensed by chemoreceptors which send many nerve impulses to the medulla. This in turn sends many nerve impulses to muscular effectors which increase the rate and depth of breathing. These processes reduce the CO_2 concentration and counteract the original deviation from the norm. This corrective mechanism is an example of negative feedback control.

(iii) It maintains the body's internal environment within certain tolerable limits.

b) **(i)** See figure A24.2.

(ii) % CO_2 in inspired air.

(iii) As % CO_2 increases, rate and depth of breathing increase.

(iv) Depth.

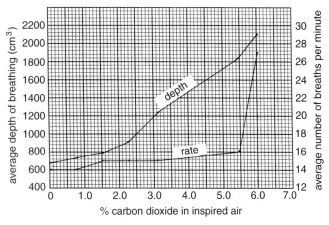

Figure A24.2

c) (i) It will decrease.

(ii) There is such a low concentration of CO_2 in the blood that for a brief period the brain sends no motor nerve impulses to the chest muscles, so breathing stops.

d) (i) It will increase.

(ii) Chemoreceptors sense the high concentration of CO_2 and send nerve impulses through the system. This soon triggers involuntary breathing movements.

2 a) (i) Hormonal messages or nerve impulses.

(ii) During exercise.

b) $CO = HR \times SV$.

c) (i) 5.76 l/min.

(ii) 100 beats/min.

(iii) 100 ml.

(iv) 120 ml.

d) Person (iv) is fitter. The larger stroke volume indicates that his/her heart muscle is more powerful.

3 a) (i) Increase.

(ii) Decrease.

(iii) The skeletal muscle is working hard and needs plenty of glucose and oxygen which are supplied by the blood stream.

b) (i) Skin.

(ii) Kidneys.

c) (i) Brain.

(ii) The energy demand by brain cells is continuous and steady regardless of the level of activity occurring elsewhere in the body.

d) (i) The skin would turn red.

(ii) Extra blood would be diverted to the skin where vessels would dilate (allowing much heat to be lost by radiation).

e) Vasoconstriction reduces blood flow to a body part because muscle in the wall of the arteriole supplying the body part contracts making the bore of the tube become narrow; vasodilation has the opposite effect.

4 a) (i) Between 07.00 and 08.00.

(ii) Homeostasis.

b) (i) 08.00.

(ii) They both increased.

(iii) Time is needed for glucose in the blood to reach the pancreas and the cells in the islets of Langerhans to respond and release more insulin.

c) Fatty acids are the breakdown products of fat and their concentration decreases as the concentration of insulin increases.

d) See figure A24.3.

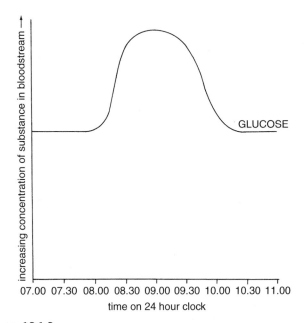

Figure A24.3

e) After ingestion of glucose the maximum value of blood glucose concentration reached would be much higher. The blood glucose level would have only shown a slight decrease by 11.00 hours.

f) The babies of diabetic mothers receive more glucose (which promotes growth). Their mother's blood is rich in glucose because she produces insufficient insulin to store her excess glucose as glycogen.

5 a) and b) See table A24.1.

hormone	endocrine gland from which hormone originates	letter(s) indicating effect(s) of hormone
adrenaline	adrenal	C, E, F
insulin	pancreas (Islet of Langerhans)	A, D
ADH	pituitary	B
glucagon	pancreas (Islet of Langerhans)	C
thyroxin	thyroid	F

Table A24.1

6 a) Hypothalamus.

b) Nerve impulses.

c) (i) It would become vasoconstricted.

(ii) Less blood would flow near the surface of the skin and little heat would be lost by radiation.

d) (i) It would produce an increased volume of sweat.

(ii) Heat energy from the body would be used to convert water in the sweat to water vapour thereby reducing body temperature.

7 a) (i) 27°C.

(ii) Shivering.

b) It increased. This was necessary to prevent him from cooling down and suffering the adverse (or fatal) effects of hypothermia.

c) Rate of sweating increased. This was necessary to prevent him from overheating and suffering the adverse (or fatal) effects of hyperthermia.

d) (i) 45°C.

(ii) It increased. Homeostatic control had broken down.

e) At these extremes, death would occur.

8 When some factor affecting the body's internal environment deviates from its normal optimum level, this change is detected by receptors. These send out nerve or hormonal messages that are received by effectors. The effectors bring about responses that negate the original deviation and return the system to its normal optimum level. This corrective mechanism is called negative feedback control.

When blood sugar level rises above its normal optimum level, receptor cells in regions of the pancreas called Islets of Langerhans detect this change and produce extra insulin. This hormone is transported in the bloodstream to the liver where it activates an enzyme that promotes the conversion of glucose to glycogen. Excess glucose is therefore stored as insoluble glycogen and the blood's sugar level returns to normal.

If blood sugar level drops below normal optimum level, receptor cells in the pancreas produce extra glucagon. On arriving in the liver, this hormone activates an enzyme that promotes the conversion of glycogen to glucose. By this means normal blood sugar level is restored.

Homeostasis is the maintenance of the body's internal environment within certain tolerable limits so that it can function efficiently. All living cells need a continuous supply of glucose from blood but the body only obtains glucose when food is eaten. Negative feedback control is the means by which homeostasis of blood sugar level is effected.

Insulin and glucagon are continuously acting antagonistically causing the blood's sugar level to fluctuate around an optimum value. Sufferers of diabetes mellitus are exceptions to this rule. They are unable to make adequate supplies of insulin and are therefore unable to exert negative feedback control. They need to be given regular supplies of insulin and to adhere to a controlled diet.

25 Brain

1 a) Elephant = 1 : 250.
Human = 1 : 50.
Gorilla = 1 : 400.

b) (i) Human.

(ii) Gorilla.

2 (1) Auditory sensory area – receives nerve impulses from cochlea and interprets these as sounds.

(2) Auditory association area – receives impulses from (1) and by relating these sounds to previous experiences, allows recognition of doorbell.

(3) Premotor association area – receives impulses from (2) and plans the motor activities needed to go to the door.

(4) Motor area – receives impulses from (3) and sends appropriate messages to skeletal muscles enabling body to move to door.

3 a) Lips and hand.

b) Foot.

c) The pinna would be much larger in relation to the rest of the body in the rabbit because its ear flaps are much more mobile than those of a human.

4 a) 3 and 4.

b) (i) Reading a book.

(ii) Reading a book out loud.

c) 3–4–1–2.

d) (i) No effect.

(ii) The person would be unable to speak.

5 (i) B. The right side of the object becomes an image on the left side of the brain which is where the speech motor area is also located.

(ii) C. The left side of the object becomes an image on the right side of the brain which also controls the left hand.

6 See page 206 and summarise the contents of table 25.1.

26 Organisation of the nervous system

1 See figure A26.1.

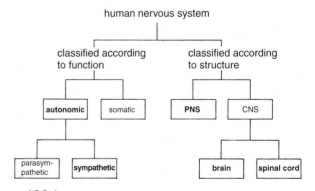

Figure A26.1

2 a) Sensory nerve impulses are received by the brain and interpreted as indicating an impending crisis. Many impulses are transmitted via sympathetic nerves to certain parts of the body. This results in preparations being made for 'fight or flight' such as increased heart rate and dilation of air passages. Extra energy becomes available to cope with the crisis.

After the crisis, many impulses are transmitted via the parasympathetic nerves. This results in decreased heart rate, constriction of air passages and increased rate of peristalsis as the body calms down.

b) It is possible that they would sink into a coma.

3 a) (i) The muscle will contract.

(ii) It will decrease.

(iii) Less blood will flow to the gut allowing more to be diverted to skeletal muscles where it is needed.

b) (i) They will make the muscle contract and close the sphincter valves.

(ii) Parasympathetic nerve impulses to the same muscle.

(iii) It would be of advantage when the body is at rest and digesting a meal because it would enable the sphincters to open and allow food to pass through.

4 The autonomic nervous system regulates the body's internal structures without the person's conscious control being involved. It falls into two parts: the sympathetic system and the parasympathetic system. Both of these affect many of the same structures but exert opposite effects on them. The two systems that make up the autonomic nervous system are therefore described as being antagonistic.

Under normal circumstances, the sympathetic and parasympathetic systems work in an equal but opposite manner and the activity of an organ under their control is mid-way between the extremes of hyper- and hypo-activity. The sympathetic system acts like the accelerator in a vehicle and the parasympathetic acts like the brake. A combination of the two allows a fine degree of control over the organ.

Stimulation of the sympathetic nerve to the heart (e.g. in preparation for 'fight or flight') brings about an increase in rate and force of contraction of cardiac muscle resulting in an increase in cardiac output of blood. Stimulation of the parasympathetic nerve to the heart (e.g. during the recovery period following 'fight or flight') brings about the reverse effect resulting in decreased cardiac output of blood. Simultaneous stimulation of the two systems results in a cardiac output mid-way between the two extremes.

During a crisis, stimulation of sympathetic nerves supplying the circular muscle in the arterioles that lead to skeletal muscles make it become relaxed. This widens the bore of the vessels and allows extra blood to be diverted to the muscles where it is needed to provide extra oxygen for aerobic respiration. At the same time stimulation of the sympathetic nerves supplying the circular muscle in the arterioles leading to the gut make it contract. This makes the bore of the vessels narrower and reduces the flow of blood to the gut where only the bare minimum is required during the crisis. During recovery these effects are reversed by the parasympathetic nerves having the opposite effect on the circular muscle.

Sweat glands are an exception to the rule. They are only supplied with sympathetic nerves. If they receive many nerve impulses, they show a high level of activity. As the number of sympathetic nerve impulses drops, so does rate of sweating.

27 Neurones and neural pathways

1 See figure A27.1.

2 a) X = sensory neurone, Y = association neurone, Z = motor neurone.

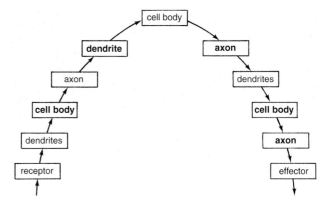

Figure A27.1

b) When the reflex action of limb withdrawal occurs, this involves the <u>somatic</u> nervous system and the type of response is described as <u>involuntary</u>.

c) Grey matter is composed of nerve cell bodies; white matter is made of nerve fibres.

d) The brain.

3 a) 1 = membrane of dendrite, 2 = synaptic cleft, 3 = synaptic knob, 4 = axon.

b) (i) Vesicle (containing neurotransmitter).

(ii) Acetylcholine.

(iii) The receptor molecules at sites on the membrane of the postsynaptic dendrite.

(iv) Right to left.

(v) Acetylcholine is broken down into non-active products by the enzyme acetylcholinesterase. (These products are reabsorbed by the presynaptic membrane for future use.)

(vi) Mitochondrion. It supplies the energy needed to resynthesise neurotransmitter.

4 a) If the neurotransmitter were not removed quickly between impulses, only a limited number of impulses would be able to pass in a given time.

b) Since curare blocks acetylcholine receptor sites, nerve impulses will not be transmitted across the neuroeffector junctions. The person's muscles will fail to respond and the overall effect will be paralysis.

c) Lack of active cholinesterase results in acetylcholine persisting in clefts at neuroeffector junctions. This allows repeated transmission of nerve impulses and responses by muscles (i.e. twitching) without the arrival of new nerve impulses.

5 a) X = cone, Y = rod.

b) 1 and 3.

c) Compared with cones, rods are much more sensitive to light and are able to transmit weak nerve impulses in dim light. (Several of these impulses from convergently arranged rods are needed for the postsynaptic membrane to reach threshold.)

6 a) (i) Car alarm.

(ii) Flashing light.

b) (i) A, B and E.

(ii) These students were able to suppress the sensory impulses from the distractions and perform as well as they had done in the absence of distractions.

c) The nervous system is made of many interconnecting nerve cells. Two conflicting types of message (one 'saying' pay attention to the distraction; the other 'saying' ignore the distraction) meet in a convergent pathway. If the overall effect at the synapse is excitatory, a nerve impulse is fired and the person pays attention. If the overall effect is inhibitory, no impulse is fired and the person ignores the distraction.

d) (i) So that only one variable factor is being investigated at a time.

(ii) The person might remember the solutions to some of the problems from the previous time thereby artificially inflating their score.

(iii) The level of difficulty of the questions might not be consistent from one set to the next.

(iv) Many more than six students could be included in the investigation. Each student could repeat the experiment several times.

7 A synapse is a tiny region of contact between an axon ending of one nerve cell (the presynaptic neurone) and the dendrite of the next nerve cell (the postsynaptic neurone) in a nerve cell pathway. It is at a synapse that information is passed from neurone to neurone by means of a chemical called a neurotransmitter (e.g. noradrenaline).

The membranes of the two neurones at a synapse are separated by a very narrow space called a synaptic cleft. The synaptic knob (axon ending) on the presynaptic side of the cleft is rich in vesicles containing neurotransmitter. When a nerve impulse reaches the synaptic knob, several vesicles are stimulated and discharge their contents into the cleft. The molecules of neurotransmitter cross the cleft and combine with receptor molecules on the membrane of the postsynaptic neurone and alter its electrical state. This allows the nerve impulse to be transmitted on through the system.

To ensure precise control of the system, the postsynaptic membrane must remain excited for only a brief moment. The neurotransmitter is therefore rapidly removed after transmission of the impulse. Noradrenaline, for example, is rapidly reabsorbed by the presynaptic membrane ready for reuse. So effective is the removal of neurotransmitter that many separate impulses can be sent across a neural cleft per second.

In a diverging neural pathway, the route along which an impulse is travelling divides. This allows information from the original source to be transmitted to two or more destinations. Divergence of pathways from a common starting point in the motor area of the cerebrum, for example, allows impulses carrying the same information to be sent to the fingers enabling them to work in unison.

In a converging neural pathway, impulses from several sources are channelled towards and meet at a common destination. Rods are receptors in the retina that are sensitive to very dim light. The nerve impulse transmitted by one rod is too weak to be effective. However converging impulses from several rods enables a nerve impulse to be transmitted to the brain allowing vision in conditions of almost total darkness.

28 Localisation of memory

1 a) He was unable to recall recent TV highlights because hippocampi are required to form and transfer new declarative memories to their storage site (e.g. temporal lobes). He could

recall old memories because hippocampi are not involved in the retrieval of declarative memories from their storage site.

b) He could remember how to play table tennis because hippocampi are not required to form and transfer new procedural memories to their storage site (e.g. cerebellum). However he could not remember the rules because hippocampi are needed to form and transfer new declarative memories to their storage site.

c) No. The formation and transfer of new procedural memories were unaffected by lack of hippocampi.

2 a) The death of many brain cells and the irreversible loss of parts of the memory.

b) Remembering how to pronounce words requires procedural memories; remembering their meaning requires declarative memories. The information supports the idea that humans possess these two different types of memory but that sufferers of Alzheimer's disease are unable to retrieve certain declarative memories due to death of brain cells.

3 a) The transport of iron ions from gut to bone marrow.

b) It mistakes aluminium for iron.

c) (i) It blocks transfer of calcium ions across the postsynaptic membrane.

(ii) Nerve impulses will not be transmitted across the synapses. Postsynaptic membranes will not undergo long term modification and memories will not be stored.

d) There may be a connection between the damage done by aluminium ions and the death of brain cells characteristic of Alzheimer's disease. If silicon were used to combine with aluminium preventing it from being absorbed, this might protect people against Alzheimer's disease.

4 See pages 230–231. Use should be made of information in figure 28.5.

29 Memory – encoding, storage and retrieval

1 a) As the number of letters in a series increases, the percentage of students able to remember the series decreases.

b) (i) 9 letters.

(ii) 2.

c) (i) 4 letters.

(ii) 5.

d) (i) No.

(ii) The graph of the results is symmetrical.

e) (i) To avoid using sequences of letters that would act as chunks and be easily remembered.

(ii) To avoid the introduction of a second variable factor.

(iii) To increase the reliability of the results.

2 Four digits can be arranged into a big enough number of combinations to make each PIN number different from the others yet at the same time short enough to be easily remembered.

3 Person b) will be faster because s/he will be familiar with the first 4 codes that will act as chunks. S/he will only need to memorise the last 4 digits. Person a) is confronted with 14 unfamiliar digits.

4 a) To prevent them from rehearsing the numbers that they will later be asked to recall.

b) (i) 35.

(ii) Attempt 4.

c) They would be allowed to rehearse the letters in between attempts to recall them.

d) (i) The effect of lack of rehearsal on memory.

(ii) It leads to a decline in effectiveness of the encoding of memories.

(iii) Lack of rehearsal allows items in the STM to be displaced and forgotten before they can be encoded and stored in the LTM.

5 a) attention

b) groups

c) repeating

d) meaning

e) visual, bizarre

f) overlearn

g) short, long

h) rest, recreation

6 To become part of the memory, selected sensory images must first be encoded. This requires their conversion into a form that the brain can process and store. Visual encoding involves forming a visual image of the item to be remembered (e.g. making a mental picture of it). Acoustic encoding involves forming an auditory image (e.g. thinking about how the item sounds). Semantic encoding involves forming an image of what the item means (e.g. thinking about how it works).

Once an item has been encoded, it must be transferred from the short term memory (STM) to the long term memory (LTM) if it is to be remembered. This transfer can be aided by several techniques as follows.

Rehearsal involves repeating over and over again the item that is to be encoded and remembered. This process extends the item's time in the STM and promotes its transfer to the LTM.

Organisation involves the grouping of items into sets according to features that they have in common. As members of easily remembered sets, the items are more successfully encoded and transferred from STM to LTM.

Elaboration of meaning involves thinking about the item to be memorised and considering in full its various features and properties. This tends to make the item more meaningful and more likely to be retained by the LTM.

To be remembered an item that is stored in the LTM must also be capable of being retrieved. This process is aided by contextual cues. Each of these is a reminder that triggers off an impulse through a 'memory circuit'. For example 'plants', 'flowers', 'clocks' etc. might all serve as cues to retrieve information about dandelions. The more categories an item is filed under in the LTM, the more contextual cues it will possess and the easier it will be to retrieve.

If an item was accompanied by unusual circumstances at the time of its original transfer to the LTM (e.g. a person's 21st birthday party), it will be easily remembered and recalled.

Retrieval can also be aided by mnemonic devices. Such a device often takes the form of a light-hearted expression where the first letter of each word helps the person to recall some more important piece of information. For example the mnemonic 'Rip Off Your Great Big Itchy Vest' acts as an aid when trying to remember the sequence of colours that make up the spectrum of white light – red, orange, yellow, green, blue, indigo, violet.

30 Factors influencing development of behaviour

1 a) E, G, D, B, F, A, C.

b) (i) Maturation.

(ii) Development of speech and cognitive abilities.

c) (i) 5 years.

(ii) 6 years.

(iii) 7 years.

2 a) Fiona.

b) (i) Susan.

(ii) Susan was older at the time of her intensive training than Fiona and would therefore be at a more advanced stage of development making her more capable of memorising the digits.

c) (i) They were lost.

(ii) In the absence of intensive training, each girl's pattern of development returned to the natural maturational level found amongst 4 year-olds.

d) Disagree. Although the gains resulting from training were lost when the training stopped, the girls returned to normal without their abilities being impaired.

3 a) Schizophrenia is a condition characterised by personality disorders often involving delusions or hallucinations.

b) (i) 74.

(ii) 12.

c) Inherited factors play a major part since there is a higher incidence of schizophrenia amongst twins sharing the same genetic material than amongst those sharing only some.

d) They not only have the same genetic material but have been exposed to the same environmental factors.

e) (i) Survey 4.

(ii) Survey 1.

(iii) Survey 4 is most reliable because it considered the largest number of twin pairs; survey 1 is least reliable because it considered the smallest number of twin pairs.

4 Love takes many forms (e.g. maternal, sexual, platonic etc.) and means different things to different people. However most people have difficulty stating precisely what love is. Similarly intelligence takes many forms (e.g. linguistic, mathematical, spatial etc.) but it defies neat definition.

Nevertheless, if given the choice, most people would opt to be intelligent and have love in their life.

5 a) (i) Scientists induced PKU by giving the rats an enzyme inhibitor.

(ii) The enzyme inhibitor would prevent the enzyme (phenylalanine hydroxylase) from breaking down excess phenylalanine. Phenylalanine would therefore accumulate as in a PKU sufferer.

b) (i) A.

(ii) In the presence of the inhibitor, the enzyme in their cells was unable to convert excess phenylalanine to tyrosine.

Instead it was converted to toxins which affected brain development.

(iii) No. The overall brain mass remained fairly constant throughout although it fluctuated slightly from sample to sample.

c) It had no effect since brain mass results for group B do not differ significantly from those for group C.

d) (i) C.

(ii) Groups A and B were unable, when necessary, to convert phenylalanine to tyrosine, an amino acid needed for growth (and gain in body weight). (Presumably the minimal supply of normal food given to the rats did not contain enough tyrosine for optimum growth.)

e) Many rats were used to increase the reliability of the results. The ten were chosen at random so that the results were not biased.

6 The factors that influence the development of behaviour are maturation, inheritance and environment.

Maturation involves the progression by an individual through a sequence of inherited developmental stages. For example, a growing infant progresses through a series of genetically 'pre-programmed' events such as rolling over, crawling, walking holding onto furniture and so on until eventually s/he is able to walk alone. Maturation also occurs in the development of speech and cognitive abilities. The rate at which such maturation occurs may be limited or enhanced by genetic and environmental factors.

The development of behaviour is in part affected by the particular set of genes inherited by the individual. Certain alleles are needed to provide the genetic material to control maturation. In addition normal development of the nervous system and behaviour depend on having the appropriate alleles of the genes that code for the proteins involved in the production of nerve cells, neurotransmitters and neuroreceptors.

Phenylketonuria (PKU) and Huntington's chorea are examples of inherited disorders that affect the nervous system and behaviour. A sufferer of one of these conditions has received one or more alleles unable to code for the necessary protein(s).

Studies of monozygotic twins are used to assess the influence of the environment on development of behaviour since such twins are assumed to have been affected by the same genetic and maturational factors. The results from intelligence tests on identical twins reared together and others reared apart suggest that environmental factors do play a part in the development of intelligence. Such studies also suggest that inheritance plays a large part in its development.

The development of any form of human behaviour is a complex process involving all three factors given at the start. No behaviour is influenced by only one of these factors. All behaviours result from a combination of all three though some forms of behaviour may be more strongly influenced by one than the other two.

31 Importance of infant attachment

1 a) (i) Type 1 = indiscriminate, type 2 = specific.

(ii) As the first decreases in intensity, the second increases.

b) (i) 29–32 weeks.

(ii) Type 2.

(iii) 0.

(iv) It makes the mother want to protect and care for the child.

2 The ones where the babies received little more than food and basic hygiene. Babies also need contact comfort to develop normally.

3 a) (i) Cloth = 18 hours, wire = 1 hour.

(ii) Infant monkeys spend more time in contact with the cloth 'mother'.

(iii) No. The overall trend shown by the graph for groups A and B is the same.

b) (i) C.

(ii) They did not spend as much time with the cloth 'mother' compared with A and B.

c) (i) Wire.

(ii) It increased.

(iii) The fear score of an infant reared with the wire 'mother' is much greater. Contact comfort reduces fear in infant monkeys.

d) The interest level shown by infant monkeys for a cloth 'mother' is almost as high as that for a live adult monkey. The interest level shown for a wire 'mother' is almost as low as that for an empty room.

32 Effect of communication

1 a) Compared with babies exposed to irregular sounds, babies exposed to the sound of a normal heartbeat spent less time crying and gained more weight.

b) It is possible that heartbeat offers a familiar rhythm that comforts the baby making it cry less and use more of the energy in its food to grow.

2 a) This is more likely to make the potential customer warm to the sales assistant and believe what is being said.

b) (i) Smiling.

(ii) Speaking clearly and using a friendly tone of voice.

3 a) (i) 14.

(ii) 2.

b) (i) It is because they feel embarrassed on finding themselves much closer to the interviewer than is generally accepted for strangers unless an act of aggression is intended.

(ii) It is because they feel even more embarrassed on finding themselves much closer to the interviewer than is generally accepted for strangers of opposite sexes unless a sexual overture is intended.

4 a) Some people are very dependent on their facial expressions and body language to communicate with others. When talking face to face, they are able to use their eyes for meaningful eye contact, their mouths to smile indicating friendliness and their body parts to make use of gestures e.g. nodding in sympathy.

b) Adopting a friendly tone of voice, varying the tone of voice and speaking clearly.

5 a) (i) Minute 14.

(ii) Minute 10–11.

      (iii) It increased.

      (iv) It decreased.

  b) **(i)** When listening, the person spends about 60% of the time gazing at the other person.

      (ii) When speaking, the person spends about 40% of the time gazing at the other person.

6 Non-verbal communication enables parent-infant bonding to occur. A newborn baby communicates with the parent by crying, clinging and suckling. These trigger in the parent a strong desire to protect and provide for the baby. After a few weeks the baby smiles in response to a feeling of wellbeing and at about 6 months uses smiling as a selective social signal to communicate with close members of the family. This behaviour is of survival value since it makes the baby appealing and strengthens the bonding process.

Amongst adults, non-verbal communication takes many forms often involving facial expressions. These are largely dependent on the use of the mouth and eyes to convey attitudes and emotions. Smiling, for example, may be used to indicate pleasure, teeth bared might suggest anger, eyes popping could mean outrage and winking might indicate friendliness.

The eyes are also used to convey signals by one person looking at another person in a meaningful way. Such extended eye contact might be intended to indicate that the person employing it would like to get to know the other person better.

People also communicate non-verbally using body language. For example, someone standing with their arms folded and their feet planted firmly on the ground might be squaring up for a confrontation; someone slumped forward in a chair with their head down may be expressing feelings of depression.

A language is a system that combines basic sounds into spoken words usually represented by written symbols. These are then arranged into words, sentences, paragraphs etc. allowing the transfer of information. Use of language enables members of a society to express their thoughts and feelings and to exchange the information needed for survival from day to day. Good communicators tend to adopt a friendly tone of voice, speak clearly and take time to listen to the other person's point of view.

Language also allows the transfer of information (e.g. knowledge and skills) from generation to generation. This accelerates learning and intellectual development since each generation is taught the existing body of knowledge without having to make each discovery for itself.

33 Effect of experience

1 **a)** **(i)** B.

      (ii) A.

  b) **(i)** Distributed practice is more effective than massed practice.

      (ii) It is thought that a motor memory is laid down by synaptic connections being formed between certain neurones following repetition of the skill. It is possible that more connections are formed during distributed practice spread over 20 days than during massed practice concentrated on the same day.

  c) To improve the reliability of the results.

  d) To prevent the introduction of a second variable factor.

  e) The investigation could be repeated with a fresh set of volunteers exposed, this time, to an auditory distraction at each trial. The results would be compared with those for the version without the auditory distraction.

2 **a)** Y. It is easier to learn a new skill by imitating an expert than by reading a set of instructions.

  b) To prevent the introduction of a second variable factor (e.g. different levels of intelligence).

3 **a)** Behaviour that receives a <u>reward</u> regularly, undergoes <u>reinforcement</u>. In theory, therefore, behaviour that goes unrewarded should suffer <u>extinction</u> and disappear.

  b) Giving him 50p sometimes would reinforce the bad behaviour intermittently (and make it even more resistant to extinction).

4 **a)** Such training involves shaping which is the process by which a desired pattern of behaviour is eventually obtained by reinforcing successive approximations of the desired response.

  b) This higher incidence was due to social imitation of parents who smoked by impressionable youngsters.

  c) This is an example of positive reinforcement. It occurred when something positive was received by the person after she had made the desired response, thereby increasing the chance of her repeating the response.

  d) Both of the children were demonstrating behaviour called generalisation which is the ability to respond in the same way to many different but related stimuli. The girl showed a narrower range of this behaviour than her brother.

5 **a)** Learning curve.

  b) The larger the reward, the faster the learning process.

  c) The rats have reached their best possible score and cannot improve.

  d) Since there are only 2 choices available, the rats would score, on average, 50% correct responses even before learning the T-maze.

  e) To eliminate the possibility that the rats have some instinctive behaviour pattern that just happened to make them choose one side of the maze more frequently than the other.

  f) **(i)** DE.

      (ii) The food rewards were stopped.

      (iii) The size of reward had no effect.

  g) Continuous. The behaviour pattern became extinct quickly. It would have been much more resistant to extinction had the reinforcement been intermittent.

6 See pages 263–264.

34 Effect of group behaviour and social influence

1 **a)** **(i)** Competing with others present resulted in a better performance.

      (ii) D.

  b) **(i)** Performance improves.

      (ii) Performance remains unchanged.

      (iii) During the repeat the task is easier because it is more familiar. In group **(i)** the competitors improve further because they are spurred on by the presence of one another. However this does not happen in group **(ii)** because they are in isolation.

2 **a)** True.

b) Provided that subjects are familiar with the task to be carried out, they are found to work faster and achieve an enhanced performance when placed in competitive situations. This is called social facilitation.

3 Deindividuation is the loss by individuals of their personal identities. This behaviour is demonstrated by the members of the Ku Klux Klan who allow themselves to fall under the influence of group pressure. As part of a faceless mob enjoying complete anonymity, they feel confident enough to carry out disreputable deeds and indulge in a level of risk-taking that they would not consider doing on their own.

4 **a)** Drugs are bad for you and eventually make your life miserable. Smoking can kill you.

b) Internalisation.

5 This type of advertising tries to use identification to sell its product. The manufacturers of the product hope that potential customers will identify so closely with the gold medallist and his/her achievements and lifestyle that they will buy the endorsed product to be like their hero/heroine.

6 Deindividuation is the loss by an individual of his/her personal identity when in a group. It can lead to diminished restraints on the person's behaviour. The person has given in to group pressure because s/he wants to be like the other group members and enjoy the gains that membership of the group brings.

Deindividuated people, when amongst the members of the group, act in a way that is different to the way that they would act when on their own. In the group they feel anonymous and indistinguishable from others. Under these circumstances they often act mindlessly and behave in an aggressive, anti-social way as part of a faceless mob. They are also willing to take irresponsible risks that they would not take when on their own. They feel that as members of the mob they are less likely to be caught and punished if they break the law.

Internalisation is the process by which people incorporate within themselves a changed set of beliefs, values or attitudes. They may obtain these from many possible sources such as their family, friends, school, the media etc. Party political broadcasts on TV and advertising campaigns are two examples of attempts to bring about internalisation by first creating a feeling of dissatisfaction and then presenting the person with a 'better' alternative.

Identification is the process by which people deliberately change their beliefs in an attempt to be like some other person whom they admire enormously. In some cases they imitate their 'hero' and even fantasise that they are that person. Advertisers exploit this process by employing much admired 'celebrities' to endorse their products.

35 Population change

1 **a)** **(i)** B.

   (ii) D.

b) **(i)** C.

   (ii) D.

   (iii) A.

   (iv) B.

situation	does this situation occur in the graph? (answer YES or NO)	if YES identify the stages(s)
br = dr	YES	D
br > dr	YES	A, B, C
br < dr	NO	–

Table A35.1

c) See table A35.1

d) D.

e) It would decrease (since dr > br)

2 **a)** Average annual rainfall and size of tribal area.

b) Average annual rainfall.

c) **(i)** To increase the reliability of the results.

   (ii) To eliminate the introduction of a second variable factor.

d) **(i)** As the average annual rainfall increases, the size of the tribal area decreases.

   (ii) The less rain that falls, the larger the area that has to be occupied to obtain supplies.

e) They are hunter-gatherers of food.

f) Few tribes still pursue their traditional way of life unaffected by modern civilisation and the population has decreased rapidly.

3 **a)** It means growing crops and rearing animals to meet your own needs and not to sell for a profit.

b) They lack access to electricity and sanitation. They use simple tools and basic methods. They only employ family labour.

4 **a)** 83.7.

b) **(i)** 44.

   (ii) 75.4.

c) Babies are especially vulnerable to disease when very young. (If they reach their first birthday then there is a good chance that they will survive.)

d) It was longer in 1960 compared with 1930.

e) Poor nutrition, disease.

f) **(i)** 54.

   (ii) 74.

g) **(i)** D.

   (ii) 420.

h) See figure A35.1.

5 See pages 279–280.

36 Demographic trends

1 **a)** 0.2 per 1000.

b) 10 per 1000.

c) 750 000.

2 **a)** Figure 36.3 charts the growth rate whereas figure 36.7 charts the total population.

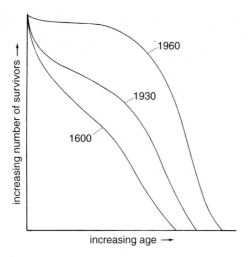

Figure A35.1

b) (i) 44 per 1000.

(ii) 42 per 1000.

(iii) 2 per 1000.

c) (i) 40 per 1000.

(ii) 16 per 1000.

(iii) 24 per 1000.

d) 12.

e) (i) 10 million.

(ii) 90 million.

(iii) 80 million.

(iv) 800%.

3 a) See figure A36.1.

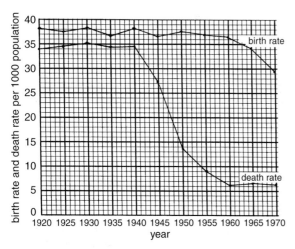

Figure A36.1

b) (i) 1 and 2.

(ii) Br = 7 per 1000 and dr = 5 per 1000 (both values approximate). This is assuming that by 2000 the model will be at stage 4. Br will be decreasing and be almost as low as dr.

c) In the absence of arranged marriages, many women may postpone marriage until later in their lives and therefore have fewer children. Improved education may provide women with career opportunities outside the home giving them an alternative option to that of continuous child-bearing.

d) Better sanitation and improved medical care.

e) In times of high infant mortality, couples need to have many children so that at least some of them will survive and work to help support the family. When the dr. drops, people feel more confident about their children surviving and are therefore willing to risk having fewer.

f) They must become equal.

4 Encouraging rigorous birth control. Reducing pollution of the planet by greenhouse gases.

5 The demographic transition model tries to relate rate of population growth with cultural development. It suggests that a developing country passes through four demographic stages on the way to becoming a developed (industrialised) country.

During the first demographic stage, birth rate and death rate are both high and about equal so the population does not grow. At the second stage, the death rate drops dramatically as living standards and hygiene improve, but birth rate stays fairly high. As a result the population starts to grow and expand rapidly.

At the third stage birth rate drops rapidly but death rate hardly drops so the difference between them narrows. The population continues to grow but at a much slower rate. At the fourth stage, birth rate and death rate are low and about equal. The population only grows slowly or not at all.

As a country becomes industrialised and wealthier, living standards improve as a result of better hygiene and major advances in medicine. These lead in turn to a reduction in child mortality. People no longer need to have large families so that at least a few of their offspring will survive. At demographic stage 4, as people feel more secure they have smaller families and the birth rate drops to its lowest level.

Lack of deadly diseases, improved health and better standards of living also bring about an increase in life expectancy. This results in people living to an older age. As a society becomes industrialised its death rate therefore continues to fall, reaching its lowest level at demographic stage 4.

37 Food as a limiting factor

1 a) During the second half of the twentieth century, the share of the world's land mass covered by:

(i) tropical forest decreased as a result of deforestation;

(ii) temperate forest remained constant as a result of reforestation.

b) (i) The people need wood for fuel and cleared woodland to grow crops.

(ii) Flooding of low-lying land.

2 a) See figure A37.1.

b) (i) As concentration of nitrate increases so does growth rate until 160 kg/ha of nitrate. From this concentration onwards the growth rate levels off (or even dips slightly).

(ii) No effect.

c) 40 kg/ha = no effect
80 kg/ha = increased growth rate overall
160 kg/ha = decreased growth rate overall.

d) 120 kg/ha of nitrate combined with 80 kg/ha of phosphate.

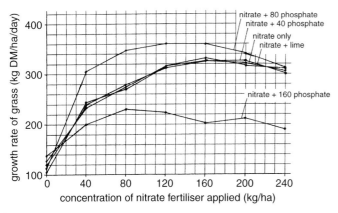

Figure A37.1

3 a) They could try crossing them and some of the offspring might inherit both of the desirable characteristics.

b) They could employ somatic fusion. Naked protoplasts from both plants would be prepared by digesting away the cell walls from unspecialised cells. An electric current would be used to induce the naked protoplasts to fuse giving hybrid protoplasts. These would be given hormones in their growth media to make them grow into plants some of which might have desirable characteristics from both species.

4 a) An average Indian eats more plant protein and less animal protein and consumes a smaller overall mass of protein per day.

b) (i) East Africa.

(ii) No.

5 a) (i) Shortage of protein in the diet.

(ii) Unlike the 'new' baby, the 'old' baby is no longer receiving the mother's milk which is rich in protein.

(iii) The child is not starving since it receives an adequate number of kilojoules but it is suffering malnutrition since its diet (low in protein) is not properly balanced.

b) Red meat. Its production involves expensive energy-losing links in the food chain as the animals are fed plant protein.

6 a) *Erysiphe graminis* and *Puccinia graminis*.

b) To improve the reliability of the results.

c) No significant effect by either A or B compared with the control.

d) Fungicide A had no effect at 5 ppm but worked to some extent at 50 ppm. Fungicide B had no effect at either concentration.

e) (i) A.

(ii) A.

(iii) 50 ppm of A.

f) (i) 99.

(ii) 38.

g) They are effective on fungi W and X (that cause mildews) but have almost no effect on the other two fungi.

h) A is more effective than B at killing spores of fungi W and X and it is less toxic to wildlife.

7 Humans make use of synthetic fertilisers. These are chemicals rich in nitrate (and other substances) essential for healthy plant growth. They replace the chemicals removed from the soil by the previous crop and create optimum conditions for growth of the next crop. This often gives enormous yields of food and may even enable the farmer to use the same piece of land for growth of the same crop continuously.

Use is also made of selective weedkillers which stimulate the growth of broad-leaved weeds to such an extent that they use up their reserves and die. In the absence of such competitors, the food crop thrives. Its healthy growth may be further enhanced by the use of pesticide sprays to kill fungi and/or insects which would attack the leaves and reduce photosynthetic yield.

Food production has also been greatly increased by humans selectively breeding plants over many years. They have chosen from each generation of food plant those with the best characteristics and have used them (and no others) as the parents of the next generation. Such selection over many generations has produced plants with useful characteristics such as higher food yields and greater resistance to disease than was possessed by earlier strains. Use of selectively bred varieties on a massive scale brought about the Green Revolution in the second half of the 20th century.

In recent times scientists have been employing genetic engineering to attempt to transfer genetic material for useful characteristics from one species to another. For example a gene in pea plants which produces a natural insecticide has been transferred by recombinant DNA technology to potato plants. Similarly scientists hope to produce crops containing recombinant DNA for increasing photosynthetic yield and ability to fix nitrogen. This last characteristic would reduce the need to spray agricultural land with large quantities of fertiliser.

38 Water as a limiting factor

1 See figure A38.1.

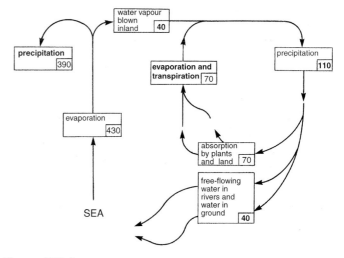

Figure A38.1

2 a) 6.

b) (i) April/May.

(ii) Variation in rainfall during the seasons of the year.

c) It has made the volume of water-flow fairly uniform.

procedure adopted	reason why land becomes susceptible to erosion	agent of erosion	possible consequence
Clearing of forest from hillsides	Top soil no longer bound to roots of forest plants.	Rain water	Silting up of rivers and dams; flooding of low-lying land.
Overgrazing of grassland	Plants die and roots no longer hold soil	Wind	Desertification
Cultivation of marginal land	Crop dies and soil dries out.	Wind	Desertification

Table A38.1

3 See table A38.1.

4 See pages 309 and 312. Use should also be made of the information in figure 38.10 on page 311.

39 Effect of disease

1 a) (i) Y.

    (ii) X.

    (iii) Vaccination began earlier and eradication was achieved earlier in X.

  b) This is supported by the fact that the start of the vaccination campaign was followed each time by an apparent surge in cases when in fact this high level probably existed all along. It is hardly likely that it was caused by vaccination.

  c) (i) Almost complete eradication of the disease.

    (ii) The organism changes from one form to another giving three phases. No vaccine (so far) has been produced that protects against all three. In addition many strains of the pathogen exist with different antigenic proteins on their surfaces.

2 a) Rural.

  b) See table A39.1

type of community	changing level of access to facility with time	
	clean water	proper sanitation
urban	○	✗
rural	✓	○

Table A39.1

  c) Dysentery and cholera.

  d) Yes, prevention is better than cure. The greater the number of taps, the greater the number of people with clean water and the greater the chance of disease being prevented. The

number of hospital beds only indicates the potential available to fight disease once it has been contracted.

3 a) (i) Diphtheria.

    (ii) Tuberculosis.

    (iii) Good food, improved quality of housing, clean water.

  b) (i) 4.

    (ii) 60.

    (iii) 1882.

    (iv) 0.8.

  c) People sleeping 'rough' in cold, damp conditions become susceptible to respiratory infections including tuberculosis since their resistance is low.

4 In historical times, fatal diseases (e.g. bubonic plague) exerted a regulatory effect on the population. As some countries became developed, their levels of hygiene and sanitation improved and incidence of many deadly diseases dropped dramatically. This success was due to higher standards of living, better food, clean piped water and mains sanitation, all of which increased the people's resistance to the disease.

This pattern was not repeated in many developing countries where standards of hygiene and sanitation are still low and pathogenic micro-organisms thrive e.g. in water which is used for drinking, washing and sewage disposal.

In recent times, advances in medicine have resulted in the production of effective vaccines for many diseases especially those that had a history of being fatal in childhood. A combination of antibiotic treatment and determined immunisation programmes in developed countries has all but wiped out these diseases. However in developing countries the story is often one of only limited success because of lack of information, understanding and financial means. Children often miss out on the vaccine or fail to receive more than one of the three doses. This leaves millions of children in developing countries susceptible to diseases and results in many of them dying every year.

A worldwide immunisation campaign by the WHO led to the complete eradication of smallpox from all countries. However the development of vaccines for AIDS and malaria still elude scientists. Although inhabitants of all countries are potentially susceptible to these diseases, it is the inhabitants of poor developing countries that suffer most resulting in millions of fatalities annually.

40 Human population effects on environment

1 a) 3.

  b) X. Its concentration dropped to zero after 40 days.

  c) Y. Some of it still persisted at 60 days.

2 a) Soil mite and ladybird.

  b) Because the spider mites survived the pesticide and ate some of the crop.

  c) The population of plant-eating spider mites underwent uncontrolled growth in the absence of predators.

  d) Secondary, web, primary, increase, producer.

3 a) seed → seed-eating bird → peregrine falcon

  b) Dieldrin is non-biodegradable and therefore it builds up in concentration along the food chain as each organism eats a large number of the previous organism in the chain.

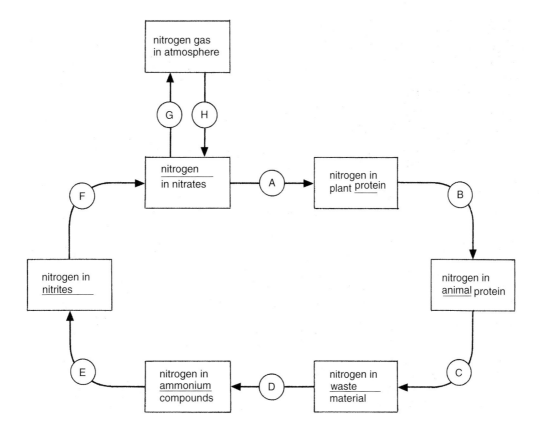

Figure A40.1

c) C.

d) 65%.

e) Many thin-shelled eggs break during incubation so fewer young survive to become breeding adults.

f) The number of breeding pairs is rising because use of dieldrin has been stopped and its effects are gradually disappearing.

4 a) They are stirred up from the deep by winter storms and build up in concentration until the growing season begins.

b) Temperature and light intensity.

c) (i) May.

(ii) Concentration of phosphate and nitrate.

d) (i) It may have been released from the cells of dead algae that decomposed.

(ii) Lower light intensity probably acted as the limiting factor.

5 a) Excessive use of fertiliser.

b) Via rivers.

c) (i) W.

(ii) It contains the least nitrate because the tidal current tends to move it away (towards the other three sites).

d) (i) Bloom of toxic freshwater algae causes a build-up of poison in the water. This can kill fish when they breathe it in.

(ii) Bloom of toxic marine algae results in those shellfish that feed on algae taking in and retaining the poison. Local community is poisoned on consuming the shellfish.

6 a) See figure A40.1.

b) Denitrifying.

c) (i) H.

(ii) E and F.

d) (i) A.

(ii) Nitrate.

e) (i) Decomposition.

(ii) D.

(iii) Reduce it. They use it during aerobic respiration.

7 a) (i) June and September.

(ii) September.

(iii) June.

b) (i) D.

(ii) During August there is no requirement for nitrate by the crop so added fertiliser would remain unused and be leached out of the soil.

c) (i) A.

(ii) B is wrong because the fertiliser would remain unused by plants and be washed out by rain. C is wrong because this would be a wasteful method as the plant can only use a certain amount of fertiliser at a time. D is wrong because the fertiliser could be easily leached out of the soil before being used by the plant in spring.

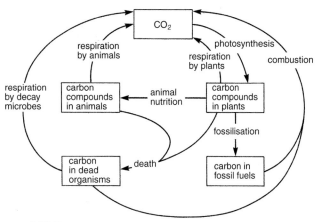

Figure A40.2

8 **a)** See figure A40.2.

b) 5.

9 **a)** See figure A40.3.

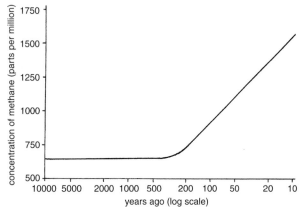

Figure A40.3

b) **(i)** 650 ppm (approx.)

(ii) 200–300 years ago (approx.)

(iii) This coincides with the start of the industrial revolution.

c) Because it traps infra-red radiation (heat) coming from the Earth's surface and reflects it back to Earth, helping to keep the planet warm.

d) Because methane is 30 times more efficient at absorbing infra-red radiation than CO_2.

10 Extreme eutrophication of aquatic ecosystems may be caused by nitrate from farms where fertiliser has been sprayed in excess on fields, running into local rivers. Similarly such over-enrichment of water by nitrate can be caused by the dumping of sewage from pig-farming into waterways.

The extra nitrate in the water promotes the growth of algae which form a bloom. When the algae die and undergo decomposition by bacteria, the latter use up the river's oxygen supply. This has a devastating effect on most of the other organisms in the aquatic ecosystem that depend on dissolved oxygen in the water for aerobic respiration.

Inadequately treated sewage in a river results in organic waste being acted upon by decay microbes. Ammonia is formed and becomes converted to nitrite and nitrate. A high concentration of nitrate leads to an algal bloom causing the disruption described above.

Excessive use of fertiliser rich in nitrate on farmland may result in some of the nitrate reaching water supplies intended for human consumption. High levels of nitrate may be harmful to babies since an enzyme in their stomachs converts it to nitrite. This combines with haemoglobin and reduces the oxygen-carrying capacity of the baby's blood. Very high concentrations of nitrate in drinking water are probably harmful to all ages.